THE SALES
PROFESSIONAL'S
ADVISOR

THE SALES
PROFESSIONAL'S
ADVISOR

DAVID M. BROWNSTONE
and
IRENE M. FRANCK

A Hudson Group Book

A Wiley-Interscience Publication
JOHN WILEY & SONS
New York · Chichester · Brisbane · Toronto · Singapore

Library of Congress Cataloging in Publication Data:

Brownstone, David M.
    The sales professional's advisor.

    "A Wiley-Interscience publication."
    Includes index.
    1. Selling. I. Franck, Irene M. II. Title.
HF5438.25.B747 1983   658.8′5   83–6532
ISBN 0–471–86352–1

Printed in the United States of America

10 9 8 7 6 5 4 3 2 1

PREFACE

Sales professionals today need a book that will help them successfully pursue their careers in what for many are personally difficult times. For without paying greatly increased attention to astute career development, lifelong professional self-development, and careful medium- and long-term personal and financial planning, many will find themselves trapped in exceedingly adverse circumstances as this period unfolds.

Our intent in writing this book has been to focus on such personal and practical career matters as career building, moving up, effective job changing, alternative careers, and how to develop a program of lifelong professional self-development. We have also focused on such very practical skills as selling, time management, and effective communication. And we have paid a good deal of attention in this book to such job-related matters as where to find business information and the changing language of selling. We have also included considerable discussion of such matters as compensation, personal financial planning, personal appearance, and how to handle some key job-related personal problems.

Although we have included a review of selling basics, our intent has been to focus on career development matters throughout, rather than on selling skills, as this is a personal career companion, not a standard sales handbook.

Please note that throughout this work we have drawn upon a considerable body of our own earlier thinking, some of it previously expressed in other published works. That is especially so in Chapter 6, where we have drawn heavily from *Sell Your Way to Success* (John Wiley and Sons, 1979); in Chapter 9, which contains substantial excerpts from *Personal Financial Survival* (Wiley, 1981); and in Part 6, which contains excerpts from *Where to Find Business Information,* Second Edition (Wiley, 1982).

Please also note that this book is part of our Career Companion Series, and therefore carries much material that also appears in other books in the series, as many kinds of professionals encounter similar problems and are aided by similar solutions in many aspects of life and work. For example, a sales professional who purchases this book and then moves into management and also purchases our manager's Career Companion will find much duplication between the two books, as will a librarian purchasing both books for different audiences. Our intent here is to cover those matters unique to each profession uniquely, and at the same time to work with those matters common to many professions in the fashion that best serves those practicing them.

Our thanks to Rosemary Guiley, whose thinking contributed substantially to the development of Chapters 7, 8, 10, and 11; to Bruce Trachtenberg, whose thinking contributed substantially to the development of Chapter 7; to Thurman Poston and Richard P. Zeldin, our editor and publisher, respectively, at John Wiley & Sons; and to our expert typists, Shirley Fenn and Mary Bunch.

DAVID M. BROWNSTONE
IRENE M. FRANCK

Chappaqua, New York
September 1983

CONTENTS

THE SALES
PROFESSIONAL'S
ADVISOR

PART I
BUILDING A CAREER IN SELLING

CHAPTER 1
CONTEXTS

Sales professionals are very practical people indeed. They have no choice, really, for success in selling is first of all a matter of consistently producing very visible, measurable sales results. Whatever else may have changed in the world of business, that has not. Today's sales professionals, like yesterday's, need to know how to effectively prospect, present, handle hurdles, and triumphantly close a sale—time after time, year after year, always with the same freshness as the first time and with increasing skill as the years go by.

In this exceedingly basic respect, the world has not changed at all since the days of the "drummers" of preindustrial America, who went from town to town selling a wide variety of wares and forming with their own kind a subculture that has since vanished, but stays on in American folk myth. Neither, for that matter, is the world very different from the time of the "peddler," now a pejorative term, but once merely a term describing those men and women who traveled the countryside—and especially the expanding American frontier—providing a wide variety of goods and services.

However, in some very significant ways, the sales professional's world has changed a great deal, first as the pace of technological change has accelerated, and then as the context within which most Americans make their livings has changed enormously for the worse.

When asked what he or she does, the career sales professional will often respond "I'm in selling," rather than "I sell computers" (or airplanes, frozen fish, furniture, or xylophones). That is not diffidence, but recognition that in the most basic sense "selling is selling," that the career sales professional is quite sure that he or she is perfectly capable of selling anything under the sun, given adequate preparation, no matter what is now being sold, or for how long that has been so. That is central to professional self-definition; without that kind of self-definition, lifelong professionalism is impossible.

Selling is indeed selling, but you must have excellent product knowledge to be able to sell. And to be able to sell the products of high technology—whether objects, services, or systems—you must be able to learn complex material. That means having the kind of basic language and concept command that is far more common among those who have had at least two, and better yet four, years of college than among those who have not had any college at all.

That is not as true of other kinds of goods and services; in fact, selling is still one of the great apprenticeship occupations, and college degree requirements, in many instances, are a matter of possessing quite unnecessary credentials. But requirements there are; someone who wants to enter professional selling today is best advised either to have a bachelor's degree or to be ready to go back to school part time for a degree in the not-so-very-long run.

Putting it a little differently, and from the point of view of those who sell, a college degree is now openers for beginners, partly because it is necessary for the accretion of some kinds of product knowledge, and partly because prospective employers require it, even when it is not necessary to do the job well and even though selling is mainly an apprenticeship occupation. Either way it is openers, and future mobility in a fast-changing business environment requires at least the mobility the degree affords.

Technological change continues to accelerate. Computers and new information and entertainment technology continue to permeate all phases of American life. Robots are beginning to be introduced in industrial processes; in a generation, they will be as ubiquitous as computers are now, and will have at least as profound an impact as the computer revolution. New forms of energy will help transform human societies in our lifetimes, as will much longer life spans and new medical discoveries. And we stand on the edge of space. Many of today's occupations will disappear; others will change unrecognizably. Yet assuming—as we do—no major changes in our basic economic system, selling will still be selling, though pursued in the considerably changed circumstances caused by modern technology, and making much more education and continuing professional development necessary for those who sell.

Men and women who sell today are also very considerably concerned with such career development matters as getting started, polishing selling skills, moving up if and as desired, job changing in an increasingly uncertain business world, and alternative and later-life careers. We also pay a great deal more attention to our physical and emotional health, to our family situations, and to personal financial matters in these difficult economic times, as well as to the development of our more basic skills in such areas as effective reading, writing, speaking, understanding and use of language, and use of sources of information. All very necessary in a fast-changing business and personal world; all requiring considerably more attention to lifelong professional self-development than was required of either the drummer or the peddler—even though selling is still selling.

It is also true that a deep and far-reaching change has occurred in the United States and throughout the Western world in the last decade or so, one that must be taken into account by people in every walk of life and in every profession. It is this: The world economy, quite particularly including the economy of the United States, no longer looks as if it is headed unlimitedly upward, as so often seemed true in the 1950s and 1960s. At that time, all was expansion and growth, punctuated by modest economic downturns that seemed only preludes to renewed expansion. Tomorrow was always going to be like today, but better. If you were a gambler, you could take a fling working with a small and untried company, or even in a company of your own; if it didn't work out, you could always find a good job and retire from it later on. If you were security-minded, you could look forward to working for a solid company all your life, and retire from it with a combination of savings, investments, Social Security income, and company pension payments that would set the basis for a very comfortable set of golden years. Oh, you might want to "keep your hand in," and do a little part-time selling in retirement, or perhaps a little inside work on the telephone, but it would not be necessary—it only might keep you more busy than bored.

Not so; it was an illusion—always an illusion. For the overwhelming majority of us, it was never going to be that good. We were figuring without the normal inflation built into our economic system, much less allowing for the possibility of the kind of protracted double-digit inflation that hit in the mid-1970s and continued through the early 1980s. We were figuring without high interest rates and huge unemployment rates; an indexed but insufficiently funded Social Security; a debilitating war; enormous federal, state, and local deficits; the unprecedentedly high cost of sending our children to college; foreign competition; oil crises; and armaments budgets. Twenty-five years ago, we spent pretty much everything we made, except for investments in securities that went bad, and homes that appreciated but had to be remortgaged to pay for college. In essence, we did not in any way anticipate that the booming American economy of the 1950s and 1960s would turn into the stagnant economy we have been living with for the past decade; nor that there would be every chance that this stagnancy will persist for much of the rest of this century, if not beyond. But that seems to be the case. The American economy in our time neither booms nor busts; it wavers around a slow and stagnant center, moving up a little now and then, providing a brief seeming recovery, only to then go down again shortly after. It inflates and deflates as successive groups of politicians in power for a little while try to find short-term American solutions for long-term world economic problems.

Several things flow from the combination of accelerating technological change on the one hand and long-term adverse economic circumstances on the other. First, we will be healthier during those longer life spans; but we will also have to support ourselves for a much longer time, as we will not be able to count on anyone—government, employers, or our children —to support us in our later years. Neither can we count on our savings and investments; inflation and long life guarantee the kind of financial erosion that will force most of us to pursue remunerative work of some kind as long as we reasonably can. Most of us will find that the combination of lower real Social Security payments, corporate pensions that pay less in real dollars than we had supposed (if they are still there at all), and interest and dividend payments that disappear as we are forced to eat up principal, add up to pauperization if we retire at 65 and live out what are now our normal life spans. But none of us want to live out our lives as de facto wards of a state that cannot and will not support us.

Nor can we reasonably expect to lead quiet, untroubled lives as long-term corporate employees, either. The time when you could sell reasonably well, meet quota and then some, and look forward to retiring from a single company after decades of productive and professional work are gone. You still may have precisely that experience—there are still many healthy companies on the American scene—but you cannot assume that anything like that will be your own experience. The proper assumption in these times is that today's employer may be tomorrow's bankrupt, or acquired, or technologically displaced company, and that you may have to take your professional skills elsewhere at any time.

This requires keeping your skills very, very sharp, your job contacts in good and growing shape, and planning the financial side of life extremely conservatively and carefully. No matter how good a sales professional you are, unforeseeable circumstances quite literally beyond your control can put you out on the street any tomorrow. If that happens, you will need financial reserves that will see you through a job-seeking period. You will also need other contingency plans, and some live prospective employers who have previously expressed a desire to talk with you should you ever become available. For generalist sales professionals—for whom selling really is selling—unemployment is not the kind of disaster it can be for others in harder-to-place professions; but it does require a great deal more planning for in difficult times than in easy times.

Adverse times and major technological and social changes have their flip side, as well, especially for sales professionals. They create new opportunities, as well as pitfalls. New industries create new opportunities; the failure of one can create a new opportunity for another. Today's fleet automobile seller may be tomorrow's mass industrial robot seller; today's top computer software seller may be tomorrow's sales manager for the same, or perhaps another, company. Today's real estate salesperson had better be professional enough, though, to be able to go into an entirely different kind of selling if construction continues to be bedeviled by high interest rates.

Which is why self-development as an all-around sales professional is more important than ever before. That means constantly reviewing and upgrading basic selling skills. It also means continually working on the underlying persuasive and communicating skills, as well as becoming "computer literate" and entirely able to learn in all but those areas requiring many years of formal training, such as engineering and some of the hard sciences.

It is a time for careful planning and a great deal of self-reliance. That is true in all seasons and never more than now. To a significant extent it has been so for those who have been in sales all along; the stereotype of the glib, lightweight, irresponsible transient has been only that. The truth is that people who fit the stereotype often fail at selling; success in selling consists of a great deal of effective entrepreneurship, which means a great deal of absolutely independent initiative, planning, preparation, perseverance, execution, and follow-up—all the things a lightweight simply cannot do.

In the long run, it is for most professionals, including sales professionals, a matter of how the game fits, how the process works or does not work for you—not the rewards taken or interim goals reached. What less independently minded people find hard to understand is that, in a very basic and long-term way, sales professionals like being out there all alone. While there are tensions between freedom and loneliness, between freedom and security, between freedom and life with loved ones, the essence of the matter is that feeling of freedom. Without that, in the long run, the work has too many drawbacks to be really acceptable. And without independent professionalism, too many limits have to be placed on the kind of selling job you will accept to allow for real job mobility in a very fast-changing world.

There is a contradiction, one that plagues many in selling throughout their working lives. It is that most people in selling work for, and are therefore accountable to, others. Only such entirely independent small business owners as manufacturer's representatives and independent distributors operate entirely on their own; however independent-minded others in selling are, they must be responsive to sales management, and to company policies and structures. That contradiction becomes central for some when they are faced with the question of moving out of the field and into sales management, for then an entirely different game has to be accepted, as well as a whole new set of skills learned.

Freedom is a central question for those who sell, and having a significant measure of freedom on the job is an essential element of job satisfaction. There is more to job satisfaction than that, certainly, including the self-respect that comes from selling goods and services you respect and being with people and organizations you respect as well. There are also money, some measure of security, future prospects, and status; they are seldom the prime motivators that outsiders think them to be, but are nonetheless very basic career and job satisfaction building blocks.

In a rather imperfect world, and in a particularly difficult economic period, why the stress on job satisfaction? All kinds of people do jobs they do not much like; some do jobs they detest, year after year, usually in far-from-quiet desperation. Why must those who sell be more satisfied than, for example, those who produce the goods and services they sell, or those who work in the management of those companies? After all, a young MBA who is $30,000 in debt after six years of schooling and is stuck in what is essentially an entry-level management job has more reason to be upset than does a young seller who had two to four years of college, has small education loans outstanding, and is making twice as much as the young MBA. Why should anyone worry about keeping the sales professional happy?

It is simple enough; all seasoned managers know the answer, from management's point of view. The sales professional is the goose that lays the golden eggs. You tamper with a successful field salesperson or organization at your extreme peril, for you do not really know what makes a superb producer or how to replicate that producer, any more than you know how to guarantee that a sales organization will keep its power and forward thrust on your behalf. And from the sales professional's point of view that is a very gratifying answer. It is nice to be looked upon as the goose that lays the golden eggs.

On the other hand, if all you see is management's point of view, rather than keeping clearly in mind at all times that in the medium and long term you have to like what you do, to make it worthwhile to be out there producing, you may trap yourself. For that is when good people can go "stale," "lose their selling edge," "overstay," and get "past it." Then there can be few golden eggs, unreachable quotas, considerable personal anguish on the way out, and an eventual involuntary job change. To consistently motivate others to buy what you are selling, you must have basic job satisfaction; it is as simple as that. In the long run, you cannot "psych yourself up" every morning to do a job you do not really want to do, and then go out and do it well. Oh, you can once in a while; we have all done that. But not every day, or even most days. Which is why it does not matter how happy management is with you and your golden eggs—if you are not happy while producing them.

Another basic matter is the professional context within which you see yourself. A sales professional is "in selling," and is at this time selling computers, steel, hot dogs, legal services, automobiles, or whatever else. Someone who is "in the computer business," or "the automobile industry" and is engaged in selling within that industry, is hardly likely to be a broad-gauged professional seller; the narrow self-definition is quite likely to defeat long-term professional development efforts and make real mobility impossible. If selling is indeed selling, then professionals must avoid unnecessarily limiting self-definition. It really does not matter how you describe your work to another, of course; but if you see yourself as limited to a single industry or group of related industries or products, you can do yourself grave long-term career damage, for you are then seeing main contexts too narrowly.

So, too, the question of long-term work and personal economic contexts. To be an effective personal planner and an entrepreneurially minded professional means seeing your economic activities as a single, lifelong enterprise, and regarding the entire economic side of your life as, whatever else it may be, a small business. Working, saving, investing, part-time businesses, major expenditures, life style, alternative careers, and ensuring productive and economically rewarding activities for your later years are all part of personal and career planning. It is wildly imprudent to believe that you will work for a single company most of your life and retire to a life of leisure at the age of 65, gold watch on wrist and economic future secure. You are just as likely to work for seven companies as one, go into business for yourself once, twice, or three times, and spend your later years selling up a storm for yourself or for an employer, working considerably smarter and a good deal less than you did earlier.

It is vital to see yourself as a highly skilled and independent professional set solidly into the context of a major and growing profession, with skills capable of carrying you through difficult times and personal crises, as necessary. For that is the truth; that is the way it is. At the same time, it is vital to understand that in the difficult times we all face today and tomorrow, it is not enough to be able to sell well; there is also a career to actively pursue, and career matters to consider every step of the way. It is to these kinds of career matters that we now turn.

CHAPTER 2
CAREER BUILDING ESSENTIALS

First things first: building a career in selling depends on being able to sell well, year in and year out, decade after decade, whatever and wherever you are selling. That is rather an old-fashioned thing to say in a world full of systems, prospecting aids, sophisticated promotion pieces, and a large variety of advices on how to persuade, negotiate, confront, wheedle, and generally sharp-angle your way to "the top." Perhaps it is so basic that it need not be said, in an era of distribution and marketing majors, MBAs headed for marketing careers, and a good deal of portal, field, and refresher sales training.

Or perhaps it is so basic that it must be said, again and again, throughout a lifetime in selling—not by others, but by each of us to ourselves, as part of the indispensable and very personal self-analysis that is at the heart of all professional self-development and career building. It is a series of interconnected questions, really: Am I selling well and consistently? Are my attitudes to life and work "on straight"? Am I doing it all, and increasingly effectively? Am I putting in enough and the right kind of time? Am I avoiding the main traps? taking advantage of the main opportunities? consciously pursuing a course of lifelong professional self-development? Do I have long-term and very real personal and career plans, and am I working my plans? Am I taking my understanding of the selling process and my selling skills into every aspect of my business life? Am I behaving like the independent businessperson and professional that I really am? All these are very straightforward, but all too seldom they are seen as an intertwined set of basics.

As seasoned sales professionals so well know, selling well and consistently most emphatically does not mean "having a good day" (or week, or month, for that matter). Certainly, to sell well today is indispensable; just as certainly, the person who does not habitually engage in the whole selling process and who does not develop a personally effective and comfortable selling style will be erratic, at best, with the bad days far outnumbering the good. To fail to prospect effectively is—sooner or later—to run out of qualified prospects, and thereby to run out of good days, no matter how effective you may be face to face. To fail to develop information and sell empathetically is to set up the conditions for failure after failure, no matter how strong a "closer" you are, and whether you try to close once, twice, or fifteen times. To come to where you have little respect for your company, management, and product, and are "sour" in a job, is to have overstayed and set up a personal disaster. To come to where you reflexively attempt to hide your distaste for a good many of your customers and prospects—and therefore for yourself, for being in the situation you are in—is at best an immediate and tremendous problem to be dealt with urgently, and at worst a career-breaker.

We deal with the selling process at length in Chapter 6 of this book, and will not duplicate that treatment here. What must be clear at the outset in any discussion of a career in selling, though, is that without demonstrated selling excellence, you have no real place in selling. You will not be able to build anything permanent in the way of a career, no matter what other personal and business skills you bring to that career. Also, you must realize that even the developed skills of a career sales professional will not withstand a long-term loss of effectiveness, although loss of effectiveness in one job should never be taken to indicate loss of professional skill and motivation; very often, what is needed is a job change, not a change of occupation. In straightforward and practical short- and medium-range terms, if you cannot sell effectively enough, then you cannot hold a job, or can hold it only so tenuously that the stresses involved make it clear that a change is advisable.

Most working sales professionals do not encounter problems that immediate and profound, though, unless they are in serious personal and career trouble. Far more frequently, it is a matter of doing the kind of job you or your manager may characterize as fair, but know very well is mediocre, and far beneath your performance possibilities. It is even possible to hang on year after year, hovering around quota, inevitably growing less and less satisfied, and more and more trapped, as others move ahead all around you. Make no mistake about this: only excellence in the field commands the attention of management. Nobody wants a mediocre seller —no matter how experienced—to take training assignments, to handle national or key account responsibilities, to introduce new products and lines, or to become an assistant manager of a region or a field sales manager. Those things are for people who sell well and consistently; that is, openers. Nobody wants to hire someone with a mediocre track record, either; some will, for good people are always hard to find, and those hiring often have to settle, with regret, for less than the ball of fire they were looking for. And nobody reaches into someone else's organization to steal a mediocre seller, either; that, too, is reserved for top performers.

Bedrock, then; you have to sell consistently and well to be able to seriously pursue a career in selling. And equally basic: you have to understand what that career in selling is and what kind of commitment is needed to build it seriously.

THE SELLING PROFESSION

Folklore and even some modern stereotyping have it that selling is a lark, and that people who sell are happy-go-lucky, smile a lot, work very little, and spend their little time on the job creating a tissue of lies to ensnare the unwary. Modern stereotypes often also include mea culpas every morning, déjà vu daily, and identification with Willy Loman on gray days in November. Nonsense, surely; and *Death of a Salesman* was scarcely about people who sell, being intended as a metaphor for the human condition in the American society of its time.

Yet stereotypes are interesting here, for they can mislead people within a profession or trade, as well as those without. Selling has traditionally attracted many people looking for a good, quick, and easy living. Most such people do not last very long, but their presence does testify to the impact of the stereotype. Beyond this obvious impact, though, there is a widespread misapprehension among people in selling that somehow it all ought to take less time, that selling should really be a nine-to-five kind of job, and that sales professionals should be able to look forward to a 35- to 40-hour week, like normal human beings; for example, like the people who work in the home office.

Which people? Certainly not professional managers, who work in company offices from nine to five or thereabouts and then proceed to work another 10 to 30 hours a week, and sometimes more, at home, on commuter trains, on weekends, and on the road. And certainly not those in other professions or businesses. Many doctors habitually work 60 to 80 hours a week, and sometimes more, as well as trying their best to keep up with advances in medicine. Most small business owners are on deck 12 hours a day, six days a week, and spend many more hours on paperwork and planning at home. And try talking to a lawyer deep in litigation or a CPA during tax season about the 35-hour week!

In truth, field sales professionals need just as much independence and commitment as managers, doctors, lawyers, accountants, and small business owners. Whether employed by others, as most are, or running their own selling businesses, they must behave like people in business for themselves. That means planning, preparing, prospecting, selling interviews, and successfully handling selling situations, often along with installation and some aspects of customer service, as well. All of that requires a very considerable and absolutely necessary time commitment.

It also requires self-definition as someone capable of selling whatever, whenever, and to whomever, and a recognition of the need for continuous professional self-development. In other words, it requires self-definition as an independent sales professional, rather than as someone employed to sell a particular product or line of products. In selling, as in management, professionalism is a question of self-definition and a body of skills. Not buttressed by certification, selling is rather an apprenticeship occupation, as were so many of the currently certified professions in earlier times. But it is no less a profession, and recognition of that is as essential to sales professionals as is the ability to consistently sell well.

KEY ATTITUDES AND SKILLS

Career building, like selling, rests heavily upon a set of positive and growth-producing personal attitudes and skills. Some of these attitudes are precisely the same as those needed and cultivated throughout their working lives by successful sales professionals; that gives sellers some very significant career-building advantages, if they are able to recognize the strengths they carry over from the selling process into other aspects of their business lives. Among these are: personal integrity; the will to win; the ability and will to function entrepreneurially; the ability to plan and execute, and to set, reach, and exceed personal goals; the habit of skeptical and searching self-analysis; the ability to refresh yourself from those around you; and the linked responsive listening, seeing, and empathizing skills that are so basic to long-term successful selling. No less important in career building is the ability to surmount the potential emotional problems caused by personal and business problems, especially in difficult times like these. Likewise, you must have the ability to overcome some of the hazards endemic to working with others in all seasons. Time wasters and rotten apples are to be found in every trade and profession, and are always quite ready to negatively color your attitudes, if you let them; the successful sales professional does not.

Not the least of these positive career-building attitudes is the will to win. No, not to be a carnivore, chewing up people all around you in an unrelenting pursuit of fame and fortune; that is the stuff of bad novels and third-rate films, not the reality created by people who must work together in organizations. A winner nonetheless, one who wins most of the contests, plans well, and quite visibly works those plans successfully, and is a natural for a difficult assignment—or a promotion.

The will to win on a bedrock of personal integrity, that is. For personal integrity is as much a bedrock career-building matter as are selling consistency and professionalism. It is odd to have to point that out, in a way; but we live in a world in which this most basic of positive personal characteristics is often perceived as something of a drawback in a business world that is sometimes—and sometimes properly—perceived as a "jungle."

When we think of others as possible business associates, colleagues, superiors, peers, and subordinates, we think first—and last—of people whom we can trust, "standup" people, people who "will be there when you need them"; in short, people of integrity. All the other positive things, too, but personal integrity most of all. For all our talk of jungles and competitive warfare, we value integrity most, and oddly enough, even while doing some things ourselves, from time to time, that give the lie to some of our most cherished self-images. It therefore seems apparent that personal integrity is the most important career-building personal characteristic of all. You are both what you are and what you make of yourself. The person who has a well-deserved reputation for personal integrity has the most important image a sales professional can have—and as actuality, not merely image.

That kind of observation seems hard to square with perceived corporate and marketplace realities. Advertisers routinely overstate, lying by omission and by exaggeration, and often by outright misstatement as well. Many books and articles counsel a wide range of cunning stratagems and artifices, claiming to instruct people on how to play all the possible games one can encounter in life and work. Some claim to have the keys to "powerful" professional and personal relations, others tout foolproof negotiating and persuading methods, and yet others offer sure ways to move ahead with enormous and unchecked speed and momentum. Indeed, people who sell professionally are sometimes urged to engage in a whole set of practices that add up to cunning manipulation of buying motives and buyers, to close deceptively and hard again and again, to use "every trick in the book" to make the sale. Nonsense, of course; those who buy are inured to tricks and deceptions, and the professional seller who develops a well-deserved reputation for being slippery and tricky, soon needs to find another line of work.

That is easy to see in selling; sound sales professionals know all about the unique importance of integrity. Yet sometimes the same people who see the importance of perceived integrity in the field do not see it so easily when dealing with career-building matters. The person who habitually "cuts a corner" by covertly offering an "on-approval" sale to the house's considerable disadvantage in terms of shipping and installation costs is making a serious personal error. So is one who pads an expense account every month because "everybody does it"; or engages in shady competitive practices; or badmouths a selling colleague in competition for a promotion. Those who do that sort of thing very often destroy both self-respect and the respect of others, to enormous personal and career detriment.

The truth is that all of us live in the same business and personal world, know the tricks as well as we know what we had for lunch 10 minutes ago, and desire nothing quite so devoutly as to work with people we trust, who do not play manipulative games—precisely the games we are urged to play by some bogus experts. Most fully seasoned sales professionals know better than to habitually play such games, recognizing the professional and personal harm they can do to themselves and to others; a few do not. Some inexperienced people are taken in by bad advice, and do try to play manipulative games, harming themselves and others in the process, and doing themselves no good at all professionally. Certainly there is tactical maneuvering in the real world; certainly we do not always reveal everything we know to others; certainly we do things that hurt others—that is the inevitable result of any competition at all. However, habitual "gaming" is extraordinarily counterproductive personally and for organizations. And the person who is seen by his or her peers and superiors as lacking in personal integrity has nowhere to go but out, if personality and image cannot be repaired in place.

Integrity and the will to win are not the only positive personal characteristics needed to sell well and to build a career in selling. You also need —we almost hate to say it, for it conjures up a wholly unwanted image —a considerable measure of personal buoyancy or optimism, if you will. Ah, shades of the smiling idiot who wants to sell popsicles in a snowstorm . . . ? No, not really. It is just that to sell well consistently you have to be up and ready for every selling situation, so that you may give it your best with as little residual impact as possible from prior negative experiences. And that sometimes takes some doing, as when you have just come into an office on the hottest day of the summer, after being stuck in a traffic jam in a car with a broken air conditioner, after two busted appointments in a town 20 miles away, and missing lunch entirely. Or when you have been moving about in a city business district on foot in a snowstorm, unable to find a taxi, and carrying demonstration materials that weigh 40 pounds, which by now feel like 140 pounds, and you have failed to close a sale all week. Not an atypical situation, by the way, and sometimes quite unavoidable, no matter how well you plan. People who sell encounter stressful situations very often, and see rejection every day, and if they allow themselves to do so, they see it as personal rejection. Stress and rejection are intrinsic. They are part of the job, which means that survival alone demands a certain amount of self-confidence and personal buoyancy; consistent sales success and astute career building demand even more.

REFRESHING YOURSELF

But self-confidence and buoyancy do not flourish untended, nor can they be tended in isolation. You can pump yourself up for a little while by doing self-confidence exercises before a mirror every morning. However, in the long run you must have sound, reliable means of refreshing yourself through others—like Antaeus touching earth mother, in a very real sense —and of growing professionally in a variety of ways.

There is nothing particularly wrong with looking at yourself approvingly in the mirror every morning, by the way. That may be a pretty good reflex, if you take the trouble to develop a sharply analytical and self-critical eye. Checking the externals is particularly important when you are pursuing a highly visible profession. At the same time, you may be able to develop the ability to check some of the internals, too, during that early morning look at yourself, and again and again as you go through your day. It is valuable to know what takes you up, and what pushes you down emotionally. You adjust, of course, and simply go on through ups and downs; but it is nice to be able to do a few modestly remedial things in a reflexive way when you find yourself down. For example, many people really do function much better at one time of day than another, which requires adjustment during the off times. For someone who functions well in the morning, that ritual mid-morning cup of coffee may be a waste of valuable selling time, as it so often is; but for someone whose metabolism is demonstrably sluggish until some time after lunch, that mid-morning coffee may be vital, its usefulness far outweighing the time spent. Yes, you can do without the coffee, or the few minutes spent freshening up between a hot parking lot and a waiting prospect, or for that matter a relaxing sit-down lunch occasionally. But it is far better to learn to reflexively schedule yourself so that such routine physical needs are routinely satisfied, if they are indeed needs.

Deeper refreshment comes from mutually supportive relationships with others, and with learning from others as they learn from you. It starts with the deeper personal relationships, really; the ability to interact fruitfully with co-workers, prospects, and customers reflects more your home and other deep personal relationships than the other way around. Putting it a little differently, a good home situation can take you through many adverse work situations, no matter how much impact those work situations have upon you and those you love. But it takes only one really adverse home situation to create a personal and professional disaster.

That argues strenuously for involving those you love in your work, as much as all of you can reasonably stand, and perhaps even a bit beyond sometimes. The best thing that can happen in this regard is for everyone at home to be interested—really interested—in your long, perhaps boring recount of the day's events, or the week's events, if you have been traveling. Bear in mind that the converse must be equally true, for if you expect interested listening from them, but are not equally interested in their long, boring recounts, you will soon lose their interest in your doings. After all, it is not that these events are intrinsically interesting; it is that they are fascinating because they are part of your life and theirs.

That means a lot of talk, often at times when you and others are tired and perhaps have some office-at-home work to look forward to, besides. And it means some forethought. Whoever is on the road—and these days it may be either spouse or both—needs to thoughtfully provide the little presents and mementos that make the return home something of an event. The same holds true for those at home. Forethought, by the way, also means mutual forbearance; the best kind of family agreement on problems is to wait to take them up until all have had a chance to unwind and reaffirm relationships.

It also means taking every possible opportunity to travel with those you love. To sales meetings, certainly; most modern managements provide these kinds of opportunities routinely, and they should be taken advantage of. On personal selling trips, besides; a longish trip with a minivacation at its other end, timed to coincide with a school holiday, a spouse's vacation, or both can be a superb family builder. And make no mistake about this: every family builder of this kind is also, in the long run, a career builder of no small importance.

Family involvement can yield a substantial additional benefit. For many Americans, not surprisingly, selling is seen as a low-status occupation, and not a profession at all. The stereotype of seller as a calculating and habitual liar has had considerable impact for some generations. In this sense, all those "traveling salesman" jokes—like all jokes depending upon occupational, racial, sexual, ethnic, and religious stereotypes for their "humor"—are in this sense very far from funny. That "Daddy sells brassieres," or "Mommy sells soap," is hardly likely to confer status upon children going to school with other status-conscious children. And when Mommy or Daddy (or both) are away from home a good deal on selling trips, it is possible for those left at home, including nonworking spouses, to feel neglected, as well. Involving family in work can go a long way toward preventing the development of problems before they even get a chance to get started. There are trinkets, travel notes, trips that the spouses and children of prosaic doctors, lawyers, and bankers do not get to share. And there is also the self-confidence that comes with a full sharing of your self-confidence and professional self-definition. Spouses share, if you let them. Children seldom seem to listen, but almost always emulate, whether you like it or not. Give your loved ones a chance to see what you are, what you do, and where you go, as shared family strengths; the benefits to all can last a lifetime.

We can also refresh ourselves daily, from customers, colleagues, and prospects. Such refreshment is a simple-seeming, perfectly obvious, positive attitude builder. Yet how you handle it can make or break your career. It is often at the heart of the problem of the "stale" seller, the "sour" seller, or the seller who's "over the hill." Those are things that almost invariably have to do with how you see, feel about, and relate to your customers and prospects; they often have little or nothing to do with age, experience, and "selling skills." The truth is that no one can continue selling year after year, with empathy a precondition for achieving success, unless there is continual refreshment from and growth with customers and prospects.

Such refreshment is pretty central personally, as well. It can be extraordinarily painful to go out into the field day after day, detesting the work and the people, unsuccessfully trying to make it on technique without the substance of human relationship. "Liking to talk to people," of course, is not quite enough. Refreshing yourself with customers, colleagues, and prospects means asking a lot of the right questions about work, product applications, competition, company, industry and community affairs; it means listening hard and responsively; and it also means expanding your knowledge in a conscious, fully rounded way.

A solid sales professional learns a great deal from customers, colleagues, and prospects, and keeps learning afresh every day. For example, you can learn a lot about current business, industry, and specific company needs and conditions, valuable information that, as you pass it on, can help you in similar selling situations. People often look to sellers to carry this kind of general information, appreciate it, and, more importantly, develop a view of the seller as counselor, advisor, someone whose opinion is worth soliciting. The day your customers and prospects begin to look upon you as a valued business advisor is the day your future in selling is pretty well assured.

You can also continually test the strengths and weaknesses of your products under actual field conditions, as well as continually re-examine their market appeal. That is like taking a combined continual refresher course in product knowledge and sales appeal. The truth is that no home office can supply you with the kind of refresher that is yours for the asking from the very expert product users and sellers you meet every day in the field.

It is a question, though, of how you view those you are selling to and working with. If you think you can learn a great deal from them, and take the trouble to try to do so, you will learn. If you think they are objects to manipulate, you will not learn and, in the long run, you will not sell very well or build your career, either.

That is one of the things that is wrong with excessively "sharp" (meaning fast, tricky, and unscrupulous) sellers. They cannot grow, their manipulative skills get progressively more empty, and they have nowhere to go but downhill, which is often an entirely avoidable personal tragedy.

So add now to this constellation of key personal attitudes and qualities the ability to consistently achieve understanding and empathy, whence comes a constant refreshment of personal warmth and continuing personal pleasure in face-to-face daily interplay with all kinds of people functioning in many different kinds of situations. "Being out there with people" is one of the chief wellsprings of pleasure for sales professionals, and for most that is the best part of the game. And game it is, in considerable part; without the game element, any profession or trade can become flat, stale, and ultimately personally distasteful.

STEADINESS

The will to win, integrity, well-founded self-confidence, and buoyancy. Also steadiness; which is another way of saying that you must know for yourself and consistently convey to others that you are the kind of person who can do anything that needs to be done as well or better than anyone else—that you are a man or woman for all seasons.

This describes a whole set of handling abilities and the attitudes consistently underlying those abilities. Sales professionals have to handle all kinds of situations and people every day, many of which involve problems that must be solved before a sale can be consummated, others involve difficult post-sales and servicing questions that may be of an emergency nature to those who raise them. In a single day, there may be potentially hostile receptionists and secretaries, personally difficult prospects, customer complaints, servicing emergencies, demanding home-office and sales supervisory staff, complicated reports to do, a balky automobile, and a sound film presentation that does not work. There may also be some sales, the opportunity to expand one or more of them, some valuable referral possibilities, a useful new home-office contact, and several firm appointments made for next week. And through it all, a sound professional maintains equanimity, and demonstrates excellent people-handling and problem-solving skills, flexibility, balance, and warmth. And is extremely bright and quick, while seeming to take it all in stride, in what to others may seem a deliberately slow-paced style. Prospect and customer relations, home-office–field matters and relationships, and scheduling problems all are treated as everyday matters, to be handled extremely well and without fuss.

That kind of steadiness stems from possession of the kinds of key personal qualities we have discussed so far, and also from firm possession of some very important personal skills, such as astute listening, careful and considerate questioning, close watching, and the ability to "put yourself in the other guy's shoes"—that is, to empathize. After all that comes the ability to skeptically and realistically analyze people and situations, while learning by engaging in critical self-analysis. These are the basic personal selling skills, and every sales professional has them and knows how to use them.

As selling skills, that is; their use by sales professionals in career building is, to put it gently, rather minimal. When that is so, it is a waste of some extraordinarily valuable skills and something to put right. The sales professional who consciously and consistently adapts and uses his or her selling skills for career-building purposes can go very nearly any distance desired, in a career sense; and those who do not, often cannot. For sales professionals engaged in career building, the key understanding is that the selling skills that we sharpen every day are entirely usable as tools of persuasion in every other part of our working lives. The key activity, therefore, is to learn how to do all the things we know so well how to do, in a wider context. All the steps of the selling process are involved in job seeking, promotion seeking, intracompany relationships, and personal network building; all the skills we use in the selling process are as equally well used in these matters as they are in selling. It is as necessary—and as fruitful—to develop and tell a benefits story in every other part of business life as it is in the field.

LISTENING

Listening is an extraordinarily important selling skill and an equally important career-building skill. Just listening; listening to what people say, and doing your absolute best to understand what they really mean. Listening to be able to understand well enough to empathize and, if desired, to persuade. As in field selling, it requires the habit of full concentration upon "the other guy" rather than upon yourself and your own needs and desires, no matter what else is happening, with as few preconceptions as possible. You have your problems; other people have theirs. To them, theirs are always far more important than yours. When a sales manager complains about how much time has to be spent on training new people, you may be hearing an attempt to divert you from your legitimate complaints about sales compensation plan changes, product defects, and territory adjustments. More likely, you are listening to someone who needs the kind of help you can offer—if you are interested in starting a move into management with successful sales training assignments under your belt. When a customer complains about the state of the business, you may be hearing a chronic complainer or someone setting up a stall or objection to buying what you are selling, but once in ten, you may be hearing someone who may need the kind of selling or sales management help you can offer.

Listening also goes beyond persuasion to self-development. We listen and learn and, if we listen well, we learn a great deal. Our associates and customers do more than refresh us; they teach us much of what we need to know to move forward. It goes far beyond formal education and product knowledge acquired from company-supplied materials. Our customers teach us about a whole field, composed of one or more industries. They also help us to keep up with a fast-developing business world, in which they function as working professionals. Our associates learn with us, and together we learn far more than any of us could learn alone, if we take the trouble to listen carefully to each other.

With listening comes astute questioning. Not adroit interrogation; that is for bad courtroom dramas and pushy people who tread on toes and alienate everyone in sight. The lifelong habit of successful questioning depends upon personal warmth and seeming indirection. We ask questions aimed at eliciting answers that inform and clarify, often as much by the way the question is answered as by the content of the answer. And the right questions almost always raise further questions, with all adding up to clues that can be used in persuasion and insight that can contribute to self-development.

If we listen and question well, then we inevitably also become very good at watching and seeing, as all good sales professionals do. We watch the entire verbal and nonverbal communications patterns of those with whom we speak. We reflexively watch the interplay between all the members of groups we are in; it quickly becomes second nature to do so. We see environments, people, and motion, and we develop the habit of picking up insights we will use to build a benefits story. That is true whether that benefits story has to do with selling goods and services or selling ourselves into a new job.

We empathize. People buy because we reach in to find their possible buying motives and then empathize with those motives; that is, understand those motives well enough to put ourselves into their shoes, show them how our products satisfy their wants and needs, and make it easy and completely logical for them to buy now. That is the process of selling benefits empathetically; in a wider sense, it is also the process of persuasion. Good sales professionals really do not need to read books on how to manipulate their way upward in the big, bad corporate world, or how to get others to do what you want. They handle people's wants and needs every day of every week.

LEARNING

To the list of career-building keys, add also now the ability to learn from experience and training, for without that, professionalism is only a dream. Learning requires the interlinked habits of analysis and self-analysis; these habits in turn are linked with skepticism and realism, those personally indispensable traits for all seasons and situations. Which is also another way of saying that self-confidence is wonderful only if accompanied by skepticism and realism; and that sales breed more sales and success builds success, but only professionalism can build long-term success and career.

From the first sales call we ever make right through a whole career in selling, we learn to sell analytically. We scribble notes on prospect cards in elevators and lobbies; have near-accidents in automobiles while reliving that last presentation, whether it went well or ill; and coffee ourselves into near-addiction in the course of "post-morteming" with trainers, managers, and often enough only with ourselves. That is, if we are any good at our trade; the sales professional who does not develop the habit of analysis and self-analysis is not worth much in the long run.

It is interesting, by the way, to watch and then post mortem with a home office visitor who has taken all or part of a presentation while visiting you in the field, whether to demonstrate something to you, try out something new on a prospect, or out of sheer desire not to lose touch. For underneath all else, and no matter how experienced your visitor, the home office visitor should be asking himself or herself the same basic personal questions you always ask yourself. How was I going in, and in those vital first few minutes? Did I see the right things, and ask the right questions? Did I get real contact and empathy? How was my presentation? my objection handling? Did I smoke out and handle the real objections? How was my timing and handling of the close? When was that sale made—or lost? If made, did I sell everything I could? If lost, what about next time? If your home office visitor is or has been a sales professional, that is; failure to ask these key questions will be a clear indication, if not.

GOAL-SETTING

Closely tied to analysis and self-analysis is the personal goal-setting habit, and the development of a pattern of reaching and exceeding the goals you set. This applies to sales goals, certainly, but goes beyond sales goals to career-building matters.

Sales professionals certainly get enough practice in goal-setting and achievement. The budgeting process often seems to go on all year every year, with seller and management continually discussing and revising quotas of all kinds. Indeed, between quotas and contests, there are often all kinds of daily, weekly, monthly, quarterly, and yearly goals to meet, for sales, resales, lead conversions, and expansions, and even sometimes for the numbers of presentations, calls, and referrals you make. It often all seems like far too much, and the paper it all generates seems part of a field paperwork blizzard.

Some of the paper generated by management really is excessive, the product of ineffective staff work and too many computer-generated information requests generated by cumbersome management information systems. Yet at the heart of the matter there are real needs here: management's need to know, control, and motivate; your need to feel that some people care about you and how you are doing out there, sometimes lonely and often rejected. Exceeding company quotas, winning contests, even writing some of those never-ending reports all provide a meaningful set of organizational attachments, even while you pursue your work as an essentially independent entrepreneur.

Company-provided goals also provide a minimum set of standards from which you can begin to set your own goals, your own quotas and standards. And that is an indispensable lifelong activity—indispensable in selling, and indispensable in career building. Yet in career building, you have none of the help so routinely available in selling. In career building, you are not an integral part of an ever-developing, continually reevaluated set of company-wide plans. No one is there to help you analyze your personal career situation as managers, trainers, and home office people help you analyze sales. You get no leads, brochures, or planned presentations; you meet no quotas and win no contests. No one continually insists that you consistently sell benefits, sharpen your persuasive skills, continually update your knowledge, plan your career and work your plan, as you do in selling. In short, no one pushes you to apply all the enormously valuable things you know how to do to the question of building a career in selling and beyond, if you wish.

It is necessary to do it all yourself, as any other independent professional does. There is a business and financial side to every professional career; and in the largest and longest-term senses, sales professionals are engaged in the development of their own businesses and professional careers, whether employed by others or operating independently. When sales professionals go fully into management, they pursue management careers; that is a whole different game, requiring new skills and approaches to be added to the existing sales career skills. When they go into their own selling businesses, they become small business owners as well as sales professionals, and that, too, is quite another game, added to the existing selling career. For major lifelong professional planning, though, the main approaches are the same: it all really starts with the understanding that you need to do it all yourself and for yourself, just as if you were a much larger business entity.

Long-term planning is much easier and more effective if, early in your career, you have developed a pretty good idea of the directions in which you want to go. Fairly early, anyway; it is rather difficult to make a meaningful long-term plan, with interim goals along the way, if you are terribly uncertain about main personal drives and goals. That is what we are discussing here: overall personal plans five, ten, and twenty or more years out, with rather carefully thought through and specific plans year by year that are fully reassessed at least yearly and, in some respects, as often as monthly. Yes, that can sound somewhat unrealistic to those who rely upon their companies to plan their business lives for them, and who plan their personal, business, and financial lives hardly at all. But it will seem only rational to those who understand that the difference between sound planning and poor planning can also be the difference between a life full of as many satisfactions as living can bring and a life that consists of a long, frustrating, exhausting stumble uphill, punctuated by endemic financial and personal crises, with later years spent as a de facto ward of an uncaring state. So we do our level best to plan as well as we can, trying to learn how to reflexively ask ourselves as many of the right questions as possible every step of the way, and counseling with ourselves as we would counsel with others.

These are difficult times for American business organizations. That has been so for well over a decade now; it will in all probability continue to be so for many more years. We have watched the dismantling of considerable portions of the American industrial system, the erosion of much of the once-superb American infrastructure, and the partial demoralization of much of the American management cadre, as most American companies have turned more and more toward the pursuit of short-term profits, rather than pursuing the traditional goals of both profit and growth. We can expect that pursuit of short-term profits to continue, with continued adverse effects. We can also expect international competitive pressures in most industries to accelerate that process of adulteration of materials and shoddiness of workmanship known as "hidden inflation," which daily debases American products and services, thereby worsening competitive positions and providing sales professionals in many industries with goods that create ever more problems and are ever more difficult to sell. Increasingly, the American economy, in both private and public sectors, fails to renew its industrial base and large portions of its infrastructure—and becomes in several very important ways antique and uncompetitive.

It may get worse, it may get better; but it will not change very substantially for quite some time. Yet, at the same time, there are very healthy American industries as well as many sick ones, and many healthy American companies—and many opportunities for career building in sales. But they are harder to find, and cannot be taken for granted. It is no longer realistic to expect to work for a few companies early in a working life, one or two more in your thirties and forties, and set yourself into a job in your late forties or early fifties, to move only for an extraordinary opportunity. That can happen; it will happen for some who are working in healthy industries and companies. For most, it is far more realistic to assume that one who enters upon a career in selling also enters upon a perpetual consideration of multiple job opportunities, inside and outside of current employment.

That means considerably more heightened sensitivity to career opportunities and pitfalls than was necessary when the perceptions of those now in senior sales jobs were formed. This, in turn, means that some advisors, who have kept up with new realities, can continue to be enormously useful, but that other advisors should be looked upon with new skepticism. It means that recruiters, who yesterday might have been thought to be terrible time wasters, today should be looked upon as indispensable adjuncts to astute career building. It also means that professional meetings, courses, and contacts of all kinds take on a new career-building significance, for each is also a job mart. One should burn no bridges at all, if at all possible. The need to build a web of long-term business friends—now called networking—is more important than ever. And the interpersonal and political skills underlying all this must be kept sharp as never before. Upward career mobility can happen almost by accident, a happy combination of being in the right place at the right time and doing an excellent job. But it is, as it always has been, rather unusual for it to happen that way. Normally, it takes a good deal more than that. And today, as never before, it takes careful and constant self-assessment and astute opportunity-seeking to protect your career and help it grow.

ASSESSING GROWTH

Opportunity-seeking starts with knowing what you wish to seek and how you wish to seek it. Putting it a little differently, we face the same basic career direction questions all our working lives: Where do I want to go? How do I want to go about getting there? The contexts and answers certainly change a great deal for most of us during the course of a life and career, but the basic questions remain the same. As age, experience, and accomplishment grow over the years, some of us come to prefer these questions cast in terms of processes: What do I want to be doing for the next five years? the next ten? For the rest of my career? For the rest of my working life?

After basic career choices have been made, many—or perhaps most—working professionals do not ask those kinds of questions systematically and repeatedly. If faced with personal or career crises, they may be forced into a re-examination of basics. But systematic and repeated re-examination of career choices is not a habit that develops out of circumstances; it is a matter of conscious planning, a habit that can only develop out of a set of self-analytical reflexes. Yet without asking and re-asking those basic questions, there can be no serious career planning. There is only a reach for each successive promotion or seemingly advantageous job change, even though our personal desires and needs may change enormously over the years, and even though career survival itself in these times may depend on careful long-term analysis and re-analysis of goals and personal situations.

Sales professionals have a wide variety of career and personal goals, and the two are intertwined. The most dedicated young college graduate determined to subsume all to career is merely failing to see personal goals. Even the youngster who announces that he or she is determined to sell up a storm, make a million dollars a year, and go on to preside over a major corporation usually carries a rather romantic view of corporate and personal power, prerogatives, and status, and secretly wants to impress his or her loving family and all the kids on the block.

These basic personal goals questions underlie all the rest. For the answers to the host of questions that add up to "How am I doing?" must always be related to the basic goals questions, if they are to make any sense at all. Personal goals change in a rapidly changing world; grabbing the brass ring on the merry-go-round does not mean much if you have decided that the merry-go-round is not where you want to be. That promotion into sales management working out of the home office of a New York-based company may not really turn out to be what you wanted if, between the time you started trying for it and the time you received it, you have decided that New York is not the place for you, and that the Southwest is where you want to put down roots and stay. The decision to put down roots anywhere may change the basic career game for you so much that you want to re-examine some seemingly basic goals. Maybe you want to find a company headquartered in the Southwest and settle into it, with a view toward developing your own independent representative operation there in later years.

Sometimes your choice of industry will restrict your mobility, overriding other concerns. Perhaps you above all want to work with books, even though you know that many portions of the publishing industry are desperately sick, that many companies will not survive, and that you could make a lot more money now and have far better future prospects as a sales professional in another, healthier industry. Then the decision to stay in publishing, which makes no sense at all without the desire to stay with books, may not only be defensible, but the only one you should make. You will still look for a relatively healthy company to work with, and try to grow with it as best you can under considerably adverse circumstances, but your basic decision has been to stay with books, and try to get where you want to go in an admittedly difficult vehicle, the publishing industry.

People have all kinds of reasons for developing and then changing these kinds of basic desires as the years go by. What is indispensable is to develop the ability to recognize your own basic desires, assume the ability to reach them, and continue to reassess them as they change, for change they will. Concentrating as Americans do upon personal relationships, it is easy for most of us to see that relationships change quite naturally as life patterns develop. We easily see that marriage relationships, sibling relationships, and all kinds of other personal and family desires and relationships change. What is not so easy to see is that, by the same token, it is entirely natural that career matters are also deeply affected by life experience and changes in personal goals. The key thing is to recognize the attitudes and assess the changes in them that do occur. How? By engaging in more or less continual self-analysis. By that we mean not psychotherapy, but rather developing the habit of continually asking oneself the right questions, again and again, throughout a lifetime. "Where do I want to go?" then properly becomes "Where do I want to go as I see myself, my needs, and my desires now?" "How do I want to go about getting there?" then properly becomes "How do I want to go about getting there as I see myself, my needs, and my desires now?"

In business, we routinely develop five- and even ten-year development plans, revising those plans yearly or even every six months. And we routinely do rolling yearly forecasts as budgets, reassessing those budgets quarterly, sometimes even monthly, or whenever extraordinary business developments make such reassessments necessary.

A career cannot be planned quite as easily as that. Nor can it be planned and kept up with as easily and as relatively precisely as the kind of personal financial planning suggested in Chapter 9. Yet, it can be planned. The principles of periodic and systematic questioning and reassessment are the same; the need to do a rolling revision of plans based on current outside and inward realities is the same. So, too, is the need to recognize the interpenetration between the "How am I doing?" questions and the more basic "Where do I want to go and how do I want to go about getting there?" questions.

Which leads us to the whole body of questions that, for serious and continuous career building, must be asked of oneself periodically. By periodically, we mean at least yearly in a formal sense; as a practical matter, these are the kinds of questions that should recur reflexively and quite naturally as career and personal events occur. Once we get into the habit, these are the kinds of matters that are under perpetual review as we do whatever else we normally do. All are in a very real sense "How am I doing?" questions; all are inextricably intertwined with the basic "Where do I want to go and how do I want to get there?" questions.

REVIEWING CAREER STATUS

Most career-related questions are incapable of being answered in hard, precise ways; in this they differ greatly from sales performance and personal financial growth questions. That is a key reason for focusing first on the easiest to answer and therefore easiest to assess career question: "How am I doing financially?" While progress in this area, year by year, is not necessarily a crucial determinant, in the long run money tells us a great deal about how we are doing. In a very real sense, we sell our time and talent in an overlapping set of national and world markets, composed of all those who might buy the use of that time and talent. In the long run, therefore, marketplace supply and demand factors tend to deeply affect levels of pay; comparative pay within an industry, and among those doing similar jobs in different industries, provides most revealing information as to how we are doing in the national and international marketplaces in which we work. And in addition to comparative pay, we can measure how we are doing in real dollars, very specifically and unsentimentally. In Chapter 9, we discuss a wide range of money matters, including the total sales compensation package and long-term personal financial planning. Here, we are limiting our discussion of money matters to the question of how to measure career progress. We use some of the same examples and cover some of the same ground in both places; what is different are breadth and context. It is important to see money matters both ways—in terms of career progress and in terms of lifetime financial planning—and therefore both sections should be read carefully, and considered separately in their differing contexts.

During the last 15 years, prices as measured by the Consumer Price Index have just about tripled, meaning that the dollar we spend today is worth about one third of what it was worth 15 years ago. (As you read this book, those basic facts may have changed somewhat, but they are unlikely to have changed very much for the better.) Therefore, a sales professional who is now making $60,000 per year is—in real pre-tax, or gross income, dollars—earning about as much as one who was making $20,000 per year 15 years ago.

That is a pretty staggering fact; it means that many people who have spent their whole careers moving up from $20,000 to $60,000 (or whatever the equivalent tripling of income has been) have in fact turned out to be marking time financially; even though they may carry far larger responsibilities now, they are making no more real money than they did 15 years ago. It was not quite that simple, of course; many made real gains until the mid-1970s, and then lost all their gains and often much more as the pace of inflation leaped ahead of increases in most incomes. Others, who did not keep up with the pace of inflation as well as this, have suffered quite substantial losses during most of the 1970s and 1980s. Someone who is now making $40,000 is making $13,000 –16,000 in the real dollars of 15 years ago.

These are difficult facts for most of us to face. But without facing them, there can be no realistic answer to "How am I doing financially?" That income went up 10% last year may signify a real increase in pay, if the inflation rate last year was 6%. But if the inflation rate was 10%, that was only a cost of living increase. And if the inflation rate was 12–14%, that was no real raise at all, but a loss, no matter how large the congratulations that came with the seeming raise, or how many sales contests you won.

If all those working in the American economy gained or lost equally, this would be an empty question. But that is not the way it works; varying rates of real increase or decrease occur, often relating less to individual merit and progress than to company, industry, and career choices. A company that is doing badly may not be able to significantly raise the compensation level of even its most successful sales professionals; it may indeed require pay cuts, which have a multiplied impact in periods of rapid inflation. In this period, many whole industries are sick; sellers working in those industries are often disadvantaged vis-à-vis managers in other industries. Sometimes whole professions are more or less advantaged than others. For example, sales professionals as a group have not kept up with the incomes and tax-advantaged practice-building possibilities of people in the health care professions, but they have stayed well ahead of the general income levels of people in such professions as social work, urban planning, and writing.

With all that in mind, "How am I doing financially?" is a little harder to answer. Certainly, if your cash compensation is growing at a faster rate than the pace of inflation, you are at least making some progress. In more sophisticated terms, more important for those with higher incomes, if your total compensation package is growing significantly faster than the pace of inflation, you are making some progress—but that is somewhat harder to assess than direct cash compensation. What a pension or profit-sharing plan will be worth at some future date is often hard to evaluate, especially in difficult times; and whether or not today's strong-looking company will be there to honor its long-term commitments when you retire may be questionable. With cash compensation needed more than ever, and with tomorrow's ability to honor today's promises shakier than ever, it is surely most realistic to look hardest at cash compensation—cash in hand now —when assessing financial progress in your career each year. Cash compensation is, therefore, by far the firmest and most determinable single aspect of career progress in this period.

That emphasis on increasing the amount of real dollars you are paid each year has some very significant career-building implications. Among other things, it means that a job move within one's current company that does not result in significantly higher immediate real-dollar income is to be regarded very warily indeed; we can no longer expect that moves into management from field selling, or moves to greater responsibility within a field organization, will more or less automatically result in higher real incomes, even when they are accompanied by moves to higher compensation grade levels within a company. More than ever before, higher compensation in current companies under these conditions becomes a matter of negotiation, rather than acceptance of a presumably beneficial status quo, in terms of established salary and organizational structure. For we are now in a time when many companies can reasonably be expected to strongly resist routine real-dollar salary increases, making every attempt to substitute status for money and promises for real-dollars now.

As sales professionals are very much on their own in compensation negotiations, a new stress must be placed on job mobility. Certainly job mobility is a must for defensive purposes in difficult times; it is also a must for those of considerable talent and skill, who can do better elsewhere than in their present companies. Putting it a little differently, we are in a period in which many companies are not willing or able to hold their best people with real-dollar compensation increases, and in which each of us must be ready to move to other companies for real-dollar compensation gains. Under these circumstances, moving from job to job rather frequently is no longer as clearly inadvisable as it was in an earlier day; instead, it becomes a necessity for many people, as companies and whole industries falter and become unable to move their people up as well as do other companies and industries.

No, we do not suggest moving every year or two to a different company; that is still properly described as sterile job-hopping, leaving you with too little time to really build anything anywhere, and raising a serious question as to whether or not you are capable of doing so. We do suggest a far more serious attempt than ever before to keep other company and industry job options wide-open, to spend time adroitly increasing those opportunities, and to come to regard job moves as quite natural and healthy, rather than fearing each move as a step off into an unknown world full of hazard. But never burn a bridge. The number of companies that see former employees as somehow disloyal grows smaller every year, as current business realities change old attitudes. More often than ever before, a move to greater real pay and responsibility in a different company or industry ultimately results in a return to a previous company at a higher level. Somehow, those who could not see you for a desired promotion when you were an employee, can easily see you for a job two steps up from that a few years later, when you are returning from a more responsible job in a different company. The career-building logic of our time is not "Stay put, and grow it where you are," but "Move, move, and keep moving until you find something to grow, unless you are lucky or skillful enough to find that early in your career."

REVIEWING COMPANY STATUS

The next career assessment question would, in other times, have been the question of one's own excellent performance. But in these times, a prior question is "How is my company doing?" Excellent personal performance, even if well-perceived, no longer can be relied on to bring desired rewards; companies and portions of companies must be doing relatively well to reward excellent performance. It must often be seen even more narrowly than that, down to "How is my division doing?" and "Does my management have the power to reward my excellent performance, or are they in such difficulty that we are all likely to be swept away in the debacle that is about to occur here?"

In a way, the larger questions are rather easier, although most of us do tend to stick our heads into the sand and refuse to recognize when our companies or operations are in trouble. For example, American industry is full of sales professionals who have had the experience of working within a company that was losing money, or was clearly vulnerable to takeover because it was not making enough money, or was about to be sold by owners anxious to retire, and who refused to recognize that their business environments were about to change, dramatically and sometimes adversely, because of a change of ownership. It is not so hard to study company balance sheets and operating statements to see how your company is doing relative to other companies in its industry, or to keep up with your company's stock as it fluctuates. It is fairly easy to keep up with ownership possibilities in a family-owned company, or with acquisition and divestiture movements within a larger corporate structure; that is some of what home office friends are for. And it is essential for your long-term career that you do all those things. If you are doing rather well, and everyone else is doing very badly, you may be seeing opportunity— but you are far more likely to be seeing a disaster shaping up, in which you will be deeply involved, unless you take early and decisive preventive steps. Not that what you do, or try to do, will always be correct or work out well; but the worst possible error is to make of yourself an uninformed ostrich caught in a corporate sandstorm.

It may be hardest of all to recognize that you are associated with a failing situation. Hope springs eternal; and inertia strongly prevents movement, especially when you are selling well and would, in normal circumstances, be enjoying good income, job security, and excellent future prospects. But it can happen that a seemingly good job situation is, in truth, anything but that—and never more so than in difficult times.

There are no easy answers in this area. Good professionals become identified with their own operations, and develop group goals and loyalties, whether or not things are going well. It is the rare person, indeed, who is able to stand back and coolly recognize that the situation all are trying so hard to save is in fact unsavable, and that it is time to add some distance, transfer, change jobs—in short, to move on. It usually happens far too late, when choices have already been severely limited. Yet, in career terms, it is desirable to cultivate just that sort of analytical ability in all seasons, no matter how deeply involved you are in the efforts of the moment or period. And in this season—a season of prolonged and intractable economic and, therefore, company difficulties—that kind of analytical stance becomes an absolutely necessary career-building and career-saving tool.

How your company is doing and how it is likely to do in the near future is an important estimate to make. You are best able to make job moves when you are doing very well, in a company that itself seems to be doing at least rather well. When a company is visibly doing badly, it often becomes much harder to move up out of it, to the kind of job that is a substantial promotion and increase in real dollar pay. Your desirability and therefore your negotiability are always best when moving from a strong company, and almost always weakest—unless you have recognizably unique or valuable things to offer—when moving from a troubled or failing company.

REVIEWING SELLING SKILLS

And then, in estimating how you are doing, there is you, your attained level of selling skills and demonstrated excellence of performance. Learning how to sell increasingly well is a lifelong enterprise, and one that continuously refreshes those who sell. To some extent, the way that ability is developing is a matter of subjective analysis, of feel, rather than only a matter of how well you are selling. Selling well is certainly basic and indispensable, but no matter how well we are selling, we are best advised to be our own most severe critics; that is the way to continuing excellence. That requires a well-developed habit of self-analysis, of taking a long, cool, critical look at personal performance, day by day, year in and year out. "I'll do that even better next time" requires the ability to make some pretty informed estimates as to how well you did it this time, whether or not a sale was made.

Selling excellence is demonstrated to others by how well we sell and how well we perform all the other tasks associated with selling, including such matters as prospecting, customer service, referral selling, paperwork, and home office relationships. We want to perform excellently, for ourselves and for our own professional development most of all. We also want our excellent performance to be recognized by our superiors and peers, and that requires exceeding quotas, winning contests, and demonstrating sales leadership in every possible form.

Beyond that, making sure that our excellence is recognized is partly a matter of politics and positioning within an organization. How one is currently doing within a company is more than that series of basic and indispensable matters having to do with demonstrated sales excellence, real pay, and the esteem of superiors and peers. Those things are musts; without them there is no progress possible or discernible, and no amount of skill in personal maneuver is likely to prove very helpful in career terms. There are exceptions, of course; only the blind would maintain that American business is free of nepotism, favoritism, sexual exploitation, and assorted bigotries. Yet they are exceptions; the general rule is that at least recognized competence and more often demonstrated relative excellence are openers when dealing with questions of career advancement in most substantial business organizations.

Yet once those basic matters are in place, a substantial number of what can only be called political skills come into play in every organization, as formal and informal organizational structures interpenetrate to form the real motor forces at work in every organization. Therefore, "How am I doing in my current company?" must also be answered in terms of essentially the same kinds of questions that occur to those involved in any other kind of political life. These are questions that involve business friends, mentors, rivals, influences, promises given and received, and the whole web of relationships that characterize every organization.

Therefore, political skills are to some extent part of the career-building side of selling, as they are in other professions, as well. The curricula of our colleges and universities are strikingly deficient in this regard; while Machiavelli is seen and taught as an historical figure, little or no attempt is made in any of the professions to develop those indispensable skills that have to do with motivating and moving the people and organizations we work with in desired directions. We teach a little about propaganda, something of selling, and sometimes (in speech departments) focus on the techniques of persuasion, but hardly at all on intraorganizational persuasion and the skills associated with that practice. It is an enormous gap in the formal education offered the overwhelming majority of professionals, sales professionals among them. True, the skills involved are hard to quantify, graph, program, and otherwise massage with mathematical tools. And true, these skills are all too often rather sanctimoniously viewed by many in academe as somehow indecent, often as the unwelcome underside of American public, commercial, and professional life. But they are indispensable skills, nonetheless; without them, one cannot in the long run function very effectively in a world full of emotional, self-interested, often irrational people, carrying all sorts of conflicting attitudes and interests—in short, ourselves and our co-workers.

In this context, "How am I doing in my company?" requires a sober periodic counting-up of friends and foes among peers and superiors, and an equally sober comparison of relationships now with those of a previous time, probably a year before. And along with that counting-up go some questions: Have I maintained and strengthened relationships with my friends? Have I done anything for each one of them in this last period, or they for me? Have we continued and strengthened our information-sharing and mutual day-by-day support? Have I paid attention to their wants and needs as I would want them to pay attention to mine, or have we let our relationship slip somewhat, assuming quite erroneously that we will "be there" for each other when needed? Have I added any friends? Have I acted as a mentor for others? Have I, in short, properly recognized that friendships must be worked at and have I continued to strengthen mine within the company?

The same sorts of questions apply for superiors, some of whom may be your long-term, in-company sponsors, champions, and advisors—your mentors. All lasting relationships are two-way streets, matters of give and take, of caring about those who care about you, and that applies to those who, at first glance, might seem to want or need nothing from you, while being willing to help you in any way they can. With a mentor, it is often as little as a note or clipping; some seemingly irrelevant talk about the weather and current state of each other's health when you get together at a sales meeting; a baby picture; a golf score; a restaurant recommendation; a shared complaint about the air conditioning—a set of tokens, signifying that you face your world together, rather than quite apart and at arm's length. It may also involve such matters as information-sharing—many a wise, corporate-level old-timer understands the value of networking at least as well as younger and less experienced people who are rapturously discovering, applying, and writing about the technique. Early, sound information delivered by those we trust can, and often does, make all the difference between timely action and far-too-late attempts to piece things together after a costly set of errors. And those who deliver timely information coupled with their own sound insights are demonstrating excellence and are seen quite properly as comers by astute people farther up the corporate line.

A subsidiary question that should accompany this kind of periodic in-company personal evaluation has to do with somewhat intangible—and therefore more difficult to assess—positioning matters. Formally recognized sales leadership is clearly a career builder. But to a lesser extent so are such things as training assignments, new presentation field tryouts, field visits from home office managers, and key account troubleshooting assignments. These bring contact with matters important to management, and considerable exposure to management, exposure that may be worth as much as any other accomplishment in a given year, even though it may be only two or three days in the field with a home office marketer anxious to try out a new presentation. Therefore, further proper questions are: Have I had any kind of fruitful or potentially fruitful special assignments and exposures in this period? How have they worked out, in career-building terms? If still in progress, what should I see and do to help them work out to my best personal advantage?

CAREER MOVES

The answers to all these kinds of questions make it possible to arrive at a reasonable evaluation of how well you and your company are doing now, and as compared with the last such evaluation. They provide the necessary basis for asking such questions as: Should I be actively seeking an in-company move right now? Am I doing all that I can to build my career in this company at this time? Is this still the right company for me, given my own changing wants and needs, and given internal company, industry, and general economic developments? Or is it really time to move on, to very actively seek affiliation with a different company, in view of current possibilities in my present company, my demonstrated skills and performance level, and the level of opportunities available elsewhere?

The answers to these kinds of major career questions rest in part upon your answers to some other questions that deal with somewhat wider professional and personal matters.

Here we turn to lifelong professional self-development, seen from the viewpoint of practical career mobility. For it is when you encounter questions like these that you really begin to see the importance of keeping up with the industry and function within which you are currently working, with the broad contexts within which you and all other sales professionals are working, and with the profession of selling as selling. When you make a move, you may hold yourself out as expert in a field or industry; of at least equal importance, you hold yourself out as a wholly mobile sales professional, to whom "selling is selling." And to the extent that you have consistently pursued lifelong professional self-development, you are able —by demonstrating who and what you are to a prospective new company —to back up your central claim to being a professional.

That is particularly important when moving from the field into management, or from one industry to another. Then all the questions about in-house and outside courses, degrees, professional association activities, and the breadth of view demonstrated in that all-important set of face-to-face hiring interviews come up; the question of lifelong professional self-development becomes central.

When we are considering the big question of whether or not to try for an intercompany move, we also find ourselves exploring how well we have pursued our network of outside contacts during our current employment. And it is extraordinarily important that we do just that, quite formally, at least once a year, as part of a substantial "How am I doing?" evaluation. Unless carefully scheduled, this question can and does easily get away from most sales professionals, who quite naturally focus on current colleagues and job-related matters, rather than making the effort to keep up with and further develop a wide network of career friends and contacts far beyond their present companies. The person who does let this kind of networking activity slip away, despite good early intentions, is in a very poor defensive position should anything go seriously wrong with current employment. Even if a decision to move has been made from strength and the realization that better opportunities exist elsewhere, such a person is in a seriously deficient job-seeking position.

This is when you test the network of professional friends you believe you have built up over the years; find out whether the potential job contacts you have cultivated are really worth anything. This is when you see if the customer or recruiter who sought you last year meant it when he or she begged you to "get in touch" if you ever changed your mind and decided to make a move. This is when you find out that you should have developed a network and cultivated job contacts, if you had not previously done so.

When the will to do so is present, a network of potential career-builders is very easy to build, the ways of going about it very easy to see. Many of our best lifelong career contacts are those with whom we have previously worked, people who were part of our internal networks over the years and who have moved up or on to other companies. It is often as simple and direct as following a mentor to another job; the new marketing director reaching back into a previous company or division for key sales personnel is a common phenomenon in the business world. Often the connections are considerably more circuitous, however. Peers who once worked together and have remained friends over the years may inform and recommend each other for job after job in an ascending spiral for decades.

So, too, can our customers and competitors become part of our network of potential career-building contacts. A satisfied and admiring customer is often, later on, an equally satisfied and admiring employer or source of employers. A competitor who has every reason to respect your work over the years may be very happy to lure you away from your current employer. A standard caution applies here, though: never engage in job-changing conversations with customers or competitors unless you are very serious about considering a move, for no matter what people tell you about confidentiality, the word soon enough gets around in an industry that you are considering a move. And that can hurt your company, and your own sales performance. People buy you, your company, and your products, all mixed together in their minds; and if you no longer think enough of your company to want to stay, and will not be there when they need you to handle a problem, they will not buy nearly as readily from you as before.

Excellent career contacts can also come from outside professional contacts. People who find themselves sharing and enjoying a weekly or monthly table at a periodic professional luncheon, quite often expand their contact and become valuable professional friends.

And then there are the recruiters. Not those who will take anywhere from several hundred to a couple of thousand of your dollars to run tests and perhaps help you find a job if you are involuntarily unemployed, but those who are engaged by companies to find excellent sales professionals to fill vacant or soon-to-be-vacant selling and sales management positions, and therefore call you. They are all too often pejoratively described as headhunters, the implication being that they will do anything to steal good people from their loving companies. Nonsense; let yourself be headhunted, recruited, or whatever you want to call it. There is no better way to turn up good opportunities; you are never in a better negotiating position than when a company comes to you regarding a new job, rather than vice versa.

Even if you have no intention of making a move, it never really hurts —and can help a good deal—to talk to recruiters. In immediate terms, you may find yourself confronted with an offer too good to turn down, and which you had no idea at all you might receive at this stage of your career. Also, you may very possibly learn a good deal about pay and conditions in other companies and throughout your own and other industries. Recruiters come to know a great deal about many things that sales professionals—and especially excellent professionals who do not move about very often—may not learn so easily in any other way. And in less immediate, but often even more important, terms every recruiter you talk to is a potential job contact should you decide to make a move in the relatively near future. By all means take the time to meet and talk with recruiters. Let them talk; listen hard; ask questions. Each such contact can, in the long run, amount to a considerable expansion of your network of job contacts.

Recruiters can be particularly valuable for a very special reason having to do with the difficult nature of the times. Many of them do tend to specialize in one or two industries, but many work in several industries and keep files reaching across many industries. In this period, characterized as it is by faltering companies and even whole industries in trouble, when you may very much need to be able to reach into other industries as well as into other companies for stable jobs, recruiters can play a considerably enhanced role. An experienced recruiter who knows you and believes in your experience and demonstrated talents can in these times become a prime career-building asset for you, as are all the key people in your network of business and personal friends and contacts.

In difficult times, most of us tend to focus on defensive career moves, as when we try to anticipate personal trouble in a failing corporate situation and attempt to make a job change while still employed and doing well, so that we can move from employed strength rather than from a visibly failing situation or an unemployed position. That is proper—but it is far from the whole story, nor should it be. In good times or bad, there will always be many selling professionals who have the ability to move ahead in desired directions, for excellent selling skills are in great demand in every season. In some ways, it is easier to move ahead in hard times, for then many companies are making sales organization changes, as they try hard to boost lagging sales. Easier, perhaps, but more chancy. To move from a good situation to another, perhaps more promising, situation in hard times may also mean a move from strength to weakness. For when you are doing well in a strong company, you may be attractive to many potential employers, but if you have moved into a new situation that does not work out and need to make another change, that change may be much more difficult to accomplish.

Still, many of us do make changes in pursuit of career goals, rather than purely defensively. Rather thoughtfully, usually; almost all of us are well aware of the potentially disastrous personal problems that can come with an ill-considered change, as when someone with small children who sells in a major metropolitan area and is home almost every night takes on a travel territory and sees the family thereafter mostly on weekends. Yet, with sufficient thought, many make quite substantial job changes in pursuit of career goals. A strong travel territory may mean a good deal more money and far better opportunities for sales leadership than a relatively weak city territory. That can be very important for someone who has children soon headed for college or who is driving toward management. A territory in one region or selling group can be far better positioned than one currently worked, if only because someone is about to retire in the new region.

Similarly, a move to special account handling, or to become part of a national account group, may be much desired, and seen as a necessary move up in terms of career goals, even though a great deal of traveling is involved.

On the other hand, someone who does not particularly want to move into management, and who wants to set down roots in an area and perhaps later move into business as an independent, may be better advised to stay put and develop wide-ranging and deep relationships throughout the business community in the area, and in the process become a well-recognized and valued part of that community. For someone with those kinds of goals, there is no particular value in moving about the country, servicing widely separated accounts, or being part of sales management. Far better then to join every local club in sight, take probably much-needed small business management courses locally to prepare for eventual small business ownership (if that is what you want), and to keep on selling, more and more effectively and lucratively as the years go by. You will, by the way; as you become a fixture in an area, the whole business of selling in that area becomes easier and easier, even aside from the fact that you are getting better and better at it.

Small business ownership, even as an independent sales representative, is a whole other thing; that is not recognized as often as it should be. Aside from capitalization needs, there are a wide range of financial and business skills that are little needed when employed by a company, even though you are an entrepreneurially minded sales professional employed by that company. Very good sales professionals can very easily fall flat on their faces as independent sales representatives running their own organizations, unless they take the time and trouble to learn what they need to know as small business owners. That is partly a matter of apprenticeship and partly a matter of formal preparation—the details are beyond the scope of this work, and the subject of another work in this series. Let it suffice that the best possible course of action for a sales professional headed for a personal independent representative's business is to go to work selling for an established independent representative organization and work at that for at least six months, or better a year, paying close attention to how the business side of the independent representative business works, including the smallest operational details. At the same time, courses at a local business school will be an excellent idea, aimed at helping you to understand how to start and operate a small business.

So, too, a move into management is a very different thing from selling —and this is fully recognized far too seldom by those who want to make that move. To a significant extent, that is a matter of relative professional prestige in organizations that are, after all, run by managers. The organizational expectation is that a very good sales professional will quite naturally want to become a field sales manager and then perhaps move into general management. That expectation is, to some extent, often also carried by family, friends, and the world at large, as management is a profession carrying considerably higher prestige value than does selling in this culture at this time.

But there is no particular reason, other than prestige, for someone who enjoys selling and is very good at it to change careers—for that is what a move into management is—unless there is real desire to do so, rather than the expectation of others to satisfy. Some management people—those up at the tops of substantial organizations—make more than do all but a very few sales professionals, but those sales professionals who move into management are usually far less equipped to move to the tops of organizations as managers than are those trained as professional managers. That will be more and more true as time goes on. Most field sales managers, and even many national sales managers, make less than the top producers in their own sales organizations, work at least as hard, see their families a good deal less, and have less job security than do their top sales producers. Indeed, since most sales managers were top producers before they became managers, many actually earn less than they did as field representatives. And they are often low people on management's totem pole, quite overshadowed by home office people of all kinds, while as top sales producers they were treated with little less than adulation for being the geese that laid the golden eggs for the whole organization.

The necessary skills are quite different, too. Ideally, a top producer is made into a sales manager so that replication can occur, with the selling ability of one turned into the selling skills of many. But the truth is that not terribly many people who are very good at selling are also very good at training and leading a sales organization. And even fewer are very good at home office relations and policy matters. Selling is selling, but management is management. It requires a considerable body of quite different training, people-handling, supervisory, and leadership skills than does selling, and a great deal more tolerance for intracorporate matters and the development of necessary intracorporate political skills. The truth is that many superb selling professionals operate as entrepreneurially minded independent businesspeople in their own territories, but are entirely misplaced as cogs in a large corporate wheel, and have little in the way of management skills when they make the mistake of becoming part of management.

So—look before you leap. And if you do decide to leap, be prepared to learn a whole new profession on top of the selling profession. A sales management person is a dual professional, just as is a computer designer, engineer, accountant, or copywriter who moves from any other functional skill into management. In a very real sense, moving into management involves a new period of on-the-job apprenticeship; it should also involve a good deal of additional formal training and the cultivation of quite new self-development reflexes. Again, the details are beyond the scope of this work and are the subject of another work in this series, but understand that you are entering a new profession when you enter management.

If you do decide to try to move into management from selling, your move is most likely to be in-company, rather than directly into another company, unless it is into a much smaller company in which you both sell and manage, typically growing a selling organization from scratch. If it is directly into another company in a full managing position, though, then you are attempting the most difficult of tasks, for you are moving into a new profession and a new company or even industry simultaneously, and have an enormous amount to learn very swiftly, all while you are charged with producing sales. Within your own company it can often be done a little more gradually, using your own demonstrated sales excellence and your web of intracompany supportive contacts—your network, that is— to help you make the move you want.

Sales excellence first, of course; without that, there is no real hope of a move into sales management, no matter how good your supportive network might be. There is no better way to bring yourself to the attention of top management than to be a consistent sales leader and contest winner. It guarantees that you will be talked about by everyone in the home office marketing group, right up to and including top marketing management. And beyond—many top management people want to know everything they can about sales results and sales leaders, quite correctly understanding that nothing at all will go right without sound and consistent selling.

Sales leaders are also those in the field force who get direct access to top marketing and general management. A sales leader who wins an all-expenses-paid trip to a watering place is also usually presented with an opportunity to spend some very personal time with top management. In that kind of situation, top management is always sizing up the winners with sales management in mind, now or in the future. Sales meetings present similar opportunities, but of a lesser nature.

Sales leadership also carries with it the top management field visit, to try out a new presentation, to get a first-hand look at how all is working in the field, or to look you over with sales management in mind. Such a visit brings with it both major opportunity and major hazard for those seeking management, and should be treated with extreme care. Which means being on your best behavior as regards such potentially disabling factors as overdrinking and complaining, and making very sure that you sell something—or several somethings—while you are working together in the field. That means setting up as many promising appointments as possible before the visit, even if it means a certain distortion of activity in the period before your visitor arrives, and a certain amount of possible overbooking during your time in the field together. Work extremely hard and effectively, do not worry about tiring your visitor, and make some sales. There is nothing quite so satisfying to a visitor (especially a top management visitor) as to be able to tell everyone in the home office, in loving detail, about the sales you made together in the field. Your visitor is likely to remember those live field sales—and you—for years, as he or she goes through all the obligatory meetings, briefings, performance appraisals, paperwork storms, and marathon telephone conversations that so characterize the life of the modern American manager.

Never ask for a move into management during a field visit. Never complain, no matter how justified your complaint about policy or personnel might be. Never attack anyone else in the company. Nobody wants to bring a pushy complainer, whiner, or backbiter into management. If asked about management aspirations, answer directly. If not, say nothing about it; your feelings will usually be quite apparent to experienced people. If not, and they want to know, they will find some way to gently ask, without necessarily offering.

If you do want to move into management, there are likely to be people who will help you along the way, some of whom you will have cultivated and some of whom came quite naturally, without much prior cultivation. First among them is likely to be your manager, who may recommend you for training assignments, which train you as much for management as they prepare your trainees for selling. Your manager is also very often able to recommend a successor on transfer, promotion, or retirement, and will be listened to very closely.

Help will also come from those of your peers who have moved into management before you, and from such sources as home office trainers and marketing people you have worked with over the years. If you do want to move into management, and are a sales leader, there are always many ways to make your desire known and listened to, and a very good chance that you will be able to move in that direction.

PROFESSIONAL SELF-DEVELOPMENT

Professional self-development is by far the most long term and also one of the most important of the career-building essentials. We refer to professional self-development, rather than professional education, deliberately. For professional education has come to be widely used as synonymous with *formal* professional education, that which is *taught,* whatever the teaching form adopted. And from a personal point of view, that tends to stand the matter on its head, to the detriment of consistent and lifelong self-educational efforts, the success of which must be measured by what is learned and applied successfully in life, rather than by what is taught. To say this does not denigrate the role of the teacher or of the school in which teaching takes place; it is only natural for institutions to measure success in their own institutional terms, rather than attempting very seriously to go deep into the subsequent practical careers of their students to attempt to measure what has been learned. In truth, that would be too much to expect—institutions should be expected, alas, to self-justify, rather than self-criticize, for that is intrinsic to their natures.

From the individual's point of view, all selling education is self-education, whether secured formally or informally, and at whatever stage of one's career. Whether you follow a course of study eventuating in a marketing or distribution degree, take a refresher course in or out of your company, or accrete on-the-job experience, the extent of your resulting development depends upon how well you learn the material at hand. Putting it a little differently, it is quite possible to take courses, secure degrees, work in the field, and learn relatively little. It is also possible to spend relatively little time in formal courses, accrete experience, and learn a great deal. For, while selling skills and attitudes can help be developed by formal courses, selling is still, and will be in the foreseeable future, one of the few great remaining apprenticeship occupations, with its most important skills and lifelong attitudes learned on the job.

We should distinguish here between education and credentials. A bachelor's degree is a necessary credential; it is now openers for most beginning professional selling jobs. But that degree, by itself, is nothing more than a credential; its holder may or may not have acquired much that will prove useful in the pursuit of a selling career.

For those who sell, professional self-development is mainly a matter of sustained lifelong attention to the self-development that can come from day-to-day practical experience, if that experience is seen as a source from which learning can flow. If, on the other hand, day-to-day experience is treated so pragmatically that generalizations are not habitually drawn from it whenever possible, very little learning results. Then it scarcely matters how much formal training is joined to practical experience, for little personal development takes place.

It is not really usual for us to think this way. We tend to think of learning as something for the classroom; the practical world is somehow different. That, too, is only natural. After all, most of us spend our early years embedded in educational establishments that develop that point of view, with very little opportunity to develop self-generating learning attitudes. Yet, as working professionals, we desperately need self-generating learning attitudes, if we are to grow as we can and should in a fast-changing world. That central contradiction between early educational modes and lifetime educational needs haunts most of us all our lives. It need not; but it requires clear understanding and considerable initiative to surmount the early disabilities we carry.

Yet even while recognizing the primacy of experience, we must also recognize the need for lifelong continuing formal education, to keep up with the pace of change in a world characterized by accelerating technological changes and a worldwide information explosion. In addition, people who visibly pursue lifelong formal continuing education are perceived as more hirable and promotable than those who have not; that is one of the facts of life and work. Also, if you may want to move into management or into your own selling business, you can profit greatly by preparing yourself for such a move with appropriate formal courses, which you will join with practical experience later on.

Many professions in this period are faced with similar continuing professional self-development needs. In some professions, such as medicine, that need stems from the enormously swift pace of change in medical science and related areas; the doctor who does not keep up may literally lose lives that might otherwise have been saved. In other areas, such as law, it is the interplay of legislative, regulatory, and judicial materials that make it absolutely necessary for lawyers in many substantive areas to keep up or fail to represent and advise their clients properly. In profession after profession, it becomes increasingly clear that competence depends much upon continuing professional self-development. For some professions and in some jurisdictions, such professionals as doctors and lawyers are legally required to take continuing professional education courses; California is one state that has been a pioneer in this area.

Sales professionals, as of this writing, face no such legal requirements. But selling shares with other professions the momentum created by both an accelerating pace of change and rapidly developing public attitudes as to the desirability of continuing education. That is why continuing education is such a widespread movement in American business, with many organizations offering it in various forms, including the American Management Association, a large number of graduate and undergraduate colleges and universities, and several thousand independent educational organizations of all kinds. They offer everything from hard knowledge courses in computers, mathematics, and financial analysis to highly questionable courses and traveling seminars on the latest fads in the manipulation of yourself and others.

Once again, it is desirable to distinguish sharply between credentials and useful learning. In the area of continuing professional education, the overwhelming emphasis is upon learning; yet even here, credential seeking often plays a part. Someone who takes courses part-time as a matriculant in pursuit of a business degree can and often does pursue learning and credentials simultaneously, with the courses completed—even well short of a degree—counting considerably in promotion plans on a present job and in a resume. Someone who secures an advanced marketing degree often finds doors opened, even on a current job, that were closed before, although the level of knowledge and professionalism achieved the day before the degree was earned is much like it the day after. The degree, in that respect, then becomes a matter of status—not your perception of self, but how you are perceived by others.

Many courses yield credits called Continuing Education Units. Such credits do not, at this writing, lead toward any kind of generally recognized degree, in the sense that the BA and MBA degrees are widely accepted degrees, granted by institutions of higher education, operating within a whole accrediting and legitimizing apparatus. Courses are given by thousands of organizations unaffiliated with accredited institutions of higher education. Many of these courses are very useful indeed; some are not. Yet even in this area credentials are often gathered, with companies viewing current and prospective employees more favorably if such courses are part of a work history and resume.

As a practical matter, however, the relative utility of such courses is the most important thing about them. Someone who takes a relevant professional education course is very often informed and made more valuable to his or her company by that course. Such courses are particularly useful where practical experience has been light, and you are not a recent business graduate who has just taken relevant courses. The sales professional who wants to move into management can be helped a good deal by showing current interest, aptitude, and knowledge, as evidenced by relevant completed courses.

A very practical and personal note here. Many companies will finance or help finance continuing professional self-development efforts on your part, all the way from the company that routinely sends top and middle managers to a business school summer seminar, all expenses paid, to the company that matches your tuition contributions in pursuit of a graduate marketing degree. Company practices in this area are important to explore when considering a job offer. And such matters can also be part of the substance of negotiation between you and a prospective new employer or your current one.

Professional association memberships also have a role to play. While they are most often seen as career-building tools, they can also be self-developmental tools. The extent to which that can be true varies greatly; an individual chapter may be moribund, or it may be an active organization, with useful exchanges of ideas and experiences, interesting speakers, and in the long term provide a good deal of valuable material. A national organization may do little more than run a showy convention once a year; or it may run a large body of continuing professional education meetings, seminars, and large formal courses, itself or in conjunction with colleges and universities. Alert modern companies normally encourage their people to participate actively in appropriate professional organizations, and often pay membership fees, encourage attendance at meetings and conventions at company expense, and act as sponsors of association educational activities. It is useful to encourage your company in this, and participate actively yourself, as part of both continuing professional self-development and career building.

Professional self-development also very much includes understanding and using the changing language of modern business. As a personal and practical matter, sales professionals must have excellent speaking, reading, and writing skills in standard (sometimes called "university") English. Let us hasten to add that we are not practicing "elitism" or "cultural imperialism" when we urge this. We strongly urge those who for good reason want to be expert in such special languages as Black English, the several regional English dialects spoken in the United States, and for that matter the different languages spoken by the many ethnic groups comprising our culture and people to pursue that goal, agreeing that plurality and diversity are essential to the unfolding of the unique American experience. At the same time, we must very strongly say that the language of business, as is true of most of the professions, is standard English, and will be standard English for the foreseeable future. All the main ideas expressed in business, all the main information, and all the sublanguages developed by specialists use standard English. All memos, reports, studies, proposals, letters, and promotion materials are written in standard English, and evaluated by people who accept standard English as "correct." The sales professional who does not have a wide vocabulary and flexible command of all the modes of expression in standard English is, in professional terms, considerably disadvantaged. And one who has poor standard English skills must either sharply improve those skills or be substantially and perhaps fatally disabled in professional terms.

There is considerable change in the language of business, even from year to year, as old techniques and objects are described in new ways, and as new processes and technologies call for new descriptors. Much of it is ephemera, here today and changed tomorrow, and it is tempting to dismiss most of it as gobbledegook, and the new terms as buzzwords.

That is a mistake, for new language, however ephemeral, must be learned, if only for purposes of communication with those who use it, pretentiously or otherwise. And very often new language does usefully describe new processes and technologies, although sometimes several different terms will be used to describe the same thing, as language evolves.

For example, a generation ago the term describing marketing efforts directed at selling goods and services to discrete, determinable, and relatively small markets was *special interest marketing*. That became, in due course, *special marketing*. At this writing, the main term describing exactly the same thing is *narrowcasting,* with some also using the term *segmented marketing*. In this period, all four terms are worth knowing, and any one of them is useful in describing the marketing processes involved.

Or take some terms out of the special sublanguage of computers, that fertile source of new and often terribly awkward synonyms for perfectly usable existing terms. During the course of a single selling interview, or in a single communication, you may be exposed to any one of the following related terms: terminal, computer terminal, editing terminal, layout terminal, video-editing terminal, videotext terminal, video-layout terminal, video display terminal, cathode ray tube, or the initials VDT or CRT, which are used even more often than video display terminal and cathode ray tube, for which they stand. The problem is that all those terms may be used imprecisely, and cause complete confusion. For a video display terminal (VDT) is a kind of cathode ray tube (CRT), which is often familiarly called a terminal or somewhat more formally a computer terminal. All the other terms are possible video display terminal uses, depending upon the programming involved. Later on, more sophisticated and therefore much simpler language will evolve; right now, you have to be able to communicate with the imprecise and overlapping set of terms available.

You must be able to move easily in standard English and through to the appropriate sublanguages. You must also have a couple of good reflexes. One is the dictionary reflex; when an unfamiliar term comes up, that reflex calls for turning to a large standard dictionary, a general business dictionary, or a special dictionary for your industry or business.

A second reflex is the keeping-up reflex. One of the most important functions performed by current business and general periodicals is to keep you abreast of relevant current language, language that is so new that it is not to be found in the dictionaries you consult. Very often, language that new is not really defined in the periodicals you read, but can easily be understood in the context of the work in which it appears, and then used and understood as necessary in other contexts.

An old saw has it that understanding the jargon is half the battle in any field. Taking away the wryness implicit in the observation, and replacing the term *jargon* with the word *language,* that old saw has it exactly right. Mastering the language of business is part of being a sales professional.

In sum, astute lifelong professional self-development provides much of the basis for sales professionalism, and helps make it possible to move freely between companies and between industries, as well as into your own business or into management. And make no mistake about it—in these times you will be likely to want to make some moves. It is to the moves themselves that we now turn.

CHAPTER 3
EFFECTIVE JOB CHANGING

Changing jobs well requires a good deal of preparation and the application of vitally important personal selling skills, whether the change sought is voluntary or involuntary, part of upward career mobility or a defensive move away from a troubled situation, inside your current company or to another company.

Professionalism, balance, integrity, personal warmth, a wealth of relevant skills and experience—all this and more we try to project to others during the course of our careers, as we move up and around in the world of American business. In one way or another, we project those images every day as we pursue our careers. When we are involved in selling situations, we are very careful to do so indeed. And when we are seeking employment elsewhere, finding and meeting people who may or may not know something of us and our work, and who have not really worked with us before, we do everything we can to sell our prospective new employers on the immense benefits that will result from hiring us. Putting it a little differently, in all these kinds of situations we engage in persuasion, with the attention, time, and effort we put into them depending largely on how important they are to us and how difficult it may be to persuade others in the situation.

JOB-SEEKING AS SELLING

The essence of job-seeking—whether within or outside your present company—is that you are involved in a selling process, with you as seller. That description in no way vulgarizes or oversimplifies the process; it is a precise description of the main content of the transaction between you and whomever you are trying to convince. Nor is the process simply analogous to selling; it *is* selling, ultimately face-to-face selling. The successful job-seeker uses precisely the same procedures and techniques as does the successful face-to-face sales professional.

Job-seeking involves several kinds of pre-selling activities, many of them alternatives that depend on where you are starting from. It also involves a set of selling processes, again often alternatives, aimed at selling someone or a group on the desirability of seeing you face-to-face. And it involves a second set of selling processes, this one rather straightforwardly applying equally to almost all face-to-face selling situations, in which you and a prospective employer come together, to sell and be sold on the desirability of hiring you above all others. In-house personal evaluations differ in that you are not always seeking to make a sale, but many of the persuasive techniques used face-to-face are indistinguishable from those used in the job-seeking selling process. In-house job seeking often involves some pre-selling activities, normally takes little interview-selling, and involves essentially the same face-to-face skills and understandings that outside job-seeking requires. Two significant features make in-house job-seeking special: you are likely to know a good deal about company, division, and operation. You also may know those who make the hiring decisions, which is a real advantage because empathy is often a good deal easier to achieve this way than with strangers or near-strangers.

Throughout these job-seeking processes, you should bear in mind some basic selling approaches. One is that what you are selling are the *benefits* that hiring you will bring. No, you are not selling *you;* it is both self-denigrating and inaccurate to think of job-seeking as a process by which you sell yourself. You are not for sale; further, nobody should have any reason to buy you. Some, in their eagerness to sell "themselves," lose both the image and the substance of personal integrity, and that is a personal and business disaster. What is for sale is not your time, loyalty, skill, or talent, either; those things have to do with you, not with the benefits that come from hiring you. That you have long and relevant experience is a *feature* of the product that is you; that your experience as part of a constellation of skills and qualities will bring profitable sales is the *benefit* that you bring with you. That you have a wide range of government contacts is a *feature* of the product that is you; how you will use your contacts to sell lucrative government contracts for your new company is the *benefit* that hiring you brings. In short, as in all selling, it is a matter of "putting yourself into the other guy's shoes," and responding empathetically and specifically to that other guy's wants and needs. Those who want to hire will say: "This is what I think she (or he) can do for us." In contrast, "This is her (or his) background and experience," is the language used by those who have not been sold on the benefits that hiring you will bring. *Will* bring, not *can* bring. People hire the sales professional they believe will do the job. If there is an element of doubt in their minds, they will probably keep on interviewing. That is especially true in hard times, when competition is keener and hiring standards stiffen.

This question of selling the benefits that hiring you will bring is central, as it is in all selling, whatever is being sold. It is an understanding that should permeate every aspect of the job-seeking process, providing a proper basis for first approaches with potential job contacts, recruiters, personnel people, and those who hire, whether those contacts are face-to-face or in writing. And it should provide a takeoff point for all self-description, as in resumes and covering letters. People tend to take you at your own self-evaluation; they see the image you habitually project, so will more easily see the truth of high self-evaluation if there is truth in it. But they need help in seeing how to apply your virtues to their business wants and needs; that is why selling benefits is so important.

These questions of understanding and personal attitude lead to another central matter in job-seeking. Put simply, you have to be up and ready for every relevant job-seeking personal contact. The old song has it that "nobody wants you when you're down and out." Quite right; nobody does. Nor when you're tired, ragged, affected in the slightest degree by alcohol, defeated, or down in any discernible way.

In one very significant way, job-seeking is not like professional selling. In professional selling, you have to be able to close sales, day after day, year after year, never losing the sparkle that professionalism brings. In job-seeking, you need only make a single sale; you may not have to make another such sale for a decade or perhaps even for the rest of your life.

The sales professional knows how to stay "up"; it is a basic career need. But as a job-seeker, even a seasoned professional is all too often in a series of unfamiliar situations, in a hurry, sometimes in urgent need of a job change or is unemployed, and easily becomes disoriented by repeated, seemingly personal, rejection. It is very easy to lose your "edge" when job-seeking, to become perceptibly negative, and to thrust yourself upon potential employers as supplicant rather than as large potential asset. All of which results in more negative responses, more self-doubt, and a downwardly spiraling attitude from which it can be very difficult to recover. For it is not so simple as "pumping yourself up" for every interview or contact; real attitudes show, whether we want them to or not.

The essential understanding is that you need only make one sale, and that each situation is new. As an excellent sales professional you know that, and take great care to treat each new prospect as a brand new ball game; the same goes for each employment interview or personal contact. In job-seeking, the last interview is just as important as the first. In each, you need to be calm and cool, warm and eager, professionally distanced and capable of being deeply involved with whomever you are dealing. You need to have researched well enough and to empathize enough so you can put yourself into "the other guy's shoes," and apply your prepared benefits story to your prospective employer's wants and needs. That is the language of selling; it is also the language of successful job-seeking.

Another basic is your physical appearance. As in all selling, appearances convey first what you are and the attitudes you carry to others. The person who arrives in an office or a restaurant on a hot city day somewhat wilted and sweaty, and who does nothing to freshen up before the meeting, will probably unfavorably impress an executive recruiter or prospective employer, stacking the deck in the direction of failure. It is far better to be a few minutes late, those few minutes having been spent in freshening up, than to move into a situation looking and feeling less than your best. It is better yet to arrive early, cool off, and freshen up, providing yourself with a chance to review your research and your benefits story.

Clothing matters are also important in job-seeking. We cover the general question of appearances in Chapter 10. In this context, we should stress only that flamboyance is out; conservatism in dress and demeanor is in. In short, the old rules still apply here, and especially for sales professionals, who must be assessed in terms of their abilities to deal with all kinds of people in many different situations.

Do not, under any circumstances, arrive with even one modest drink under your belt. For some hirers, the slightest hint of alcohol having been taken before arriving at a job interview is a complete disqualifier, the kind of red flag that cannot be disregarded. It is good to remember that, from the prospective employer's point of view, there are all too few personal keys to be perceived in an interview, and many have learned to treat alcohol as the kind of key negative that should not be disregarded.

At a luncheon or after-hours interview, it is wise not to drink anything alcoholic, if possible; stress may cause even one drink to have an unusually strong impact upon your system, and especially on an empty stomach. Sometimes abstention turns out to be impractical, as when a prospective employer really presses you to take a drink as an "ice breaker," and you assess that it is he or she who really wants the drink and would probably feel uncomfortable drinking alone. Then the lightest drink possible is indicated—a glass of wine, or perhaps a tall scotch and soda, to be sipped, rather than swallowed. A second drink can and should almost always be refused. Even if it soon becomes apparent that it is not you, but your interviewer, who may have a drinking problem, it is entirely inappropriate to have more than one drink. That may sound a little rigid, but interviews are easily spoiled by drink, and it takes too much time, trouble, and expense to get an interview with a qualified prospective employer to let a couple of drinks ruin a job opportunity. Even when drink seems to be helping the situation a great deal, as you and your interviewer seem to get on extraordinarily well in an alcohol-induced haze, you are probably ruining your chances; many a job offered the night before has been withdrawn the morning after.

Smoking is not indicated, either, unless your interviewer makes it perfectly clear by smoking that it really is all right. The nonsmoker who gamely invites you to smoke is highly likely to remember only that you did smoke, and that it was bothersome. That is especially true of the virtuous, recently converted nonsmoker, who may be particularly bothered when you smoke. And if you generally smoke cigars, do not do it during an interview; the smell lingers and sours, and all too often so does your prospective employer's recollection of you.

PRE-SELLING MOVES

A great many things can happen before you even try to sell a prospective employer on having you in for an interview. Depending on such matters as positioning and career status, it can be as easy as showing up at a recruiting session or responding affirmatively to an executive recruiter's or friend's call. Or it can be as hard as instituting a full-scale approach to hundreds of strangers via letter and résumé, while answering as many advertisements, some seemingly appropriate, as can be found.

The best way by far to look for any kind of job is from a position of employed strength. That is something that "everybody" knows. On the other hand, it is not something that everybody, or even most of us, take as a guide to action. Again and again, in these times, we see people "hanging in there," in situations that they know very well are fragile, to put it gently. We see companies that have been doing badly for years finally going under in generally worsened economic circumstances, their assets sold off, their employees, including their sales staff, given rather brief notice, and thrown out on the street to make their way as best they can. Our comment is often some equivalent of "Ain't it awful!" Yes, it is.

For sales professionals, staying on is one of the avoidable disasters of modern life. Some will, of course, but you need not. It is far better to seek new employment from the strength of current employment. The same applies for those who are facing adverse circumstances that may block advancement or lead to firings. And so, too, for those who want to make a move as part of career-building, rather than defensive, strategy. The key idea is to move from a position of strength.

Under such conditions, pre-selling moves include activation of previously made contacts outside the current company, and in some instances cultivation of new contacts, as when you very carefully arrange to exhibit at industry meetings and shows, become active in local industry and professional organizations, and attend professional development courses —*after* making the decision, or tentative decision, to seek new employment. Those are all things that should be done routinely in all seasons and in all years; but, being human, many of us tend to do them less than we should, so swift catch-up is indicated. It can be done in that kind of catch-up way, and work well; but it is hazardous, given the pace of business change in these times. The danger is that you will be caught unprepared by recognition of adverse business circumstances and, when you should be activating a host of contacts to swiftly move out of a bad situation while still employed, events will overtake you, while you are still trying to catch up. Then, as so many have found to their painful surprise, the contact who would gladly have recommended you yesterday as a prime acquisition will suddenly find that no openings exist, and will warmly urge you to "keep in touch." The old saw has it that "success builds success." In terms of job recommendations and referrals, that is certainly true. People like to hire and recommend success, or at least seeming success, and all too often have doubts today about unemployed people that yesterday they would have loved to "steal."

Bear in mind that—as every sales manager knows—good sales professionals are hard to find. So hard to find, in fact, that it is often necessary to settle for someone who seems fairly competent rather than the top producer you are really looking for. When you arrive on the scene, highly recommended by another known and respected professional, most good sales managers will feel remiss unless they talk to you. It is part of the sales manager's job to search constantly for people just like you. If you look strong enough, the astute sales manager will make a place for you. But also bear in mind that referral selling in this area usually takes time and planning. And it almost always requires being employed while you are looking.

Pre-selling moves from an employed position often include talking to professional recruiters. It is best here to be talking to recruiters who have called you, rather than approaching those who have not, although most recruiters will assure you that it makes no difference at all who approaches whom first. The fact that previous conversations did not lead to a job is not a bar here; for most recruiters, it only means that the valuable time and effort expended to get to know and sell you can now be made to pay off. And if you have previously turned down job offers obtained through recruiters who have approached you, so much the better. You are often viewed as a commodity of greater value under those circumstances, as long as you are still employed.

All this places a considerable premium upon talking to recruiters who approach you, even though you have no current inclination to seriously consider a job change. You can never know what career-building offers may be out there; and in these times, you never know when you will have to change your mind about the desirability of making a move. An approach to a recruiter is as easy as a phone call, whether to someone you know or to a stranger. So is a broadcast letter approach to recruiting firms, although that is usually an unnecessarily time-consuming approach for people currently employed.

Some of your closest business and personal friends—outside your current organization—can also be approached directly, as they would expect to be able to approach you. But job-seeking contacts with less close business and personal friends and acquaintances require considerably more care. They are not casual matters, for a bad first impression, a bad introduction, or the choice of a bad time may destroy an otherwise promising job contact. Most people know very well that these are difficult times for many, and know that although the basic thrust of your job approach may either be career-building or defensive, it is quite likely in this period to have strong defensive aspects. Even so, and even with most business and personal friends, it is wise to remember that people feel most comfortable selling and hiring strength. When one of your friends recommends you somewhere, it feels far better to be able to say something like "I have someone really great for us; hope I can convince him (or her) to move" than "One of my friends is in real trouble over at AYZ Corp; think we might have anything open?"

If your friend is willing to say anything at all, that is. Or if that treasured job contact you've been associating with week after week at chapter meetings of your professional organization is really eager to hire you. You will seem more desirable to both if they see you as an asset ready to make a move up than as someone about to be fired. A caution here: Even your best friend may have second thoughts about hiring or recommending you if your approach comes over a couple of drinks at the end of a long, dispiriting day, week, or month, and in the form of a desperate plea for help. *The job-selling situation starts at the moment you raise the question of a new job face-to-face with a friend, recruiter, or prospective employer.* Therefore, it has to start when you are entirely up for a new situation, have thought through your benefits story, look your best, and are in all respects ready to make this sale the one—and remember, you only have to sell one.

As a practical matter, that often means making a very difficult decision in private, often in considerable anguish and in a state of mind quite closely approaching despair; or, if it is a basically career-building move, in a state of considerable excitement, accompanied by a couple of celebratory drinks. It is not every day you decide to make a major job move; the day that you do so is not usually a good time to try to do anything about it. Wait, at least until the next morning, before you tell anyone, except perhaps those so close to you that they have helped you make the decision, such as spouse and closest friends. Then think it over again, in the cold light of day. If it still looks like a good decision, it then becomes time to update your résumé, develop a benefits story adapted to each of your current best job prospects, re-examine your wardrobe and the rest of your personal appearance, and begin to make your moves. For while it is true that you only need to sell one, your first few moves are likely to be toward your best prospects, and any one you lose early because of inadequate preparation may have been your best opportunity. In some ways, then, the first few job contacts may be more important than most of the others you may have to try farther on down the line.

Beyond existing networks, possible referrals, and known recruiters are a great many easily qualified prospects; they are as close as the host of newspaper advertisements and the employment agencies. A good sales professional is indeed hard to find, and there are always a great many people out there looking for some.

Many companies believe it best to hire sales representatives directly through newspaper advertisements. Some of your best prospecting will therefore be done directly from the want ads.

Many will be blind ads, with a number to call. (Sometimes these numbers may be in a different city and can be called collect.) The number will often be that of a hotel or motel, and the person you're calling may well be your prospective hirer and perhaps future sales manager, out in the field on a hiring trip.

Thousands of American companies sell nationally, have offices in very few places, and rely on far-flung selling organizations and sales managers who travel a great deal of the time. These managers often hire, train, supervise, and handle some major accounts. In short, they are the marketing organizations of those companies in their sales regions.

When you call that kind of sales manager in answer to a direct advertisement, you're calling a prime prospect. Moreover, you're calling a prime prospect who has held up his or her hand and asked for help. That sales manager wants to hire a solid sales professional, preferably someone who will be a star. Someone who will require little training and retraining, a magnificent closer who will stay on for years and years, making money and building careers for everyone. In short, a money-making top producer —you.

Convincing that sales manager that you're precisely the right person for the job starts the moment you pick up the phone. Yes, you want to know a little more about the job, and the manager wants to tell you more, but the main object of your call is to start the process of selling yourself into that job. You need to sell the interview when you pick up the phone—not yourself, the interview. You can always turn down the job later if offered; what you want is the opportunity to meet that sales manager face-to-face in a selling situation, just like any other prospect.

The sales manager, in turn, is trying to find out whether your experience and telephone personality warrant further investigation, whether or not the face-to-face selling interview is worth going into. Over the phone, he or she will want to know a little about you and your experience, be listening hard to what you say, even harder to how you say it. Your clarity, maturity, and vibrancy are all capable of being communicated over the phone, and can be key factors in selling the interview. There are always general knockout factors a manager has in mind over the phone—too little and the wrong kind of experience chief among them—but most such knockout factors evaporate when a seasoned sales manager hears someone over the phone who sounds good. It's usually rationalized by the manager with "A little light on experience, but sounds great! Can't hurt to take a look." And you've sold the interview.

A few direct advertisements will ask that you send a résumé. By all means, do so, although it is usually an inexperienced manager who goes about hiring that way. If you do get a callback in response to your résumé, respond to it as if you hadn't sent a résumé at all; sell the interview as if you were starting a brand-new selling situation. You probably are.

Managers with open selling jobs also often place them through employment agencies. Many employment agencies specialize in sales and marketing jobs; others have specialists within general agencies who deal exclusively with sales and marketing openings.

Agencies often advertise selling jobs. Promising-looking jobs advertised by agencies may turn out well. On the other hand, they may be come-ons aimed at getting you in to offer you a far less desirable position which the agency is finding hard to fill. In any case, it never hurts to treat agency ads as you would leads supplied by a home office, which must be investigated and qualified. And, as with any lead, the sale starts as soon as you enter the agency office. Although the strength of an agency recommendation rests mainly on the placement person's desire to make a commission by filling the open job with you or someone else, you are the one who supplies the agency person with what to say about you.

Agency representatives, in most instances, are commission sellers, working either on straight commission or on a draw against commission. If they are agency owners, they get income from results, just as do their representatives. They want to sell you into a job and need some selling tools to work with. It's up to you to give them those tools—the ability to describe your appearance as superb, your experience as just right, your motivations as those of a winner. And very often, agency representatives are not as good at selling as the sales professionals they're trying to place; they need a lot of selling help from you. Therefore, when you move into an agency situation, move in ready to sell.

Some agencies are worth prospecting for leads even when they haven't advertised any jobs that look right for you. The right ones to visit are easy to find. They are those that advertise that they specialize in sales jobs. They are the agencies that obviously specialize in the industry you've been working in or want to enter, and that clearly have a sales and marketing specialist. You'll find the right agencies to visit in the general newspapers, in the business newspapers and magazines of your region or city, and in the trade magazines of your industry.

Most agency-advertised selling jobs today are fee paid. That is, the employer picks up agency charges in full, at no cost to you. Others split fees between you and the employer. Others charge agency costs entirely to you, usually to be paid as a percentage of salary over a specified period of time. Be very, very careful to understand precisely what the agency fee basis is for any job possibility you're sent out on. Know just how much you'll have to pay the agency, if anything, should you get the job. Be particularly careful not to get caught with a fixed agency fee that must legally be paid even if you quit the job soon after you get it.

Some "agencies" are really executive-search organizations, which will charge you a fee, often a rather large one, for helping you look for a job. Such organizations often render real service, with tests aimed at identifying your most salable talents and skills, and offer real help in finding the kind of selling job you want. Others are of questionable value. Occasionally, one will turn out to be an outright fraud. If you do hire this kind of help, treat it as you would any major purchase—check directly with others who have used it, or with the Better Business Bureau. Ask a lot of questions and be skeptical as to the answers. Above all, don't be stampeded into signing anything you don't understand. The foregoing seems like odd advice to have to give to sales professionals, but a great many sellers are very easy to sell, and too many sales professionals with their buying hats on turn out to be victims.

Often, your knowledge of the industry you've been working in can often supply you with the names of several companies you might like to prospect for a selling job. Research will often turn up more.

When you do have the names of some companies you want to prospect, treat them as you would other prospects. Get the name of the national or regional sales manager from directory sources or from the switchboard operator at the company. Call the right prime prospect, using much the kind of telephone interview selling approach described earlier. Do your best to sell the interview. Usually, some variant of "I'm calling you because you're the best" works well.

Again, as with any cold calling, you may find yourself with some time between other calls, and may want to do a little cold calling on company employment offices. It's generally the least fruitful of job-hunting techniques, but occasionally turns up a reasonably good prospect you might otherwise have missed.

RÉSUMÉS

Another pre-selling requirement, really part of the nuts and bolts of job-seeking, is a good basic résumé, which will properly include work and personal history cast in a selling form attractive enough to help you secure an interview. Rather too much is made of résumés, really. They do not ever get you a job; at best they help you, with appropriate covering letter and other approaches, to get in the door and face-to-face with a prospective employer.

Résumés have a basic role to play, however. A good résumé certainly does not merely tell an amorphous group of potential employers something about you, so that they will be able to see whether or not they want to interview you. A résumé that does only that—and that includes by far the overwhelming majority of résumés—does you an enormous disservice. Such a résumé performs approximately the same function as an operating manual or a similar piece of background or how-to-use material; and you do not sell very well from that kind of material.

A good résumé *sells.* It is not general, for all possible industries or functions, but directed at specific industries or functions, and sometimes both. It aims to cast you, your previous training, and your career to date into the most favorable possible light for the kind of job you are seeking.

It tries to provide specifics that can be alluded to in your covering letter, which will cause a prospective employer to want to see you in relation to a specific job. But both should sell. The résumé and your covering letter are a single selling package, rather than your résumé being a straight broadcast document, leaving your covering letter to do all the selling.

That is why the general broadcast résumé, with or without broadcast covering letter, is generally ineffective. By its very nature, it is very hard to develop as a selling tool, being general. Its frequent rejection by prospective employers tends to make you think that you have used up possible employers, when in fact you usually have not even begun to approach them. And it can make you think that something must be wrong with you, when in fact what is wrong is that you have not begun to sell. To send broadcast résumés to hundreds of potential employers can be a waste of time and effort; to cover them with letters that in no way specifically reach for the employer's wants and needs may merely waste good prospects. The broadcast résumé should only be considered in two types of situations. If you are rather well known in a field or industry, the broadcast letter and résumé serve to alert your contacts quickly to your availability; even so, the technique is to be used very cautiously. However, one who has used up many of his or her best prospects might lose very little by using it.

Rather than a broadcast résumé, you should develop a series of résumés tailored to the different industries and responsibilities that interest you. There is everything right about developing more than one résumé, whether you are looking for your first job or have years of experience as a sales professional. As a practical matter, it will in most elements be a single basic résumé, with adaptation to different kinds of employers and, in some instances, to a single employer, when time and situation allow. A basic résumé will be used for certain purposes; for example, it may be sent in response to advertisements asking that applicants include résumés or to prospective employers turned up through research on whom insufficient data has been developed to "customize" the résumé. But whenever possible, and however much work it entails, that basic résumé should be adapted for a particular purpose. And the résumé should always be topped by a personal letter to a prospective employer, unless your résumé has moved through a recruiter or some other employment organization, in which case they will supply the covering letter.

Here is an illustrative résumé, one that does its best to sell, rather than to merely list. This résumé is not done in the only form we think workable; there are several available résumé forms and approaches, and some works focused solely on job hunting suggest as many as a dozen. It is illustrative only; Vaughn Smith might be a man or a woman, is a composite, and is not a real person.

What follows here is the résumé of a sales professional who has had considerable practical experience in several different areas. It starts with name, address, and telephone numbers; moves immediately to a summary statement of objectives cast as benefits resulting from the hiring of Vaughn Smith; moves into a chronological account of work history, which continues to stress achievements and imply benefits; and then outlines education, nonwork accomplishments, and relevant personal data, ending with a promise to furnish references and supporting information as necessary on request.

It is as long as it happens to be. The many who counsel short résumés and the few who counsel relatively long résumés are reminiscent of those advertising people who interminably argue about whether ad copy should be "short" or "long," for maximum effectiveness. The truth is that excellent copy sells, whatever its length, and that bad copy does not work, whatever its length. If a résumé is intrinsically interesting—if it sells well —then it will be read, no matter how long or short it is, or how busy its reader. A too-short resume may not take the time to sell as well as it should; a long, badly written résumé may not be read at all. What does matter is that a résumé be written clearly, tell its benefits story, and serve as a basis for an interview. You are wisest to adopt the selling style that works best for you, however short or long the resulting résumé.

This example is a basic résumé, attempting to specify a sufficiently varied array of accomplishments, so it can be turned in whatever the desired direction by recruiter, by business friend, by Vaughn Smith's own covering letter, or during the face-to-face interview.

It does not state age, although age is implied by length of work and related history. "They're either too young or too old," is a response you need not court. The résumé helps sell the interview; a prospective employer's preconception about age (which might be a knockout factor, if age is stated in the resume) can often be easily dealt with face-to-face. It states nothing about sex, race, religion, or ethnic origin, recognizing that those matters are irrelevant to the central selling questions involved in the hiring situation. Nor does it include earnings history; the question of price is here entirely premature, as the sale has not even started. If absolutely necessary, you can include some earnings history data in your covering letter. It does, however, include data indicating a high level of energy and community involvement, matters of considerable importance to many in making interviewing and then hiring decisions.

This is the résumé of a seasoned sales professional, who has taken great care to accrete wide experience and build success on success. This is a person who very clearly and from the first has been successful and growth-oriented, unafraid to move into new areas and take up new challenges, and who can be relied upon to make a substantial contribution to any company.

RÉSUMÉ

Vaughn Smith
2222 Smith Street
Chicago, Illinois, 11111
(987) 1212
(987) 3131

Objective:

The opportunity to help profitably grow a substantial company into an even more substantial one, using the proven skills developed during the course of a very successful career in sales and marketing. Major qualifications and experience include over 15 years of senior sales leadership while profitably developing companies all over the country. Have very successfully accomplished national account, regional, and territorial selling functions, as well as regional sales supervisory functions. Fully equipped to apply the tools and techniques of modern selling and marketing to the widest possible range of problems and opportunities.

Experience:

1975 to present   PRS Corporation, San Francisco,
                                         California

Senior Representative, National Accounts Representative, and *Field Sales Representative* of this large, multiline industrial equipment manufacturing company.

As midwestern regional Senior Representative, headquartered in Chicago, handled a wide variety of special account and sales promotion functions, as well as many field training functions. Was Acting Sales Manager of region in absence of regional sales manager. Helped plan and execute regional expansion from 10 to 18 representatives, while introducing several new lines and products and increasing regional sales by 34% over two-year period.

As National Accounts Representative, headquartered in San Francisco home office, was responsible for expanding sales to existing national accounts handled by over 50%, opening up many new accounts in the process.

As Field Sales Representative, handled Atlanta, Georgia, territory. Was National Field Rep of the Year in 1977, and sales leader (top 10 in country) in 1976, 1977, and 1978.

1970 to 1975   TPT Corporation, Atlanta, Georgia

Senior Field Sales Representative and *Field Sales Representative* for this well-established regional distributor of office equipment.

As Senior Field Sales Representative, worked out of Atlanta home office selling and servicing major accounts throughout the Southeast. Increased major account volume in this area by over 20% in each of three years, for a total of 68%, and increased number of major accounts sold by 41%.

As Field Sales Representative, handled New Orleans territory. Was contest winner and sales leader throughout period in which territory was handled.

1966 to 1970   GHI Corporation, Detroit, Michigan

Field Representative and *Sales Support Liaison* for this regional restaurant equipment dealer.

As Field Representative, handled Chicago Center City territory. Grew territory billings by a total of 54% over three year period, and was sales leader every year.

As Sales Support Liaison, handled a large variety of sales administrative and support functions in Detroit home office, including the development of promotional materials and sales contests, and assisted in the preparation of several sales meetings and training classes.

Education:

B.A., Michigan State University, 1965, top 10% of class, majoring in Business Administration, with special emphasis on Sales and Marketing.

Continuing Professional Education includes courses in Advanced Selling, Modern Marketing, Public Speaking, Speedreading, and Persuasion, for a total of 24 Continuing Education Credits (CEUs).

Community Activities:

Vice-Chairman, Community Fund, Skokie, Illinois, 1982, 1981
Vice-Chairman, Toastmaster's International, Atlanta, Georgia, 1977, 1976

Hobbies:

Tennis, golf, public speaking

Personal:

Married, two children, excellent health
References and personal data on request.

Note the continuing emphases on profitable growth, sales professionalism, and continuing sales leadership. These are the key matters, underlying all the mechanics of résumé, covering letter, contacts, and appearances. The promises you make and the attitudes you bring with you are
central hiring matters. Your success in job-seeking depends in large measure upon how well you convey those promises to others, first while selling
the interview, and later face-to-face in the direct job-selling situation.

PREPARING FOR THE INTERVIEW

However the process of selling the interview starts—whether through
your mailed letter or by telephone, as in response to an advertisement;
through the referral of a business friend; by action of a job searcher in your
employ or recruiter engaged by a prospective employer—there will be
some interviews.

Before those interviews, however, two other things are likely to happen.
The first is a phone call, which may either set an interview or serve as a
screening device, and you cannot know which it is when you pick up the
phone. The second is your own research on the company and, when
possible, on the individual with whom you will be meeting.

The screening call is easy enough to handle, if you bear firmly in mind
throughout the conversation not to go off the deep end and try to sell
yourself into the job while on the phone. That hardly ever works, and very
often sets up barriers between you and your prospective employer that
either cause cancellation of the projected interview or make the interview
far more difficult than it should have been. On the telephone, just as when
you are answering an advertisement, all you are doing is continuing to sell
the interview, and after that has been done, trying to leave the most
favorable possible personal impression, as preparation for the actual face-
to-face interview. Be as brief as you reasonably can, answer whatever
questions are asked as best you can, make it clear that you look forward
to the interview and the possibility of working with the company and

individual enormously, but never take that one step beyond and try to sell yourself into the job on the phone.

With the interview sold, it is time to do some research. When the firm involved is one you have been interested in, you may already know a good deal about company, key personnel, strengths, weaknesses, future prospects, and where you would like to fit in. Otherwise, all that must be accomplished between the time an interview is set and the time it takes place. Try to leave yourself enough time for that kind of research. Clearly, if someone you want to see is eager to see you immediately, you will make the appointment, scant the research, and hope that your prospective employer's eagerness to see you can be used far more effectively than the selling tools any research would have yielded; but if some research time can be arranged, take it.

Some of your most valuable insights may result from a series of calls to your business friends, inquiring about the company, its situation, and its people. It is not at all unlikely that one or more people in your web of contacts will know a good deal about your prospective employer. You may also get a good deal of hard and detailed information relating to what your prospect may be seeking, information that can help you turn your background and skills into a solidly effective benefits story, which you may use to sell yourself into the job. Indeed, you may find yourself talking to a good friend who is capable of paving the way for you with a glowing recommendation to a friend of long standing who is about to interview you for that job.

On the other hand, your friends may be able to make it clear that you would be unwise to touch prospective job and employer with a 10-foot pole and that, too, is extraordinarily valuable insight, although you are likely to want to make up your mind for yourself by going through with the interview. You cannot know what you will get from your business and personal friends until you ask, and you should never be shy about asking for information. That is what friends are for, and a lot of what networking is all about. And if you ask them now, they will be encouraged to ask you later, which only solidifies friendships.

There are formal sources of information, too. One of the best of such sources is really not a single source, but a vehicle more and more in evidence on desks and in libraries. It is the computer terminal, hooked into one or more massive distributed data networks, such as Lockheed's Dialog, which taps hundreds of massive databases. Through such a terminal, it is possible to secure corporate disclosure statements filed with the federal government pursuant to the securities laws; yearly and quarterly financial statements, such as profit and loss statements, cash flow statements, and balance sheets; lists of directors and officers; business press articles relating to the company and its people; and a wide miscellany of other quite relevant materials capable of helping you build a job-getting benefits story.

There is another such vehicle, too, the time-honored one. It is the nearest specialized business library or large public library, which will have many similar information sources in their print-on-paper forms, and sometimes on computer terminals, as well. They will also have trained business and general reference librarians, who can be invaluable in helping you frame the right questions to ask about your prospective employer and in finding the answers to those questions. Here, as with your friends, you must not be shy about asking. Librarians will help a great deal, if you let them.

These on-line and print sources can yield a great deal of basic information, and even sometimes yield—as through an astutely researched and written article on the company—a lot of what you need to know about the company, as to both selling yourself into the job and whether or not you want the job. A series of financial statements and accompanying materials can tell you how the company is doing and is likely to be doing in the near term. Company people are likely to paint a rosier picture than is justified by the hard facts; you need to try to learn something about those hard facts before you go into that interview.

HANDLING THE INTERVIEW

And so to the face-to-face interview, where it all comes together, and where you and your prospective employer are involved in the process of deciding whether or not you want to work with each other.

The best job interviews involving two sales professionals—one as seller and one as buyer—are also a good deal of fun, as the best-selling interviews always are, but in a sense even more so. For good job interviews have a certain resonance, a kind of double impact. You are presenting the benefits that hiring you will bring; at the same time you are both sizing up your potential employer and assessing how well he or she appreciates the art and craft you are demonstrating in the selling situation. Your prospective employer is assessing the benefits you are describing, and at the same time watching you sell, perhaps with appreciation for the art and skills of a real professional, perhaps with some dismay. That all makes it interesting, as much as any selling situation you will ever be in. All the more so if you successfully close; interesting either way.

We have so far cast this discussion in selling terms. That is proper;

when you seek a job, the essential transaction that continues to take place throughout the process and until a job offer has actually been made is a selling process, with you as seller and prospective employer as buyer. The fact that seller is sizing up buyer quite as actively as the other way around is not relevant to the central transaction. Be aware that if you spend too much time and attention probing and sizing up a prospective employer, it may indicate less than the active interest in the job you may otherwise be expressing, possibly harming your ability to close the sale. There are questions to raise, many of them, but they should be seriously raised only after a job offer has been made, so as not to interrupt the flow of the selling process before and during the face-to-face interview.

That face-to-face interview may be one or many. You may meet with the person to whom you will report only once, and get a job offer. Or you may meet with someone from a company personnel department, then several members of sales and marketing management one at a time, and finally even with a member of top management, who can make or break a decision tentatively made by others—and all before you have a firm job offer. Aside from the personnel department screening interview, it matters little how many times you are interviewed, and by whom; the basic situation changes little from interview to interview. You still need to "put yourself in the other guy's shoes" in order to empathize successfully and thereby become able to adapt and focus your benefits story so that it properly speaks to the wants and needs of your prospective employer. Achieving empathy is really the key to the face-to-face job interview with someone who will be your superior or peer in a new company, just as empathy is the key to all selling success.

In job-seeking, as in all selling, empathy-building is more than anything else relaxed and responsive listening, signaled to others by every nonverbal and verbal means at our command, and conveying that we care a good deal about what they have to say, and want to hear it. It requires knowing what you plan to say extremely well—at least in its general outlines—so that you can focus hard on what "the other guy" is communicating to you verbally and nonverbally. Then it is relatively easy to find the specific insights you need to fit yourself so well into the situation that you are clearly the person for the job. And underneath, it requires real human sympathy for those with whom you are meeting, for sham almost always is apparent, and especially to people who are just as experienced as you. Real empathy requires real human sympathy.

Operationally, it starts with as simple a move as a calm, warm, friendly handshake, and an icebreaking comment about the restaurant you are meeting in, a trophy on the office wall or outside in the reception area, and a straightforward query about what the company and interviewer have in mind for the job in question. After all, the interviewer has your résumé and may know a good deal more about you besides. Many will respond to that kind of approach; people do like to talk about their work, their companies, and their own careers, and it is always a good idea to encourage them to do so. For then you stand a very good chance of learning what you need to know to later secure the job offer. You are also likely to painlessly pick up much of the basic insight you need to make your own decision as to whether or not to take the job if offered. All depending, of course, on whether you listen responsively enough so that the flow of talk will continue.

Then, and usually fairly soon, it will be time to tell your story. The opportunity then lies in casting your personal and work history as a series of potential benefits which will derive from hiring you, each facet meeting employer needs and desires as squarely as possible. The hazard lies in forgetting about benefits, and merely telling your story as a series of incidents in which you are the prime figure, thereby ensuring that you seem narrowly self-centered. It can be compounded by focusing on negatives, such as how unfairly treated you were on this job or that, but few of us are so naive as to do that. The main danger is self-absorption in the telling, rather than careful focus on what hiring you will do for your interviewer's company and, if possible, for the interviewer as well.

You are best advised to "assume sale" throughout. When you walk through a prospective employer's door, you expect to get the job. You really do; it sticks out all over you. You are relaxed, but ready to go, eager to get started on what promises to be the job of a lifetime. You want to hear all about it, are ready to tell your interviewer all about yourself, but regard all that as a mere formality, because once the company understands what you can do for it, you will be offered the job. No, not as rawly ebullient as that, but almost. A quiet but firm assumption that you are going to get the job will very often during the course of an interview build precisely that view in the mind of your interviewer.

You will be ready for such standard questions as "Why are you leaving your present company?" or "Why do you want to come and work with us?" or "Where do you see yourself in five or ten years?" or "What do you see as your key strengths and weaknesses?" Those kinds of questions are easily handled, if prepared for; their answers should be as much a part of your planned presentation as your basic résumé and covering letter story, as adapted during the interview. As a sales professional, you sell with a completely thought-through presentation complete with the basic answers to the standard questions, stalls, and objections raised by prospects; so, too, when you function as a seller in a job situation. By all means write the answers to what you feel will be the basic questions you will be asked; memorize those answers, if you feel that will help. At the very least, memorize the key words and phrases you will need in dealing with such standard questions.

It will help to learn how to "take the prospect's temperature," that is, to trial close. It is not really an attempt to get a firm decision; in an interview, that is rarely appropriate. Rather, it is such a query as "Does that make sense to you?" or "Does that square with your view of the matter?" It is an attempt to find agreement between you and prospective employer on matters key to the hiring decision; to the extent that you successfully find common ground, you have moved closer to a favorable decision.

From a selling point of view, the interview generally consists of an early introductory and empathy-building period; a presentation period in which you tell your benefits-laden story; a wide-ranging discussion period, in which you handle questions and possible reservations about hiring you, while continuing to build empathy and find areas of agreement; some trial closing along the way; and the close, in which you get as close as you can to a firm job offer. As to the last, this situation differs somewhat from that encountered in most selling situations. In selling, you usually try very hard to close the sale during the interview, knowing that the sale deferred is usually a sale that has to be made all over again later; in the job interview situation, it is quite likely that no decision will be made on the spot— unless you are at the end of a whole selection process, in which instance you will be best advised to fight hard to close the job then and there.

We are not describing a fixed sequence of events. You may find yourself engaged in a wide-ranging discussion of business events from the moment you move into the interview, never sequentially present your benefits story, and find yourself with a firm job offer half an hour after you meet for the first time. You may meet a compulsive talker and self-aggrandizer, who hardly lets you get a word in edgewise, talks uninterruptedly about his or her own family matters for two hours, ultimately regrets that you did not have more time together, and does not hire you because you somehow "failed to impress." Or you may find yourself in the middle of a well-oiled, multimeeting hiring process, in which you never really get to first base with whomever counts, although you meet with a whole series of sales managers and personnel people over a period of months.

When you are talking to someone who will make a hiring decision, it is quite often the first few minutes that count the most. These are those utterly crucial moments in which you make a first impression, begin to develop empathy with your prospective employer, and begin to show to an experienced eye who and what you are. That is what the experienced eye looks for first, after all: who and what you are, not where you have been, what you have done, how you have been educated, and what you know. All those things can be put on paper, weighed, and analyzed, but they are not why you hire sales professionals. From the viewpoint of the experienced manager who is deciding whether or not to bring you on board, all the paper is background—essential background, but only that. It is the face-to-face interview or series of interviews that tells the experienced manager who and what you are, and determines whether or not you are the one for the job.

As always, the first few minutes are crucially important. Putting it a little differently, most job offers are lost in the first few minutes; most real contenders for jobs are born during the first few minutes of the face-to-face interview. Yet whether or not those first few minutes go well or badly is not a matter of chemistry (often used as a synonym for accident), as so many think. The kind of chemistry that occurs between seller and buyer has little to do with accident, and much to do with the seller's art. Those first few minutes together provide—or fail to provide—an excellent first impression and the beginning of empathy, and that is the formula that gets job offers.

You should bring to the interview copies of your résumé, letters of reference, and key supporting documents, and be prepared to use the résumé as the basis for a connected life history. Very often, you will not present that life history, or any large part of it, during the interview. On the other hand, you may find yourself being interviewed by someone who wants you to do just that; when that happens, you must have the best-prepared presentation you can muster. There are those who will want to hear you talk about yourself for a while, while they orient themselves and "size you up." Others will come to the interview unprepared, and need to hear your story to even begin to assess your possibilities.

The interviewer who says, "Why don't you tell me a little about yourself?" should not then be treated to an off-the-cuff, undirected discussion of family, childhood dreams, and miscellaneous unconnected professional accomplishments. That question should never be treated casually in an interview; it should be seen as opening up an opportunity to tell your carefully prepared benefits story, in which personal and business histories together point to a series of substantial benefits flowing from your hire for the job in question. An experienced interviewer will normally expect you to be able to do that, and failure to at least start to make a highly professional presentation can weigh heavily against you.

That presentation should clearly show a career-building line of previous jobs, with you going to continually greater pay and responsibility. Where there are breaks in that line, clear, sharp, and positive explanations should be ready. For example, trying to go on your own and failing can be seen as a negative—but if cast properly can be seen as proof that you are entrepreneurially minded and, in many ways, are therefore better able to make a contribution than many who have played it safe and never struck out on their own. A caution here, though: those who hire are usually at least as experienced as those who come to be hired. If you have had a bad career break and it shows, say so, indicate how much the experience helped you to learn proper career directions, and move on. It will seldom then be seen as a negative in the hiring situation.

Your presentation should include the reasons you made each move, and focus strongly on your reason for leaving your current or last employment, if at all possible casting that move as a positive career-builder. Here is where the desirability of moving from currently employed status to a new job becomes particularly apparent.

It is enormously important not to be seen as a restless job-hopper, one who moves around from job to job not for good career-building reasons, but rather out of impatience, boredom, and perhaps incompetence, never stopping long enough to build anything anywhere. Nobody really wants one of those around, no matter how good the formal educational and work records look on the surface. Even if you have made a fair number of moves—as many as four or five in 10 to 15 years—you may have been pursuing a firm career-building line rather than job-hopping. Here it is the explanation that makes all the difference. The prospective employer who is convinced that you are basically stable and capable of moving ahead strongly will usually have no difficulty with several previous job moves, if they make good career sense. On the other hand, if those moves convincingly indicate a pattern of instability, and you are unable to dispel that impression face-to-face, your cause is probably lost.

Throughout your presentation, you should find opportunities to link up what you have learned during the first portion of the interview with your past history and current job objectives—that is, if you have properly developed information and started building empathy in those crucial first few minutes. Bear in mind that the job presentation that goes most smoothly and with the fewest interruptions is the one that is probably going worst. Without interruptions and the ability to build areas of agreement, you are probably not making any significant contact and are getting nowhere. Contrary to how it is normal to feel while presenting your story, interruptions are good for you and passive and seeming acceptance is bad. If you have done your early work well, and started to build empathy early, you will be interrupted, be unable to finish your story, find yourself building agreement, be able to assume success easily throughout the interview, and stand a good chance of getting the job.

Similarly with questions, especially during and after you have told something of your story. The engaged prospective employer will very often ask searching questions, demand clear answers, and go back again and again to matters of particular interest, hearing you on the same subjects from different vantage points. When that happens, what you are getting is enormously important insight that can help you get the job, for then what you are seeing is exposure of the employer's own concerns and interests, which makes it possible for you to sharply adapt your selling story to perceived employer needs.

Although most job interview situations will not result in an opportunity to try to make an on-the-spot close, some will. There are times when you may find yourself meeting with someone who can make the hiring decision and is ready to do so, then and there. On rare occasions, it will be at a first interview; but the manager who hires that way will seldom hire well. But it can come on a callback interview, when most applicants have been weeded out, and it is down to you and very few others; or at a time when there are still many applicants under consideration, but you strike someone who has a hiring decision to make as particularly right for the job and perhaps personally very compatible.

Sometimes it is quite clear that the person you are meeting with cannot make a hiring decision, as when you are meeting with someone from a personnel department, rather than a sales manager. Often, though, you do meet with someone who can hire, and the question is whether or not he or she is willing to make a hiring decision now. Often, the question seems to be "When do I ask?" Well, if you have done your selling job well, and built real empathy between you and your interviewer, it never hurts to ask, and it never hurts to ask again and again. On the other hand, if it has not gone well, and your first asking runs into a stone wall, you will know it. Then it hurts a good deal to ask again and again, for then you are likely to be regarded as pushy. There is never any magic about closing, no foolproof technique that works particularly better than any other technique to get a job or make a sale, no way to force or trick anyone into hiring you, and no optimum number of times to ask for a job during an interview. Closing techniques in this context consist only of a few ways of asking for the job, some of which will be more appropriate in one situation, or with one person, than another.

Sometimes it is most appropriate to simply ask. If you have built empathy, told as much of your story as seems desirable to both of you, discussed whatever needed to be discussed, agreed a good deal on important matters, and have been together doing all this for a good while, it may be perfectly natural to say something like "It all sounds wonderful to me, and it's beginning to sound to me as if you feel the same way. Do I get the job?" Or it may seem better to put it a little less baldly, given the situation and the people involved. Then you may simply assume sale, and ultimately say something like "Great! When do I start?" Alternatively, you may want to put it in terms of a post-decision choice, assume that a favorable decision has been made, and say something like "Fine. I can start on the first of next month, if that suits you. Or, if you like, I can give a little less notice, and start two weeks from today. Which would you prefer?" A caution here: The choice close works well in selling goods and services, but should be used cautiously in the hiring situation, and only if you are quite sure you are dealing with someone very close to a favorable decision and yet so indecisive as to need a bit of a push in a direction he or she really wants to go. For the really undecided, this kind of push may be counterproductive, causing an almost committed interviewer to back up and want to think about it all over again.

Sometimes, you will not say anything at all, using the weight of silence —and silence has a great weight—to work for you. For example, far down the line at the end of a hiring interview, you might say something like, "It looks good to me. How does it look to you?" and wait. Then, as silence grows between you, so does a certain kind of confrontation, and with it considerable pressure to make a decision. A caution here, too: these are pressure tactics, and can rebound to your disadvantage.

On balance, it is usually better to play this kind of close rather conservatively, with "Do I get the job?" or "When do I start?" or "Which would you prefer?" the better closing choices, when you do have a chance to try to close.

And close you will, whether during or after the ultimate hiring interview, for if you learn how to move from job strength to strength, build your network of contacts well, research and prospect effectively, develop sound written materials and prepared presentations, and above all to sell empathetically as well in the job-seeking situation as you do in the field, you will be far better equipped than most to build your career through a series of increasingly satisfying jobs.

NEGOTIATION AND DECISION

As a prospective employee, you will have many questions about job, company, and related matters. Many of these will be answered during the course of the interview or series of interviews, often as part of the interviewer's discussion of the job in question. Some will not, and will need to be answered before you can decide on acceptance or rejection of the offer. It is often tempting to raise some of those questions during the course of hiring interviews, but it is wiser to wait until you have a specific offer, even if it means going on through and spending time that might ultimately prove to have been unprofitably spent. It is very difficult to put questions so well that none of them will be seen as objections or premature negotiations, and the last thing you want to do during the job selection process is to shift focus from the enormous benefits to be derived from hiring you to your own possible objections, or to begin to negotiate terms before receiving a firm offer. If there are really major objections, such as a mandatory relocation when you will not relocate, or an income range that at its top is far too low for you to even consider, then you should stop the job selection process as soon as that is known, which will usually be very early. But if the job is worth considering, then let the focus continue to be the hiring decision, and that means going through to the end of the hiring process and receiving a firm offer.

Once you do have a firm job offer, then negotiations are very much in order. For then all has reversed; you are wanted, rather than wanting. The seller has sold and, with firm offer in hand, has become the buyer. Prospective employer is now desirous employer, engaged in selling you on the wisdom of taking the proffered job, and therefore almost always willing to make some concessions on top of the firm job offer in hand. Now the company has time and money invested in you, and a decision has been made that no one is likely to want to remake. And whoever has made the hiring decision has ego and hopes invested in you, too. It is very much like dealing with someone who has spent a good deal of time agonizing over which of several boats to buy, who then waits with ill-concealed impatience for delivery. Your bargaining position is small before the hiring decision has been made, but it is never better than just after, and before you have accepted, the job offer.

Note that this is a time when you may have new bargaining power in your current job, as well. Some current employers will not negotiate against a new job offer, as a matter of policy; but many will. A good sales professional is hard to find, and just as hard to keep; when someone else has recognized your worth, the new offer may remove blinders and unlock previously locked doors in your current company. No, we do not suggest soliciting an offer from another company to use as a lever in negotiations with your current company. That is a very dangerous game indeed, and can rebound to your very great disadvantage. But when you do have a firm offer and are quite ready to take it, then by all means consider giving your company a chance to make a better counteroffer. The way to do it is to be very simple and straightforward. With satisfactory new offer firmly in hand, tell your current company that you have an offer and that, although you hate to leave, you are very seriously considering taking it, and plan to respond affirmatively tomorrow or the next day. Say no more; your attitude will indicate clearly enough that you might respond favorably to a counteroffer. Then wait. If no counteroffer is forthcoming, take the new job, for you have very likely burned your bridges by informing your current company of your readiness to make the move. On the other hand, you may get a counteroffer; if so, it must be specific and immediate, rather than a general promise to somehow take care of you later on. Of course, if you cannot wait to get out of an uncongenial situation, the whole question is moot; then it is a matter of going when the going is good.

Negotiating ability varies, of course, as does available flexibility on the part of a prospective employer. For most experienced people, though, it is possible to do a good deal of negotiating between the time you say, "That's wonderful! When can we talk about the details?" and when you say, "Okay, that's it; I'm satisfied if you are. I'm giving notice Monday morning."

A prospective employer will usually go to considerable trouble and expense to see to it that you have the kind of information and incentives you need to be able to make a favorable decision on the job offer. We discuss the total compensation package at considerable length in Chapter 8; many elements of that package will be negotiable between offer and acceptance. Here we will discuss the kind of information you need to be able to make a balanced decision to accept, reject, or negotiate an improved job offer.

Some of that information is precisely the kind of insight you may have been able to discover through business friends and published sources before going into the interview. Whether before or after the interview, though, you will certainly want to know as much as possible about prospective employer and company prospects before accepting a job offer. That may involve trips to home offices and sometimes other locations at company expense, to see facilities and talk with company people. It may, in the instance of international relocation, mean a trip abroad, again at company expense. It is very difficult to size up a job offer from a distance;

the possibility of making a major mistake becomes very large if you are interviewed, negotiate, and accept a job offer far from your eventual operations base. And even when your job move is within your present geographical area, or to an area you know well, it is wise to size up company and people on-site, rather than taking anything at all for granted. That is particularly true in difficult times, for yesterday's affluent, growing company may be today's company in deep trouble, and yesterday's "plum" of a job may be today's personal and business disaster.

Relocation questions can deeply affect both your basic decision as to the desirability of a proffered job and your negotiating stance on several elements of the total compensation package. Sometimes it is as basic as being delighted by the prospect of a move to San Francisco or Phoenix from New York or Detroit, or dismay at the thought of trying to cope with New York's extraordinarily difficult living conditions and cost factors. Sometimes it is a matter of realizing that one area may be far more expensive than another, in terms of your quality of life requirements, whatever the Consumer Price Index indicates as to relative price levels, generating the need to negotiate a higher income offer before an otherwise desirable job can be accepted. Sometimes it is the quality or kind of schools available, or cultural life, or recreation, or professional opportunities for a spouse. All require careful examination before effective negotiation and decision making can eventuate. No, you will hardly ever have as much insight as you would like in accepting or rejecting a job offer involving relocation, but you can try very hard to get as much insight as possible before making a decision.

Happily, the corporate job-moving styles of the 1950s and 1960s are less and less prevalent. Few corporations in this period attempt to routinely move their people from installation to installation every few years. Some do; whenever possible, those should be avoided, for they provide only a fragmented, corporate-dependent life, with little opportunity for real professional growth and no opportunity to put down satisfying personal and economic community roots. That corporate transfer style causes enormous personal difficulties; rootless families are, far more than most, disoriented and may have deep problems. So are rootless employees, for that matter.

One large reason for the demise of the corporate transfer style is the emergence of the movement for women's liberation and sexual equality. Many women today reject the role of nonworking wife and mother, much preferring to pursue satisfying and lucrative careers. Many transfers that formerly would have been accepted are now refused, because the career dislocation and loss of income resulting to a working spouse is often an unacceptable price to pay for a corporate transfer, even when that transfer involves a substantial promotion and raise in pay.

It makes very little sense to trade two careers for one by accepting a corporate transfer that effectively puts one spouse out of work or sets back that spouse's career development by many years. A psychologist or lawyer who has spent many years developing a practice cannot redevelop that practice at will and quickly in another location, perhaps even in another state with different certification requirements, and should not be asked to do so just because her husband has been transferred or promoted. That goes either way, of course; women in business today find themselves facing the same transfer and promotion questions as do men.

In terms of family and professional security, two careers are far better than one. Two professionals in one family can together build some savings and investments, and thereby develop a "cushion" against such adversities as the loss of a job or serious illness. Two professionals with such a cushion can afford to make job moves that involve a certain degree of risk, or venture into their own businesses; the result is a flexibility rarely available to one worried person with a mountain of bills, children to educate, and a nonworking spouse. With fewer transfers, companies may have somewhat more difficulty meeting changing staff requirements, but for individuals it is usually far better to stay in place, develop two lucrative careers rather than one, and reap the benefits of setting roots into a community, as well.

Sometimes, though, a relocation seems right, as for a promotion within your own organization, a step up to a better job in another organization, or a move from unemployment to employment. When that occurs, you will want to explore personally several related cost and quality of life factors, if at all possible on the spot and, if you are married, with your spouse. For even your best friends—sometimes especially your best friends—will shade the truth when they are trying to convince you to make a move. Before deciding to accept a job offer, you will want to see for yourself several things:

• Where you and your family, if you have one, would like to live, within reasonable distance of your home base. Within reasonable distance, that is; the community that is "only" an hour away in the suburbs of a big city may turn out to be an hour and a half away in rush hours and two hours away in rush hours in midwinter. There may be several such communities; there may be only one; there may be none. There is often a balance to be struck between quality of life and cost factors, and negotiations that must be undertaken before a job offer becomes acceptable. It can also happen that careful examination of an area makes it clear that you want no part of it, and then it may not matter how good the job offer is in other ways; you will either reject it, or spend some very, very unhappy months or years before you decide to give up on what turns out to have been a bad job-changing decision.

Within compatible communities, you will have some quite standard, quite indispensable explorations to pursue, including:

• The nature and cost of the housing available. That means consulting with local realtors on home and mortgage prices and availability. By all means, visit some homes for sale, so that you can see what is really available at indicated prices. The same for rentals, if you plan to rent rather than buy, including the visits to available rentals. And since realtors are in the business of selling homes, it is wise to doublecheck their information on mortgage rates and terms at some local banks.

Some of this information becomes important when finally negotiating the job offer, if you indeed decide to take the job. You may need to negotiate sale of your current home guaranteed by your transferring company or new employer, with purchase of your old home at a guaranteed base price a condition of employment. You may need mortgage assistance in your new location to get any mortgage credit at all, with company payment guarantees if mortgage rates and points are over guaranteed maximums. You will be very wise, for example, to try to get the company to pick up mortgage interest payments over a guaranteed maximum interest rate, if you take a flexible rate mortgage, which can rise over the years and ultimately become far more expensive than you had anticipated.

• What the schools are like, if you have children. That, too, needs a personal look, which can usually be arranged without any trouble with local school officials, who are quite used to such requests. The schools may indeed look fine to you; on the other hand, you may decide that expensive private schools will be necessary or desirable for your children, with the very large additional costs that are involved. Such costs, measured in after-tax rather than pre-tax income dollars, can make a big difference as to income needs, and may have to be figured into negotiations.

You may also find that no available schools are acceptable, and that may be a knockout factor, making the job offer unacceptable. That is especially important if you have a child who needs special education that may be available in your current location, but is unavailable in the area into which you may be relocating.

- What the cultural and social amenities, which have so much to do with the quality of life, are like. Concerts, theaters, sports facilities, local libraries, churches, and synagogues—such organizations can have profound impact upon the quality of life as perceived by you and your loved ones, and therefore upon your job decision.

- What commuting conditions will be like from compatible communities. A long, difficult commute from the nearest compatible community in an area can be daunting; perhaps it should be daunting more often than it actually is, for in the long run, it can disastrously affect the quality of your own life. Once again, there is no substitute for actually doing it; take the drive or the bus or train, and more than once if possible, and carefully consider it as a major job-decision element.

- What educational opportunities are available in the area and state for you, your spouse, and your children. You may want to pursue additional formal professional education, for example. The existence of a major business school nearby then can have significant impact upon your job decision. Or your spouse may want to either pursue additional education or get some basic education; what is available can become very important in career development terms. And one state may offer your children fine state colleges, at small cost, while another has a rather poor state college system, necessitating large college costs at private colleges. The difference to them and you can be tens of thousands of dollars.

- What professional and other career opportunities are available for your spouse. That lovely home in a parklike setting may turn out to be very lovely indeed—but if it is located 50 miles from the nearest fair-sized city, your tax accountant or psychologist spouse may have an impossibly difficult time making professional connections, making the move unacceptable. On the other hand, you and your spouse may long have dreamed of doing some farming, and a move into a country setting may be an opportunity to make that dream come true—and perhaps an alternate career for one or both of you as well. A major job move requires considerable self-analysis on the part of all those moving.

Relocation is a particularly difficult problem when it involves an international move, and especially for those with families. For then a spouse's career can be in very serious jeopardy, and the related quality of life and cost of living questions as well as tax and foreign exchange factors must be examined with extraordinary care. Before you accept a post abroad, by all means take at least one trip to the proposed location, as an indispensable part of the decision-making process. Accept with thanks the advice and materials furnished by your prospective employer or current company, and then read and discuss the proposed place and situation with everyone you know and respect, including your accountant and lawyer, before and after you make that trip abroad and before you make the job decision. Then, if your decision is affirmative, seriously consider going on ahead by yourself for a considerable period, to pave the way.

Many do decide to hedge their relocation bets, whether they are going abroad or staying in their home countries. Some commute long distances to their new jobs for a period. Some return home only for weekends for a rather extended period of as much as a year or more. Others come home less frequently, as in the instance of an international move. That is often a quite necessary set of arrangements, as when it is important for children to finish a school term or year in place, rather than suffering the dislocation of a mid-term move; or when the process of selecting, closing, and readying a home for occupancy takes months, and begins only after the job has actually started. It is also often a very prudent approach, for no matter how carefully a job move is considered before it is actually made, many a move goes sour soon after. Unanticipated internal moves, business difficulties beyond your control, even allergies surfacing in new climatic conditions—a score of things can turn a job move bad, even if the original decision was a correct one. Sometimes the move is simply recognized too late as a mistake, for whatever the reason. When a job move does turn out badly early in the game, the ability to return to your previous community and business environment can make a relatively painless correction out of what might have been a family disaster, if you had picked up stakes and moved entirely to the new job and community.

For those who travel alone, relocation questions are often just as difficult as for those with family ties. Even those just starting out, having been hired for their first jobs right off college campuses, can face difficult and potentially very expensive career decisions—and before they have any experience to fall back on.

Some of the potential problems faced by beginners are economic. A 25-year-old may be single, but is rarely unencumbered, in these times of huge college costs and shrinking family abilities to pay. Young people are quite likely to have large debts; have little or no capital with which to acquire such goods as automobiles, clothes, and furniture; and command not-very-large after-tax incomes. It may be difficult, under those circumstances, to make ends meet anywhere, and particularly difficult in such expensive cities as New York and Houston. Yet housing must very often be obtained in the most expensive portions of center cities, as working hours for beginners may be extraordinarily long during the years of apprenticeship, and commuting costs and the automobiles necessary to live in suburbs in themselves add large expense items to modest budgets. And beyond the pure economics of the matter, it can be terribly lonely, and therefore demoralizing, to be young and virtually friendless in a new town, and stuck out in the suburbs. Most young people need to be where other young people are to be found, and where the action—such as it is— functions as icebreaker and group-maker for people like themselves. It is not at all unusual, therefore, to find young people living over their heads in center cities, while seeming to command rather large incomes which should guarantee immediate solvency. The young person who "can't save anything" is not to be censured; that is merely normal in our times.

But lack of solvency can cause career problems, for this is a time when mobility is a must, and early solvency therefore is far more than a prudent approach to savings and investment. Young people need money to be able to move from job to job and from industry to industry, as apprenticeship needs and desires on the one hand, and defensive needs on the other, demand. A young person who has been fired because of company cutbacks or failure, and who has neither a strong track record nor financial reserves, can be someone in deep personal trouble, for he or she is probably also carrying a sizable education debt and may need to relocate to find a new job. A young sales professional who clearly sees that a move should be made, and wants to gamble, for example, on a move to a small, untried company in a growing new industry, must have some savings to fall back on if the gamble does not work out. Otherwise, in all probability, he or she should not and will not make what might otherwise be an excellent career move.

Given the economic conditions of this very difficult period, it may be unwise to go heavily into debt to finance graduate business education. Some may profitably continue to do so—an MBA from a top business school, such as Harvard or Stanford, may lead to a fast and very lucrative career track—but many may be better off to take their MBAs after moving into the business world. Many companies will pay all or part of tuition for employees, and will cooperate in other significant ways to help their people through graduate school; as credit becomes even more difficult to get, the high cost of education may indeed make company assistance essential for many.

Similarly, economic factors may cause young people just starting out to reach for jobs in major metropolitan areas, where many potential employers exist, and where job moves may not require relocation. It is all very well to get relocation help when taking a job, but when leaving a job you may have to bear the costs of relocation yourself, and those costs may prove prohibitive. A recent graduate who took a job in a single industry town, lost that job, and has had to relocate to a big city, broke and jobless, has little bargaining power. Without realistic severance arrangements— and that means more than a return airplane ticket to the campus from which you were recruited—the enticing job in a fine but isolated physical location may be a career and a personal mistake.

For any single person, and for a good many married people as well, relocation can bring loneliness. The easiest and most attractive country or small-city life style may be a personal disaster for someone who is a confirmed city dweller used to the cultural and social amenities available in a major metropolitan area. The church-centered social life so attractive to some may be a stone wall for the agnostic or atheist. For the devoted small-town churchgoer, on the other hand, life in a big center city may be wholly unacceptable. For all of us, a long, searching look at the social and physical environment within which we are going to work in a proffered new job is just as important as our assessment of the job itself. We are whole people, and must try to view business and personal needs and desires as an intertwined whole.

In sum, then, it is wise to regard most aspects of an offered job as negotiable, including income, moving expenses, house-selling and mortgage assistance, insurance plans, club memberships, and vacation arrangements. All after the offer and before acceptance, none before the firm offer; and all cast in terms of helping you to best do the job you are now setting out to do. You should not have to be worried about a less-than-adequate income in inflationary times, about being unable to sell an old house or properly finance a new one, or about inadequate incentives—not when you are setting out to do the job of your life in the opportunity of a lifetime.

CHAPTER 4
EFFECTIVE CAREER CHANGING

Sometimes it is more than a job change—even more than a change from selling to sales management—that is being considered; it is instead a major career change. When that occurs, and whether a matter of choice or perceived necessity, it is wise to take a long, careful look at motives and alternatives. For whether you are looking for an alternative career in mid-life or seeking a satisfying, productive later-life career, such a change requires extremely careful assessment and planning.

Sales professionals have a good many excellent alternative career choices, made possible by their selling and marketing skills, varied experience in people-handling, and wide exposure to all kinds of problems and opportunities. In embarking upon new careers, some of them require as little as a change of self-definition over a period of years or a move from full-time to part-time work. Others require the addition of capital to established skills to achieve a change of self-definition and career. Some new careers require little in the way of new skills and experience, while others require a period of apprenticeship and additional formal training, to fill gaps and develop new skills. Still others require a great deal of new formal education and sometimes certification, and often a period of apprenticeship and investment of capital as well. Almost all are helped enormously by what an excellent, experienced sales professional brings to them.

As applied to careers, there is little operational difference between the terms *alternative* and *later-life.* The entrepreneurially minded person who literally becomes an entrepreneur and goes into his or her own business at the age of 55, staying in business full-time and later substantially part-time for 25 more years, until the age of 80, has engaged in an alternative career that eventually became a later-years career. The 30-year-old who opens a hardware store in a small Maine coastal village is, in operational terms, doing quite the same thing, although perhaps with considerably different motives.

It is the motive that supplies the distinction between alternative and later-life careers. Those who seek alternative careers are usually people who want to leave the corporate world, sometimes in favor of careers and life styles that seem far more attractive, and sometimes simply because they wish to take flight from a career that has become intolerably burdensome. Those who seek later-life careers, on the other hand, usually see pretty clearly that they want to continue in productive work for many years beyond retirement and often for the rest of their lives, or for as long as possible. An increasing number of those seeking later-life careers also understand that productive and lucrative work far beyond retirement is a necessity in these years of greatly increased life expectancies, constant inflation, and continuing erosion of the real value of all personal savings and investments, as well as of private and public pension plan payouts.

The distinction between alternative and later-life careers is important because you will explore, assess, and plan quite differently for one than for the other.

ASSESSING A CAREER CHANGE

In exploring the possibility of an alternative career, you must first ask one basic question: Do I really want something other than a selling career, or do I simply want a change? Beyond this are a number of corollary questions: Do I want out of selling or do I just want to do something different from what I am now doing? Is there something better that I want to do —and is there anything about a particular other career that I so strongly seek that I am willing to undertake a complete career change to get it? Is there anything intrinsic to selling that I detest? Is career choice the central issue confronting me, or are other matters far more central to my current discontents? Are my discontents truly job-related, or do they go back beyond the choice of management career? Am I, then, really talking about a career choice here, or a great deal more?

Those are hard questions. It takes a great deal of deep, unsparingly honest self-analysis to begin to answer them; even then, we can often only be very subjective in our approach to them. Others can help; but all too often those who in other situations help most—our spouses and other loved ones—are so much part of the problem, whether we or they know it or not, that their assistance is generally of little use. Close friends can help a little. So can counseling assistance, sometimes. Mostly, however, we are thrown back upon our own resources for analysis of our motives in these very difficult areas of career motivation, just as we were as teenagers starting out many years ago.

There are some very significant differences, though. We know a great deal more about ourselves, our personal situations, and the world than we did when making our earliest career choices; and we are far better equipped to do some astute problem-solving for ourselves than we were many years ago. There is another rather significant difference for most of us, as well: we are far more encumbered than we were then. Making decisions involving others is a good deal harder than those involving only ourselves as young people just starting out. Our material encumbrances, especially debts and other obligations, also force us to plan a great deal better than we once did and to take longer to implement any career-changing plans we make.

You may wake up one cold, wet December morning in Michigan, look in the mirror, and find yourself saying something like: "This is it. I've always wanted to be a lawyer, and defend the poor and helpless," or "I can't imagine what I'm doing here, getting ready to go into plastic places to sell to plastic people." If so, you may be seriously starting the process that eventuates in a career move. Caution, though: you may find yourself some years later, older and poorer, considering the same mirror in the same place, wondering what you are doing there, and beginning to realize that what you really wanted was a different job in a different place. Lawyers, after all, have to eat, just as do sellers; for every lawyer who spends a substantial amount of time in social service work, there are dozens who would like to, but spend most of their time in sober, dull commercial work.

It is very easy to misunderstand the nature of the problem. For example, a new career in the same geographical area will not solve the constant respiratory problems faced by people who work for years in cold, wet climates; post-nasal drip and sinus headaches can make life utterly miserable, no matter how well other aspects of life are going. A job change, accompanied by relocation to a warm, dry climate can and often does handle the problem, though.

Along similar lines, but less mundanely, a career change is highly unlikely to change a marriage that does not work into one that does. Yes, less travel and more agreeable living conditions can ease tensions. Certainly, more time to spend with one's family can have a beneficial impact on family relations. But marital problems are usually deeper and far more complex than that, and the strains caused by the process of seeking, preparing for, and entering a new career are often merely different, not less, than those that existed while you were pursuing your selling career. The existence of a difficult marital situation should not accelerate the seeking of a new career; just the opposite. It should act as a warning signal; the personal situation, not the career situation, may be the root cause of deep discontent, no matter how much the career situation seems to contribute to the problem. In such situations, family counseling can help a great deal more than career change, for the strains caused by career-changing may destroy a marriage that might otherwise have been salvageable.

For some of us, career change motives are as simple as realizing that the careers we originally wanted to pursue are now open to us. The young college graduate who wanted to go to law school, but had no money and many obligations on graduation from college, may have gone into selling, done an apprenticeship, made some money, and now may feel able to finance a legal education and a startup period in the practice of law. The woman who wanted to be a doctor 20 years ago, and was unable to enter medical school because of sex discrimination, may today leave the selling career she pursued as an alternative and seek to become the doctor she never stopped wanting to be.

Some of us develop new interests and new career drives during the years in selling, causing moves into new careers after years, and sometimes even decades, in selling. The person who becomes deeply involved with his or her own children and then far more widely interested in children over the years, may develop a strong desire to work with them professionally, and become a psychologist, reading specialist, or social worker. The city person who comes to live in the country may be so strongly attracted to the land that nothing but farming will do. The sports buff who pursues a career in selling may turn out to be most of all, a sports buff; more than a few skilled sales professionals have turned their talents to the development of racquet clubs and ski resorts, only partly in pursuit of business opportunities, mostly in pursuit of a sports-related career. Likewise the hobbyist chef who opens a restaurant, the publishing marketer who moves over into a writing career, and the boating enthusiast who winds up running a marina—all these are people who are running to new careers rather than away from old ones.

Later-life careers have much in common with such alternative careers, in that they are positively, rather than negatively, inspired. Here, too, whether the contemplated later-life career involves substantial investment and full-time commitment for many years or modest investment and part-time commitment, the move is being made to reach new goals, bringing with it productive work and usually much-needed income for the later years.

Whatever the reasons for wanting to make a career-changing or later-years career move, careful assessments and specific preparations must be made before alternatives can become choices and before moves are actually made. For without realistic planning and effective implementation of plans, such career moves may become little more than opportunities to go broke.

Therefore a caution: never burn your bridges when you move out of a selling career, for the move may prove temporary. Yesterday's dream may be today's bankruptcy; it may also prove to have been today's crashing bore. That wonderful restaurant you always wanted to start may prove a drain on both financial resources and patience. You may find that cooking is a wonderful hobby, but that arguing about the price of provisions and finding the money to pay your staff after a couple of bad weeks is quite a different game indeed. And cooking for friends once or twice a week may prove quite different from working 12 hours a day, six or seven days a week, in a hot kitchen. That selling job you found so unrewarding may look perfectly wonderful after a couple of years of running your restaurant, or hardware store, or farm. Many who headed for the country during the 1960s stayed in the country, pursuing new careers; but many others stayed for a while and then returned to their former careers. So do not broadcast what you think of your company and its president over too many drinks at your going-away party. Do keep all the people in your various in-company and wider business networks informed as to your whereabouts, activities, and plans, no matter how inconvenient all that letter writing may be on a kitchen table out on the farm. And do keep a little rainy-day money, which will enable you to go back to your previous life and career in relatively orderly fashion, if that is what you ultimately feel you should or must do, no matter how committed to your new career you are at the start.

PLANNING A CAREER CHANGE

Whatever the nature of your contemplated new career commitment, you will need to plan well if it is to succeed. And good planning in this area starts with a sober assessment of assets, liabilities, and possibilities, in terms of skills, resources, aptitudes, and drives.

Let us first discuss the mid-career full-time change. Here current and near-term realities come first; and first among these your financial resources. (The personal financial statements you develop in Chapter 9 will be especially helpful here.) In this context, what you are looking for most of all is not personal financial worth, or how much you can realize when selling a home that must in one way or another be replaced almost immediately. You are looking for spendable liquid assets, in the forms of savings and investments that can easily be turned into cash to apply toward living expenses, any necessary formal training or apprenticeship, and any other necessary investment in your new career. Those assets will not include such personal pension plans as Keogh and IRA accounts, for the cost of converting these into cash prematurely is too high.

It will then be necessary to subtract current debts from those liquid assets. You will have to include all debts on which payments are being made or that will become due in the years in which you will be moving into your new career. These will be drains on liquid assets in those years, not necessarily offset by current income if you are likely to be making less money in those years than you are now. Even if your new field is as lucrative as selling, it is unlikely to pay you as well in the early years as does selling now, after some years as a working sales professional. This must be taken into account in planning the financial side of an alternative career move.

Next, it is necessary to take a very sober look at predictable major expenditures for the coming few years, especially the coming cost of educating children (if any), as well as those costs that may be associated with formally educating yourself in a new career. Even a modestly expensive four-year college education will cost $6,000–8,000 per year, or $24,-000–32,000 for four years, in this period, while expensive schools cost $50,000–60,000 for the four-year period; both will soon cost a good deal more, and all this without graduate school costs. Someone who attempts a major career change in mid-career without soberly taking into consideration coming college costs will probably be unable to complete that career in the long run.

In a way, it seems a bit unkind to dwell upon the financial necessities inherent in a major mid-career change; what usually makes such a change so attractive is the feeling of coming freedom it engenders. But for serious people, and usually family people at that, financial considerations are basic. As always, the money does not seem very important when you are a relatively well-paid working sales professional, but it becomes crucial when you do not have enough of it to provide for yourself and your loved ones. That is always true; but in difficult times, it becomes even more important to be financially prudent, for getting where you want to go requires more astute planning and execution than in easy times.

Now, with real liquid assets in hand, and identifiable major expenditures defined, it is wise to conservatively estimate your probable after-tax, or spendable, income in the years just ahead, including income from your own new work, that of others in your family, and anticipated savings and investment earnings. Be sure to allow for any periods in which you will be earning little or no income because of formal education, apprenticeship, or startup requirements. Then estimate your normal personal expenditures for that period.

With all these factors in mind, and with figures in hand, you can begin to make realistic estimates as to the financial feasibility of those alternative careers you may have in mind. If the net of anticipated income and expenditure for that coming period is a minus, as it usually is, that minus factor must be carefully taken into account. Caution: Do not, as is perfectly natural, begin to trim the figures unrealistically, in order to make them work. Anyone can play with figures; certainly sales professionals know how to do so. But do not. The figure play that we must sometimes engage in during sales forecasting is entirely inappropriate when projecting alternative careers, for here you are normally dealing with all your personal reserves. In a corporate situation, a misestimate may be embarrassing, but within reasonable limits will not particularly harm you or your company. But a personal misestimate in alternative career planning can sink you, and by destroying your financial position can make it very difficult to seek alternatives for many years to come. Then you may indeed be trapped. Yes, it happens all the time, and especially when the chosen alternative career is a business that requires personal investment and loans secured by personal signature. It may even happen to you; but it is not likely to happen if you plan your move soberly, using all your professional skills.

Very often, the net of all the figures you generate at this stage of the alternative career planning process is a stunning and daunting minus figure. That should not be surprising. In this period, few mid-career people with family responsibilities have much in the way of savings and investments; and most have large and quite predictable expenses ahead, whether or not they change careers. For some, the size of the additional stake needed for serious pursuit of an alternative career is an insurmountable barrier, at least in the current period. If so, it is better to reach that conclusion rationally than either to embark upon a ruinous and impossible enterprise or to regret for the rest of your life not making a move that, on analysis, would have been a disaster. The business world is full of those who wish they had tried various alternatives in their earlier years, but did not. For those who find romantic yearning sustaining, it may be useful never to know whether a cherished dream was possible or a pie in the sky made impossible by previous personal—usually family—commitments. For most of us, it is far better to reach rational conclusions, know why we have or have not made a move, and then proceed to make the most of what we have.

More often, however, the minus figure is not insurmountable in the long term, although it may require considerable adjustment of our initial desires. Adaptation to reality may consist of deciding to wait before making an alternative career move, meanwhile building up savings and investment and fulfilling responsibilities to others. It is not at all unusual for a planned alternative career move to take years to accomplish, as people take formal courses while continuing full-time work, trim living standards to allow for the building of a financial stake, and often defer action until college or other educational expenses are paid or accounted for.

The selling profession being what it is, and sellers being as flexible as they are, adaptation also often consists of moving into jobs closer to the proposed career change. For example, those wanting to leave the cities and move into ranching and farming will often look for jobs that allow them to live in rural areas; then the process of developing a new country life can proceed quite rationally as the years go by, with land purchase and the start of work paralleling the selling career. Such a gradual approach is especially effective if both partners in a marriage desire the same career change; first one spouse and later the other can be "liberated" to do the new kind of work. The seller who wants to be a lawyer may attend law school part-time, making sure to live in an area in which this is possible. The seller who wants to become an entrepreneur will very often seek work as a sales manager in a small company in the desired industry, or move from sales management in a big company to a small company, with an equity stake in the small company the vehicle for a move into an entrepreneurial position. Sales professionals, far more than those in most other professions, can move directly toward many other careers, while still working in selling.

What new career you would like to move into is a matter of motivation. When, where, and how you move are largely matters of resources and adaptive ingenuity. How well you will be able to make a go of your move rests upon all of the above, and also upon your skills and personal characteristics.

If you are personally unsuitable for a projected new career, and if no amount of preparation and skills-building can make you so, then you are pursuing a will-o'-the-wisp, and should desist forthwith. That most sales professionals are excellent people-handlers and personally quite adaptable is of no help at all if you are unable to handle the organic chemistry necessary for pre-medical study, or the mathematics necessary to become a physicist, or do not have the physical ability to become a professional athlete. Those kinds of things are quite obvious reality sandwiches, to be consumed with good grace, if somewhat ruefully.

Other disabilities are less obvious. For example, it is quite possible to become a very successful sales professional without having much of a head for numbers. You can go on for years without anyone, including yourself, quite understanding that. But if you want to become the owner and general manager of a small business, that lack of numbers sense is a fatal disability. You can ease the problem by spending an apprenticeship period in someone else's business; by trying to pay a great deal of attention to the financial management side of your own small business; and by securing and spending time with a good accountant. For many that is enough to cure the early weakness. But for others, all fails; the numbers sense just is not there, and then a seemingly good career move proves to have been a mistake. Sometimes, it is still possible to make a go of it, even then; many a family business moves along quite nicely with one spouse handling the numbers and the other handling other aspects of the business.

Questions of aptitude and skill should be faced as squarely as possible before alternative career decisions are made. They are often curable afterward, but only if perceived in time; all too often they are perceived far too late for the failing situation to be saved.

Similarly, many successful sales professionals are superb people-handlers, as long as they can roam free, and need only persuade people to buy. When it comes to such mundane matters as buying penuriously, training workers, organizing production, and making sure that everybody gets paid on time, their skills are less than minimal, and their motivations even less. Many good sales professionals are no more fitted to go into business for themselves than they are to go into sales management or any other kind of management. Many recognize this over the years, and therefore stay happily and lucratively in field sales—but somehow fail to link up with current hopes when they go into their own businesses and lose their shirts. Once again, the problem may be curable either by the accretion of new skills or by the securing of a partner to handle that side of the business. But if the problem had been understood early, perhaps a different kind of alternative career would have been chosen—or perhaps no alternative career at all. Some of us are far better off continuing to do what we do so well; the grass may only *seem* greener elsewhere.

Our strengths, too, are important to assess. What is weakness for one course of action may be enormous strength for another. One who should think carefully before going into a production-oriented business may do extraordinarily well as an independent investment broker. The manager with little numbers sense may make a superb restaurateur, as long as someone else handles the numbers.

Successful alternative career choices require sizing up your skills and aptitudes as astutely and unemotionally as you would if you were evaluating someone else's. The ability to analyze the strengths and weaknesses of others is a prime selling skill, and is to be applied to ourselves as well, as best we can.

MAKING A CAREER CHANGE

If your decision is to go ahead and seek a new career, then the key actions are: going toward strength and desire, rather than moving away from weakness and unhappiness; going when you have the financial resources to make the decision stick through what may be some difficult times; going when the family situation is supportive and good, rather than in a probably doomed attempt to save a bad situation; going when the going is good, that is, when health and drive and energy level all will contribute to your success at whatever you try; and going intelligently, ready to get the formal and apprenticeship training you may need, fill gaps in your skills as needed, and repair or make up your weaknesses as necessary for the new kind of job you are setting out to do.

For some alternative careers, additional formal training is a must. Law, medicine, accounting, the sciences, engineering, college teaching, and architecture, among others, require years of formal education and some kind of certification. The time and cost of formal education must be taken into account when considering these careers. For other alternative careers, such as agriculture, the performing and visual arts, writing, broadcasting, and many kinds of business ownership, a very considerable amount of additional education and apprenticeship may be needed, but little in the way of formal degrees or certification. For such careers as business ownership and agriculture, which is for these purposes mainly business ownership, some capital investment is also needed.

But even when formal education and certification are not required, many alternative careers, in practice, do require considerable additional formal education. One who wants to move into the arts or farming, for example, is very well-advised to take appropriate formal courses before moving into the early years of work in the new career.

Where educational gaps exist, formal courses can help a great deal. Someone who is weak in finance, for example, should not go into business without attempting to fill this gap in knowledge by taking courses in business mathematics and the use of small computers programmed to meet small business needs.

For almost all alternative careers, a period of apprenticeship is no less necessary than it was for the original careers pursued. It is odd indeed to see a sales professional who has spent many years really learning his or her profession—years that may or may not have included much formal training, but certainly did include a great deal of early practical work that can only be described as an apprenticeship—then proceed into small business ownership with little more than a modest amount of cash and a great deal of hope.

No sane business owner hires a general manager to run a subsidiary or division who has had no hands-on experience at all with a business carrying a similar set of functions and responsibilities. When you hire such a general manager, you pay a great deal of attention to demonstrated skills, relevant hands-on experience, size of operations previously managed, the extent of previous profit responsibility, and track record in that area. You pay considerably less attention to formal training, and especially that which has been completed many years ago. You pay some attention to previous functional responsibilities, but not much, for a superb staff person will usually be totally unqualified for a general manager's job.

Yet new small business owners "hire" themselves to run small businesses all the time, using precious and often irreplaceable personal capital to fund their businesses, and going into debt besides, without taking the trouble to train themselves properly to run their own businesses. Putting it that way makes it sound absurd—and so it is—but it is done every day, and with our own money and future prospects.

For example, a sales manager may reason that "management is management," and "selling is selling," and that the same skills that have been successfully applied to a career spent in large corporations can be applied equally successfully to the management and growth of that hardware store on the Maine coast, or a suburban restaurant, or the running of a farm. Not so—or at best only partially so—for the missing skills and experience elements will generally cause business disaster. In the hardware store, lack of knowledge of the basic stock and resulting inability to advise customers on the use of that stock, coupled with the need to hold and manage a large inventory turning over at low margins may, and probably will, cause the inexperienced to fail. In the restaurant, the need for astute, low-margin buying as well as selling, coupled with the need to continually hire, train, and manage new people in a labor-intensive industry characterized by high staff turnover, will often turn the novice's promising restaurant into a failure. On the farm—well, by golly, on the farm you need to know how to farm, no matter who you are or what else you know, and that requires hands-on experience.

All require development of the kinds of knowledge that come from experience. That experience may be gained in several ways, all the way from deep involvement for a year or more—which is optimal, if you can arrange it—before taking a full entrepreneurial plunge, to several varieties of part-time involvement. One way to gain experience is to work part-time in someone else's operation, perhaps on evenings and weekends, often for small pay, the main compensation being what you learn. Another is to buy a share in a going business, learning while your partner manages, and later taking fuller operating responsibility or buying out your partner, perhaps by prearrangement. For example, it is very often possible to buy a going business, and make an arrangement with an experienced owner to stay on as manager for a while, perhaps six months to a year, while you learn the business and perhaps wind up your responsibilities elsewhere. Or you might buy a share in a growing business, using your capital and increasing knowledge to expand the business, as for example to open a second jointly owned restaurant or to begin a franchising operation which links your selling skills with the specific skills of your new partner.

Some apprenticeship periods can last part-time for years, as when you develop a farm or service operation as a part-time business, only gradually moving to a full-time business. A classic and often-successful pattern is for one spouse to move into the business and begin to grow it while the other stays put, supplying part-time assistance, learning as both accrete experience, and continuing to supply much-needed business capital and living expenses from a continuing management career. When both spouses are involved, this can be a most fruitful way to go, coupling the accretion of needed skills and experience with a relatively safe continuing supply of personal capital. In periods of high interest rates, that supply of capital alone can mean the difference between success and failure. And that experience can mean the difference between success and failure in all seasons.

Even if you are likely to hire others, hands-on experience may prove invaluable. The entrepreneur who wants to open a print shop in a local community, which will employ others as copying machine operators, printers, and artists, will be very well-advised to learn how to run the basic machines before stepping off into the business. The computer service business requires some basic knowledge of computers and programs, as well as how to sell and manage.

Other professions often require considerable lead time before becoming economically viable, as they would have if you would have pursued them as your first profession, and no matter how much your skills help you to expand the business side of the profession. For example, if you become a lawyer, you will need time either to develop a practice, or to develop enough skill to command a salary anywhere near what you commanded as a sales professional. Likewise, as a new doctor, and aside from any residency requirements, you will need time to develop a practice or command a good salary. When and if you do decide to go into practice, you will need a good deal of setting-up money.

The details differ, but the same is true for business enterprises. The capital you initially invest usually must be joined by more—often a good deal more—if your new business is to have a reasonable chance to succeed. Most new businesses fail, and the single largest reason they fail is undercapitalization. This translates into inability to stay the normal course, through the necessary months and sometimes years of business building, the years in which experience is accreted, "tuition" thereby paid, and proper foundations laid for success.

For those coming out of the corporate world, it is often not so much a question of foolish optimism or burning desire to leave that world, as it is a misestimation of financial scale. On the financial side, small business requirements, and especially cash-flow requirements, can seem minuscule in comparison with even the smallest corporate budgets. Alas, small expenditures do not seem so small later, when they must come out of smaller revenues and personal, rather than corporate, resources. And corporate people, no matter how profit-conscious, rarely pinch pennies, as beginning small business owners must; what in a large business might be thought by all to be counterproductive in morale terms may be simple survival necessity in a smaller business. In a large business, one does not tend to literally count paper clips; in a small business, one who does not quickly learn how to count paper clips, packets of seed, napkins to be cleaned, and the number of 10-cent widgets in inventory is soon out of business.

Similarly, scale can defeat proven skills, if care is not taken to adjust them to small business needs. A kind of attention to detail is necessary that may never have been required before. In small businesses—and here we include professional practices, which are to a considerable extent also small businesses—individuals must be trained far more carefully than in larger businesses, for much more rides on each individual trained. Similarly, small business owners must personally buy, price, and sell with the right margin in mind for each item or service sold. Here there is no formal market testing, skilled purchasing department help, or professional management group at work. Only you, with the skills and care you bring to the situation. The importance of a proper transition from large to small enterprise cannot be overestimated; as with undercapitalization and insufficient apprenticeship, it can cause failure where success might well have been achieved.

Moving into a new career takes planning and can take a good deal of time, what with family responsibilities, training and apprenticeship needs, and necessary capital accumulation. As always, though, it can help enormously to know where you want to go—or at least a range of alternative possibilities—for then you can prepare, fruitfully using the time between decision and new career launch.

For example, it is often possible to use current activities and affiliations for positioning purposes. The sales professional who wants to become a restaurateur will be well-advised to try to find selling work in the hotel and restaurant industry, perhaps then even being able to start the new career part-time or with one spouse leading the way, ultimately to be joined by the other.

LATER-LIFE CAREERS

Like mid-career changes, the successful development of alternative later-life careers requires astute long-term planning and effective execution, especially in difficult times. Planning and execution in this area can and should be a very long-term affair, involving capital formation, formal preparation, and apprenticeship, all often occurring while your earlier career is in its most productive and lucrative period.

Most sales professionals achieve greatest job status, personal prestige, and income levels late in their careers; yet this is the period in which later-life careers are most actively planned and started. That is as it should be. No matter how much responsibility you carry late in your career, and even though the latter part of your career is quite lucrative, the odds are that you will *need* to pursue gainful economic activity long after your sixty-fifth birthday.

We put this in terms of need, rather than desire, quite advisedly. Yes, many of us may correctly perceive that it is far healthier to continue in some kind of productive work as long as reasonably possible, which for some of us will be well into our seventies, eighties, and even into our nineties. But, in fact, most of us will really have little choice in the matter —inflation and long life will see to that. As our retirement incomes erode, we will have to find gainful work—and not entry-level work, but the kind of lucrative, satisfying work that we are capable of generating with our seasoned skills.

There will be exceptions to this increasingly evident rule, certainly. Some who have done exceedingly well financially and perhaps have gained a substantial entrepreneurial share in a company that continues to be successful, may be able to live on pensions and the interest and dividends generated by their capital, without invading capital and with earnings enough beyond yearly expenditures to grow their capital and keep up with inflation. Others will not do quite that well, but will have enough at 65 to provide for all foreseeable needs for their lifetimes. But those who will be able to retire at 65 without continuing to earn are now few and far between and will become even fewer in number in the decades ahead. Fixed pension plan payments that look large now will seem and will be very small later, as inflation effectively devalues the dollar. Corporate stock in good, growing companies may hold and increase its value, but today's sound company may be gone tomorrow. Government pension payouts can be relied upon only to diminish in real dollar value.

Were you to retire tomorrow, at age 65, with $50,000 per year in income from all sources, you would still be well-advised to develop lucrative later-years work. For in less than 10 years that $50,000 will be worth only $25,000, if the inflation experience of the last decade continues into the next. When you are 85—and many of us will live that long or longer, and often in good health—that $50,000 is likely to be worth $12,500 or less in today's dollars. Actually, if you have no other income, you will probably long before then have found it necessary to invade capital, thereby further diminishing your future income. Putting it sharply and clearly, then, all but a very, very few of today's working professionals had best plan to use their skills to make money far beyond today's normal retirement age of 65. It is probably better to do so for reasons of physical and emotional health, anyway; but for reasons of economic health, it will be indispensable.

For many, that will first of all mean not retiring at 65, but staying on in place or with somewhat reduced responsibilities. In a period in which many heads of state and others in government around the world are in their seventies (sometimes in their very late seventies and even in their eighties), it makes very good sense for those in reasonably good health to plan to stay on, acquitting their responsibilities increasingly well. In selling, experience—when accompanied by continuing good health—counts for a great deal; seasoned professionals in their late sixties and on into their seventies can continue to make major contributions, and will be doing so more and more in the period ahead.

Sometimes, in-place, later-years work will be accompanied by shifts in responsibility. A traveler may trade the best and one of the most arduous travel territories in the company for much less wearing, but sometimes as lucrative, city territory. A hard-charging national accounts representative may wind up working behind a telephone in the home office and making just as much money as before. Later-years work in place may mean somewhat less money, but not necessarily.

Many will choose to retire, collect well-earned benefits, and stay in selling. There is no reason at all for someone who has spent decades selling in an industry and knows that industry inside out to quit it, as long as there are independent representatives selling in that industry. And many a sales professional looking forward to the later years has bought into a lucrative distributorship, dealership, or franchise, turning existing selling skills and contacts into far greater income than was ever enjoyed during the selling years.

Staying in selling, one way or another, is worth considering carefully, when thinking about a later-years career. It may be that if you see it properly, you need look no farther than your own backyard.

But even when a continuing career in selling is possible, many of us do not wish to continue doing what we have done for most of our lives, instead looking forward to changes of location, life style, and occupation in our later years.

Under those circumstances, a wide range of alternative later-life careers are available; the same wide range of alternative careers that may be chosen by those seeking mid-career changes, plus many part-time occupations that might not yield enough income to be pursued in mid-career, but are entirely satisfactory later in life.

We speak here of occupations, of careers—not of entry-level time-fillers. There is no reason in the world for a skilled professional to work for even an hour as a school crossing guard, a night watchman, or a babysitter. A later-years occupation has nothing to do with "making a few dollars to help you through the later years," as well-meaning bad advice so often has it. Far from it. If you take the time and trouble to prepare properly, and enter a later-years career as an independent professional or businessperson, you will command the same kind of respect and hold the same kind of prestige—though often in a much smaller geographical area —that you did during your earlier career. And simultaneously you will earn far, far more than you could possibly earn as a school crossing guard, a night watchman, or a babysitter.

For later-years occupations, lead time is the key, and the longer the lead time, the better. You may choose a later-years career that requires little more than moving from a sales career into a related business, as when you choose to be a franchisee, or a manufacturer's representative in a familiar industry. In such instances, the main requirements are likely to be some investment capital and some small apprenticeship time in the specific kind of business. On the other hand, you may choose a later-years career that requires many years of preparation, as when you decide to enter a whole new profession, requiring years of formal training followed by apprenticeship.

Starting the decision-making process early allows you to consider the widest possible set of choices. Most of us start planning for such careers far too late to be able to consider many of the choices available. At age 54, you can easily and seriously consider amassing the considerable skills needed to become a farmer, lawyer, or financial planner, and do so some time between then and reaching 65. But at 64, you may have enormous difficulty moving into such occupations from a standing start, even when capital is available.

Unfortunately, many of us do not even start planning later-years occupations until after retirement. We retire somewhere between the ages of 60 and 70, live on our pensions for a while, sometimes for many years, and then find that we are bored and restless—and are running out of money. By then our choices are very limited, our financial resources small, our web of contacts long gone, our physical and emotional stamina often greatly impaired. Then we can indeed find ourselves working for next to nothing, if we can find any work at all.

It is far better to start thinking hard about how you can productively employ your talents and skills while you are in your forties, move into specific planning soon after (certainly no later than your mid-fifties), and into execution of your well-laid plans in plenty of time to guarantee success. Although most other professions, such as law and teaching, easily define necessary lead times in terms of education and certification requirements, many other later-life occupations also require considerable preparation.

Even turning hobbies into lucrative part-time and sometimes full-time second careers can require a good deal of lead time. You may decide, for example, that coin or stamp collecting, which you have done for many years as a quite casual hobby, can be the kind of second career you want. That may not require any formal education or certification, but it certainly will require a great deal of study and professionalization on your part. The difference between the casual amateur and the professional in any field is a whole world of learning and experience. The casual collector can attend an occasional show or auction, browse in a collector's magazine now and then, make a good buy here and a bad buy there, and come out more or less decently, partly by accident and partly through the impact of inflation over the years, which provides seeming gains in the value of what was collected. The professional collector and dealer, on the other hand, knows just as much about his or her trade as you do about selling. That means a great deal of reading, studying, and immersion in the field, leading to astute, consistently knowledgeable and advantageous buying, selling, and holding; in this, the astute collector and trader is much like the professional securities trader.

The same holds true for those who plan to spend a good deal of their time managing their own financial resources. That is no more an affair for amateurs than is collecting or selling. It all requires immersion, development of skills and experience, and the working of an apprenticeship period, preferably with a seasoned hand at the business to show you the ropes.

For most who move into other careers in their later years, it will be best to plan early and well to become a small business owner or independent professional. Age discrimination, no matter how rigorously prohibited by law, will continue to be a fact of life in hiring for some time to come. But the same company and people that will find some reason not to hire you as an employee at age 70 will often rather easily enter into a business relationship with you as accountant, tax preparer, bookkeeper, lawyer, stockbroker, or vendor of any of the scores of items they need to conduct their business. And people will buy your goods and services at retail equally readily whether you are 73 or 37.

The difference between working as an independent businessperson or professional, and working as a poorly paid "retiree" are enormous. The truth is that people at the top of their trades find it very difficult to go to work at or near entry level in any other trade—nor should they. The truth also is that the difference between what you can make as an independent professional and what you can make as a relatively unskilled later-years employee is very large. Forgetting about fringes for the purpose of this example, the difference between payment at the rate of even $30,000 a year —and that is low for retiring sales professionals—and the perhaps $5 per hour you might make as a relatively unskilled worker, is the difference between about $16 per hour and $5 per hour. Even working half-time, that difference of $11 per hour comes to $10,000 a year. That $10,000 more a year is like going into your later years with an additional $125,000, assuming you could net even 8% on your investment money yearly, and like having the money grow right along with the pace of inflation over the years. Inflation will erode your pension, dividends, and interest earnings, but the reverse will hold true for professional earnings. Your $10,000 more per year, now worth $125,000 in investment money, may in 20 years be worth four times as much in the dollars of that year, growing to $40,000 per year as your other payments diminish in value.

In sum, those of us who develop a real second career for our later years in a timely and well-planned way, are likely to live out our lives well-respected, relatively affluent members of our communities, while those who plan too little, too late, or not at all, risk living ever closer to the edge of poverty, as unwilling and increasingly helpless de facto wards of the state. Clearly, it is necessary to exercise the quite obvious choices before us, to prepare and execute plans for later-life careers.

PART II
CAREER SKILLS

CHAPTER 5
MANAGING YOUR TIME AND WORK

Managing time and work well is a matter of developing sturdy techniques, based on sound work habits, into lifelong reflexes that will see us through all kinds of situations and jobs, in and out of selling. We are whole people, after all; a fragmented and erratic approach to the personal side of life will inevitably be reflected to great disadvantage on the working side.

A life in selling really requires a great deal of self-management, and backup piled upon backup. For the truth is that without astute and consistent work planning and execution, even the best face-to-face selling skills in the world will not suffice to build selling success and your career. And that excellent self-management is increasingly necessary; prospects and customers, faced with extremely difficult personal and business lives, are all too often pressed and somewhat demoralized by the blizzard of paper, telephone calls, and people in which they find themselves, so we must be better organized than ever before to maximize our field effectiveness.

Sales professionals can all too easily be pressed and demoralized, too, if they let control over their working lives slip away from them. It can happen in a score of ways on any day—a couple of missed appointments, a fire to put out way over on the other side of a territory, a mislaid prospect file, a flood of telephone calls because of a widespread service problem, a maladjusted carburetor, an unanticipated dinner engagement and consequent inadequate preparation for the next day, an insistent home office call about some long-delayed and entirely insignificant reports—and all these only begin to tickle the negative possibilities. On top of these kinds of very real external problems, there are the sour apple who manages, over time-wasting morning coffee, to sour your day, too; the argument at home over the time you are spending on paperwork and planning; the complaint from your children last time you set out on the road; the missed quota; the unpaid bills; and myriad other negative emotional possibilities. All of which—the concrete and the emotional—can harm your concentration, your ability to plan and execute, and your sales success, thereby making matters that much worse. Sales professionals depend upon attitude, skill, and consistency; the out-of-control tailspin is the greatest of all short-term hazards, and can grow into a career breaker, if you let it.

That, in the largest sense, is what organization is for: to help you to concentrate, plan, execute well, and build success on success, whatever the negative factors might be in work and life. Efficiency builds sales and makes money; that is a prime result of the proper organization and management of time and work. Beyond that is the control that excellent self-management gives you, which builds your professional career—and that is the most important result of all.

It starts with some basic understandings of what it takes—in time, attention, and skill—to manage a selling career. No, it does not start with organizational forms, complete with neat time charts and boxes to fill in; it starts with understanding, the most important of which stems from analysis of what we must do, and how and when we must do it.

One of the greatest enemies of selling effectiveness is the concept of *prime selling time.* Not only when carried to absurdity, as it so often is by the least effective (and often the laziest) of us; that is easy to see. When a field representative solemnly assures you that the best possible time to sell them is between 10:00 and 11:30 A.M., and between 2:30 (when "they" get back from lunch) and 4:00 P.M., you know that you are looking at either an amateur or someone who thinks you are an amateur. And it is absurd; people will buy what you are selling at any time they are willing to make a firm appointment and place themselves in what they know will be a selling situation. That is axiomatic; all sales professionals know that, whether admitting it to others or not.

But even some professionals fall for the prime selling time concept in a different and quite damaging way. What grows is the seemingly self-serving notion that some times really can be better than others for selling, and that so much other work is connected with selling that some time has to be spent during the working day doing the nuts and bolts kinds of things: prospect file updating, telephone service calls, call reports, pre-heat letters, and a wide-ranging miscellany of time-consuming trivia. That can mean a good deal of office time, whether in the company office, the office at home, or a motel while on the road. Usually, it means starting the actual selling day "just a little later" and ending it "just a little earlier." Except that just a half hour spent on this sort of thing every day, when you should be on the way to your first—and very early, if possible—appointment of the day, can be very, very expensive in the long run. And just a half hour at the end of the day can be equally expensive; so can a half hour spent each morning having coffee with a group of failing time wasters from your office. The fact is that prime selling time is any time your qualified prospects are at work—or elsewhere—and are willing to talk to you in a selling situation. And every possible hour of that prime selling time should be spent setting up selling interviews, getting to those interviews, selling, taking care of existing customers, and refueling self and vehicles as necessary, and the less time you have to spend on getting to them and refueling, the better it is. The paperwork and all that is for another time, when your prospects and customers are not willing to be sold. They are just as likely as you are to be working in nonprime times, by the way—just not ready to be sold.

Time, work, and career building are all aspects of a single professional life; all are a single seamless web and all must be managed together, within the context of a satisfying personal life. The controlled weaving together of all these elements adds up to successful self-management; and all depend on constant evaluation and reevaluation, setting and resetting, of personal and professional goals.

In the area of time management, for example, it is always very tempting to start by pointing out that there are only 168 hours in a week; to proceed by setting forth a series of mechanisms which will in the aggregate help us to use our time most effectively and then to embellish lovingly what are essentially a series of simple techniques with scores of checklists, charts, graphs, and other visual materials designed to help drive home the simple points made. Useful, certainly; but by itself utterly misleading. For without a deep understanding of your own personal and professional goals, and of the work within which you are to a considerable extent encased, these simple techniques will take you nowhere, no matter how effectively and attractively presented. In this instance a picture is not worth a thousand words; quite the opposite. A few well-chosen words, reflecting your own hard analysis and illuminating the nature of your goals and environment, are likely to be worth a thousand graphs, checklists, charts, and cartoons.

Our main long-term goals are least likely to change as our careers develop. To put it a little differently, jobs, tasks, environments, and career goals may change, but we will continue attempting to keep our home situations stable, maintain our physical and emotional health, build our skills and careers, make our organizations successful, and provide for our later years, no matter how much else changes.

Except for relatively brief periods, as in the early years of selling, or in such unstable periods as those of marital breakup, most of us will insist on trying to develop and grow healthy home situations, no matter what the demands of our work. That is not new; however, the extent and bedrock nature of that insistence is new, and reflects the expectations and emphases developed by two generations of concentration upon such matters as mental health and sound interpersonal relations. It is even quite likely to be true of the "liberated single," who is very often, underneath the appurtenances of life style, just a rather traditional American man or woman who demonstrates the need for stability by attempting to build long-term relationships out of some very unlikely material and situations.

For sales professionals, that bedrock insistence often seems in sharp contradiction with professional needs and job demands. For the truth is that most of us do not work even nearly the hours we seem to work. You may work a 35-hour week—in the field—but aside from holidays you are highly unlikely to have devoted as few as 35 hours a week to the practice of your profession in all your working life. There is always work to do at home, much of it vital to job success. There are always networks to be cultivated for career-building purposes, on the job and also most significantly on your "own" time. There are professional publications to read and assess, and professional organizations that quite properly require a good deal of attention. All these on personal time.

Personal time? Nonsense. That is the conceptual error that creates the seeming contradiction between the very real 50–80 hours a week you spend pursuing your career and your bedrock insistence on a sound personal life. To think of the time spent during the "normal" business day as paid work time, and the rest of your professional time as a set of unpaid and deeply resented encroachments upon your personal life, is purely and simply to set yourself up for a life of continual personal resentment and abrasion at home, and for a foredoomed lifelong attempt to somehow cut your out-of-the-field professional time demands as close as possible to zero.

PROFESSIONAL LIFE

It just does not work that way. It never did. A sales professional can no more avoid "after-hours" professional responsibilities than can a lawyer, who must keep up with current professional developments and develop and sustain client relationships for much of each working week, far beyond the time actually spent in office, court, or library. Or a doctor, who must keep up with professional developments and association activities, even though a direct working week may be as long as 60–80 hours, sometimes even more. Or a manager, who may leave a clean desk at the office after spending a seven-hour day there, but then goes home with a briefcase full of planning and paperwork, and spends large amounts of commuting, evening, and weekend time on work and career-related matters.

Putting it that way, there is no reason to expect that your professional life should be less busy than the lives of other kinds of professionals. Real adjustments must be made between professional and home matters, but they need only be adjustments, rather than the kinds of seemingly unmanageable contradictions that stem from misunderstanding the nature of a professional life. You do not simply sell time, on an hourly, weekly, or yearly basis; you pursue an entire career, with field time and current compensation only part of that career. With that understanding clearly in mind, expectations can be realistic; so can be moves aimed at improving total effectiveness, saving valuable time, and increasing control over both professional and personal life.

In any event, sales professionals should expect to spend a good deal of valuable working time at home, on the road, and in some cases while commuting to and from offices. The nature of the work and the need to pursue a career makes it so. Your after-hours work is vital and normal, and to be planned for, no matter how effective your selling style may be.

Once the professional practice of selling is seen this way, the seeming and real contradictions between business and home life come into focus. The real contradictions remain; they are the same time choices caused by the practice of any work requiring long hours and close attention. However, the seeming contradictions—and these are the ones that cause so much trouble at home—disappear. They are replaced by recognition of the need to organize effectively that part of the work that is properly done out of the field, so that it may be done well and within time bounds you have consciously set, rather than expanding to fill and thereby destroy your own personal life and the lives of others with whom you live.

That requires most of all the will to do so, which can only come from shared understandings. It does not matter how efficiently you may have set up an office at home if those you live with expect your almost undivided attention at home. For example, a woman in selling whose family expects her to come home to cook, clean, nurse, and in general watch and ward for them during all the rest of her waking hours is a woman whose career and home life are in probably disastrous conflict. Not because she is spending too much or too little time with either business or personal life, but because her family does not understand that her profession demands that she continue to practice it at home as well as in the office.

Similarly, a man or woman who is heavily and continually criticized at home for "not spending enough time with the family" may indeed be a compulsive and self-destroying person; or may be simply a working professional trying to practice that part of his or her trade that must be practiced at home, under terribly adverse conditions. There are work compulsives, of course; but there is also widespread misunderstanding of when and where the profession of selling is practiced. Someone who works 60 or 70 hours a week, and sometimes even more, including many hours at home, may be a "work compulsive," who is in the process of destroying home and family; he or she is far more likely to be a quite normal, considerably overworked sales professional, trying to pursue a difficult profession in the twin maelstroms of home and field.

And there is the key. You have to be able to think, plan, and organize somewhere, whenever you want to. It is a must; it is indispensable to the practice of the profession. It cannot be done during a day in the field; it must be done before or after hours, and elsewhere. Usually that means at home. Usually—but not always. Some who travel a lot accomplish a great deal of "office" work on the road, and some who commute accomplish much while traveling to and from work.

OFFICE AT HOME

In the long run, however, most sales professionals need an office at home. Nothing else will do. A real office, as carefully organized and equipped as any other professional office. For most of those living in their own homes, that is not terribly hard to accomplish, with a little investment and foresight in home selection. For those living in necessarily crowded city or suburban apartments or condominiums, that is often much harder to accomplish; harder, but not less necessary.

A real office at home is a separate space, preferably a separate room, as isolated as possible. It is a dedicated space; offices at home have nothing to do with kitchen or dining room tables co-opted for work while families either continue their normal activities and thereby make it impossible to work properly, or tiptoe about resentfully, making it impossible to have a normal family life. As this is being written, federal tax laws afford favorable treatment to such a dedicated space. Tax laws do change and this favorable treatment may be canceled or diminished in the future. If so, it will be no less necessary to have such a space—only more expensive, in terms of real dollars.

Beyond the basic understanding that selling is also practiced at home, and that an office at home must be private and dedicated to its working functions, offices will vary as widely as do working styles, mechanical skills, needs, and available technology. For some, an office at home may be a very small room, containing little more than a desk, a filing cabinet, good lighting, and a telephone. Some will add such machines as calculators, typewriters, dictating machines, and personal computers, or will be tied into substantial computer systems through terminals at home. Some, where such possibilities exist, may choose to set up working quarters in separate structures, much as an artist sets up a studio in a barn or other outbuilding. Whatever the home office setup is, the physical rules are basically the same at home as at any other office: an adequate table or desk; such other surfaces as are needed; letter- or legal-size files; good-to-excellent lighting (a must); decent heat and ventilation; high-quality machines that work consistently; a comfortable rolling chair; adequate book space; and a reasonable set of office supplies.

Your office-at-home telephone requires a good deal of careful control. For without close control and careful handling, your business calls at home can significantly damage your personal life. It is not difficult to prevent an uncontrolled flow of business calls into your home, calls that must be answered by you or other members of your family at times that may be very, very inconvenient. That is where a separate line, that rings only in your home office, and an answering machine are so valuable. Together they can completely insulate your family from your business calls, and make it possible for you to take calls only when you wish, stacking the rest and returning them at your own convenience.

Get a machine that can be set to ring only once; better yet, look for one that can be set not to ring at all. And get one with a monitoring device, so that you can listen to incoming calls if you wish, and decide whether or not to pick up before the caller finishes putting a message on your machine. Don't worry about people who are uneasy about talking to answering machines; they are fewer and fewer, especially in the business world. You may also want to get a machine with a remote device, so that you can call from outside for messages, without bothering your family or depending on family members to be home when you call for messages.

Telephone control is one very significant aspect of what must be a lifelong drive to control the seemingly uncontrollable, to work effectively in what can all too easily become a maelstrom of ringing telephones and demanding people, an avalanche of problems, and a storm of paper. Effective telephone control succeeds in significantly limiting and organizing your exposure to others.

Note that many modern companies—even in difficult times—clearly recognize the stake they have in making it as easy as possible for sales professionals to pursue job-connected matters in a well-equipped office at home. Such pieces of equipment as computer terminals tied in to large, main-frame computers and distributed databases, minicomputers, dictating equipment, answering machines, typewriters, office supplies, and even some items of standard office furniture are routinely supplied by some companies. Others will supply these kinds of goods and services if you take the trouble to ask, and press the point. Still others will do so only if you have made it part of the whole body of items negotiated when you took the job. These items should not be regarded as fringe benefits, by the way; they are essential working tools for professionals who are doing their jobs properly, and should be supplied as readily to offices at home as they are to offices on company premises.

Those working at home cannot always tightly schedule and ration time spent on business matters. On the other hand, it is quite possible to set aside recognized periods in which others can expect you to be working at business matters, and to stay generally within the patterns established. Your work at home then becomes expected and mostly predictable. Without that kind of predictability, someone working at home is always cast in the role of a villain who can be relied upon only to frustrate family plans, and any work you have accomplished at home seems to have been done at the expense of others and against strong family resistance.

These may easily be seen as trivial matters; taken one by one, they may be. But in the aggregate, proper understanding and handling of professional work needs and of work at home is a central matter in terms of both relationships with others and satisfaction of our own lifetime goals and expectations.

When seen clearly, such matters as long-term work time commitment and bedrock insistence on a healthy family life are most fruitfully perceived as processes, whether or not so stated. There are milestones along each of the intertwined ways in which our strategies work themselves out; shorter-term goals achieved or not, desires reached or not, battles won or not. That much of your professional life will be pursued at home must be a shared long-term understanding with those you love, whatever the changing physical and time arrangements are over the years.

Similarly, and intertwined, is the question of focus. Or, to put it a little differently, the question of at least seemingly unbalanced focus.

A standard, and only sometimes useful, bit of folk wisdom is that if you spend most of your time at home focusing on work-related matters, and perhaps spend an unnecessarily large part of your time traveling, you are conveying a clear signal that something is very wrong with your personal relationships, and that you may be getting ready for a change of partners.

Perhaps; perhaps not. It is at least equally likely—in the early years, anyway, before one-sided focus really can destroy relationships—that you are in the process of being caught by a set of job and professional needs, in a set of games you may not know how to play terribly well. After all, winning objective after objective does not bring you any nearer to the end of the professional game; only time does that. While the game is being played—and that is for a whole career—it can expand to fill every bit of time in your life, if you let it.

Except for that other bedrock personal goal, so sharply demanded by the people of our time and place: insistence on trying to find and build long-term personal relationships. For we are, in the long run, desolate if we are unable to do so, and almost equally distressed if we are unable to do so in our work. All of which sets a considerably amended set of contexts within which we pursue our careers in this last portion of the twentieth century, and helps explain our focus on such matters as interpersonal relations, time management, and several kinds of people-handling matters.

The current focus upon time management is quite appropriate, seen in this set of contexts. For without excellent personal organization and priority setting within a clearly understood body of long-term goals, all of life can very easily become a maelstrom, and few, if any, long-term personal or business goals can be consistently pursued.

The main thing is to keep those goals firmly in mind, continually assessing and reassessing them in light of events. Beyond that central and indispensable activity, there are a few simple time-, people-, and task-handling techniques that can make life relatively easier and can enhance efficiency considerably, if they are developed into habit. None of them have to do with time alone, for all are inextricably intertwined with tasks, people, tactics, and strategies; as is usually true in life, time-saving and efficiency are means rather than ends in themselves. All are simple enough, as sophistication is simple; all taken together add up to cultivation of a set of excellent working reflexes, which begin to make it possible to consistently translate long-term goals into the stuff of everyday life and work.

ORGANIZING YOURSELF

The most important working reflex of all is to develop the habit of continually putting to oneself two related self-management questions, and of having the answers to those questions before you constantly, written down in the form of ever-changing lists of tasks and priorities. The questions are: "What do I want to get done?" and "What needs to be done?"; and "When?" is implied in each.

These are the essential self-organizing questions. Note that they do not lead to exploration of a wide range of alternatives; that is part of longer-term decision making and planning. In contrast, day-to-day effective self-management requires limitation of alternatives and development of current action from proven skills and strength. A list of possible actions, rather than a list of specific actions to be performed, is likely to be quite useless, a waste of time to prepare, and a worthless self-organizing tool. A good deal of effective thinking must precede preparation of a list of things to do; it is the process of preparing the list that is the key act of self-organization.

Very few of us need to be convinced that listing is a necessary device. It is axiomatic that no one can remember more than a modest fraction of all that needs to be done in business and personal life; it is equally axiomatic that five undone things bouncing about unlisted "inside your head" feel like 50 undone things. Indeed, the best way to convince someone of the value of listing is to go through the process. Almost always, that person's "I always seem to have so much to do" results in a far shorter list than he or she had imagined. The listing process also often turns up vital matters that had not been on that person's mental list.

Listing always seems simple enough. You take a sheet of paper, or a notebook, or a personal computer, for that matter, and write what needs to be accomplished. You include everything from "Get haircut," to "Explore job change," to "Do major prospect list analysis." Then, as things get done or proceed toward accomplishment, entries are crossed off or updated; and as new items develop, they in turn are listed. The result is an all-inclusive, undifferentiated list; it takes the least possible time to prepare and update, and you do not have to spend half your time listing, updating, excising, adding, and thinking about lists. Simplicity itself; but not nearly enough.

For listing is a key act of personal planning, and many of the matters with which you routinely deal are not intrinsically simple and easy to accomplish. Oh, you can and should keep the trivia of the day and week before you at all times on a running list; given the complicated lives most of us lead, to do otherwise can be maddening. But if all you do is keep an undifferentiated list, you are quite likely to find yourself dealing superbly well with trivial matters and perhaps filling your life with nobly handled trivialities, while missing the main matters with which you should be dealing, except as they are forced upon you by outside events. "Get haircut," is easy; "Do major prospect list analysis," is a lot harder and more time-consuming, and the kind of indispensable forward planning that is all too often deferred or even abandoned, as far less important day-to-day events crowd it out.

The main thing to understand about listing is that it is only the basic and indispensable start of effective planning. Certainly you will start with a relatively undifferentiated mass of items, but you will need to develop several special-purpose lists adapted to your particular needs. Once these are in being, you may quite routinely update and study several lists simultaneously—perhaps as you sit down on a Sunday night to plan your coming week's work—rather than making a single list and then transferring items out to special-purpose lists. As you proceed through each day, you are quite likely to enter items on several running lists, although some people prefer to keep an undifferentiated list and transfer items once a day to special-purpose lists. For many kinds of items, such as interview appointments and timed customer and prospect calls, you will use such calendared devices as appointment books and desk diaries, which you will carry with you routinely, and use both in the field and in home and company offices. For these purposes, lists kept on personal computers are difficult to use. It is a physical problem; you need to be able to carry lists into many different kinds of places and situations, and plain old paper and print are better for that than computer screens. That may change in coming decades; later on we may all find ourselves carrying small computer devices hooked into remote memories. But that kind of change will be measured in decades, not in years; for now, lists are best done in paper and print. You will develop a series of lists and listing tools that suit your personal preferences and needs, so lists and listing devices will vary considerably. But whatever the mechanical devices used, well-organized sales professionals are likely to find themselves using five general kinds of lists, with considerable overlap between them: prospect files, customer lists, day-by-day item lists, datebook lists, and major project lists.

How you hold and update your prospect file will to a considerable extent depend on your company's practice and your own approaches to organization. If your company has a standard way of keeping prospect files, it may supply company-generated prospects in a standard way into its own standard system, and you will feed your prospects into that system. If there is no company form, you will need to develop your own, which will probably consist of large cards or a looseleaf notebook. Whatever form you choose, it must be one that allows you to capture a fairly substantial and growing body of information about your prospects in one easily reached place, so that it may be seen easily during a telephone call or in an automobile you have just parked in a company parking lot prior to a selling appointment. In many instances, your prospect card will also function as a customer card; keeping your prospect and customer cards in the same basic form can save paperwork, if the products you handle and your company paperwork arrangements make that solution possible.

Whatever the form of your files, they must be capable of being reached easily and being used effectively over the phone and in the field. That means keeping them entirely up to date at all times, and making sure that they carry all the relevant facts you need to help you sell the prospect. You will often want to refresh yourself on a prospect before a contact of any kind, and that makes it necessary to keep at least the following body of information about each of your prospects in the file.

• The full name, address, and telephone number of each prospect. Where individuals within a firm have separate telephone numbers, they should be included.

• As much basic personal information as you have or can develop about the prospect, such as current business title and business interests, schools, prior jobs, family, hobbies, and whatever else that can help provide some basis for empathy.

• As much relevant material as can be developed about those around your prospect, such as others who may participate in buying decisions and such support people as assistants, secretaries, telephone operators, and receptionists.

• How the prospect was developed and when, complete with prospect source, date of first contact, and any other relevant information.

• What has happened so far—a record of every prospect contact, whether face-to-face or by telephone or mail, and the result of the contact.

Many people who sell seem to spend a great deal of time—or so it seems to them—in shuffling prospect cards. They are usually alphabetized, and often further sorted and alphabetized within sorted groups. Many are taken out of the main file when appointments are made, and put in a chronological file, which acts as a "pop-up" file for appointments, and uses the cards as an alerting device. When the appointment has been completed, the card will then either be put in place in a chronological file for callback of some sort or put back in the prospect file, to wait for another day and another try at selling the prospect.

Many travelers take all or substantial portions of their prospect files on the road with them. If you do that, you may want to seriously consider making a duplicate set of prospect files and leaving it at home. It is a good deal of extra work to either maintain two sets of prospect files, or periodically photocopy your card file, but the thought of losing prospect files or any substantial portion of them is enough to make a sales representative's blood run cold. The truth is that loss of your only set of prospect files, "safely" locked into the trunk of your subsequently stolen car, may effectively put you out of business for quite a long time, and cost you far more than the car itself. You can insure a car, but you will have a very hard time insuring prospect files for any more than the slightest fraction of their real worth. Because for you, as for all sales professionals, that real worth is enormous.

But prospect files can be reconstituted, if necessary. What is really most important is the development of the prospecting skills needed to create them, and the consistent application of those skills throughout a selling career, which are matters discussed in Chapter 6.

A second kind of basic business list that must be carried in usable form by selling people on the move is the customer list. In earlier times, that list would be carried as a looseleaf notebook or set of cards, one or more pages or cards to a customer, with updating done by hand. Today, it is far more likely to be carried in the form of a mammoth, computer-generated printout on accordion-folded paper, impossible to add to a bulging briefcase and arriving in updated form monthly or weekly. Indeed, field representatives sometimes feel as if those printouts arrive every other day, for the sole purpose of straining already overstrained storage spaces in home offices, closets, and basements. But not so; if used well, as reference material, those printouts can save a good deal of laborious hand entry into your own records.

But computer printouts are no substitute for a customer file that is a current selling file, rather than a reference file. You should still have every customer on a looseleaf page or card, with the same kinds of information you carry in your prospect file, for customers are, in most instances, also your best prospects. And it still takes some hand entry; for example, when a customer buys a relatively small item from your company by mail, you will want to note that on your customer-as-prospect file, for the mail sale is very often the key to a much larger personally achieved field sale.

There is good reason to carry prospect files and customer-as-prospect files in the same form, if possible, whether as cards or looseleaf pages, as you will probably want to mix them in your chronological files, with both kinds of prospects popping up on the same day and in the same geographical areas or zones for further selling efforts.

The third kind of basic list is the day-by-day, rather undifferentiated item list, which will contain mostly trivia, but will also include recent additions not yet added to other special-purpose lists. That list is probably best carried separately and constantly, as on a pad or looseleaf memo book. For selling people, who move about a good deal, such lists should be pocket-sized, and therefore easy to carry and use in most situations. When something occurs to you in an elevator or train, on a street or in a restaurant, during "working" hours or at other times, it is important to be able to jot it down, to capture and set the thought. That is true whether what occurs is a task to be listed or some other thought you will want to pursue later; you will therefore want to be able to use a single memo device that allows you to add to a running list or make other notes.

This is a raw list; some of the items you add will be crossed off on reflection. Others will prove to duplicate items already on this or other lists. No harm. That will become apparent when you stop to consider the items you have added, which you certainly should make every attempt to do daily. A caution: Do not triumphantly excise items as soon as you think they have been accomplished; all too often you have accomplished only part of an item, or must verify later to make sure that something has, in fact, been accomplished. Premature excision can cause you to lose items; that is a bother at least, and sometimes can cause real problems.

Some people carry these kinds of raw lists in their pocket appointment books. That is attractive, but the sheer mass of trivia often causes unnecessary duplication, with many items carried over and rewritten day after day, until accomplished. On balance, it seems more efficient to carry the raw list separately, making or updating diary entries only if timing elements are involved, either from the start or at various stages of accomplishment. For example, "Get haircut" will be part of a raw running list until it is either done or you make an appointment to get it done. If done, it is removed from your list. If an appointment has been set, it leaves the running list and is put in place in your appointment book, at the time indicated. Similarly, "Call prospect on June 30," may first go on your undifferentiated running list and then, at the end of the day, be put on a prospect card and that card placed in the chronologically organized portion of your prospect file.

Effective planning demands that major personal projects be listed separately, not just in those raw and calendar lists through which they enter and are worked out within your planning system. No matter how active you may be—or how overworked you may feel—it should be possible to place every one of your substantial projects on the fourth kind of list, which is a single ever-developing major planning list, with key elements and project status always in clear view.

And that project list must be viewed and reviewed continually and critically, for that major planning list is one of the key differences between the career builder and the time server. It is a device through which you can place business, personal, and career-building tasks and goals side by side, all in one place, continually evaluating progress, making connections that work for you, and setting and resetting your view of the context within which you are functioning.

A project list will certainly include "Do complete prospect file review," as well as "Open up widget market," and "Start next year's sales forecast." It will also include such skill-building items as "Develop better computer literacy. Explore possible sources." And such career-development items as "Become more active in Sales Executives' Club this year"; "Cultivate Mary, Joe, Tom re: field training assignments"; and "Explore and consolidate sales recruiter contacts; weak here." This is a comprehensive, personal, and very private project list, and should be for your own eyes only.

Your project list should be all in one place, and if possible on one sheet of paper, to help you to reach and hold most easily a complete view of your personal situation and priorities. At the same time, it needs to contain outlines of the main tasks to be done to help make projects move along. That can usually be accomplished with a combination of your own abbreviations and appended materials as necessary. This is a list that provides an overview, but it is also a working list, and you must have enough detail to be able to note progress and revise as you go.

As a working list, your project list will indicate priorities, often by the order in which you place projects and also by your appended comments. Similarly, you will probably use such marks as asterisks and underlining to call attention to priority matters. Priorities change; so will those marks and comments.

You will need to provide yourself with a fresh copy of this list periodically, as your neat, clean copy gradually turns into a mass of hand-scribbled additions, updates, and excisions. How frequently you will need to do so will depend largely upon how actively you pursue your projects. Planning tools like lists are meant to be worked with; if any of your lists are as clean at the end of the week as at the beginning, your progress in the areas covered by those lists has probably been negligible.

The fifth kind of general list is the calendar, which may occur in such various forms as pocket-sized appointment books, day- or week-at-a-glance desk diaries, looseleaf memo books, pop-up files or ticklers, and desk and wall calendars. Whatever form or forms you use, you will want to provide ample space for notetaking and changes, for the most efficient way to handle timed matters is to attempt to put them all together in one place. For example, a single page of a day-by-day appointment book, with one page for each day, may contain business appointments, personal appointments, timed calls to make, personal and business trivia, and personal and business events, such as professional meetings, birthdays, trade shows, anniversaries, and due dates of several kinds.

With that kind of information in hand, all in one place, it becomes possible to do what should be done and to avoid the kind of surprise and dismay that so often occurs when you forget things important to others —and sometimes to you, too. That argues strongly for keeping a fair-sized day-by-day book, with enough space to hold all those items, and the accompanying inevitable mass of changes. You may also keep more complex tools, as dictated by preferences and job needs; some people buy and use quite elaborate planning board devices; others use computers to help them master their timing needs, and expand such uses to include personal and business planning materials. Most of us, though, will find the appointment book enough, if we use it well and consistently.

That appointment book should travel with you, from home to field to office and back again. With you, and not in your luggage, by the way; its loss would be a small disaster. It is as much part of your personal equipment as a watch or eyeglasses, and is far more important than either, for watches and eyeglasses can be easily replaced.

MONITORING PROGRESS

The appointment book technique makes some extraordinarily important self-analysis possible, for it enables you to consistently track how and with whom you spend your time. And keeping track of your time on a regular basis is one of the most valuable planning-related activities in which any sales professional can engage; it can help you convert or partially convert a seeming maelstrom into a set of manageable sequences in business and personal life.

Let us stress the central importance of consistency here. As elsewhere, consistency is essential when you seek to turn well-reasoned approaches into good reflexes, and repeated actions into habits. It really does not do to carefully log your time once in a while; to make a few remedial moves to attempt to make better use of your time; and then slowly to sink once again into a sea of trivia, time-consuming chores, and callbacks that seem to take up all available time. That is all too often the norm. Repeated, it is disheartening and can become demoralizing.

Some counselors on time management may be contributing to the problem, rather than the solution. The difficulty lies in the complexity of the self-analytical material and techniques offered, and the special attention that must be paid to them. If, to manage your time effectively, you must develop and learn how to use new and complex tools, replete with forms and flowcharts, the odds are that you will not do so, continue to do so, make it all over into habit, and then do what every good professional does—make it look easy. If complex materials are needed, then the odds are that you will read a book, take a course, or both, and apply what you have learned once, if at all. The application will seem to help, though you will not be sure whether that is because the techniques are helping or because you are momentarily paying close attention to time management matters. But it will not help enough for you to make the extra effort needed over a long period of time to develop it all into habit. It is usually too special, too complex, too time-consuming.

It is far more to the point to use a time-oriented tool already at your disposal for other purposes: your appointment book. If you develop the habit of noting in it precisely how you spend your time, day after day, throughout a career, you will be able to begin exercising as much control of your time as is possible in your specific circumstances, whatever your job, company, and personal contexts.

That means using your book as both planner and time log, not only in field and office, but also at home, while traveling, and perhaps while commuting. Your whole time situation can come into proper focus when you record all your time expenditures; to record only what you do during your field working day is to miss much of your professional life.

It is impractical to suggest logging every minute of every day of the year, but it is entirely practical—indeed, vital—to suggest doing exactly that at stated periods throughout the year. You can very easily pick one week in each quarter of each year for close time-logging, note those weeks in your book at the beginning of each year, and then proceed in very orderly fashion to do just that, as the prescribed date pops up. That, too, is a good habit. Scheduled, it is anticipated and easy.

For most of the year, your book will serve as a basic time log, if you get one that devotes at least a full page to each day, and breaks up the day hour by hour. During close time-logging periods, you may need a little more space than that, adding additional space and entries as necessary, or even keeping your time log separately. But do try to keep your time log in your diary, if at all possible, even during such periods, however you must compress your notes to do so.

No matter how long and consistently you record your time expenditures, you are likely to find each successive time log reevaluation rewarding and surprising. Very few of us really know how we spend our time, and most of us, when asked, will respond with substantially inaccurate estimates. When closely analyzed, far too many days turn out to have included little time spent with qualified prospects in real selling situations; likewise far too many hours spent "lining up prospects" and "cementing customer relations" turn out to have been wasted trying to reheat old leads over the telephone and stuck deep in a set of callback traps. All of us waste travel time at one time or another zigzagging about a territory to make unanticipated selling and servicing calls. All of us sag at one time or another, and find ourselves spending time with colleagues or customers who are chronic time wasters. But close and consistent analysis of how we spend our time can make those kinds of instances exceptional, rather than usual. With analysis, patterns become apparent, and success patterns can be reached for, held, and turned into reflexes.

With long-term goals in order, and a full personal and business project list before you, thoughtful time log analysis can yield excellent—though not necessarily unpredictable—results. Most of us find ourselves wasting enormous amounts of time on trivial matters; spending far too little time on projects; barely touching some of our most important long-term strategic goals, particularly in career- and skills-building areas; and tending to fill our personal lives with the same kind of trivial business matters that occupy so much of our workdays. No matter that much of the trivia is generated by our own companies, prospects, customers, and families; our job is to manage our time and work so as to minimize waste and maximize both effectiveness and the satisfactions to be gained from living rewarding personal lives.

That takes a great deal of thought and attention, and often necessitates sharp limitation of some kinds of time demands placed upon us by our situations and by others. All the personal planning, replanning, listing, relisting, logging, and analysis we have been discussing takes valuable time —a good deal of it—and it is in the long run only worthwhile if it can be made to pay. That requires a good deal of action, some of it not always acceptable at first to those around you, as you move to control the seemingly uncontrollable in your life and work.

CONTROLLING TIME WASTERS

"I'm just spinning my wheels . . ."

"Spent all day running around putting out fires; I feel like a dog chasing his tail."

"Went out for a cup of coffee with Anne this morning, and she chewed my ear off for an hour about how awful it all is . . ."

"Awful nice guy, but every time I go in there I lose half a day. Don't want to offend him . . . and you know, they're big customers . . ."

Controlling the uncontrollable is first of all a lifelong dedication to the elimination of time-wasting attitudes, actions, and people. Yes, there are times when you cannot seem to make a firm selling appointment to save your soul, no matter how well the same basic telephone technique has worked for years. And times when you call in from one end of your territory and find that there is a real emergency that must be handled today, requiring that you drive 50 miles out and then 50 miles back to resume—if you can—your busted selling day. But these are exceptional kinds of things; when they happen often, you may either not be taking enough care to avoid time-wasting traps or welcoming them. Or a little bit of both, of course.

Unproductively spent field time is the great enemy of the sales professional. As a stoutly resisted exception, it is normal, and merely sometimes frustrating—part of the game. As a set of unfolding patterns, it is a career-breaker.

Unnecessary moving about through failure to control your territory is one of the greatest of all time-wasters. In these days of high travel costs, it is also a very expensive time-waster. Much of it is avoidable, though, with proper zoning and telephone use.

Zoning is quite simply a matter of breaking up your selling area into bite-size pieces, and trying your very best to spend usable chunks of time in one piece at a time, rather than racing around between the various pieces. If you are on the road for some days, it also means organizing your moves so that you move from piece to piece in as efficient a fashion as possible. It is as simple as keeping a map of your territory with you at all times, setting up your chronological customer-as-prospect and prospect files to conform with the zones you have set up on that map, and making every effort to schedule appointments of all kinds in a single zone on a given day. Then, aside from real emergencies, you will not find yourself spending needless and expensive hours traveling that should better be spent selling. Caution: It is always tempting to make a promising out-of-zone selling call, particularly when you do not yet have a firm set of appointments for the only day all week your prospect is willing to meet with you. But it is usually a mistake, although it may occasionally eventuate in a sale. Most likely, it will only result in a broken-up and inefficiently spent day. Nobody sells them all, prospects cancel scheduled appointments, and appointments made later, many miles away, may be even more promising. It is best to keep to your zoned plans, if at all possible, rather than running off to seek pie in the wrong part of the sky on the wrong day.

There are also a great many friendly people out there, and especially friendly, long-term customers. Some of them will like you so much that they will do their best to ruin your career, by encouraging you to waste inordinate amounts of your time and theirs in fruitless conversation. Beware of the too-friendly time-wasting customer; remember, anyone who has a great deal of rather pointlessly spent time to spend with you is likely to be a time-server and time-waster on a larger scale, as well. Those who treasure time-wasters as valued business contacts are quite likely to find their friends gone one day when they come to call. Looking at it that way, it is appropriate to see a time-waster as someone likely to be in trouble, and view the situation as one in which you should without delay cultivate others in the firm if you want to safeguard the account.

There is also the callback trap, always the refuge of the slumping field representative. When someone calls again and again on the same few prospects and customers, trying to warm up potential sales that have long since ceased to have any immediacy and current possibility, that someone has fallen into the callback trap. Certainly, some sales require several selling calls, for all kinds of reasons. There can be several buyers and buying decisions involved, interrupted and therefore unconsummated selling interviews that have to be entirely re-done, more information to be secured from a home office, and even some stalls that somehow cannot be broken through on the way to the close. But when your appointment book shows call after call on the same prospect over a period of weeks or even months, you may truly just be "spinning your wheels," and deep in a set of callback traps. And that is one of the worst time-wasting patterns of all, often requiring a deep look at your whole prospect file and set of selling attitudes; sometimes even a look at whether or not you are in the right selling job. No, not a look at whether or not selling is the right career— that is hardly ever the problem, though it is perfectly natural to have it cross your mind when you are in the middle of a long slump, deep in a set of time-wasting callback traps, and perhaps long since ready for a job change.

All quite controllable, if the effort is consistently made. As are some of our time-wasting colleagues, who might like us to coffee with them every morning, for "just a few minutes." That few minutes, of course, becomes anywhere from 15 to 45 minutes, and the time wasted thereby may be anywhere from a little over an hour a week to nearly four hours a week. Or putting it a little differently, the convivial coffee-ers in your office may be wasting as much as 200 hours a year having coffee with each other for "just a few minutes" every morning. That is well over a month of good selling time wasted every year—lost, never to return. The direct costs to those who so waste time may be some thousands of dollars a year; the indirect costs, in terms of career-building, can be much higher.

Goal-setting, developing a sound office at home, listing, self-evaluating, zoning, prospect and customer record-handling, avoiding the standard time-wasting traps—all these begin to add up to astute self-management of time and work. Now add consistent control of the mass of paper that often seems about to drown us. We get computerized customer lists, sales leads, customer complaints, home office requests, memos, contest bulletins, questionnaires, in-house newsletters, brochures, technical manuals, and miscellaneous product and promotion information; and we reach out for a mass of professional and general information aimed at helping us to effectively pursue and build our sales and careers. We are expected to produce considerable quantities of call reports, expense statements, memos, letters, prospect information, and a wide miscellany of forms and reports aimed at helping sales management and marketing people do their jobs as effectively as possible. We need to ingest and produce it all on the fly, so to speak. Sales professionals spend as much time as possible selling; all the rest of it gets done in other-than-selling time, and in a wide variety of "offices," including company offices, home offices, motel rooms, commuter trains, airplanes, restaurants, and traffic jams at raised drawbridges. But all that paper must be handled, and handled well.

That calls for selectivity and consistency. Selectivity first. If you are not selective about what you read, what you put aside to use as reference material, and what you quite ruthlessly discard, you will spend a whole lifetime in selling and in the business world hopelessly trying to catch up with all you think you should read, and hopelessly behind in handling all the business matters you should very definitely be handling.

Selectivity means scanning newspapers, professional journals, manuals, brochures, newsletter articles, and other broadcast printed materials, rather than attempting to read everything literally in sight. You will follow general matters as a responsible and interested citizen and as you like, but scan the business, industry and company news for matters of direct interest and significance to you, and ruthlessly jettison the rest. You will read as much as you feel appropriate of company-generated materials, but scan whatever you can, putting much aside for use as reference material. You will be likely to use computer-generated reports mainly as reference materials, after a quick scan and study of any summaries provided.

Consistency means promptly disposing of anything that can be disposed of easily and quickly. To let your desk disappear under a river of unanswered memos and letters is, to put it very gently, counterproductive, in that it will only result in more memos and letters, with small and routine matters becoming problems that grow large as time goes by. To let undone call reports and expense accounts pile up is only to guarantee that you will do them at difficult and inconvenient times after requesting and then demanding letters and calls urging you to do so.

Selling people are always people in motion, and often are people on the road, whether in travel territories or holding regional, national, or international selling responsibilities. For sales professionals, effective time and work management often depends on finding and setting personal styles that enable them to handle a wide variety of paper and planning tasks while on the road. For if you hold a great deal of your reading, planning, and office work until you return home, you will find yourself trying to catch up with a mass of tasks and materials that grows faster than you can handle it.

USING TRAVEL TIME

For many of us, time spent "on the road" is dead time, aside from actual field work and the most routine paper-handling tasks. Yet the truth is that travel time offers multiple and high-quality time-expansion possibilities, if we take care to develop good working reflexes. In the short run, effective use of travel time can help you avoid drowning in a mass of paper. In the long run—if you put your mind to it—it can be a real career-builder, for long, potentially very lonely evenings can turn into evenings full of plans; notes to a wide network of career-building contacts, including and far beyond your current colleagues, customers, and prospects; and other self-development activities.

Not at all incidentally, this is also the best possible way to prevent the kinds of problems that can and so often do beset people who travel a good deal. Loneliness and disorientation can trigger very difficult personal problems, and empty conviviality with strangers in a motel bar is far more likely to create problems than solve them. Most women who travel do not even have that motel bar to go to; and when you feel trapped in a motel room on the edge of a strange town, you can become very lonely indeed. Which is one of the kinds of things that make closet alcoholics, by the way. There is nothing quite like waking up at 4 A.M. in a motel with no facilities open, with a television set that presents only a blank, buzzing face when turned on, and without a working radio. Or the first, jaggedly disorienting time you find yourself walking down a windowless corridor in a hotel or motel and realize that you do not have the slightest idea of what city you are in, or for that matter what time of day or day of the week it is. Travel —if you let it—often becomes little more than an endless series of motels, restaurants, appointment-setting telephone calls, sales interviews, and roads; also boredom, loneliness, drink, sometimes casual and entirely unrewarding sexual partners, and the condition of disconnection from time and place technically known as anomie, which can signal the onset of very serious emotional problems.

Not much fun, and a lot of hazards. But it is all controllable, and capable of being turned into growing time. The best solution to travel problems is work—sound, fruitful, consistent career-building work, with travel time viewed as opportunity time rather than dead time.

Clearly, attitude is the key in this area. But astute traveling also requires some selectivity, preparation, and skill. Selectivity starts with the travel decisions themselves. The right cost-and-time-efficient question is always "Is this trip necessary?" There is no magic or virtue at all in making a quarterly trip to a set of remote locations because you did so last year and the year before, or because that was "what was done" by your predecessors. There is no reason to reflexively exhibit at a convention or trade show because "we've always been there," or because it is important to "show the flag." Do people expect you, and look forward to your coming? Perhaps, and that may be reason enough to go, even though the trip is not directly cost-effective. But is satisfying their expectation enough reason to make the trip and spend thousands of dollars in out-of-pocket expenses and wasted time? Have you taken a zero-based look at the trip, by costing it out and trying to make a reasonable cost–benefits estimate?

Selectivity extends to the detail in travel plans. When you are in an area, it is always very tempting to make every possible customer relations call, without stopping to reflect on the time costs involved. It is possible to spend a day making such calls, sell very little if anything at all, and bed down in a motel, convinced that you have somehow spent a fruitful day. More than likely, it has not been so; what was missing was only the heart of the matter: selling effectively to qualified prospects in selling situations.

Most sales professionals work very hard when they travel. Days start early, traveling times are often long, and the end of the selling day is often only the beginning of a trip to somewhere else, so that the next day can be started fresh and rested. Working harder is seldom needed advice; on the other hand, living smarter on the road is very often possible. That means planning your itinerary so that you will not routinely court exhaustion because of too-long driving distances; staying away from nightcaps that can turn into long, sleepless nights; eating decently and regularly, rather than gulping junk foods at odd hours; and in general taking care of yourself at least as well on the road as you do at home. You have to be able to develop a deliberate, effective personal pace on the road, containing the kind of self-regenerating reflexes that will last a whole career. By all means locate and use recreational places; a swim, run, or tennis game at the end of a long day in the field can mean a great deal to mind and body. Cultivate some friends, if your road is a repeated swing through familiar territory. Real human contact can make a great deal of difference. Work and self-development are the keys; recreation and friends can help a great deal, too.

People who travel long distances, such as those handling national accounts, face some very special hazards, for jet lag is dangerous, both physically and to the successful consummation of our selling plans. Most of us have come to understand—intellectually, at least—the physical aspects of jet lag in recent years, but very few really act upon that knowledge. Many are still capable of working all day in field or office, jumping aboard a flight to a time zone several hours west, and coming off the plane to keep an appointment which may go on into dinner and even later. Then, after having effectively stayed up all night working, they compound their error by dropping into bed for only a couple of hours of sleep, before starting to work again, perhaps handling delicate and demanding matters.

Some personal and work problems accompany that kind of pattern. First, it is extraordinarily hard on the body. To work all day and all night, spending many hours in transit while doing so, places enormous short-term strain on some pretty important and sometimes fragile organs, including heart and nervous system. To wake in what, for us, is the middle of the night, because of time zone differences and the way our bodies are attuned, creates enormous additional strains. It is perfectly clear by now that it is exceedingly short-sighted and dangerous to work our travel in this way; yet many of us continue to do it, figuring that "the next guy" will be the one who has the heart attack. Well, it may not be the next guy.

And a perfectly obvious set of working problems are created, too. You stack the deck against yourself when you go to work exhausted. Exhausted people tend to sell impatiently, and to antagonize those they are there to persuade. And exhausted people fighting jet lag and working full days in a quite different time zone stay exhausted.

It is far better for the body and for work objectives to take exhaustion and jet lag into account in planning long-distance trips. If you must travel at night, arrive quietly, go to your lodging, stay up until you are quite tired —but relaxed—and go to sleep. You may wake up rather early the next morning, but you will be well on your way to conquering jet lag, and will not be exhausted. If you must work the night of the day you travel, by all means travel early on that day if you can, so that you may arrive, acclimate, and perhaps fit in a nap before you have to go to work in what, for you, is the middle of the night.

The converse is also true. If you are flying from west to east any considerable distance, your problem will arise the next morning. You will not have been able to go to sleep until the middle of the night in your arrival time zone, and should not attempt to schedule anything until the afternoon of the first full day in the new zone; otherwise you will find yourself fighting to stay awake all that day, rather than being in top condition for whatever has to be done. If you stay on, bear in mind that you will still be attuned to a different time zone; try not to schedule very early morning appointments until your body has had a few days to acclimatize.

If working effectiveness is to be maximized and working opportunities used, considerable care must be paid to other early timing-related questions, as well. When and how closely to schedule planes and other transport; how closely to schedule appointments on the same day; and whether or not to travel to dinner at that wonderful French restaurant just 40 miles down the coast after a five-hour flight—these are all matters to consider carefully.

Proper physical preparation for "office" work is far more important when traveling than when working at your office or home. Small working tools that can be taken for granted in a familiar environment can become vital omissions on the road. Some basic working tools are apparent and part of the working equipment of almost all business travelers; but some equally basic tools are often overlooked. On the road, you should have:

- A properly flexible, small wardrobe, as washable as possible.

- Adequate writing instruments, and paper to write on. If you normally use a typewriter, then by all means take along a small electric portable, with paper and carbon sets, so that you can send your originals and keep the carbons as safety copies.

- A small calculator, with a paper tape. Some may prefer the kind of hand-held calculator that is easily carried in pocket or bag, and without the tape attachment, but serious work is much easier with the tape, which can be removed and attached to the work done.

- A cassette recorder, for dictating notes and communications. Some of the very small models are quite attractive, but will take only 15- or 30-minute tapes. On balance, it is desirable to carry the smallest sturdy recorder you can find that will take 60-, or at most 90-minute tapes.

Beware of tapes taking over 60 minutes of material—that is, more than 30 minutes a side; these tapes are more fragile and have much less chance of standing up to the rigors of travel. Caution: Do not take your tapes through airport detecting machines, which can scramble the information you record on magnetic tapes; instead take them out of your carrying case and have the attendant pass them around to you. Note that many companies now have order-processing dictating equipment in their offices that can be used by remote entry over telephone lines. Your orders and some or all of your communications from the road can be sent directly in that fashion, if your company is so equipped.

• A small, high-intensity lamp and bulb, so that you can convert almost any dimly lit hotel room into a workplace. Many otherwise completely acceptable rooms are designed as bedrooms rather than as offices and are therefore inadequately lit for working purposes. Bear in mind that without adequate light you cannot work effectively; also that your eyes age faster than the rest of you, and need much care.

• Two 3-socket conversion plugs, so that you can convert a single socket into three sockets, and thereby accommodate the equipment you are carrying. If you are going abroad to where electrical systems are different, then you also need appropriate conversion units.

• A heavy 12-foot extension cord, which should be long enough to reach from an available plug to that part of the room where you are using your equipment.

• An extra pair of reading glasses, if you use them, as emergency spares. These should be obvious, but are often omitted.

• Your working lists of all kinds, which should always travel with you.

• A small quantity of precisely the same office tools and supplies you normally use: a small stapler, a staple remover, paper clips, rubber bands, small scissors, and the like.

It will help a great deal to outline your needs to hotelkeepers wherever you are going. It is often as simple as specifying "a room suitable for working in, with table, chair, and good light." People who do not do that risk arriving at hotels and motels that might have been able to accommodate modest working needs if they had been informed earlier, but are now fully booked and cannot. On the other hand, a hotel may ignore your careful specifications; if so, it is still sometimes possible to get a proper working place on arrival, if you ask, rather than taking the luck of the draw in a randomly assigned room. Hotelkeepers can and should be pushed as necessary in these areas; most will try to be helpful without pushing, but some will not, and you cannot know which is which until you try. By all means, force the situation a bit if you must; it will be worth it in terms of being able to take better advantage of work opportunities on the road.

Reading for information and insight is prime work to do while traveling. The road can be a real opportunity for reflective reading of periodicals and of some of the longer-range and deeper works you might otherwise have difficulty finding sufficient time for. The same holds for some of the longer reports and memos that we all too often put aside. Better take along some light reading, too, if only as a kind of security blanket; the world can be a lonely place in that airport motel at 4 A.M., far away from home.

Not all travel time expansion opportunities depend on long evenings away from home. Many sales professionals work out of offices, especially those working in major metropolitan areas. When it takes an hour—or sometimes even two—to commute to work, and you are not doing the driving, you find yourself with two or more hours every day that are not otherwise committed, in which a great deal can be accomplished. That woman or man who obviously works hard to and from work every day, rather than playing cards or sleeping, is not necessarily a compulsive worker. What the card players and sleepers—when they wake up—see every day may be a very effective professional, using what might otherwise be dead and boring time to read, write, and think in what can very easily be made into a totally private environment, with no ringing telephones, happy and noisy children, or traffic to fight. As many have found over the years, you can get an enormous amount of work done during commuting hours, if you see your career commitment needs properly.

To work successfully while commuting, all you need is a supply of relevant materials to carry back and forth; a hard flat surface to write upon, such as a briefcase; and basic writing (or dictating) materials. And a seat. All is lost here if you have to stand on the way, which makes unremitting agitation for adequate commuting facilities far more than a matter of comfort. If you cannot sit and work, you are being robbed of productive work opportunities for from two to four hours a day, and that is a few hundred to a thousand hours a year, depending on the length of the commute and the away-from-office travel time. Not a small amount, and the work many can accomplish while commuting is not a small matter.

Successful management of time and work makes it possible to identify and reach for selling and career-building opportunities; it is well within the competence of, and very much a career "must," for sales professionals.

CHAPTER 6
A REVIEW OF THE SELLING PROCESS

This chapter could just as easily be called "A Review of the Buying Process" as "A Review of the Selling Process," for buying and selling are two sides of the same coin. We focus here on the selling process because that is what you are able, to some extent, to control, to move; but it is easiest to understand what is happening between buyer and seller if we first examine buying motives and then examine selling approaches and actions.

Don't be alarmed. We are not now going to embark upon a long, tedious, and ultimately sterile discussion full of psychological jargon—what has so aptly and cuttingly been described as *psychobabble*. Our approach is not theoretical, either. We are concerned here with discussing lifelong successful selling, rather than with the development of a body of motivational and marketing theory, however useful that may or may not be in other contexts.

Sales professionals can benefit greatly from the operations of economists, market researchers, psychologists, corporate planners, direct marketing people, marketing managers, advertising people, public relations practitioners, and a wide variety of other professionals engaged wholly or partly in analyzing buying behavior. It is broadening and refreshing, in the long run, to keep up with what is being done in related areas. But at the same time, it is necessary to "keep your eye on the ball"; for sales professionals that means focusing sharply on the essence of the individual transaction between buyer and seller, understanding it so well that it can be applied to scores and perhaps hundreds of different situations encountered in the course of a selling career. For if, indeed, "selling is selling," it is because the essence of the sales transaction can be captured, and we can therefore become able to generalize well enough to see and apply insights reaching all selling situations.

People do seem to buy for all kinds of reasons. They buy insurance against potential catastrophe and sports vehicles that cannot help but bring catastrophe closer. They buy foods that they know will make them fat and chemical preparations aimed at making them thin; paintings of great beauty as investments and extraordinarily ugly bric-a-brac of no artistic merit because they think it beautiful; sound houses to live in and absurdly uncomfortable and expensive houses for show. They soberly shop for bargains in order to save, while conspicuously consuming luxury goods. They buy because they need, and they buy because they want— quite rationally and entirely irrationally. They buy on a hard sell and they buy on a soft sell. They buy for a very wide and mixed variety of emotional and rational reasons that intertwine and move toward purchase or rejection in what can be called either the buying process or the selling process, depending on the point of view adopted.

In the end, they buy because they feel—consciously or unconsciously, and often a little of both—that their purchase is somehow satisfying, the right thing to do, something they want to do, something from which they derive benefits. That, not at all oversimplified, is the essence of the matter.

SELLING BENEFITS

The essence of the matter to sellers, therefore, is to convert all the features of what you are selling into benefits that, on some conscious or unconscious level, will be regarded by your prospective purchaser as reasons to buy. In shorthand, the essence of the matter is therefore to sell benefits.

Consistently selling benefits is one of those very easy things that can be extraordinarily hard until mastered, and then you wonder why others have any trouble at all understanding a concept that is so obvious and mastering such an easy approach to selling. And consistently selling benefits is also the single most important key to lifelong selling success.

All it really takes is the ability to "put yourself in the other guy's shoes," and to do so reflexively and completely, time after time, with much of your attention devoted to gaining the information and insight necessary to make that possible. Among other things, it requires understanding what the benefits are in each situation, and not confusing product features with your prospective purchaser's benefits. It requires reflexively asking yourself the same question about your prospect in each selling situation: "What benefits can you get out of what I'm selling?"

That is a very simple, direct question, and consistent selling success requires that you be able to answer it fully and well in the vast majority of selling situations. Oh, there will be a few situations in which you make the sale without the answer to that question—the prospect who "takes it away from you" before you even get halfway through your presentation or the prospect who buys for reasons you cannot fathom after you have quite given up and are ready to pack it in—but those situations are few and far between. To be able to identify and sell benefits is the simplest, most basic skill in selling, and the most important.

Features are not usually benefits, though occasionally they are so perceived by prospects and therefore become so in fact. A loving description of all of the outstandingly advanced technical features of the small business computer system you are selling will very rarely sell that system; you must convert those features of the system into benefits recognizable by your small business owner prospect, such as ease of use, economy, increased speed of collection, and improved inventory control. There may seem to be exceptions; the small business owner who is also a computer buff may be fascinated by your technical descriptions and be eager to describe the advanced features of that system to his or her envious computer buff friends. You still will probably need to convert features into benefits to make the sale, but the features then are also benefits, for the status the system brings becomes a buying motive, which is a synonym for benefit.

It is very easy to confuse features with benefits, and thereby confuse the selling situation as well. It happens most often in technical areas, but in all other selling areas as well, and is the hallmark of the novice. Unfortunately, it is also a habit into which experienced professionals can and do also slip on occasion. The computer system seller who is entranced with hardware, software, and the rest of the jargon of the computer world has an exact counterpart in the life insurance seller who loses sales with interminable talk about settlement options, cost per thousand of term versus life and vice versa, and new interest rate schedules—all after an easy close could have been effected.

Benefits must be put simply and clearly to prospects. We must remember that we are extremely familiar with both our products and the kinds of selling situations that develop around our attempts to sell them. Our prospects are not; it is all new to them. Even the most astute prospect needs the clarity provided by our interpretation of features into benefits. To state features and benefits in complex, difficult-to-understand language does not elevate the product being sold in any way; rather, it normally betrays lack of the kind of complete product knowledge that is needed for simplicity of statement. As all writers and teachers understand, you have to know a great deal about a matter to put it simply and clearly, yet fully and correctly. In this, as in so many other things, simplicity is the essence of sophistication.

PRODUCT KNOWLEDGE

Product knowledge consists of a great deal more than the ability to demonstrate and explain the workings of your products. Certainly you will be able to effectively present, answer basic questions, and compare product or products presented with other products in your line, if any. You also, however, often have to discuss product uses and possibilities far beyond the limit of your prepared presentation, and be ready to discuss very knowledgeably the products of your competitors, as well. In almost all instances, those who sell must know their products intimately, in terms of real strengths, weaknesses, uses, and competitive position.

In a fast-changing world, you must also keep up; certainly with your own products, as they change and develop, but also with those of your competitors. Beyond products, it is quite necessary to keep up with developments in your field. There are a number of ways to accomplish this. One of them is through careful study of company-provided materials, such as sales materials, technical manuals, and house-generated newsletters and magazines directed to internal staff and to customers. You should read and reread these materials very carefully until their contents are fully understood, for sales will often depend on your understanding of them. That means the company has a stake in your understanding them; therefore sales management, production people, and home office staff will, in most companies, be responsive to questions from the field, which you should not hesitate to ask.

Company training and retraining sessions can be excellent sources of updated product, competition, and industry knowledge. Many companies run such training sessions as ongoing schools, passing field staff through retraining courses periodically. Many others include training sessions in regular sales meeting agendas. Experienced professionals use those sessions for the accretion of needed information, and therefore often regard sales meetings as opportunities—which they usually are—rather than necessary evils.

If you work out of an office with others, those you work with and report to can often be excellent sources of information, particularly on selling approaches that are working well and on competitive matters. For some, this opportunity turns into a trap, consisting of endless talk over second breakfasts and too-long lunches, while prime selling time is wasted. But it need not be so; controlled exchanges with co-workers can be very useful.

Customers and prospects can be extraordinarily important sources of information and insight, if you take the time to listen to what they have to say. These are people in your field, who are spending a great deal of time using your products and those of your competitors in the field. They can be an endless source of competitive information, third-party selling material, new selling ideas, and practical knowledge as to the strengths and weaknesses of your own products.

When it comes to customers and prospects, sometimes it is hard to separate the useful material from the rest, and it can take a good while to learn what is worth your attention. It is very easy to block out the chronic whiner and complainer, ignoring the kernel of information buried in the mass of minor complaints. Sometimes that is the right thing to do; chronic complainers waste a great deal of valuable time, and are best treated as briefly as possible, as long as their real complaints are satisfactorily handled. But there are also many customers and prospects from whom you can learn a great deal, if you listen.

It is also a good idea to keep up through subscription to one or more industry publications; such periodicals normally keep up rather well with industry developments and trends, and also include new product and service announcements that can prove useful. Many people in selling also take formal courses, such as those offered by local adult education courses and area colleges, in order to better understand the basics of their fields. Many companies encourage this, and provide tuition assistance or even full tuition payment in recognition of the value of such outside self-development activities.

EMPATHETIC SELLING

One can be extremely well-armed with up-to-date product knowledge, understand the importance of identifying and selling benefits, know the difference and be able to sharply distinguish between features and benefits —and still not be able to sell. And without the ability to consistently turn it all into sales, this is all interesting, but merely academic. The proof of this pudding is wholly in the selling, which largely depends on the interaction between buyer and seller, an interaction that must be generated and controlled by you, the seller.

Face-to-face with a prospect in a selling situation, the probable general sequence of events is predictable. With minor variations and transpositions within the sequence, you will try to develop information about the prospective purchaser and his or her relevant needs and desires; present your product or products; attempt to handle stalls and objections; and ultimately attempt to move into a successful close. But if it is as mechanical as all that, you are hardly likely to close successfully very often. That is scarcely selling, and is about as useful as some of the canned presentations handed to sales professionals by a small number of relatively unskilled marketing management organizations.

Successful selling, like all successful persuasion, is what is happening underneath all that. The mechanical moves are easy to see; the interaction and processes underway between the players—seller and prospective buyer—require more insight. Observing seller and buyer at work with each other, you may see the seller speaking, and strongly reinforcing and amplifying what is said with body language, relaxation and tension, pace, and timing. Meanwhile, you may see the buyer saying one thing and nonverbally showing that something else is so; you may see a buyer back away, not necessarily knowing why. An experienced seller will reach forward to find out why—often to help the buyer find out why—so that whatever is really there can be made explicit and can be dealt with, and perhaps be handled as a lever with which to move toward the close.

If you are watching a good sales professional, you will see someone at work who understands very well that it is crucial to be able to put yourself, as much as possible, into a prospect's thought processes, to understand how another is thinking and feeling in the middle of the situation. The essence of the matter is to be able to move with your prospect toward solutions of problems, toward satisfaction of needs and desires, adding your own insights so that you share in the process and reach conclusions together. That is, after all, the essence of all face-to-face persuasion; it is also a description of the processes involved in empathetic selling. It works somewhat differently with groups, and very differently with multitudes. We are speaking here, and in the main throughout this book, of face-to-face, one-to-one persuasion, the processes involved when one seller attempts to persuade one prospect to buy.

Empathetic selling—or, to put it a little differently, successful selling —is the ability to put yourself into your prospect's shoes every step of the way and move ultimately to the close in complete agreement. It requires early *concentration* on the prospective purchaser, and his or her expressed problems, needs, and desires, rather than on yourself, and your own need to present and sell. It requires the ability to concentrate while projecting —and feeling—*relaxed,* so that you may best be able to draw out your prospect. It requires the ability to *see;* yes, literally to pick up visual clues from your prospect's appearance and business or personal environment. It requires the ability to *listen,* to really hear what your prospect is saying to you. An astonishing number of sales are lost because sellers do not bother to listen to the basic information and clear selling clues that prospects provide early in the interview. And most of all, it requires feeling and projecting personal warmth and real interest in what your prospect has to say, so that you find yourself developing a *sympathetic stance* and *empathy* with your prospect. And it better be real. On the one hand, people are very used to detecting phony sympathy and rejecting it; on the other hand, and much more important, it is in the long run extraordinarily dangerous and self-defeating to try to project a false image rather than develop long-term empathetic attitudes. There is no surer way to turn yourself sour, and ruin both your career in selling and your personal outlook. But when the approaches and techniques that add up to achieving empathy with your prospects are fully accepted and become reflexive, the act of selling can become the rewarding fun it can and should be.

People who sell goods and services face-to-face outside and by telephone spend a good deal of their time identifying and finding prospective purchasers who are qualified to buy by virtue of their needs or desires, and who further are qualified by their ability to buy. Some astute retail sellers —especially those selling rather specialized goods and services—also prospect, seeking to find and attract specific kinds of qualified potential purchasers into their establishments, there to be met face-to-face and sold. And selling organizations of all kinds use advertising and several kinds of direct marketing approaches to both sell directly and find qualified prospects that can then be sold face-to-face.

If you are fortunate enough to be associated with a company that develops large numbers of qualified prospects for you—often as an adjunct of direct mail marketing and couponed advertising—your job will be made much easier, and your sales production considerably enhanced. Even in that company, and throughout your sales career, you will still need to know a great deal about how to generate your own qualified leads, for that is an indispensable set of career skills for every selling professional. Even if your company generates large numbers of qualified prospects one year, it may not do so the next year. Or you may change jobs, and find yourself in a company that relies upon you to generate qualified prospects. The truth is, if you have not mastered the prospect-getting skills, you are not the complete selling professional and sales generalist you must be to pursue your career in a fast-changing business environment. Nor are you properly able to consider striking out on your own, either during your younger years or in a post-retirement occupation, for identifying potential buyers enables you to assess the possibilities—or lack of them—in a projected business move, while finding and reaching them are often essential to business success. Prospecting then is properly seen as an essential entrepreneurial tool throughout a lifetime in selling, whether you work for someone else or for yourself.

It is also true that you will be able to generate some better qualified prospects than any of your home office marketers can generate for you, because you will be generating some of them—the best of them—face-to-face. That is what referral selling is, after all; the process of generating highly qualified prospects face-to-face, while simultaneously creating third-party selling material from the referring source.

The best qualified and most receptive prospects you will ever encounter are your own satisfied customers. Even when they are not "your" customers, if they have a history of doing business with your company, they are predisposed to do further business with you. A satisfied customer is a good deal more than someone who has bought goods and services from your company. Such a customer has also "bought" your company, and trusts it to do what it promises to do and make good, one way or another, on promises it has been unable to keep. When the crucial question of trust has already been solved, it is certainly far easier to sell more of the same, upgrade, sell different goods and services, and introduce new products than it is to an untrusting stranger. A properly untrusting stranger, by the way—buyers are wise to deal with strange or untried sellers at arm's length until those sellers have proved themselves; that is a fact of life in the field.

When you yourself have sold goods and services to a satisfied customer, and especially when sales have been face-to-face, rather than "service" sales over the telephone, the status of that customer as prospect takes a quantum leap. For from then on you are dealing with someone who has accepted house, product, and you, and the importance of that personal relationship cannot possibly be overestimated. It can be the key to an unending chain of sales to an individual with whom you have an increasingly excellent relationship, to others within the same organization, and to an unbroken succession of business friends and acquaintances over the years. Key buyers and referral sources are indeed the stuff of which successful careers in selling are made. They take a good deal of development—that means time, and time is precious in the field—but they are quite worth the time spent.

Unless you use them as a crutch and fall into the callback trap, of course. As every experienced professional so well knows, it is very comfortable to call on the convinced; they do not really need to be sold, and they will often buy enough—or almost enough—to make the call seem worthwhile. But effective servicing of an account, coupled with constant sale and resale (all of which is right and proper) can all too easily degenerate into profitless continuing callback, wasting precious field time that should far more profitably be spent in effective prospecting and the development of new accounts. It is nice to spend time chatting with an old friend on a snowy or steamy day, but it does not necessarily build a territory or a career.

Satisfied customers will themselves often buy more, especially when they have recently bought from you; very often when they have just bought from you. That is euphoria working in your favor. When you have just sold a customer he or she is usually "high" after making the "right" decision. You, your company, and your products will never look better than the moment after the close. Which is why your just-sold customer often becomes a highly qualified prospective purchaser immediately after the close of the previous sale. A self-congratulatory customer will, at the moment following the sale, often seriously consider add-on sales, related products, and even quite unrelated product purchases. Your customer will, in the period of euphoria following a buying decision, be very likely to want to help you, and at the same time will want to help some of his or her best business or personal friends (depending on the nature of the product) to be able to make the same sound buying decision.

If handled properly, your just-sold-and-therefore-self-congratulatory customer will provide excellent *referrals,* with the aggregate of your satisfied customers therefore supplying you with a literally endless body of qualified prospects. The keys to securing referred prospects are asking at the right time, if at all possible after you have made a sale; asking for a limited number of referrals at any given time; being careful not to mix the referral request with product recommendation requests; and handling product recommendation requests very gently.

When after sale you ask for referrals will depend on the specific situation. You are likely to move from the sale just made into an add-on sale try, saving the referral request until after you have tried to make the additional sale, before you gather up your materials in preparation for leaving. But in some instances, you may want to ask for referrals after the initial sale itself, using a question about whether or not one of those referred might be interested in other products as a lead-in for your additional sales attempt. In no instance should you try for a referral with your coat on, your briefcase packed, and ready to go out the door, any more than you should seriously try for an additional sale then. By then, the game is likely to be over, the selling situation gone; you and your customer will both be looking forward to whatever is next in the day.

By asking for a limited number of referrals you are asking for a favor that is very easy to grant, requiring only the recommendation of a couple of friends down the hall, in the same building, across the street, or a few miles away, rather than a serious decision followed by a time-consuming search for addresses and telephone numbers. The right number to ask for is two, as in "Ms. Jones, I'd like a chance to discuss these systems (or products, services, policies, or whatever else it is you are selling) with other people in the industry (or locally, in the city, or around here). Do you know two other people you think it would be worthwhile to talk to?" Note that you have asked for two, rather than one, for a single referral may be easily misconstrued as a recommendation as well as a referral. But only two, rather than "a few," or anything that might be seen as work-creating, and therefore as an unwarranted imposition. And note that you have not asked for any kind of product recommendation, but only for people with whom to discuss specific products.

You will often get two referrals if you ask for them this way. Sometimes you will get more, as you take the two names, and then sit, pen poised, obviously waiting to see if more will be volunteered. If no more are volunteered after a moment, it is best to let it go at that. There will be another sale to the same customer another day, as well as service contacts.

When you do get referrals, your customer will also often offer to call those being referred, to tell them that you will be calling. Whether or not that offer is made directly to you then, your customer will often inform friends that you are going to call. If possible, therefore, give your customer a chance to contact his or her friends about you before calling. And bear in mind that busy people may not make the contact immediately, or even on the day they first call each other. If you can hold off calling on referrals for a couple of days, you will have maximized chances that your customer has made an all-important call ahead of you, and that you can call your new prospect for an appointment and get it easily, often with a personal and product recommendation already in place.

Product recommendations are a delicate matter. Think carefully before asking your customer to tell friends how good your products or services are, for a refusal to do so can create an awkward and possibly damaging situation. Putting it a little differently, try not to ask unless you are pretty sure your customer will agree to do so. Some have a second chance to try for referrals from satisfied users; others do not. It depends on whether or not what you have sold requires any kind of installation in which the purchaser is directly involved, as when you have sold an office machine in a small office and install it personally or together with a service representative. For then if the installation goes well, post-sales opportunities may repeat, with add-on sales and referrals possible from a self-congratulatory customer. Such installations are sometimes quite wrongly seen as nothing but time-consuming chores; they can be that, but they can also be excellent opportunities to create a brand new sales and referrals situation.

Referrals secured may in some instances be outside your territory or for products that you do not handle. Alert sales organizations therefore often supply incentives for those who generate referrals resulting in sales for others. However, even when organizations fall down on this vital sales-building technique, alert sales professionals find ways to generate leads for each other, in the sure knowledge that swapping prospects so generated will pay everyone handsomely in the long run.

Good referral prospects can also often be generated from satisfied customers who are happy to help you because they think highly of you and your company. Often it happens within the context of a routine service or troubleshooting call. Customers rarely volunteer referrals, though; you must ask, gently, diffidently, and above all consistently.

That is true of family, friends, and even other prospects who have not bought. There are products, such as securities and life insurance, that are sold quite often through the referrals of family and friends. There are prospects who will refer you to others, whether they are still in the buying decision-making process themselves, or have reluctantly deferred purchase until a later date for financial or other business reasons. All will generate good referral prospects; all must be asked to do so.

A reminder: the tricky sales professional is not really much of a professional at all. Claiming business or personal friendships that are merely passing acquaintanceships, or claiming referrals or product recommendations that have not, in fact, been given, is asking for trouble. Somehow the word percolates that there is someone out there selling who cannot be trusted. It does not take much of that to threaten a job and damage a career.

While the prospects generated by current customers can be excellent sales leads, there are many other prospect sources as well. Former customers, if properly cultivated, can be excellent prospects for resale. Every publisher selling periodicals by direct mail knows that; lists of former customers, called *expires,* are second only to current subscriber lists as prospects for other publications. It requires time and attention, usually consisting of a prolonged, systematic effort to rekindle interest, and to develop existing proven needs into new desire for what you are selling.

The essence of the matter is the continued existence of those proven needs. When someone has already bought from your company and perhaps directly from you as well, the all-important question of need no longer must be established before the question of buying your products and services can even be addressed. Of course, if the entire nature of a prospect's business has changed, needs may disappear completely, but that is an exceedingly rare situation. It is far more likely that a former customer may have gone over to the competition, or may even have dropped only part of your product line. A resale under those kinds of circumstances is far easier than a new sale to a stranger. That may be true even when relations have been ruptured between your former customer and your company, as over an unpaid bill or an alleged major quality or customer service failure. It is usually far easier to redevelop selling relations with a former customer than to sell a new prospect.

Rekindling interest may be as easy as making sure that all your former customers continue to receive those company promotional and customer relations mailings you consider relevant, whether through formal company channels, or directly through you. Many seasoned professionals regularly mail prospects, and especially former customers, items aimed at stimulating felt need for their products, along with company-generated material. Some also mail items they pick up that seem particularly relevant to the individual or company they are trying to resell, following up with telephone calls periodically. Some take advantage of special promotions and discounts to attempt to rekindle former customer interest, as well as to kindle interest in other prospects.

Buyers of your competition, like former customers—and many of them often are former customers—are also prime prospects, no matter how deeply entrenched your competitors seem to be and how unsuccessful you and others have been in selling to them over the years. That lack of success in selling them, however, often has a great deal to do with continued failure to do so. For the prospect who continues to reject our approaches can easily be seen as rejecting us—not only as businesspeople, but as human beings—and nobody likes continued rejection, even seasoned sellers who know how to handle it maturely. The truth is that most of us stop, if rejected often enough and firmly enough. We mask rather effectively what is really happening, of course—we are spending too much time on a lost cause, have to move on to more fruitful prospects, cannot get appointments anyway, maybe ought to try them again later on sometime. Anyway, if we keep on pushing, we are just going to poison relations and kill any hope of eventually selling them.

Yes, we may indeed. Continually calling and being rebuffed may indeed build up a wall of rejection between you and your prospect. But a continuing set of contacts, such as the contacts you maintain with former customers, coupled with judicious follow-up, may serve your purposes very well indeed. It requires consistent, long-term follow-up, which often in the long term succeeds extraordinarily well. You cannot know which new product announcement, third-party recommendation, or cost-saving tip you mail to a competitive buyer will do the trick; but you can properly assume that sooner or later one of your follow-up calls will result in a face-to-face selling situation.

For the law of life is change. Wants, needs, relationships with competing companies and sales representatives, buying personnel, product lines, pricing arrangements—all these things change, creating new situations which you may take advantage of, if you are properly positioned to do so. Your constant contact with competitive buyers does that positioning for you. It may be a promotion or company change, moving someone who is deeply committed to a competitive product, seller, or company, and removing the block caused by that commitment. It may be that the same kind of product, service, or personal relationship disaster that caused one of your customers some years ago to become a decidedly unfriendly prospect, is now occurring with the company to which your customer went. With the shoe now on the other foot, and proper contact having been maintained, the move may be back to you rather than to a third company. It may be a story in a newspaper or told over coffee in a commuter train that morning, about how much better your new product is than a competing product. Do not fall into the negativism trap here, by the way, or at any time when you are handling competitive situations. The right assumption is that your product is always uniquely able to stand on its own merits. Surely you will make sharp competitive comparisons, when they are called for by the situation, but if you let the sale rise or fall on a competitive comparison before you have properly told your unique selling story, you have weighted the decision against yourself. It is one of the oldest basics in selling: sell the positive aspects of what you have to sell, eschewing the negative as much as possible, and never, never, never make a personal attack upon a competing seller, company, or product. That can be construed as dirty pool, and there is nothing better calculated to destroy a growing trust in you, and the selling situation with it.

Prospects may also come as leads generated by advertising, direct marketing, or a trade show exhibit. Many companies generate large numbers of leads for their field representatives in these ways, with the quality of the leads ranging all the way from very poor to excellent, depending on such factors as how wide the advertising copy net was cast and the nature and price of the mail-sold products purchased. Because direct mail leads are buyers of some sort, direct mail on the whole tends to supply somewhat better quality leads than does advertising. But that is more a tendency than an inflexible rule. After all, an advertisement-generated lead for a specific and rather expensive product is likely to be a far better prospect than the mail order buyer of a $5.00 item, who winds up in your hands as a prospect. And your company may not be very adept at helping you qualify the prospects sent; you may have little more than name and address to start with. In that sort of instance, you can only ask, attempt to reach prospects by telephone, attempt to determine the nature of their potential interest and ability to buy as best you can without being face-to-face, and, when appropriate, try to set up a selling appointment. At worst, you will present to unqualified prospects; at best, you will make some wholly unanticipated sales to people you did not even know existed.

Some of the best company-generated leads you are likely to get will be the names, addresses, and sometimes information on prospects who have seen your company's products and expressed interest at a trade show or some other kind of exhibit. These will often be people who have rather carefully studied your company's sales material and often the products themselves at the exhibit, and may have had considerable discussions with your people as well. Such prospects must be reached as soon as possible after receiving company-generated leads.

On the other hand, you may also find yourself receiving all the names of those who registered for a convention or trade show, neatly typed for you on a lead form, without any other information and with no way to determine which of them are superb prospects and which are wholly unqualified. When confronted with that kind of all-too-common situation, you can only try to separate the real prospects from the rest by telephone, once again being ready to waste selling calls on a few unqualified prospects if you must, but not letting the good ones go. The trap here, by the way, as in all mass-lead situations, is that you will let the good ones go. Twenty fruitless telephone calls in a row can sometimes daunt even the hardiest, most experienced "old pro," who should know better—and really does, most of the time. But in the long run it is right to go ahead and make the twenty-first call, and then the forty-first and the fifty-first. Good new prospects can be hard to find, and consistently pursuing home office leads can, in the long run, be an excellent career-building habit.

Consistent prospecting is also a matter of keeping up with some readily available sources of current information. For example, the real estate section of a city or regional newspaper is must reading for many sales professionals; knowing about move-ins in a timely way can make the difference between a substantial sale and the resulting new customer relationship and a late and disappointing contact after more alert competitors have sewed up a new firm in town.

A good deal more than move-ins can be derived from such sources. Between the local press and the trade publications in your field, you should be able to get a good deal of vital updating information on promotions and job changes, company developments, and new technology; all can be prospect-creating, if the information is timely, and if you are ready to move in a timely way to take advantage of it. A bit of job-change information can result in a call to a key new executive who is considering —and indeed may have been brought in to accomplish—a set of major changes substantially affecting buying patterns and vendor relationships; that person can become a major new customer for you. The promotion of someone you have cultivated may result in a timely call and sale, rather than a late call and no sale at all. A technological development or move by a company into a new line of business may open up substantial new prospects you may have missed had you not taken the trouble to keep informed.

Prospects are also to be found merely by looking, rather than unobservantly passing by. The tenants' listing in the lobby of an office building may inform you of move-ins even more effectively than the local press, if you take the time to look when you are making a call in the building. Your customers will tell you about new people in the town or area, if you take the time to ask when you are calling on them. There is usually not much sense in spending large amounts of time in cold calling, though; normally it is far better to try to develop information about such "found" prospects and then using the telephone to try to sell a firm appointment.

Some people do enjoy cold calling, though; it can be part of the fun of selling, if it is not carried to wasteful extremes and made a substitute for systematic prospecting and information gathering. Sometimes, between appointments or after a busted appointment, it can be enjoyable and rewarding to turn the handle on the door of a strange office, do your best to find out what you can about the company and its people from the receptionist you then encounter, and even proceed to try to make a cold call upon someone you are not at all sure will turn out to be a qualified buyer. You may sell a later appointment to someone you think may be a qualified buyer; you may even make a totally unexpected sale on the spot, depending on what you are selling and the breaks of the game. All if you have the time, that is, and nothing better to do in that place at that time; cold calling on strangers can be a terrible time-waster, and should not be relied on for very much in the way of sales. When you walk into a selling situation without any information at all on your prospect, you are making it harder to sell than it needs to be. Even the telephone call in which you have sold the appointment can yield enough to begin to develop the information you need with which to first qualify and then empathetically sell the prospect; a cold call often does not even take you that far, much less give you an opportunity to develop vitally important prospect information before the selling interview actually takes place.

There are a wide range of sources from which to derive such prospect information. Your own company files may yield some, if the prospect is a former customer. So may your own prospect files; you cannot remember everything in them, and a new prospect may turn out to be not new at all once you consult your files. Your selling colleagues may be sources of information, if the new prospect is a move-in. And so may your own customers, who may have vital information for you available merely for the asking.

Beyond those kinds of sources are a wide variety of published sources of information. In Part 6 we supply a quite substantial selection of business information, derived in large part from Brownstone and Carruth's *Where to Find Business Information* (John Wiley and Sons, 1982), which is to be found in almost all business libraries and very many public libraries as well. We there discuss your own basic needs for and sources of information, and include most of the major sources of current information you will be able to consult as needed. Some of the sources will not be available in every library, but many will be available in both business libraries and substantial public libraries. Most sales professionals have or can gain continuing access to such a library, sometimes as a matter of right, as in the case of public libraries; sometimes as a matter of local policy, as when a college, university, or business college opens its library to local business-people and professionals; and sometimes, if necessary, by special arrangement with the librarian of such a school.

It takes a considerable amount of time and attention to learn how to use published sources or prospect information efficiently. But it is very much worth the effort. Financial and other relevant information on tens of thousands of companies is available, as is biographical information on some millions of Americans. And there are scores of special directories, looseleaf services, books, and newsletters containing information that may provide needed prospect information.

Learning how to use all these sources develops a long-term career-building kind of skill, which makes it possible for you to generate much of the information you need, whatever your selling job and whether you are working for another or on your own. And it is not really very hard to learn what you need to know to use the library effectively, especially if you let the skilled reference librarians you will find there help to the best of their considerable abilities. It is foolish to wander about in a library, trying to figure out how to find the information you need. Even if you ultimately do, all by yourself, you will have wasted a great deal of time, and probably settled for far less than is really available. Ask the librarian, if necessary again and again; and the more intelligent questions you ask, the better most reference librarians will like it. Learn how to use the wide variety of printed sources you will encounter; also take the time to learn how to find needed information in the other forms in which it is stored, as on microforms and in computer memories. More and more we are storing information in computer memories now, and calling forth specific pieces of information as needed. That is the shape of the future, a future in which enormous masses of information will be available in computerized forms, and capable of being reached—accessed, as computer people are fond of calling it—through viewing devices in your office and home.

The net of all of the above prospecting and information-gathering activities, assuming consistent and skilled work on your part, is a constant flow of highly qualified prospects, all of whom find their way into your prospect files. To develop files full of prime prospects is to provide yourself with one of the building blocks you need for long-term career success in selling. As so many before us have said, "A good prospect file is like money in the bank." It provides you with resources you can dip into as needed, with a reserve of prospects you reach for to build a productive day, week, or month. Without it, you are reduced to a great deal of cold calling, over-attention to a narrowing group of customers, and constant callbacks on a small and increasingly inhospitable group of prospects. Putting it a little differently, without knowing how to build—and consistently building—a good prospect file, you are very likely to be a former sales representative for a good number of companies, and headed for eventual long-term unemployment. In Chapter 5, we discussed how to organize your prospect and customer files for maximum efficiency. Here we will maintain our focus on the selling process.

INTERVIEW SELLING

Converting a stack of prospect cards into selling appointments requires bringing another group of selling skills into play. For after finding prospects and gathering information about them, you must sell them, and before you can sell them your products you must sell them on the desirability of making a firm appointment to see and discuss your products with you.

The key to successful interview selling is understanding what is happening between you and your prospect. On the telephone, trying to make a firm appointment with your prospect, you are not selling your product—you are selling the interview. All you want to accomplish on the telephone is to sell your prospect on the desirability of talking with you face-to-face. You will often have to explain something of yourself, your company, and your product so that the prospect can make the interview decision. You might have some questions to ask the prospect to help you determine whether an interview will be worthwhile. But to the extent that you step over the fine line between explaining and selling you will harm your chances of getting a firm appointment with your prospect.

Even for some experienced people that fact can be hard to accept. Once you have a live prospect on the phone, the temptation is to glowingly describe the product, prepare the way for the face-to-face encounter, and go as far as you can to get information and prepare the close. Unfortunately, it just does not work that way. The harder you try to sell your product over the phone the less chance you will have of selling the interview. And being human, the less you succeed in selling interviews, the harder you are likely to try to sell the product over the phone, creating a kind of downward spiral. It is best to reserve product selling efforts for the face-to-face interview.

The main problem is that when you try to sell your product over the phone you are selling into a partial vacuum. Face-to-face, you have had a chance to size up the firm, the prospect, and the selling situation. You have asked some questions, given and received both verbal and all-important nonverbal communication, and begun to establish empathy and focus on the prospect's problems. On the phone, all you have is the instrument and a disembodied voice on the other end of the line. You cannot see, feel, empathize; you are just playing cards with the deck stacked against you, and by your own choice. If the situation begins to go bad, your chances of recovery are very slim.

On the other hand, when you sell only the interview, you are presenting your prospect with a very limited decision—see you or not. And by setting it up as a firm appointment, both you and the prospect know you are going into a selling situation.

Many companies provide their field forces with prepared telephone-interview selling presentations. If you have one, use it. It has been developed, redeveloped, and honed down fine with the problems and opportunities of your company and its products in mind. It will usually contain a basic presentation and several alternative ways to go as you and your prospect reach choice points in your conversation.

If you do not have such a presentation, it is not too hard to develop one for yourself, as long as you keep your concentration on the goal of the telephone conversation: you are selling the interview, not the product. The opener of one such presentation might go something like:

"Hello, Mr. Smith. I'm Mary Tate of the Hummus Company. I'm calling this morning to try to set up a meeting with you to discuss how our new line of widgets might be helpful in your production line operations. Would it be possible to get together tomorrow at ten, or would after lunch be better?" (Of course, if you have a referral it will be "Jack Jones of Jones and Jones suggested that I call you this morning . . .")

Mr. Smith is likely to want to know a little more about your line of widgets, perhaps about your company, before he can decide whether or not to see you. Answer the questions and then come back to a quick closing question as early as you feel you can. A time-choice close that focuses the prospect's attention on when to see you rather than whether or not to see you will usually work better than a straightforward "will you see me" approach. "Will you see me?" courts a straightforward "No!" which ends game, set, and match.

Your prospect will often counter with an early objection, something like, "Oh, yes, I've heard about those widgets. Aren't they pretty expensive?" That is when your resolve to stick to selling the interview gets tested. If you respond quite naturally, "Oh, no, Mr. Smith. Our widgets are not really expensive, when you consider their durability and design excellence," you have just fallen into a trap. Instead respond with something like, "That's just the kind of question I want to discuss with you face-to-face, Mr. Smith—costs, savings, durability, design, and how our new widgets can fit into your operations. How would Monday at 10 A.M. be for you?" You have deferred the too-early objection, focused on the interview, and stand a far better chance of selling that interview than if you had fallen into the trap.

Your prospect will often simply stall. Then it is a question of continuing to stress the potential value of the interview, reaching again and again for the close. You probably will not want to try to smoke out the hidden objection under the stall over the phone unless you have been stalled with something like, "Sorry, I don't have time to see you . . . try me next week," again and again.

Quite often, you will have to get through a secretary or administrative assistant before you can get to your prospect. And that person is often responsible for screening just your kind of call.

If you have a good referral, you are likely to get right through. "Hello, I'm Mary Tate of the Hummus Company. Jack Jones of Jones and Jones suggested that I call Mr. Smith this morning. Is he there?" That is pretty straightforward, and "Is he there?" sidesteps the screening function of the person you are talking to. The only decision to be made is whether or not to put you through.

Without a referral, you still may get right through with "Is he there?" If you do not, you may have to explain why you are calling, in much the same words as in your basic telephone presentation. Then your final phrase can be, "Do you make all Mr. Smith's appointments?" In the unlikely event that the screening person does make all appointments, you will try to make one. Much more likely, the answer will be no, and then you will ask to speak with Mr. Smith.

Selling interviews over the phone can be a difficult and annoying chore for field sales professionals, unless it is done skillfully. But, just as failure at it spirals downward, so does success build success.

THE SELLING SITUATION

Here we deal with you and your prospect or prospects—seller and buyer —in direct encounter and interplay. Now the prospect has been identified and the interview sold—or has been self-identified, as in retail selling— and buyer and seller are in the same place at the same time, soon to be face-to-face in a selling situation that will or will not result in a sale being made now. Let us stress that *now,* for each selling situation is unique. The sale that is not made in one selling situation should never be seen as merely deferred until another day; it is far more likely that it will have to be made all over again another day, in what is another and different selling situation.

In that sense, every selling situation is new. And that is true in a personal sense, as well. Every sale is, in some ways, the same: the same motives on both sides, the same approaches, sequences, techniques, key words and phrases. Yet every sale is also brand-new, as every game is brand-new, no matter how well the players know the rules. To some people outside your particular game, it can all seem deadeningly stale and boring—but it is not their game. The truth is that most professionals in every game find their work fascinating, and those who sell are no exception. Those who like the game find a great deal of enjoyment in selling, and the best people in any field do it as much for the fun as for any of the other rewards attached to success.

For analytical purposes, it is probably best to distinguish between outside selling and retail selling. Even though the essence of the interplay between buyer and seller is the same, there are some very substantial differences between the two kinds of selling situations.

The most important difference has to do with environment, for in outside selling, you come to the buyer and work in the buyer's environment, and in retail selling the buyer comes to you. In outside selling, therefore, you are likely to be dealing with a qualified prospect in an environment very familiar to the prospect and unfamiliar to you, but one in which you will be able to pick up many selling clues. You will also most likely be selling to an individual, rather than a group, and will usually know in advance if it is going to be a group presentation. You will be approaching; often rather formally presenting, perhaps with sales aids, although usually without the product itself to show; handling stalls and objections; and, if all goes well, moving to the close.

In retail selling, however, you will be dealing with self-identified prospects, but will need to qualify them on the spot and while moving into some sort of presentation, which will often feature a direct product demonstration. Your environment will be entirely familiar to you, but not to the prospect. You will therefore have fewer selling clues; you may have to deal with a certain amount of prospect disorientation; are unlikely, due to the retail environment, to be able to put together anything more than a rather brief presentation; and can almost count on even that being interrupted. You will also very often be presenting to a group, rather than to an individual, or find yourself presenting to a group after starting to present to an individual. Who said retail selling was easier than outside selling? Prospecting is easier, not selling; selling is only different, each with its own environmental imperatives.

Most sales professionals are involved in outside, rather than retail, selling, and the nature of the selling processes and many of the products involved do make outside selling considerably more complex than retail selling. We will therefore discuss outside selling first, and then more briefly discuss some of the special features of retail selling. We will discuss telephone selling only as an adjunct to face-to-face selling, as when you sell a prospect on an interview; telephone selling is normally so canned as not to need or be willing to pay for the services of sales professionals. For that reason it is also quite unattractive to most professionals.

THE CONTEXT

When you move into someone else's environment, the selling situation starts as soon as you enter that environment. That is not necessarily the prospect's office or other place of business, either. It may be a parking lot, a reception area, the lobby of a large building, or for that matter a restaurant across the street, where your prospect just happens to be having lunch or taking a coffee break.

Times change; social expectations change. The stereotype of the sales professional as a gold-cufflinked male in an expensive suit driving a big new car is long gone in most places and in most fields. But some axioms do remain. It remains axiomatic that if you drive into your prospect's company parking lot in an automobile that looks as if it is ready to be compacted into scrap, your prospect is highly likely to be idly looking out an office window directly at you, and wondering what kind of person might be willing to drive that kind of wreck. If you arrive in a reception area hot, tired, dusty, and in desperate need of freshening up, the receptionist that announces you—who may have been with the company for 30 years, and may be informally charged with a certain kind of screening—may in tone and telephone manner prejudice your prospect against you before you ever come face-to-face. And that prejudice is very likely to remain, at least as a question, even though you freshened up after making your disastrous first impression on the receptionist. If you are somehow discourteous to whomever is waiting on the table or the counter across the street in the diner, you may be creating the same kind of first impression; nobody likes a two-faced hypocrite, who is polite to buyers and nasty to those who are powerless. Sales professionals make no mistake about this —the selling situation starts as soon as we enter what even *may* be the prospect's own environment.

That environment can yield very important selling clues to those who take the trouble to cultivate looking and listening reflexes. And reflexes are what are needed, for there is a great deal to ingest and turn to advantage when you have the opportunity to spend a few minutes waiting for a prospect. Some of the questions you may ask yourself—quite reflexively, and without necessarily knowing that you are doing so—are:

• *How does the place look?*   Is the office small, dingy, full of tired-looking furniture and peeling plaster, or spacious and prosperous-looking? Is the plant in need of a paint job, with some long-broken windows, or is it modern, efficient, and in good repair? Is the store clean, well-lit, with fresh windows and signs? Many an old-fashioned office is prosperous and forward-looking, but it is much more often true that appearances do not deceive.

• *How's business?*   That is a question you are going to ask, one way or another, before you are very far into the selling situation. But it helps to try to size up business a little before you walk into your prospect's office. Do many offices seem untenanted, or is the place bursting with people and action? Is the parking lot crowded? What does the receptionist answer when you ask how business is?

• *How do the people look?*   Tight ship or loose rein? Happy or grim? A good deal of time-wasting from what you can see or a solidly businesslike atmosphere?

• *Any products or trophies in the reception area?*   Companies often use their reception areas as showcases, supplying valuable information on what they consider important by the products they feature and what they are proud of by the trophies they display. That is valuable empathy-developing information for you, and can start your conversation with your prospect. Sometimes it can be direct selling information as well.

• *Any promotional materials in sight?*   Many companies display their own promotional materials in their reception areas; valuable information indeed, when you are trying to fit your goods and services to the needs and desires of an unfamiliar firm.

• *What periodicals are in the reception area?*   You may find only last year's general interest magazines, but you may also find highly specialized materials reflecting the interests of your prospect—and you are eager to amass as much information as possible about those interests.

Receptionists can also be valuable sources of such information. Even more, they can help supply the "feel" of a new environment, and sometimes valuable clues as to the persona of your prospect. Clearly, if a receptionist obviously does not want to or cannot speak with you, it will not do to force it. Someone working hard to handle a busy phone, receive live callers, and perhaps handle a typing assignment as well may be unable to speak with you, no matter how willing to do so. On the other hand, most people like taking a break, and always respond to a little warmth and news of the outside world. It usually starts with the weather or a balky typewriter, and often very easily turns to work matters, for people love talking about their work; they need only be given the chance to do so. A skilled sales professional can learn a great deal about a prospect in a few minutes with a receptionist. It is always in order to try to secure and remember the receptionist's name—request it if it is not displayed—as you may be calling and coming back personally on other occasions, and remembrance of a name is always appreciated. Basic advice? Certainly. Too basic to be worth mentioning? Certainly not. Even the most experienced of us sometimes find ourselves moving away from sound selling reflexes occasionally. It is always worth reviewing the basics. And equally basic: If you and the receptionist are in the midst of a conversation when a prospect or a prospect's assistant or secretary comes to collect you, break off your conversation apologetically, as you would with anyone else you respected. To end a conversation abruptly is ill-mannered, and will be perceived as such; you will then seem manipulative and insincere, and will have been better off if the conversation had never taken place.

Whether you are collected and taken to the prospect or directed to the prospect's work area, your next contact is likely to be the prospect's assistant or secretary. Either way, you have very little time—important time, not for information-gathering, but for communicating warmth, for making contact. You may have spoken with the assistant or secretary over the phone, perhaps when setting up the appointment. If so, contact is easy and necessary, and as simple as a "Thank you." If not, contact is still very easy—as easy as a smile of appreciation and a thank you for having been guided to the right place. Another basic, for people who sell in all seasons: if you treat people like people, rather than like inanimate objects, they respond in kind. If you shake hands, get someone's name, take the time to write it down so that you get the spelling right, and say goodbye later with a smile, however the interview worked out, you are very likely to make a friend. That friend may swing an undecided sale for you, for many an assistant or secretary does just that—either way. And that friend can make it very easy—or close to impossible—when you call again for an appointment. It is also well worth bearing in mind that yesterday's competent assistant or secretary may be tomorrow's up-and-coming executive, in this or some other firm, willing to listen to an old friend's selling story, or ready to turn a deaf ear to someone who once treated a lowly assistant or secretary badly.

FACE-TO-FACE

And now you are face-to-face with the other player. A whole human being first; also a prospect, buyer, customer. A bundle of contradictions, just as complex as you are, full of concerns, operating on several levels at once, under many and quite diverse pressures. Possessor of a unique personal history, yet sharing many interests and problems with others you meet and work with every day. Ready to hear what you have to say, but simultaneously considering a good many other matters, both business and personal, and highly unlikely to be ready to concentrate on buying the way you are prepared to concentrate on selling. Someone whose attention you will probably have to catch and hold long enough to be able to present coherently, and then someone who must become engaged enough to want to buy. Someone with whom you can achieve empathy and with whom you can move toward a buying decision.

Your prospect is also someone who may be rather outgoing and friendly, or reserved and defensive, decisive or indecisive, attentive or distracted, tired or fresh, sharp or fuzzy—that day, that hour, that moment when you first meet. All are tendencies, all differ with the impact of a wide range of variables, and all require sharp analysis on your part in the selling situation.

For, in essence, you have to control the selling situation, from beginning to end, no matter how the situation was initiated. That is as necessary at the beginning as at the close, in that extraordinarily important first few moments of the interview, in which the whole relationship between you and your prospect is first cast. Those first few moments face-to-face are so important that they are worth dissecting, move by move.

It is interesting and revealing that the first and by far the most important context-setting move you make is nonverbal, the conveyance of basic attitude toward the prospect with body language. Your set of basic attitudes is first and quite lastingly conveyed by how you move to meet the prospect: relaxed, warm, friendly, intelligent, confident, entirely up to meet and welcome a new person and a new situation; or hot, cold, tired, perhaps a little defeated and unsure, quite down, and ready for another rejection. You project who and what you are both by design and quite involuntarily; real attitudes cannot be masked enough to fool the experienced eye, and your real attitudes will in the long run always show and support or defeat you. You project a whole person, to whom others will naturally move as they learn to respect, like, and trust you, and from whom others will withdraw if they perceive falseness and self-defeat.

The second move is also nonverbal; it is a matter of eye contact and close attention to the person you are meeting, who happens to be your prospect, but is first of all a whole human being, just like you. That people who run confidence games look at their victims squarely as a means of cultivating misguided confidence has nothing to do with it; confidence game people are emulating you, not the other way around.

You are then likely to shake hands, because most Americans do. You may run into someone from Great Britain, who does not normally shake hands, or someone who, for personal reasons does not like to shake hands; that poses no problem as long as you come close enough to allow your prospect to do so if desired. Most of us never did any variant of the hearty, bonecrushing "salesman's" handshake and backslap; that is a perennial comedy staple, and quite out of style. Just a firm, quite brief handshake will do.

The rest of the mechanics are straightforward, basic, and worth mentioning only because some who are not sales professionals will be reading this book. If you are carrying a coat, it may already have been taken from you, or the prospect will tell you where to put it. If neither happens after greeting the prospect, look around the room, find a likely place, ask if it is all right to put your coat there, get assent, and do so. The sight of someone who should be a sales professional standing awkwardly holding a coat and not knowing what to do with it is enough to make a sales manager's blood run cold. But it happens.

You will be asked to sit, and will not sit until you are asked. Of course, if some time goes by and you are still not invited, you will surely find some reason to be asked. When you do, try to sit reasonably close to the prospect, in a place that allows you some surface on which to spread sales materials later in the interview. Usually that will be the prospect's desk, and you will probably sit on whatever side of the desk a second chair has been placed. If there is a choice as to which side of the desk to sit on, choose the left side if you are right-handed, the right if you are left-handed. That will allow you to place your briefcase between the desk and your chair so that you can pull materials in and out of it with your best hand, and allow you to use the end of the desk for handling materials, rather than your lap.

During the course of the interview, you are likely to pull a good many materials out of that briefcase. Be sure to leave them out only as long as needed, and then put them away to avoid distracting clutter. As to the briefcase—make sure it is in good condition. A badly scuffed, dirty briefcase can be fairly unobtrusive in a reception area or on the floor of a prospect's office. But the moment you have to put it on your lap, on a table, or on the prospect's desk to get something, it becomes shockingly obtrusive.

You will continue to study the prospect's working environment throughout the interview. It is not a contradiction in terms to give the prospect your complete attention and keep looking at the environment. It merely takes getting used to—and a lot of practice. Mechanically, it is mostly a matter of peripheral vision. Just as you see off to the sides of the road while focusing on the road itself, so you can see a good deal of the office environment while focusing on your prospect.

It is important to do so. There are a great many clues in a workplace —products, trophies, photos, books, decor, repair, windows, office placement—and any or all of them can be useful in making the sale. Bear in mind that although each one is a new environment for you, you are in hundreds, even thousands of them. Once you get used to looking for clues, you will find them everywhere, find them more easily as time goes by, and eventually not even have to think about looking for them. Many sales professionals see everything worth seeing with a single, quite automatic glance, and use what they have seen all during the interview. It is simply a matter of training yourself to be observant and getting a good deal of practice.

Beyond the simple mechanics, the key things that are happening in those vitally important early moments of the interview are the beginnings of empathy; you are beginning to be able to put yourself into your prospect's shoes, and are gathering vital information regarding prospect needs and desires that can later lead you to a successful close. You can deliver a presentation carefully calculated to appeal to the wants and needs of the "average" or "typical" prospect, but each prospect is, in some most significant respects, unique; therefore, the early information you gather and later adroitly use is very often the difference between closing or not closing the sale.

The early conversation between you and your prospect, then, is vitally important; it is far from the trivial interchange it so often seems to an unperceptive observer—and often also to the prospect. If it is controlled well, that is. If not, it can indeed consist of little more than useless, situation-deadening trivia, with your prospect becoming restless and you then plunging prematurely into your presentation, with neither the beginnings of empathy nor the vital information you need to take the prospect to the close later on. In that case, you will have fallen into one of the classic early traps, be well on your way to both losing the sale and convincing your prospect that you are someone to be avoided in the future.

It is never really difficult to avoid this kind of trivia trap, as long as you are exercising conscious control over the situation and moving it somewhere, rather than sitting back and letting the situation go. Directionless "friendliness" takes one nowhere. The trivial, friendly opening must quickly be taken in a solid business direction. This is where all your preparation begins to pay off, for your knowledge of the industry, and of specific companies, people, products, and processes will make you an interesting person to your prospect, and possibly a valuable source of future insight. When it is clear that you know a good deal about matters your prospect needs to know about, you become more than a seller; you become a counselor as well, meaning that your prospect will often rather eagerly open up and discuss problems, needs, and desires with you—just what you need to reach empathetic understanding and develop information. For then you are giving as well as getting, and developing what can be a mutually advantageous and personally satisfactory business relationship—a real two-way street.

Some opportunities also create their own pitfalls. Beware of the prospect who seems to open up and deluge you with problems before you have had much more than a chance to smile and say hello. That is, after all, another classic early trap: the crier, who will, if possible, cry you right out the door, deeply sympathetic over the sad plight of the crier's business—and without a sale.

After not very long, it becomes time to present. When? Oh, when it feels right, when your prospect clearly wants you to do so, or when you feel that enough empathy and information have been generated to make it time. Or, of course, when you are not sure, perhaps having run into some early stalls and objections or seemingly impossible-to-penetrate defensive shell on the part of the prospect. When talking around the main business of the day seems inappropriate, or when you have done pretty much what you wanted to do in the early stages, then it's time to "look them right in the eye, speak your piece, and listen just as hard to them as you want them to listen to you."

PRESENTING

Presenting is rather an expensive business. By the time you total up all the costs involved in placing yourself before a qualified prospect—including prospecting time, research time, travel time and costs, other out-of-pocket costs, and presentation materials—you are faced with the sometimes daunting fact that you have spent anywhere from $40–50 to as much as several hundreds of dollars merely to place yourself into a situation in which you can effectively sell. That is a great deal of money spent for the privilege of speaking your piece, and makes it not at all inappropriate to think of your prospect as someone in whom you have already invested a good deal of money. Now it is time to get that investment back, and then some.

The presentation does several things:

- It completely and clearly lays out the major buyer benefits associated with purchase of your products and relates those benefits to the product features being shown.

- It organizes and tells the whole product story, fully and specifically, so that the prospect can fully understand those features you are turning into benefits.

- It relates the early information you have gained on prospect needs and desires to the specific benefits and features of your product.

- It handles, often anticipates, major prospect stalls and objections, including competitive objections.

- It provides a sound basis for handling stalls and objections successfully and moving to the close.

Every effective presentation is prepared, one way or another. Nobody really sells entirely "off the cuff," pulling words and concepts out of the air. Anyone who thinks selling happens entirely spontaneously just has not stopped to think through what is really happening. Even if you sell without any kind of consciously prepared presentation, you are working from product descriptions prepared by others—advertisements, brochures, manuals, handbooks, visual materials of several kinds—and developing your thinking around those standard materials.

No matter how creative you are in thought and language, you will still describe benefits and features basically the same way to the same kind of prospects in the same kinds of situations. Anyone doubting this need only tape his or her own presentations for several weeks. The words, the tone, the appeals are always strikingly similar from situation to situation, and so are the gaps, especially if you have not given sufficient thought to preparing your presentation. It is always startling and often pathetic to watch sellers who have spent hundreds of dollars getting before qualified prospects and then muff the selling opportunity by presenting an incomplete, badly put, totally inadequate products features story bereft of the necessary benefits.

On the other hand, watching someone race letter-perfect through a canned presentation without once making human contact with the prospect is even more painful. Many sales organizations provide fully worded presentations for their sales representatives to memorize and present as is. Some sales management people even provide several long, fully worded presentations at once for their hapless sales representatives to try to memorize and keep memorized, complete with obligatory pauses, head motions, and other body language. That, of course, never works for very long —the pressured representatives memorize in training sessions as best they can, then quite properly jettison the impossible presentation load as soon as they are in the field.

Sometimes sales managements provide their field forces with fully worded, visualized presentations in the forms of slide–audio and motion picture presentations. That kind of presentation has a real place in some highly technical product areas, but little place in most product areas.

Canned presentations were the last generation of sales management's answer to the off-the-cuff approach, and in many situations worked effectively. In this generation, though, given some of the presentation aids available, it is clearly possible to fully prepare effective presentations without losing the crucial ability to sell empathetically.

Most sales managers who insist on fully memorized presentations expect them to be used with some degree of judgment. That means human contact, questioning, listening in the early stages of the interview; pausing to handle a question or objection while going through the canned presentation; moving away from the presentation when the prospect's eyes begin to glaze and breathing becomes too regular. Of course, there are a few sales management people whose incompetence expresses itself in excessive rigidity. They are to be borne if you feel you must, and fled from into more rewarding jobs if their demands become onerous.

Use the canned presentation flexibly and add a personal component, even if you are dealing with a motion picture complete with soundtrack. If you are using only a script, usually with some visual materials, take care to analyze it to find places where you will be able to plug in the personal element. For example, you will find some benefits that repeatedly appeal to specific kinds of prospects. You will be looking for that kind of benefit appeal in the early stages of the interview, and often will get verification of your guess that the specific benefit is one of the selling keys for that prospect. Then, when you reach that benefit in the prepared presentation, you can call the prospect's attention to that benefit, drive home how much that benefit can mean. It is as simple as pausing and saying something like "That's the sort of thing you were talking about before, Mr. Smith. These widgets can be used in four different ways, and may solve the setup problem that has been bothering your engineers." Look for a little agreement from Mr. Smith, but do not pause to discuss the whole matter; move on with the presentation.

In a slide–soundtrack or motion picture–soundtrack presentation, it is clearly harder to introduce the personal and empathetic component. But you can still study the presentation and find places for a meaningful look, a nod, and a few words relating what is being shown to the needs and desires earlier discussed with your prospect. And in almost all cases, it is desirable to do that kind of benefit-relating as soon as the presentation is over. It provides an excellent way to start handling objections and move toward the close.

The most important thing to know about the canned presentation, or about any presentation, for that matter, is that the presentation does not make the sale. You do. No presentation will establish empathy, illuminate prospect needs and desires, handle objections, and use all these things to move to the close. Those are your skills, and they are much of the fun of selling.

Very often, it is possible to develop very effective presentations by combining fully prepared visual and script materials with your own characteristic style and the insights you have gotten from the prospect. It may be as simple as using a company-prepared visual presentation book, with both illustrative visual material and key words and phrases right there on the page before you and the prospect as you are presenting. Or it may be less fully developed, as when you have a whole product line to present, with many alternative ways to go. Then you may be presenting around a single brochure for each product, using the photos and other visual materials in the brochure, the language of the brochure to talk around, and your own language.

The talk-through technique allows you maximum flexibility of expression, and guarantees that you will not leave out anything substantial, or inadvertently mix up the logical order of presentation, or improperly weight presentation elements and so give a distorted benefits picture to the prospect. For most products and in most selling situations, the talk-through is the most effective way to go.

Sometimes you really do go in almost barehanded as regards presentation materials. It can happen when you are selling for a very small company, or handling several commission lines, or perhaps relying very heavily on samples. It happens less and less, but it still happens.

You cannot very well write a brochure to sell from or develop a talk-through visual presentation. What you can and should do, though, is try to put every significant benefit and feature of each product in writing in the order you think most logical and effective. Figure out where to drop in product samples and any other visual materials you have. Then talk your basic presentation simultaneously into a mirror and a tape recorder. Do it several times before you use it in the field, refining as you go. When you begin to be satisfied with what you have, use it in the field. After each use, jot down some notes on possible refinement. Over a period of time, you will develop a presentation, much as a presentation is developed by any competent home office marketing department team. It may have some deficiencies, but at the very least you will be presenting a complete, clear benefits-and-features product story and moving effectively toward the sale.

Developing a highly professional presentation and group of presentation materials is a job for promotion writers and visual artists, working hand in hand. And while some sales professionals may also be writers, a few may be visual artists, and a very few are both, it is quite unusual to find a field representative developing an excellent presentation. If you are able to do so, fine; but when professionally developed materials are available, they will usually do the job far better—though sometimes with minor modifications suggested by your style and field experience—than you will be able to do yourself.

At the same time, it is vitally important that you know how to build at least the modestly effective presentation described above. Without the ability to do so, your lifetime career mobility as a sales professional is seriously impaired. For without the ability to build a coherent selling story, you will be unable to sell effectively in situations where you must go it alone, as when you are employed by a very small selling organization, or have gone on your own, either in your own selling organization or in some other kind of small business which requires that you develop a sound selling story.

A good many things can happen in a selling situation; and in the course of a sales career, everything that can happen will happen, usually more than once. There are times when distractions seem to multiply, and other times when it all goes so smoothly that you wonder when and what axe will fall just before the close, frustrating all that has gone before. Some interruptions and distractions will be just that; others will seem so to the neophyte, but will be recognized by the professional as paths to the close. Sometimes smooth sailing will be just that; but often going fluently and uninterruptedly through an entire presentation means only failure to engage the prospect in any way, leaving you with a blank wall where a close should be.

A sound presentation is a story with a beginning, a middle, and an end. For that story to be told well, it must be told more or less in sequence, although not at all necessarily in exact sequence and entirely whole, as conceived by whoever wrote it. At the same time, a sound presentation is one that helps engage the prospect, who if engaged can be counted on to behave like a lion, rather than a lamb. Someone who is right with you while you are presenting is likely to interrupt, ask difficult questions out of sequence (your sequence, that is), disagree, cut you short, discuss entirely irrelevant matters, and generally behave the same way you would in his or her shoes. To the beginner, and especially a beginner stumbling along trying to remember a completely canned presentation, a really engaged prospect often seems a disaster, rather than someone providing a multitude of closing tools. Of course, the prospect who is far more considerate, and says nothing at all, is quite likely to look a little puzzled after all has been fully recited, and say something like "Thanks; I'll think it over. Good day," or "I'm not entirely sure I understand all that. Would you mind going over that once more; I can give you 10 more minutes."

The good professional knows how to stay on the presentation track, while at the same time seeking to engage the prospect. That means being ready for all the interruptions, being poised to handle them well and then move on. The seller has an immense advantage over the prospect in this: the seller has been there before, a thousand times, and knows what to expect and how to handle it. To control the pace and focus of the situation is to control the whole situation, and much of success or failure in the selling situation—most obviously during the presentation—rests on who controls pace and focus.

Control depends significantly on composure. All of us are familiar with the prospect who plays power games—interrupts to raise purposely misleading questions, attacks your company, accuses you covertly or even overtly of misrepresentation—the kind of person who reflexively attempts to dominate all situations in which he or she is a player. But even that kind of very difficult person can be handled and sold, as long as professionalism is maintained throughout the interview. Professionals do not lose their temper or argue with prospects. They may disagree, even sometimes quite sharply, and express that disagreement, but with composure. Rarely, professionals may even walk away from a particularly disagreeable prospect. Mostly, professionals routinely handle whatever comes up, stay on track, and use seeming interruptions as tools to further the close.

During the presentation, an early question or objection is often encountered, one that you quite routinely expect but want to defer until you have spoken your piece and have laid the foundations for handling it and turning it in the direction of the close. For example, you have just launched your presentation, and the prospect stops you with "Before we go any further, I think you ought to know that we've been buying widgets just like these from Smith and Smith for the last 10 years—and we like them fine."

Ah, Smith and Smith; your main competitors, and a set of products you are quite ready to meet head-on when you must. But not now; it's premature. You do have some idea of what you are up against, though, and that can be helpful later. Your response is likely to be something like "Yes, they're a good company. As we go on here, I think you'll see how some of the unique features of our widgets make them especially suitable for you." And on with your presentation, ready to meet Smith and Smith directly later, when it is more appropriate.

Even more often, the prospect has a much-too-early—for you, that is —price question. You are three minutes into your 15-minute presentation, and he or she says, "Excuse me, but how much will the basic system cost me?" That may be an early, casual question that can easily be handled with "Far less than you might imagine," or "I think you'll find them very affordable," then adding to either "particularly with the kind of savings (or whatever other kinds of benefits apply) you will realize from their use. Let me show you how that works as we go along here." And on with the presentation.

The early price question may be just a question, or it may be a crucial question in the mind of the prospect, and one from which the prospect may not so easily be turned. If so, it is still worth trying hard to defer it until later, for if the price question comes up before the product story is told fairly, it may dominate the selling situation, destroy your pace and your focus on the unique benefits of what you have to offer, and kill your sale. If, in the long run, you come to believe that not answering the price question directly will fatally harm your ability to build empathy with your prospect, creating a wall of mistrust between you, then you certainly must answer it—but not until you must.

You may also get an assertion of fact that must be handled with a direct answer. Your prospect may say, "I'm afraid you're barking up the wrong tree here. I believe that your whatsit is incompatible with our whosits." Then it must be a matter of agreement and switch to another product or go on back out the door, or "I think you'll find they are compatible; our engineers have seen to that. Let me show how that works as we go along here." And go back on the presentation track, informed as to a potential problem, and supplied with a closing tool for later.

Interruptions also occur; the prospect who is interrupted five times during the course of a rather brief presentation by secretary, colleagues, and telephone may find it hard to properly attend to you and your selling story. That can destroy a sale; if it is really impossible, you may have to break off and come back to sell another day. More typically, though, you will patiently wait through the interruption, review a bit before going on, and then move back into the presentation. Trying to sell through an interruption does both you and the prospect an injustice.

Only neophytes seriously try to close during the course of their presentations. Occasionally, a prospect will "take the product away from you," cutting the presentation short with questions and comments that so clearly indicate an intent to buy right now that you would be remiss in not closing on the spot. But that is, regrettably, all too rare an occurrence. What does sometimes happen, however, is that a "trial close," that terribly misnamed and entirely right attempt to engage the prospect and simultaneously see how well you are succeeding in doing so, is misunderstood—by seller, prospect, or both—and taken to be a serious closing attempt.

A trial close is only a device—a reflexive question put by the seller— that attempts to get some kind of modest agreement, as when you say, "Doesn't that make sense to you?" "Don't you agree?" or any other such question as you proceed with your selling story. A blank stare or perhaps the tiniest shrug is a pretty clear indication that you are not getting through; a thoughtful nod or encouraging smile is an indication that you are at least mutually engaged in the selling situation. The trial close is therefore a device aimed at building empathy and agreement; nothing less, but nothing more. To go from the agreement gained in a trial close into a serious attempt to close may destroy whatever empathy you have so far developed, and that is the kind of setback that can cost a sale.

In developing a presentation technique, it is vital to understand that form must in this instance follow function. A demonstration or installation can be achieved in a darkened room and using wholly standard and literally canned (or filmed or cassetted) presentation materials; but a sale can rarely be achieved under those conditions. Marketing managements are sometimes hypnotized by visual and machine-assisted presentation materials, insisting that their sales representative use them to the exclusion of empathy-building techniques—but not for long, because canned techniques standing alone seldom work for very long. They may work during a new-presentation introduction period, when all else in the selling organization are focused upon them, and while they have the virtue of novelty. And many kinds of visual and audio materials can be extremely useful in selling situations, especially when highly technical products are being sold. But in the long run, no matter how much pressure is applied to a field force by a temporarily wrongheaded marketing management group, skilled sales professionals find ways to use canned materials as adjuncts, rather than the main motor forces of their selling stories. This is because effective long-term personal selling depends on empathy and mutual problem solving, and that must be done on a person-to-person, situation-by-situation basis, with seller applying products and services to prospect problems, needs, and desires.

That is true even in a group presentation situation, where the need to present to more than one prospect may vitiate the impact of your one-on-one approach, and where you must consider the dynamics of the group in presenting and selling. We are here discussing formally presenting to a group, rather than the kind of informal group presentation retail sellers very often encounter, which we will discuss later.

To a considerable extent, successful group presentation depends on your ability to make and develop one-on-one empathetic selling relationships with one or more of the group's members, while at the same time avoiding the potential trap of falling between contending group members. That means attempting, during the early stages of the interview, to identify the relationships between group members. Sometimes that is very easy; a primary influence in the group self-identifies or is identified by the other group members. When you are presenting to an executive who has brought in several subordinates, your working hypothesis has to be that you are selling primarily to that executive, though you will be watching carefully to see who else in the group may be in a position to seriously influence the buying decision.

On the other hand, you may find yourself presenting to several relatively equal prospects, some of whom are pursuing disagreements that have little to do with you and your product. Then it is a matter of doing your best to get agreement from two or more key prospects, a far more difficult but not at all improbable achievement. It is often tempting to try to play one prospect or group against another in such a situation, forcing the issue by making it turn into a demonstration of power by the most powerful in the group, and making it part of whatever set of internal battles your prospects are involved in. That may force a sale, once in a long while. More often, it will destroy it, and with it your future possibilities with all or some of the group members. People inside an organization may squabble bitterly among themselves, and even let an outsider see them doing it, but they bitterly resent an outsider who attempts to take advantage of their divisions, and they often close ranks against that outsider.

It is often worthwhile in group situations to try to spend more time than you normally would on the early empathy-building stages of the interview, even stalling a bit as you attempt to sort out the structural and power relations between group members, so that you can try to begin to build empathy with the right people in the group before moving into your presentation. That kind of sorting out can be an indispensable adjunct to group selling.

A group presentation is often longer than your normal one-to-one presentation, partly because of the need to sell to more than one group member, but mostly because you may need to repeat yourself a great deal. What is clear to one group member may be absolutely opaque to another. Someone may have missed a basic assumption, been a little shy about saying so, and then demonstrate incomprehension later on, forcing you to review a substantial portion of your presentation. Two group members may have engaged each other in conversation, forcing you to review for them. Several people may listen to your answer to a question during the presentation, and start a lively discussion that you find hard to control, or may ask the same question again and again in slightly different ways. The generally correct thing to do is to treat each question or comment with as much close attention as you would if it were coming from the most influential member of the group, answering again questions that have been asked before, re-presenting briefly as necessary.

Whether fully memorized and using completely canned materials, or done in a talk-through fashion with a minimum of presentation materials —and any of the gradations between—the great enemy of effective presentation is routine. In this, the seller is like an actor in a long run; unless new meanings and depths are found day after day, in the same role or making the same basic presentation, it is highly likely to all turn flat, stale, and boring to you and your prospect. To the neophyte, the great enemy seems to be loss of memory and failure to "get it all in"; but quite the reverse is true. Learning to get most or all of it in is easy; keeping it fresh and therefore effective can be very difficult and challenging.

Keeping it fresh and effective depends to some extent on developing technique and a variety of alternative moves within the framework of the presentation. It depends to a much greater extent on making real contact with the prospect in those vital first few minutes and building that contact and empathy all during the presentation. That is what keeps the presentation—and you, the presenter—fresh, interesting, and effective, both in the short run as regards the specific sale, and in the long run, throughout a career.

Technique itself comes with practice. An exceedingly good presentation is a matter of combining complete familiarity with presentation materials and the language of your selling story with a great deal of product knowledge, and joining all that with the early contact and empathy you have started to build with your prospect in the early stages, before a word of presentation is uttered. Those who can consistently do that, and place themselves before enough qualified prospects, will sell successfully, whatever their other selling weaknesses may be. If they combine the foregoing with the ability to handle stalls and objections, using them to move toward the close, they will sell even more successfully. And if beyond that they know how to use all that has gone before to close consistently, they will be top professionals throughout their careers, whatever they sell and to whomever they sell.

STALLS AND OBJECTIONS

Handling stalls and objections well depends on several prior understandings. The first of them is that effective selling is, by the nature of the human interactions involved, a rather untidy process. Prospects ask all kinds of questions and make all kinds of comments out of sequence, irrationally and often irritably. Even worse, some of them do not question or comment at all, leaving you to go through an entire presentation and come to a close that just is not there, because you never really got started on the selling process. Some prospects tease, nitpick, and—if you let them—provoke you to fury. Bad for the digestion, even worse for the sale. There are interruptions, distractions, latecomers who force you to re-present; a dozen different things can happen in the course of a selling interview that can cause you to lose your pace and control. Yet that is a great deal of the fun in selling—controlling the pace, the flow of the action, moving into greater and greater empathy with your prospect, through whatever comes, all the way to the close.

Another main understanding is that it is perfectly natural for people to stall and object, no matter how rejecting that may seem to you. It is not realistic to expect prospects to be able to easily understand what you have to say, trust you, and make up their minds to buy. There are quite legitimate questions to be answered, reservations to be surmounted, fears as to making a wrong decision to be dealt with, and skepticisms to be overcome.

Beyond the entirely understandable, there is also the deep distrust of people who sell carried by so many Americans in this period. That is a fact of life, and there is no use in turning a blind eye to it, as so many in selling tend to do. Nor will it be overcome by piety or time; the techniques of gross overstatement used so widely in some print and broadcast advertising will guarantee that. Unfortunately, it is not just a matter of a few unethical mass marketers—far from it; it is woven into the fabric of our commercial life. Every time a pharmaceutical maker sincerely advertises a product containing an unnamed wonder ingredient that the overwhelming majority of doctors recommend—which turns out to be plain old aspirin—several somebodies somewhere shake their heads and know that they are seeing or hearing a plain old distortion of the truth, so grossly as to amount to a lie. Every time a financial firm touts a product that is highly speculative without really saying so, people are once more reminded that skepticism is a healthy thing. Every time people hear inflated claims of the excellence and reliability of some ultimately nonworking appliance, automobile, toy, or other piece of hard goods, in this era of shoddy work and inflated prices, the honest sales professional's work is made harder. No, we don't lie; but most of the people we see are subjected to a barrage of broadcast lies every day, and are conditioned to expect that we will do the same. That creates an extraordinary need to build trust in you, your products, and your company, a need that must be satisfied if the sale is to be made and the relationship built. Formal sales presentations and accompanying materials can be helpful, but what you do with empathy and how you handle stalls and objections on the way to the close is indispensable.

When that is clearly understood, each successfully handled stall or objection can properly be seen as a milestone on the way to the close, and therefore welcomed, rather than as annoying rejections to be evaded in the hope that they will somehow go away. Certainly, some are to be deferred and others will go away as you proceed, but when and how to handle a stall or objection is then a matter of timing and judgment, rather than an expression of anxiety on your part.

Some kind of fear is very often at the heart of the matter in stall and objection handling. It can be as simple as the fear that you will not know enough to supply the right answer to a question, or that even the factually correct answer you do have will somehow create unforeseen difficulties. It may be a matter of over-concern about your own products and company, resulting from your own magnification of internal problems. Or—and by far the most common reason here, as it is in closing—it may be a fear of rejection. After all, no matter how good a closing average you have, there are often many "no's" on the way to a "yes," as well as many failures to make a sale at all. It is not very professional to convert failure to sell into a fancied personal rejection, but we would be less than human were that not to happen occasionally.

Yet it is precisely the ability to combine professional distance with empathy that adds up to effective long-term professionalism in selling. Putting it a little differently, we need to be able to see ourselves and others with whom we are involved in a selling situation as players in a game, while playing that game and empathizing with the other players. Once that basic understanding is achieved, and has grown into a set of reflexive responses, handling stalls and objections becomes a simple, rather enjoyable part of the total selling situation and game. And the seller has a great advantage in that he or she handles the same basic stalls and objections every day, and is therefore far more familiar with them than the buyer. Sales professionals expect and are therefore ready for stalls and objections, and know how to use them to move to the close.

It is the way you handle a question, a stall, or an objection that conditions the interaction between you and your prospect, and shapes what can be either an antagonistic confrontation or a confidence-building step on the way to the close. Here are some basics that can easily be forgotten:

- *When the prospect talks, listen hard and responsively.* Your attitude toward whatever matters the prospect raises will be conveyed by the way you listen. If you are handling paper or rummaging around in your briefcase, you will not seem to be paying much attention to what the prospect is saying, no matter how hard you are really listening. When the prospect says something, stop what you are doing, relax, and listen attentively. And listen responsively. Do not sit forward in your chair, move restlessly while the prospect is talking, or seem ready to speak as soon as you can. Sit back quietly, hands at rest, and nod or otherwise indicate thoughtful response to whatever is being said. That cannot be just an "act" either. False interest in others shows. The truth is that if you really listen attentively you will often get much of what you need to move to the close, then or later.

• *Respond thoughtfully.* When the prospect is finished talking, you are going to speak. At that point, you are confronting one of the greatest hazards in selling—the glib-seeming response. When you sell, one of the worst potential hazards you face is the stereotype of the "drummer who talks a mile a minute and has the answer to everything before you get the words out of your mouth. Can't trust any of them . . ."

Even when your prospect is asking you a simple question that you have answered completely and correctly hundreds of times in a hundred other situations, be careful to respond thoughtfully. Remember—it may be a simple enough question and answer to you, but it is a new and perhaps important question to your prospect. A quick answer indicates that you do not think much of the question, and perhaps not much of the questioner, either. A slower, more thoughtful answer is always more reassuring on both counts. It requires no more than following hard and responsive listening with a pause in which neither of you is talking and you are obviously concentrating on framing your answer, then a carefully considered, moderately toned, clearly put response. That pause need not be more than a second or two and may be preceded by some sort of nonverbal response—a thoughtful look, a nod, anything that is natural and true when you are thinking about and framing a response.

• *Respond empathetically.* There is all the difference in the world between a short, sharp "No!" and a thoughtful, friendly, "I can see your point. It may work a little differently here, though." Or "I see what you mean, but I don't believe so." Or even a nonverbal nod, pause, and quiet, "No, I don't believe so."

The key to a confidence-building response lies in your ability to separate your regard for and empathy with the prospect from any potential disagreement over what the prospect is saying. It is the basic difference between argument and friendly discussion. You may disagree with a good friend over any number of substantial matters without losing—and often actually deepening—the friendship. You may find that you and your prospect are far apart on many specific business and product questions, yet you will make the sale. Once the prospect has grasped the idea that you are a warm, friendly, helpful, well-informed professional, many seeming obstacles disappear.

You need not agree, though much standard advice to neophyte sellers revolves around getting immediate agreement or seeming agreement followed by going off in one of several turn-the-conversation-to-your-advantage directions. The trouble with blindly following the "seeming agreement" advice is that sellers who do that often run head-on into the "insincere" stereotype. "Sure, they agree with everything you say to disarm you, then twist it around to make it seem as if you really agree with them."

Selling is selling, but as selling has permeated every aspect of American life, prospects have changed a little, often with good cause. People with their buying hats on are a little warier than they were 30 or 40 years ago, when the main reflexes of many now in senior sales management were formed. The advice to agree easily, disarm the prospect, and then move on to handle the hurdle was good advice a generation ago, but today those tactics often run into a wall of skepticism. It is far better to focus on how you listen and respond than to rely on mechanical agreement.

Often, your response will be neither agreement nor disagreement, but a question of your own. You may want to clarify the prospect's question or objection. You may simply want to understand the prospect's comments better, so that you can best frame satisfactory answers. Or you may want to use questions to help the prospect better understand the matters raised. People often frame questions imprecisely. They sometimes ask questions quite different from those they have in mind, questions that can use a little clarification before your answers might confuse an already confused situation.

You may want to determine whether re-presenting is called for. Sometimes you will go through much or all of your basic presentation only to find your prospect asking questions and expressing objections that make you feel you may not have communicated on some key points. You will probe then, trying to see where you went wrong. You may very well answer the question or handle the objection by a considerably wider re-presentation than would seem to be called for by the prospect's comments. Often, answering the prospect simply and directly is far from enough; what is called for is going farther back into the benefits story and placing your answer within the context of that story.

For example, you may tell the whole benefits story and immediately find your prospect raising competitive price objections. You thought you had anticipated those objections by stressing quality, durability, and cost-effectiveness. Obviously, it did not take. You can restate your conclusions and follow up with proof materials. Or you can restate your conclusions, back up into that part of your presentation, and then come forward to the proof stories.

Answering a question with a question can be a good clarifying technique. Alas, all too often it is not a clarifying technique at all, but rather an argumentative technique. The trouble is that it is very easy to go over from clarifying to arguing. And even when you are quite careful and do not step over that line, your prospect very often does not know it. And what can be very funny on stage can be a disaster in a selling situation. Arguing with questions is a much used, properly avoided objection-handling technique.

There is also the matter of raising questions in the prospect's mind. Anticipating possible objections is a perfectly valid technique, if used with discretion. And discretion consists of stressing the unique benefits you and your product have to offer without making the mistake of raising potentially damaging questions that might not otherwise have occurred to your prospect.

It can happen rather easily, as when you stress the quality of your products, and mention that they are also "a little more expensive" than those of one or more of your competitors. You have perhaps quite properly anticipated a possible price objection on the part of your prospect by stressing quality, but have also raised the price question, which your prospect might not have seen or raised, and you may have created wholly unnecessary problems for yourself by so doing. Or you may decide to meet a competitor head-on, and sell directly against it right from the start, as so many mass advertisers do. But in so doing you may cause your prospect to seriously consider your competitor—which might otherwise not have happened—and perhaps seriously harm your own possible sale. When price, competition, or any other kind of objection, is raised by your prospect, you will handle it, in your own way and in your own time. But when you cause the objection to be raised by something you say or do, you have made a possibly costly error, but one that can be easily avoided, with care.

Stalls and objections are easy to identify and deal with—in a book. For in a book we separate them and deal with them individually for study purposes. But in life they come in groups, inextricably intertwined. People often have complex reasons for making buying decisions, and seldom say exactly what they mean in selling situations; indeed, they often do not know precisely what they mean and why they buy. That is up to us to figure out in the course of selling to them.

Here are some of the most common stalls and objections. They may come early, before the presentation. They may come during the presentation, or after the presentation. They do come, one way or another, at one time or another, throughout a career in selling. There are relatively few of them, though to the beginner, who has not yet had a chance to get used to them, they may seem legion. To the seasoned professional, they are all a little different, because each situation and each prospect are a little different, but at the same time they resolve themselves into a few basic hurdles to handle on the way to the close.

The three most common kinds of objections encountered in the field have to do with price, competition, and your own product. The price objection cuts across most other potential hurdles. Competitive objections, need, and product questions are all often put in terms of price. Many hidden objections add up to price, as do many outright stalls and evasions.

There is no easy answer to the price objection—but there is one essential way to handle it from the start. That way is to see your product as a unique benefits story and to tell that story fully and well. If prospect needs and desires are well enough stimulated by your benefits story, price will often play a minor role in the buying decision. That is why price is one major objection you will try hard to defer, no matter how sharply it seems to be raised early in the interview. Occasionally you will have to put price forward early, but even then you will try to proceed immediately with the presentation to show how well your prices are justified by the benefits attached to product purchase. No matter how straightforwardly and sincerely the prospect raises the question of price as the key to the buying decision, if you let in the question of price too early, you run the risk of price dominating the entire discussion, and pushing aside your benefits story before it can be told. Then the odds become great that you will lose the sale.

Many sales professionals have whole lines to sell, with a number of models, styles, and price options. Therefore, when you move into a selling situation, it is often a little difficult to decide precisely which product to present. In those situations, part of what you are doing in the early stages of the interview is trying to develop information that will help you decide which product or products to present.

When that is the case, and you run into strong price objection, early or late in the interview, it is often tempting to move with the objection and step down to a lower-priced product. That is usually a mistake. You have partially or fully presented a benefits story, and at that point can expect your step down to result in a discussion that turns almost exclusively on price, rather than on the benefits connected with the lower-priced product. You may even find that the lower price is acceptable, but that some key benefits available with the purchase of the higher-priced product are make-or-break for the prospect. Then you are trapped, and you probably can't close the sale either way. You may also find, after stepping down, that price is not really the main issue at all, and that the sale swings on other factors. Then you still have not presented a full benefits story for any product, are in a discussion that hinges on price, and are quite unable to recover.

If you should run into a strong price objection very early in the interview, before you have presented any benefits story, it is possible to step down without significant penalty as long as you can move into a full benefits story without having the new story aborted by another price objection. But if you are committed and presenting, it is far better to present and re-present on the benefits of the higher-priced product than let yourself fall into the price objection trap.

You may have some price flexibility. If so, do not let it get away from you early in the interview, in response to a price objection. Hold it for the close. It may be an especially important tool where price is a central question to the prospect. Even in closing, though, use price flexibility very carefully. Any sale that depends on price concessions is intrinsically weaker than a sale that closes on customer benefits. Benefits can be stated, restated, and worked with at the close. Price flexibility, once used, again turns the sale on too narrow a ground, and makes the close fragile and easy to lose if the price is not good enough or if the objections turn out to be more than price-related.

Competitive objections can appear at any point in the selling interview. They are almost always best deferred as long as possible, and then dealt with as necessary, rather than anticipated and prematurely discussed. Usually, you will run into competitive objections when you are in a selling situation trying to replace entrenched competition. And the normal reaction of many sellers and sales managers, therefore, is to go head-on into competition, right from the start, making highly comparative presentations and closing on comparative matters.

That is usually a mistake. Replacing competition seldom rests on comparing features and benefits, if for no other reason than that entrenched competition is indeed entrenched. The prospect is accustomed to the competition; there is an existing set of working relationships with the competitive company and selling staff. And remember, the prospect has bought the competition and is satisfied that good judgment was shown in the purchase.

A competitive presentation is best handled like any other presentation, but with more sensitivity to inevitable competitive comparisons as you handle objections and move to the close. That means presenting your products as a unique benefits story, not with competitive comparisons from the start. Competitors need not even be mentioned until, and if, the prospect brings them up.

When competitive objections are raised, however, you had best have done your homework. You need to know the nuts and bolts of your competitor's products as well as you do your own. You need to know strengths and weaknesses, prices, applications, main selling approaches, and the main competitive arguments used against you and your products. Your company will usually be very helpful in this area; so will your multiple contacts with prospects who buy competitive products.

You will always get far more mileage out of stressing and restressing your own benefits than in attacking the weaknesses of competitors. Do not worry about the prospect not knowing competitive weaknesses. Just as your customers know many of the weaknesses of your product, so competitive customers know the weaknesses of what they are buying.

Product objections can arise around anything you sell. A prospect may say something like: "I don't think this is for us. It won't do the job we want done," or "No, it looks a little too fragile to me. And I'm not too sure the styling would suit us." There are a good many entirely honest, straightforward product objections. They are expressed in terms of product deficiencies, but they are always to be answered in terms of benefits. You will normally answer the honest product objection with re-presentation of features and translation of those features into user benefits. You will often follow with proof stories that tell of customers satisfied in just the areas in which your prospect has doubts. Those doubts, once put to rest, can often become the levers you will use to close the sale. If you can prove to the prospect's satisfaction that your product is not fragile, but very strong and durable, and if that is an area of major prospect concern, then you have probably also found a major buying motive.

Product objections are often comparative. People often buy whatever they think is the best choice available, and rarely wait for the "ideal" product to come along. If the prospect feels that your product "won't do the job," there is probably some thought that a competitive product will.

Your astute questioning will often be able to uncover the hidden competitive objection, and enable you to deal with it.

Occasionally, there are expressed reservations or even open hostility toward your company. "We bought a gross of widgets from your company two years ago, and none of them worked right. Tried to get credit, and had to go through a lot of red tape to get it."

That is not too hard to straighten out. You will try to find out what went wrong, and let the prospect know that your company has a wonderful customer service department, especially since the new complaint processing system was installed. You will also have several happy customers the prospect can call to prove how well your company handles complaints these days. Your prospect has gotten what was probably a very minor complaint, that has become magnified over the years, off his or her chest. You have responded soothingly, and you can both get down to business.

More often, it is a matter of vaguely remembered problems with your company, or bad word-of-mouth in the industry, or even competitive badmouthing. Then you must empathize, present, and re-present your benefits story, and let the hidden objection either be forgotten or eventually surface. If the objection is a tough one, it may be at the root of the stall you have had a hard time handling, and may give you a good deal of trouble at the close. But it may be the kind of hidden objection that is overcome by the warmly empathetic relationship you and your prospect develop during the interview. Convinced of the potential benefits, but unsure about the company, the prospect buys your honesty and the kind of guarantees that that honesty brings.

Once in a great while, the problem is not a matter of price, competition, product, or company, but of the relationship between you and your prospect. Sales professionals very, very rarely trigger adverse personal reactions with anything they say or do. Your chances of generating that kind of reaction are remote. But your chances of running into someone "who got up on the wrong side of the bed this morning" are far from remote. Your chances of selling to people who are under severe personal and business pressures of many kinds are quite good. Your chances of running into people with ego problems, who are personally abusive to those around them, are excellent.

No sales professional should take personal abuse—and those who refuse to take abuse get the respect of all those they meet. That does not mean meeting abuse with abuse, emotion with emotion. It means developing and keeping a friendly, businesslike approach in every selling situation. If possible, a descent to personalities is to be ignored, while you get on with your business. If it cannot be ignored, then it is time to leave. Do not argue or get emotional; just leave.

It is also possible to run into prejudice, which by its very nature is unreasonable, irrational, and destructive. Women can run into sexual prejudice. Blacks can run into racial prejudice. People have all kinds of language, ethnic, age, and appearance prejudices. Young people can run into something as absurd as strong distaste for the way they cut their hair, or a stocky person may be treated with contempt.

You are there to sell, not to try to change the social attitudes of your prospects. You are there to sell, not lose your composure. And you do not have to take any abuse at all. Do what you are there for, ignore covert prejudice, and do whatever is necessary to keep your self-respect in the face of overt prejudice. If that means terminating the interview, do so. Most of the time, it will mean selling right on through, by your very composure and professionalism effectively removing the problems caused by prejudice. Prejudice springs from ignorance, and your prospect's working contact with you and other targets of prejudice will do more to bring about attitude change than all the arguing in the world.

Many objections are unspoken. They are often called *hidden objections*—but they're hidden only to the unprofessional eye. When you have presented fully, clearly, and well; answered some questions; turned some objections into closing tools and seeming product weaknesses into product strengths and the prospect is still cold, you know it. You know that somewhere along the way you missed some vital clue or clues, missed some unspoken central objection. You will probe, re-present, and try to smoke out what it is you have missed so far. It might be anything, or a combination of factors. It may be as simple as general uneasiness, resulting from an inadequate grasp of the benefits picture. It may be an unspoken competitive objection. It may be that you have misassessed the rightness of the prospect; you may be talking to someone who cannot make the buying decision.

The unspoken objection is often part of a stall—I won't buy now, but I won't tell you the real reason why. The key to smoking it out usually lies in the first few minutes of the interview, before you have even begun to present. If you have handled the empathy-building stage of the interview well, most of what might have been unspoken objections will be spoken. And if you have built empathy well, those objections that remain unspoken will be spoken for the asking.

There is some debate among sales trainers and managers about whether or not to come right out and ask for the unspoken objection. Those who are for it in essence say, "Why not? If you are deep into the interview and still have not smoked out the hidden objection that is holding up the close, you have little to lose by asking for unspoken objections, even 'putting words in the prospect's mouth' to try to smoke out the objection." Those who oppose it in essence say, "Don't do it. You may raise objections that were never in the prospect's mind. Even if you don't, you'll lose control of the interview."

Unnecessary debate; it misses the point. If you have no real empathy, and have not smoked out the real objection, it does not matter whether you ask or not. You will not get what you want, and you will not make the sale. Conversely, if you have real empathy, there will be very few unspoken objections, and your prospect will be glad to tell you what the problem is if you ask. The truth is that the prospect often has no more idea of what the hidden objection is than you do, and needs to figure it out with you before it can be dealt with.

Note that unless you have made a prospecting or early information-gathering error, and are trying to sell something entirely inappropriate to your prospect, "I don't need it," is never to be taken as literally true. It always means something else, like, "I'll keep the one I have. You haven't convinced me yours is worth the money," or simply "I'm not convinced." The main tactic then is re-presentation and careful questioning to determine the real set of hidden objections. "I don't need it," may hide any kind of objection or stall.

Stalls are scarcely diabolical plots aimed at frustrating your best efforts —though they often seem so. There is nothing quite so frustrating as the prospect who goes all the way with you to the close, and then responds with some variation of "No, not right now. I'll think it over. Don't call us—we'll call you," or "I'm just not convinced it will do the job. Maybe I ought to think it over a little while longer."

Here are some major reasons for stalls:

• *Unwillingness to make a buying decision.* Most people dislike making decisions, especially buying decisions. No matter how well everything else has gone, there is often that final hurdle to surmount. That is much of what closing is about, and why closing merits very special treatment in any book on selling. The stall is almost always directed at avoiding the buying decision, often at forestalling any attempt on your part to close. It is sometimes a conscious maneuver on the part of the prospect, but much more often quite unconscious.

• *Inability to make a buying decision.* Sometimes you are talking to someone who cannot make a buying decision at all, as when an assistant is "screening" products for a superior who will make the buying decision. If you find that to be true, you will have to make an on-the-spot, sometimes difficult, decision as to whether or not to press for an immediate interview with that superior. It is often preferable to come back another day to present to the real prospect rather than spinning your wheels and perhaps being eliminated by the unqualified assistant.

On other occasions, you may find yourself with a thoroughly qualified prospect, but one who finds the size of the buying decision larger than anticipated. When that happens, you may not really know whether you are being put off by the "I have to talk to my partner (or company president) about this" stall, or whether it is simply fact. In the vast majority of instances, it is just a stall, and it is worth trying to move through to the close. Very often, your prospect will be unwilling to admit inability to make a buying decision, feeling that this somehow diminishes his or her standing in your eyes. Then you may get all kinds of stalls and evasions, and try to reach through to the hidden objection, which is simply pride.

•   *Lack of conviction.*   Sometimes the stall just means, "Sell me some more. I'm not convinced." Then the prospect is not really saying no, will not say yes, wants you to somehow do it all again, without literally redoing the whole selling interview.

When you perceive that kind of motive for the stall, you will want to re-present on strengths, use agreed-upon strengths to move to the close. You will "review" whatever seemed most important to the prospect, get agreement again and again, question to try to find hidden objections, try to build further upon the confidence in you, your company, and your products that has been developing throughout the interview. Often it is a matter of giving the prospect a little more time to get used to an idea and move to the buying decision. Re-presenting on strengths supplies that time in the most constructive possible way.

CLOSING

And now to the close, to which all that has gone before is prologue. All the attitude-building, preparation, prospecting, approaching, presenting, and objection-handling add up to one thing: success or failure, sale or no sale, home run or strikeout. None who are sales professionals make any mistake about that—in every selling situation, you either close the sale or you don't. Whatever the reasons and no matter how well you may have positioned yourself to come back and try again another day, no sale is only no sale. Even if you have done everything superbly, you still have not made the sale. Conversely, you may not have done nearly as well as you would have liked during the course of the interview, and still made the sale—and that is ultimately what matters most. However a sales professional works, whatever they do on the way to and at the close, they all share the ability to close successfully, day after day, year after year, all during their selling careers. For without that ability, there is no career in selling.

There is no secret formula that unlocks the secret of successful closing. Nor is there a bag of tricks, a single set of words of art, or a preset number of serious closing tries that works best. All that is pure nonsense, and has nothing at all to do with you, the selling process, or that part of the process that is closing.

There are keys to successful closing, though; and there are techniques that many have found useful at the close. The techniques are quite simple, easy to learn, and, in the right hands, rather effective. But they are the least portion of the matter; what is far more important is your attitude going into and throughout the selling process, and how you have conducted the selling interview throughout. The truth is, if you have seen yourself and the selling situation properly, and moved empathetically throughout the selling situation, the close will be there when you and the prospect are ready for it, and there will come a time in the interview when you will close the sale. The truth is also that if you have not been able to move the whole situation properly throughout the interview, no closing technique or combination of techniques will do. It will not matter whether you try to close one time or 10 times. The harder you try, the weaker your position will be, and the farther away your prospect. There is no successful hard sell, soft sell, or any sell at all if you have not moved toward agreement throughout the interview.

You cannot very well build confidence in yourself, your company, or your products without having that confidence yourself. And, as we have previously discussed, there is no way to fake it; your real attitudes permeate every step of the selling process.

We all dislike being rejected by others and dislike repeated rejections most of all. Yet if we develop real fear of rejection, we generate a downward spiral in which rejection feeds fear, fear develops hesitancy which is communicated to prospects, failure builds on failure. Fear of rejection often turns into a self-fulfilling prophecy, in selling and throughout every aspect of our lives. Fear of rejection feeds fear of failure. In a culture that values success as much as it values anything, the will to win and its flip side, the fear of failure, are extremely powerful motivators. The will to win and fear of failure exist side by side. While the will to win is stressed and is held consciously as a major goal, the fear of failure is the dark, hidden side that exists in every powerful, competitive winner. In a very real sense, then, fears of rejection and failure are perfectly normal—everyone has them. And like any other fears, they are not to be suppressed and overridden. That leads only to stiffness, rigidity in personal and business matters, and unnecessary and counterproductive personal pain.

In selling, fears of rejection and failure can best be handled by the kind of professional excellence, in every aspect of selling, that guarantees success. In a way, that sounds absurd—you handle your fear of losing by winning. But it is not at all absurd when you consider how a sound sales professional wins. The winning sales professional is much like a star scorer in any sport. When the puck goes into the net, the ball through the basket or between the goal posts, it is not a fluke. When you see a superb athlete working, you know the skills and the moves are there. Yes, success builds on success, scoring on scoring, close on close. But the really skilled sales professional knows that whatever the product, the company, the competition, the advantages and disadvantages, there are going to be a lot of successful closes. The reasons are internal, not external. You sell or fail to sell mainly for those internal reasons.

Winning attitudes and fears show up most clearly in closing. It is in closing that direct success and direct rejection come. And, because you cannot expect to hit 1.000 or even .500 consistently, there are usually more rejections and failures than there are successes. A lot more. Even when you make a sale, it may be after several rejections or seeming rejections on the way to the close. In selling, you often seem to be fighting uphill against a wall of rejection or failure, even when you are an outstanding selling success.

The strong closer is simply someone who makes contact with the prospect, builds confidence all the way, and confidently asks for the order again and again when it feels right. The weak closer usually has problems in developing empathy. He or she compounds these problems by sliding away from rather than handling stalls and objections for fear of rejection, and then is afraid to try to close. For the strong closer, there are many right times to close. For the weak closer, no time is the right time.

There is really no magic time to close. Nor is there a magic number of times to close. Those who say you must close at least five (or four, six, or ten) times are simply wrong. That is incompetently rendered advice, and not an act of either leadership or friendship, for it misinterprets the nature of the selling process, and leads up a blind alley to frustration and failure.

Once developed, you keep the habit of listening, seeing, putting your-self in the prospect's shoes, continually sizing up where you and your prospect are in the selling situation. Once you learn how to read, you do not forget how to do it. When you have been handling the interview well, you will see and correctly read the closing indicators. No matter which of you is talking, you and your prospect will continue to com-municate in many ways, and the prospect's state of mind will be crystal clear to you in most situations. Even when you run into a prospect who habitually masks reactions, you will see signs that will tell you what you need to know.

Watch most for attitudes expressed nonverbally and in tone of voice. Look at the prospect's body set. Is the prospect sitting back, uninterested, covertly glancing at some papers or is he or she leaning forward a little, following your comments, fully engaged? Make real eye contact. Eyes go pretty blank and expressionless when you are not getting through. They involuntarily respond when you are. Eyes tend to narrow a little when the prospect concentrates, blink when you make a particularly telling point, and visibly focus and become more alert-looking when you have complete attention.

Watch the prospect carefully. Boredom is often accompanied by a head that is immobile or sags a little, legs that cross and uncross nervously, fingers that imperceptibly and unconsciously tap or play with a pen or paperweight. As real interest develops, the body becomes more focused and still, leans forward. Hands often open and move a little in tune with your gestures; the head nods imperceptibly in agreement. Not the full, studied nod that is used by many as a defensive tic—the imperceptible nod that means real agreement.

Tone tells you a great deal. Personal warmth usually means you have gotten through at least partially; studied coldness usually means you have not even made contact, no matter how long you have been in the room. Of course, sometimes a cool, dry style can merely be a good defensive stance, so that coolness alone does not mean rejection. Tone is best consid-ered in terms of how questions are asked or answered. "Did you say these widgets will last 10 years on average?" can be a strong closing indicator or an expression of complete incredulity. You are not about to try to close someone who has just come very close to calling you a liar; you will re-present on strengths.

Some specific questions are prime closing indicators, if their tone is right. A price question late in the interview, with your prospect starting to write down the figures you supply is often a message to ask for the order right now. Late-interview questions on delivery time, service contracts, customer relations policies, and other post-sale matters very often mean you should close now.

Assuming sale is often described as a closing technique. In that context, it simply means getting to what you think is a right time to close, assuming that the customer is with you, and moving right past the buying decision. When you assume sale, you shift focus to such matters as choice of options, delivery, installation dates, and other minor considerations, and away from the possible barrier created by focusing on the buying decision itself. It is usually done with the order form, or some such device aimed at focusing attention on post-buying decision mechanics. And when well done, it is an excellent closing technique, that technique most favored by sales professionals.

It is the most favored and widely used technique for an excellent reason: it is far, far more than a closing technique. In fact, the "assume the sale" attitude permeates the entire selling process; it is an attitude that favorably affects every step of the process, every aspect of the developing relationship of confidence between you and your prospect.

When you move into a selling situation, you will assume that you are there to close a sale. Not to meet someone or to present your products; to close a sale. Every move you make will spring from that assumption. And it is not a matter of whether you will close the sale, but only of when. That means understanding that every step toward prospect confidence is a step toward the close, that every "yes" develops further yeses, every "no" breeds more nos.

You will be looking for verbal and nonverbal yeses, avoiding negatives. You will try very hard not to ask questions that can be answered with a simple "no." You will want affirmation on a minor matter rather than triggering a "no." For example, early on you are unlikely to ask: "Do our widgets look right for your operation?" You are much more likely to ask: "How might these widgets fit into your operation?" It is really the same question, but not one the prospect can simply answer "no." That is why you will look for the "how, which, when" kinds of questions, rather than the "yes-or-no" questions. It is also the reason for avoiding the "why" kinds of questions if possible. The answers to "why" questions often take you so far off the track that you do not reach the affirmation you are looking for at all.

In a very real sense, "assuming sale" describes much of what you are trying to do, and can be your most powerful tool throughout the selling process. It is natural to move from a well-handled question or objection into a close. You have told the benefits story, gotten a good deal of agreement, answered some questions, and handled some objections. At this point, you have a pretty good idea as to where you and your prospect stand, and you think it is time to start asking the prospect to buy now.

For example, you have just successfully handled a major price objection late in the interview. Your prospect seems satisfied, interested, untroubled by any other pressing questions at the moment. However you choose to ask for it, what better time to ask for the order? If the prospect is not ready to buy, nothing has been lost. You have sized up the situation well enough to bet that "no" will really mean "not yet" or "sell me a little more—I'm not quite convinced." On the other hand, if you have guessed wrong about the prospect's state of mind, it is time to learn about the error. If it gets too late, you will run out of re-presenting time.

People are used to being asked to buy. Your prospect would not be talking to you if he or she were not considering buying what you have to sell. It is only when the closing attempt is entirely inappropriate, when you and the prospect just have not gotten together, that resentment can arise.

When they do buy, it is likely to be when they have developed real confidence in you, your company, and your products. The well-handled objection converts what the prospect thought might be a substantial weakness into a strength—sometimes a substantial strength. That develops confidence, and provides a closing opportunity.

It is important to distinguish between removing an objection and developing confidence. It is one thing to point out successfully that your price is competitive. That removes a price objection, and is desirable. But it is far more important to make the competitive price point and then move forward to advantage, the kind of advantage gained from combining competitive price and longer wear. "Ms. Jones, we estimate that our combination of competitive pricing and far greater durability will save you between 20% and 25% of the money you now spend for widgets over a 10-year period. Given your widget consumption, that should come to between $80,000 and $100,000, or $8,000 to $10,000 per year. Would you like delivery March 1, or would April 1 be better for your planning purposes?" Converting the well-handled objection into a close is a natural, sound way of moving to success in the selling situation.

Beware the *trap close*. It happens every day in automobile agencies. Seller has some price leeway, prospect has a price objection. It is late in the interview. Seller feels that giving way on price without pinning the prospect down is a waste of what may be the only closing tool left. Seller finally says: "Well, I just don't know. I guess I can try knocking $500 off this price, but I don't know if I can make it stick. Let's write it up on that basis, and give it a try." Prospect agrees, and they write it up. Of course, the order goes through, being well within the price leeway the seller has.

Aha! Trapped the prospect. That is one good way to do it. Nothing tricky or sneaky about it—all's fair in love, war, and selling.

That's what you think. In this suspicious age, the prospect is much more likely to have snapped to mental attention when the seller tried out this hoary old chestnut and said something like: "Wait a minute. Why don't you go right on back to the office over there and see if you can sell the car at this price. If you can, let's talk about it some more. If you can't, tell me so. And if no one here can settle the price, I'll just take a walk for myself. Saw some nice cars a little way down the street." And then the seller has lost whatever confidence the prospect had been building up all during the sales process. The odds are that any price concession then will not be enough. Previously handled product reservations and objections will suddenly resurface. The prospect will want more time to think the whole thing over. No sale.

That is called the trap close. Sometimes it is described as the boomerang close. Occasionally, it is dressed in new jargon to hide its true nature. And it is the kind of thing that sometimes gives selling a bad name. Don't use it. For every "successful" use, you will have many of the worst kinds of failures, the kinds of failures that alienate prospects and create the kind of bad word of mouth that ruins sales careers. Your integrity and credibility are crucial success factors, and that kind of shoddy trickery destroys them.

A closing technique is just a way of asking for the order. It is valuable to have several good ways of doing it, if only because you are very likely to ask for the order several times in the course of the interview, and it sounds and feels forced to ask the prospect to buy now again and again in exactly the same way.

One prime technique is to assume sale. Your assumption of eventual sale has been your central attitude all during the selling process. Now, at the close, you want to make it easy for the prospect to hurdle the final barrier—the buying decision itself. The easiest way to do that is to avoid forcing the prospect to say, "Okay, I'll buy it." The decision is made just as surely if it is a silent one, but it is easier to make.

It is often done with the order form. At some point during the interview, seller has the order out and ready to be filled in. Often, the form is placed at the end of the presentation materials, so that it is naturally out and open at the end of the presentation and stays there during the rest of the interview. Then, at an appropriate closing time, pen poised, seller says, "Ms. O'Brien, how do you spell your name?" gets an answer, and proceeds to fill out the form, quietly and completely, as they continue to talk. Then the seller places the order form before the prospect with the place to sign clearly indicated, and waits.

The filled-in order form sometimes generates a startled, "Wait a minute. I'm not ready for that yet." Fine, then it is time to re-present and tell the benefits story a little more. The order form still stays right there, waiting for signature, is often picked up, studied, and signed as the discussion proceeds.

The assumptive technique sometimes works best with simple silence. You have filled out the order form, have it before the prospect ready to be signed, and have stopped talking. The prospect says nothing, is thinking it over. The silence lengthens, deepens, acquires a weight between you. Somehow, you both know that whoever breaks that silence first is at a great disadvantage. What can happen is that the prospect ultimately picks up the pen and signs the contract.

Silence does have a great weight, especially in a room with two people who have been talking for some time. It develops decision-making tension, seems to stretch out, and can fool your sense of time completely. Twenty seconds can seem like a minute, a minute like ten. Use silence as a closing tool if you have the strength to keep quiet. If you are too nervous for it, leave the technique to others; you have plenty of other ways to go.

You can also close on smaller alternatives. This approach is often called a "choice" close or "closing on a small choice," and can provide another good way of helping the prospect avoid the overt, spoken buying decision. In a way, it is like assuming sale, and can often be done with the order form and silence techniques. Choices can be in any post-sale area—options, colors, delivery dates, styles—anything that assumes the sale has been made, the buying decision is behind the prospect, and there are only some minor choices still to be made.

"Good. Would you like delivery March 1, or would April 1 be better?"

"Fine. Would you like it in black or red?"

"Excellent. Do you want it with or without the case?"

You can also close on a special offer basis. "We have two dozen of these punchpresses left, and are selling them at 25% off their list price. When they're gone, that's it. We're discontinuing this model."

"We're bringing out this book at $18.95 list until Christmas. After December 25, the list price goes up to $22.95."

"We have a special introductory price . . ."

"For a limited time only, we're offering . . ."

There is nothing wrong with a bargain-basis closing. It can move a wavering prospect to make a buying decision now and act as an effective closing tool. The technique has to be used carefully, though. For the sake of your credibility and that of your company, be sure that what you say is true. The "limited offer" that turns out to be standard is seen by prospects as a trap close, and resented. It guarantees that you will run into price objections early and often in the future, finding them terribly difficult to handle successfully.

If you sell one punchpress at 25% off and 10 others at 30% off, the odds are pretty good that the prospect who bought at 25% off will feel "taken," even if the 25% discount made the press a superb buy. You will create needless difficulty for yourself by offering varying discount arrangements, and once again will guarantee very serious price objection and credibility problems in the future.

Watch out for the bargain-basis variant known as the *get on board* or *standing room only* technique. It goes something like: "We only have five of these left . . . don't know when we can get any more at this price, or any more at all for that matter . . . have to have your decision right now." In a circus sideshow, it starts "Hurry, hurry, hurry. . . ." Whether it is a con game or not, it is very likely to be looked upon as one by your prospects. Don't do it. Leave it at a bargain-basis offer, and do not try to ram the sale through with these kinds of pressure tactics. Prospects resent it, it hardly ever works, and even when it does work, it creates ill feeling that costs a lot more than the sale can possibly be worth.

Almost anyone can close "on approval" because it is hardly even selling at all. All that such a *trial sale* does is place your merchandise in the hands of the prospect. It bypasses a real buying decision, and all too often defers it to your very great disadvantage. The worst part of it is that when you sell on approval, the real buying decision is almost invariably made in your absence. You have no real ability to influence the decision from a distance and are not in a face-to-face selling situation with your prospect when the decision is made.

In some kinds of mail sales, especially on low-priced items, selling with "money-back guarantees," "on approval," and on a "trial basis," works very well. It is also a standard arrangement between manufacturer and retailer in a few industries, such as book publishing. But for the kinds of goods sold by most sales professionals face-to-face with qualified prospects, "maybe" sales like these are not worth doing. It is almost always far better to stick with it, go for a real close, than to settle for a trial sale.

One closing tool that is sometimes neglected is simply asking for the order. At the right time, there is nothing wrong with doing just that. It is often just a matter of saying, "Good. Will you please put your name here?" Note: "put" your name, not "sign" your name; people often have a well-developed aversion to signing anything, but will "put" their names on pieces of paper quite readily.

In some situations, direct asking can be better than either the assumptive or the choice closes. There are a good many direct, businesslike, sometimes rather sophisticated people around who do not like being asked for the order indirectly. They do not want any part of what they think of as selling tricks. They want to make an open, hard, and fast decision and get on with their business. When you are selling to that kind of person, you will know it, and may want simply to ask for the order.

AFTER THE CLOSE

The selling situation is not over after the close. It does not end until you are out the door. What has changed is your relationship with the prospect. That prospect is now a customer, and a new set of obligations and opportunities opens up.

Here is the situation. You have closed the sale. There is a signed contract on the table between you and your customer. You have some post-sale details to cover and some selling opportunities as well. You certainly will not want to try to "sell up" at that point. The buying decision has been made, the order signed, and that's it. On another day, you will raise questions relating to more expensive versions of what was just bought; you do not want to upset the sale now.

But that does not mean you will avoid all additional selling now. You know that right after the close there is often a period of euphoria, which, if handled properly, can result in an expanded sale. Most dictionaries define *euphoria* as a blissful feeling, a feeling of great happiness. That is exactly the situation you often find yourself in just after the close. You are happy that you have made the sale; the prospect is happy over the decision, often over having made any decision at all. As long as you do not try to sell something new and large or introduce a whole new set of buying decisions, you can sell some more.

You may want to try for an increased quantity. You may have been talking during the interview about one dozen or two dozen widgets and have wound up with an order for one dozen. For now the prospect is a customer and may look upon adding another dozen widgets as just a sensible supply economy, when 10 minutes before it was twice as large a buying decision. And you may be able to make it a little easier to buy, with quantity discounts that look better now than they did before.

You may want to sell options. The outstanding instance of option selling in America is the automobile agency, which closes a car sale and then proceeds to load on additional sales as *options*. It is by no means limited to the automobile industry. All kinds of products, from copying machines to computers, have options, which are really additional sales made after the close.

You may also want to sell replaceables. When you buy a ballpoint pen, you may buy several replacement cartridges. When you buy a copying machine, you have to buy supplies to feed it. After the close is the best possible time to add a substantial replaceables sale to the sale you have just made.

The sale and customer relationship can often be badly damaged when the post-sale mechanics are badly handled. Even if you feel your prospect becoming a little restless after the close and before you have risen to leave, it is worthwhile to spend the small amount of time necessary to guarantee sound post-sale handling of the order.

Be sure that you really know what delivery times to expect on whatever you have just sold. Be doubly sure that your customer knows approximately when to expect delivery, that you will keep close watch over the delivery situation, and will keep your customer informed as to any changes in anticipated delivery dates. Many a promising new customer relationship has foundered on the delivery date question, with euphoria giving way to annoyance and then bitter anger as promised delivery dates go by, a far-off home office makes pledges that are not kept, and the seller is nowhere to be found.

Beware of extra charges. Absurdly enough, a $1,000 sale can be ruined by a $5.00 unanticipated charge. When there are any extra charges at all, be very sure to call your customer's attention to them, whether or not they are plainly printed on the order form for all to see. That means everything —taxes that must be added, normal shipping charges, extra charges for requested rush deliveries—anything, no matter how small the amount, how trivial the extra charge seems. Beware the customer who will cheerfully buy at full price, but somehow feels "taken" by an unstated 50-cent charge.

Whether you install whatever was sold or your company arranges for installation by others, by all means make sure that what you sold is properly installed, that customer and staff know how to use and maintain it, and that guarantee and repair policies are clearly understood by all. Sound installation and explanation build the customer relationship, paving the way for future sales as well as guaranteeing that current sales stick.

Checking on installation and use is often best done personally. But even when your schedule, as in a far-flung travel territory, precludes a personal appearance just after installation, you are still as near as the telephone.

The call to "see that everything's okay" is always much appreciated; failure to make that call has ruined many a customer relationship that could have been saved with a little attention at the right time. Be sure that your customers understand service charges, if any. When you state service charges clearly right at the start of a customer relationship, you are guaranteeing against unpleasant, disruptive surprises. If there is a service contract of some sort, sell it, and make sure it is completely understood, including any extra charges or service exclusions in special situations. You certainly do not want to be identified in the customer's mind with hidden service charges.

Service calls are sales opportunities, and should be treated as such. Every time you service an account, you build up credits and make the customer relationship just a little firmer. A service call may provide an opportunity for making an appointment for a product presentation, turn up a referral from a grateful customer, provide a quick add-on sale.

The party's over—almost. You have done it all and are about to put that signed, option-added, expanded order in your briefcase. Then you are going to rise, shake hands with your happy customer, and leave the premises after smiling at assistants and receptionists.

Once you put that order in your briefcase and rise, it is over. Making an additional sale or getting a key referral after turning dramatically away from the office door to reconfront the customer sounds wonderful. It makes a great training session or sales meeting story. Trouble is it hardly ever happens—which is why it makes such a good story. It is far better to keep the order on the table, cover it with your hand, pick it up preparatory to putting it away, or just look away from it.

Then ask for referrals. "There is one more thing before I go, Ms. Jones. I'd like to get these widgets the widest possible distribution, feeling as I do about their unusual value for people like yourself. Do you have two business friends I might see about them?"

Word it yourself, in whatever fashion best suits your personal style and the situation. But do ask for referrals, at precisely that time and generally in that way. That technique alone can supply you with a literally endless supply of qualified prospects.

RETAIL SELLING

Mostly, selling is selling. If you are successful at selling business services, the odds are good that you will be successful at selling automobiles. If you are good at selling retail furniture, you will probably be good at selling wholesale groceries. The main face-to-face success factors are the same, selling inside or outside, tangible or intangible. In retail selling, the successful seller makes contact with the prospect, questions, listens responsively, empathizes, learns what needs and desires to satisfy, presents, answers, handles objections, and closes.

There are some special aspects worth noting, though. In outside selling, a great deal of time and attention must be devoted to getting to qualified prospects. You need to organize, prospect, sell interviews, make cold calls —all the time-consuming necessities connected with coming face-to-face with substantial numbers of qualified prospects.

But retail selling starts with the prospect coming through your front door. A great deal of time, concentration, and cash is spent to get that prospect through the front door, starting with site location and including advertising, promotion, and astute business-building, but ultimately the retail prospect comes to the retail seller, rather than the seller to the prospect as in outside selling.

That means the prospect is coming into your totally familiar daily environment, just the reverse of the outside selling situation. The prospect is in new surroundings and needs to ingest the unfamiliar place and its contents. It also means that you often have an excellent opportunity to observe the prospect while letting that process of adjustment proceed.

Prospects come into retail establishments looking to buy. Very occasionally, someone comes in to keep warm for a few minutes on a cold day or spend a few minutes pleasantly browsing, but that is not the main reason most people come in. And even the casual browser, as all bookstore owners know, can be a fertile source of impulse buys. But because they need a little time for adjustment and do not want to be harassed by over-eager sellers, they often adopt the "I'm just looking" attitude when approached.

There is nothing wrong with letting them look before making a real first approach, but let them know you are aware of their presence, if only by a smile and nod while you are taking care of another customer.

Here is a typical situation. A prospect comes through the front door of your appliance store. You are on your feet checking stock a little way back in the store. Your habit of close observation comes into immediate play. In less time than it takes to tell, you mentally register: "Woman, probably mid-forties, casually dressed as people are around town on an ordinary workday, but expensive coat and handbag."

She stops just inside the entrance, blinks, adjusts to the light. It is a sunny day; people need a moment to get used to the dimmer lighting inside the store. She scans the store, sees you, half-nods, keeps looking. You nod, smile, make no move toward her. She is in motion, anyway, is looking at some dishwashers a little to the left of the door. She spends a few more moments looking at the dishwashers, studying one medium-priced machine rather carefully, then moving on to another higher-priced machine, then back to the medium-priced machine. You keep on "checking stock," actually watching as carefully and unobtrusively as you can manage.

Finally, she looks up, seems a little puzzled—still not looking at you. But that's your cue. You stop checking stock, make eye contact across the store, focus absolutely full attention, and move to greet her. "Good morning. Can I help you?" At that point, you are fully into the selling situation. From the moment you start moving across the store to greet her, nothing exists for you but the prospect. If you were interrupted in your move across the floor by another customer, you would have said something like "Excuse me, I'll be right over," and kept on going. At the moment you made eye contact, you were committed. The process of empathetic selling had begun.

What you say in greeting is not very important; when and how you say it is. If your approach is easy, open, and natural, rather than bright, artificial, and false, your prospect will respond favorably, whether you are selling outside or inside.

It is easy to assault and thereby insult and alienate your potential customer. The overly aggressive move to the front door with an effusive "Hello. What can I do for you today?" while someone is blinking and getting used to the difference in light can be unsettling and offensive to the prospect. The "merchandise" approach, in which seller accosts unwary customer by flashing a piece of merchandise and extolling its virtues, is great for a circus sideshow, but wildly inappropriate for selling in America in this part of the twentieth century. For just as in outside selling, retail prospects are very, very way of being "taken," and respond with aversion to what they think are pressure tactics. And remember: they have a very easy answer to pressure tactics—they can simply walk back out through the front door.

When you see a group of people come in together, one of the earliest questions you have to ask yourself is: "Are they buying as a group, or as two or more individuals?" When a couple comes in, starts looking at merchandise together, and within a very few seconds one wanders off and idly strolls the aisles while the other focuses on some merchandise, you are most likely going to be selling to the focuser. On the other hand, beware the stroller. He or she may come back after the presentation and damage the sale.

When two or more people come in and start discussing the merits of some specific merchandise together, you are probably in an informal group sales situation. Then there are some special things to consider during the selling process.

• *Identify the primary buyer.*   You want to come as close as you can to knowing who is the primary buyer in the group before you get very far into the presentation. That is accomplished by closely watching who seems to be dominating the conversation, leading the group, before you even approach. You may even want to hold off that approach as long as possible to try to understand the group dynamics as well as you can before going face-to-face. After the approach, skillful questioning will often make the primary buyer apparent.

• *Include all group members in your presentation.*   While you are selling to that primary buyer, it pays not to ignore the other group members, perhaps by keeping good eye contact with all group members and moving your eyes to meet each member as you proceed with the presentation.

• *Let the group members argue among themselves.*   Groups, and especially family groups, are capable of arguing about anything. Sometimes, the arguments seem trivial and the outsider is tempted to comment off-handedly and move on with business. Don't do it. Squabbles often mask much deeper disagreements. It is very easy to get sucked into a family argument and lose the sale. And even if you make the sale, you may not see that family group again.

• *Don't use group members against each other.*   Along similar lines, avoid the temptation to use group members against each other when handling objections. It may seem very easy to look appealingly at a husband while a wife objects to a product feature, or at a wife when a husband has doubts about service policies. Again, don't do it. Faced with those tactics, groups will often unite against you.

• *Handle all group questions and objections, even if redundant.*   In a busy retail establishment, it is very easy for a prospect to be distracted. The environment is unfamiliar, people are moving about, other products suddenly attract and distract. You may be focusing on the primary buyer, and be suddenly confronted by a question you have fully answered some time ago from another group member. When that happens, it is best to answer it all over again, without reference to the previous answer. It is a chance to re-present, and it guarantees that you will not be floored by a late ill-informed objection from any member of the group.

• *Treat children as part of the group.*   It is always be-nice-to-and-patient-with-children week in retail selling. If you possibly can, treat them as adults and include them in the presentation. In doing so, you will often find that children can exert a good deal of positive influence on the buying decision. If you do not, they can distract the prospect, cut short the interview, and ruin the sale.

All too often in retail selling, interruptions occur. The phone rings and must be answered, a deliverer has a question, another customer breaks in with question or comment—your conversation is broken and the selling situation invaded. It will happen. When it does, all you can do is try to keep the interruption brief and keep focusing on the prospect. You can often return a telephone call later, rather than handling it while selling; hold off the deliverer's question or refer it to someone else, do the same with the interrupting customer.

If you must turn away from your prospect, do it with a smile, and make it clear that you are handling the interruption so that you can focus more fully on the prospect when you return. That is particularly effective when you decide to try to handle more than one customer at a time. It is not usually a good idea to try to do so, but occasionally you find yourself somehow boxed into doing it. When you must, the difference between a smiling temporary interruption and an abrupt, harassed break-off is often the difference between returning to make the sale and finding the prospect long gone when you do return after the interruption.

When your retail establishment has had a quiet day in the middle of a quiet week in a very quiet month, it is very easy to start making weak sales. There are two major kinds, with many variations on the main themes:

• *Inconsistent bargains.* Price concessions are a standard, entirely acceptable way of moving stock that you want moved at less-than-usual profit margins. In a bargain sale, a store offers stock at a discounted percentage or at firm below-list prices, and can often generate business by doing so. The trouble starts when the bargains are not uniform, when sellers in individual selling situations show prospects that their prices are anything but firm. Then everything turns on price, very detrimental words get around about your price policies, and you are in trouble. Your good customers feel cheated for having bought at full price, and your prospects want to talk about price rather than hear your product benefits story.

• *Money-back guarantees.* Anybody who offers money-back guarantees is looked on with considerable suspicion in the marketplace. The people you want as customers are unlikely to come in because they regard that kind of "guarantee" as just a come-on, which it usually is. Those who do buy on that basis are merely gullible.

But what often happens is that a seller will say something like "Look, Mr. Smith, why don't you try it? We've been in business a long time, and I can't remember us turning anybody down who was dissatisfied with this product and wanted to return it with full credit. It's nothing I can offer you formally, and I know you'll understand that. But just between us, why don't you try it?"

The temptation for a weak seller and weak closer to try that one is obvious. Many succumb, at one time or another. Don't do it. A combination of dissatisfied buyer and outraged employer can play havoc with your job and career.

In retail selling, as in outside selling, it is strong, consistent empathetic selling that builds a successful sales career.

CHAPTER 7
EFFECTIVE COMMUNICATION

Sales professionals must be particularly sensitive to the need to communicate with others clearly and persuasively. They, more than most other professionals in the business world, spend a great deal of each working day reaching for understanding with others and then moving from understanding to persuasion. Therefore, anything that continually hinders clarity of expression must be excised, and anything in an existing personal style that customarily helps move forward the twin processes of understanding and persuasion is to be encouraged. Effective communication and persuasion mean clear speaking; clear nonverbal communication that enhances, rather than detracts from, clear speaking; and clear writing. Clear and mutually enhancing speaking and nonverbal communication are basic to both successful selling and career building. Clear writing is basic to career building and in conducting business affairs, and is useful in selling, as well.

Because of the very nature of the selling process, most communication with customers and prospects is one-to-one, and at root informal, no matter how well-prepared the set of presentations we deliver. Beyond prepared presentations is selling; people in selling who cannot understand that usually find themselves in other lines of work. That is also true when selling to small groups, and when using the telephone. All of which means that sales professionals are not actors or politicians, able to operate from a distance and use techniques that convey personalities that are not their own. In a very real sense, we usually convey to others what we are, warts and all. And if what we are is any great distance from what we would like to seem to be, then we have problems—especially in selling and career building.

In this sense, *effective communication* is more fact than aim; in a mixture of verbal and nonverbal ways, which add up to a great deal more than the sum of their parts, what we are comes through to others, whether we like it or not. And what we are is not very much changed by cosmetic work on speech, body language, appearance, or close attention to manipulative techniques. People who are arrogant or very defensive can do a good deal of work on speech, body language, and appearance, and still not be able to soften the kind of closed coldness that makes it impossible for them to empathize, thereby find buying motives, and sell. Nor will sharpening personal communications skills help very much when basic attitudes are worsening—the sour and personally defeated will not sell and build their careers well, no matter how much they are exposed to training in verbal and nonverbal communication.

That said, however, there are some ways we can help ourselves to communicate and persuade more effectively. Each of us develops a unique personal style, a characteristic mode of expression that reflects both basic attitudes and communicating and persuading skills; that develops and changes as our personalities and skills develop and change; and that sums up the whole face we present to the world. As long as they are not loaded down with self-defeating attitudes, these personal styles can be sharpened in many ways. Clear thinking and lucid expression can, to a considerable extent, be learned. Body language can be consciously molded and re-molded, and made into a set of good habits. Appearances can be adjusted rather easily.

SPEAKING

First—and most important for sales professionals—are speaking skills. People who develop the lifelong habit of speaking in a clear, relaxed, and thoughtful fashion go a long way toward selling and career-building success. In the informal set of contexts that characterizes most selling and other business situations, that basic speaking—and thinking—approach is the one most likely to wear well in the long run.

This style starts with an old childhood admonition: Think before you speak. Yes, it is as simple and basic as that; developing and maintaining the habit of thinking before you speak is the most important single key to effective spoken communication. For the habits of speaking before you have quite collected your thoughts, of filling silences with words, and of responding too quickly in conversation, can be lifelong impediments to career success, and especially so for sales professionals. These are habits that cause you to speak unclearly, no matter how well you are physically able to form and speak words and sentences; unclarity of thought brings unclarity of expression.

There are physical speech flaws that come with unthinking talk, too. Unthinking speakers tend to talk too fast, in a higher pitch than they need to, and louder than they should. They often compound the error with body language pressure and succeed in conveying that they do not really know what they are talking about, and are trying hard to make sales any way they can.

Like so many other bad habits, this is fairly easy to change once you know what is wrong and what you want to do about it. All you really need to do is to listen hard and responsively when in conversation. That listening process alone will cause you to take a mental "deep breath" before saying anything. And if you are starting a conversation, take that mental deep breath before opening your mouth. One key thing to remember is that hardly anyone you are likely to meet, in or out of selling, will be offended by your habit of fairly slow-starting, very thoughtful speech. Quite the contrary. Thoughtful, careful speakers are highly prized in our culture. You will be listened to, and respected, and will communicate and sell even more effectively.

A second lifelong effective speaking habit to cultivate is that of relaxation—and we mean that quite literally. Relax your whole body while you speak. It will do you, your speaking style, and the entire communicating situation a world of good. There is nothing quite like relaxation to provide the basis for clarity, empathy, and persuasion. If you are tense, you will communicate that tension, and will often cause others to develop tension. Tension builds walls, which is exactly the opposite of what you want. If your voice communicates real warmth, ease, and relaxation, you are quite likely to be met similarly by others. Relaxation does good physical things for your speech, too. A relaxed speaker usually speaks more effectively than a tense one. The voice is deeper and more resonant; the words are often much more clearly spoken. There is more variety in the voice, with a much wider range of volume and better breath control. The total result is far more effective communication.

A third key effective speech habit is that of speaking rather slowly. That is something easy to advise and sometimes very hard to do. Use the mirror, time yourself, and press family and friends into service as volunteer listeners. Those who speak quickly are often startled at how much better they sound and how much more clearly they communicate when they slow their speech down even a little. Forming words fully helps slow speech, but the main thing is to consciously speak slowly. At first, it sounds to you (never to others—they appreciate and respect slower speech) as if you are dragging out words and sentences. In a short time, the slower, clearer, more effective speech will become a valuable new habit.

A fourth very basic habit to cultivate is that of speaking clearly. Many people do not. Relaxation and slow, thoughtful speech help clarity a great deal but, by themselves, are often not enough to achieve the clarity you want.

Often we develop unclear speech habits simply because those around us speak unclearly. Sometimes it is the effect of a regional speech pattern, as when New Englanders leave off the "r's" at the ends of syllables and words, and the words "order" and "Harvard" come out "awduh" and "Havahd." That is fine in New England, but may require some minor speech adjustments when talking to Midwesterners, who pronounce a very hard "r" in the same circumstances.

More often, though, it is a certain laziness and sloppiness that creeps into our language over the years. After all, we are understood perfectly well by friends and family, aren't we? True, but in selling we are often speaking to people with a much wider set of backgrounds than those normally close to us, and we have to make ourselves understood by people from all over the country.

It is usually fairly easy once you know what to look for. Practicing before a mirror can be very useful. Listening to a taped recording of your voice or watching and hearing a video recording of yourself can help even more. When you talk quickly and carelessly into the mirror you will see common sentences come out startlingly unclearly. When you talk slowly, carefully, and clearly into the mirror, opening your mouth and forming the words, you will see yourself looking the same, taking what seems to be just about the same time (time it, the difference is insignificant) to say the words, but speaking a great deal more effectively.

Do not worry about regional, national, ethnic, or any other "special" accents and influences in your speech, except for such minor adjustments as indicated above. You need not and probably should not try to change the speech patterns of a lifetime in your search for effective speech. When you try to change your normal patterns and rhythms, without the trained eye and ear of the professional performer, you may very well achieve only affected, stilted, phony sounding speech, which is far more disagreeable, and for that matter, far more noticeable than any regional accent you may be trying to change. Speak slowly and clearly, form your words fully, and you will be understood and respected.

Sometimes, as when the New Englander we mentioned earlier relocates in the Midwest, or when a Southerner relocates in the North, people want to make long-term changes in their regional speech patterns. Usually, it simply happens. When you talk with people every day, listen responsively, and are in the business of communicating your thoughts to others, your speech patterns are likely to change to meet the normal patterns around you.

If you want to move the processes of change along a little faster, you need only to listen to the vowels and word endings a little harder. A great deal of regional and other special speech is a matter of how the vowels are pronounced and how the word endings are handled. We are a collection of regions and a nation of immigrants, with languages from all over the world still being fused into the American language, but the language is indeed in the process of fusing, and it is easier and easier to move your speech into the main patterns of the region you are in.

Your voice is an instrument of considerable range and variety. It can be used to create music, to speak poetry, in a theater or on a platform. It can be used to communicate clearly, sharply, and persuasively; and misused so that it will stand in the way of selling and career-building success. One major hazard lies in the area of pitch. A voice that is pitched high, coming out of a tense, tight throat, often offends the ear of the listener. It is described as "grating," "shrill," "unpleasant," and often causes listeners to want to escape. Sometimes it is associated with a high, aggrieved whine that seems to multiply its offensiveness.

Like most other such problems, the trouble can be cured once you know what the problem is. But you often do not even know the problem exists. You talk a certain way all your life, are understood and accepted by friends and family, and have no reason to believe there is anything wrong with the way you speak. That is literally true—there is nothing "wrong" with the way you speak. It is just that other people may find it somewhat unacceptable. That is not much of a problem, unless you are in a profession that requires good personal communication, like selling. Then a high, tense whine can be a major disability.

To improve your voice, you need a little help from family, friends, and co-workers. Especially co-workers, who are less accustomed to your speech patterns than family and friends. Normally, people will not tell you if they think there is something disagreeable about your voice, or for that matter any other aspect of your personality. But they will do so if you ask for purposes of self-improvement. Your manager and other sales professionals can tell you about any pitch control problems and can help you practice your way out of them.

The answers are very often in areas already discussed. Relaxation and responsive listening loosen the throat, which results in a lower, softer pitch. Slowing too-rapid speech and using clear word formation often seem to bring down the voice a whole octave, softening hard, rasping edges in your speech.

Those are the normal solutions to problems of too-loud speech, as well. Too-soft speech, which is rarer, is usually a question of self-confidence, and cures itself as the deeper question of self-confidence is solved. Too-loud speech sometimes has a simple physical basis. You can be a little hard of hearing and not know it. Family and friends tend to accept us as we are, do not think about the fact that we talk louder than they do, or perhaps discount it as some kind of personality need.

Once again, it is not much of a problem unless you are in a communications-related profession like selling. And once again, co-workers can be very helpful. If you do have a hearing problem and need some sort of mechanical aid, it is far better to have and use the aid than to go without it—better for your career and a great deal better for you personally. The chief reaction of people who have not known they need hearing assistance who have then secured some help is: "This is great. I didn't know what I was missing."

Many of us have speech habits that get in the way of effective communication. Usually, we are not aware we have them and are often surprised and somewhat embarrassed to discover them. Here are some of the most common verbal "tics."

"Like, y'know."

"Like I was driving to the store last night and like this other driver like cut me off and like we nearly had like a real bad accident." "You know, I really think he was nearly sold, but you know it didn't work out quite right" and "you know I'm going back in there next time though and you know I'm really going to sell him then." Except that it usually comes out "y'know" rather than "you know."

Not many sales professionals talk that way, but millions of other Americans do, and no one is immune to the development of that kind of bad speech habit. Words and phrases such as "like" and "y'know" seem to fill in the pauses in speech. They seem to impart a certain rhythm and structure. If you have the slightest tendency to develop a case of the "likes" and "y'knows," fight it hard. These examples are not just "bad speech" in academic terms, they are the enemies of clarity and effective selling.

The a . . .

"A . . . . ., Ms. Jones, I a . . . want to a . . . show you our a . . . new line of a . . . green a . . . widgets from a . . . Afghanistan. They're a . . . some of the best a . . . widgets we've a . . . ever a . . . shown." This is a disastrous habit, and the most common one in the world. It is also something that is almost impossible to hear yourself doing. You literally do not hear the "a . . ." and are enormously surprised to learn that you are doing it. This one calls for a tape recorder. If you have any thought that you are an "a . . .-er," tape yourself talking and listen carefully. If you have any tendency in that direction, cure it.

Throat-clearing.

We often develop the habit of literally or figuratively clearing our throats before we speak. That can take the form of compulsive throat-clearing before launching into conversation, or, more often, it can take the form of a meaningless word or phrase repeated again and again. For example, you may habitually respond, "Well, Ms. Jones," when the word "well" has nothing to do with anything you are discussing. Or you may preface with a "Yes," even when you are really about to say "no." It happens often, and is worth guarding against.

Throat-clearing is both a verbal and physical "tic." There are other physical tics as well. Most of us develop some in the course of life and career, and can fix them fairly easily—once recognized—unless they reflect deeper tensions that must be analyzed and handled in more basic ways. These kinds of tics are all the little unconscious, repeated physical moves that can so distract others while face-to-face with you. They can range from head scratching to finger tapping, and often involve the hands. For example, there is the kind of tic that involves playing with something while in a selling situation. You may continually handle your glasses, pen, presentation materials, tie, handbag, or order form, without realizing you are doing so. You may also be a nose rubber, head scratcher, or chin scraper. Or you may fold and unfold your hands a dozen times during a conversation, shift about in your chair, or even be an arm folder or finger tapper. All indicate tension, all impede communication and persuasion, and all are normally rather easily fixable, with proper attention.

BODY LANGUAGE

Effective face-to-face communication and persuasion depend as much upon nonverbal as upon verbal communication. In practice, verbal and nonverbal are intimately intertwined, part of the same set of processes, each occurring side by side whether we like it or not. We communicate with our whole bodies, and it is our bodies that usually convey the subtle emotional signals that are so important in any kind of persuasion.

Each of us has spent a lifetime developing a style of personal expression, a combination of words and body language that serves to communicate and persuade. As with speech, it is best not to try to make large changes in that basic style when dealing with matters of body language, but rather to shape natural style to career building and selling needs. For example, if you move a little too quickly, slow down a little. Speed makes people nervous; moving a little more slowly makes for easier, more empathetic communication and relationship.

It is also appropriate to do your best to adopt a reasonably relaxed body set. When you are listening responsively, you will probably lean forward just a little, perhaps cock your head, sometimes smile appreciatively, often nod when a telling point is made. All these movements can and should happen quite naturally if you are really listening and responding. If you are tense and force your responses, people will usually know it, realize that you are faking warmth and response, and they will close up tight. It is always your natural style that works best—with modest improvements and avoiding basic errors—but still your own open and natural style.

Some sales professionals are a little afraid of using their own natural expressive styles. It usually predates going into selling and indicates a rather defensive attitude toward the world and the people in it. Their usually unspoken thought is that, by avoiding body language as much as possible, they will preserve their privacy, keep up their defenses against the world and others, be able to stick to business, and avoid personalities. But it does not quite work that way. Quite the contrary: carefully controlled people reflect tension, tightness, and the presence of a wall between themselves and others. The personal attitudes projected are often tension, coldness, arrogance, even distaste for others. The physical results are often tightness of face and body, constricted motion, voice tension, and inability to relax and responsively listen.

Body language has a great deal to do with success or failure in selling. The only way you can avoid using body language in selling is to avoid face-to-face selling situations. And anyone who needs to do that needs to find a different line of work. Far better to learn to relax, use, and improve on your own personal expressive style, and move ahead.

By all means talk with your hands—or any other part of your anatomy, for that matter—if that is part of your natural style. "Don't talk with your hands" is nonsensical advice. Of course it is all right to talk with your hands, your shoulders, and the angle of your head, as it is all right to talk with your lips, tongue, and the air that flows from your diaphragm to be shaped into words.

One of the most common problems faced in speech is that of the "stiff upper lip." Try talking with your upper lip held purposely as stiff as you can. Difficult, isn't it? You come out like Humphrey Bogart playing one of his early gangster roles. If you have a stiff-upper-lip problem, you will want to cure it, to achieve more mobile, effective speech.

Similarly, the main problem in body language is not "Don't talk with your hands." Quite the opposite. It is the problem of stiffness, inability to loosen up, get the tremendous expressive advantages that flow from free and fluid use of your body along with free and fluid use of your voice. Do talk with your hands, if that is your style. If you study yourself as you talk, and find your gestures so broad, sharp, and strong that they rivet the prospect's attention to your hands rather than on what you are trying to communicate, then you must moderate your gestures. That is very easy. Once you are aware of the problem, you will be able to turn the sweeping gesture into a shorter, equally communicative, less distracting motion. The sharp, hard, cutting gesture can be turned into an equally useful, much less distracting aid in making your point.

And do talk with your whole body. Just sensitize yourself to what you are doing. Study yourself in the mirror as if you were a stranger. See the main natural things you do, and moderate them, rather than try to force yourself into rigid, uncommunicative patterns of "acceptable" behavior.

HANDLING THE TELEPHONE

On the telephone we are unable to use body language, so effective communication and persuasion become far more difficult than they are face-to-face. Most sales professionals know this very well; that is why they so much prefer face-to-face selling, and strongly resist the temptation to sell products by telephone as long as face-to-face selling is possible. That is not merely habit, as some who favor telephone selling might suppose; rather, it reflects understanding of the role that nonverbal communication can and normally does play in the selling process. It would be nice to be able to sell by telephone; no more traffic to fight, no day-destroying broken appointments, just a string of sales interviews adroitly conducted by telephone. The trouble is that field selling is much more effective when conducted face-to-face. That is why telephone selling—and some kinds of telephone selling can be quite cost-effective—is usually done not by sales professionals but by rather modestly paid people, using fully canned presentations, complete with alternative ways to handle the most common stalls and objections encountered.

Sales professionals do communicate by telephone a good deal, though. We sell appointments, handle customer relations matters, talk to our home offices, sales managers, and colleagues, and do a wide variety of other things on the telephone. It all adds up to a good deal of time spent relying solely on our voices for effective communication, using an instrument that is inherently not capable of handling a full range of communication. That places a premium on such purely verbal matters as roundness of tone, low and pleasant-sounding pitch, moderation of volume, relatively slow delivery, careful pronunciation, and control of regional and ethnic accents. On the telephone, you must first of all be understood, clearly and completely, and there is no way to check nonverbal response to see if you are being understood, much less being persuasive.

Telephone conversations must therefore go more slowly—often much more slowly—than you would like, to become effective communications. Even when conducted very carefully, you still cannot be as sure as you can be face-to-face that understanding—and, if desired, persuasion—are actually taking place. It is not at all unusual for agreements reached over the telephone to become, in practice, partial or even total disagreements, with both parties to the conversation thinking the other at least rather stupid and at worst unforgivably dishonest.

Because of the frustrating nature of the human contact possible by telephone, many of us talk too long, wasting valuable time trying to develop some kind of rapport, and simultaneously causing those with whom we are speaking to dearly wish the conversation had never started. We also sometimes talk far too brusquely, quite antagonizing others, and behaving in what is perceived by others as insulting fashion. No, sales professionals are rarely insulting, by telephone or face-to-face; but they can be inept on the telephone, and seem to be insulting. Unfortunately, whatever the reason, unskilled telephone behavior conveys lack of control and arrogance to others. Handling the telephone badly is a sales-losing and career-harming reflex; it is also discourteous, and the old axiom is still right: Those who give no respect deserve no respect.

Professional telephone handling includes getting the mechanics right. The telephone instrument should be placed to the left of those who write with their right hands, and vice versa, with the wire coming from that side, rather than trailing over your desk from the wrong side and impeding your prime reading and writing area. Writing materials and appointment book should be next to your writing hand, rather than requiring a reach every time you want to write during a telephone conversation. The telephone instrument should be easily reached, held a few inches away from your mouth, and you should speak into it naturally and easily, rather than raising your voice. If you find it comfortable, by all means get a shoulder cradle that lets you operate hands-free, or a desk microphone, that lets you speak and listen without using a receiver, if you find one that works well enough. Such advice is simple and basic, certainly. But it is honored only in theory by many people who pay less attention to organizing the mechanics of personal telephone-handling than they do to buying a tennis racket, even though they spend hundreds of hours each year on the telephone. Good telephone handling focuses on using the telephone primarily for what it does best, and doing your best to sell face-to-face. But when we do get on the telephone, we want to do our best to handle it well.

WRITING

The same is true of writing. For, while most face-to-face sales professionals do not in the normal course of events need to be polished professional writers, they do find themselves putting a surprising number of words on paper—and on tapes and discs, as well—in the course of even a couple of months in the field. There are letters to customers and prospects, memos to management and regional and home office people, letters to professional and personal acquaintances and friends, and sometimes even a personally written piece of sales material, although that is rare. Whenever possible, field people should rely upon trained promotion people for written sales material, as promotion writing is very much a writer's special task. It is the sort of thing that, like selling, looks easy from the outside, but in fact requires a good deal of training and focus to come out well. Proposal writing is also a special skill, and those whose selling responsibilities include a good deal of such work will be well-advised to seek the necessary special training, from their companies and from published work on this special skill.

From the point of view of career building, good writing skills are a considerable asset, especially for those who want to make the move into management. Managers write a great deal, and need to be good at clearly and persuasively putting their words into written forms. Assessment of the suitability of prospects for a move into management always includes a close look at their writing skills.

Good business writing is just that—a skill. It requires a proper set of attitudes, careful preparation, organization, work, rework, attention to detail, and practice. It does not require a great deal of talent, and it most emphatically does not require long-winded multisyllabic language full of professional jargon. In this, good business writing is like good business speech—it is clear, easy-flowing, relaxed, and friendly. The best possible approach a sales professional can take to writing is to think before writing, organize those thoughts into a coherent whole, and then write the way you speak. No, not the way *other* people write, or the way you might think you should write—the way you speak. Then, after getting it on paper, rework it for clarity and friendliness, again and again as necessary until you have it the way you want it. Then type it or have it typed and do a final proofreading and editing, if necessary typing it again. Worry about such matters as grammar and word agreement during rework and editing, not during the basic writing. The key to the whole process is to let it flow, get it down, and then spend whatever time you need to fix it up in final form. Conversely, the main enemy is fear—of being misunderstood, of being laughed at, of somehow saying less and being less persuasive than you know you can be face-to-face, of exposing ignorance, of not being able to "fix it all up" with body language as you do face-to-face or as you do with extra words on the telephone. A good writer learns to relax and let a personal style—an individual and authentic voice—emerge in writing, just as a good face-to-face selling professional does in the field. For both, the main enemy is "freezing up"; for both, the best approach is turning learned skills into lifelong reflexes.

Effective business writing is aimed at the audience it addresses. Your letter confirming an appointment with a prospect is likely to be written differently than your letter to a complaining customer, and both are likely to be written differently than a letter to the marketing management of your company. But whatever your audience, it is usually a good idea to keep your writing free of jargon and shop-talk terms. A letter or memo that cannot be understood does not accomplish the writer's purpose and wastes everyone's time. When you are uncertain about the audience, aim for a general lay level. There are times, however, when the shorthand of shop talk is appropriate. Reserve shop talk for internal memos, when you are absolutely sure of your audience and its understanding of the subject.

The purpose and audience of your communication will guide you in setting the tone. How do you wish to come across to your readers? Are you handling a complaint or making a pitch? Do you want your voice to seem authoritative, friendly, or sympathetic?

Consider your relationship to the reader (is it formal or informal?) as well as any biases the reader may have toward you or your subject. Choose words that will communicate the right attitude. It is not always easy, especially if the subject is a delicate one. Since you cannot see the reader, you cannot judge any reaction to your words by watching facial expressions, and change your tone accordingly. Sometimes factors beyond your control or knowledge—such as political or personal sensitivities, or differing interpretations of the meaning of certain words—will make a reader "hear" the wrong tone.

Your best approach is to try to place yourself in the reader's position and anticipate how that person is likely to react to what you say in print. For example, a customer with a complaint may want empathy and assurance that a problem is being resolved. Notice the difference in tone between these two letters.

Dear Mr. Raymond:

Pursuant to your letter of June 30, we have shipped you one wide-angle lens #A58, which you ordered from our catalog. We are sorry for the delay, and thank you for bringing it to our attention.

Dear Mr. Raymond:

The wide-angle lens #A58 which you ordered from our catalog has been shipped to you by Parcel Post.

The delay in filling your order was due to a clerical oversight. We customarily process orders within one week of receiving them.

I hope you have not been inconvenienced. Thank you for doing business with us, and please consider us again for your future optical needs.

Both are perfectly correct, but the first is wooden and brusque, while the second communicates understanding and personal attention. The recipient of the second letter is much more likely to place repeat business with the company.

Above all, remember that writing is communication between human beings. Too many of us think business writing must be formal, dry, and riddled with ornate prose, rather than clear and friendly. Where it is appropriate, stay in touch with your audience through the use of personal pronouns such as "I," "you," and "we." Imagine you are having a conversation with the reader. Face-to-face you would never say, "ABC company wishes to extend its appreciation for your introduction of our new widget line to your customers." Instead, you would say something more like, "Thank you for joining in the introduction of our new widget line, for which we all have high hopes." Set a warm, human tone that will help you accomplish your purposes.

It is also important to be aware of timing. If you are setting your own deadline, consider whether purpose or content hinge on a time factor. Then you should plan your writing schedule to meet the deadline with time to spare. Be sure to build into your schedule time to conduct necessary research or obtain information from other sources. Do not count on wrapping up your communication at the last minute, because—as in Murphy's Law—something is bound to go wrong. An emergency will sidetrack your attention or your typist will get sick. You also will need time for revising and editing. Few good writers ever stop with their first, or even second, draft. Even one-page letters and memos need a once-over for corrections and polish.

Your writing environment is also extremely important. Wherever you write—whether in office, home, airplane, or hotel room—make your working area as comfortable as possible. Have all your notes and reference materials at hand. It is annoying, as well as counterproductive, to stop writing to search for a piece of information. Most offices are reasonably well set up for writing work, but sales professionals, who often write elsewhere, must carefully create the proper environment. Otherwise the task is not as productive as it could be—and far more frustrating than it should be.

At home, do your writing away from main family activity areas, especially where a television set or radio is on. If you have not yet set up a full office at home, at least shut yourself in a bedroom or study and request that you not be disturbed. Writing at the kitchen or dining room table or in a living room easy chair invites interruption. It is best to work at a desk or table with a chair of the right height for your working surface. A chair that is too low or too high causes muscle strain. Metal folding chairs are unsuitable for long periods of writing work. If you do a lot of work at home—and sales professionals should expect to do just that—it would be wise to invest in a good quality office chair; the added comfort will be well worth it. Otherwise, try your kitchen or dining room chairs, adding a cushion if necessary. Above all, you need adequate light to avoid straining your eyes; overhead lights are not enough. Compact, high-intensity desk lamps are inexpensive and portable, and some models have clip-on features for attachments to furniture.

The same comfort considerations should be given to your hotel or motel accommodations. Ask for a room with a desk or table and chair and try them out as soon as you check in. If the furniture does not feel comfortable or the lighting is not good, request another room. You will get far more accomplished with less fatigue in an adequate work area.

You can also make productive use of flying time by carrying on writing work. The small meal trays are not well suited to be writing surfaces, however, because they usually force you to lean forward to write. Use an attaché case in your lap as a writing surface; or if you carry a soft portfolio, include in it a clipboard or hard notebook binder. If you plan to work throughout a long flight, minimize mental and muscle fatigue by taking an occasional walk down the aisle.

Effective writing also requires good writing habits. That means disciplining yourself to write, whether or not you "feel" like it and in spite of minor distractions. If professional writers wrote only when they "felt" like it, newspapers, magazines, and books would never get published.

WRITING EFFECTIVE LETTERS

A good business letter, whether it accepts, rejects, tells, or sells, has warmth and a human touch. It is direct, polite, and sincere, and tells the recipient what he or she needs to know. Above all, letters should have a pleasant tone, even if you want to complain about something. Angry letters do not accomplish nearly as much as firm, reasoned ones.

Before you write a letter, think first what you would say to the recipient if you were communicating in person. Would you ever really say, "I am sending forthwith . . ." or "re your letter of August 18 . . ."? We hope not. Certainly you should avoid such cumbersome, overly formal phrases in your writing. A pleasant tone is not conveyed by awkward, stilted phrases.

The use of personal pronouns, such as *I, we,* and *you,* helps set a pleasant tone in letters. Avoid using harsh negatives and commands. Instead of saying, "we cannot fill your order," say "we are unable to fill your order." Do not tell the recipient that he or she "must" or "has to" do something. Instead of: "You must sign the enclosed form letter before we can issue the title," say: "We need your signature on the enclosed form before we can issue the title." For an informal tone, use contractions, which are more conversational.

Letters should come right to the point. Give the pertinent information and sign off, not abruptly, but without digression or padding. One significant exception to that rule, though, is a letter replying to a complaint, in which you are trying to soothe someone, and in which you may not want to come to the point quite so quickly.

Whatever their subjects or purposes, all letters have in common a salutation and a closing. Each must be chosen to suit the tone you have adopted—formal or informal—and the relationship between you and your reader. The most common salutation is "Dear _____" followed by a comma (informal) or a colon (formal, and most commonly used for business purposes).

Dear Mary,

Dear Mr. Jones,

Dear Ms. Randall:

Very formal salutations are "Dear Sir" and "Dear Madam"; reserve those for persons of very high rank or eminence. You may wish to use "Dear Sir or Madam," "Dear Sirs or Mesdames," or "Dear Ladies and Gentlemen," when you are uncertain who will receive your letter. While none of these choices is terribly attractive, they are preferable to *To Whom It May Concern,* which has a legalistic, antiquated sound to it.

What if you are uncertain of the gender of the recipient? Say you are writing a formal letter to a Leslie Smith, but you do not know if the person is male or female. Do not use *Sir/Madam* or *Dear Mr./Ms. Smith.* Above all, don't guess. Instead, write out the full name:

Dear Leslie Smith:

It may sound a little cumbersome, but it is far better than risking an insulting error. If you do not know the marital status of a woman, use *Ms.* The neutral title has lost its militant image and is now widely used and accepted. Many businesswomen prefer it, regardless of marital status.

Closings are simpler. The choice is simply between informal and formal. The best all-purpose closings are *Sincerely* and *Sincerely yours.* Some good informal closings include:

Cordially	Regards
Best wishes	Warmly

Some more formal closings are:

Respectfully	Respectfully yours
Yours truly	Very truly yours
Very cordially yours	Very sincerely yours

Avoid being cute or clever in closings. In general, avoid extremes, like the too-casual *Yours* or the somewhat archaic *Respectfully submitted.*

As all sales professionals know, mistakes do happen. If you are on the receiving end of a valid complaint, own up to it with a polite apology.

Dear Mr. Southwell:

Since we received your letter about the improper printing of the last issue of *Bird News,* our vice president of production has met with our press foreman to determine what the problem was.

Apparently, a press person loaded the paper feeder incorrectly. The error was spotted, and the bad copies were pulled out of production. Evidently a few slipped through—we think it could not have been more than 30 copies.

This was a human error, and all personnel have been alerted to be much more careful in the future. We apologize for the mistake and wish to assure you that all precautions will be taken in the future to deliver a product of which we can all be proud.

If the complainer is in error, or if you cannot comply with their request, be polite but firm.

Dear Mr. Calder:

We have doublechecked our records and find that our last billing was correct. Your last payment was received on March 17, and your account shows that $54.29 is still owed us.

Perhaps your payment envelope was misplaced or lost in the mail. If so, you may still avoid a finance charge by remitting the above amount by the next billing date.

Whatever kinds of letters you routinely have to write, you will benefit from developing your own standard "form" letters. Examine your own files for a certain period, isolate the various types of letters, and analyze the contents, retaining what you think—on reflection—worked well, and replacing what did not. You will save yourself a good deal of rethinking for those parts of your letters that are relatively routine. A caution, however; avoid form letters when you are dealing with a single person or company over a long period of time. They would surely be insulted by such letters.

SOME WRITING CAUTIONS

Bear in mind that jargon—nonwords and often-meaningless gibberish—is a bane to clarity and conciseness. In government agencies and businesses large and small across the nation, people are "solutioning" problems, "dollarizing" new production processes, getting "oriented" to situations, and "throughputting" suggestions. While some corporate publications have taken up a "ban the jargon" standard, and many seminars and books tackle the subject, jargon still thrives.

We are guilty of using jargon when we turn nouns into verbs, create nonwords, and otherwise mangle the English language. A favorite in the business lexicon is *escalate.* Used properly, it means "to increase in extent, scope, or volume." Used as jargon, it means taking an issue to a higher authority, as when someone dislikes a decision and announces, "I'm going to escalate this to the vice president." Not surprisingly, lawyers are among the worst jargon offenders. Legal mumbo-jumbo renders inscrutable many contracts, laws, regulations, and applications.

Jargon and obfuscation have long been problems in the bureaucratic ranks of the federal government—so much so that an internal campaign was launched in 1979 to fight them. Members of the Document Design Center, a division of the private, nonprofit American Institute of Research, have been instructing government employees how to write in plain English. Alas, thousands of confusing regulations and application forms still are churned out every year. Ironically, the campaign has created some new jargon: "good paper" and "bad paper," which describe the clarity of government writing.

Much jargon comes from plain laziness. It is faster to say "dollarize this" than to say "estimate how much it will cost to do this." Some jargon comes from ignorance: *solution* is a noun, *solve* a verb. Problems are solved, not solutioned. A quick check with a dictionary would save many a writer the embarrassment of an improperly used or nonexistent word, like the sales executive who reported that sales of a certain product were "denigrating." (He meant declining.)

Some jargon-users sincerely believe that jargon makes them sound impressive; quite the opposite. At worst, jargon will reduce your writing to gibberish, and make you appear uneducated; at best, it is annoying clutter. If some jargon has crept into your draft, excise it. Do you really mean "electronic mail" instead of "electronic document distribution"? Are you "offering" suggestions instead of "inputting" them?

An active voice, rather than a passive voice, will contribute to your clarity and conciseness. In an active voice, the subject of a sentence performs an activity or takes action. In a passive voice, the subject receives action. A passive voice, which is used far too often in business communications, weakens sentences and dilutes their meanings. Because it can provide an anonymous cloak, it is a favorite of writers who wish to blunt their words or evade responsibility for a statement.

See how much stronger the following sentences are when written in an active voice.

Passive: Replacement of existing copiers with newer, faster models is being planned for the next fiscal year.

Active: We plan to replace all copiers with newer, faster models next fiscal year.

Passive: It is recommended that our prices be increased by 10%.

Active: I recommend a 10% price increase.

Note that the active voice sentences are shorter, more concise, and more powerful, and have more impact on the reader. If you find that your writing is largely passive, rewrite your sentences in the active voice during editing.

It is also important to establish a smooth pace and pleasant cadence for the written word, just as for the spoken word. Sentences that are short and choppy give the reader an unsettled, stop-and-go feeling. Long sentences, which must be reread and deciphered, leave the reader feeling exhausted and confused.

Here is a single sentence published in the U.S. Department of Agriculture's October 1981 telephone book. Fill your lungs and try to get through it in one breath:

> To ensure that the information on all USDA employees on file within O&F is current, it is essential that all employees promptly notify their designated agency contact of all changes to any of the information contained in the alphabetical listing section of the directory, i.e., name, room number, building location, and telephone number, so the contacts can transmit this information to the AMLS and Telephone Directory Section of the Production and Distribution Division which maintains the data base for this information from which the alphabetical listing section of the USDA Telephone Directory is prepared as well as periodic updates of the telephone directory information on USA employees which are transmitted to the GSA Locater Service here in Washington, D.C.

Do you know what that says? There are 135 words in this sentence, counting the abbreviations as single words.

These two possible revisions are more understandable and save the reader considerable time in reading and rereading.

> Please submit promptly all changes of name, address, and telephone number to your agency contact in order to keep federal directories up to date. (One sentence, 24 words.)

> Please help keep federal directories up to date. Submit promptly all changes of name, address, and telephone number to your agency contact. (Two sentences, 8 and 14 words, respectively.)

For your readers' sakes, keep your sentences of a manageable length. If your sentences *average* 17 to 20 words in length, you are in the right ball park. Some sentences will be shorter and some longer, of course. You should vary the lengths to avoid monotony. Calculate the lengths of a few sentences you have written. If they *all* run longer than 20 words, break several of them into shorter sentences. Your information should be evenly paced throughout your document, too. Do not drop too much on the reader at once, but do not skip over something too lightly.

Give your material a test by reading it aloud. Do any parts of it sound jerky, as though you are missing a transition link? Can you combine two choppy sentences into a single sentence? Does your material look pleasing to the eye? Is information neatly packaged in manageable paragraphs? If it is a long memo, have you used headings and subheadings to break up chunks of type? Most often, editing involves dealing with several types of problems at once. Be ruthless in chopping out unnecessary words and jargon, and in changing sentences from passive into active ones.

Take considerable care to de-sex your writing. It is acceptable to use *him or her, his or hers,* and *he or she,* but do so infrequently, because they are clumsy. Similarly, avoid *he/she, his/hers, s/he and (s)he.* In those rare instances when you want to use masculine pronouns to represent everyone, be sure to announce that choice in the beginning of your text. In most cases, though, it is best to try to write around gender.

Find neutral substitutes for words that traditionally have been masculine, such as *chairman, mailman, stockboy, manpower, manhours,* and *salesman.* Here are a few examples of neutral nouns:

Chairman	chair
mailman	mail carrier
stockboy	stock clerk
manpower	workforce
manhours	workhours
salesman	sales representative

It is best not to substitute *-person* or *-woman* in masculine words, such as *chairperson* or *chairwoman,* although you may do so in a pinch.

Along similar lines, avoid describing women by their personal appearance, unless it is essential to what you are saying and you are treating men the same way.

If you said this about a woman:

Senator James, an attractive redhead . . .

would you say this about a man:

Senator Harris, balding and broad-shouldered . . .

Personal appearances rarely have anything to do with a person's professional ability or standing, and such descriptions have no place in business writing.

Please note that Part 5 of this book (Language for Sales Professionals) includes a section of notes on some of the most troublesome areas of grammar, punctuation, and usage; a checklist of commonly misused and misspelled words; a phonetic alphabet to help you in dictation; and a list of proofreading and editing marks.

Clear and persuasive speaking, body language, telephone handling, and writing are essential career-building skills for sales professionals, and are well worth the time and attention it takes to learn to do them well. With them, professionalism is enormously enhanced, and you are more readily able to move anywhere and handle almost any kind of work in the world of selling—which is pretty much what professionalism is all about.

CHAPTER 8

WOMEN AND MINORITIES IN SELLING

Despite all the movements for affirmative action, equal opportunities, and equal pay, and despite substantial advances made by women and minority group sales professionals in recent years, the world of selling is still dominated by white males. To a considerable extent, women and minority group members seeking to enter and move up in selling careers are still seen as novices by many seasoned sales managers and field sales professionals, and are very likely to continue to face unthinking prejudice as well, for a long time more. It continues to be true that women and minority sales professionals must generally work harder and be more skilled and competent than their white male counterparts to achieve full acceptance and equal opportunities for advancement. Similarly achieving white male sales professionals often have a much wider range of action; they can often "get away with" behavior that would be devastating to the career of a woman or minority sales professional. With all the changes of recent decades, women and minorities must still work doubly hard and overprepare to meet and overcome social obstacles to successful careers in selling. For sales management, this state of affairs implies the need for extra attention, not to provide special support for any one group, but to see that an operation is run in a fully professional manner, unaffected by sexual or racial questions. This chapter is primarily directed at those minorities, women included, who are still working to gain that fully neutral, professional acceptance in the selling world; and secondarily to those sales, marketing, and general management professionals who wish to run organizations free of discrimination.

In selling, the heart of the matter is empathy. Yes, prospecting, selling the interview, approaching, presenting, handling stalls and objections, and closing are important. But underneath it all—empathy. The ability to put yourself into the other guy's shoes, to find the buying motives, to come together to the close.

That poses a problem for women selling to men in this society. For men selling to women, too—but much less so, for men have not been sex objects in the same way, have not been sexually exploited in the same way, and do not run the same risks that women do of being misunderstood in selling situations.

The problem is that the reach for empathy can very easily—and very often quite willfully—be misunderstood as a sexual approach. And sex and selling do not mix. The selling situation that becomes confused by sexual signals, undertones, overtones—any tones at all—is a selling situation that is headed in the wrong direction and is highly unlikely to result in a sale. It is much more likely to result in a totally unwanted and thoroughly insulting sexual approach by prospect or customer to a woman sales professional.

Most women in selling know how to avoid this, and more and more men being sold to are coming to quite well understand that selling situations are not also sexual situations. Still, it does not take too many sexual approaches or near-approaches to sour a day or week, and women in selling usually take great care to dress and groom in non-sexual-signal ways, and to project entirely businesslike attitudes in business situations. We discuss the dress and grooming aspects more fully in Chapter 10.

The less obvious, but in the long run the more important, sales success question is that the heart of the selling process is still the achievement of empathy, and that the need to back away from any action or attitude that might trigger a sexual approach in a selling situation can make it considerably more difficult to achieve empathy in cross-sex selling situations. Yes, tens of thousands of women do sell successfully to men—just as successfully as men sell to men—but only by surmounting the sex and empathy problem. It takes care and skill not to project what may easily be interpreted as a set of sexual signals while reaching for empathy—but to be able to do so is also an indispensable selling skill.

There are still double standards routinely applied on and off the job to women and minority group members in every profession and trade, and selling is no exception. That is odd, in a way, for selling is so results-oriented a profession that it would seem logical to assume that it would be very easy to see who was successful and who was not regardless of sex. Indeed, that is a very attractive aspect of the profession for many; either you sell or you do not, and all the political maneuvering, nepotism, and plain old bootlicking in the world is useless if you cannot sell. The trouble is, sex prejudice and other bigotries are by their nature not at all reasonable or logical, and women and minority group members often have to prove themselves in the field over and over again, as sales leaders, trainers, customer relations experts—whatever it takes to demonstrate professional excellence—before that excellence will be recognized. They are all too often not even considered, much less considered and rejected, for senior status, top territories, national account jobs, and management, even though they may be by every rational standard top contenders for advancement. All too often, the woman, black, or Hispanic somehow "doesn't fit," "is a little too independent," "may not really be a team player," or "might cause some problems out there." Of course, management itself never carries the virus of bigotry—not much.

All to be expected, dealt with, and turned into a better set of attitudes over the years. It may have seemed otherwise to some during the very hopeful early years of the modern movement against business bigotry, but the truth is that bigotries die hard and deeply held attitudes take generations to change. Laws have helped—and helped a good deal—by providing a new set of contexts within which the move toward real equality in the business world continues to work itself out. But experience, not laws, changes attitudes. New experiences now accrete; attitudes are slowly changing as women and minority group members move into and become fixtures in selling and other professions; but it still changes very slowly, sometimes hardly even seeming to change at all. When a woman moves into a male prospect's office, and he immediately first-names her, and goes on to call her "honey" and "dear," all the while visibly sizing her up as a sex object; not too much has changed in the mind of that prospect, whatever else has occurred in the larger society. Nor will it, for him; his son may feel quite differently, though. *May*, not *will;* the returns are by no means in yet on the rate of change regarding those bigotries built into American society.

Meanwhile, all this has to be dealt with. And although women and minority sales professionals seem to have gained considerable ground in recent decades, much remaining prejudiced behavior is not overt, but very subtle; often it is even unnoticed and unrecognized by those who feel they are relatively enlightened. That very subtlety poses real problems for women and minority sales professionals trying to establish the kind of recognized professionalism that will serve them so well both in the field and within their own companies.

How to establish that kind of professional status? Most of all, by looking and acting the part of a sales professional at all times and in all situations. Many customers, prospects, and colleagues will not take women and minorities seriously without a special effort; they often have to earn the respect that white male sales professionals may be accorded almost automatically.

Appearance is often crucial in quickly establishing the proper professional image. People form first impressions based on appearance, and those whose dress is not conservative and professional may be automatically discounted.

Whatever else they do, women and minority sales professionals must maintain their composure, even when faced with difficult situations in the field and in their own companies. This is especially important for women, who are often expected to be emotional and flighty. A male may succumb to pressure in the field and let impatience with a difficult customer or prospect show without risking loss of professional status and the respect that comes with it; a woman who does so runs great risks. Similarly, a male may fly off the handle in a difficult intracompany situation and be regarded only as a "little off his feed today," while a woman who does so may all-too-easily be seen as unstable, and in need of coddling and coaxing. This fits perfectly into previously held stereotypes and becomes a stone a woman may have to push uphill for years.

Profanity, likewise, should be used with extreme caution, especially by women. Better yet, not at all. Yes, an occasional well-placed expletive may get proper attention and help restate strength of character. On the other hand, many are likely to be shocked and strongly disapprove the use of profanity by women, using that also to reinforce their previously held prejudices. Profanity can also backfire, drawing attention to itself and away from the point you are making; that continues to be true for all of us.

It is also important to speak up at sales meetings. As a sales professional, you are likely to have to attend many sales meetings; do not take them lightly. Field people are constantly being sized up for possible advancement at such meetings, and those who do not speak up may considerably harm their chances of moving up. It is especially important to take the time to prepare for each meeting and to do your best to contribute something of value. Merely agreeing with others or offering thoughts that do not add to the matter under discussion will not do, however; to be meaningful, the contribution must be substantive, or you may be seen as a lightweight and a time-waster.

ENTERTAINING AND TRAVELING

The double standard pervasive on the job also applies to the social side of business life. Behavior that is tolerated, sometimes even admired, such as an ability to socialize at a bar for hours, is scorned in women and minority group members. They must always be aware that, whether it is apparent or not, their behavior is being observed and noted, and negative impressions are formed easily.

Women have a particular problem in business entertaining, such as over lunch. It does not matter who does the asking, what their status is, or how big their expense account is, many men still do not like women to pick up the check. It makes them feel very uncomfortable and embarrassed. Increasingly, men are coming to accept equality in check-paying, especially when the woman puts the whole situation on a firmly professional basis. Occasionally, however, a man appears to be truly distressed at the idea of having his lunch paid for by a woman. In that case, after a gentle protest, the best course is to smile graciously and thank him. A fight over the check will only increase his discomfort and undo any goodwill established with him in the business relationship.

Many women avoid such scenes by making arrangements with the waiter or waitress in advance to have the check placed on their side of the table, so the check will not automatically be given to the man. In that situation, it is a good idea for them to have a credit card ready in advance, in a handy pocket or right on top in a purse, so they can immediately place the card on the table when the check comes. It is far better to pay with plastic than with cash, for riffling through bills seems to make men even more uncomfortable. The guest may still protest, and if he insists, the businesswoman will have to judge whether the price of lunch is worth his distress. Many businesswomen, especially those working in city business districts, have learned to avoid the check scene altogether by arranging to pay in advance, so that a check never reaches the table. They search out one or two restaurants to patronize, go there regularly, and get to know the staff. Generally they present their credit card in advance of a lunch date, specify the tip percentage (a generous one, so there are no slip-ups), and sign the check. If they patronize an establishment and tip well, the staff will be only too happy to accommodate them. The same procedure holds for entertaining while traveling out of town. It is wise to check out in advance restaurants where you will likely eat, introduce yourself to the maitre d'hotel or head waiter, and explain how you want things handled when you bring your guest in.

Women also have a special problem with dinner dates, because they too often can lead to something else. People tend to be a little more relaxed over dinner, and after a few drinks or a bottle of wine it is all too easy to retire to the bar or a nightclub for a nightcap—and perhaps a proposition. If a male business acquaintance suggests dinner, the wise woman will decline and suggest lunch or drinks instead. If she meets someone in a bar for drinks at the end of a working day, she can always excuse herself after one or two drinks, citing other plans or an appointment. In a place where there is music and dancing, she should decline invitations to dance, for then she would become a sexual object, not a businesswoman.

The area of social drinking poses hazards for all sales professionals, but especially for women and minority group members. Even the practice of meeting associates for drinks after work should inspire caution. Whether you are drinking with your peers, superiors, customers, or prospects, never try to keep up with the others, and never allow yourself to get intoxicated. If you match them drink for drink, they may cheer you on at the table, but remember you as a hard boozer the next day at the office or in the field. The last thing you want is a reputation as a barfly. That caution applies especially to women. It does not matter that Charlie downed six doubles without looking any worse for it; the standards that apply to him and his male associates do not apply to women. If you feel yourself getting intoxicated, excuse yourself immediately and leave. It is far better to leave early than to risk slurred speech and sloppy coordination.

What you drink is as important as how much you drink. More and more people are steering clear of hard liquor. It's a good idea—let others drink scotch and bourbon if they wish. One alternative is sherry, a drink you can sip and nurse for a long time. Beware, however; sherry's alcoholic content is greater than wine, and will affect you more quickly. Beer is another alternative. Wine is probably the safest alcoholic drink, and can also be sipped very slowly. A wine spritzer, which is wine mixed with soda or seltzer and served with ice, is even better, though you should be careful not to drink it quickly just because it is diluted. Of course, you need not drink alcohol at all, either at lunch or after work, and many today do not. Mineral water with a slice of lemon or lime is perfectly acceptable and health-conscious. Not only will you keep your mental alertness, you will be doing your figure and your health a favor.

As a sales professional, you may be expected to attend evening functions or to entertain at your own home. If you are entertaining at home, such as a dinner party or a cocktail party, do it in style with hired help and a caterer. Nothing reduces your professional status faster than to run around fixing and serving food and drinks. Besides, you cannot really entertain your guests if you are preoccupied with kitchen and bar details. Hiring help will enhance your image and is well worth the cost. A single woman should never invite a lone male business acquaintance home for dinner, because it implies seduction.

Single businesswomen always have the dilemma of whether or not to bring an escort to business–social engagements. Wives may tend to resent single woman, and if she is alone, she may appear to be even more of a predator who will snatch their husbands away. Yet, an escort may be a handicap, requiring introduction, entertaining, and inclusion in business-oriented conversations. For these reasons, many businesswomen have decided it is best to forgo the escort. However, it is a good idea for single businesswomen to go out of their way to meet the wives of co-workers, of superiors, and sometimes of their best customers, and to try to put them at ease; they will seem less of a threat that way.

Although wives have the freedom to dress up for evening functions, and some of them will go out of their way to look sexy, conservatism should be the rule of thumb for businesswomen. That does not mean wearing a navy blue business suit, but it does mean wearing modest, high-necked, and nonclinging clothes. Anything remotely sexy will counteract a professional image—and increase resentment from wives.

Traveling also requires special attention for women and minority group members. If they are traveling alone, they may well encounter some discriminatory treatment in service establishments, which are used to catering to the white male business traveler. Hotel clerks may slight them, reservation clerks may put them in rooms they would never dream of giving their preferred customers, and restaurant help may treat them like pariahs. It may be infuriating, but getting angry will accomplish little. If you are placed in such a situation, be polite and firm; do not accept second-class treatment. Refuse the table by the kitchen door, speak up when the service is slow, and do not hesitate to insist on another room if you do not like the one you were given. It will help if you always dress like a professional and tip well.

For women, traveling alone on the road can be an extraordinarily lonely experience. All too often, the end of the field selling day is also the end of all real human contact. You cannot have an "unwinding" drink alone in the hotel or motel bar; that only invites unwanted attention. You dine alone, often with a book, for invitations to dine with customers and prospects have almost always been very wisely turned down during the course of the day in the field, and invitations to dine with strangers are turned down reflexively. You then go up to a very, very empty room, to a pile of work, a television set, a book, some personal letters, and perhaps an all-too-brief long distance conversation with those left at home. Then to sleep—if you can. Tomorrow it will be the same.

All of this can make the most stable of us do some very foolish things, such as going down to the bar late at night just to be with people; and even winding up spending the night with a perfect stranger in a fit of extreme loneliness. Like finally accepting a dinner invitation from a very nice male customer or prospect, and ending the day fighting off his advances in the politest possible way, and perhaps alienating him, as well. Worse, not fighting him off, and winding up with a "reputation," in his small town —or the county, or state. People talk; men talk about their "conquests."

There are no easy solutions to the problem of isolation women face on the road. You can help yourself somewhat, though, in two ways. First: cultivate women friends. Men cultivate men friends to overcome the problem of isolation, and often make a beeline for friends and a home-cooked dinner in every town in their territories. Women are wise to cultivate women similarly. There are more and more women in business, and women sales professionals are just as capable of making friends with women customers and prospects on the road as men are with men.

Second, be sure to work nights, setting yourself in attitude, tools, and hotel or motel environment to do just that, as we have discussed at length in Chapter 5.

Traveling with males, whether they are superiors or equals, is often a touchy situation for women in selling. Men often feel ill at ease, and some are downright resentful that they cannot really "cut loose" while they are away from wife and family. Because some men will naturally feel obliged to look after women companions while traveling, women must make it clear, politely, that they can shift for themselves. They should not drag along too much baggage, but pack the minimum and make sure they can handle it easily themselves. If they are fearful flyers, they should not admit it, no matter how terrified they are and no matter how much their traveling companions may rattle on about their own flying jitters. Women's behavior must be impeccably businesslike for the entire trip.

The woman who does not wish to dine with her male associates should decline with a simple but vague "I've already made plans for the evening," even if it's only eating alone in the hotel room. If dining with one or more associates is unavoidable, she should do so, but excuse herself at the end of dinner and not be enticed into going out on the town for a night of drinking, which is asking for trouble. At some point in her career, almost every woman will take a trip with someone who assumes that an out-of-town trip is reason for a one-night stand, someone who would never think of propositioning her back at the home office, but does it quite matter-of-factly on the road. If you are a male, such behavior should be considered strictly off limits. If you are a woman in that situation, do not puff yourself up indignantly and make a big deal of it, for you may have to travel with this person again. Decline politely and firmly in a nonpersonal way. You might add either that you are happily married or, if you are single, that you are involved with someone else, even if you are not at the moment.

THE BUSINESS ROMANCE

That raises the question of the business romance. No matter how you look at it, those who engage in business romance, no matter what their professional level, stand to lose more than they gain. The risks are enormous. News of such romances has a way of getting around, no matter how careful or secretive people think they are. It is gossip that spreads easily and quickly, especially because people are still all too willing to believe that women in selling routinely try to make sales and advance their careers through the bedroom.

In selling, the business romance is most damaging when it occurs between people selling in team fashion, or between sales manager and sales representative. At the very least, such a romance can be distracting and disruptive, not only to you and your partner, but to those you work with. Corporate policy may severely discourage such sexual entanglements; both the man and the woman—although sometimes only the woman— may be disciplined, let go, or transferred. Even without such action, the affair may run out of steam and leave both parties feeling extremely uncomfortable at having to continue to work together. Many people argue in defense of such romances, saying they are inevitable as long as men and women are frequently thrown together. Attraction and sexual tension naturally result. While it is true that some people manage to successfully carry off an office romance, affairs still backfire far more than they succeed. In general, you are better off leaving sexual tension unacknowledged, for acknowledgement requires some sort of action, either acceptance or refusal.

While affairs among peers are difficult, affairs between superiors and subordinates are even more so—for both parties. The superiors risk at least loss of professional image, which can be disastrous for a woman or minority group member. Subordinates in such affairs are in an even more precarious position. Some think this will benefit their careers, and sometimes it does temporarily, although the benefits may be undone in the end. Co-workers will resent them for having an unfair advantage over others. If the lover departs, for another division or company, the new superior may swiftly throw out the remaining party. Or, if the affair dwindles, a superior may get rid of an ex-lover, who is an embarrassing reminder of a former dalliance. By far the worst kind of romance involves partners who are married to others. The gossip can be far more malicious, and the consequences worse.

But, say some single women, how is it possible to have a social life without dating those you work with? What if you do not like to go to bars, and your job keeps you too busy for involvement in clubs or organizations? It is a dilemma, and a tough one, without a ready answer. Still, the risks of such romances must be carefully weighed before you become involved in one. If you do become romantically involved with a co-worker, you are better off with someone with whom you do not work closely every day.

No matter how attracted you are to someone you work with, do not react impulsively or rashly. Keep a cool head and carefully assess your situation, lest you undo a lot of hard work and years of effort to advance your career.

If you work for a company in a highly competitive industry, you also must be careful about seeing people who work for competitors. You may never breathe a word about business when you are together, but if your company finds out about your relationship, you may be out on the street before you know it; at best your position may be compromised.

HANDLING PREJUDICE AND CHAUVINISM

Women and minorities may have come a long way, but chauvinism is still pervasive in the business world. Some of it is obvious and overt, and some of it is very subtle and difficult to counter. Some of it is even disguised as chivalry, as with the strongly prejudiced man who believes a woman cannot handle responsibility as well as a man, that she must be closely supervised, that she is just "biding time" in the job until she quits to have children or to spend more time with her family, and that she is really just a sex object. Other men may not have such extreme sentiments, but may still treat women differently due to upbringing and years of cultural conditioning that have taught them that women are not equal to men. These attitudes may be irritating, even enraging, but taking an aggressive posture against them will get you little more than an "angry feminist" label. That does not mean that women should have to put up with any demeaning behavior; just be cool in their counterattacks.

One of the most common sexist behaviors is the use of endearments, such as "honey," "sweetheart," and "doll." It may seem harmless enough, but every time a woman lets someone get away with it, she has allowed herself to be reduced to a sex object. She should stop it immediately and firmly with a reply such as, "My name isn't honey, so please don't call me that," or "My name isn't doll, it's Susan," repeated—always coolly—as often as necessary. Some men are chivalrously chauvinistic. They constantly remind a woman that they are not equal through little courtesies such as helping her on with her coat, holding open doors, and making comments in meetings such as, "Well, Roberta's here now, so clean up your language," or "Here comes Denise, now we can't tell any more dirty jokes." Women on the receiving end of such remarks should simply smile pleasantly and tell them it is not necessary to alter their behavior for her. If someone holds her coat or opens a door, she should accept the courtesy graciously but say, "Thanks, Tom, but that isn't necessary." She should never make a big deal out of it, especially in front of others. Men who have these habits are not even aware of what they are doing; they are not deliberately attempting to demean women. Some even think they are being casual and friendly, which is why it is inadvisable to leap down their throats. Attitudes do not change overnight; that takes a long, slow process of re-education. It is up to women —and really to all enlightened professionals—to see that the re-education takes place. Laws alone will not do it.

Fortunately, laws have gone a long way towards reducing sexual harassment in the workplace. Once it was quite pervasive, and women who complained about it were usually fired, while the offending men were unscathed. However, demanding sexual favors—regardless of whether a man or a woman is doing the demanding—is against federal law, and many companies today are swift to react to it and stop it, punishing or firing the guilty party. Alert managers should be sensitive to any such harassment in their organizations, and should take steps to stop it, rather than leaving a victim to handle the situation alone.

Sexual harassment usually occurs at the lower levels in a corporation, and most often is directed against the lowest level of female employees, such as secretaries and clerks. Women sales professionals will probably experience propositions, but little overt and persistent harassment. If, despite a professional attitude and dress, a woman receives a proposition, she should try to deflect it without striking out at someone's ego or personality, no matter how much she would like to; she can always plead that she is married or involved with someone already—and then change the subject. Even if the situation turns more difficult, the harassed party should always try to handle it on a one-to-one basis. He or she should remind the offender that asking for sexual favors is against the law; if that still does not work, the situation should be referred to the offender's superior. Court should be the last resort in seeking redress for sexual harassment. Court suits take a long time to settle and create many bad feelings on both sides. The parties involved should ask themselves if they can continue to work in an organization together, as the proceedings get messier.

In recent decades, minority managers have become less subject to overt kinds of harassment. But both women and minorities are subject to a wide range of covert actions stemming from prejudice or chauvinism.

What if you are in a meeting or a group and someone deliberately tries to embarrass you with an insulting joke or remark, for example? You are in a tough spot, because you can lose either way—if you speak up and challenge the offender or if you meekly let it go by. One response will make you look like a militant with no sense of humor, and the other will make you look like a spineless jellyfish. If you are lucky and smart, you will have cultivated some allies who will speak up for you. It is far better for an offender to be censured by others, making clear that that sort of behavior is unprofessional and unbecoming. If you have no such ally present, the best thing you can do is ignore it. You may be being baited, and your refusal to take the bait may make others uncomfortable enough to discourage such remarks in the future.

But what if someone persists in trying to discredit or embarrass you with rude remarks? You would be best advised to speak to that person privately, and say something such as, "I'd like to establish a good, cooperative working relationship with you, but I'm a bit put off by the remarks you make about _____ (you fill in the blank) whenever I'm around." This approach is risky, because it can make the person very defensive; if the person is nasty enough, he or she may keep trying to undercut you in that or some other way. But a direct approach may jolt the person out of that behavior.

Another form of chauvinistic treatment that can be quite frustrating is to be discounted or even ignored. It usually happens in meetings. A woman or minority group member speaks up with a suggestion or idea, and no one seems to pay much attention; perhaps no one even responds directly to those remarks. Then, a few minutes later, someone else pipes up with almost the same idea, and everyone applauds the suggestion. That person takes the credit, and the originator has been discounted. If that happens to you, there is not much you can do about it but keep silent. If you try to point out it was your idea originally, you will only antagonize people and look like a whining poor sport. Instead, try to prevent it from happening in the future. That means making sure that others notice you when you speak. Women, especially, are often easy to overlook or ignore because they speak softly, sometimes even timidly. Practice projecting your voice, as you would do in a group field presentation, so that it commands more attention. Be careful not to raise the pitch because your voice will begin to sound unattractive or screechy, and others will tune you out in self-defense. Keep the pitch low, but your voice strong. Get right to the point. If you are sitting in an audience, stand up when you begin to speak so that others can see you and focus their attention on you. And on days when you know you will be attending important meetings, wear a dark-colored, conservative suit, which will lend seriousness to your image.

The position of women and minorities may be undercut in other ways, too. For example, they may be assigned secretarial duties at a business meeting. If asked in advance to take notes during the meeting, to be written up as minutes, the best course is to demur, citing lack of shorthand knowledge and suggesting a secretary might be more appropriate. If that is met with the insistence that they "just jot down a few notes," you may agree to do so, if the duty is shared by others at future meetings. If asked at the start of the meeting, in front of others, they should agree pleasantly, but should tell their superior in private that they do not wish to be exclusively delegated the task. Similarly, you should not accept a "fetch-and-carry" role. If asked to see to the coffee before a meeting begins, you should turn that job over to a secretary or assistant. But whatever you do, never bring in the coffee, and never clean up the empty cups and dirty ashtrays after a meeting.

MOVING UP

All professionals must actively pursue their own career interests. Women and minorities must do so even more than most. It not only is acceptable to actively seek raises and promotions, it is expected. No professional should for a minute sit back and think that his or her strong performance will be noticed and automatically rewarded. Even if noticed without assistance, they may not be rewarded financially. Companies try to hold personnel costs down as much as possible, and if people are willing to work for less than their true market value, so much the better for the company. That is the employer's gain and the professional's loss. Do not be shy about tooting your horn, because no one else is going to do it for you. The longer people work for less than they should, the more it hurts them. It does not take long for percentage raises and bonuses to widen the gap between what you earn and what you *should* earn.

In order to make the most out of opportunities for advancement in pay and position, you must have a clear idea of your own career plans. What are your goals with your company? Do you want to change territories? Move into national account selling? Move into sales management? Once you know exactly where you are headed, tell your superior and remind him or her periodically of your aspirations. Do it in a low-key fashion at the right moments, of course, such as when you sign up for a training course. If your advancement hinges squarely on your superior's advancement, you must be especially sensitive about making your plans known.

No one likes to think that someone is out to get their job—especially while they are still in it and perhaps uncertain of their own promotion prospects.

If a slot opens up that you want, and you qualify, do not hesitate to speak up for it; otherwise no one may think of you as a candidate. Women and minorities are far more likely to be overlooked for advancement than are white men, who more or less take upward movement for granted. Many males still have a hard time thinking of women as ambitious. Be able to explain, with concrete examples, why you deserve the job and (as we stress in Chapter 3) what you have to offer. Saying you have been in your present job long enough, or that it is time to move on, will not suffice. Cite your past performance and accomplishments, and the contributions you have made to the company's operations.

Even so, you may find yourself held back for no apparent reason. If you are routinely skipped over, and management seems to turn a deaf ear to your pitch to move up and on, give notice that you are going to take the matter up with higher levels of management. If you do take your case to the next level again and again, and still get no results, prepare yourself to look for another job—you may be working for the wrong company.

If you are basically a salaried employee, and if it is a raise in your current position you are after, be aware that there are good times and bad times to ask for more money. The best time is right on the heels of a major accomplishment, which has earned you favorable recognition or attention. Do not wait for the glory to grow cold, hoping that you will be rewarded; step up and ask for it. Make your request at an appropriate moment, when conditions are favorable and time is available to consider the matter—not right before a major meeting or near an important deadline.

No matter how much you may deserve a raise, your chances of winning one will be sorely diminished if you choose to ask just when the company's earnings are down. Better to wait a few weeks. Never, however, let more than a year go by without asking for a performance review and raise. Most companies have regular schedules for such matters, but some smaller ones do not; as long as you let it slide, an employer is likely to let it slide, too.

On the other hand, mistrust excuses that put you off until another time, or justifications for small raises. Arguments that company profits are down or that a ceiling has been placed on raise amounts are often not completely true. Management somehow always finds a way to adequately reward the good performers. Chances are, the gullible employees will buy the argument and settle for less or nothing, while the funds available for raises go to those who make a strong case for them. Be persistent and firm. Do not, however, be hasty in delivering an ultimatum—"If I don't get a raise, I'll quit!"—because an ultimatum may backfire and work to an employer's advantage. Do not deliver one unless you are prepared to follow through on it. As with promotions, be sure you can back up your argument for more money by citing examples of performance; never plead financial difficulty or give the lame reason that you just "deserve" more money.

When discussing salary for a new position, do not be afraid to negotiate. Many relatively inexperienced people fear that if they try to negotiate, they will lose out altogether, but negotiation is a natural and expected part of the process for setting salaries. Know what your market worth is. You can keep current on this in a number of ways: through classified job ads in the Sunday newspaper, professional organizations, and executive recruiters. In order to negotiate effectively, you must know what your general market worth is.

Decide on a minimum figure you want to accept, and then ask for a figure higher than that. Give ample room for negotiations but do not name an astronomically high figure; remember, both sides will want to feel they have won something. As always, be prepared to show why you should be earning the amount you are seeking.

If you are interviewing for a new position and your interviewer asks what you expect to earn in that job, never reply, "What does it pay?" Such an answer starts you off in a weak bargaining position. State firmly what you expect to make. Do not be surprised if the other person protests that your sum is too much; that is a common negotiation practice. Once the other person has named a figure, you can work out a compromise in between. Women and minorities often get caught in a low-pay trap in salary negotiations. Most of them are underpaid for what they do; some are severely underpaid. An interviewer who asks what they are currently earning as a basis for calculating an offer will keep them in a low earnings trap, claiming the size of increase they are looking for cannot possibly be justified. Make it clear that your compensation must at least equal the compensation of others doing comparable jobs in your own company and throughout your industry.

If a salary ceiling on a job is firmly lower than desired, it is always possible to try to negotiate extra perks or a salary review within three to six months. Whatever arrangement is made should be confirmed in writing; otherwise a promised review can easily fall by the wayside because of a personnel change or for any number of other reasons or excuses.

Remember that the more money you command, the more you are valued by a company. People who work cheap do not get the same respect as those whose price is high. If an employer has to pay well to get a sales professional, everyone will feel that he or she must be good at the job. It is automatic for the men who still do most of the hiring in the nation's corporations to expect women and minorities to be happy working for less than other sales professionals. A prospective employer should know right from the start that competent, serious professionals expect to be paid fair market value for their worth.

PART III
PERSONAL MATTERS

CHAPTER 9
THE MONEY IN YOUR LIFE

One of the major results of a successful selling career can be financial success, and with it lifelong financial security, sometimes within the context of a rather affluent life style. On the other hand, one person's financial success is another's entrapment in a consuming life style, bringing with it a lifetime of overspending at every income level achieved, constant insecurity, and eventual near-poverty late in life.

Which is true for you depends to a considerable extent on how you see your wants and needs, how well you understand some essential facts and trends, and how consistently and well you plan the financial side of life.

The times they are always a'changing. In any "now," the present looks extraordinarily complex, the future terribly chancy. As the old saw properly puts it, hindsight is always a great deal easier than foresight. All true —but a little misleading. For some times are indeed more volatile than others, and in some periods a number of the assumptions with which we grew up may no longer be valid, making it far harder for us to plan than even a little while before.

This is one such period. The heart of the matter is that unprecedentedly long life, coupled with a worldwide long-term high rate of inflation, wrapped around a stagnant economy, has created a new situation for us all. Like it or not, yesterday's dreams are only that; we face new economic and personal financial realities.

The most obvious, and for many the least palatable, of these new realities is that most of us will not be able to retire and live whatever is our version of the good life when we reach 65. And not at 68 or 70, either. We are not likely to be working in demanding travel territories in our mid-seventies, but one way or another, we are likely to be working as long as we reasonably can, as a matter of simple economic necessity. There will be no other way to continue to live reasonably well; complete cessation of work will not come to most of us as long as we are reasonably healthy. Those of us who plan well, and learn how to turn our skills into later-years substantial sources of income will probably thoroughly enjoy our work, live well, and live longer than we might have if we had retired earlier; those who plan badly or not at all may find themselves working at difficult and uncongenial unskilled jobs, and living very modestly indeed.

It is a matter of long life, inflation, stagnation, and consequently changed expectations. The odds are that you will live 20 to 40 years past retirement. It is extremely imprudent to expect that the government will be able or willing to provide more than minimal Social Security benefits for that length of time. It is highly unlikely that private pension payments, no matter how attractive-seeming now, will provide more than a small portion of your needs for that length of time. For most managers, savings and investments will help a good deal, but will be insufficient to meet lifetime needs. The net of it all is that expectations change to meet reality. For most of us, it is not a question of whether or not to work after retirement from our jobs, but at what we will work. We discussed the matter of later-years work in Chapter 4; here let us only point out that revised expectation as to the probable length of your working career is a key element in financial planning.

A second not-very-palatable new financial reality characterizing this period is that most of us are, in real salary dollars, doing little better than marking time, and in many instances we are falling behind the pace of inflation. In these years, the financial sky is no longer the limit. Small wonder, then, that most of us are hard pressed to maintain what previously were considered modestly satisfying middle class living standards. That makes saving and investment extraordinarily difficult, and places a premium on astute long-term financial planning, to meet current wants and needs as well as those of the later years of life.

A key fact to bear in mind in terms of savings and investments is that those working in companies are not the main logical beneficiaries of the American economic system. That system favors owners far more than it does employees. The successful business owner accretes value in his or her business over the course of many years of operation; competition, necessary growth, and our tax system literally force savings and investment upon business owners. Employees have no such major accumulation forced upon them, although they can and do often gain tax advantages and accumulation through pensions, profit-sharing plans, and stock options.

But pensions may provide fixed-dollar benefits that turn out to be pathetically inadequate later on. Profit-sharing plans need substantial profits to share, and may also be very small in real dollars later. And stock options are not always available in meaningful amounts. It is necessary to plan consciously and carefully to save and invest, on a lifelong basis, for nothing in the employee's basic situation forces adequate saving and investment.

Whatever else you are—and we are far more than mere economic animals—you are also an economic entity, with many of your most cherished goals dependent upon your economic circumstances. And as an economic entity, you must of necessity strive to reach economic goals through the development and working out of economic plans, just as do the organizations within which you spend most of your working life. You must seek to:

• Maximize income, taking the widest possible view of what income really is, which means seeing your income as a total compensation package containing both short- and long-range components, and simultaneously seeking to generate income through activities not connected with work.

• Guard against the statistically predictable, though personally unpredictable, economic crises of life.

• Minimize expenditures, within the context of a flexible, ever-changing body of personal goals. Aside from a relatively small body of expenditures to provide basic necessities, all other expenditures involve choice, and the nature of our choices must be the subject of considerable and lifelong attention.

• Learn how to continuously evaluate and reevaluate your personal financial position, constantly sharpening the skills you need for financial survival.

• Generate income for personal savings and investment, and then use your resources as astutely as possible to develop further resources.

CASH AND THE COMPENSATION PACKAGE

In the long run, it is vital to view compensation not as a matter of cash compensation and fringes, but rather as a complete package composed of many elements. In that complete package, direct cash compensation must play an important role, but tax considerations and long-term financial planning goals may make other forms of compensation quite important. A dollar in direct compensation may be subject to combined federal, state, and local income taxes amounting to 60–65%, even after the federal tax changes of the early 1980s. The same dollar, in a tax-advantaged pension plan, may accrete without taxes until many years later, and the ultimate difference can be enormous.

Having said that, let us hasten to point out that cash is scarcely out of style. Far from it; current adverse economic conditions make it far more important than at any time since the Great Depression. Accumulation through tax-advantaged instruments is vital; making enough in direct compensation to make ends meet and satisfy current obligations is indispensable. And, since the same early-1980s tax changes, federal taxes on higher-range incomes have diminished somewhat, in terms of top tax brackets and the size of the brackets themselves.

Yet, assuming a basically acceptable minimum income level, it remains true that the progressive income tax and the complicated nature of the American tax system place a very high premium on tax avoidance. Those who can shield income from taxes through tax deferral and avoidance techniques can maximize real income. It is therefore necessary to pay a good deal of attention to *all* of the elements of the compensation package, certainly focusing hard on maximizing direct compensation, but also recognizing that other elements in the package may be of extraordinarily important long-term value.

For the overwhelming majority of us, cash is by far the most important element of the compensation package. For a while, in the 1950s and 1960s, that seemed less and less to be so. In a period in which the real value of the dollar eroded very little, real wages were rising sharply, taxes were on the increase, and the use of meaningful personal tax shelter devices was confined mainly to the rich, it seemed to make sense to focus on tax-advantaged and estate-building aspects of compensation.

But in the 1980s, with many real incomes declining sharply, and far more personal tax avoidance devices available than in earlier periods, the focus has shifted decisively to direct cash compensation—and that is as it must be, now and for the foreseeable future.

That does not mean adoption of a job-hopping personal style; a series of quick job changes for small income gains is still bad career strategy. It does, however, mean fighting hard within your own company to keep your direct compensation at least in line with the pace of inflation, and fighting equally hard to do better than that. If you are making $30,000 this year, and the rise in the Consumer Price Index for your area this year is 10%, you need a $3,000+ increase in direct compensation just to keep up. The $3,000 is a 10% increase; the "plus" is whatever additional amount is needed to pay the additional taxes due from your arrival in higher tax brackets. And if you are making $50,000 this year, and the Price Index rise is 12%, you need a $6,000+ increase just to keep up. Under those circumstances, a focus on direct cash compensation is absolutely necessary.

Looking at it that way, the income levels achieved in the last decade by such diverse occupational groups as doctors, unionized factory workers, secretaries, and some lawyers no longer look quite as large as when they are looked at comparatively. These groups have kept up with and in some instances pulled ahead of the Consumer Price Index. Some sales professionals have done so, too; many have not.

Many cannot; it is unrealistic to expect that average sales incomes in troubled industries will keep up with the pace of inflation. No matter how skilled and valuable, sales professionals in deeply troubled sections of the automobile, steel, and publishing industries cannot look forward to long, happy, prosperous careers. Quite the contrary; they can look forward to insecurity, worsening real incomes, and increasing dissatisfaction. Prudent people will, in those circumstances, not only seek the soundest companies in the industry, but will give very serious thought to changing industries, with increased cash compensation in mind.

It is easy enough to make a rough, but basically accurate and extraordinarily telling, analysis of where you have been headed in terms of cash compensation in previous years. All you need do is compare the Consumer Price Index, still popularly known as the Cost of Living Index, with your cash compensation. It is simplest, for these rough calculation purposes, to omit tax considerations, and compare the Index with your pre-tax cash compensation. It should be recognized, however, that most taxpayers have paid increasingly higher proportions of their pre-tax income as taxes during the last 15–20 years, as a consequence of increased tax rates in the higher tax brackets in which they have found themselves; the term used to describe this is *bracket creep*. It should also be recognized that this comparison does not take into account the pronounced decline of quality and durability we have experienced during this period; these are the chief elements in what is called "hidden" inflation. Therefore, these comparisons are, if anything, somewhat understated; the situation is even worse than the comparisons indicate.

Using 1967 as a base year, which is what the Bureau of Labor Statistics does, 1967 becomes 100, and all changes in the Consumer Price Index are related to that year. Using that yardstick, the Consumer Price Index in 1982 stood in the middle 270s, and has moved from there to whatever level it now stands at. That means that for all practical purposes you had to earn about $2.75 in 1982 for each dollar you earned in 1967, just to keep up with the pace of inflation!

Using that rough but effective comparison, someone earning $20,000 in 1967 needed to be making $55,000 in 1982, just to keep up with inflation. Someone making $25,000 then needed to be making $68,750; and someone at $30,000 then needed $82,500 to break even with inflation.

Most sales professionals did not do anywhere near that well, even if they moved well in their careers, steadily stepping up to increasing status and responsibility. The net effect is that in the last decade and a half most have suffered a net loss in cash compensation, even as they pursued what seemed to be highly successful careers.

The picture became even worse in the mid- to late-1970s, as inflation accelerated. Between 1973 and 1981, a period of only eight years, the Consumer Price Index doubled, meaning that if you made $30,000 in 1973 you had to make $60,000 in 1981 just to keep up with the pace of inflation. And very few indeed did that.

All of which makes it very clear that direct cash compensation is a more important element of the total compensation package than at any time in the last two decades. It will probably continue to be so in the foreseeable future, and will need to be fought for, as companies try to survive and grow in very adverse economic conditions.

That cash compensation may be straight salary, straight commissions, or any of the wide variety of sales compensation arrangements in between these two ends of the compensation spectrum. For most sales professionals, it is likely to be a combination of salary (or nonreturnable "draw," which is operationally equivalent to a minimum salary) plus incentive pay tied to individual or group sales performance, or both. Incentives are likely to be paid, at least in part, monthly, with some incentive pay often depending upon quarterly and annual performances.

Most successful sales professionals have traditionally liked compensation tied in large part to prices, and that is especially so in periods of considerable inflation. When pay depends on commissions figured basically as a percentage of sales dollars brought into the house, then an automatic escalator is built into sales compensation. When prices go up, those who can keep unit sales even at current levels get more money, and if the company is able to raise prices enough to keep up with the pace of inflation, that amounts to a cost of living increase in income. And if unit sales are increasing, or product lines are developing, or renewals and step-ups to larger quantities are increasing average sales, compensation goes up accordingly. When compensation is tied to sales dollars, there is no need to negotiate salary increases or to resist constant management pressure to maximize profits by not raising sales salaries to reflect sales dollar increases.

There are attacks, however, on sales incomes in many companies that do tie compensation to sales dollars; that is inevitable in good times and bad, and particularly to be expected when companies are not doing well. Those attacks may take the form of direct slashes in percentages of sales dollars paid as compensation, but are far more likely to arrive as new and "fairer" sales compensation plans, which will in the not so very long run actually trim sales incomes. Sales and marketing managements often resist such attacks on the sales force, however, reasoning quite correctly that it is they who will have to take the blame for consequent defections of star sales professionals and worsened overall sales performance. Astute top managements worry about these kinds of attacks, too, for they very well know that you tamper at your own peril with the geese that lay the golden eggs—which is exactly what good sales professionals are for any company.

All by way of pointing out that incentive arrangements based in large part upon sales dollars as well as unit sales performance are most easily defended against attack, in the long run are likely to yield more compensation dollars, and should continue to be a preferred form of compensation for sales professionals.

For many in selling, though, the main element of direct compensation is salary, which is not directly tied to sales dollars. Then it is a matter of consistently expecting to be paid what you are worth, not being at all afraid to ask for justified increases, and making it clear that you are indeed the goose that lays the golden eggs, and must be compensated accordingly. Which means not waiting for increases, but asking for them, and doing your best to make sure that those increases really do bear a significant relation to the increased sales dollars you are producing, whether or not compensation is directly tied to those sales dollars.

INSURANCE

For most sales professionals, some kinds of life and health insurances are part of the total compensation package. Both insurance terms are of course triumphant euphemisms, for the basic life insurance transaction is the payment of premiums to protect others against the catastrophe of *your* death, and the basic health insurance transaction protects you and others against the adverse consequences of your illness or incapacity.

Except for life insurance amounts over a legally set limit, such employer-provided insurances are exceedingly tax-advantaged, being taken by the employer as business expenses and nontaxable to employees. Premiums paid on life insurance coverage over the legal limit (at this writing $50,000) are taxable as income to those covered, however.

In a very real sense, then, such tax-advantaged insurances are government subsidized, for the tax monies that might come from them must come from elsewhere. And the premiums paid are therefore worth far more than they would have been as wages, for wages are taxable. If you are in a total federal, state, and local top income tax bracket amounting to 50%, for example, and are paying for life insurance out of after-tax earnings, every dollar you pay in premiums is equal to two dollars in pretax earnings. By the same token, every dollar spent by your employer on your life insurance coverage is worth two dollars to you in direct compensation. The tax savings on employer-provided health insurance work out somewhat differently, but the tax advantages to you are still very considerable.

Employer-provided group life insurance, however, can also result in personal disaster, if you fail to plug an almost universal "hole" in such coverage. The nature of the coverage causes the problem. Employer-provided plans are normally group plans providing term insurance; that is, insurance without savings or investment features, which provide only for the catastrophe of the death of the insured. They are also plans that average risk over the lives of the entire group insured, which usually includes people of all ages, including many who are quite young. When you terminate your employment, and with it your group life insurance coverage, you will usually be able to convert the group coverage over to individual coverage; however, it will often be at a much higher rate of premium payment than before. That is because the insurance company will often be able to insist on selling you individual coverage that includes savings and investment features—the "whole life" or "straight life" policy —which is therefore far more expensive to you than the group coverage was to your employer. Further, you may be considerably older than the average age of the group you have just left, and will be subject to much higher premium payments on that account.

For most, the practical alternative would seem to be to buy individual term insurance, which is less expensive, and perhaps to take somewhat less of it than the previous employer's coverage, until a new job carrying group life coverage as part of the compensation is secured. *But that is when the trap may be sprung*—for you may then be found uninsurable. Then your only alternative may be to convert to ruinously expensive individual straight life coverage, or to buy far less of that expensive insurance than you had and really need.

The only sure way to avoid this possibility is to buy basic life insurance coverage of your own, whether a term policy, or a whole life policy purchased early in your career and therefore carrying relatively small level-payment premiums. How much to buy depends entirely on your perceived needs. A single person with substantial other assets will clearly need far less life insurance than someone with a large family and small other assets. A young parent will need more than will someone whose children are grown and out on their own. You will certainly want to carry enough life insurance of your own to guard your loved ones against destitution for at least a couple of years if untimely death should take you; you may want to go as high as five or six times your current annual earnings.

In considering the question of life insurance, it is wise to go beyond the question of the total compensation package to the underlying question of how much life insurance you think you need to protect others. Even when life insurance premiums paid by an employer for you over a legally prescribed limit are taxable to you as income, it may be desirable to have as much life insurance as possible provided by your employer. That is sometimes a matter of negotiation between you and your employer, part of the entire set of negotiations attendant upon offer and acceptance of a new job. The premiums paid by an employer as part of group life insurance coverage will probably be much smaller than you would have to pay as an individual. A combination of a good deal of employer-supplied group coverage and minimum basic personal coverage of your own should best suit most insurance needs at the least possible cost.

Employer-provided health insurance coverage can also be a highly desirable and tax-advantaged portion of your total compensation package. Coverages provided may include only the basic Blue Cross–Blue Shield coverage provided to tens of millions of employees by employers, in itself desirable and tax-advantaged; but coverages may also include far, far more. Some basic hospital–surgical group plans provided by insurance companies contracting with employers include far better hospital and surgical coverage, as well as such otherwise personally expensive features as complete or very nearly complete payment for dental, psychiatric, obstetric, doctor's office, and several other kinds of pre- and post-hospital health care. Many also include major medical coverage, which takes over where the basic insurances end, and covers employees for 80–100% of costs, sometimes up to as much as one million dollars for each covered illness. A few include disability insurance, providing payments when you are disabled and off the employer's payroll for an extended period.

Given the enormous and accelerating costs of health care, major medical insurance is truly catastrophe insurance. We live in a time when a single illness not covered by catastrophe insurance may wipe out a family's assets. It is not at all unusual for combined surgical, hospital, intensive care, and nursing home costs over a two-year period to go up into the $100,000–$200,000 range, far beyond normal ability to pay out of personal assets.

Given these facts, you should carefully assess your company coverage. Many employers provide coverage up to only $50,000 or $100,000 per covered illness. That was quite enough 20 years ago; it is not nearly enough today, and should really be supplemented by an excess or "piggyback" major medical policy, which takes over where employer coverage ends. Many such policies have very high deductibles; that is, they start paying only after $10,000–$25,000 in other benefits have been paid by the employer's coverage. And, as most major medical policies "coordinate" benefits, premiums are often very small, since as a practical matter many such policies start paying benefits only after $50,000–$100,000 have been paid by employer insurance. Today's health care cost crisis makes such personal coverage mandatory, unless company-provided insurance provides major medical coverage up into the $500,000–$1,000,000 per covered illness range.

However, some basic personal major medical coverage is necessary in any event, *for there are two potentially devastating traps here,* which are present in most employer-supplied major medical insurance plans and some basic hospital–surgical plans as well.

The first is the pre-existing conditions trap, which works this way. An employee is covered by an employer's insurance plan during the period of employment. On termination of employment, the insurance coverage ends, usually after a period of 30 days after formal termination. If the coverage in question is basic Blue Cross–Blue Shield protection, then either a new individual or family plan or a new company-sponsored plan will take over without problems, with all coverages in place as if there had been no break of any kind. On the other hand, some basic plans and most major medical plans provide only for continuation of plans on an individual basis, usually at prohibitively high costs and often at much lower benefit levels coverage than the previously held group plans provided. Under those circumstances, even if you convert your health insurance to individual insurance on termination, you have only inferior, high-cost insurance. Yet if you do not convert, and are carrying no other health insurance—and very many are in this situation—you will have a gap in your coverage, which can conceivably cost you everything. For if you, or anyone in your family, have any kind of major illness that can be traced to a pre-existing condition, either during a period of unemployment or during a period of six months to two years (depending on your new employer's coverage) you may not be covered at all. That can be expensive and disheartening when basic coverage is involved, and an illness costs thousands of dollars; but that is usually something that can be handled. However, when the illness involves major costs—the kinds of costs major medical coverages are designed to handle—lack of coverage can be a financial disaster.

The other trap here lies in the area of potential uninsurability. Suppose you work along for many years, covered by an employer's basic and major medical health insurances, and then leave your employment not for other employment but to strike out on your own. You may be able to secure basic coverage, with or without the presence of the pre-existing conditions trap, as that coverage is available without a physical examination. But you may find yourself uninsurable as regards personal major medical insurance, and therefore wide open for catastrophe, for after a major illness today you may heal physically far more quickly than you will financially.

To avoid both traps, it may be wise to secure major medical coverage of your own. Often group coverage is available through membership in such organizations as alumni associations and fraternal organizations, and that is especially valuable if you are otherwise uninsurable, for such group policies do not usually require medical examinations. And if you are in good health, individual and family coverage may be available. Unfortunately, such insurance will be rather expensive in any case, if issued by a substantial and well-funded insurance company. Whatever the type of insurance, it is vital that it be on a guaranteed renewable basis, meaning that the company cannot cancel your policy as long as premium payments are up to date, and they cannot raise premium rates unless they are raised on the whole class of policies of which the individual policy is part. Anything less than that kind of coverage is not worth paying for at all, for personal catastrophe insurance is one of the bedrocks of personal financial planning, and catastrophe insurance has to be there if you ever need it.

Some employers also provide disability insurance as part of the total compensation package. That can be a very worthwhile element of compensation, and once again a tax-advantaged one. Many purchase disability policies on an individual basis as well, although individual policy premiums are usually rather expensive. Unless family responsibilities seem to make this kind of coverage quite desirable, it should be viewed cautiously, as possibly adding an unnecessary personal expense element.

PENSION AND PROFIT-SHARING PLANS

Most sales professionals have some kind of company or institution-supplied pension plan, as well as the insurance plans just discussed. Many companies also supply profit-sharing plans. Both pension and profit-sharing plans can be greatly tax-advantaged, if they meet minimum legal reporting and administrative requirements—and most do. They therefore can be extremely important elements of the total compensation package.

The essence of the taxing arrangements involved is that employer contributions are treated as business expenses when incurred and not treated as income to employees until some later date; in the interim they are allowed to compound tax-free. That is no small advantage. Current tax and interest rates make a dollar saved in a tax-advantaged pension fund or a profit-sharing plan worth a good deal more than a dollar received in direct compensation, from which taxes are then deducted. If you are in a combined federal, state, and local 50% income tax bracket, you must earn $2 in direct compensation to net $1 for spending, savings, or investment. If you save one net after-tax dollar per year for 20 years, compounding at a seeming 12%, you will really be compounding at 6% with a total yield of $38.99 over that period, for you will have to pay taxes on your interest earnings over the years. But if you are accumulating in a tax-advantaged pension or profit-sharing plan, your real 12% compounding will yield $80.70 in that 20 years, well over twice as much. And if your pension or profit-sharing earnings are truly equivalent to your after-tax earnings, your employer will be putting $2 into the plan every year, not your after-tax $1. The difference between $1 in after-tax savings compounding for 20 years at a fully taxed 12%, and $2 in pre-tax earnings so accumulating is the difference between $38.99 and $161.40. To accumulate, then, $2,000 per year in pre-tax earnings at 12% for 20 years will create a fund of $161,400, while to save the net proceeds of $2,000 in direct compensation at the same rate of interest over the same period will create a fund of $38,900. In terms of total long-term compensation, therefore, an employee in these circumstances will create a fund more than four times as large as otherwise might have been possible, and the net effect of $2,000 put into a retirement plan every year is as if it had been well over $8,000 in compensation, figured in constant dollars. You will have to pay taxes on your long-term gains in later years, but in all probability at much lower long-term capital gains tax rates than you would pay now, and at a time when your income may be much lower than it is now.

It all sounds wonderful. And it is, for very long-term employees of companies that are doing well and will continue to do well over the course of our very long working lives. But there are a lot of pitfalls here, so many that you would be imprudent to depend on corporate pension and profit-sharing plans for long-term financial security. Many allow themselves to become that dependent, thinking that a combination of long-term corporate plans and government-sponsored social insurances will take them through their later years comfortably.

One major pitfall has little to do with corporate and other institutional plans, but rather stems from the mobility of many sales professionals in pursuing their careers. It is not at all uncommon to move from job to job, freely making advantageous moves as they become possible. You may work for two companies while in your twenties, two more in your thirties, another in your forties, and make what may or may not be a final career move in your fifties, steadily moving up all the way. If so, you may never stay anywhere long enough to have any significant long-term pension rights "vest," that is, entitle you to some payments out of the corporate plan when you retire many years later, even if then employed by another firm. Or you may have some vested rights in one or more company plans, but your tenure may have been only long enough to vest, not long enough to accumulate significant benefit sums.

In addition, corporate pension and profit-sharing plan funds are quite outside your control, depending upon management initiative or union–management negotiations as to size of employer contribution, fund management, and benefit amounts. Some plans provide for voluntary employee contributions, but since such contributions are from after-tax income, the incentive to do so is small. Tax-advantaged plans are federally regulated, and to some extent federally insured, so that the chance of total default on the part of an otherwise bankrupt employer is minimal. That has happened, however, and can happen again, at a time when conditions have changed and regulation has loosened.

Default, however, is only one adverse possibility. If a business is doing badly, a pension plan's benefits may in the long run be greatly reduced. And there have to be profits to pay into a profit-sharing plan. Badly managed corporate plans—and there have been and are many such—may invest badly, depleting funds that should be available for employee retirement benefits.

Even when a fund is well managed, and its sponsoring company is doing rather well, pension plan payments are very often in fixed amounts, with no provision made for inflation during the retirement years, and that is all too often a financial disaster for retirees. Ten to twenty years after retirement, benefits that seemed adequate on retirement may be pathetically inadequate to support even a modestly decent living standard. Inflation guarantees that. Actually, a pension plan may ultimately turn out to be an illusion, for a plan paying a fixed sum and coordinated with Social Security benefits, which are somewhat indexed to inflation, may ultimately pay no benefits at all, with all benefits coming from the Social Security component, which will be far too small in real dollars to meet basic needs.

As is true of all kinds of deferred payment compensation package elements, the larger and better established the company, the better the chance of eventual payout as promised. American Telephone and Telegraph is more likely to be there and paying pension benefits in 20 years than is a small, lightly capitalized company in a sick industry.

Profit-sharing plans are found in companies of all sizes, but most often in small companies, sometimes in conjunction with and sometimes without an accompanying pension plan. Such plans are often used to create substantial incentives for employees, to defer taxation on some corporate earnings because of owner contributions to plans, and to provide a flexible means of building retirement funds. While pension plans require regular employer fund contributions, employers may contribute to profit-sharing plan funds only from profits, and only up to 15% of wages paid. In years of loss or low profit, there may be no contributions at all, while in profitable years, the foregone contributions of previous years may be added to the year's 15%.

For some, the corporate deferred compensation plan is an excellent tax deferral vehicle. Such plans provide for the withholding of a stated portion of what would otherwise be direct compensation, on which income taxes are thereby deferred until later payout, usually at retirement or on leaving employment. Funds so held for an employee by a company are normally placed in some kind of funding vehicle, so that they may accrete tax-free until payout. On payout, the gain on the withheld money is treated as ordinary income, but is often paid after years of tax-free accretion and at lower income rates than might have been paid earlier.

While you will normally be unable to control any major aspect of most pension and profit-sharing plans, deferred compensation is often a matter of choice, and sometimes a matter of negotiation during the job selection process. It can be extremely useful as a tax-deferral device, but at the same time should be seen as little more than a company's promise to pay you deferred earnings at some future date. Again, if the company is American Telephone and Telegraph, your chances of receiving promised payouts are good—not certain, but good. If the company is a small and struggling one, however, you may want to look for tax-deferral elsewhere, and take all your direct compensation as soon as it is earned.

STOCK OPTIONS

The same kind of thinking applies to the question of stock options. Even though in 1976 they were made far less tax-advantaged than they had been before, since the 1981 tax law they have once again become far more attractive as part of a total compensation package. As of this writing, the basic transaction consists of a corporation's grant to employees of the right to buy company stock at a fixed price, which may be advantageous if the stock has risen when the employee exercises the option. Capital gains taxes only are paid on stock sale, and are due only on sale. To qualify for such a tax-advantaged treatment, corporations must meet applicable statutory and regulatory requirements. As a practical matter, you can normally safely assume that your company has met those requirements, and that the option you are offered as a qualified stock option is that.

You can substantially add to long-term total compensation by exercising proffered stock options—by buying company stock—if the stock is up over the option price and if there is substantial reason to believe it will stay over the option price during any specified minimum holding period, and if there is a ready market for the stock and your sale does not depress its price. You cannot sell the option itself; it must be exercised by you within the number of months or years provided by its own terms or it becomes worthless.

In a depressed market, stock options in most companies are not worth much. But even in a depressed market, some companies do well, and can reasonably be expected to do well in the future. If you work for such a company, stock options can be valuable. On the other hand, if your company's stock has been very sluggish, and you have stock options available, you may not choose to exercise them, even if that stock has made a temporary recovery. By the time you are able to exercise the option, you may find that the stock has gone down again, and that you will suffer a loss if you sell. All too often, as so many found when the boom markets of the mid-1960s became the depressed markets of the 1970s and early 1980s, optioned stock then becomes just another bad investment. In the late 1960s, many corporate employees borrowed substantial sums to finance stock option purchases, only to find themselves saddled with enormous debts rather than with appreciated stock. That is a very considerable hazard in stock option situations, for many substantial options require investment far beyond the current means of those exercising them. If you decide to borrow to exercise a stock option, consider the debt and debt service you will thereby incur, the possible future movement of the stock in question, and carefully think about whether or not the risk is anywhere near the possible reward.

The one kind of long-term, tax-advantaged investment plan that every employee should have, beyond all company arrangements, is an Individual Retirement Account (IRA). At this writing, federal tax law allows individuals to place up to $2,000 per year, married couples with a nonworking spouse up to $2,250 per year, and married couples with both spouses working up to $4,000 a year into an Individual Retirement Account. Sums placed in such accounts may be subtracted from gross income and funds in such accounts accrete tax-free. In essence, the tax advantage is much like that offered in most company pension plans, but has few of the hazards and lack of control associated with company pension plan participation. You will be taxed on the gain in the account later in life, when you begin to draw money out of your account, but at capital gains rates and after many years of tax-free accumulation. The advantages are so obvious that those who do not open such accounts are missing a truly enormous capital accumulation opportunity. Only one caution here: be very careful to evaluate which of the very many plans available, from all kinds of financial organizations, offers you the best terms and best suits your investment approach. In this area, professional advice will be most helpful.

EDUCATION AID

Another often-encountered element of the total compensation package is education aid. It may occur as continuing professional education paid for by your company, as when the company sends you to an outside course for anywhere from a day to several months, and with a direct investment in you of anything from less than $100 to well over $10,000, plus your fully compensated time. It may also occur in the form of tuition reimbursement, as when you take night courses at a local business school, or as an education loan at favorable rates for you or to you for other members of your family. However education aid occurs, it can be and often is a notably beneficial element of compensation, well worth seeing clearly as such.

PERKS

A considerable body of other compensation package elements are often lumped together and described as *perks,* or *perquisites,* from the British usage. Some are quite useful, some are merely unproductive exercises in conspicuous consumption.

Among the most useful are the whole body of negotiated matters around a relocation, including such matters as company payment of moving expenses, home price guarantees, and mortgage assistance. Also very useful are holiday and severance pay arrangements, company-funded and -assisted low-interest and interest-free loans, professional association dues, and the provision of free financial counseling. These are quite valuable additional elements of compensation, and are well worth seeking.

For travelers, company-provided vehicles and payment of associated expenses are particularly valuable elements of compensation, as are per diem or item-by-item expense account arrangements. Although travel territories often pay higher percentage commissions than do metropolitan territories, the cost of doing business on the road has in recent years gone up so steeply that the higher commissions that once adequately made up for higher travel selling costs now no longer offset those higher costs.

Somewhat less useful—but much sought—are those perks that have to do with "expense account living," including such matters as some kinds of entertainment expenses and country club memberships. From the sales professional's point of view, these are properly seen as elements of compensation, although—like the other "perks" mentioned—they are largely business expenses from a tax point of view.

In fact, some are very much elements of compensation, and not to recognize them as such involves little more than legal and tax fictions. A country club membership may demonstrably be for business reasons, and so recognized by tax authorities, but we would be remiss if we did not identify it as in the main a matter of compensation.

But this kind of compensation is not really worth much in the long run. The manager who lets these kinds of "perks" become important is merely hooked on conspicuous consumption. Cash now, meaningful long-term, tax-deferred compensation arrangements, and many fringes and perks are economically useful, and help meet needs and develop savings and investment now and for the future. But some perks are merely waste.

CONSPICUOUS CONSUMPTION

In a way, these kinds of perks are the worst kind of overspending trap. The sales professional who lives "high on the hog" on company money is all too often a man or woman who takes that kind of wasteful overspending into the personal side of life, where conspicuous consumption is in the long run little more than the traditional one-way ticket to the poorhouse.

Conspicuous consumption—the "keeping up with and going one better than the Joneses" trap—is just that. The habit of overspending destroys the possibility of effective lifetime personal planning, by making saving and investment impossible. It makes us vulnerable to adverse but predictable economic events, guarantees that we will spend our most productive years paying off old debts and incurring new ones, and that we will face the prospect of spending our later years as de facto wards of the state.

While much conspicuous consumption is easily recognizable, a good deal of what is in reality overspending is not so easily perceived. In these times, someone who buys an expensive sports car and pays for it in 60 mammoth monthly payments at enormous rates of interest is clearly engaged in conspicuous consumption. So is the male or female clothes horse, who has closets full of expensive clothes and drawers full of unpaid bills to match.

But overspending is not only a matter of conspicuous consumption. It consists even more often of converting what are really only personal wants into perceived personal and family needs. The family that lives in a "good" neighborhood or suburb, lives "well," entertains often, vacations expensively, buys new cars frequently, and sends its children to the "best" private schools and colleges often sees itself and is seen by others as a family in the process of fulfilling the American dream, as long as it does not go too deeply into debt while doing so—often even if debts are quite substantial.

But surely it must be easy to see that for many such families the American dream will in the long run turn out to be little more than a nightmare. Even in the short run, a family with substantial debts and little in the way of assets is entirely vulnerable to a single job loss, a single major illness, a single period of unemployment lasting for a year or more. Often, with both wife and husband working full time, the loss of either income for a considerable period brings on a financial crisis. Even in the medium term, the onset of college costs often brings on an effective financial wipeout, to be painfully surmounted over many years of payback, with both parents and children in debt for a decade or more after college has been completed. And in the long term, failure to save and invest during the most productive years, coupled with long life, virtually guarantees many years of poor and hard living later in life.

For most sales professionals, who are after all people working productively at rather good jobs and with reasonably good economic possibilities, it is a matter of current life style and short-term expectations. Much of what is thought of as reasonable expenditure is in reality overconsumption, once saving and investment are viewed as current necessities, rather than future possibilities.

Two examples make the point somewhat more concretely. The first is that classic personal financial trap: the more-expensive-than-necessary home purchase.

When one or both of the partners in a marriage are bringing in what seem to be reasonably good incomes, buying a relatively expensive home in a community that cares a great deal about its schools, about keeping out industry, and about the status of its citizens seems a perfectly sound idea; once again, a piece of the American dream. Of course, that kind of home is going to be somewhat more expensive than a home in a less affluent, but caring, community, which has allowed light industry to move in, and which all in all is not really as good an address.

Somewhat more expensive? No, *much* more expensive, once the costs are clearly seen. Let us assume that you buy a home for $150,000 in a rather affluent community (not an extremely expensive home by current standards) and that you are forced to make a one third down payment of $50,000 and secure a mortgage loan of $100,000. Let's also assume that your average interest rate over the 30 years of your mortgage is 15%, whether you have a fixed-rate mortgage for that amount or a variable-rate mortgage that so averages out over the term of the mortgage. Although you may have to secure a second mortgage to be able to make that enormous down payment, we will leave that interest out of our calculations.

Your level payments on that $100,000 mortgage over a 30-year period will come to $1,264.44 monthly, for a total of $455,200. Your taxes in that affluent community are hard to estimate, but assuming a current $3,000 per year in taxes and a 7% per year increase, your taxes will average about $12,000 per year for the 30-year mortgage period—and let us stress that this is a low estimate. You will also probably continue to get tax avoidance on mortgage interest and taxes during the period, which we do not include here because it is so individually variable, as in the instance of second mortgage interest above.

Roughly then, but sufficiently for purposes of this illustration, your $50,000 down payment plus your $455,000 in mortgage payments, plus your $360,000 in tax payments totals $865,000 during the 30-year mortgage period add up to quite a lot more than the seeming $150,000 purchase price.

Assume now that you had purchased a home in a neighboring community—probably as large or nearly as large as the home you bought in the affluent community—but not nearly as prestigious. You might have had to pay $120,000 for that home; that is 20% less, and probably not very far from the going price of prestige.

Assuming all other factors being equal, but a 20% smaller purchase price and 20% less in taxes—though the tax reduction would probably be greater—you would then have a down payment of $40,000, a mortgage of $80,000, and average taxes of $9,600, with a monthly mortgage payment of $1,011.56 and a total 30-year price of $749,761, or *$115,000 less* than you would pay for the house that seems to cost only $30,000 more at the start. That $115,000 saved can be a substantial chunk of the family's needed education money, or the start of a substantial retirement fund. Prestige, in this instance, turns out to cost a great deal more than it seemed.

Clearly, the over-expensive home in the over-expensive community is a huge financial trap. Another such pitfall—one of truly enormous proportions for most middle- and upper middle-class American families—is the "best college" trap. For reasons having to do far more with status striving and upward social mobility than with comparative educational quality, some of the most expensive private colleges in the United States have come to be widely identified as the "best" colleges in the country.

The truth is that in terms of educational quality no one has yet satisfactorily identified that constellation of elements that can be used to so classify colleges. In fact, looking at such factors as faculty salaries, seminar sizes, library availability and size, and Graduate Record Examination scores, many public colleges are at least as educationally sound as their private—and far more expensive—counterparts. It remains true that on a few—a very few—fast career tracks, an undergraduate degree with honors from Harvard will help greatly in getting into graduate school. And it is also true that a graduate degree with honors from a "top" school will help entry into some fast career tracks in the professions. But that's all. For a few highly and specifically motivated young people, therefore, relatively enormous private college expenditures may be justified. For the vast majority, they are quite unnecessary. Such expenditures are all too often undertaken to satisfy parent status needs rather than student educational needs, and result only in draining the family of funds and plunging it deep into debt. It is not at all unusual for parents to run out of money and credit as well, long before even undergraduate school is completed, forcing students to borrow heavily and mortgage their futures; even then students sometimes fall short of the ability to finance their needed and desired graduate school educations.

Taking all expenditures into account, supporting a student in an expensive private college such as Harvard, Yale, Amherst, or Bard, or in graduate school (not considering medical schools, which are even more expensive), costs in the $12,000–$15,000 per year range as of this writing. Taking the lower figure, that means $48,000 for a four-year undergraduate education. A family sending three children to college, with an average of one year of graduate school each, would therefore have to spend $12,000 per year times 15 college years to get its children through college. That is $180,000. An absurd number? Yes, indeed, but a real one. Families are doing it today, often with disastrous long-term economic results for both parents and children. And the impact is even greater than it seems, for this is all after-tax income; at a 50% tax level, roughly two dollars would have to be earned for every dollar paid out in college costs.

Contrast this enormous sum with what it would take to send all three children to college and graduate school on a less expensive—but educationally just as sound—basis. The average total cost per year in a publicly supported college is likely to be in the $4,000–$5,000 per year range, varying somewhat with state of residence and in-state or out-of-state student classification. Assuming the lower rate, as we did above, and assuming that graduate school will cost as much as $8,000 per year on this basis, the total anticipated cost of getting all three children through college becomes $4,000 per year times 12 college years for undergraduate school and $8,000 per year times 3 college years for graduate school—a total of $72,000. That is still a very great expenditure for most families, and means working, saving, and a great deal of borrowing, but it is *$108,000 less* than it would cost in expensive private colleges and graduate schools! And that $108,000 is not money the family has; it is money that would have to be borrowed, if the loans were available, carrying very heavy long-term interest costs on top of the principal repayments due.

For most of us, then, avoiding the personal consumption and status traps can mean the difference between being able to save and invest, and a lifetime of entrapment in a mountain of high-interest-bearing debt. And that, in turn, can make the difference between being able to function freely in our careers, taking chances when we think we should, and being forced to stay with stale, dead-end jobs because they are safe, and because we desperately need the current income just to make ends meet. It can make the difference between going to work for a promising young company or staying with a big company; between going into business on your own— with all the promise and risk that entails—or not; between one or both of the partners in a marriage trying an alternative career, or not; between semiretiring at 65 and not being able to retire at all; or in the long run, between being old, sick, and broke, or being able to take care of yourself reasonably well for the rest of your life. High stakes, indeed!

PERSONAL FINANCIAL PLANNING

Effective personal financial planning carries with it very high lifelong rewards. Conversely, failure to plan consistently and work your plan brings with it high lifelong risks. What is astonishing to many personal financial planners is that most sales professionals, who are so used to thinking of themselves as independent professionals in their own small businesses, fail to do anything like effective planning for themselves.

Your financial life is a small business; it deserves to be treated as such. Effective personal planning has very little to do with counting pennies at the supermarket (though that's not a bad idea) any more than in your company it has much to do with counting and dispensing paper clips. But it has everything to do with ensuring a constant flow of good information;

securing good advice from trusted advisors; continually and correctly assessing and tracking your personal situation; properly organizing your personal financial life; becoming completely and skillfully familiar with available financial alternatives; guarding against the impact of unforeseen catastrophes; and engaging in informed decision-making within the context of your personal and financial goals. That is exactly what good small business owners do; it is just as necessary and valuable for your personal life.

INFORMATION AND ADVICE

Good information upon which to base personal financial decisions can come from a variety of sources. To a very considerable extent, such information will come from the same sources you use to obtain good business information, many of which are described and discussed in Part 6 of this book, on Sources of Information.

Beyond such general business information sources—some of which, like *The Wall Street Journal,* also serve as good investment information and insight sources—you will probably want to secure some materials that focus on financial information and advice. One such tool will be a basic financial planning guide. Much of the material in this chapter is based upon the book *Personal Financial Survival,* by David M. Brownstone and Jacques Sartisky (Wiley, 1981). Another standard work is Hallman and Rosenbloom's *Personal Financial Planning* (McGraw-Hill, 1979). Both attempt to provide integrated approaches to personal planning, rather than the potpourri of financial advice provided by most "money books."

You probably should also have an up-to-date investor's dictionary. As of this writing, that need is satisfied by the Brownstone and Franck's *Investor's Dictionary* (Van Nostrand Reinhold, 1981), although other such books may appear in the future that will satisfy the need equally well.

You may also want to subscribe to one or more general investment publications, such as the Barron's, Value Line, Janeway, or Holt advisory services. Some people who are interested in closely following specific kinds of investments may want to reach for sources that focus sharply on such areas of interest as options, collectibles, gold, and real estate.

Only by carefully securing and maintaining such sources of continuing information and advice can you hope to become at least the "semipro" you need to be to adequately take care of your financial planning needs. At the same time, you will be well advised to reach equally carefully for financial advisors, finding and holding those you trust and respect for many years. Your financial advisors are some of the most important people in your life, and should be chosen with that fact in mind, rather than being casually acquired through chance recommendation and the accident of physical proximity.

The overwhelming majority of sales professionals cannot afford even substantial part-time financial planning advice, but must instead depend on those who offer such advice as part of other services rendered. The accountant who handles your taxes, the stockbroker who handles some of your investment transactions, the insurance seller, the banker, and the attorney all render financial planning advice. Some of the advice given is excellent and right in line with your goals and game plans; some is so self-interested as to be misleading and harmful; some is well-meant and incompetently rendered. The trick, as is always true in both business and personal management, is in your skill at people-picking.

Someone whose main business it is to sell you something may not always be an impartial advisor, for even the best intentions in the world can—and usually do—succumb to the advisor's own self-interest. Often that is not a matter of shrewd calculation at all, but rather a matter of attitudes formed by what there is to sell. It is the rare stockbroker indeed who has the objectivity or personal breadth necessary to be able to counsel a customer to make investment decisions in which the broker will have no financial participation at all. As between purchase of local real estate for investment purposes and participation in a syndication, for example, the broker is quite likely to have the syndication to sell, and not the local real estate. Similarly, it is unrealistic to expect a life insurance seller to tell you that you do not need any more life insurance, or that by dropping some of your life insurance you can liberate some cash for the professional education of a nonworking spouse. And the day of the small-town banker, who functioned as a full-time financial advisor to the whole community, is long gone. Your banker is quite likely to be a few years out of school, eager to put you into whatever financial vehicles the bank is currently selling, and poised with one foot out the bank's door in the course of pursuing a career in banking, being a young manager on the move. The truth is that it is not easy to find excellent advice on a modest budget; but such advice is indispensable. And when something is that important, you do it, however difficult, in personal management as in corporate management.

Your main advisor most likely will be a Certified Public Accountant (CPA), although in some states your prime advisor may be a public accountant, and in some rural areas it might be an attorney. If you have the resources to do so, you may seek out a Certified Financial Planner or hire a bank's financial planning department.

Over the years, your accountant can and should be far more to you than a tax preparer. Indeed, that is why you should use an accountant, rather than a tax preparer, to prepare your tax returns. For, in the process of preparing your tax returns, year after year, your accountant can develop a rounded view of your entire personal financial life and help you to build a lifetime financial plan. An experienced accountant with sound financial planning experience can be an enormous asset, if you take the time to work with your accountant on financial planning, and are not content merely to dump a box of records on his or her desk once a year barely in time for tax returns to be prepared. In the hands of a good accountant, tax return preparation soon grows into effective tax planning, and tax planning into total financial planning—and that is what you need. Your accountant will reach out to other professionals as well—lawyers, bankers, insurance people, brokers. So will you, quite independently. Some of them, with or without self-interest, will be sources of valuable financial planning assistance, but you will very often want to check their advice with your key financial advisor before making financial decisions.

The best way to find an excellent key financial advisor is to solicit the recommendations of those you trust in other contexts. Someone you respect in a business context—one of your peers or someone further along in a career—may be able to recommend his or her own accountant or financial planner. Your banker, broker, insurer, or lawyer is quite likely to be able to do the same. Then it is a matter of asking those who recommend why they are recommending, as in any business situation, and going ahead to interview those accountants or financial planners who seem most likely to be both astute and personally compatible.

In selecting a key financial advisor, it is wise to opt for experience. Inexperienced advisors may be "sharp," and eager to help you make a quick "score," but that sort of thinking should be a danger signal rather than an inducement to proceed. In tax and other financial matters, caution and mature judgment are to be prized. The only quick speculative "killing" you are likely to achieve is your own, and bad tax advice can haunt you for many years.

Whatever financial decisions you make should be your own; never blindly take someone else's advice, no matter how well you respect the advisor. A good financial advisor will want you to understand the advice being offered, and will understand that, in the long run, there is no substitute for helping you to develop the ability to make thoroughly informed financial decisions. If you have an advisor who sees it otherwise, get a new advisor. If you have to go through several advisors in several years, until you find one who commands your respect and with whom you are personally compatible, then so be it. The goal in this instance is well worth the effort.

On the other hand, anyone, no matter how skilled and committed to your interests, can give bad advice on occasion, and staying with "the devil you know" is sometimes better than striking off into the unknown. When you do find sound professional advisors, cultivate them.

PERSONAL FINANCIAL ASSESSMENT

Basic to all financial planning is a clear assessment of current financial status. In assessing your personal financial status, you will rely very heavily on the records you keep and on the changing goals you develop. Those goals depend considerably on the real facts of your financial life. Sometimes those facts seem hard to ascertain and to hold clearly in mind for planning purposes as life proceeds. All too often people have no real idea of their net worth, their real liquidity, their potential tax liability, or the extent to which they should be insured in view of their circumstances and goals. In trying to establish these basic financial facts, it is useful to take a lead from standard business practice.

A series of well-established and widely used financial statements indicate the current status and financial health of enterprises. The balance sheet, showing current assets and liabilities as of the time of its preparation, acts as a still photograph of an enterprise's financial status. The cash flow statement illuminates the movement of cash and cash equivalents in and out of the enterprise during a given period. The profit and loss statement shows the net, plus or minus, of business activities for a given period. The budget or forecast shows anticipated cash flow and projects profit and loss for a given period. Most of the very same tools can and should be adapted to our personal businesses; these are the best tools yet devised to help us see our real financial situations and can enable us to do effective financial planning on the basis of real information and realistic objectives. We explore some simplified, personalized versions of some of these statements shortly.

Most of the data we need for personal financial statements and realistic budgets is developed yearly for tax preparation purposes. Just as an accountant should be far more to you than a tax preparer, so the process of doing a yearly tax workup should be even more. It should be a time not only for summation of the previous year's economic activity, but also for reassessment of that year's planning and the preparation of the next year's plan. No less than once a year should you evaluate how well the previous year's economic plan worked out and consider any new factors that may cause you to revise your financial plans for the next year.

Even your monthly bank statement reconciliation should not be just a time to discover if you forgot to enter a check. Except for payment of bills and monthly reconciliation of the checkbook, many people look at their financial status only at tax preparation time. However, you should plan to assess your standing monthly. Use this time to do such things as allocate money you plan to add to your investment and savings account, check on investments, or see if a bank certificate or dividend payment is coming due. You may find that an investment was not wise or that it can be improved upon; a monthly review will allow you to make changes promptly.

The main elements of your tax workup should be in place before the turn of each year, assuming that you are a calendar-year taxpayer; this should be early enough—often in October or November—to enable you to make any possible advantageous tax planning moves, with counsel from your financial advisors, for the current year before it ends. Your main financial reevaluation should occur then, too. Most accountants and other financial advisors understand very well the value of such tax and financial planning; they will be happy to meet with you every autumn to review your plan. They usually wish that more of their clients would call on them for that kind of help. An alert financial advisor may suggest a number of transactions prior to the year's end that may reduce your taxes without fundamentally changing the nature of your financial situation or your portfolio. Always remember that the less you pay in taxes in a given year, even if you recapture that tax payment in later years, the more favorable to you, since you can put those tax savings to work, earning for you. This kind of yearly tax and financial workup and planning session is central to the health of your personal financial business. To try running your financial life without it is extraordinarily unwise, much like running a business without financial statements of any kind—a sure prescription for financial disaster.

It is not very easy to assess your own financial progress. You are earning, consuming, investing, and borrowing, while the value of the dollar continues to erode because of inflation. The answer to the question "How am I doing?" is often "I don't really know."

One useful way to approach the matter is to attempt to estimate yearly, as closely as you can, the value of your controllable assets. This estimate would not include all of your assets, as would be included in the balance sheet of a business, because your consumable personal property, aside from certain collectibles, disappears as it is consumed, ultimately to be resold, if at all, for something very close to its scrap value. Nor would your estimate include your Social Security and employee corporate pension plan shares, for these are things over which you have no control. Your estimate *should* include all substantial assets of continuing, if fluctuating, value. The Yearly Asset Growth Estimate (Table 1) gives one simple form you can use in making this estimate; you may wish to modify it to suit your individual needs.

The Yearly Asset Growth Estimate will take a little time to calculate, especially the first time, but it is relatively simple and should take less time

Table 1. Yearly Asset Growth Estimate

	Start of Year	Year-End	Change
Asset Value			
Savings accounts			
Short-term			
Long-term			
Securities			
Stocks			
Bonds			
Other			
Own business			
Real estate			
Personal			
Business			
Insurance			
Own pension and profit-sharing plans			
Other (gold, collectibles, etc.)			
Total			
Debts			
Mortgages			
Personal			
Business			
Other business			
Personal			
Total			
Net apparent yearly asset growth			
Impact of inflation			
Net real asset growth			

in succeeding years, becoming more valuable as your experience develops. You should start by entering the value of your assets and debts at the beginning of the year; the calendar year is an easy period to use, since your tax workups will serve as partial bases for these computations, but any 12-month period will do. Then enter the current values of your assets and debts at the end of the year, and find the net gain or loss in each category. Total the net gains and losses for your assets and also for your debts. Finally, subtract the net debt change from the net asset change, and you have an estimate of your net *apparent* gain in asset value. To make that figure a meaningful comparison, you must then adjust it to find your net real asset growth: multiply that figure by the annual rate of inflation, and deduct the result from your apparent asset gain.

Note that no attempt is being made to further adjust for the ultimate tax consequences of transactions made, because many kinds of offsetting transactions and tax-bracket differences would need to be estimated many years before they may occur. For example, a house that appreciates 15% in value in one year must ultimately be sold—but will it be sold and will tax be paid on the gain? Will it be sold with the seller's taking advantage of a large, one-time tax exemption, as is now the law? Or will it be sold after the death of its present owner by an heir operating under entirely different tax laws, after passing tax-free, or very nearly tax-free, because of deductions available under estate and inheritance tax laws? Will a tax-sheltered investment result in substantial taxes on deferred taxables later on? Or will those potential taxes be forever avoided by the use of offsetting devices and the operation of estate and inheritance tax laws? Such questions are far too complex and unpredictable to be included in this general estimate. The estimate can, however, be a useful guide for you and your financial advisors in assessing what tax moves might be advantageous and how your long-term capital accumulation is progressing.

Note that this approach measures only asset growth, not investment return (that measurement is taken up a little later), and that for individual items, only change in asset value is being measured.

Note also that we have not computed "net worth" here, feeling that it is not a very useful personal financial planning concept. Should you want to estimate your net worth, you would add an estimate of the value of your personal property and of your vested pension and profit-sharing plans.

Once you have your financial status laid out, you can make some basic decisions (in consultation with your financial advisors) about what changes would allow you to increase your assets at a faster rate.

Just as you estimated your yearly asset growth, you can estimate the yield of a specific investment or kind of investment. Only one essential modification is necessary: the splitting apart of growth and cash yield, so that you can estimate the after-tax cash income resulting from an investment during a period.

After-tax cash yield on investment is often very difficult to estimate, because a number of factors must be taken into account, including the proportion of income that is derived from such primary sources as employment or ownership of one's own business, the amount of investment income that is tax-sheltered, and the proportions of consumption and investment occurring within a body of discretionary spending. Therefore, it is safest to estimate the impact of income taxes at the level of the top tax brackets in which your taxes are paid, while in practice you attempt to reduce that as much as possible.

For example, a common stock worth $100 might pay 4% in dividends and grow 4% in a given year, a year in which the impact of inflation is 10%. A rough estimate of the resulting net investment return to a taxpayer in a 50% bracket is as follows.

Value of stock 12/31	$104	
Value of stock 1/1	100	
Gain from 1/1 to 12/31		$4
After-tax value of 4% cash dividends in 50% bracket		2
Net apparent gain	$ 6	
Impact of 10% inflation	(10)	
Gain or *loss*		($4)

In this case, the 10% inflation rate multiplied by the $100 value of the stock at the beginning of the year caused an apparent $6 gain to be a real $4 loss. The loss here might be even larger, because whenever the stock is sold, taxes will have to be paid on that apparent gain.

Here is another instance, which makes the same assumptions, except that the asset is a parcel of real estate that has appreciated in fair market value by an estimated 15%—an estimate only, which can be put to reality's test only on eventual sale, if that should occur.

Value of house 12/31	$115,000
Value of house 1/1	100,000

Net apparent gain from 1/1 to 12/31	$15,000
Impact of 10% inflation	($10,000)
Gain or loss	$5,000

Here the net gain is 5%. These are, of course, rough estimates, far from what would be acceptable for planning purposes in corporations. For individuals, they meet the tests of rough accuracy and ease of use in planning, supplying a bird's-eye view of individual investment and asset growth progress.

Effective budgeting is an essential financial planning tool. A budget is merely a forecast, yet it is such an essential management tool that companies spend enormous amounts of highly compensated management time making the guesses that go into budget forecasts, and whole departments are devoted to the development of computerized forecast models and to the forecasts themselves. Companies estimate both cash flow and profit and loss. Forecasts are detailed at least month by month for a year, and forecasts for a full year ahead are normally revised every quarter. Longer-term plans are developed as a context within which to develop shorter-term plans and forecasts.

Individuals, whose economic lives are very much like small businesses, should do the same. They are best advised to pay careful attention to the development of yearly cash flow forecasts, as the context within which to run their economic lives most effectively and with the least possible personal strain. Why say *cash flow forecast* instead of *cash budget?* Because even to many sophisticated people, the word *budget,* when used in personal life, conjures up a series of nitpicking arguments as to whether or not to buy a steak, a chuck roast, or a can of beans. To many people, *budgeting* means hard times, and to others it means retreat from the unrestrained consumption thought to be such an important part of the American dream.

But that is not what budgeting, or cash flow forecasting, is really about. Budgeting is, to a large extent, seeing long- and short-term choices clearly, taking alternative courses of action, and fighting your way free of entrapment in a consuming society. Oddly enough, budgeting does not straitjacket, as so many think; it creates freedom by making financial independence more than a dream and by making rational asset growth something that can occur in the here and now, not out somewhere in the indefinite future. When you are creating savings for investment, which is what budgeting makes possible, you can take advantage of opportunities and have a chance to beat inflation. As a trapped consumer, you are free only to worry about an increasingly uncertain future.

Table 2 gives a form you can use for developing your cash flow estimates for each month. If you make such estimates every three months for the 12 months ahead, you will have built in a self-adjustment technique. Record the anticipated major expenditures in the months in which they will occur; do not forget such special matters as tax payments or refunds, expensive vacations, lump-sum education payments, and insurance premiums, and adjust all items for the impact of inflation. This recording is done most easily by spreading out all 12 months—with a *Projected* and *Actual* column for each month—on a large sheet of accounting paper, which can be purchased in any stationery store. It provides a model to use each month.

This kind of cash flow forecasting can be as helpful to you as it is to your company. It can tell you well in advance when you will need more cash than you are currently generating. If you have a cash buildup from previous months or years, it can tell you when to hold that cash for coming short-term needs and when to invest for the longer term; by matching current needs and available cash, you can maximize the productive use of investment money. It can tell you when you will need to tap current assets for anticipated cash needs or to borrow to meet those needs, giving you ample time to convert longer-term holdings into cash or to look for financing, if necessary. The quick cash emergency sale is very often a sale at a loss or at less profit than could have been realized; the emergency loan is usually harder to get than the timely loan and is often more expensive as well. In the long run, the matching of projections with actual results, month after month, then year after year, develops the habit of extremely effective cash management, a skill that is central to the development of a healthy financial future.

FINANCIAL RECORDS

Financial transactions generate paper. That paper must be kept and should be filed so as to be easily retrievable; some paper, in the form of valuable documents, must be kept safe. Therefore, effective financial planning requires two very obvious physical things—a good place to work and a safe-deposit box. Your office at home, or at least a portion of a room separate from all other household activities, should provide adequate

Table 2. Cash Flow Forecast

	Projected	Actual
Cash in		
Direct compensation (each full-time job, part-time job, or business salary separately)		
Dividends and interest (each source separately)		
Rental and royalties (each source separately)		
Alimony and child support		
Other[a]		
Total		
Cash out		
Mortgage repayments or rent		
Other fixed monthly payments		
Utilities (each separately)		
Taxes		
Insurance		
Alimony and child support		
Education		
Medical and dental		
Food		
Clothing		
Transportation		
Household maintenance		
Personal care		
Contributions		
Recreation		
Major purchases		
Other		
Total		
Net cash flow for month		
Net cumulative cash flow for year to date		

[a] *Note:* Possible additional sources of income this month (bonuses, gifts, sales of assets, second job not yet held, tax refunds, etc.).

worktable space and sufficient, well-organized file space, with some files being lockable; even if no children are about (and in many households they are) other people are often present, including guests, the children of guests, and sometimes cleaning people. It is worth setting yourself up properly for an activity that will extend throughout your lifetime.

You will want to keep careful, detailed, and long-term records of financial transactions, often far beyond the minimum times necessitated by tax law. For tax purposes, you should hold all materials relating to items on your tax returns for at least four years—three years to satisfy the normal statutory requirements and one year more, because the facts embodied in your return stem from the year before the return was actually filed. On the other hand, there is no statute of limitations on tax fraud, and in certain complex tax situations your accountant may advise you to keep some kinds of tax-related documents indefinitely.

Personal financial statements and the worksheets used to develop those statements should be held indefinitely. They constitute a running record of the financial side of your life and can be quite valuable financial review tools later on.

No matter how much paper is involved—and it can be a good deal— be very sure to hold indefinitely all materials relating to investments, pensions, insurance, estate planning, and tax planning. How and when a pension plan contribution was handled can be a matter of considerable tax and benefit significance 30 years later. What you originally paid for a collectible can be of great tax significance to you or your heirs when tax authorities are trying to set a realistic basis for computing gain on an eventual sale decades later. Knowing precisely when a financial transaction took place can save you a lot of money in future years. Receipts for valuable personal items should also be kept to indicate the value of objects in case of fire or casualty loss for which you are filing an insurance claim.

Some papers, such as deeds, copies (not originals) of wills, stock certificates, and contracts, are best kept in a safe-deposit box, often with copies in your possession at home or business for day-to-day checking purposes, if necessary. The original, witnessed copy of your will should be kept in some other safe place, such as in the office of the lawyer who prepared it. Your personal safe-deposit box will, on your death, be sealed in anticipation of estate settlement, and if your will is sealed with it, unnecessary legal difficulties may result for your executors and heirs.

In general, overplan and overkeep. Ask your professional advisors just a few more questions than you need to ask, rather than several fewer; you will learn and keep learning that way. When in doubt as to whether or not to keep papers, keep them; you can always throw them away later, but you cannot recover them once they are gone.

Organizing the financial side of life is prosaic and time-consuming and involves constant questioning and paperwork. In the course of pursuing a busy life, often full of other personal chores and work-related paper of all kinds, it is very easy to let personal affairs slide; to let the papers pile up; to send your tax preparation work-up to your accountant by mail, thereby missing a yearly tax and financial planning conference; and to find years later that your personal affairs are in a mess. Try not to let that happen; the lifestyle you desire depends on the state of your finances, and in an increasingly uncertain world, organizing the financial side of life is a must, an essential part of long-term personal financial planning.

ASSESSING YIELD AND GROWTH

Effective long-term financial planning depends largely on an understanding of the mechanics of compound interest and on applying that understanding to the relationship between net after-tax (not pre-tax) earning and growth and the rate of inflation. *Net after-tax* is the key phrase. The comparison must be between everything you net from savings and investment, including what you have and what you add every year, and the rate of inflation. If you can add substantially to your real assets every year, after taking into account the rate of inflation, no matter how high it is, you are going in the right direction, moving ahead in the strength of your financial position—in a sense, in the growth of your own personal business. If you fall behind again and again, or gain a little in some years and lose a little or more than a little in other years, it is reevaluation time.

The heart of the matter is the way interest compounds—for you as your investments grow and earn, against you as inflation takes down the value of the dollar. Table 3 illustrates how $1 compounds over 50 years at different interest rates. That is for just $1. If you can add $1 every year and have that compound, too, so much the better. Table 4 shows how interest accumulates, assuming you start with $1 and add $1 each year, reinvesting all interest.

Your actual gain in interest is far smaller than it seems to be in Tables 3 and 4 because of the progress of inflation, which erodes the value of dollars just as inexorably as the mechanics of compound interest cause them to grow. The essence of the matter is to have some dollars working for you, and, if at all possible, netting enough after taxes to keep up with or even surpass the rate of inflation.

In the 1970s and early 1980s, 3% has not been a high rate of inflation or a high net after-tax return. Yet, for many, 3% is all that is netted, after taxes, on a savings account paying 6%, while inflation has moved at a double-digit yearly rate often in this period. The figures do tell a good deal

Table 3. The Value of $1 of Principal, with Compound Interest Accumulated over 50 Years at Various Rates

Number of Years	Interest Rate					
	3%	6%	9%	12%	15%	18%
1	1.0300	1.0600	1.0900	1.1200	1.1500	1.1800
2	1.0609	1.1236	1.1881	1.2544	1.3225	1.3924
3	1.0927	1.1910	1.2950	1.4049	1.5209	1.6430
4	1.1255	1.2625	1.4116	1.5735	1.7490	1.9388
5	1.1593	1.3382	1.5386	1.7623	2.0114	2.2878
6	1.1941	1.4185	1.6771	1.9738	2.3131	2.6996
7	1.2299	1.5036	1.8280	2.2107	2.6600	3.1855
8	1.2668	1.5938	1.9926	2.4760	3.0590	3.7589
9	1.3048	1.6895	2.1719	2.7731	3.5179	4.4355
10	1.3439	1.7908	2.3674	3.1058	4.0456	5.2339
11	1.3842	1.8983	2.5804	3.4786	4.6524	6.1759
12	1.4258	2.0122	2.8127	3.8960	5.3503	7.2876
13	1.4685	2.1329	3.0658	4.3635	6.1528	8.5994
14	1.5126	2.2601	3.3417	4.8871	7.0757	10.1472
15	1.5570	2.3966	3.6425	5.4736	8.1371	11.9737
16	1.6047	2.5404	3.9703	6.1304	9.3576	14.1290
17	1.6528	2.6928	4.3276	6.8660	10.7613	16.6722
18	1.7024	2.8543	4.7171	7.6900	12.3755	19.6733
19	1.7535	3.0256	5.1417	8.6128	14.2318	23.2144
20	1.8061	3.2071	5.6044	9.6463	16.3665	27.3930
21	1.8603	3.3996	6.1088	10.8038	18.8215	32.3238
22	1.9161	3.6035	6.6586	12.1003	21.6447	38.1421
23	1.9736	3.8197	7.2579	13.5523	24.8915	45.0076
24	2.0328	4.0489	7.9111	15.1786	28.6252	53.1090
25	2.0938	4.2919	8.6231	17.0001	32.9190	62.6686
26	2.1566	4.5494	9.3992	19.0401	37.8568	73.9490
27	2.2213	4.8223	10.2451	21.3249	43.5353	87.2598
28	2.2879	5.1117	11.1671	23.8839	50.0656	102.9666
29	2.3566	5.4184	12.1722	26.7499	57.5755	121.5005
30	2.4273	5.7435	13.2677	29.9599	66.2118	143.3706
31	2.5001	6.0881	14.4618	33.5551	76.1435	169.1774
32	2.5751	6.4534	15.7633	37.5817	87.5651	199.6293
33	2.6523	6.8406	17.1820	42.0915	100.6998	235.5626
34	2.7319	7.2510	18.7284	47.1425	115.8048	277.9638
35	2.8139	7.6861	20.4140	52.7996	133.1755	327.9973
36	2.8983	8.1473	22.2512	59.1356	153.1519	387.0368
37	2.9852	8.6361	24.2538	66.2318	176.1246	456.7034

Table 3 *(Continued)*

Number of Years	3%	6%	9%	12%	15%	18%
			Interest Rate			
38	3.0748	9.1543	26.4367	74.1797	202.5433	538.9100
39	3.1670	9.7035	28.8160	83.0812	232.9248	635.9139
40	3.2620	10.2857	31.4094	93.0510	267.8636	750.3783
41	3.3599	10.9029	34.2363	104.2171	308.0431	885.4464
42	3.4607	11.5570	37.3175	116.7231	354.2495	1044.8268
43	3.5645	12.2505	40.6761	130.7299	407.3870	1232.8956
44	3.6715	12.9855	44.3370	146.4175	468.4950	1454.8168
45	3.7816	13.7646	48.3273	163.9876	538.7693	1716.6839
46	3.8950	14.5905	52.6767	183.6661	619.5847	2025.6870
47	4.0119	15.4659	57.4176	205.7061	712.5224	2390.3106
48	4.1323	16.3939	62.5852	230.3908	819.4007	2820.5665
49	4.2561	17.3775	68.2179	258.0377	942.3108	3328.2685
50	4.3839	18.4202	74.3575	289.0022	1083.6574	3927.3568

Table 4. The Value of $1 of Principal to Which $1 Is Added Per Year, with Compound Interest Accumulated over 50 Years at Various Rates

Number of Years	3%	6%	9%	12%	15%	18%
			Interest Rate			
1	1.0300	1.0600	1.0900	1.1200	1.1500	1.1800
2	2.0909	2.1836	2.2781	2.3744	2.4725	2.5724
3	3.1836	3.3746	3.5731	3.7793	3.9934	4.2154
4	4.3091	4.6371	4.9847	5.3528	5.7424	6.1542
5	5.4684	5.9753	6.5223	7.1152	7.7537	8.4420
6	6.6625	7.3938	8.2004	9.0890	10.0668	11.1415
7	7.8923	8.8975	10.0285	11.2997	12.7268	14.3270
8	9.1591	10.4913	12.0210	13.7757	15.7858	18.0859
9	10.4639	12.1809	14.1929	16.5487	19.3037	22.5213
10	11.8078	13.9717	16.5603	19.6546	23.3493	27.7551
11	13.1920	15.8700	19.1407	23.1331	28.0017	33.9311
12	14.6178	17.8821	21.9534	27.0291	33.3519	41.2187
13	16.0863	20.0151	25.0192	31.3926	39.5047	49.8180
14	17.5989	22.2760	28.3609	36.2797	46.5804	59.9653
15	19.1569	24.7825	32.0034	41.7533	54.7175	71.9390
16	20.7616	27.2129	35.9737	47.8837	64.0751	86.0680
17	22.4144	29.9057	40.3013	54.7497	74.8364	102.7403

Table 4 (*Continued*)

Number of Years	3%	6%	9%	12%	15%	18%
			Interest Rate			
18	24.1169	32.7600	45.0185	62.4397	87.2118	122.4135
19	25.8704	35.7856	50.1601	71.0524	101.4436	145.6290
20	27.6765	38.9927	55.7645	80.6987	117.8101	173.0210
21	29.5368	42.3923	61.8733	91.5026	136.6316	205.3448
22	31.4529	45.9958	68.5319	103.6029	158.2764	243.4868
23	33.4265	49.8156	75.7898	117.1552	183.1678	288.4945
24	35.4593	53.8645	83.7009	132.3339	211.7930	314.6035
25	37.5530	58.1564	92.3240	149.3339	244.7120	404.2721
26	39.7096	62.7058	101.7231	168.3740	282.5688	478.2211
27	41.9309	67.5281	111.9682	189.6989	326.1041	565.4809
28	44.2189	72.6398	123.1354	213.5828	376.1697	668.4475
29	46.5754	78.0582	135.3075	240.3327	433.7452	789.9480
30	49.0027	83.8017	148.5752	270.2926	499.9569	933.3186
31	51.5028	89.8898	163.0370	303.8477	576.1005	1102.4960
32	54.0778	96.3432	178.8003	341.4294	663.6655	1302.1252
33	56.7302	103.1838	195.9823	383.5210	764.3654	1537.6878
34	59.4621	110.4348	214.7108	430.6635	880.1702	1815.6516
35	62.2759	118.1209	235.1247	483.4631	1013.3457	2143.6489
36	65.1742	126.2681	257.3760	542.5987	1166.4975	2530.6857
37	68.1594	134.9042	281.6298	608.8305	1342.6222	2987.3891
38	71.2342	144.0584	308.0665	683.0102	1545.1655	3526.2991
39	74.4013	153.7620	336.8824	766.0914	1778.0903	4162.2130
40	77.6633	164.0477	368.2919	859.1424	2045.9538	4912.5913
41	81.0232	174.9506	402.5281	963.3595	2353.0069	5798.0378
42	84.4839	186.5076	439.8457	1080.0826	2708.2465	6842.8646
43	88.0484	198.7581	480.5218	1210.8125	3115.6334	8075.7602
44	91.7199	211.7437	524.8587	1357.2300	3584.1284	9530.5770
45	95.5015	225.5082	573.1860	1521.2176	4122.8977	11247.2610
46	99.3965	240.0987	625.8628	1704.8837	4742.4824	13272.9480
47	103.4084	255.5646	683.2804	1910.5898	5455.0047	15663.2580
48	107.5407	271.9585	745.8656	2140.9806	6274.4054	18453.8250
49	111.7969	289.3360	814.0836	2399.0182	7216.7162	21812.0930
50	116.1808	307.7561	888.4411	2688.0204	8300.3737	25739.4500

of the story in this instance. If you have $10,000 in savings accounts and leave that $10,000 in those accounts at 6% for 20 years, reinvesting all interest, and if at the top of your income you pay 50% in combined income taxes, you are netting 3% on those savings. You will have netted only $18,061 (from Table 3, $1 after 20 years at 3% is $1.8061, multiplied by $10,000) after income taxes at the end of those 20 years. That same $10,000 accreting at an after-tax net of 9% would have grown to $56,044; at 15%, to $163,665. At the 3% level, you would have lost much of the $10,000, measured in real value, because of inflation. At 9%, you might have stayed a little ahead or fallen a little behind, depending on the average rate of inflation over those 20 years—but you would, at least, have a far better chance of holding your savings. At 15%, your chances of making meaningful investment gains are rather good.

Tables 3 and 4 can be very useful to you over the years as you make such analyses and comparisons between various investments.

Yield and growth expectations measured together with taxes subtracted, add up to the single after-tax number that you must estimate in order to evaluate the probable worth of an investment. In finance, "yield" is the measurable amount of value returned by an investment, not including the worth of the investment itself. If you put $10,000 in a savings account at 6% yearly interest (without worrying about compounding for the purpose of this example), the yield is $600 in one year. If placed in a savings certificate carrying an interest rate of 10%, that $10,000 yields $1,000 in one year. A bond worth $10,000 when originally issued and carrying a 9% interest rate, yields $900 per year. However, if the bond's value has declined to $9,000 by the time you buy it, it still pays $900 per year; in that case your yield would be 10% of a $9,000 investment, or $900.

Let's take a different example. Some common stock you bought for $10,000 pays after-tax dividends of $500, or 5%. Suppose that common stock goes up in market value to $11,000 one year from the time you buy it. If you sell it then, you have gained $1,000 in growth and $500 in dividends, for a total gain of $1,500, or 15% on top of your original investment. Part is growth and part is direct yield, which is money actually paid out. The two are sometimes lumped together for purposes of description, but in personal financial planning the two should be distinguished; combining them confuses further analysis, particularly with tax factors in mind.

But when evaluating alternative savings and investment vehicles, you must take into account more than possible after-tax total yield and growth combined. The degree of risk involved and the liquidity of the funds used must also be considered. An investment in gemstones in a rising market may offer extraordinary possibilities for speculative gain—but you are also very likely to lose your shirt. An investment in raw land may be both relatively safe and potentially quite lucrative—if you can hold it for decades if necessary. But if you need to get your money out of that land, you may find yourself unable to sell it at any reasonable price, if at all; under those circumstances, the initial purchase was little more than a speculation.

Speculation is indeed a great trap, and an enemy of effective long-term planning. In truth, mastering the mechanics of compound interest and after-tax yield will take you toward economic self-sufficiency far more surely and quickly than will speculation. And when an investor-speculator discovers the joys of "leveraging"; that is, investing with borrowed money and building a larger and larger economic castle in air with increasingly large amounts of expensive borrowed money, effective planning for long-term economic health is far, far away—and effective bankruptcy is right around the corner.

Ignorance is an equally great trap. There is really no substitute for becoming a good semiprofessional in financial matters; the old saw that "nobody watches your business as well as you do" remains true in personal financial matters. You may—and should—get good professional advice for personal moves, as from a skilled stockbroker, or you may buy professional management of your funds, as when you buy a mutual fund or hire a financial planning organization. But in the long run the decisions you make must be your own, backed by your own knowledge of the investment vehicles in which you are putting your long-term planning money.

You will need every bit of knowledge, caution, and skepticism you can muster, every bit of sound professional advice you can gather to accomplish long-term planning in this most difficult period. We live in an investment world turned quite upside down, with yesterday's blue chip stocks often today's losers, and with yesterday's scorned pedestrian short-term, safe savings devices and debt obligations today's most widely used investment vehicles. It is a world in which nothing less than a commitment to continuing information, skills growth, and informed flexibility will suffice.

SAVINGS AND INVESTMENTS

The savings and investments vehicles available to reasonably modest savers and investors—like most working managers—are unusually diverse in this period. Many vehicles effectively available to only the wealthy as recently as a decade ago are quite routinely offered to smaller investors in this period.

The main savings and investment vehicles currently available include savings instruments such as demand deposits and certificates of deposit; debt obligations, including federal, other government, and privately issued bills, notes, and bonds; ownership shares, including common and preferred stocks; mutual funds, including money market funds; commodities, including gold, silver, gemstones, and other extracted, grown, and gathered substances; collectibles; and real estate. Transactions available include both current and future interests in that which is being traded; several tax-advantaged modes of trading and forms of ownership; and a number of insurance forms and policies that carry investment and tax-advantaged features.

We will now discuss some of the major vehicles and forms, assuming that readers will also have at their disposal one or more of the basic financial works previously recommended.

All of us have some working cash, which we use for short-term expenditures. And the question of how to use your working cash as a source of revenue is precisely the same question your corporate controller faces every day on behalf of your company. The traditional—and worst—way to handle the question is to hold your working cash in a non-interest-paying demand deposit checking account. Your corporate controller may have done that, too, some decades ago, but has long since learned that there are far better ways to handle company working cash.

You can get some income from your working cash by keeping it in a checking account that pays interest, or by keeping part of it in an interest-paying savings account, which the bank often holds in tandem with your checking account, passing your money back and forth efficiently between checking and savings, and maximizing available interest. Such demand deposit accounts are federally insured, and are liquid short of national economic disaster. And, if you believe that such insurance is necessary for your short-term cash, that is the way to handle it.

On the other hand, if you believe that money market mutual funds, invested in high grade short-term debt obligations, are sufficiently safe vehicles for your short-term working cash, there is a better way to proceed. Then you will keep a very small amount of working cash—perhaps enough for a month's bills—in interest-paying bank accounts, and the balance in a money market mutual fund. We will discuss the mechanics of such funds shortly; the essence of the matter for your short-term funds is that you can treat the money market fund as a supplementary, uninsured bank account, moving money into it in increments of as little as $500 after setting it up with a purchase of $1,000 to $5,000, taking money out of it by writing a check for as little as $500, and taking it down to almost nothing, as you can a bank account. Such money market fund accounts are entirely liquid, and have the great advantage of paying far higher rates of interest than do ordinary bank demand deposit accounts. An average of $4,000 held in money market funds at a net after-tax 7% rate of return for 30 years grows to $30,449. The same $4,000, held in an interest-bearing bank account at a net after-tax 3%—and that is all it really yields for most working professionals—grows to $9,709, less than one third as much. The loss in opportunity cost to you—that is, the difference between what the money earned and what it could and should have earned—is a whopping $20,740. Quite a sum to lose through inattention!

Some longer-term funds may also be held in time deposits, on which banks may offer much higher rates of interest than on demand deposits. You may withdraw your money from some such accounts—normally called certificates of deposit—at any time, if necessary, although you would lose considerable interest from premature closeout. But note that some such deposits—especially the longer term deposits, often running for as long as five or six years—may be held by the bank for the full stated term, even though you may want your money out earlier. Be very careful to know the terms of the bank's offer, or you may unintentionally tie up funds far longer than you plan, and at far lower interest rates than you might otherwise secure. For many of us, the money market mutual fund, with its combination of liquidity and high interest rates, may provide a better vehicle than the bank certificate of deposit. Please do note very carefully, though, that federally insured deposits and certificates of deposit should be turned to when current economic events are so alarming as to raise a serious question in your mind as to impending economic collapse. However relatively safe, money market funds are uninsured mutual funds run by fallible humans; in a disaster, you would have a better chance of coming out whole or nearly whole with federally insured instruments.

Let us assume that you have the personal financial basics in place. You have an adequate store of working cash. You have an adequate habitation; not necessarily an owned home—to buy or rent is an investment decision, within the context of our financial planning discussion. You have secured adequate personal life and health insurance, recognizing the company insurance traps we have previously discussed, and have adequate property and liability insurance as well. You are, at least to some extent, avoiding the overspending trap. You are generating discretionary income available for investment.

One of the first investments you are likely to consider will be an investment in the common stock of your own company, either by exercising stock options or by using discretionary funds to buy company stock at current market prices. You will probably be able to develop a better informed opinion as to the yield and growth prospects of that stock than of any other; you may even be able to see how your own efforts and the efforts of those around you may be able to directly affect the progress of the stock—to take a hand in the game.

At the same time, you will want to subject your own company's stock to the kind of searching scrutiny you would give any stock you would consider buying. For the American stock market has not done very well in recent years, as compared to other investment alternatives, and cannot be expected to do very much better in the near term. The general level of stock prices has not even nearly kept up with the pace of inflation in well over a decade. The Dow Jones common stock average, that most widely used barometer of stock market health, hovered at or near 1,000 in the late 1960s; a decade and a half later, it does the same, or even worse. Given the rate of inflation in the intervening years, it has in real dollars gone down—disastrously—and is worth only about one third of what it was worth in the late 1960s. Dividends have in some instances risen somewhat in those years, but at nowhere near a rate that would compensate for inflation. Meanwhile, yields on several other kinds of investments, and especially on interest-yielding debt obligations, have risen dramatically in those years.

However, your own company stock may present an entirely different picture, especially if it is unduly depressed by general downward pressures on stock prices. Exercise of your stock options may provide substantial profits, sometimes on considerably tax-advantaged terms. You may participate in a dividend reinvestment plan, buying more stock with dividends received; while the dividends will be taxable, it may be a worthwhile way to accrete stock. A word of caution on stock options, though: If you work for a small company, you may find that the options you hold in the stock of that company have gone up in value, but that you cannot sell them easily or at all on the open market when you want to, because they are not listed on a major exchange and are very thinly traded. Your only choice may be to hold them or sell them back to your company, which need not purchase them from you. Widely held and traded stock in a large company is a much more desirable stock to hold at option.

The stocks of other companies you know something about may be "buys," too. You are likely to know some of the other companies in your industry nearly as well as you know your own; purchase of their stock may be a wise investment move. You may also want to study and invest in the stocks of companies far outside your own field, in such new technology areas as robotics and computers, or in any other area you feel can result in profitable stock investments—as long as you take the time and trouble to learn about the companies you are investing in. That is the key— investing in companies you know a good deal about, rather than on the basis of tips and rumors or in a large, amorphous something called "the market."

You may also speculate, but do not call it or think of it as long-term financial planning. Buying stocks on as much margin as is legally available is a form of speculation. So is looking for and buying into "special situations," which are usually the low-priced stocks of companies in deep trouble, which someone is trying to turn around, usually without much success. So is betting on a takeover situation, called *takeover arbitrage*. The "hot tip" on a stock that is "about to have an extraordinary runup" is usually worth about as much as a "hot tip" on a long shot that is "about to win" a horse race at the nearest racetrack.

While the overwhelming majority of stocks did very badly in terms of real dollars during the 1970s and early 1980s, many debt instruments did comparatively very well. Many investors in this period have quite astutely turned to three basic kinds of debt instruments: United States government debt obligations, state and local debt obligations, and the debt obligations of privately owned organizations.

The United States government is a truly enormous spender and borrower. Now, after decades of annual deficits, it is also an enormous interest-payer, with carrying charges on past debts one of the largest items in every yearly federal budget. Political rhetoric set aside, it is highly unlikely that the basic situation in this area will change, at least for the balance of this century. Inflation, energy costs, continued and at times accelerated massive military expenditures, and a Social Security system that at some time in that period will run out of money and need to be financed out of general tax revenues will all see to that.

Governments repudiate debts, including those owed to their own citizens. They do not always do so directly; that can bring down a government and even change a whole social system. But very often they do so indirectly, by paying back debts in dollars that are worth a great deal less than those lent the government by unwary lenders in previous years.

That is clearly what has been happening—not through any grand conspiracy, but in fact—to long-term debts solemnly incurred by the United States government in the past and maturing in these years. Long-term federal government bonds issued many years ago and paying interest in the 3–6% range at a time when the rate of inflation was in the same range continue to pay those rates of interest to maturity, guaranteeing substantial losses for their holders. Federal savings bonds, which are non-negotiable, can only be cashed in, in order to cut losses. Negotiable long-term federal obligations can be traded on bond markets, but trade at far lower prices than those at which they were originally sold, reflecting the constant tendency of bonds to adjust their prices to current interest levels. Such bonds are as safe as they ever were in terms of receiving principal at maturity date, being backed as they are by the full taxing power of the federal government, but they are worth a great deal less than at time of issue. Technically, that is not repudiation of debt; practically, it works just as surely as partial debt repudiation would. That is why investors in the late 1970s and early 1980s have turned to short-term federal debt obligations, and why the government has had to turn more and more to that kind of obligation to meet its enormous and growing cash needs.

You can buy some kinds of federal obligations from your bank, paying small service charges. Most kinds will be available through your broker. Some you can buy yourself, avoiding charges, if you are willing to take considerable time and trouble to do so. Information on direct purchasing is available from your bank or broker or directly from the Treasury Department in Washington, D.C. Such debt obligations are also part of many mutual fund and bank fund portfolios selling participations to investors.

Treasury bills are the most common short-term federal debt obligations. The United States Treasury issues 3-, 6-, and 12-month bills that pay fixed interest for the period of issue. The bills are discounted in advance, meaning that you will pay less than the face value of the bills and at maturity will be repaid the face value, the difference being your interest payment on the obligation. In periods of rapid inflation and great financial uncertainty, the three-month bills have been widely purchased by both institutions and individuals. In periods of somewhat greater stability, the longer-term Treasury bills may be somewhat more convenient to handle, necessitating fewer transaction fees and less attention. Interest can be lost on these and on all other short-term obligations if they are not rolled over quickly, meaning that, immediately upon sale of one short-term obligation, another must be bought with the proceeds of the first.

In more stable times, Treasury notes, which mature in 1 to 10 years, are a safe way to soak up surplus funds, although they do not necessarily have a high enough yield. These bear coupons, as do many other kinds of bonds, which are clipped and presented for fixed payments at stated intervals; the term *coupon clipper,* in fact, has come to describe someone living on the interest from his or her bonds. Like all longer-term debt obligations, these notes may appreciate in value if interest rates go down after purchase and may lose value if interest rates go up after purchase. If held to maturity, the fixed interest is paid periodically, and the principal is returned at maturity. Treasury notes and longer-term federal debt obligations are as safe as debt obligations can be in terms of interest and principal repayment, but during their lives are as sensitive to fluctuations in the interest rate as are other high-grade obligations.

Federal bonds are those federal obligations maturing in more than 10 years. Except for savings bonds, which are discussed subsequently, they are mainly traded in large blocks by institutions, rather than being proper instruments for personal financial planning.

In addition to Treasury-issued debt obligations, there are an increasingly large number of debt obligations issued by federal agencies of all kinds, such as the Government National Mortgage Association (GNMA, known as Ginnie Mae); the Federal National Mortgage Association (FNMA, known as Fannie Mae); the Federal Land Banks; the Small Business Administration; and the Tennessee Valley Authority. Federal agency debt proliferates very quickly. These agencies are funded by legislation, and their debt-incurring activities are carried out on their own. Therefore, although backed by the United States government's promise to pay, they are not direct Treasury issues and thus have, at times, been considered slightly less safe than Treasury obligations. As a result, they have sometimes paid somewhat higher interest than that paid by Treasury issues, making them attractive to those who realize that they are very good risks indeed. However, in uncertain, high-interest-rate periods, many have chosen to invest only in the shortest-term issues of these agencies, some of which run as little as three months. Agency debt obligations are purchased through brokers and banks.

Federal savings bonds were very popular during World War II, when purchasing them was the patriotic thing to do, and when their interest rate was only a little below that available from other vehicles. Even today, they are sold quite aggressively by the federal government. They are usually purchased by people who have only small amounts of dollars at a time to put into savings or investments, since they can be purchased through periodic payments of small amounts, as in a payroll deduction plan. We would certainly not advise anyone who wanted to buy them for patriotic reasons to hold back for a second. But anyone buying them for financial reasons should think very carefully before doing so in the economic climate of the 1980s. They are non-negotiable and cannot be used as collateral. Their low interest payments are fully taxable, but only at maturity, thus affording only a small tax break, however that does not even come close to making up for their negative investment characteristics. For someone looking for tax breaks, state and local debt obligations may prove far more rewarding, if one is careful.

State and local obligations are the debt obligations of all other governmental bodies in the United States outside the federal government. These include tens of thousands of state and local governments and their multifold agencies, which together form what is commonly called the municipal bond market, even though they include many bodies that are neither municipalities nor in any way related to municipalities.

Their major financial attraction is that, as a matter of national policy, their interest is by law exempt from federal income taxes. Where a purchaser is a legal resident of an issuing locality, that interest is in many instances also free of state and local taxes, as a matter of state and local taxing policy. Tax rates vary widely and tax laws change continually, but the tax breaks provided by these state and local obligations offer a very substantial attraction indeed.

Wealthy people have long taken advantage of the tax advantages inherent in municipals. Even during the 1950s and 1960s, with stocks enjoying a historic boom and bonds paying relatively low interest rates, municipals offered real advantages for many high-income people. In that period, municipals tended to be quite safe, as well, with very few defaults or moratoriums. Defaults are failures to pay interest or repay principal when due, with bondholders getting some of their money back much later. Moratoriums are failures to repay principal when due, with interest payments extended. In either case, bonds tend to lose a good deal of their market value in such situations.

As individual investors tended to move out of the stock market in the late 1960s and early 1970s, and as interest rates began to soar, making bonds generally far more attractive investment vehicles, people in the upper-middle income tax brackets began to buy municipals. Some of those who began to buy might have advantageously invested in municipals long before, but neither knew nor were advised properly as to their net after-tax yield possibilities. As more and more investors began to be interested in municipals, however, brokers began to follow their customers in that direction. Some began to strongly recommend municipals; others began to form and aggressively market mutual funds composed of municipals. What investors and brokers were learning about municipals was that, although the interest rates paid on them were almost invariably lower than the interest rates paid on corporate bonds, and even lower than the rates paid on most federal obligations, the tax exemptions they carried enabled some high-income investors to secure higher after-tax yields than were available with any other bonds.

The resulting rush to municipals unfortunately failed to take into account the fact that the same economic factors that had made the stock market unattractive operated throughout the economy and that many of those issuing municipalities were in serious economic trouble. That oversight became common knowledge when New York City ran into enormous financing difficulties in the mid-1970s, as did many other issuers in the same period.

In the late 1970s and early 1980s, another problem became apparent. Medium- and long-term municipals, like all other bonds, declined sharply as interest rates rose, and those holding them suffered substantial paper losses. That is, if the municipals were sold before maturity, they had to be sold at a very substantial discount from their face value; if held to maturity, the municipals would pay their face value then, but would pay interest until maturity at rates considerably lower than those currently available. Either way, the municipal holder experienced a real loss in the long run.

Yet the tax break remains. Maturities shorten, lessening the risk of long-term interest rate rises. Insurance is placed on some municipal issues, lessening the risk of default or moratorium. Interest rates on new issues rise to meet the current level of interest in order to compete for buyer attention. Some issuers are still excellent risks and will continue to be so for the foreseeable future, as in the case of some substantial localities in energy-rich Sunbelt states. It is necessary, however, to view municipals as discrete investments, rather than as a kind of tax break. It is just as unwise to invest in municipals as it is to invest in "the market." The wise investment is in the specific municipal issue, just as the wise investment is in the specific company. Although a municipal may carry insurance against default and moratoriums, there is no way to insure against market decline.

There are several kinds of municipal issues. Although they offer somewhat different degrees of safety, investors should, in deciding whether or not to invest in a specific issue, consider primarily the safety, or lack of it, afforded by the total economic situation and the issuing locality's ability to pay.

Issues called *general* carry a direct and unlimited promise to pay on the part of the issuer and therefore are described as being backed by the "full faith and credit" of the issuer. These are backed by the taxing power of the issuer, which is subject to federal and state restrictions. Only the federal government can create an unlimited balloon of credit; that is not possible for municipal issuers, which is why such obligations, as a group, are not nearly as safe as federal obligations. The federal government can and routinely does raise its own debt limits; lesser governments in the United States cannot.

Short-term tax anticipation notes, sometimes called *warrants,* are borrowings that pay interest for the privilege of using your money now, to be repaid in tax receipt money later, and that are intended to be used as smoothing-out devices for government income and expenditure. Tax receipts do not usually follow even collection patterns, with equal amounts collected each month. Instead, receipts wax and wane with tax collection due dates, whereas expenditures tend to be more regular. Since these notes usually carry a prior claim upon receipts and are relatively short term—usually six months or less—they are both relatively safe and less vulnerable to changes in interest rates than are longer-term debt obligations. They tend to be sold in very large denominations to institutional investors and not be directly accessible to individuals, but they are an important part of some mutual funds composed of money market instruments and are thereby accessible.

Revenue bonds carry a promise to pay interest and principal out of the revenue coming in from a specific source, for example, from bridge tolls in relation to a bond issued in order to raise funds to build the bridge. They are not backed by a general promise to pay on the part of the issuer. Making the point with an extreme case, the destruction of the bridge by earthquake might bring bridge tolls and bond interest to an end for many years, if not forever. Recently there has been a proliferation of revenue bonds to raise funds for purposes far less secure than bridges and roads. For example, a municipality may issue revenue bonds for an industrial park in order to attract new businesses into the community. The investor must be aware, however, that while interest rates may be higher than those on other municipal bonds, they really pose a far greater risk, for the industrial park may fail in its purpose, leaving the investor with worthless revenue bonds even though the municipality may continue as a viable entity.

The special assessment bond is, in a sense, a kind of revenue bond, although it is usually classified separately. It carries a promise to pay interest and principal out of special taxes levied in connection with whatever is to be financed with the proceeds of the bond; for example, assessments to a group of homeowners for building a sewer system.

Municipals will continue to be interesting to savers and lenders in upper-middle and high income tax brackets for the foreseeable future. As a group, they are a trap for the unwary, but that may be said of almost any group of investment instruments. As individual investments coupling substantial interest rates with large tax savings, and therefore as proper vehicles for personal financial planning, some can prove quite attractive —as can some of the corporate bonds we will discuss now.

Private industry generates several kinds of short- and long-term obligations that may be directly or indirectly purchased by investors. The short-term obligations are *commercial paper;* the longer-term obligations are *bonds.*

Short-term corporate debt obligations are traded on national and international money markets, take several forms, and may be secured or unsecured, usually the latter. As of this writing, these corporate debts usually run from 90 to 180 days, are the debts of well-known "blue-chip" companies, and are traded in minimum denominations of $100,000.

Until the late 1970s, investors could not participate in the purchase of such short-term obligations because of the $100,000 minimum size of the instrument, although rates of return and safety factors made these instruments attractive. In recent years, however, investors have been able to purchase participations in money-market mutual funds (of which more is said soon), which provide indirect participation, with the funds buying large participations and selling smaller participations to the public. In future periods of even higher interest rates and even lower stock market prices, companies may turn more directly to the public to satisfy short-term borrowing needs; but they may continue to satisfy those needs by issuing commercial paper bought by banks, mutual funds, pension plans, and other purchasers in large denominations.

Coming as they do from very highly rated major companies, these short-term corporate debt obligations can indeed be quite attractive, usually paying 1.5–2.5% more than federal short-term obligations, and carrying low risks. But for those who are very concerned about the American economy and the possibilities of a major depression, it should be pointed out that there have been some (not many, but some) defaults on short-term corporate obligations in the 1970s and 1980s. Also, the size of the instruments makes it impossible to pick and choose the companies to which you will loan short-term money, since the small investor must buy them through mutual funds. At the same time, the fact that the individual investor buys these obligations as mutual fund shares spreads the risk and minimizes the size of potential default-related losses.

Bonds, on the other hand, are normally issued in denominations that make it possible for most investors to purchase them directly. They are the direct medium- and long-term debt obligations of privately owned companies, including industrial, transportation, utility, and financial organizations. Many of the investors who left the stock market during the 1970s and early 1980s moved into corporate as well as government bonds.

Corporate bonds pay fixed interest rates for specified lengths of time and repay principal at maturity. Like all bonds, they tend to fluctuate with

changes in interest rates, declining in value as interest rates rise above their
set amounts and increasing in value as interest rates decline below their
set amounts. Many companies include call provisions in their bonds,
allowing the companies to recall the bonds should interest rates decline
below a specified point, so that the issuing company can issue new bonds
at lower interest rates, thereby cutting company financing costs.

Corporate bond values, like all bond values, fall sharply when interest rates rise quickly, as they did, for example, in 1979 and 1980. That
is a considerable hazard for investors. At the same time, bonds issued
by highly regarded American corporations and rated at least "A" by
both Moody's and Standard and Poor's are likely to be excellent risks
throughout the 1980s. But again, you should not invest in "bonds," but
in the debt obligations of specific companies, and you should learn
enough about the companies and bonds you have invested in to be able
to follow them over the years and make informed decisions about them
as necessary.

There are several kinds of corporate bonds. One very special variety,
which became popular in the 1960s, is the convertible, which provides for
conversion of the bond into common stock at the option of the bond-
holder, within bounds specified on issuance by the bond itself. The right
to convert is exercised by a holder when the preferred or common stock
into which it can be converted rises far enough to make it an attractive
move. Until then, the market movement of the stock causes the bond itself
to fluctuate somewhat more than other bond market factors, such as
interest rates, might do by themselves. Convertible bonds have not been
attractive in the 1970s and early 1980s because of the move away from
the stock market and into other investment vehicles, although they may
become attractive again, as the situation changes.

Corporate bonds may be unsecured by any collateral. In that case, they
are often called debenture bonds, or debentures. They are then backed by
the "full faith and credit" of their issuer, constituting a promise to pay
based upon the future business prospects of the company. For some
companies, that promise to pay may be enough to create an attractive
investment possibility, if coupled with relatively high interest to make up
for the lack of collateral. It is quite reasonable, for example, to suppose
that American Telephone and Telegraph will be able to honor its commitments in the foreseeable future. But for most companies some kind of
collateral, securing the promise to pay, provides better security for bondholders, especially because many corporate debentures are subordinated;
that is, they are not unlimited promises to pay, but, rather, promises to
pay only after certain other kinds of debts, such as those owed banks and

insurance companies, are paid in a business crisis situation, such as bankruptcy.

The collateralized bonds issued by corporations come in several forms. Most of them involve securing the debt instrument with corporate physical assets, such as realty, sometimes directly and sometimes through the creation of intermediary trust instruments, which hold the land and guarantee payment out of assets held. No matter what device is used, the thing to look for is a clear, unambiguous, unencumbered use of physical assets that are likely to hold their value in the event of corporate disaster. That is what any competent lender would look for when loaning you money with your property as collateral; so it should be when you loan money to others.

First-mortgage bonds can be good bond collateral if the property used to secure the mortgage will be able to withstand corporate troubles. For example, a large parcel of improved land in suburban Houston may be excellent security, with the underlying value of the property carrying the value of the bond issue easily. In contrast, a factory near the center of a depressed northern industrial town may be next to worthless if closed, and hardly worthwhile security at all. In the latter instance, the bond is still a general promise to pay out of future corporate earnings, just as is a debenture, and should be treated for investment purposes as if it were a debenture, rather than a first-mortgage bond.

General mortgage bonds are often misnamed. They might better be called second mortgages, for that is what they often are: mortgages on property that is already wholly or partly mortgaged. Often property has appreciated in value, if only because of inflationary factors, and a second mortgage—a borrowing against the additional value of the property— becomes possible. Existing mortgages take precedence for payment, however, and general mortgage bonds should generally be viewed as if they were debentures.

The main thing to bear in mind when buying corporate bonds is that you are lending money to a corporation mainly upon your estimate of that corporation's current and future strength. If the corporation is strong now and in the future, you will be paid interest and will be repaid principal; if not, you are likely, one way or another, to lose all or some of your invested money. If you invest directly in bonds at all, that argues strongly for investing in the bonds of very strong, major companies with excellent future prospects. And it requires watching those companies, just as if you had bought shares in them. Bonds and other debt instruments are investments to be watched, not to be tucked away. There are not really any "annuity" stocks and bonds, or "widows' and orphans' " investments, to be bought and put away and to sit unexamined over the years, yielding safe, excellent interest and dividends for generations. There never were, but it is more apparent now, in this time of financial concern and chaotic financial market conditions.

COMMODITIES AND OPTIONS

The worst personal financial problems people experience during difficult times stem from the panic that such a period engenders. It is easy to mistake some kinds of speculations for hedges against inflation and depression. Under certain circumstances, some such hedges can be advantageous, but only if they are handled conservatively, not speculatively. Even so, you should explore carefully the particular investment situation, assess soberly the risks involved, and commit only a small percentage of your assets to such ventures.

Gold is a classic example of a hedge against inflation that has far greater risks than most investors anticipate. Because of price swings, gold often becomes a speculative instrument for buyers and sellers, rather than the simple long-term hedge against inflation that many purchasers desire.

Gold is a commodity, and in many ways its market behavior is little different from that of most other commodities. When supply is relatively large, and when world and national economic conditions are relatively stable, it tends to diminish in price. When those conditions are chaotic, and when supply does not increase, or the freely traded supply actually diminishes because of hoarding, it tends to rise in price. Because of hoarding, supply conditions, economic and political sensitivity, and the mystique that surrounds gold, its price in our time tends to rise and fall somewhat more sharply than that of many other commodities. Stated in these terms, gold market behavior is neither full of mystique nor very complicated. What is complicated—and extraordinarily so—are the vagaries of the international gold markets, which depend very heavily on political priorities and the actions of large commodity traders, speculators, hoarders, and users.

In dealing with gold, it is crucial at all times to know that governments, notably those of South Africa, the Soviet Union, and the United States, and such international bodies as the International Monetary Fund, can sharply affect the price of gold by either withholding gold from the world's supply or dumping stocks of gold on the world market in pursuit of national and international policy aims. South Africa and the Soviet Union, as major gold producers, can both withhold and dump; the United States and other national and international holders can only dump.

Traders, speculators, and hoarders can also affect the prices of gold and other precious metals considerably. Hoarders—and they are to be found all over the world, not only in the Middle East and other extremely volatile areas—buy and tend to hold indefinitely, diminishing the amount of gold in trading circulation and tending to drive prices up. Industrial users, such as the jewelry industry, diminish supply by taking gold out of trading circulation. Traders and speculators drive the price of gold up in a rising market as they buy, with a multiplication effect caused by their use of borrowed money.

On the way down, that multiplier can work in reverse, as was most spectacularly demonstrated by the experience of Nelson Bunker Hunt and his associates in early 1980, when their silver purchases turned into very bad speculative investments. They had purchased massive amounts of silver, using both cash and borrowed money, and in the process had driven the price of silver up from about $6 an ounce to about $50 an ounce in a little over a year. As market conditions changed, and as interest rates on borrowed speculative money went up very sharply all over the world (more than tripling in the United States in a short period), other speculators and the Hunts themselves found it increasingly difficult to hold their speculative positions. Ultimately, the bubble burst. Silver went down to a little over $10 an ounce, banks withdrew financing, brokers sold out positions to meet margin requirements and save themselves from bankruptcy, and the speculators lost hundreds of millions—by some estimates, billions—of dollars. Many unrelated buyers and sellers of silver were caught up in the downturn, with disastrous results.

Yet the mystique of gold, resulting largely from gold's historic role as the hardest store of value and medium of exchange, brings with it an inevitable tendency toward both hoarding and speculation, encouraged by gold's long-term tendency to hold and even increase its real value as compared to all other stores of value. There is one very well-defined investment school, that of the "gold bugs," who insist that in the long run gold is the only reliable store of value and that governments inevitably debase their own currencies and repudiate their debts, even to their own people.

That may or may not be true, but does not inevitably lead to the conclusion that gold is the ultimate store of value. The truth is that no major modern government anywhere in the world backs its currency with gold. All major governments, in a closely interconnected set of world economic orders, back their currencies with only their full faith and credit, which is merely a naked promise to pay, backed by the power of the state. Any government can prohibit—and in this century many have prohibited

—ownership of gold and other precious metals by its citizens, and confiscate privately held stocks of precious metals. Without notice, any tomorrow.

Looking at it that way, gold as a refuge against political and economic catastrophe might make sense for people living on the edge of political disaster all over the Middle East and South America. But for Americans, the saving of gold as such a refuge supposes the ability to store gold in a "safe" foreign country and the ability to go get it and to live on it elsewhere in the world, under conditions of crisis and complete political and economic breakdown in the United States. What is sometimes not so clearly understood is that the kind of breakdown that might destroy the United States' economic system would also destroy that of much of the rest of the world and would probably be accompanied by the kinds of conditions that would make canned goods, pound for pound, quite as valuable as gold. Something you cannot legally hold or trade would not be much of a refuge under such conditions. It might be of some use at a later time, assuming that crises were surmounted and a new political and economic system emerged, but that is a very tenuous reason for burying gold in your backyard.

Putting the classic hoarding reasons aside, then, gold must be considered fundamentally as an investment. As an investment, it has some strengths and some weaknesses. Its outstanding strength is that, in our time, its value does tend to grow at or better than the rate of inflation and should continue to do so over the long run—even if governments do some dumping of gold stocks. Such dumping might have disastrous short-term effects—but on speculators and traders, not on long-term financial planners.

Gold does tend to hold its value in relation to other goods. In a period of inflation and fear, it will probably rise somewhat in relation to other goods. At the same time, it yields no income of any kind until it is sold. That makes it necessary for you to be able to hold the gold for long-term investment purposes until a right time to sell—which may not be when you are ready, but as long as a year or two later.

If you have some money to put into gold—and it should never be more than a small proportion of your investment money—the ideal thing is to buy "against" the market. The only thing you can be sure of in the world of investments is that market prices of all kinds will fluctuate, and gold will fluctuate a great deal, as mystique and panic force its price up in bad times and as a turn to other, seemingly more attractive, investment opportunities forces its price down in good times. Like many other long-term investments, gold is best bought in good times, when it seems least attractive, and best sold in bad times, when it seems most attractive. The worst possible time to buy it is in a time of panic and fear.

As to speculating in gold and other precious metals—don't. The rationale that there is little "downside" risk, meaning that you will not lose too much of your money if it goes down because of the intrinsic value of the investment, is just that—a rationale. Speculating in gold in a rising market puts you into competition with professional traders and speculators all over the world, who watch gold and other precious metals every hour of every day, as you cannot possibly hope to do. If you buy precious metals high in a rising market and are forced to sell low, you may lose your shirt. If you hold the metals, waiting for long-term factors to reassert themselves, you may sell out your holdings years later at the dollar amounts you paid for them, but lose much of your money anyway, because of the inexorable loss of value of the dollar due to inflation. In the interim, you will also have lost the income that might have been generated by your capital.

There is very little virtue and much danger in speculating "a little," by taking a small percentage of your investment money and putting it into gold or other speculations. Another name for speculation is gambling, especially when it is indulged in by amateurs. Gambling has its own laws of development, being a fever that rises with a little exposure and that can lead to total financial destruction. And gold is particularly seductive to speculators, as it was to alchemists for more than 2,000 years.

The development is simple enough. First you take a couple of thousand dollars and put it into gold or some other speculative investment in a rising market for that kind of investment. You make some money and then reinvest it. Sooner or later, and usually with the help of an obliging broker, you discover the delightful possibilities of "leverage" and expand your investments through use of borrowed money in a margin account. Then, as other investments seem less and less attractive in comparison to the one you are riding with, you convince yourself that it is not a speculation at all, but a perfectly sound, sane, and conservative investment vehicle—and further, one that is paying far better than some of your other investments. At that point, entirely seduced by the money you are making, you put yourself wholeheartedly into the speculative investment vehicle, leveraging as much as possible; that is, borrowing as much and putting in as little cash as possible. Ultimately, as even such wealthy, professionally advised people as the Hunts found out, the bubble bursts.

Gold, silver, platinum, uranium, diamonds and other gemstones—all are precious metals and minerals that can be invested in, used, saved, speculated in, and traded. One way of investing in them is to buy and take physical possession of them. Another is to trade in the stocks of companies mining, selling, and trading in precious metals and minerals. These stocks are part of the stock market, but have a special character because of the nature of the goods handled; very often they respond more to the market price movements of the goods these companies produce and sell than to longer-term evaluations of the companies' corporate performances and prospects.

In a sense, that is as it should be; the long-term world price rise in gold in the 1970s and 1980s, for example, changed the profit prospects of gold-mining companies enormously, as it did current valuations of their stocks of gold on hand and their mining properties. Similarly, a sharp drop in silver prices after a speculative price rise may considerably harm the profit anticipations of silver-mining companies for the following year.

However, such market fluctuations are only part of the picture. Normal stock market investment rules apply to precious metals and gemstones stocks. You should not invest in a kind of stock, but rather in a company, no matter how attractive the kind of stock seems at the moment. One company may be better managed than another. One set of mining properties may be nearly exhausted, another may carry decades of proven reserves. One mining company may be located in Canada, whose political situation would be stable enough even if the country split into French- and English-speaking nations; another company, perhaps a leading world producer of gold and diamonds, may be located in South Africa (as so many are) and be a very questionable investment indeed in a period when intense pressure is being exerted upon that white-dominated country by a number of other African nations. "Buy American" is not particularly astute investment advice, carrying with it, as it does, a load of emotion that has nothing to do with analysis; but "buy North American" may be a sound approach to investing in companies in the mining industries. The political questions may be more and more important as this century draws to its close.

For the individual investor, some precious metals and gemstones differ from most other commodities in that they may be purchased and held. An ounce of gold, a pound of silver, or a diamond may be bought, physically taken, and put away somewhere. Industrial users of these kinds of commodities also buy for use or holding. Kodak, for example, buys hundreds of tons of silver every year for use in its photographic products. For that kind of industrial user, it is imperative that future supplies be assured, and at determinable prices. Therefore, over several centuries of dealing in commodities, a worldwide set of futures markets has developed, which deals in both current commodities sales, called *spot sales,* and in contracts to buy commodities up to a year in the future, called *futures contracts.*

Organized commodities exchanges exist all over the world, on which there is trading of a wide variety of spot and future commodities contracts. Some of the commodities traded are corn, wheat, soybeans, pork bellies, cattle, sugar, cocoa, cotton, and precious metals. In addition, in recent years trading has become active in such noncommodities as currency and other financial instruments. What is being traded is a contract specifying future delivery or receipt—stemming from sale or purchase—of stated amounts of the commodity or other item of value at a specific time. Each contract specifies identical quality, quantity, and terms of trade as do all other such contracts; because all are identical, they are tradable on a commodities exchange.

Most commodities trading in which individual investors participate is trading in futures, but that trading is very different from the trading done by industrial users. Such users may sometimes speculate, but basically they buy futures to provide for future use needs; in contrast, individual investors buy futures as pure speculations and do not even contemplate delivery on the contracts they buy, since the quantities involved are appropriate for large industrial users and not for individuals. For example, the standard unit of trade on most exchanges will be several thousand bushels of an agricultural product, scarcely an amount an individual investor is equipped to handle. For the individual investor, the game—and that's what it is, a particularly fast speculative game—involves buying and selling these large contracts on margin, in the hope of making large profits on the "leverage" created by the borrowed money. As always, leverage works both ways, and the possibility of gain must be weighed against the possibility of loss.

Individual investors can speculate in futures themselves or can arrange for others to manage such speculation. Just as in the stock and bond markets, both mutual funds and managed individual accounts are available. Either way, you would need to immerse yourself in this kind of speculative investment to have any chance at all of success in the long term. Oh, you may be able to make a little money—or perhaps quite a lot —as an unknowledgeable gambler in a booming set of futures markets; some have done so, usually losing their gains and their original investments as those markets fluctuated. But in the long run, making this kind of investment requires substantial skill and commitment and thus is not for the amateur.

The rising futures markets in the late 1970s encouraged development of an options market in futures, in which the basic transaction was the purchase of an option to buy or sell a stated quantity of futures at a specified time and price, with the option itself an instrument of value. Such trading had been prohibited in the United States on certain regulated commodities since the mid-1930s, although options trading in several commodities had continued uninterrupted on London commodities exchanges. However, because of the existence of loopholes in United States regulation of such trading, some commodity options could be traded in the United States, including silver, silver coins, sugar, cocoa, platinum, and copper.

Whenever a market yields quick profits to speculating investors, it becomes a magnet for sharp operators and some outright swindlers. The atmosphere surrounding a currently "hot" kind of speculative investment creates precisely the kind of situation in which it is possible to steal from the gullible. So it was with commodities and commodity options for some years, as it was with Florida real estate in the 1920s and is with Sunbelt real estate today. People bought nonexistent "London commodity options"; they bought "managed accounts," in which commissions of all kinds turned out to be more than 50% of the amounts they had invested; they even bought gemstones worth very little, in packages they agreed not to open until some time in the future in order to ensure the inviolability of the contents and to safeguard the "guarantees" of promoters.

Yet not all commodity options were bad investments. For some speculative investors, they afforded a way to speculate small, with losses limited to the amounts paid for the options and with large gains possible. Commodity options trading is not, in all hands, a bad speculation; it is not, however, a long-term financial planning vehicle.

Stock options are another kind of speculative investment, one considerably used in rising stock markets and avoided in falling stock markets. The option itself is the instrument of value, consisting of the right to buy or sell something of value at a specific price and within a certain time, which is the option period. Options to purchase land or commodities work the same way as tradable stock options. Up until the time specified for exercise of the option, that option is a legally enforceable right and may itself be a thing of value. After the period has expired, an unexercised option is worthless.

Such an option is a legally enforceable right; that fact can lead to considerable confusion, as the term *rights* is often incorrectly used as a synonym for stock options. Rights are only one kind of stock option, occurring when current common shareholders of a company are granted the right to buy, in proportion to their current holdings, newly issued company shares set at fixed prices for a specified time. If the price of company stock goes up before expiration, the newly issued rights are valuable and may be exercised or sold by their holders. If the price of company stock does not go up, the rights issued are worthless. Such rights, when issued to holders of debt obligations and preferred stock, rather than holders of common stock, are called warrants. They are negotiable if issued alone and non-negotiable if issued as coupons attached to the debt obligations or preferred stock.

Those who trade in stock options often are described as trading in puts and calls. A *put* is an option to sell for a set amount before a set time; a *call* is an option to buy for a set amount before a set time. One who buys an option to sell—a put—is speculating that the stock on which the option was purchased will go down more than the difference between its current market value and the price of the put. If so, the speculator will sell at a profit—a large profit, if the stock goes down a good deal. Often, however, the put is bought to hedge against such a sharp drop, with the buyer reasoning that the ability to sell the stock at current market levels is worth the price of the hedging put. If the price of the stock goes up, the price paid for the put is only a small subtraction from profit, and the downside risk is considerably less.

One who buys an option to buy—a call—is speculating that the stock on which the option was purchased will go up more than the difference between its current market value and the price of the call. If so, the speculator will buy at the low price guaranteed by the call and will resell at a profit—sometimes a very large profit. If not, the speculator will lose some or all of the money paid for the call; some, if the stock's price goes up a little, but not as much as the money paid for the call, and all, if the stock's price does not rise.

Taken as part of an overall stock market investment strategy, stock option trading need not be a speculative tactic. For an individual investor who wishes to buy common stock, stock options may be a hedge, using the price of the option as the risk investment toward the purchase of the common stock at a future date. Stock options can effectively limit risk if used in this fashion, but only if the investor is considering the purchase of the common stock as part of long-term financial planning. Risk can also be minimized by the very sophisticated use of straddles, which involve the purchase and sale of options virtually simultaneously, but this method should be avoided by anyone who is not an expert in that investment area.

In short, stock option trading can be used effectively as one of the tools in the professional's kit of tactics, as part of a long-term financial planning approach. Such trading by itself, however, is little more than speculation —modest speculation, but speculation all the same—for the entire amount invested may very easily be lost. All depends on the turn of the short-term stock price wheel—and markets do fluctuate.

COLLECTIBLES

These markets include collectibles markets, as recent experience has so clearly demonstrated. The term *collectibles* embraces a wide variety of tangible items that are bought, held, and traded for reasons other than use and for which trading markets have developed. In its investment sense, the term includes antiques, works of art, and tangible items of any age, including some that are brand-new, such as newly minted coins and newly printed stamps. It may even include items attached to realty, and legally part of realty, such as ironwork and barbed wire. It may include items collected partly because of their precious metals content, such as silver plates. The main investment aspect of a collectible is not what it is, but that a market exists or is thought, by many, to exist for it.

People trade in all kinds of things. There are well-defined markets for ancient and modern products of all the visual and decorative arts, such as paintings, furniture, glass, utensils, and sculpture; for everything printed or written, such as books, stamps, periodicals, autographs, theater programs, and photographs; for what were originally industrial products, such as old automobiles; really for everything under the sun, from matchbook covers to comic books to used clothing once worn by celebrities. As long as people collect and trade these items, they are, in an investment sense, collectibles.

In hard and uncertain times, worried individual investors tend to rush into the collectibles market, just as they rush into gold, silver, other precious metals, and gemstones. That rush lends a certain buoyancy to all collectibles markets—a buoyancy that may disappear as better times come and as other investment vehicles regain lost favor. Even worse, the ready market that exists for some kinds of collectibles in hard times may dry up in better times, and investors who bought high may find themselves holding on to items for which there is no market and which therefore may have to be sold at ruinous losses.

There are other possible disadvantages, too. Collectibles yield no dividends and are potentially quite illiquid. They must be sold to realize profit and often must be held for sale at the right time, rather than when you are ready or need to sell. Fads and styles in collecting change, as well, and this decade's fancy for a certain kind of painting, piece of furniture, or kind of printed matter may turn into disinterest in the next decade, when you are ready to sell. In truth, you can lose your shirt in many ways by investing in collectibles.

In light of these facts, can collectibles have a place in your long-term financial planning—even an important place? Yes, indeed, if you know what you are doing. That is the heart of the matter. Collectibles investing can provide you with some extraordinary opportunities, as long as you take the time and trouble to learn everything you can about what you are collecting and trading. Putting it a little differently, the most effective way to lose your shirt in this area is to invest in the collectibles market, as is true of investing in stock, bond, or commodities markets. The key to successful investment in collectibles is concentration on a single kind of collectible at the start, often on a single small area within a certain kind of collecting. It is quite possible to expand one's set of collecting and trading interests later on, as long as the new interests are mastered as fully as the old.

If this is done, collectibles offer both long-term profit and an opportunity to develop a sideline business to take with you into your later years. If, as we believe, it will be necessary for the overwhelming majority of us to work as long as we can, which may be a very healthy thing to do as well, then developing a collecting hobby that can become a sideline and then a retirement business is one of the few ideal ways to go in terms of long-term financial planning. Collectibles businesses can range all the way from multimillion-dollar international enterprises, such as Sotheby Parke, Bernet, to quite respectable and profitable enterprises run out of a single room at home. A skilled mechanic can collect, maintain, rebuild, and sell antique and classic cars on several acres out in the country; a skilled stamp or coin collector-trader can do what is, in investment and financial planning terms, essentially the same thing out of a small retirement home.

In trying to advise young people on their career choices, it is often fruitful to ask them what kinds of things they most enjoy and to try to build from there to an understanding of what they would like to do with their lives. After all, most people will do best what they like best; motivation is half the battle. So, too, with collecting. If becoming expert is far more than half the battle of investment success (and it is), and if collecting can be a major opportunity for long-term financial planning and a second career (and it can), then it is important to move into your collecting career as carefully as you would move into any other career. That means seeking out several areas of interest, settling on no more than one or two at the start, reading, subscribing to specialist periodicals, taking courses if possible, and haunting any available shows and sales in your chosen area; in short, finding a second vocation.

It sounds like a lot of work, and it is. It can also be tremendously rewarding, in terms of both money and enjoyment, if done properly. To build an investment stake and a second career simultaneously is an opportunity to be grasped, once understood.

Some cautions are necessary in this area, however. One centers on confusing collectibility with precious metal or gemstone contents. If you buy a silver plate, for example, thinking that the silver content of that plate will always guarantee you resalability and a reasonably good price, you may be sorely disappointed years later when you want to sell it. You may find that you have put investment money into a plate containing silver worth only a small fraction of the money you paid for it, and you may be forced to sell for the value of that silver content alone, receiving no dividends at all on the money you tied up in the plate. The net of such a transaction, after the impact of inflation, is a whopping loss in real dollars. Investors in such collectibles have often failed to assess soberly the real value of the precious metals and gemstones in such manufactured goods as silver plates and gemstone figurines. And though the astute promoters of these kinds of items have, in most cases, under government pressure, ingeniously managed to disclaim underlying value as a reason to buy, they have actually stressed resale value and ready marketability.

The truth is that, as long as markets for the kinds of precious metals and gemstones used in such goods are going up, resale value and marketability are generally excellent, buoyed partly by those rising markets and partly by the expectations of those buying and holding the goods. However, as soon as those markets go down for any period, measured in months or years, expectations disappear, many sellers appear, and marketability at any price much higher than the underlying value of the goods becomes impossible. It suddenly, and far too late, becomes clear that those who promoted these manufactured goods included large promotion costs, substantial manufacturing costs, and a very large profit in their sales price and that they have no intention of making good on their implied, nonbinding promises to make resale markets at high prices for those goods.

Other cautions center on fads and quality. Collectibles sometimes fall out of fashion, which results in a severe impact on prices and sometimes on marketability as well. Yesterday's voguish modern painting by a relative unknown, which sold for $1,000 and was sure to triple in value in a few years, may now be worth $200—if you can find a buyer at all. On the other hand, medium- or high-quality stamps, coins, antiques, books, and jewelry seldom lose much of their value, as their markets tend to be well established and worldwide. You can make a collecting specialty of something unusual or relatively new to the collectibles world and make a lot of money at it, but it can be risky, converting what can be long-term income and second-career building into long-term speculation and loss. It would seem far wiser to become expert in a well-established collectibles area before moving into more speculative activities. Of course, there are always exceptions to such a rule. Sometimes interest overcomes prudence. Some people who were fascinated by baseball cards, comic books, or science fiction magazines collected them when they had no great intrinsic value and seemed very unlikely ever to acquire such value. Ultimately, their interest was translated into very valuable collectibles and in some instances into lucrative sidelines and even full careers.

Collecting and trading in collectibles can be very profitable, the genesis of a whole new retirement career, and great fun, too. The trick is to become expert and to keep on sharpening your expert knowledge as long as you live. It will probably also help you to live longer.

REAL ESTATE

The last of the major kinds of investments we will deal with here is real estate, which as an investment can be conservative, speculative, or anything in between, depending upon what is being invested in and how that investment is handled. Evaluating real estate in terms of long-term financial planning requires identifying and analyzing several underlying factors and facets of the huge and intertwined real estate and real estate investment markets.

One such underlying factor in the early 1980s is that the demand for dwellings continues to rise, while the stock of available dwellings continues to diminish, relative to demand. Although birthrates have declined, people are living longer, and the high birthrates of the 1950s and early 1960s have brought many new renters and buyers into the housing market. At the same time, a complex of cost and credit factors has severely limited growth in the nation's housing stock, while existing housing continues to age. The net effect, and it is a long-term one, is that in most areas demand outstrips supply and will continue to do so, building a long-term escalator into dwelling values.

Another underlying factor is that national tax policy continues to favor real property ownership. The twin concepts of depreciation and depletion continue to be woven into the fabric of the tax law and therefore into the values of real estate and natural resources. These concepts must be understood clearly if the tax-sheltered nature of ownership investments in those areas is to be fully appreciated. A tax-sheltered investment literally protects income from taxation, allowing its natural growth in value to compound unimpeded by taxes. The concept of depreciation for non-owner-occupied residential or commercial property builds such protection into real estate ownership investments, while depletion does the same for natural resource ownership investments.

Depletion is the concept that natural resources can be and are used up. As reflected in the tax law, the concept results in substantial tax deductions for owners of such resources and is much of the reason for the development of many huge fortunes based on oil and natural gas.

Depreciation, now called *accelerated cost recovery* (for federal tax purposes), is a concept applied to business assets. It is the lessening of an asset's value because of use and age. As reflected in the tax law, it makes possible large and repeated tax deductions for the same property through owner after owner, each new owner beginning the process of depreciation again. Simultaneously, it makes it possible to take those tax deductions very quickly.

Even for nonbusiness property, tax policy much favors ownership, as all homeowners know. Tax deductions for property taxes and mortgage interest have long benefited owners of single-family homes, and now benefit millions of condominium and cooperative apartment owners as well.

The tax deferrals achieved by the use of depreciation of property are later recaptured and must be paid at a future date, but in the interim years the tax savings incurred may be used for additional investments, which is an extremely efficient use of money. Also, the taxes that will eventually have to be paid will be computed at a lower rate as long-term capital gains taxes, not as ordinary income taxes, which is a major benefit to real estate investors.

In the residential housing market in the 1960s, 1970s, and early 1980s, the nature of the mortgage transaction combined with a sustained rise in dwelling values led—quite by accident—to an extraordinary mass example of leverage.

When you buy a dwelling, you pay a certain amount down—normally 10–25%, depending mainly on the age of the dwelling and on credit factors—and borrow the rest, in the form of one or more mortgage loans secured by the value of the property. Given the relatively low mortgage rates of the 1960s and 1970s, the fixed nature of those rates, the very favorable tax treatments granted to homeowners with regard to interest and property tax payments, and the steep rise in housing values, millions of homeowners found themselves enjoying truly enormous rates of return on investment during the period. For example, an investment of $10,000 down on a previously owned house in a stable suburban community in the mid-1960s often bought a $50,000 house. In the early 1980s that house might be selling for $250,000—a fairly normal quintupling of market value but not of investment. For the investment was $10,000, not $50,000.

Assuming that payments on the house, taxes, and maintenance costs are offset by owner occupancy, with rental not being paid elsewhere, the true return on investment is not 5:1 minus any tax impact on sale, but 25:1. The real net effect was that the owner-occupier of a dwelling achieved a 2,500% return on investment, as compared to whatever that $10,000 might have earned elsewhere over roughly the same 15-year period. In the stock market, for example, it might have earned nothing.

That is leverage in a rising market. Of course, as always, leverage can work both ways. Hundreds of thousands of Americans bought homes in the 1920s, but lost those homes and the money invested in them when they could not keep up with mortgage payments and suffered foreclosure during the Great Depression; foreclosing lenders in that deeply depressed housing market resold the houses for less than the outstanding mortgage loans or were forced to hold them unsold. That was leverage, too.

For very high income investors, leverage with interest deductions can work wonders, if the investments they go into are even modestly successful. For homeowners forced to borrow large sums to swing home purchases, leverage can work either way, usually for reasons beyond their control. For the small and medium investor speculating in real estate, leverage can bring wealth—or ruin. However, the decision as to whether or not to refinance is much informed by an understanding of how leverage really works.

Real estate investment can take many forms. Most of those forms range from very safe to highly speculative, depending on how financing is handled. In that respect, real estate is little different from other investment vehicles. Investment in relatively "safe" common stocks can be highly speculative if required margins are very low and if borrowed money is used and pyramided upon, as was precisely the case during the 1920s, when those "safe" stocks began to fall, and margin calls forced them much farther down than they would have gone had not leverage worked against them.

Investments in commodity futures, stock options, precious metals, and real estate all become highly speculative when highly leveraged, but may be relatively safe when the leverage is taken out of them. Bear in mind, however, that the leverage has to be taken out of the whole market. It does not do to buy for cash in a market made volatile by highly leveraged speculators, for the market is still volatile, and you still may lose much of your investment, however safe you try to play your gamble. A closely regulated stock market with high margin requirements may be less exciting, but is intrinsically safer than a commodities futures market requiring 10% margins.

Real estate investment uses many vehicles, all variations on a few basic forms—the same forms encountered in other kinds of investments. You can buy, hold, and trade real estate yourself; you can go, with others, into a kind of business based largely on real estate ownership; you can buy an ownership interest in a real estate company; or you can lend money to real estate owners, directly or through funds managed by others.

At its most basic, real estate investment can consist of your purchasing a dwelling in an area unlikely to suffer economic catastrophe, living in that dwelling, and selling it after you reach the age of 55, to take advantage of the very large, one-time tax forgiveness allowed on such a sale. If possible, allowing for such noneconomic factors as the quality of schools and cultural advantage, that house should be located in a relatively low tax area, which speaks strongly for buying in a well-established community, rather than one with large numbers of child-raising families. That community may also be relatively low taxed in direct relation to the amount of industry that has been let in by local zoning policy. Many communities, afraid of industry, have sacrificed economy for exclusivity. A few have found that policy economically beneficial in terms of resale values, but others have found that long-term difficulties are created by the policy, as people find it increasingly difficult to make ends meet.

Dwellings purchased in cities should be carefully examined in terms of neighborhood stability and the possibility of spreading urban decay. Some neighborhoods in some cities offer excellent prospects for long-term living and capital accumulation, and other areas may increase in value dramatically, due to rehabilitation programs, but the long-term trend in residential housing in most major American cities is still downward, as jobs erode, housing stock deteriorates, migration of people and industry to the suburbs and beyond continues, financing grows increasingly difficult, and federal policy continues to look the other way.

If you choose with care, however, and constantly view and evaluate that dwelling as an investment as well as a place to live, it can be a superb investment. Return on investment can scarcely be expected to continue to be 2,500%, with the advent of variable-rate mortgages, but there is every reason to believe that the impact of favorable tax laws and long-term upward trends in housing markets will provide returns far better than those possible in almost any other kind of investment and rivaling those available from a successful business of your own.

Sole or substantial ownership and management of your own property, whether personal residence or business property, is not the only way to invest in a real estate ownership interest. Another, and very widely adopted, mode of real estate ownership is that of the limited partnership.

The essence of such an ownership interest is that the limited partner is part owner of the property invested in, but shares in profit and loss possibilities only to a specified extent, in contrast to the general partner, who carries unlimited personal liability and possibility of gain, as in any regular partnership. The corporate form would provide limited liability to common stockholders, rather than the unlimited liability to which general partners may be subjected. However, tax laws, as currently written, usually dictate that many real estate transactions use the partnership rather than the corporate form.

A properly constructed limited partnership provides limited liability to the limited partners, while allowing the losses and gains of the partnership to be passed through to the limited partners. This is especially important in those real estate transactions which, by their nature, will show losses in the early life of the partnership, because these losses can be passed through as desirable tax deductions to the limited partners. The partnership form also has value later, when income or profits are earned, because it avoids the effects of the double taxation that exists under the corporate form, where first the corporation is taxed on its profits and then the shareholders are taxed on the earnings they receive from the corporation.

The essence of the matter is that profits and losses in partnerships pass through directly to the partners, making it possible for the losses generated by accelerated depreciation and high interest payments in the early years of ownership to pass through to the partners; these losses are used as personal income tax deductions. That leaves general partners able to minimize tax payments, although their personal positions are more vulnerable because of the absence of the limited liability shield carried by corporate stockholders. But for limited partners, both limited liability and tax deductions are available—a classic case of having your cake and eating it too.

That is the basic tax and investment situation that has made participation in limited real estate partnership so attractive to many high income taxpayers. For the affluent, it has for decades been possible, using the device of the limited partnership, to finance real estate investments at little risk of liability and wholly with government money in the form of taxes which otherwise would have had to be paid on income. For many years it was actually possible to make a good deal of money in unpaid taxes, even if the real estate investment yielded no profits at all at any time—sometimes even if it was a total loss. In recent years, however, some limits have been placed on this basic transaction.

Such an arrangement sounds like a fine way to take a good deal of risk out of investment and to maximize return on investments actually made

—and so it is. A few words of caution are in order, however. A poor investment is still a poor investment, no matter how tax advantaged. An office building occupied by a single tenant in a small town or city may look wonderful on initial investment, but the same building a few years later may be a white elephant, its tenant gone and no other tenant in sight, its mortgagor foreclosing and all investment lost. Commercial property on a well-traveled highway may lose its value overnight if a new highway is built nearby that bypasses that property. An inventive and unscrupulous set of general partners may find ways to milk a property, leaving the limited partners high and dry, somewhat tax-advantaged, and wholly shorn of invested capital. Here, as with all other investment forms, one should invest in a property, not in a market; in a specific real estate investment, not in "real estate."

Other possibilities also exist for tax write-offs in real estate investment. Real estate investment firms constantly seek to develop new ways of enhancing the tax advantages available in real estate financing and management. The Internal Revenue Service constantly seeks to limit those tax advantages. The result is a constant small "war" and a good deal of contention and litigation between private investors and federal regulators in this area, as in so many other areas of government–business interface. That makes it absolutely necessary for anyone wishing to invest in limited partnerships in real estate (and in any other tax-sheltered transaction, for that matter) to seek professional counsel before investing. That means counsel beyond that provided by sellers of tax-advantaged investments. The best of such sellers routinely and properly advise prospective purchasers to seek tax and legal advice from their accountants and attorneys before investing. Real estate consultants may also be called in to evaluate the property. Whatever your real estate investment plans, you would be wise to seek professional advice.

In personal financial planning, professional help can be of enormous value; every aspect of your financial life can benefit from the kind of astute long-term analysis and advice that a good financial planner can bring to your personal matters. At the same time, it continues to be true that nobody will watch your business as closely as you will, which means that you must keep on top of your financial affairs every step of the way, all your life. Whatever advice you get, the real decisions are yours to make, and yours alone. Get professional financial advice, by all means. But bear in mind at all times that the financial side of your personal life is just as important to you as the financial side of your company's life is to your company. For whatever the other satisfactions stemming from a successful career in selling, success on the financial side of life is make or break.

CHAPTER 10

APPEARANCES THAT COUNT

Matters of dress, grooming, and equipment are matters of personal "packaging"; as such, they are important, though not nearly as important as what we are and how we convey what we are to others. And we project what we are with speech and body language far more than we do with appearances. That successful sales professionals are always people who look as if they had just stepped out of a Fifth Avenue show window is a myth; many seasoned and very successful people in selling look about as fashionable as an average middle- to upper-grade civil service employee anywhere in the country.

That said, appearances do still deserve careful attention, for while excellent appearances can help sales results and career development only a little, poor appearances can cause sales and careers a great deal of harm.

A good—meaning rather conservative, classically styled, and fairly expensive—personal appearance can help others to accept you as a working professional, in the field and in your company. Conversely, an appearance that is too far from current behavioral or stylistic norms can jar, and set up unnecessary barriers between yourself and others. In extreme instances, when grooming and dress are very far from current styles, it is even possible to severely harm sales and career possibilities. These are only matters of current style, of course, and have nothing at all to do with professional skills. Yet they can be important, if current norms are bent too far. The main thing to understand about dress and grooming is not so much that you can do yourself a great deal of good by dressing and looking well, but that you can do yourself a good deal of harm with a poor appearance. That means keeping up with current standards, looking clean, cool, and alert at all times, and in all climates and conditions; and it means dressing comfortably and classically, and not worrying too much about how you look to others.

Although such matters as how to dress are enormously overrated as selling and career-building factors, it is possible to make situations—and particularly new situations, with new people—far more difficult than they need be, by conveying wrong signals about yourself with manner and dress. Most experienced people have trained themselves to pick up useful clues from a quick first look. Such minor grooming matters as uncombed hair, scuffed shoes, or not-quite-fully-cleaned fingernails can easily be seen as evidences of a general carelessness that may show up in other, more serious ways. The person who seems unwilling to tend to such small matters may not care enough about much more important matters; such a little thing can tip a buying or hiring decision the wrong way. Similarly, those who dress quite inexpensively are all too often seen as people who may not quite be making it financially; that can jar others enough to make them somewhat uneasy about them as buyers, as employers, and as co-networkers over a period of years. We want those we do business with, and our associates, protégés, friends, and allies to "look good"; it makes us look good, and it makes our company look good.

Similarly, the sales professional who dresses too trendily or too sexily, or who uses too much cologne, perfume, hair tonic, lipstick, or whatever else is not *in* this year, tends to jar others. Among business professionals, the least questioned and most accepted image is still basically that created by Gregory Peck in *The Man in the Grey Flannel Suit,* in the period following World War II. This image, however, is no longer solely a white, Anglo-Saxon, Protestant male image, but now encompasses female, black, Hispanic, Jewish, East Asian, Native American, and a score of other national and ethnic images, as well. But all of them share this: they are still conservatively and traditionally dressed and groomed, and in every verbal and nonverbal way convey that they carry upper-middle class status. This is not upper-class economic status and the social attitudes assumed to go with "old money," which are thought by so many others to be rather nastily condescending. The main American business image of this period continues to be that of the small-town boy—or girl—who made good, and now occupies one of the big houses on the good side of the tracks.

PLANNING A BUSINESS WARDROBE

What constitutes effective business dress varies somewhat regionally and by industry. A southeastern regional representative may wear a white suit in midsummer quite easily; so may his or her clients. But those working on Fifth Avenue or Wall Street in New York City are not very likely to be found wearing white suits in any season; nor will their clients in the New York area. And when *you* go to Atlanta on business in midsummer, you will be unwise to don a white suit, although you may leave your dark, pinstriped suit and Ivy League tie behind. A white suit would properly be perceived by local people in Atlanta as a phony, while the pinstripes and Ivy League tie would make you seem too alien to be comfortable with; the solution is somewhere in between.

You will find the most conservative business dress on the East Coast, especially in the corridor that runs from Boston to Washington, D.C., as well as at most corporate headquarters, regardless of geographic location. The basic business colors of blue and grey will work well virtually anywhere in the country, but clothing styles loosen up a bit in the Midwest, where more browns and tans are worn by men, and more brighter colors by women. Short sleeves and light dresses are common in the South and Southwest. And the West Coast is far more casual than the East Coast, with California being the most relaxed of all. In general, it is best to stay within the conservative range for your region and industry, avoiding sartorial extremes.

Some basic guidelines are helpful when you are planning and upgrading a sound business wardrobe. Perhaps most important is to learn the look and feel of quality. Many people, when they shop, go through the racks until something catches their eye. If it looks all right and the price is acceptable, they buy it. They may check the label for fiber content as a second thought; they may never inspect the finishing and stitching.

If you are shopping for your professional "uniform," you should shop more carefully, with a purpose and plan. Do a little window shopping first. You will find the best quality in better stores; visit them and inspect their merchandise. Read the labels for manufacturers and for fiber content, and note prices. This will help you get the best value and quality at the best price, when it comes time to do your actual buying.

Good quality garments are well finished. Most clothing is machine-stitched, with the exception of the finest suits, which are tailored and stitched by hand. Machine-stitching should be small and even. The pieces of a garment should be well joined; that is, collars should lay flat, sleeves should not pucker, and lapels should not pull. Buttonholes should be well finished, without loose threads. Check the inside of the garment for seams that are ample and finished, and that will not begin unraveling with wear and cleaning. Linings should not pull or pucker or droop below hemlines. Buttons, if not bone, should at least be a good quality plastic or a nontarnishing brasslike metal.

For quality, look for the real thing—natural fibers or blends with natural fibers for clothing, and leather for accessories such as wallets, gloves, shoes, belts, and briefcases. In general, avoid garments that are all synthetic and any material that is shiny or semitransparent. Some synthetic fibers have a shininess to them that looks cheap; they also feel rough to the touch. Above all, avoid all polyester knits, especially for outer garments. They are distinctly not upper-middle class, and tend to snag, stretch, and bag. The real thing costs more than substitutes and imitations, but it is far better to own a few good quality outfits than many cheaper ones. The difference in quality speaks for itself.

The best natural fibers are wool and cotton. Wool can be worn year-round, particularly if it is blended with polyester. Wool breathes and keeps its color and shape well. It adds richness and texture to a blend. Wool will keep you warmer in the winter and, believe it or not, cooler in the summer than synthetics. Polyesters, rayons, and acrylics, for example, do not breathe well. A lightweight suit that is 45% wool and 55% polyester is cooler during hot months than is an all-polyester suit. When buying wool-blend garments, be sure to check the fiber contents label; 45% wool is the minimum for optimum wear, durability, appearance, and texture.

Cotton is comfortable on the skin, breathes well, and is cool in the summer, but it is a fragile fabric that is much better blended with polyester. By itself, cotton shrinks, fades, wrinkles, and wears out quickly. In a blend, you can have the comfort of cotton with the durability of polyester. Some of the best and most expensive men's shirts, however, are all cotton. Buy these only if you are prepared to foot a weekly cleaning bill. Because of the way cotton wrinkles, you will need to send your shirts out for cleaning and pressing in order for them to look crisp.

Silk is a natural fiber that has been enjoying renewed popularity, especially in more fashionable clothing. Silk is especially appropriate, even preferable, for accessories such as ties and scarves. Good silk has a rich, quality look, but the fiber has significant disadvantages in clothing for business purposes: it is expensive, can soil and stain, generally requires dry cleaning, and wrinkles easily. In addition, the rich, lustrous look of silk may give garments—particularly suits—more of an evening wear look than a business look. However, many women have made silk dresses and blouses staples for business wear. Silk dresses may be better left for evenings, but silk blouses are certainly acceptable with suits and with skirts and blazers, if one is willing to bear the expense of caring for them properly.

Silk—good silk—can be wonderfully soft and comfortable and rich and shiny in appearance. Even though it is a thin fabric, it can absorb up to one third of its weight in moisture, which makes it very comfortable to wear on hot days. Not all silks are equal, however, and unfortunately, most labels do not tell enough about the quality of the garment. Italian silks tend to be the best, generally very soft and quite lustrous—and they are the most expensive. Dyes vary greatly in quality; some are actually water-soluble, a disaster if they ever get wet. Others stain easily, and many will fade when subjected to strong sunlight. Many stores will tell you that you can avoid heavy dry cleaning costs by washing silk in cold water detergents meant for woolens, lingerie, and other delicate garments. But that may not be as practical as it sounds. Depending on the quality of the fiber, washed silk may wrinkle considerably and may not iron out well. It is safer to dry clean brightly colored silks and textured silks, such as crepe and taffeta. Some silk garments may wrinkle considerably in washing, and ironing out the wrinkles may be more trouble than having them dry cleaned. If you do opt to handwash your silks, take care not to rub or twist the fabric, because the yarns can break and stretch easily. Also, be sure to iron the garments on the wrong side.

Since you can invest a lot of money in silk, it would be worth your while to do some research on the various silk weaves before buying any—there are nearly two dozen of them, all with different qualities and properties. When shopping for silk, remember that good silk is expensive. The popularity of silk has brought many cheap silks to the market, and a cheap silk is just that: cheap. It may not be dyed evenly, it may discolor unevenly, or it may separate or tear easily. If you cannot buy silk, look for silk and polyester blends, or good polyesters that look like silk. If you shop around enough, you will soon be able to recognize polyesters that are good imitators of silk.

Accessories are where many otherwise smart shoppers fall down. They pay top dollar for quality clothes, which they then ruin with cheap accessories. Your entire appearance must convey quality; do not skimp, thinking you can "get by" with something pulled out of a bargain basement. Do not buy imitation leather; buy the real thing. Be especially careful with shoes—inexpensive leather shoes look only marginally better than vinyl ones. Any jewelry should be simple, functional, and fashioned from real gold or silver. If you have an inexpensive watch, you may wish to dress it up with a leather band instead of a plastic, fabric, or metal one. Always carry and use a good gold or silver pen—never a cheapie, no matter who else around you may use one.

As you do your window shopping, note brand names and their various levels of quality and cost. While you will find top brands in better stores, you will also begin to notice the brands that come next in quality and are less expensive. You need not buy the most expensive of everything you need. It is perfectly acceptable—and wise from a budget standpoint—to buy more moderately priced goods, as long as they look high quality. You will find some good quality, more moderately priced brands in department stores, but avoid discount chains. Discount chains often stock imperfect goods and overruns that have missed the market in their style. The same caution applies to factory and warehouse outlets. Many do sell name brand goods at marked-down prices, usually with the labels ripped out, but others sell seconds and imperfects which are not marked as such.

A word about name brand labels: as you become more familiar with the quality of certain brands, you will probably develop a list of favorites that you will trust. Many stores have their own labels, and these are often good bets for quality merchandise at moderate prices. Stores generally are careful when it comes to their own labels, as it is bad advertising to put your name on something that falls apart after one or two cleanings. A discount chain, however, may put its own label on an inexpensive loss leader item designed solely to attract traffic to the store. You must discover for yourself which stores are the most reliable.

A designer label once ensured good quality. With some designers, that is still true today, but other designer labels have become so diluted through mass manufacturing and merchandising that they really offer no guarantee of quality at all. In fact, the clothing may even be poorly constructed. Such designers license manufacturers to produce their designs, but they cannot possibly monitor quality. They sit back and collect royalties while you pay a premium price for their name without necessarily getting premium quality. The proliferation of designer labels in department stores, discount houses, and outlets has also reduced their status. Wearing such items is no longer a sure mark of upper-middle class status and wealth. In fact, in the business world, designer labels can work against you, if the designer's name or initials are plastered all over your garment. Traditional, classic apparel is understated, and is not a walking billboard for someone else.

A second basic in wardrobe planning is to consider the importance of color. For people in most business situations, dark colors work best because they convey authority and power. The all-around general business suit color for men and women is dark blue or navy blue. Charcoal grey and medium grey are good, but dark browns are not universally acceptable. If you have limited funds for your wardrobe, it is best to build it around blues and greys; beige is an acceptable third color.

Women have more latitude to wear bright colors than do men; still, both sexes should take care to avoid trendy, fashion-oriented shades and styles, which make their wearers look frivolous in the conservative eyes of the business establishment. Women should also strike red from their business wardrobes—it is a boldly sexual color. At the other extreme, be careful with black; it is a very severe color, and can cause as much negative reaction as a frivolous color, like pink. Some colors—

such as gold, pink, lavender, and certain greens—are best avoided in suits altogether.

The quieter your outfit is, the better. Solids work the best, especially for women. Pinstripes function well for men (as long as they are not reminiscent of the wide, "gangster look") but less well for women. Muted plaids and tweeds are acceptable if they are of very good quality; make certain that plaid patterns match where garment pieces are sewn together. Both sexes should avoid fabrics that have busy, dramatic, or distracting patterns, which diminish professional appearance and, consequently, status.

Shirts and blouses should contrast with suits; white and pastels (except pink) are the most acceptable shades for men and women. The pastels should not blend into the color of the suit, for that can create a dull, lifeless look. While women can wear dark shades with light-colored suits (a maroon blouse with a light grey suit, for example), men are best advised to stick to white with light-colored suits.

For important occasions, such as job interviews and key group presentations, it is wise to dress especially conservatively. The best colors for job interviews are suits in charcoal or light grey and navy blue, with contrasting shirts or blouses. When job hunting, women should forgo their freedom to wear darker colors in shorts and blouses, and stick with white or pastel blue, the most accepted contrasting colors in the business establishment.

The only kind of clothing for which bright colors are not only acceptable, but expected, is sportswear. You should not go overboard, however, and show up looking like a neon sign at your company's summer sales refresher workshop. Upper-middle class sportswear colors tend to center around white, navy, maroon, and khaki, although many bright plaids are also acceptable. Beware of light blue, which can look cheap, and bright yellow, which can look gaudy.

When selecting colors and putting together outfits, take into consideration your weight and build. Fortunately for most of us, the dark, "power" colors also tend to be slimming, while brighter colors tend to make people look larger. A plaid over a paunch can add to the rotundity. Dark colors on tall, large men and women can make them look too imposing, almost unapproachable, however, so if you fit into this category, you may want to build your working wardrobe around lighter shades such as light grey and beige.

The color of your overcoat is just as important as the color of your suit or dress. Camel and beige are good all-around colors in coats, followed by dark grey, navy blue, and black, which are somewhat more formal and severe. Furs may be a bit pretentious in the workplace, except for fur collars on coats, so women should save their fox and mink coats for evening wear.

When planning your business wardrobe you should carefully assess your professional environment. Your company, industry, even your geographic locale will influence your latitude in building your professional wardrobe. If you work for a conservative company such as IBM you would be wise to stick to very traditional dress habits. Whenever you are in doubt when shopping for clothes, it is safest to go with the most conservative choices. You may have more freedom of expression if you are in a trend-oriented industry such as entertainment, fashion, or advertising, but in most corporate circles, you cannot be too conservative.

Dress customs vary around the country, too. Drop in at a mid-Manhattan restaurant during lunch time and you will see mostly dark suits. But in Los Angeles, you will most likely see brighter colors on both men and women, and even shirts open at the neck on men.

Look around you and note carefully how your peers and superiors are dressed, particularly the key sales management people at your company. You may want to pick out one or two successful superiors, to analyze their styles of dress and use them as role models to emulate. That does not mean you should copy them—you can make mistakes that way. For example, monogrammed shirts may be seen as fitting for a senior marketing vice president, but not for a youngish field representative. And certain affectations, such as linen handkerchiefs in breast pockets or diamond lapel stick pins, may work wonderfully for one person and look pretentious or silly for another. Use your role models as guides, wear nothing that makes you feel uncomfortable, and add your own distinctive personal touches.

Once you have planned what your business wardrobe *should* be, you should carefully and critically assess your present wardrobe. This is the moment of truth. How does your closet stand up to the test? Divide your clothes into seasons and assess each item—each suit, dress, blazer, pair of slacks, accessory, shirt, blouse, and pair of shoes. Be honest and ruthless, even though it may be painful to see just how much of what you own does not meet critical standards. If you are like most people, you have accumulated your wardrobe in a haphazard fashion, buying this on sale here, that on impulse there, including items which may not fit you quite right, but they were such a terrific deal you could not pass them up. Well, reform time is at hand. No point in lamenting past mistakes—just vow not to repeat them. Give everything in your closet a meticulous examination and be firm in setting aside everything that does not measure up. And that means *everything*. All of those items will eventually disappear from your working wardrobe; how quickly will depend on how much you have to replace, and how much money you can afford to spend over what period of time. What will you do with all your discards? Save what you can to wear around the house, donate them to charity, or—if they are in excellent condition—take them to a thrift resale shop.

As you assess your wardrobe, keep in mind that you will want to build your clothing around one or two main colors. Group those items that go together and then determine what you still need to round things out. Limiting your color schemes will help prevent you from buying something on impulse, only to wear it seldom because it does not go with many of your other clothes.

What if you feel you must almost start from scratch, but have a tight budget for clothes? In that case, at least eliminate the most unsuitable items from your wardrobe and gradually replace the rest. Work out a timetable with what you feel you can comfortably afford to spend, and start with a few basics that can do double duty for you, such as a dark, solid-colored suit that can be worn twice in one week but will look different with varying shirts and ties or blouses.

Then you are ready to begin reconstructing your wardrobe. You should start by making a list of the things you need and ranking them by priority. Concentrate on the season at hand—if it is summer, focus on your lighter clothing needs. You should also make a list for your fall and winter needs, but you can postpone buying for the next season until it actually arrives. Eventually, when you get your core wardrobe established, you can begin buying for seasons in advance, in order to take advantage of sales. You can get some very good mark-downs on clothes at the end of seasons.

But you must be careful, because it is easy to get carried away with sales. Do not buy something that is of mediocre quality or that may go out of style in a season or two just because it is on sale. Do not buy something that is not quite the right color or something you merely *think* will coordinate with clothes hanging in your closet, just because the price is right. The price may be appealing, but chances are the garment will not be quite right, and it will only go unworn—a quite expensive purchase when you consider the small use you get from a particular piece of clothing. A suit marked down $80 is no bargain if you only wear it once or twice a season. You may find that the labels you like to buy seldom go on sale (as is often the case in premium clothing), although you may get lucky and find something you are looking for at a reduced price. The important thing is never to sacrifice quality and practicality for price.

Your general rule of thumb should be to buy the best possible quality you can afford. If you cannot afford a Brooks Brothers suit, buy a less costly brand that comes closest, in your estimation, to the quality you seek. If you cannot afford a good-quality silk blouse, buy one made from a polyester that closely imitates the look and feel of real silk. It is far better to have a smaller wardrobe of high-quality clothes than a large wardrobe of medium-quality or cheap clothes.

When shopping for shirts, ties, and blouses to go with suits or jackets, buy the items together rather than separately. You cannot rely on your memory to tell you accurately the shade of something in your closet; you may get something home and find it does not match at all. If possible, pick out shirts, ties, and blouses at the same time you buy a suit. Or, take a swatch of suit material with you. Better yet, wear the suit when you go shopping, or take the jacket with you. That way, you will be certain of picking out items that complement each other. The same idea applies when shopping for shoes. Do not try on business shoes while dressed in jeans or dungarees; wear an outfit you plan to wear with the shoes. It does make a difference. Remember, you are striving for a well-thought-out, unified, *total* look.

If you have done enough window shopping, and have examined the quality of merchandise offered at various stores, you will probably know which ones you want to patronize. You will probably get the best, most personalized attention at smaller shops that carry top quality lines, because part of their business is knowing the individual needs of their clientele. Most of these salespeople will not try to pressure you into quick sales; if they see you are serious about your shopping, they will generally take the time to help you assemble well-integrated outfits. Explain what you are looking for and what you can spend. Many of these shops will keep a card on file with your measurements and color and fabric preferences, and experienced sales representatives will keep an eye out for new arrivals that match certain customers' requirements. Many department stores also offer personalized consultants to help you with your year-round clothing needs. Some such services are free, while others carry charges; they can be very helpful for busy people who have little time to shop.

At warehouse and factory outlets, however, you are on your own. Such outlets may have personnel available to direct you to the right racks, even assist you with a fitting, but beyond that, do not look for much advice. If you know what you are looking for, you can sometimes find good bargains at outlets. But you must know your outlets; be sure they sell store-quality goods and not seconds or irregulars.

When shopping for any type of garment, be sure to try it on and carefully check the fit, because no two manufacturers make the same size the same way. Even two garments of the same size, made by the same manufacturer, may vary slightly. Whether you are purchasing a suit, skirt, blazer, or dress, chances are you will need alterations. Although many women simply wear garments as they come off the racks, it is highly unlikely that clothing will fit well enough without changes. Do not just "make do"; have it altered. Unfortunately, many stores still charge women for alterations that they give men for free. Even so, the extra charge is worth it to get the best possible fit.

When the alterations have been made, buyers should always ask for—and insist on—a second fitting. You should check the fit from all angles in a three-way mirror, walk in it, and sit down. Be exacting in your assessment of the job done, and accept nothing that looks merely passable but not quite right. You, not the tailor, are the one who has to live in the suit, and you want to look and feel your best in your clothing.

Unless you have a lot of money to spend at one time, it will probably take you awhile—a year, maybe even two—to acquire what you feel you need. But your investment will pay off handsomely in a well-planned image, and your quality garments should last for several years, with proper care and cleaning. Even so, you will probably want to add a little to it each season.

The general guidelines discussed in this chapter apply to both men and women. But each sex faces some special considerations regarding business dress. First, the women.

BUSINESS DRESS FOR WOMEN

Unfortunately, dress standards for women are often vague. While a company may have clear-cut, unwritten guidelines for men, women often have few or no female role models in higher positions from whom to take cues. Women have only recently entered selling in any significant numbers, and have in the process been confronted with conflicting advice on how to dress.

In the 1970s, when women began moving into the professional job market in earnest, they were admonished by consultants, both male and female, to adhere to conservative, tailored, mannish dress—dark, skirted suits, often with vests, which were cut in a masculine fashion. Many women, however, looked like imitation men rather than professional businesswomen; mimicking the dress of their male peers sometimes proved more distracting than helpful in establishing a proper business image. Such dress can be very comfortable and effective for some women, however. The key is for women to choose such styles only if they feel comfortable with them personally and in their work environment.

Toward the end of the 1970s, the female dress pendulum began to swing the other way. Women were told that they had established themselves in professional roles and could loosen up their conservative dress standards and be more "feminine." What that meant was the reintroduction of fashion in business dress. Women who were lawyers, securities analysts, and corporate vice presidents—among the most conservative positions in the business world as a whole—were pictured in women's magazines wearing new "business fashions" of bright colors, and high-fashion styles of skirts, dresses, pants, and even pantalets. But these kinds of clothes harm more than help, too. Fashion is distracting, and the message it conveys is one of frivolousness. It is hard to take someone seriously if her attire does not look serious, or she looks like she is ready for an evening date.

Furthermore, fashion clothes have two additional disadvantages. First, they do not identify the wearer as a businesswoman. The classic, conservative suit identifies a man as a businessman, and he is treated as such wherever he goes. The well-dressed businessman is accorded respectful—often preferential—treatment at restaurants, hotels and other service establishments. But any woman, regardless of her professional status, can dress herself up in the latest rage. And when you do not look like you mean business, you will not get the business—or the service or the respect.

Second, fashion clothes tend to be short-lived, holding sway for a season or two and then being replaced by something else that is completely different. That, of course, is how fashion designers and manufacturers stay in business. If their clothes looked the same year after year, women would have no incentive to replace them every season. So, it is to the fashion industry's advantage that clothes for businesswomen carry seasonal marks. The short-waisted, belted skirt suit in electric purple that looked so smart one season will definitely be *out* the next, and no one would be caught dead wearing it. Likewise with skirts and dresses that go up and down in length.

Changing your wardrobe every season is both costly and foolish. The smart professional woman builds a long-lasting wardrobe, adding to it each year. The well-constructed, high-quality man's suit lasts about five years, on the average, and sometimes longer. The same should be sought in women's business suits; in fact, in all garments. Clothes should be selected for their classic timelessness, quality, and durability. The professional woman who builds such a wardrobe achieves a polished, consistent, upper-middle class look; she is not surprising her co-workers each season with whatever "look" the fashion designers have decided will rule the day.

While women should not let fashion dictate what they wear to the office, they need not totally ignore it. Many women pay homage to trends through their accessories—scarves, belts, shoes, and handbags. They should not, however, let fashion hold sway in choosing eyeglasses. Designer eyewear, as it is often called in advertisements, comes in odd shapes and colors, and can be as frivolous-looking and as distracting as fashion clothes. A simple plastic frame that complements face and coloring is the best choice. Many businesswomen, particularly those who are petite or very young, find that glasses *add* to their authority; in fact, some women who do not need vision correction have been known to wear spectacles with plain glass lenses, just for the appearance of gravity and intelligence they impart.

Skirted suits, followed by skirts and blazers, are still the best all-around items of apparel for the professional woman. A tailored suit or blazer still communicates business and professionalism. Solid colors offer the most flexibility for combinations. Dresses tend to be too fashion-oriented, but they can combine very well with a blazer. A dress with a blazer can solve the problem of going right from the office to an evening social function; a woman can wear the blazer at the office and take it off for the evening. While men can still wear their daytime business suits on into the evening with ease, a woman is still better off with a tailored dress. Some women prefer to wear pantsuits, although such styles have, to some extent, become associated with clerical and secretarial help. While many companies find pantsuits perfectly acceptable, others do not. Again, the key is personal comfort and an assessment of your environment. If pantsuits are frowned on, you may wish to avoid them as potentially distracting; remember that you are striving for a neutral, professional appearance, not one that calls attention to itself. Vests can also backfire for women, by looking either sexy or too masculine, and sweaters and sleeveless or short-sleeved dresses are definitely not professional.

For skirts or dresses, the best hem length falls right in the middle of the kneecap, which will not hike up excessively on sitting and will not look dowdy when standing. Pantyhose should be neutral, skin-colored shades, not opaque or dark, and certainly not covered with stitched designs.

Women should be sure that jackets do not bunch or roll across the shoulders or pull across the bust. Vents should hang straight and not stick out, and sleeves should end at mid-wrist. Skirts should allow plenty of room around the hips so that zippers do not pucker. And jacket lapels should lay flat; if they do not, a pressing will not help—the lining will need to be readjusted.

When choosing dresses and blouses, stay away from anything semisheer or sheer. The best blouses or shirts have a clean, tailored look, which can be dressed up with scarves if desired. A little bit of lace is all right if it is not excessive and frilly. Necklines should be modest, never low. Dressy blouses are certainly appropriate for evening business functions, and can transform a dark tailored suit into evening wear.

Accessories should be selected similarly. Plain, leather, low-heeled pumps are the best, most practical shoe for women, and are healthier for the feet than high heels. Avoid open-toed shoes and sandals, even during hot weather, because their casualness detracts from a managerial appearance. Your shoes should be at least as dark as your clothes, not lighter; that includes white shoes in the summer, which should be avoided unless white also dominates your clothing. Silk scarves and leather belts can add nice touches to an outfit, as long as they do not bear designer names or imprints. Many women tend to go overboard on jewelry, as though more meant quality or status. However, jewelry—and that includes watches—is most effective when it is spare and functional, so resist the urge to drape several gold chains around your neck and put a series of bracelets on your arm. Women are better off with a few distinctive pieces of good jewelry than a multitude of less expensive pieces. It is often effective to have a "signature" piece of jewelry that you wear all the time, such as a tasteful locket, an unusual ring or a single bracelet (one that does not dangle or clatter). Such a piece can add to your own individual look or style.

Briefcases signal business, and women sales professionals should carry one, even if it only contains the morning paper or their lunch. Brown leather is best for women as well as men, although women may wish to avoid extremes of either a distinctively "masculine" attaché or a flimsy "feminine" envelope-type portfolio. With a briefcase, a handbag is unnecessary, although many women purchase a small, flat bag to put inside a briefcase. A handbag carried separately should be simple in design, made of good quality leather, and just big enough to carry a minimum of personal items. Nothing looks less professional than a luggage-sized bag dragging on someone's shoulder. The handbag should match—or at least not jar with—the shoes and the rest of the outfit.

Other aspects of appearance deserve similar attention. Hair should be short to medium in length, in a simple cut that tends to stay in place and requires little fussing. Long hair left to fall around the shoulders may diminish a woman's authority; conversely, hair that is too short can look mannish. Long hair may be pulled up on top of the head, as long as the bun or knot is neat and not odd looking. Hair pulled back from the face this way can give a woman a sterner, more authoritative appearance. Hair that tends to get mussed at the slightest breeze calls for a light hairspray or perhaps another kind of cut. Hairdressers at top salons can cut hair to complement the way it grows, which helps it fall into place naturally. It may be worth spending a little extra money to get a good cut.

While grey hair usually makes men look distinguished, particularly if the grey is premature, it generally only makes women look older. If desired, many rinses on the market can cover up the grey and keep hair looking its natural color. But frizzy permanents and offbeat tinting jobs, such as streaks of different color, are usually out of place in the business environment. Similarly, lacquerlike hairsprays, especially heavily scented ones, should be avoided; so should perfume. They have no place in the business environment.

Likewise, the less make-up the better. Make-up should never be obvious. Many people find elaborate eye make-up especially distracting. The last thing a woman should want is for someone to be wondering how long it took her to "put on her face" that morning instead of listening to what she has to say.

Polished talons may be in vogue in the fashion magazines, but they are very impractical for business. Long nails prevent people from grasping things properly and can impair handwriting; also one broken nail on a hand of long ones does not look good. Polish requires time-consuming maintenance, and even a few chips give an ill-kempt appearance. It is far better to keep nails filed to a short or medium length with cuticles manicured. Nails may be buffed for a sheen; if nail polish is desired it should be a clear polish, which will not show nicks or chips as colors do.

Because there are few reliable guidelines, women must experiment and learn through trial and error just what works best for them. Note that what works well in one area or company may not at another, not only because of differences in corporate standards, but because perceptions and impressions created by dress are so subjective. Many men, sadly, are still threatened by the idea of a woman seller; a woman who sells to many such men may get far better results by softening her appearance. But whatever the situation, women will be safest in sticking to tailored, classic, conservative styles that have the look of quality workmanship.

BUSINESS DRESS FOR MEN

Men, luckily, do not face the confusion that women do in dressing for corporate success. Since men have always dominated commerce and industry, clothing standards have always been readily apparent and nearly universal; indeed, the business "uniform" has evolved over a considerable period of time. Even within the confines of customary male business dress, however, there is a great deal of latitude, and some men dress to better advantage than do others.

The key is to have a tailored, subdued, well-integrated look. That means colors and patterns should be complementary and not clashing; belt and shoes should match; tie, shirt, collar, and lapels should be at neither fashionable extreme—too narrow or wide; and nothing should stick out in an obvious or odd way. All parts of the outfit should blend together in a tasteful, but not monochromatic or dull, way.

Unlike women, men are generally provided with a free fitting, unless they buy suits at an outlet or on sale in a department store. Even if they must pay extra for it, the fitting is vital and should be done carefully and thoroughly. Never let the tailor try to hurry you through a fitting. Places where alterations are most commonly required include:

- Shoulders—there should be no bunching or rolling of jacket between shoulder blades;
- Lapels and collar—they should lay flat;
- Sleeves—they should hit at the middle of the wrist bone;
- Jacket vents—they should hang straight and not stick out;
- Trouser crotch—it should fit comfortably for sitting, walking, and standing without pinching or bagging.

Trouser waists and lengths, of course, usually are fitted. When shopping, be sure to wear a pair of shoes you intend to wear with the suit so the pants can be accurately measured for the proper break over the shoe tops.

Except for people who are prepared to care for all-cotton shirts, the best bet for shirts is a cotton and polyester blend, in white, pastel blue, or ecru (a yellowish beige or light grey) with either button-down collars or collars with removable stays (stays that are sewn into collars turn the fabric shiny when ironed). Broadcloth and Oxford weaves are among the most common shirt material, as well as end-on-end, in which white threads are woven among colored threads. Solids are best for business shirts. Shirts that combine more than two colors should be avoided. That is, stripes should be of a single color—preferably dark—against white; likewise, tattersall, which is a kind of check, should also be a single dark color against white. Stripes or tattersalls that combine colors, such as red, blue, and white, or black, yellow, and white, should be reserved for sporty, casual wear.

In recent years, fashion has invaded men's shirts. Collar lengths change, from very wide to narrow and rounded, or collars and cuffs may contrast, as with solid white against a striped shirt body. These shirts go in and out of style and should not be part of your business wardrobe unless you are a high-fashion dresser, and are willing to bear the extra cost of replacing them as fashions change. French cuffs are certainly acceptable, however. White shirts with French cuffs have an elegant look, provided they are not diminished with cheap cufflinks.

Think twice before you have monograms added to your shirts, even if the monogramming is free or advertised as a low-cost special, for fashion has taken over this former mark of distinction, too. First, assess whether or not monograms are appropriate within your company and for your position. If no one else in your company or at your level of responsibility wears monograms on their shirts, you might only look pretentious, or you may stand out for reasons other than your ability. Also, monograms have become fashionable in many circles and can appear on everything from crew neck sweaters to a secretary's blouse. Catalogs and department stores advertise monogramming free or nearly free with a purchase, thus you may have little to gain by monogramming your shirts. If you do elect to have monograms, they should be small and tasteful, and stitched in uniform size above the left breast pocket or area. Avoid elaborate stitching or initials encased in diamonds or circles.

While putting together your suit ensembles, do not neglect your socks —they always show whenever you sit down. Sock colors should fit in with the color scheme of the rest of your outfit, of course; never wear brown socks with a blue suit, or vice versa, for example. And white socks are out for business wear. Skip the cheap, all-synthetic socks, which have a tendency to pull after several washings. Also, avoid short socks. Make sure your socks are over-the-calf length, and are the kind that will stay up. Nothing looks worse than socks that have fallen down around the ankles, allowing bare flesh to poke out from under trousers.

The most important male accessory, which is really a part of daily business dress, is the tie; like many accessories, it can make or break an ensemble. Ties should be selected with great care, but unfortunately, they are much abused. They are often purchased as gifts with little or no knowledge of what they will match, or what they are made of; or they are picked up en masse at sales and bargain tables. It is time to treat the tie with more respect.

Silk is the best material for ties, although thin, shiny silk will not hold a knot well unless it has a thick enough lining. Polyester and silk blends are the next best material, followed by polyester, provided it looks like silk or a silk blend. Textured or knitted wool is also acceptable, although these ties look more casual. When knotted—the half-Windsor knot is the most common knot for business—the tie tip should just reach the belt buckle.

Solid colors or solids with small polka dots are the most versatile ties, followed by rep ties, which usually have stripes running in a diagonal pattern. Club and Ivy League ties—those with small emblems, sports symbols, or geometric shapes—are distinctly upper-middle class but also can convey an Eastern stuffiness or snobbishness. If you are an Easterner, you may not want to wear such a tie when traveling to other parts of North America. Paisley is also a fine choice, as long as the pattern is not large and wild, although some people regard paisleys as less serious looking. Save bow ties for sports clothes and tuxedos. Avoid ties that mix patterns or have borders along the tips. Try to purchase tie, shirt, and suit or sports jacket together in order to get the best possible match. Do not put similar patterns right next to each other, as with a striped tie against a striped shirt. Solids on solids are fine, however.

Shoes should be constructed of good-quality leather and of simple design, either tie or slip-on, without fancy stitching or a lot of metal doodads. Wingtips are a staple in the business world, but they are a heavy-looking shoe, and a large, imposing man might look better in a more streamlined slip-on. Loafers are too casual, and higher heeled shoes are best avoided as a passing fashion. Half-boots are acceptable in many quarters, but shoes are more traditional. The shoe color should be as dark as your suit, if not darker; never lighter. Black is the safest bet because it goes with everything. Always make sure your belt color matches your shoes; do not wear a brown belt with black shoes, for example. A slim, leather executive wallet that fits in your inner suit breast pocket is better (and safer from pickpockets) than a hip wallet; neither should bulge, in any case.

Conservatism is the rule with glasses, too. Steer clear of trendy, over-sized designer shapes and wire rims in favor of dark-colored plastic frames. Glasses should not call attention to themselves. The same is true of jewelry, including watches, collar bars, and tie bars. Jewelry has become more and more acceptable for men to wear, but it is best reserved for casual social time. A simple, masculine ring (in addition to a wedding band, if you have one) is fine, but do not risk putting someone off with a bracelet. Watches should be simple. Resist the urge for digital gadgetry, like those thick diver-style tanks that glow in the dark and tell what time it is anywhere in the world. If you do buy a digital watch, keep its functions unobtrusive. Most digital watches can be set to beep on the hour, which can be most offensive and annoying. Meetings invariably suffer a minor disruption when a dozen watches start going off, never in unison. And if you are in a one-on-one situation, a beeping watch gives the impression that you are either anxious about time or have something more important to do.

Hair requires the same approach of simplicity and unobtrusiveness. Hair should be neatly trimmed around ears and never extend below the collar in the back. If your hair musses easily, try holding it in place with a light spray; never with grease, pomade, or a lacquer-type spray. You should also avoid curly permanents, unless you want to look like a rock musician. Many men do not mind if their hair is all or partly grey, feeling that it enhances their image. Those who wish to trade a distinguished look for a youthful one, however, will find many preparations that will cover the grey, restoring the natural color.

Loss of hair calls for different steps. If your hairline is receding at the temples, part it at the point of greatest recession for the neatest look. Never try to grow hair to cover bald spots and receding hair lines; invariably you will not succeed, and your attempt will look obvious and vain. Many good quality toupees are on the market, and a surprising number of men are choosing them over their own thinning hair. Shop carefully, however, because even good hairpieces are fairly easy to spot, and bad ones look ridiculous. A bad toupee may curl strangely at the nape of the neck or stick out from the neck; it may not match the natural hair; it may have an unnatural, synthetic sheen; or it may have a part that looks artificial—or no part at all (everyone's hair parts in some fashion).

For the face, a clean-shaven look is still the most widely acceptable choice. Eschew cologne, however; it is distracting and inappropriate in a business environment. Moustaches have become more commonplace, especially among younger men. If you wear a moustache, keep it neatly trimmed above your lip, and do not extend it beyond the corners of your mouth. Waxed moustaches, as well as handlebars that extend up to sideburns, are not advisable for managers. Sideburns are best when they are short and trimmed. You need not look like an Army recruit, but do avoid muttonchops and cuts that extend far out onto the cheek or are slanted in a diagonal. Beards and goatees have more variable acceptance, being sported widely in some industries and rarely in others. Those considering a hirsute look will want to carefully assess their business environments before growing a beard—and then only on a long vacation, to have time to pass beyond the "scruffy" stage and to judge its effect privately, before putting it on public view. On some faces and in some settings, a beard can enhance a person's authority and intelligence; but sometimes a beard can make others uneasy, since it hides the face and can make it harder for a person to gain the confidence of others.

For all professionals, the key to "dressing for success" is using the same type of discipline they apply in their daily business affairs—knowing their objectives and putting together a program designed to accomplish them in the most efficient, effective way. You should approach building your business wardrobe with the same diligence you might apply to preparing for a major presentation. Your business wardrobe can be your enemy, or it can be a most helpful ally for achieving your career goals. The right clothes and the right accessories, in the right combinations, can help you create and maintain a positive image, one that can influence others to respect you, listen to you, trust you, and buy from you.

EQUIPMENT

Sales equipment is an extension of personal appearance. You should no more appear before a prospect or customer carrying a worn, misshapen briefcase than you should wearing a stained, torn blouse or old, baggy pants. And you should no more reach into that briefcase and pull out tired, faded presentation materials than you should hold out a hand to be shaken that is in desperate need of washing and a manicure.

Sales equipment has to be new-looking, clean, crisp, and capable of being used to lovingly demonstrate the top of your line. It presents your company and product; it also quite significantly casts light upon and presents you to your customers and prospects. All marketing managements budget for sales equipment wear and breakage; no sales professional should be deficient in this area.

It extends to all the seemingly minor details, too. For example, the pen you work with when using an order form to move to the close should be one of recognizably good quality; inexpensive pens may write just as well, but a good pen is more reassuring to the buyer.

Similarly, but not quite as directly, your car, if you use one in the field, is an extension of your personal appearance. And although the stereotype of the successful sales professional as a cigar-smoking, fast talker driving a big car is long gone, what you drive and especially what condition it is in can, in some situations, make a difference to your prospects and customers, and can stand in the way of developing the kinds of relationships that build sales.

Unfortunately, in these days of high automobile prices and unreliable new automobiles, a battered 10-year-old station wagon that needs a new coat of paint but runs like a dream just will not do in the field. What will minimally do, though, is a well-cared-for, smallish automobile as much as four or five years old, that gets good gasoline mileage and has an excellent repair record. If you travel a good deal, you are unlikely to get more than four reasonably trouble-free years out of a car anyway, and the cost of missed appointments because of automobile troubles is usually far larger than the cost of a newer automobile.

Newer; not necessarily new. Hardly anyone cares any more about trading in a car every year or two; in these times, economy has to a significant extent become virtue, and conspicuous consumption is now rather suspect. The car you drive out in the field need not be new, or large, or expensive; but it must be clean, look well cared for, and be of a reasonably late model.

All of the above argues strongly for getting a well known and rather traditional American or foreign automobile just under the extra-laden top of whatever line it is part of, and one that is not in its first model year. It also argues for maintaining it well and preventively, and planning to retire it from field use in the 80,000–90,000 mile range, at the outside. Many of us have second cars, and a car used in the field is often perfectly usable as an additional family car for years after it is no longer suitable for work purposes. It is quite possible to buy or lease a car every three or four years, and have two usable vehicles out of that pattern of purchases at all times.

Dress, grooming, sales equipment, automobiles—all the appearance elements together present a single image of you to prospects, customers, and colleagues; an image that can, if properly worked with, considerably enhance sales and career success possibilities.

CHAPTER 11

HANDLING PERSONAL PROBLEMS

Most discussions of personal problems are conducted at about the level of a conversation between a rear-echelon colonel rapidly passing through a front-line battle area, and an exhausted, scared, private on the front lines, with the colonel urging the private to keep a good attitude, pray a lot, and think often of how much the folks at home appreciate the sacrifices being made at the front. After which the colonel departs—as quickly as possible—and the private goes back into battle, just as exhausted and scared, trying hard to stay alive a little while longer.

Take one tired, sour, demoralized, depressed sales professional, who sells too little, drinks too much, smokes too much, is deathly afraid of losing a job, and is revolted by the thought of staying on. Advise that person to "handle stress," and "avoid burn-out," by jogging, meditating, taking up needlecraft, getting along better with the family and with people at work, and seeing a psychiatrist. You may get attention; you may even get a real try at personal turnaround—for a while. In the long run, what you are likely to get is precisely nothing.

It is not stress that is the problem; nor will bromides do. Some problems are very real, and cause stress and a constellation of other quite negative emotional and physical results, which then proceed to trigger more problems. To help ourselves, we are best advised to tackle causes as much as possible, and symptoms only as necessary. Much of this book is aimed at helping create the career and personal conditions that will keep personal problems from arising, our view being that much of the seemingly uncontrollable is really controllable. Yet there are events and deep-seated problems beyond our immediate control, and many of us do encounter groups of related problems that can, quite literally, drive us to drink or to any of the other attitudes or problems briefly discussed in this chapter.

Depression, fear, money trouble, alcohol, tobacco, divorce, loneliness, stress, and profound alienation are problems encountered by many kinds of people, not more by people in selling than by others. Indeed many exhausted police officers, social workers, and slum doctors may encounter such problems in far more profound fashion than all but a very few sales professionals. So may a factory worker who has lost a job a year or more ago, and cannot find another; or for that matter a terribly lonely and increasingly alienated "homemaker," with small children and a mountain of bills. Indeed, for all of the many and real personal problems they face, sales professionals are still among the most privileged and highly rewarded people in the United States and the world. We shed no tear here for the poor, neglected seller. Rather we attempt to see what personal problems are related to the practice of selling, and what can be done to ameliorate or even solve some of these problems, just as we would if this work were directed toward police officers, social workers, slum doctors, factory workers, or homemakers.

Too often, people perceive their personal problems as matters to be resisted, rather than understood and dealt with. Many of us try to move on through personal problems, hoping that somehow they will go away or solve themselves, and reserving our problem-solving abilities for business matters. In business, sales professionals see themselves as astute entrepreneurs, running their own small businesses; in personal matters, however, many otherwise astute people become little more than pawns, swept along by events over which they feel they have little or no control.

Similarly, most of us try very hard not to perceive that many of our personal concerns and problems result from and, on the other hand, can powerfully affect job and career. All this while nodding soberly as others carefully point out that "no man is an island," and that career and personal matters are inextricably intertwined. "Yes, right . . . but not for me . . . " is often the response of the manager who agrees that stress, alcohol, smoking, work compulsion, damaged family life, insecurity, demoralization, dislike of travel, staleness in and dislike of current job, loneliness, and financial troubles, among others, are problems that can deeply affect every aspect of life and career.

Some concerns and problems are society-wide, and there is little we, as individuals, can do about them—the threat of nuclear war, hard economic times, and the plight of our young and old, for example. Yet even in these kinds of areas, it is a mistake to stick your head into the sand, and to deny the existence of problems that, by their very nature, force their way into our consciousness, affecting our perception of our lives and times. The truth is that in hard and difficult times it all seems—and is—harder, in both career and personal terms. When there are not as many alternatives as we would like, and as we have been led to expect by our earlier experiences; and when an unusual number of those available alternatives seem rather grim; and when people used to the idea of building careers are in a period when building anything at all is extraordinarily difficult, our buoyancy, our confidence, our "will to win" are in many instances severely impaired. Franklin Roosevelt suggested many years ago that fear itself was the great enemy; not so, then or now, although it was a marvelous slogan and a means of moving a country in deep trouble. But fear and drift are great personal enemies and never more so than in hard and difficult times, when more intelligence and personal initiative are required than in easy times. We should not underestimate the effect of working and living in an adverse climate; it is crucial to recognize the effects of that climate and move ahead in spite of it, conscious that we have to face and solve more—and often considerably more difficult—career and personal questions in these times.

CONTROLLING YOUR ENVIRONMENT

As in career matters, it is sound and consistent planning, coupled with the development of excellent personal reflexes and habits that stops major problems before they can get seriously started. By learning to control a wide variety of sometimes seemingly uncontrollable matters, we both prevent a drift into serious personal problems and create the ability to weather personal crises, as well.

Much of this work is devoted to exercising control and developing sound reflexes in such directly job-connected matters as fear of job loss, boredom, dislike of work, and the demoralization that can creep up upon those who fail to exercise control in such seemingly mundane and quite uncontrollable areas as traveling, work at home, and paper handling. In the largest sense, the development of a sturdy professionalism provides the best possible basis for prevention of these kinds of problems. No matter how difficult the times, a sound professional should not accept insecurity and adverse job conditions; rather, the aim should be either to change the game in place or to make a move to a more congenial and secure working environment. Putting it a little differently, our current jobs must never control reactions, attitudes, and reflexes. Just the opposite: in the not-so-very-long run, we either control our work and careers or we move on. And what we do to improve current situations or to create new ones are matters of choice. On the personal side, the trick is to make those choices overtly, after due consideration, and in timely fashion—not to wait until work-connected questions have stimulated and merged with personal problems to create personal crises than can be solved only with tremendous difficulty, if at all. For, given our focus upon work and career, an adverse work situation and the attitudes then generated can mightily contribute to the development of very severe personal problems.

More general environmental factors must also be taken into consideration. Most of these, too, in the long run reflect choices—either deliberate or de facto—and have considerable career impacts. Climate, city, travel needs, schools, housing, cultural possibilities—usually several interacting factors at once—can and often do conspire to make an otherwise agreeable and worthwhile job in the long run absolutely insupportable. Conversely, some such factors turn an otherwise marginal job into one that you will leave only if fired or faced with a job move so good you feel that you cannot possibly refuse it. The impact of these various factors are matters of personal preference; the point is to see and exercise choices, rather than ignore them.

Sometimes, though, career building seems to demand the acceptance of considerably adverse environmental factors. The most obvious example is that of the New York metropolitan area, in which nearly 10% of all Americans live and in which far more than 10% of all major American corporation home office staff live and work. For tens of thousands of business professionals of all kinds, including sales professionals, the New York move is both a major promotion and a move into the home office, a logical step in the building of a substantial career. It is also a move into one of the most difficult and expensive major metropolitan areas in the industrial world; certainly in the United States. Very little about New York City works. Its streets and highways are full of potholes; its subways are hot, unventilated, noisy, obsolete, uncomfortable, overcrowded, and dangerous. Social services are eroded, crime substantial and growing. Housing in Manhattan is crowded and extremely expensive; many middle class parents send their children to private schools, guaranteeing enormous drains on take-home pay for the basics of living. If you want to live in anything approximating a semi-rural or exurban setting, you must commute from two to five hours, door to door, every day. But commuter railways are expensive, overcrowded, slow, and unreliable. If you try to drive to work from even fairly near suburbs, it may take hours on jammed highways and cost large sums for parking. If you live in northern New Jersey to try to cut costs, you find yourself in the middle of a large, smoky, smelly, health-endangering chemical industry. In short, in terms of the standards and life-style aspirations of most American managers, New York is truly a terrible place to live and work.

Some companies, in recognition of this, have moved away, often to the near suburbs, where life is a little less difficult. Some professionals have, reluctantly, taken to refusing transfers and even substantial promotions into the New York area—and have more and more been making those refusals stick without prejudicing their futures in their companies. Yet, year after year, people take their promotions and home office moves, come to live and work in the New York area, and subject themselves and their families to environmental strains often far greater than those they ever before experienced together. Quite often, it is the working members of the family who suffer the strains most directly. It is not at all unusual for a sales manager or national accounts representative to leave a "bedroom suburb" outside New York at 6:30 A.M. and return at 7:30 P.M., during home office days, while traveling many weeks a year out of New York's airports, which are some of the most difficult airports in the world to get into and out of. Small wonder, then, that family life often suffers a great deal, with damage to children and all family relationships. And small wonder that the deterioration of family life that occurs in New York and other such very difficult areas has substantial impact on the morale of many working professionals. And small wonder that people in difficult environmental and family circumstances all too often round out the constellation of problems by turning small doses of the narcotic alcohol into an alcoholism problem.

Is New York worth it, once the hazards and probable damages are anticipated? Perhaps not, for some; yet the career choice more often than not still tips in the direction of the move to the home office. If you see New York as an overwhelmingly negative choice, it is far better to see the negative elements in the choice early; if home office is where you want to go in the long run, make home office location one of the factors you take into account in your choice of company.

New York is obvious; but the comment holds true for other unwanted environments, as well. For some, any cold, wet northern environment is in the long run anathema. For some, any major industrial city, such as Chicago or Detroit, is unwanted. For others, it is not the negative side, but the positive. A skier and boating enthusiast may love the idea of living and working in or near Boston; a music-, art-, and theater-lover may want to live nowhere else in North America but in New York. The main thing is to take the environmental factors seriously into account when evaluating and periodically reevaluating your career stance and when making and remaking career choices.

But if you are effectively bankrupt, it is very hard to see job and environmental choices as really controllable. To see and exercise real choices, you must have some financial reserve; one who is constantly about to drown in a sea of unpaid bills, while being mesmerized by an even larger sea of coming obligations, is usually in no position to refuse a transfer or promotion, or to leave even the most disastrously uncongenial job. Security becomes all, whatever the enormous personal price that must be paid for it.

Yet financial woes are not a must; for working sales professionals, they are far more often a matter of poor career planning, imprudent life-style choices and spending habits, foolishly expensive college education choices, and lack of effective and sustained financial planning. Yet hapless financial behavior yearly destroys careers, breaks up marriages, drives drinkers to alcoholism, and quite unnecessarily bankrupts vulnerable people who are unemployed for even a short time. It happens in good times and bad, but far more often and noticeably in bad times, as bad or nonexistent planning catches up with those who, given their skills and training, should have known better. In the business world, there is nothing quite so pathetic as the sight of a once-effective professional without personal financial resources, hating to stay and afraid to leave, marking the years to retirement day by day, and worrying each day about being fired, as sales attempted in that frame of mind prove harder and harder to close. Personal financial matters are very much controllables; we deal with how to handle them in Chapter 9 and throughout this work. And the truth is, if you do not control the personal financial side of life, there is really not much point in speaking of choice and personal freedom, for then there are likely to be only an unending series of personal pressures and eventual crises. In a therapy-oriented world, we tend to underestimate the emotional impact of continual money troubles; to do so is a major personal error.

In these times, though, we do tend to give full weight to the potential adverse impact of family problems upon life and career. Intellectually, that is; the world is full of people who talk a good deal about healthy family relationships, yet go right on paying far too little attention to building those relationships. Small wonder; many professionals of all kinds allow the profession's very great demands on time and attention to crowd out all else, with the result that very manageable personal problems grow into big, quite unmanageable ones. When two professionals do that in a single family, breakup is always just around the corner, even though it may be deferred for quite some time.

Although simple and so often stated as to have become a bromide, it is nonetheless true: healthy families, like healthy careers or healthy bodies, require a great deal of care and consistent attention. Otherwise, they develop problems, and, in extreme instances, break down. For people to whom family means enormously much—as is true of most of us—severe family problems almost inevitably trigger a whole set of other personal and career problems. No, we cannot avoid all severe family problems with caring attention; some problems run too deep. But we can prevent many problems from arising; in this area, even a little care goes a long way.

PHYSICAL AND EMOTIONAL QUESTIONS

So, too, the very deeply intertwined physical and emotional factors. A lack of customary energy level may be due to exhaustion or illness; but it may result from boredom, or staleness, or discouragement, or a job that has somehow turned very, very sour, and needs to be changed. Along with the periodic physical checkup and the need for physical recreation, there is a need for careful, consistent analysis of our own attitudes toward job, environment, family, and contexts. Rather standard wisdom still applies here: if you do not feel well, you will not work very well; if you do not work very well, you are not likely to feel well. Chicken and egg are, as always, intertwined; part of the same processes, to be examined separately and together.

And the evaluation should be equally focused on physical and emotional factors, as should any remedial action. If you find you have a specific illness, of course you deal with it. None of us think that it is best to leave cancer alone, once discovered, in hopes that it will somehow go away. Instead we treat it as quickly and effectively as we can, understanding that "if you don't have your health, you have nothing." We set broken legs, bind sprained ankles, even replace knees and other defective or worn-out parts in these times. It is odd that we do those things so readily, while continuing to treat other equally serious problems as if they were not diseases at all—until it's too late, that is.

There are some preventive things we all know we "should" do to take at least minimal care of our bodies and states of mind. A torrent of advice has poured over all of us in the last two decades, aimed at helping us exercise; eat properly; eschew tobacco and other narcotics; court calm rather than stress; take care of our eyes, chests, feet, and everything in between: sleep properly and well; think sound thoughts; and generally behave so as to prevent the ravages caused by living and working here now.

Yes, we should slowly eat sound, balanced breakfasts, after seven or eight hours of sleep, rather than bolting nutritionally worthless sweet rolls and scalding our mouths with great gulps of caffeine-full coffee, in a foredoomed attempt to become alert achievers after four hours of sleep. Surely, we should walk, jog, or run (or all three), as long as we take care not to provide a bonanza for the next generation of orthopedists by ruining our arches, ankles, and kneecaps in the process. Indeed, we should watch our weights very carefully; overweight is a slow killer, as are cigarette smoking and too much alcohol.

But no, we will not solve our problems unless we go to roots, as well as results. We must take good care of bodies and minds, abusing neither; but we are not in the long run likely to do so if we lead lives and careers that, in and of themselves, generate enormous physical and emotional strains. In the long run, it is necessary to practice problem prevention in life and work, as part of a wider plan, including physical and emotional problem prevention of the conventional sort. Stress is not, in and of itself, a bad thing; it is part of the process of living, working, and playing fully and satisfactorily. It is stress coupled with enormous personal frustration that ties us into very unhealthy knots and creates constellations of problems that can lead to major difficulties.

Some problems can go either way. The death of a spouse or other loved one, a major illness in the family, job loss, job-related stresses so powerful as to become self-feeding, and the alienation that comes out of extreme loneliness are all examples of the kind of problem that can be either disabling or surmounted. Which way it goes will depend to some extent upon specific circumstances, and at least as much upon your physical, emotional, and financial resources at the outset. These are very much the kinds of things that throw you into a tailspin, and for which no single handling mode is better than any other. For many of us, working right on through, and doing essentially what we have been doing all along, is the best possible approach. Scheduled time—large amounts of it—can take many people through a difficult time and out the other side. Not always; one may react to the death of a spouse by going back to work a week later, while another may take far longer to get over the shock, in privacy and near-isolation. One may react to unexpected job loss with shock and dismay, and take a considerable space—perhaps a month or two—before starting to look for another job. Another may have a résumé ready to go two days after severance, and treat the job-seeking period as merely another kind of full-time work assignment.

Loneliness, though, seldom responds well to benign neglect. The constant traveler; the young person on a new job in a strange town; the recently divorced suburbanite suddenly living poor in a one-room apartment in center city; and the recently bereaved person suddenly alone after decades with a spouse all need to pay a great deal of attention to making new friends and finding new personal institutional ties, as in special-interest organization, church, synagogue or temple, and mosque. Isolation feeds isolation; it really does not take care of itself.

Nor does enormous stress that generates even more stress tend to take care of itself. When enough stress is piled on, it can become a self-generating phenomenon, greatly exacerbating real problems and staying on and growing even when problems have been solved or very nearly so. Do not pay too much attention to analytical schemes that classify you by "personality style," such as the rather well-known Type A and Type B constructs. Stress can create much greater stress, and it can be a very long-term development; but it is very easy to mistake a controllable problem for a presumably immutable personality type, and, therefore, not really try to control and direct a recovery from such a high-tension stance. For make no mistake about it—a pattern of long-term and growing stress can be a not-so-very-slow killer, and never more so than when it is fed by very real crises, such as job loss and bereavement.

Out of control, that kind of stress pattern becomes an emergency, and should be treated like any other serious health emergency. If you find yourself quite literally getting out of control—the kind of out-of-control behavior that results in shouting, extreme nervousness, insomnia, depression, and resorting to much-larger-than-usual quantities of such narcotics as cigarettes and alcohol—the likelihood is that you have an emergency. Then perhaps it is time to turn to a trusted friend or a psychotherapist functioning as a professionally distanced, and, therefore, rather trustworthy counselor. And it is probably also time for a change of scene—in the short term, a holiday, perhaps; in the long term, if necessary, a job, location, or career change.

ALCOHOLISM

Several other patterns indicate out-of-control behavior that should be treated as needing emergency attention, often with as much help as possible from others. That is nowhere more true than in the case of alcoholism. The truth is that, in career terms, alcoholism can be fatal; it may also be so physically in some instances, but that is usually a somewhat later matter. And anyone with a continuing alcohol habit is far more at career risk in difficult times than in easy times.

That is important to see clearly, for it may change the game for some managers who have been skating along for years as closet alcoholics, tolerated and often "carried" by their long-time peers and superiors. Most of us have, during the course of our careers, known a "good old Charlie," who "drinks a little too much, but doesn't do us any real harm, and anyway we're working on it with him." Good old Charlie may have been on the job for a long time, and may have started in the company with some people who by now have gone quite a long way and are quite willing to protect old Charlie. But sometimes hard times can provide new reasons for doing what should have been done long ago. No, not firing good old Charlie, but getting some real help, and in the course of doing so helping him become a productive human being and professional manager again.

In all seasons, though, alcoholism—which we should understand to be any habitual drinking that cannot be turned off at any time for as long as desired—is a disease, an addiction with physical and emotional aspects intertwined, requiring very serious and often protracted treatment.

If you have any kind of problem with alcohol, you will know it; whether or not you will admit it to yourself is another matter. But even if you have a hard time admitting it to yourself, it is quite likely that in these days of considerable sensitivity to the problem, others will raise the question with you. Your spouse, your closest working peers, perhaps a sympathetic superior; somebody is quite likely to raise the question with you before the matter becomes a major problem and a career destroyer.

If someone—anyone—does raise the question of your perhaps having an alcohol problem, you should stop dead in your tracks and really take a cold, hard look at yourself. If your first impulse is to reject the suggestion out of hand, stop all the faster and look all the harder, for that is the characteristic reaction of the alcoholic. A suggestion that you may be an alcoholic or incipient alcoholic should, in all rationality, function exactly as if it were a suggestion that you might have cancer. It should immediately cause you to stop, consider, and reevaluate; nobody who would suggest you might have cancer would be ignored—instead you would sincerely thank the suggester and probably seek professional diagnosis. Seeing it that way, it is simply not at all sane to reject the idea that you might have an alcohol problem. The suggestion itself calls for close examination, once raised; its careless rejection raises a presumption that you may indeed have a problem.

Unless the question is sharply raised by your superiors, at a late date in what is seen all too clearly as a serious alcohol problem, it is wise to seek diagnosis and, if necessary, help outside company channels. Companies and other managers are far more enlightened in this area than they were a generation ago, when an "alcohol problem" might cause instant dismissal, but they are still not usually so enlightened that the question, once raised, might not cause career damage. It is a chance you need not take. If diagnosis or help is wanted, your family doctor or Alcoholics Anonymous can provide the way to go, and no one but you, they, and your family need ever know there was a problem.

It is very much worthwhile to go to your family doctor for diagnostic help in this area. Some of us are more vulnerable than others to even a small quantity of alcohol. Some of us take medications that are harmless enough in themselves, causing little or no side effects, but which magnify the impact of alcohol—and of other medications and drugs, for that matter. Sometimes, a seeming alcohol problem will be something else entirely; for example, a chronic and variable inner ear infection can cause quite as much disorientation as a considerable alcohol problem. Usually, though, if it seems to be alcohol, it is. And usually, if you seem to need help, you do. The trick is to see that yourself, treat any mention of your possible problem by others as a very welcome early warning, and then move decisively toward cure of the illness.

WORK COMPULSION

Drinking is not the only habit-forming activity in which we may indulge. For many, the work itself is addicting, the behavior toward work compulsive. We use the term *compulsive* here in somewhat the sense that we use the term *alcoholism*. If you cannot stay away from work; if you let it fill every nook and cranny of your life, at home, on the job, and in between; and if the need to work at your trade incessantly continues over a substantial period of time—far beyond a single contest, campaign, or period of adjustment to a new job—then you have a work compulsion problem. And if such a problem does indeed exist, it can destroy personal life, create enormous stress in every part of life, and will in the long run ruin most of us just as surely as alcohol. Not all of us, however. There are people who have no personal lives at all after years of compulsive work, and who have adjusted to their work in such fashion as to make it their entire lives. Some of them live just as long as the rest of us, although very few of them have anything at all like a fully satisfying personal life. For most of us, though, that kind of work-compulsive life is a recipe for disaster.

In some ways, our own work compulsions are harder to deal with than such socially unacceptable vices as alcoholism. The difficulty lies in the area of self-perception. Work compulsion seems to and does work well for some people over long periods of time, but for most it does not really work at all, although it may seem to for a while. Compulsive attention to work matters often appears to be a personal style that brings sought-after rewards, including recognition and advancement; under those circumstances people who achieve seeming success have difficulty seeing that they are in the process of being ruined by their work compulsion. They often respond with anger and frustration to those who seem critical of their personal work styles; they especially accuse their concerned families of wanting the material rewards of unremitting labor without accepting the breadwinner's "doing what has to be done" to secure those rewards. And they are deaf to those who counsel that they ease up a little, take up some hobbies, and spend some time with a spouse and with children who are growing up without a father—or in these times without a mother, for the disease affects both sexes.

Work compulsion can, like alcohol, be a disaster. It is also a life-threatening activity, as the stresses engendered by this style can very easily destroy physical health as well as personal life. And although it is thought to be career-enhancing, it can create a career disaster. Work-compulsive people are rarely flexible, often do not build up networks of professional friends outside the current company, and are often terribly vulnerable in the face of adverse business events beyond their control, as in hard times.

Those who are work compulsive also often do not pay enough attention to personal financial planning. They cannot be bothered with "personal" matters—as if a career were not also a personal matter—and, therefore, tend to do far too little of the kind of planning, for present and future, that is absolutely necessary for survival in these times. That usually extends to post-retirement planning as well. With little or no later-years work planning and small financial resources, the compulsive is usually high and dry soon after retirement, if he or she lasts that long. This is the kind of person who is disconsolate soon after retirement, and often lasts only a short time after the motor of work compulsion has been shut off. All of this is quite unnecessary; long-term work-compulsive behavior, though not an illness like alcoholism, is for most people an illness nonetheless. Unfortunately, there is no widely known and respected Work Compulsives Anonymous one can turn to for help; the family doctor might only prescribe tranquilizers, which in these instances rarely turn the trick. We need to recognize the problem ourselves, often with the help of our families and closest personal friends; see it as a problem to be solved rather than as the destruction of a beneficial working style; and move ahead toward a cure basically on our own. It is difficult to do so; it is usually done successfully only after the kind of sharp warning provided by a heart attack. But it can be done short of that, and is very much worth doing in personal and career terms.

PROFESSIONAL BEHAVIOR

The professional practice of management is made far more difficult by such illnesses as alcoholism and such style problems as work compulsion. Both make proper distancing from and solution of problems very difficult;

both also make relationships with others at work very difficult. Professionalism requires a constant balancing of deep involvement and distance toward those with whom you work. Involvement by itself is never enough; alone it clouds judgment, and makes difficult people-moves far more difficult. But too much distance makes leadership impossible. The cold-blooded technocrat, who sees everyone else through a microscope, is quite properly mistrusted by all. Both leadership and working in tandem with others require that the balance between personal involvement and distanced analysis be maintained. In business terms, personal problems are most damaging when they get in the way of maintaining that essential professional balance.

The same is true of some of our opinions, lusts, and bigotries, if we let them show. The very "conservative" or very "liberal" company officer who attempts to impose his or her political views upon subordinates is being thoroughly unprofessional, and the work will suffer for it, as disaffected key personnel make their displeasure felt.

The bigot who does not even realize that his or her attitudes are indeed bigoted can do an operation or a company a great deal of harm, with co-workers, customers, suppliers, and other contacts. When a manager expresses hatred or disdain for women, Blacks, Hispanics, Jews, or members of any other such group while on the job, that manager is quite probably committing acts that are in violation of the law of the land, as well as engaging in stupidly unprofessional conduct. Your attitudes off the job are your own business; what you say on the job is very much your company's business; and the business of your co-workers. And what you say on the job is very much personal career business; the manager who behaves unprofessionally in these areas is merely proving himself or herself unfit for advancement.

Similar, in career terms, is the question of sexual activities with co-workers. No moral judgments in this area here; that is not the real business of this book. Only the comment that the oldest of rules applies here as never before: People who involve themselves again and again with co-workers—and particularly managers who use their superior positions to take sexual advantage of their subordinates—are engaging in highly unprofessional activities, which can only in the long run rebound to their disadvantage. In these times, it may not take very long, either. Women, the chief victims of sexual harassment, are increasingly aware that they do not have to stand for it, and are taking action against those who attempt it.

The key to successfully approaching personal problems continues to be the matter of preventive attitudes and practices. If we function consistently and reflexively in a sound career-building way, we are hardly likely to run into major personal problems of our own making, and are more likely to be able to handle and control seemingly uncontrollable crisis situations. The main danger is entrapment in frustrating and barren personal and career situations. Only then are we likely to build up the kinds of strains and habits that we cannot handle; the main solution lies in the simultaneous development of professionalism and personal freedom.

PART IV
PERSONAL SITUATIONS

To make all that has gone before in this book even more tangible—and even more helpful—here is a series of personal situations, the kinds of practical situations that working sales professionals face during the course of life and career. The people and specifics are largely constructed for purposes of illustration, although they are drawn from the joint experience of the authors. The names used are in all instances fictitious, and any resemblance to living persons is entirely accidental.

By any reasonable measure, most of these stories involve people who have done rather well in career and financial terms, yet most of these are also people who are encountering, or are about to encounter, very serious problems. Some will plan and execute their plans well, win and keep on winning; others will find these personal and financial crises insurmountable, at least in the short and medium term.

There can be no iron-clad guarantees for any of us, now or in the future. What we do hope to make clear in these examples—as we have stressed elsewhere in this book—is that those who plan well stand a far better chance of long-term personal satisfaction and material success than those who do not. Clearly, there are as many specific personal situations as there are people, but just as clearly many basic situations have striking similarities, and the number of basic situations and solutions is limited. We have tried to present a reasonably wide range of ages, backgrounds, work experiences, and situations here, hoping that you will therefore be able to find people and situations that speak directly—at least in part—to your needs and desires.

PERSONAL SITUATION 1
ELLEN COMO WEISS

Twenty-odd years ago, when she married Sidney Weiss, Ellen Como gave up her own name. That was the style then; at the time, she never thought she would miss it. She was all of 19 at the time, with one year of college under her belt, and thought she wanted nothing more than to be in love with Sid, make a home for him, and have children.

Which is what she and Sid did. Ellen quit college after the next term, when she was six months pregnant with her first child, and then had two more children in the next three years. After that, she, Sid, and the kids had a very happy and then-conventional 12 years of domesticity. Sid sold books out of Cincinnati, and was away a good deal of the time, and Ellen was therefore necessarily the main parent of the family; but they all managed to surmount the resulting strains rather well.

In the early 1970s, facing looming college costs and also responding to the temper of the times regarding equality of opportunity for women, Ellen decided to go back to school to finish her undergraduate education. On the whole, Sid thought it might have been better to wait longer, for the sake of the children, and perhaps to forego the college education in favor of developing some earning power through a fast course in secretarial skills. Ellen didn't want that, though; her desire was to complete her education; in a sense, to finish unfinished personal business and enter the wider world again as a credentialed, educated person. She promised Sid, the kids, and herself that no matter what else happened, the kids and Sid would not suffer, and that she would continue to be the superb wife and mother she had always been.

Yes, of course—Supermom; but hindsight is easy. In those years, that too was the thing to do. But she also took her own name back the day she registered for school, and has since been known as Ellen Como, rather than Ellen Weiss.

She finished her college education; cum laude in business administration, as it turned out. Then she took a look at college costs for her children, her own college costs and foregone income if she went on to take an MBA, and her probable aptitudes—and decided to go into selling. Which she did, and with great success, picking the computer industry as the best place to be and proceeding to grow with a small company headquartered in Cincinnati.

Nor did her children or husband suffer in the process. She traveled a good deal, but was home many evenings and almost all weekends. She hired a full-time housekeeper, but when in residence continued to cook all the family's meals, clean up, help the children with their homework, and do all the things Supermoms did in those years, things which were—and still are—quite considerable.

There was one casualty after all, though. Her husband. Not through neglect, really; it is just that in the last analysis he found himself unable to handle the fact that she made more money than he did, had greater responsibilities, and—hardest of all to take—was better at selling than he was. For business is business, but selling is also an art, and artists are at bottom rather sensitive people. They lasted until their third child went off to college last year, and then split. Amicably, but irretrievably.

That left Ellen with three mostly grown children—who fill the house with themselves and their friends when they deign to come home from college—and a career. She is senior national accounts representative for her company, and limited only by the number of hours in the year. She criss-crosses the continent, spends as much as she needs to spend on entertainment, and brings home the bacon again and again.

She also works all the time, except for those rare occasions when she goes up to one of the kids' colleges or when they are at home when she is, which is equally rare. Her life on the road is totally monastic, except for work-connected entertaining and conferencing, and that is all "on deck" selling work. At her Cincinnati office, it is all work, too; there is always so much catching up to do back in the office that she seldom even goes out to lunch there, unless it is for a local selling call or for intracompany purposes.

Catching up; that is what she has told herself she was doing, ever since she went back to college over a decade ago. Just a Supermom catching up with all the things she gave up for her family, while continuing to take care of the family. But now the family is gone, and with it her Supermom role—and she is still running hard. Harder now, really; for it is all in one direction, and accelerates without the brake of other vital interests.

Now, predictably, she is beginning to hurt, just as the work-compulsive men she has competed with hurt. She had a touch of influenza last month, and her doctor found, along with some other danger signs, that her blood pressure was up. The doctor told her she might be in for trouble, and began to raise a question about her life style. She then told the doctor about the headaches, and the sleeping pills, which didn't seem to work very well any more. Ellen wondered if she might possibly prescribe some sleeping pills that were a little stronger, and perhaps a somewhat stronger painkiller for her headaches.

Her doctor, an old and trusted friend, reacted as might be expected, with a considerable lecture on the life-threatening hazards posed by work-aholism and possible drug abuse, and some very strong recommendations as to easing up, joining a health club, and developing some other interests. Then, knowing the family history, she talked about how easy it had been for Supermom to simply replace one kind of work with another, and how dangerous a pattern that was.

Very timely advice; very sensible. On the spot, Ellen promised to change her ways. She joined a health club the next day, bought tickets to a concert series, and called a man she knew and made a dinner date. All at top speed, of course, and in between work-connected tasks, one of which was to get up in the middle of the night to take some aspirin and not get to bed until she had jotted down a few notes for a presentation she is developing, which will be delivered some time next month.

Ellen will be back to see her doctor friend. Her doctor expects her, and is ready to begin a protracted and probably rather complex series of treatments and related events which will result, some time down the line, in either Ellen's serious impairment or a real change in her working and life styles. Workaholism is a difficult problem to combat; its roots go deep, and it requires much self-examination and often a great deal of help from those in the healing professions. The main thing is that Ellen is beginning to deal with it, probably before she has been seriously damaged.

PERSONAL SITUATION 2
GEORGE MARTIN

When you are good at selling, you get offers. George has had quite a few over the years; one yesterday, for that matter. But 12 years in one place is a long time, and sometimes fighting the good fight is a matter of self-respect, and takes precedence over other motives.

Eighteen years of selling; but in all honesty, only 11 as a sales professional. Kicking around selling everything from used cars to encyclopedias door-to-door may make a sales professional, but it didn't in George's case. All it made was someone who was looking for a job—any job—after his fifth selling job in six years didn't work out. Then he was lucky enough to meet Sam Ginsburg, then midwestern regional sales manager and on a hiring trip to Milwaukee. One very cold Friday in February, with a busted hiring trip staring him in the face, he interviewed George. Whether he saw something nobody else could see in George, or just couldn't face the prospect of doing the whole hiring trip all over again in March, nobody will even know, for Sam will never tell.

What is incontrovertible, though, is that there was something there, and that Sam was the right manager to bring it out. George spent a very difficult first year with Sam, learned a great deal about selling in the process, and became a professional. That was 12 years ago; Sam has retired since and George now works the Loop out of the company's home office, and handles some major national accounts besides.

George and his wife, Sarah, had started a family four years before he met Sam. George, Jr., Anne, Joanna, and John arrived at two-year intervals; they will start entering college in two years, and someone or other in the family will be in college for at least 10 years after that, and probably longer, as some will probably go on to graduate school. That means money —lots of it, which is part of the reason Sarah went back to school some years ago and is just starting her own career as a nutritionist.

Not-very-large companies that make machine parts for automobiles, farm equipment, and airplanes needed to be very well funded and managed to make it through the 1970s. George's company was, and made it through, barely—but in terribly impaired shape financially, and in need of every order and every bit of credit it can muster to keep on making it now.

It is a situation in which George is very definitely a factor, for his customer relationships contribute strongly to business retention and business building. It is also a situation in which George can be a profoundly negative factor, for if he ever leaves, it will in all probability be to join a competitor—and he will take a lot of business with him if he goes that way.

George hasn't really expected to have to face that kind of question. He has had every intention of staying right where he is for the rest of what would be a long and successful career, perhaps moving into sales management later on, as Sam did before him.

On the other hand, he is not an ostrich—far from it. After 12 years in the field, he knows a great deal about his industry and the companies in it, through a wide network of sources and friends. And the word is that his own company is in trouble, deep trouble. The kind of trouble you can get through if everything falls just right, but will not survive if any of several major negative possibilities eventuate. He has checked it out; for once, it may be as bad as rumor has it.

That poses quite a problem. For just to consider leaving, when all the people he has worked with for most of his career are in trouble, makes him feel like a rat about to desert a sinking ship. It is not so much a matter of company loyalty—though there is that—but rather a matter of loyalty to and consideration of the people he has worked with and liked so much all these years. Sure, George Martin can leave for another good job—he is a top sales professional, and can sell anything, anywhere, any time, and do well—but what about the people in the factory and in the office, who will not have that option? For that matter, what about the pensioners, like Sam, whose pensions are not fully funded and are therefore to a considerable extent tied to company fortunes?

Not so easy, for there are other people to consider, too, named Sarah, George, Jr., Anne, Joanna, and John. The day George becomes unemployed his bargaining power goes down precipitously, and those who want him so badly now will be willing to pay much less for him than they are today—if they want him at all. He very well knows that the time to find another job is while you are successfully employed, for then you are most attractive and can bargain from a position of strength. Employed, you are sought; unemployed, seeking. That's the way it works, and no amount of wishful thinking, or "putting jobs on the back burner" can change that.

If George is wise, he will move now, for the truth usually is that by the time a company is in really deep trouble it matters little whether or not a single sales professional stays, no matter how much it might seem to matter to that person at that time. And the home responsibilities do come first; to sacrifice the education of your children because you want to fight that kind of good fight is little more than a foolish and damaging gesture.

On the other hand, he may not move on, citing loyalty and consideration for others as his reasons, but perhaps it may be inertia. Perhaps mostly inertia, for most of us tend to make the mistake of thinking that somehow things will work out all right just once more if they have worked out well on other occasions. They don't though; each evaluation has to be made afresh, with possibly disabling inertia figured into the equation every time.

PERSONAL SITUATION 3
MARTHA JONES

By any reasonable set of measures, Martha Jones works in a very, very sick industry. In a fairly stable company, it is true, but still a company that pays someone as good as she is at selling about half as much as she should reasonably expect to make as the star professional she is. Deeply depressed industries are like that.

But Martha sells books to bookstores on behalf of a substantial publishing house, and is as deeply committed to books as she was the day she walked into her tiny, hometown library and decided to read everything in the library, from A to Z. She was seven years old at the time, and nearly foundered on *Anthony Adverse,* but persevered, and had by the time she left that town 11 years later just about done what she had set out to do —in principle, anyway.

After college, which started in the tumultuous 1960s and finished in the sober 1970s, she headed for New York and the publishing trade, B.A. in hand and carrying what was for her an enormous load of college-related debts. Prudently, she had taken typing in high school; that and her ability to sell the benefits that hiring her would bring got her a job as an administrative assistant to the marketing vice president of a publishing house.

She loved it; all of it—even the typing. (Well, maybe not the typing.) But New York is a very expensive place and debts must be repaid, and what she made as an administrative assistant in a publishing company was not enough to handle her financial needs.

She had thought to go into editing, but editorial jobs were then few and far between, with hundreds of experienced editors in her sick industry out on the street looking for work. So what she did instead was to try to move into the selling side, as a field representative. There was an opening in the metropolitan New York area of her company, and she applied for it—and was turned down. She was never quite sure whether it was because she was seen only as an administrative assistant or whether it was because she was Black, or because she was a woman, or all three. Actually, she thought it most likely that it was because she was seen as an administrative assistant; her company was by then hiring women and Blacks for its sales force, though it is true that she would have been its first Black woman representative.

She tried again, a few months later, this time for an opening in New England, working out of Boston, and was again turned down. That was enough; she started looking elsewhere. Eventually she found a selling job in the New York area, handling a territory for her current employer, which is by the way a thoroughly enlightened company, as companies go.

Yes, that's right; she was a star. It took her about six months to get her feet on the ground, and then she was a star. Not just a star in rather limited competition, but someone good enough and increasingly professional enough to make her way in any selling organization.

That was five years ago, and she is still a star and still with the same company and still in the same territory. Now, quite predictably, she is ready to make some career moves. The trouble is that her company has passed her over twice in the last two years. The first time, someone else, who was in no way her professional equal, was promoted to the national accounts representative job. She was the one who had been at the top of the sales force three years in a row, won all the contests, and was rolling right along; he was the one who got the promotion.

The second time, someone else was promoted to a regional manager's job; again he was in no way her professional equal. In the first instance, she thought it might be in part due to her age; the man who got the job was five years older than she. But in the second case, the man who got the job was about her own age, had been with the company only two years, and had no particularly relevant earlier experience. Further, she had made it clear that she wanted to be considered for the job, and was not even interviewed.

This time, she thinks it likely that she is being discriminated against, perhaps because she is a woman, perhaps because she is Black. She has no way of knowing whether it is a matter of management simply not being able to "see" her or whether she is encountering a hidden bigot or two somewhere farther up in her corporate hierarchy. Either way, she is being blocked, and not even being considered for an entirely deserved promotion.

Martha has a pretty good idea that she has no case, in terms of legal redress. There are antidiscrimination laws that might apply to this kind of situation, but proving discrimination would be nearly impossible; and the length of time it would take and the intracompany situation such an action would develop make that course of action unacceptable. On the other hand, she has no intention of either leaving it alone or quietly fading away into another company with better growth possibilities. She likes her company and most of the people in it, and wants to make an effort to grow where she is.

She thinks that what she will do is take the matter up very openly and as sharply as necessary with her national sales manager, making it clear that she thinks she was unfairly passed over and very much wants a chance to prove herself in the next management job that comes up. Actually, she has a pretty good idea it will be the one that was just filled; the new manager already gives some evidence of having regretted the decision to go into management, and is developing home problems over the amount of travel required.

So Martha will wait. Not for years; but until the next opening comes. When it does come, she will talk quickly and directly with the national sales manager; if necessary, she will go right over his head to the president of her division. For that matter, she is quite prepared to go as far as her company president and the chairman of the company's board of directors on this one. She has little to lose; with her skills, she can always get just as good a job as the one she has in publishing, and a far more lucrative one in any of several other industries if she decided to go that way. She is unlikely to leave her chosen industry, though; if *Anthony Adverse* didn't daunt her when she was seven, neither will a little thing like fighting through to management in an industry that desperately needs to hold on to whatever good people it has left.

PERSONAL SITUATION 4

HARRY SMITH

After Vietnam, there were a couple of bad years. He had gone in right after high school; it was the excitement, and leaving the little town in southern Indiana where he was sure he would have no future. At the time, he told his family that it was an opportunity to get a trade and maybe an education after it was all over. But the only trade he learned in the war was killing, and it was two years before he even tried to finish his education.

Eventually, though, the shock of Vietnam wore off; he did go to school. Two years of college, and an associate's degree in something called distribution, which was enough to get him started as a sales trainee with a company selling office supplies wholesale to retailers. At the start, he was just so-so at it, but then somehow Harry started to enjoy selling, enjoy it more than anything else he had ever done. He read up on it, picked the brains of the old-timers, learned everything he could about the products he was selling, and kept right at it. Long hours, days and weeks on the road—his first territory covered the whole state of Indiana and parts of Kentucky and southern Illinois, too—but he enjoyed it. Somehow it gave a focus to his life that had never existed before. Most of all, he loved the feeling of independence, of constantly being on the move, of meeting and developing hundreds of friends as a respected professional person. And five years into his selling career, he had become just that—a sales professional past his period of apprenticeship, making sales and making money, and with nowhere to go but up, even in difficult times.

Some other good things have happened, too. A girl named Mary Reilly, for one thing, who is now Mary Reilly Smith, and mother of their one-year-old daughter. And a house, just outside Indianapolis, bought with all their savings for a down payment and a huge mortgage carrying an enormous rate of interest. Their own home, nevertheless.

The traveling hasn't been nearly as attractive since the baby was born. The truth is that Harry still loves selling, but has been seriously thinking about the possibility of trying to find a job in a major metropolitan area, where he could be home most nights, rather than only on weekends. His current job is a bird in the hand, though, and he and Mary spend everything he makes, but not foolishly; it is just that prices are so high and the house costs a great deal to maintain. Selling costs on the road have gone up, too, and his commissions have not kept pace.

His current job *was* a bird in the hand, that is. He lost it a month ago. Not his fault; the company failed. He had seen the signs and ignored them, but Harry is young and in those respects quite inexperienced.

The problem is that jobs are few and far between, and he and Mary have no reserves at all. And right now, the only job he seems to have any chance at all of getting is precisely the kind of job he was thinking of leaving—and it offers less pay, at that. Harry feels trapped, betrayed. The whole thing reminds him of coming back from Nam, for the truth is that nobody cares about him, Mary, and the baby; it has to be self-help all the way.

No, he won't go off the rails; and yes, he will take the job. Professionalism will, in the last analysis, save the situation. He will take the job, and make a success of it; until he finds a more suitable selling job, that is. He will do that soon enough from a successfully employed position, as he could not while unemployed. Some astute sales manager will snap him up, or a customer will "steal" him, or one of his former colleagues will recommend him to a new employer.

But it is likely to be the last time in his life that he ignores signs that an employer may be on the rocks, and the last time he and Mary trap themselves by using all their available cash—and then some—for a house or for anything else. No matter how good you are at selling, you can't keep your head in the sand and hope to survive in the long run.

PERSONAL SITUATION 5
INGRID HANSEN

Like so many others, Ingrid Hansen got into selling almost accidentally. The truth is that when she graduated from college with a very nice but perfectly useless B.A., back in the late 1960s, she didn't have a clue as to what she wanted to do. No desire to go on with her education, either; no calling at all, in fact. Just a desire to put 16 uninterrupted years of schooling behind her and to go out into the world and live.

Which she proceeded to do, in several places, and in quite a number of dead-end, low-paying jobs, from restaurant work through a little modeling to demonstrating a new kind of processed cheese in supermarkets.

In San Francisco, in the early 1970s, some of her friends started to move into the business world more seriously. One of them talked her into applying for a very straightforward entry-level job selling copiers and copying supplies to offices, mostly to downtown lawyers, accountants, and financial people. She was broke; took the job because it paid a little better than anything else she might come up with.

She had planned to stay for a few months; selling anything to anybody was scarcely the kind of thing she had pictured herself doing during her college years. A commune in Oregon seemed somehow more to the point; but she had tried that, and it had not really been very appealing.

The months became years; a career began to emerge. She received some home office training before she went into the field, and then was lucky enough to be assigned to an excellent field sales manager, who really trained her, selling side by side with her in the field. She spent two good apprenticeship years with that manager, making money and learning her trade, and came out of it a good young sales professional, still with a lot to learn, but learning all the time. And making money, a lot more money than she had ever made before. Enough money to move into a decent apartment, buy a few things, and save a little.

At first, she complained to her friends about selling, mostly because in her circles at that time selling was looked down upon, and complaining was the thing to do. Later on, as more of her friends moved seriously into the business world, she let herself admit to herself and others that she thoroughly enjoys selling—the game as much as the rewards. She likes the independence, the freedom, and the measurable set of accomplishments; but most of all, she likes to sell, to close a sale and win the game. In short, she has turned out to be as close to a natural as anyone ever is—someone who reaches for empathy, for buying motives, for hurdles to handle and convert into buying reasons, and then knows when and how to close.

She is good at it; very good. So good that she has carved out quite a career for herself. First it was copiers, then larger office machines, then substantial systems to much larger companies. She has had success all the way, and a good deal of money and recognition, too.

For the past two years, she has been headed toward sales management. She is in her early thirties, has 10 years of solid professional experience, is accustomed to a good deal of travel, and has demonstrated her ability to learn. And her ability to train others, too; she has an excellent record as a sales trainer, having successfully handled several training assignments in the last year.

Yesterday, her friend and co-networker Janine, who is already a manager, told her that she was about to get that long-awaited offer. The company's national sales manager is arriving from Chicago on a periodic swing west, and plans to offer her the mountain states region, with headquarters in Denver, which is about to become vacant due to a promotion. Not unexpected; she had trained new representatives in Salt Lake City and Pocatello last year.

The trouble is, now that she is faced with it, she is not so sure she wants the job. No, not the mountain states job—the management job. For, all of a sudden, she has realized that management and selling are two entirely different things, and that although she has been well trained and has trained herself in selling, she has absolutely no training and not necessarily much aptitude for a career in management. The thought of leaving the day-to-day practice of the selling profession makes her feel a little odd in the pit of her stomach. It is, after all, the only profession, the only set of skills, the only career she has ever had, and she loves doing it.

Going into management means learning a whole new set of skills. To be an effective manager she is going to have to learn a great deal more about the language of numbers, budgeting, marketing, hiring and firing, supervising, internal political maneuvering—all the things that managers do just as reflexively as selling professionals prepare, approach, present, objection-handle, and close. She has none of those skills. Furthermore, she has none of the skills learned by MBAs in academe, and will have to compete in a new world full of people with formal management training and much greater experience.

All very difficult, now that she is beginning to think hard about the possible negatives in the situation. Most difficult, though, is the prospect of leaving selling. Or is it just fear of going into a new profession? She has learned selling well enough to become a top professional; why not management, too, becoming a very mobile and highly paid dual professional in the process? She knows that her company will send her to in-house and short-term outside professional development courses; also that they will pay her tuition if she enrolls in a graduate business program and goes after an MBA on her own. It is very hard to know whether these late doubts about the move are to be ignored or taken very seriously indeed.

The offer will come, probably tomorrow. She will probably take it; that is the logic of the situation and the nature of her own drive and curiosity about her own powers at this time in her life. As she is, she will probably either make an outstanding success of it or break her heart trying. On the other hand, it may be a mistake; she will have to find that out as she goes. Either way—and in the last analysis this is probably what will swing her thinking over to taking the proffered management job—she can always go back to selling, with this or another company. You don't forget how to sell, no matter how long you may be away from it. Now that she is a sales professional, she can always get some kind of selling job, in good times or bad. And she is good; if ever she must, she will be as able to sell soap, used cars, financial services, books, or anything else just as well as she was able to sell office copiers and systems.

PERSONAL SITUATION 6
INGRID HANSEN REVISITED

The plane touched down at exactly 9:13 A.M., exactly one hour and two minutes late. Two hours and a little to make a one-hour run. The start of a happy February day in Boise. Walking to the terminal from the airplane, she could feel the bitter wet cold beginning to reach through her heavy coat; it was going to snow again.

Jim Smith was not there to meet her. Strike two for Jim Smith; strike one being his abysmal sales record for the last two months, which had led to her changing her carefully planned itinerary and go to Boise in the first place, at the "suggestion" of her national sales manager. Nor did he answer his telephone at home; perhaps he was on his way to the airport, or had some kind of car trouble on the way. She waited.

And waited; and called again; and waited some more. At 10:15 she rented a car. At 10:46, she arrived at the Smith residence, and found it occupied by Jim Smith, sodden with drink, and somewhat indignant underneath his profuse apologies, because he had been wakened from a sound sleep by her insistent ringing of his doorbell. It seemed that he had turned the telephone bell off the night before on retiring, and had overslept. From the look of him, he had risen once or twice to have just one more, and then fallen into bed again.

At 10:55 or so, Ingrid had a newly vacant territory and a briefcase full of sales material to cart away with her. And a very heavy load of dismay and unhappy anticipation. For Jim had been a hiring error; she had done all the right things mechanically—asked all the right questions, done all the telephone reference checks—but had ignored that last lingering doubt that should have been listened to. Why? Because she had hired him in October, after coming away empty-handed from a busted hiring trip in August, and the territory had been untenanted then for three months. And because she wanted to get him through training class at the home office to do field training with him before the snow flew. He had been all right at the home office, and in the field with her, but then those wrong-looking call reports began to come in, and the sales results didn't. Now she was going to have to make another hiring trip—Boise in February in an airport motel in a snowstorm—and then field train in late March at best. Bad timing, and a territory effectively empty for six months. And two other territories like that, besides; she kept on going with her hopes, and coming down flat on her face.

Not really; after two years as a field sales manager, she was actually doing pretty well. Fairly well, anyway. Mid-range performance nationally last year; less hiring errors than the year before; and a couple of pretty promising new representatives. Good at handling trouble accounts, but perhaps a little too ready to handle trouble herself, rather than helping others learn how to do it. Not bad on budgeting, for a beginner; and the AMA finance for marketers course she went to last summer helped some. No chance to go for an MBA in a systematic way, though; too much travel connected with the job. She was going to be a pretty good run-of-the-mill sales manager in a few more years; maybe a national sales manager for somebody 10 or 15 years down the line. As to moving into a full scale management career—well, maybe, but that would require a good deal more formal general management training, the way things are now, and she is not enough of a ball of fire as a sales manager to make anyone want to take much of a chance on her right now.

The truth, which she has come to recognize (and never more than today), is that she has worked hard and become a competent sales manager, but is hardly likely to become a stellar performer in this or any other sales management job. And she was and still is a star sales professional; every time she works with someone in the field, they make a lot of sales, her sales. She trains decently, but cannot yet and may never be able to replicate herself. That, in turn, is because she is only fair at hiring. Oh, there are all kinds of reasons for not being a star at something; the net of it all is that she has become convinced that although she has proven that she can do the sales management job, she has also decided that she will be a lot happier and more productive back in the field.

Back to San Francisco, too. She had become used to traveling, but had seriously underestimated the importance of having a compatible home base and friends to come home to. A single woman who lives in a city in which she has no base, and travels all week, 40 to 50 weeks a year, is not footloose and fancy free. She is lonely. Life becomes an endless round of planes, cars, buses, restaurants, and very, very lonely hotel rooms, with no opportunity at all to build any kind of meaningful personal life. At least that is her experience—and that of many others like her.

She is going back into the field; today decided it. She will think about it some more; but she has been thinking about it all winter, and has quite firmly made up her mind. It will mean less money, but not much less; as a star in the field she made almost as much as she is making as a mediocre-to-fair sales manager. It may mean less status in her company—or even a move to another company, if nothing is open or can be made open in San Francisco for her—but that is nothing that bothers her very much. Perhaps later on she will try management again—but she doubts it.

PERSONAL SITUATION 7
HUGH McDONALD

His back hurt again. That was partly because it was another hot, wet, smoggy, in-every-way-ugly summer day in New York, and it caused all his joints to swell. At least it felt like all his joints; his doctor had said it was a tendency to have lower back pain, which would come on worst in this kind of weather. By lower back pain, the doctor of course meant that he didn't have the slightest idea of what was wrong, or what to do about it beyond taking aspirin. And it didn't help at all that his briefcase weighed a stripped-down 40 pounds, and that he had been carrying it back and forth across midtown Manhattan all day, from one busted appointment to another. No cabs, no way to lighten the load any further, no way to make his back stop hurting.

No way to make his post-nasal drip stop, either. His doctor had recommended staying inside in air conditioned offices, and buying a dehumidifier for the apartment, to supplement the air conditioner there. The specialist told him to go cold turkey on nasal sprays, and wanted to try something experimental on him. She said to stay indoors and get a dehumidifier, too. He had paid both doctors some hundreds of dollars for their advice, and was out here on the street right now trying to make the money to pay them and keep eating, because that is what outside sales professionals do. They get out on the street and sell.

He had always wanted to come to work in the Big Apple; get a plum territory in midtown selling home offices and be home with Joan and the kids every night. Only it took two hours each way on the train from the nearest suburb with good schools they had been able to afford, and Joan now commuted, too, to get the money to pay for college and all the rest, and two kids were in college and two more were headed for college in the next three years. The truth is they had no life, really; just trains, and bills, and carrying around a case weighing what felt like 400 pounds and slowly dying of asphyxiation.

On the corner of 52 Street and Fifth Avenue, while waiting for a light to change, he turned for a moment and saw himself in a shop window.

And there, at 3:10 P.M. on a quite-typically-nasty Friday afternoon in midsummer, at the center of Manhattan's pulsing corporate heart, he decided to leave the Big Apple forever. There are some things that have to come to an end, or they finish us.

Not to leave selling, though; he would have had to do that only if he had stayed in New York and tried to fight it out for some more years. Then the pressures would probably have become too great, with liquor, exhaustion, and physical problems ultimately leading to insurmountable emotional and marital problems. No, not to leave selling; to go back to what, for him, will be a livable and workable environment. He is not the only sales professional in the world who needs to work out of a car or sell out of a very light briefcase; or the only one whose post-nasal drip makes a hot, wet climate literally intolerable. He knows that he needs only a change of jobs, not a change of career.

That may mean some considerable personal and family dislocation; perhaps even a term of separation, for Joan's career is not necessarily as movable as is his, nor are teenagers in their last years of high school so easily moved. It may even mean staying on in New York for as much as another year or two, as things are worked out. He is far too experienced to simply quit and look elsewhere; to maximize employment opportunities, it is best to seek a job while successfully employed, which he is.

For him, it may be as simple as waiting for the right intracompany opening, in the southwest or the mountain states. He doesn't want a wholly travel territory at this stage of the game, though; he spent years traveling all week and being home only on weekends, and the move to New York was partly a move away from that. What he wants now is a metropolitan or combined metropolitan–travel territory, perhaps in an area like Phoenix or Denver. And those are areas where a relatively new but highly qualified personnel manager like Joan might very well find a job. Indeed, it may be that she will find a job first, and he will follow, if necessary changing companies to do so.

Luckily, Hugh sells high technology products to commercial accounts and is, because of his current experience, in considerable demand. However, if he has difficulty placing himself in that kind of work and simultaneously in a suitable geographic area, he is ready to change industries, as well as jobs. Selling is selling, after all; and he is a sales professional who knows that certain physical and life-style needs take precedence over what before seemed like career necessities.

In the long run, he and Joan are quite likely now to set roots somewhere, something they have never done before, with his traveling and their corporate transfers. Hugh may be quite happy to take a territory in the right area, perhaps the kind of territory and at the kind of pay he graduated from some years ago, and then proceed to go a different way, into business for himself. He certainly has no capital now, and is unlikely to develop any significant amount of capital as long as all those children are going through college, even though he and Joan both work. They and their children will be lucky to come out of the college years only moderately in debt. But he may be able to move into an independent representative's stance some years down the line, perhaps going to work for an independent representative and then into business for himself, after he learns the business side of the independent representative business. Or he may use his excellent selling skills and relatively little capital as his contribution to a dealership or distributorship partnership in one of the fast-developing high technology product areas in which he sells. Once the decision has been made to set roots in a compatible area, sales professionals can make the other solutions come.

PERSONAL SITUATION 8
LORNA DUBOIS

Three strikes and you're out. It happened again last night; the third time in a year. After dinner—one drink, light meal, fairly early night—she had gone up to her room to do some paperwork. Got on the elevator, pressed the button for six, got off at six, and headed for her room, 641, way down at the far end of the building.

It was an ordinary hotel corridor, standard width, standard lighting, standard beige walls, doors every few feet. Nobody there but her. Suddenly, she felt detached; it all looked the same, but she was looking at it from inside and somehow outside at the same time. And she did not have the slightest idea of where she was, or what day it was, or what time it was, or why she was there.

It had been one of the worst moments in her life—jarring, frightening, physically sickening. She had stopped, then forced herself to keep walking, and had come out of it very quickly in real time, perhaps 10 seconds. But subjectively it seemed entirely out of time, and impossible to measure.

Reflexively, she went on, ordered a drink from room service, and did her paperwork. She is a professional, after all, with a professional's moves. But sleep came harder than usual, and she needed a pill, the first one in a week. And next morning, she took care not to block it out. She thought about it, and has been thinking about it all day.

Reflections like that go deep. Lorna hadn't started out to go into selling; in fact, anything in the business world was the last thing she wanted. She had gone out to San Francisco after high school in Chicago in the 1960s, enrolled at Berkeley and then dropped out and into the Haight-Ashbury scene in San Francisco. Not for long, though; she had soon discovered social movements, gone back to Berkeley, and set out to change the world, as had so many others of her college generation.

That had lasted a lot longer than being a flower child. Two and a half movements, one war, and one busted marriage longer, to be precise. In the early 1970s, with her then two-year-old child, Susan, a completely uneconomic M.A. in English literature, and no resources at all, she had gone back to live with her parents in Skokie.

She had not drifted into selling then; her drifting days were over. What she had done was to examine the available alternatives, decide that she would not go back to school, reason that selling was one of the few great apprenticeship occupations left, and set out to become a successful, highly paid, well-respected sales professional. She had a lot of company; she moved into selling at a time when sex barriers were being broken down, and women were beginning to come into selling in very large numbers.

Lorna did exactly what she had set out to do. In not too many years, she had moved through a series of office equipment and then computer industry selling jobs, and is now a national accounts representative for a substantial computer products company, working out of the home office in Chicago. She travels a great deal, but is home most weekends, and shares a house and a housekeeper with two other professional women, both of whom also have children. She is in line for management soon, and will take a management job when offered, even though it will mean just as much traveling as before, for the foreseeable future.

Except that it has happened three times in the last year. And that she misses Susan terribly, every day, and has missed her every night she has been on the road for the past eight years. And that she is terribly, terribly lonely, because she is a woman on the road alone, and all the right professional moves in the world cannot make up for lack of human companionship.

She really has tried all the ameliorative road moves. She has submerged herself in work, made as many women friends as possible in places she normally visits, kept up with her professional and personal reading, spoken with Susan every night; but in the long run, for her, it has not been enough. In desperation, she has even tried a few one-night stands with near-strangers; all have been disasters. Lorna has managed so far to block most of it out. The work has been paramount over the years, an effective-seeming substitute for a great many other things. That has been one of her great career strengths; but it is not enough.

She is committed to her career, though; and tenacious. To her, giving up on the road has seemed weakness, and somehow a denial of her ability to freely pursue her career. It is not that, of course. But she is willing to seriously reevaluate the question only now because she recognizes the threat of emotional problems that are beginning to go out of control. For the truth is that she has alternative selling career paths that can take her where she wants to go, without having to spend so much time away from home, in what for her are entirely inimical environments. That she cannot "handle" road problems is neither tragedy nor weakness; the selling world is full of excellent and highly successful professionals who are as unable and far less willing than she to even try traveling 30 to 50 weeks a year.

Jarred into looking at it sensibly, Lorna sees that she might very well be able to transfer into a metropolitan regional territory with no loss of pay or status. Several regional managers in her current company would love to have her, and to use her as a trainer, besides. Indeed, the road to management—if that is what she decides she really wants—may be far more open from such a regional base than from a national accounts representative's position. She can also change companies, if she must, going either into a senior metropolitan regional sales position, or directly into sales management. She is good, and many people in her industry know it. The odds are that her present company will do everything possible to hold her, once she makes her desires clear. It may not happen overnight, but it will happen. Then there are unlikely to be any more such incidents in hotel corridors, or pills to get to sleep, and Susan will have her only parent, to help her through some crucial growing-up years, for the first time since she was two years old.

PERSONAL SITUATION 9
JOHN NOVAK

Once, in about 1962, when he and Emma had been visiting Adam at college, John had gone to see *Death of a Salesman.* It was a student production, with most of the flaws you might expect; but it was interesting, anyway, as much for the audience's reaction as for anything else. Adam kind of apologized for taking them, but John said no, it was well worth doing, a very good play, although he thought the playwright wasn't talking so much about salesmen as about a certain kind of man in that time and place. John's only real criticism of the play was that the author didn't know much about how selling really worked, and neither, therefore, did Willy Loman. No sales professional he knew would survive that many years selling the way Willy Loman sold; amateurs like that, who think they are selling themselves, and fooling their customers and prospects into buying, soon self-select themselves out into another line of work.

Quite true, but when your company goes bust and leaves you high and dry at the not-so-tender age of 61, and you haven't come up with a new job after six months, you begin to wonder. That is what has happened to John, and he is beginning to think that his 40 years of farm machinery selling experience have more than anything else locked him into a troubled trade, much as buggy and harness makers went out of style and out of work when cars came in.

He can't seem to connect. Probably too specialized, and not enough contacts with people outside the industry. Well, there hadn't seemed any need to cultivate people outside farm equipment; not after that many years as a sales leader for one of the top companies in the industry. He used to tell Emma that if anything ever really went wrong, all he had to do was pick up the phone and make a few calls, and he would come up with something right there in Minneapolis, with one of the people who had been after him to come over for years. It had been true then; no longer. Most of the people who might have hired him in the good years were unemployed themselves, retired early, or long since out of it.

Hard times; it seemed to him he had actually begged that young woman in the employment office this morning for a chance to talk to the national sales manager of that computer company. She had handled it all right, though, you have to say that for her. She had been kind, and respectful, and had pointed out very calmly that the ad had stated they were looking for people with a certain amount of computer industry experience, and that they were doing that because they were not prepared to do much training. She had even suggested a couple of other companies he could try, companies that did a good deal more home office training. Sure, for entry-level jobs, in which he might make a quarter of what he was making when his own company folded.

His own company; that was the trouble. Somehow, he had thought it was his, and that it would go on forever. Now even the pension plan was in question; it seems they had invested a good deal of the pension funds in the company's common stock, as a gesture of faith in the company. Faith, hell! The stuff wasn't worth a damned thing now. It wasn't even traded any more; the creditors would get just about everything on liquidation of the company's assets. And the same for his own stock, so attractive that he had borrowed money again and again to exercise options as they came up.

He brought himself up short. Too much of that lately; you set yourself into that kind of mood and you can never sell anything. Maybe a cup of coffee would help, like after a busted sale, when you had them down to the wire and somehow blew it.

He went into a diner across the street, sat over coffee in a booth. He went blank for a little while, then looked up and happened to see a man and a woman dressed for business, sitting and earnestly talking, a couple of booths over. Man about 40; woman in her mid-twenties. He was doing most of the talking, she was listening hard. She looked a little down, then seemed to perk up a bit as she got some coffee and what looked like advice poured into her.

It took John back, a long way back, maybe 30 or 35 years. The man reminded him of somebody back then, somebody he couldn't quite place. Then he remembered; it was Bob Harris, his first and as far as he was concerned his best sales manager. Bob Harris, with his earnest face and waving finger emphasizing every point, post-morteming every single thing that had happened that morning over lunch in some small-town diner, and both showing and telling a very young John Novak just how to get it all done.

And it came to him then; Bob would have been ashamed of him this morning; maybe a lot of mornings in the past few months. Bob always said, "Remember, you only have to sell one! And that makes it possible to sell another one, and another, and another, and turn a good day into a good week into a good month into a good year." He drummed it into all of them every day; they used to laugh about it and at him a little, but they all remembered it for the rest of their lives.

Except for John Novak, who had forgotten it for a little while. And who really did only have to sell one—just one job. The John Novaks of this world aren't Willy Lomans. They don't go out and beg for jobs, or show people how much they need jobs and how discouraged they have become. They don't come on as single-industry experts who won't fit into other industries. They sell themselves into jobs, by empathizing, finding motives for buying; that is, hiring, presenting themselves, handling stalls and objections, and using them to move successfully through to the close: the job offer. If they want to move into a new industry, they focus on that industry, learn something about it and its language and trends, and take anything they can get in that industry, even if it is way below their income levels and needs. Then they move, either in the companies they have sold themselves into, or elsewhere. Sales professionals need very little knowledge to move from industry to industry; but sometimes those hiring them do not know as well as they do that selling is selling.

John need not sell farm equipment. He can move into computers, the health care industry, the selling of any kinds of vehicles, and a dozen other kinds of selling jobs. At 61, he is a thoroughly seasoned sales professional, and will be recognized as such if he presents himself that way, rather than as a washed-up has-been. The truth is, if he had been thinking this morning, instead of just going through the motions, he would never have been talking to that nice, entirely inappropriate young interviewer. Instead, he would have looked up the national sales manager of that company in any of the standard sources he has been familiar with for over 40 years, called him, and sold himself into an interview. John Novak is available, for the first time in 40 years, and ready to move into the best and fastest-growing company in the computer industry—yours—Mr. or Ms. National Sales Manager.

John will get a job and make a success of it, now that he has solved his main job-seeking problem. That never was age, or one-industry experience. It was simply that he had not properly made the connection between selling himself into a job and selling products other than himself. He hadn't looked for a job in a very long time, and had not thought through the need to prospect properly, approach, present, handle, and close, all empathetically and always selling the benefits that hiring him would bring. It may be that he forgot; it may be that he never knew how to do that for himself, although he certainly knows how to do all that consummately well on behalf of any products he will ever sell, in any industry. Either way, he now knows what he has to do, and has known all his working life how to go about it. Goodbye, Willy; hello, John.

PERSONAL SITUATION 10
SALLY TAKEDA

Only lack of money kept Sally from going right on through to her MBA. As it was, she had to be satisfied with a BS in distribution, which she then proceeded to parlay into a marketing—that is, selling—trainee job for a big food company. With a metropolitan Philadelphia territory, she could be home every night, and that meant she could enroll in a graduate business program; she did that two years ago, and is halfway through now.

Her real aim is not to stay on as a corporate employee, but in the long run to develop some kind of business of her own. Not surprising—her family runs to small business people; her father and mother still operate the "mom-and-pop" restaurant that has supported them for the last 30 years, and that has put Sally and her two brothers through college.

Last month, she received a signal honor; she was invited into the "club," after two years on the outside. It was something she had long hoped for, but really little expected—to be invited to coffee every morning with four of the most seasoned representatives in the office, Mike, Thomas, George, and Shirley. Actually, Shirley was almost as new as she; the others had been coffeeing together for years, every morning from about 9:15 to 10:00, after leaving the office and before seeing their earliest appointments.

It had been everything she had hoped for. They talked about the trade, people in the company, what kinds of people to sell and whom to avoid, the sharp angles they used to sell the tough ones—all the things that can come only with years of experience. In truth, they helped her to begin to see something she had missed—that a lot of what she was doing was hard and unrewarding, and that there were a lot of ways to work smarter and a lot easier, and to do it all in a lot less hours. That can be extremely useful when you are going to school at night and living with someone you care about very much, as well.

Yesterday, opportunity may have knocked. Over coffee, the others in the club started talking about something they seem to have had in mind for quite some time. It seems that Mike has a client that wants to go the independent representative route; he wants Mike to take on Pennsylvania, Maryland, and New Jersey, with parts of a couple of other states. Mike has been thinking it over, and has proposed a partnership with Thomas, George, and Shirley, with all of them borrowing some money to capitalize a new firm. They are all willing to include Sally in their plans if she can come up with a little cash and take low pay—as they all will—for the first few months, until they get a few more accounts and begin to really pay their way. They know that Sally has been going to school, and feel that she can contribute not only her selling skills to the joint enterprise, but some needed business skills as well, as all the others are good at selling, but none has ever really run a business of his or her own.

Sally does have a little money; not much, but she has managed to save a little in the last two years. And she has a great deal of desire to go into her own business. The trouble is that she is not quite sure that these are the right people to go in with, and she cannot talk about it with any of her friends in the company without compromising all their positions.

She couldn't talk about it intelligently with Roosevelt Jones, either. He is lover, confidante, and friend, but has no business sense at all, having self-selected out of a job in the business world some years ago and become a recreation supervisor in a nursing home. But she could and did talk about it with his older sister, Clara, who has been making her way in the business world for quite some time now as a somewhat harried and extremely effective management consultant.

Clara listened hard, pondered, and then asked several questions; even the asking of them was rather devastating. The first was: "What do they want you for? You have never run a business of your own, either." The second was: "What in the world are they doing wasting three quarters of an hour every day having coffee? That's three and three quarters of an hour a week of prime selling time." Then, after whipping out a calculator, "Ellen, do you know that those people are wasting 187.5 hours of prime selling time every year, assuming that they work 50 weeks a year? That's well over a month of selling time wasted every year! What in the world is their sales manager thinking of, letting them do that and then letting them suck you and Shirley into it?" The third comment wasn't a question, but a very flat "Those people are born losers. I wouldn't touch them with a 10-foot pole if I were you. If you want to go into the independent rep business, go into it as you would any other small business. Go to work selling for an independent rep, learn the business, and then go out on your own after doing your period of apprenticeship. Pay your dues, and then maybe you'll make it the way you want."

Oh. Yes, quite right. Sally felt like a fool; it was all so obvious. She quit the club the next morning, by the simple expedient of claiming the pressure of business, an early appointment. Shirley quit the same way a few days later, after she and Sally talked it out one day after hours.

Mike, Thomas, and George never did go into business together; they didn't know the first thing about going into a business of their own. Mike was fired a few months later; he had been a time-waster and sour apple for years, and his production had been steadily going downhill for quite some time. Thomas and George are still with the company, still talking about pie in the sky, and still turning in mediocre performances and on the edge of failure. Shirley is doing rather well, and is looking toward management at some future time.

Sally? Oh, Sally moved on quite some time ago. She finished her studies, and received her MBA, with honors. On the strength of that and Sally's marketing experience, Clara helped her sell herself into a job with Clara's consulting firm. Now Sally and Clara are talking about setting up a little consulting firm of their own, and developing it into a big one. They probably will, too.

PERSONAL SITUATION 11
JIM KELLY

At the ages of 70 and 68, respectively, Jim and Mary Kelly are thinking about going home. Home to Boston, and to cold, cold winters, cars that won't start, urban sprawl, smog, crime, racial violence, and decay. Also to children, grandchildren, one great-grandchild, lifelong friends, and the chance of making a little money once again. And to Boston, which, in spite of everything, they very much miss.

Jim had a fine career in selling, 45 years of it, as field representative, manager, and then again in the field. Mary had her beautician's business in her later years. Between them, they did rather well. Well enough to fulfill a lifelong dream five years ago.

They did it right. On the day Jim turned 65, he went into his office downtown, cleaned up his desk, turned in his briefcase, and quit. His sales manager then returned Jim's empty briefcase to him, and his national sales manager—whom Jim had trained in the field nearly 25 years before—made a mercifully short speech, gave him a fine set of golf clubs, and then took the whole office out to a banquet at the best restaurant in town. Jim had retired.

So had Mary, completing the sale of her business the month before. They sold the big house they had raised the whole family in, bought a house in a lovely St. Petersburg retirement community, and decamped. No more Boston winters and no more work. Just a lot of good years in the sun, fishing, gardening a little, playing cards, cooking, and growing old together. And as long as they had each other, they were not going to be bored, any more than they had been since they got together in the old neighborhood, back in the 1920s.

And it was so. This is no tale of two old, tired, bored people who aged all too quickly when put out to pasture and faced with each other every hour of every day. Far from it; it only got better as the years went by. They even convinced some of their oldest friends to come and join them. Convinced is not quite the right word here; they were so happy in retirement that others wanted to emulate them.

There is a problem though. It began to surface a couple of years ago and became quite apparent last week, when they did their yearly tax return workup, which also serves as a financial status review. The problem is that they are beginning to eat up their capital, as inflation cuts the real dollar value of their pension payments and investment yields. And, as capital erodes, investment yields will diminish even further. What they all too clearly see happening is that within five years they will be deep into capital; within 10 unable to support even their current modest life style; within 15 living at the bare subsistence level provided by wholly inadequate private and public pension payments. It is not a problem that can be solved by living more carefully, either; they have been doing that, and nothing they can do along those lines will help very much.

Being realists, they know that some moves have to be made; they also realize that the move they made five years ago has very seriously narrowed their options, making what could have been easy back in Boston five years ago very difficult in Florida today. Five years ago, at home, it would have been easy for Jim to keep right on working, if necessary later going to easier and then perhaps part-time work for the company. Mary could have kept her shop, as far as that goes; she might even have taken in a partner, and eased off into part-time involvement over the years. By continuing to earn, they could have built a much larger body of capital for their later years, and might have been able to work their retirement plans as they did, but 5–10 years later. On the other hand, they might never have had five wonderful years in the sun—and Jim is still the crackerjack sales professional he always has been, and is still in excellent health. No, he will never again travel three states, winter and summer, out 50 weeks a year, the way he did back in the 1930s; but then again, he will never have to.

They may be able to work it out in Florida. Even after five years out of it, Jim may be able to use his national web of selling and business friends to find a suitable job in the St. Petersburg area. For that matter, he may answer an advertisement in the area and find a job, but that is unlikely; his age, even in this relatively enlightened period, is still against him. And Mary might well be able to find part-time work as a beautician; her skills are all in place, after all.

But there are very many people like Jim and Mary in retirement communities and areas like St. Petersburg; inflation and longer lives have seen to that. The odds are that Jim and Mary will simply go home. Someone in the family is likely to have an in-law's second house on their property or a rentable apartment in a two-family house; Boston is where their roots are. And the odds are that Jim's company or some other company in Boston will welcome Jim back with open arms; he is still the kind of goose that lays golden eggs, especially in a trade and area in which he is well known.

If that is not so, Jim will still be able to cope. His alternative plans include picking up a few lines as an independent representative, going on with an independent representative's firm part- or full-time, or going on a straight commission basis with a single firm. He has entirely warranted confidence in his continuing professional skills. And the truth is, he and Mary kind of look forward to going back to work and back to Boston and everybody. Five years in the sun have been wonderful, but maybe it is time to go home again.

PERSONAL SITUATION 12
WALTER KONWICKI

It was the bottle in the suitcase that did it. Before that, Anne had been as unwilling as he to admit the existence of a problem. After, she thought there was no way to avoid it; the only question was how, when, and where to raise it with him, and who should do the honors. She couldn't do it; there were too many other open questions between them, and whatever she said would inevitably be seen as an attack. Not his boss; Charlie Johnson had the same problem. And not any of the people he worked with; people gossip, and that could hurt him—and them both—a lot. All right; it had to be Myron Siegel; he had been quoting Myron on everything under the sun for the last 20 years. She reached for the telephone.

From May through July, Walter traveled a great deal. Partly, it was a matter of selling when people were ready to buy, and that was when they most heavily bought giftware for their Christmas season. He also liked traveling then; when you have sold for well over a decade in a territory that starts north of Milwaukee and goes way out to the Dakotas, you learn the value of getting your traveling done during the warm weather months. When the snow begins to fly, you want to do as much as you can close to home and on the telephone. It is lonely sometimes, but there are quite a few friends out there when you have been traveling a territory that long. Which is why Walter and Myron didn't get together for nearly a month after Myron called about lunch, since Myron couldn't very well tell Walter what he had on his mind.

And why Walter was so surprised when, right in the middle of catching up with each other, and after only one drink, Myron somehow rather pointedly declined a second drink—which he had never done before, as far as Walter could remember—and then looked a little strained when Walter went ahead and had his second. For a moment, Walter thought that Myron had run into some kind of drinking problem; Walter had always been sensitive to this; he had certainly dragged poor old Charlie Johnson out of enough places over the years.

But then Walter ordered his customary third martini, and Myron very

378

pointedly told him that he didn't need it—and the fat was in the fire. The truth is that at first Walter thought Myron was joking, making believe he was the kind of holier-than-thou hypocrite they had both detested ever since they got together in high school.

But it wasn't like that; Myron was dead serious, which first annoyed Walter and then made him very angry. Oh, he didn't show it—or at least he thought he didn't show it. In fact, he thanked Myron for his concern, while assuring him that there was no problem, and never had been a problem, the implication being that Myron should know that without having to be told.

Myron stuck to it, though, for a bit. He didn't mention Anne, but told Walter that he felt that he owed it to him to raise the question, and made it clear that he thought it was probably the pressure of so much travel that had caused what he thought was a problem. He apologized, too; he didn't want to lose Walter after all these years.

So they finished their lunch, somehow, and parted; still good friends, but with their friendship a little dented, at least from Walter's point of view. Not from Myron's; he viewed Walter's reaction as complete verification of Anne's observations—and he had been a little concerned for Walter in recent months, too. On return to his office, it was his turn to call Anne, who had of course been waiting for his call.

That weekend, Anne found an opportunity to raise the same question with Walter. As they headed for their car to drive home after a local Saturday night party, she quickly moved to the driver's side of the car, got in, took out her key, and waited for Walter to get in on the other side. He looked at her for a moment, a little nonplussed, and offered to drive, as he always did. She ignored his offer, started the car, and waited. He went to the other side of the car, and they then proceeded to have a rather acrimonious ride home, that acrimony continuing until they both retired —to separate rooms, something that had happened only rarely in their long marriage. Yes, the bottle in the suitcase came up, and quite a few other related matters, as well.

The next morning, they talked for a long time about making their lives together better, doing some of the things they used to do, taking some trips. And Walter promised to do something about his drinking, although he said so mainly to appease her; he didn't have a drinking problem, never would.

Walter did try to stop drinking, but it didn't last. Of course? No, sometimes it can, if sharply taken up early enough by those you love and respect. Not often, though, for it is usually seen too late, and acted upon even later. The truth is that this is a very difficult question to take up. If you've ever tried to take up a perceived drinking problem with spouse, child, best friend, colleague, superior, or subordinate, you know how difficult it is even to get a hearing. Disbelief, evasion, anger, and suspicion of malign intent are all commonplace reactions.

But after 20-plus years as a sales professional, Walter Konwicki is far from stupid about alcoholism. Between them, Myron and Anne got his attention, which in this instance was half the battle. And when he was unable to make it through the problem on his own, they were still there, ready to help. Ultimately, some months later, Anne convinced Walter to consult their family doctor, who in turn was able to put Walter in touch with appropriate professional help. He needed that help, too, and later the help of Alcoholics Anonymous; it was not a small or simple problem. It hardly ever is.

There was nothing specific that anyone could point to that brought it on. Loosely speaking, perhaps it could be attributed to "midlife crisis," whatever that is, but if so, it was a mighty mild crisis. Walter had always worked hard and generated a good deal of tension. He had always had a martini before lunch and another before dinner, and perhaps two or three at lunch or dinner once in a while, especially when out on the road. Other than that, he and Anne both drank moderately on social occasions. Sometimes, as at the party that Saturday night, the drinks were the foundation of the social occasion. Nothing odd about any of that. It was all moderate, and hardly anybody ever got more than a little high. It was part of the business and social setting within which Walter and Anne lived. Yes, sometimes someone came up with a real alcohol problem, but you could usually tie that to such problems as job loss or marital breakup.

Except that when Walter thought about all that a little more deeply, he found that some of those breakups and job losses were intimately intertwined with a drinking problem. As his marital breakup might have been if he had not been brought up short to Anne and Myron.

And as his job loss might have been. He was not aware of it—problem drinkers hardly ever are—but some of his colleagues were becoming a little concerned about that second martini at lunch. And especially about his third martini, when they had rather pointedly stopped drinking after a first. There was no movement afoot to "get" good old Walter; his business friends were real friends, and his company rather modern and enlightened on the matter. But there had been a few quiet discussions about "finding out how to help Walter through this one."

That kind of help would have been fine, if it had come to that. Modern companies are able to offer significant help to their managers and other employees on these kinds of problems. The recovery rate is all too small when the problem surfaces late, as it so often does; but there is a perceptible recovery rate.

That kind of help would also have been something of a career disaster, as Myron, Anne, and Walter's business friends knew. In career terms, it is far, far better to handle a drinking problem outside a business framework than through a company. That is one of the key reasons that business colleagues are so often very late in seeming to recognize and raise the question with a problem drinker; we are all quite aware that problem drinkers can be seriously disbarred from future advancement, no matter how "enlightened" the current business environment on this matter. Certainly, company help is better than no help at all; just as certainly, that very help all too often becomes part of a permanent personnel file, and as such is a millstone to be carried over the years.

Walter solved his drinking problem for now; perhaps for the rest of his life, but perhaps not. And he has stayed in Alcoholics Anonymous, as he knows that it may recur, as it so often does, although he quite correctly believes that it need not be so. He is not shy about telling others he had a problem, but does not particularly volunteer the information, either, unless he thinks it may be helpful to someone else. He is the sales professional he was before, and carries no significant disabilities as he pursues his career.

PERSONAL SITUATION 13
SYLVIA VAN DYKE

Sylvia felt that it hadn't been her fault that Cathy Fine had been a ball of fire. If they breathed, Cathy sold them, whether they wanted to buy or not—which created quite a record in the field, but left Sylvia with a great many inherited problems when she took over Cathy's territory.

In fairness, quite a few of Cathy's sales stuck; but quite a few came unstuck, too. Which meant that whoever followed Cathy into that territory walked into an oversold situation, a lot of cancellations, and had to sell an awful lot of new accounts to make up for the ones Cathy had oversold.

That someone was Sylvia. Cathy moved on—promoted, actually; Sylvia found that promotion hard to believe—and Sylvia was transferred in to take over the territory. At the time, it seemed like a promotion, with more existing accounts and a lot more dollar volume to handle, and a prime downtown territory instead of the half-suburb and half-city territory Sylvia had been handling for the previous two years.

The only thing is—the territory is absolutely mature. It went all right for a while, but then it became perfectly clear to Sylvia that Cathy had sold all but a very few of the marginal ones, that competition was entrenched in the rest, that the whole damned thing is oversold, and that nobody in management is willing to admit it.

Sylvia sells—oh, it scarcely matters what Sylvia sells. Every experienced manager has heard this kind of excuse for substandard performance, and most sales professionals have thought these kinds of self-defeating thoughts at one time or another. There is something like a 1% chance that a territory is saturated or oversold, and that management is unwilling to admit it and to try to do something about it. The possibility is so slim that it is in no instance proper to accept it as a working hypothesis. The proper working hypothesis is that what looks and feels like a slump *is* a slump, and that the proper place to look for solutions is in one's own personal attitudes and operation.

But considerations of different kinds of slumps have different starting points. The seller who "can't seem to close" most likely has early empa-thy-building problems, and may be selling interviews well enough and often enough, but striking out early in the interview by failing to connect with the prospect. The seller who is in an "oversaturated" or "oversold" territory isn't even selling the interview successfully, and getting a chance to sell face-to-face. That kind of seller may not know how to prospect well, or may not be putting in the necessary prospecting time, in terms of the necessary research and telephone work. He or she may not even know how to mount a referral prospecting campaign, reaching for referrals and recommendations from satisfied customers to their business friends, who very often turn out to be not-so-enamored of only seemingly entrenched competition.

In short, Sylvia needs to stop making alibis for herself in the middle of a slump. Every sales professional should recognize the importance of not fooling yourself; it only impedes your recovery.

PERSONAL SITUATION 14

MARY WU LOPEZ AND RALPH LOPEZ

Ralph and Mary got together when they were high school kids in a little New Mexico town, back in the late 1950s. Not very rich kids, by the way; Mary's family ran a little restaurant in town and Ralph's people had a little place a few miles out of town, where they raised some livestock and made it with a tourist shop about half the year and whatever they could pick up in the off season.

Aside from each other, they both shared an outstanding priority: getting out of that town and moving on to family, career, and whatever their shared piece of the American dream was going to be. Mary was a very good student, Ralph only fair. But there was no money at home, and neither of them would have made it through the University of New Mexico without guaranteed student loans, federal and state aid, and a great deal of part-time work during the school year and full-time work every summer. They both made it through to bachelor's degrees with business majors, accreted a pile of debts, and needed to go to work as soon as possible after graduation. Graduate school, if any, was going to be a matter of part-time study later.

At that time, Ralph's BA and the experience he had accreted selling encyclopedias during summer vacations were enough to land him a job selling office supplies, working out of Phoenix and covering much of the Southwest. The women's liberation movement had not then made much headway in the business world, though, and certainly not in the Southwest. What Mary was able to get with her degree was a job as an administrative assistant in an insurance agency in downtown Phoenix.

Ralph did well, so well that within two years he was selling major accounts for his company, and thinking about moving into the growing office copier industry. He did that, and developed a very substantial selling career, with promotion after promotion and raise after raise, ultimately becoming a highly valued—and highly paid—national accounts repre-

384

sentative working out of a major company sales office in New York City.

Mary worked for a while, and then began to have children—three in a five-year period. Near the end of her first pregnancy, she quit her job, and did not go back into the job market for 14 years. She had intended to resume her career a little earlier, but Ralph had been doing so well and there were so many demands on her time that she waited until her youngest had entered high school.

Their oldest is now 18, and in her first year at an excellent private college. All the kids are going to college, the best colleges money can buy; and graduate school after that, if that is what they want. Ralph and Mary are determined to do that for them.

That is going to cost a great deal, of course, and Ralph and Mary have always managed to spend everything they had and borrow just a little bit more. But they have always met their obligations, and are sure they will be able to do so again. Especially since Mary is making money now, too. With the 1960s now long in the past, and women having long since moved into selling in large numbers, she was able to get a job selling in the computer industry. She is not making as much money as Ralph—yet— but she is doing very nicely indeed.

They need both incomes, certainly. They are carrying two high-interest mortgages on a very expensive home; the second mortgage was necessary to meet the down payment. They have a live-in housekeeper and three cars —after all, children need wheels, too. They pay high taxes because they live in a bedroom town with good schools and little industry, and take rather expensive vacations every year. There is also the cottage, a lovely little place in good skiing country, which they use weekends much of the year, and which of course carries a mortgage of its own, though not a large one.

Mary and Ralph have been able to carry it all, though, or almost carry it, anyway. Like most other people they know, they have a considerable amount of other credit in use, including automobile loans, personal credit lines, and a bank loan Ralph had to take out to exercise some stock options that were about to expire next year. They are not worried, though; their net worth, including their fast-appreciating real property and a substantial amount of personal property, considerably exceeds their total indebtedness. They figured it out together last year, after listening to a local stockbroker friend expound on the importance of financial planning at a party one Saturday night.

The truth is that they are walking bankrupts. Economic basket cases. A financial disaster waiting to occur. And they have not ceased to be typical, even in these rather difficult times. Their assets are largely illiquid.

Their equity in real property is illusory, for they would need a place to live under any circumstances. The value of their personal property is an illusion; on liquidation, it would bring little more than scrap value, if it were salable at all. They are paying large amounts of interest every year, rationalizing it as tax-deductible, never really amortizing their personal debts at all, and rolling around an ever-larger and less manageable amount of personal debt. And they are about to start putting three children through expensive colleges and graduate schools. Some of the money for that will come from remortgages, which will add to debt repayment needs, and most will come from student loans. That means saddling their children with large and probably unmanageable debts as well. When public colleges would probably have done as well as enormously expensive private colleges, and at perhaps less than half the cost, their parents' status strivings are going to cost those children dearly.

Mary and Ralph are people trapped by a consuming life style. No alternative careers or chancy, interesting job choices for them; they can't afford to do anything but keep their noses to the grindstone. If they are lucky, they will be able to educate their children and pay off their debts before normal retirement age; then they will face their later years in seriously impaired financial condition, with pensions that may or may not be adequate. But if either of them is seriously ill or unemployed for a substantial time during their prime working years, they stand a very good chance of losing what little they actually have. They have no reserves, no economic staying power in adverse circumstances, and are far more vulnerable than they should or need be.

Mary and Ralph are—in their working lives—quite sensible, competent people. As working professionals, they would express disbelief and contempt for anyone who would run a company the way they run their personal lives. But as people (good, kind, rather nice people, at that) they have very little common sense, and it is their lack of common sense that is the nub of the matter here. Which is another way of saying that their perception of the American dream has led them up a blind alley, and they are just as truly addicted to status and consumption as any addict is to alcohol or other drugs.

If they somehow acquire some common sense—which may occur if one of them is jobless for a while, or when enormous college bills make their true financial position clear to them—there are several things they can do that can help themselves and their children a great deal.

For openers, they can try their level best to convince their children that except for certain special "fast track" graduate school needs served by such undergraduate schools as Harvard and MIT, state schools are usually at least as good as private schools, and often less than half as expensive. The student who wants a fast track MBA from the Harvard Business School may profitably go to Harvard as an undergraduate, as the student who wants a physics fast track may properly go to MIT; for the rest, it is usually pointless expense to go to such high-prestige, high-cost colleges. The cost differences involved, for both parents and children, can be enormous.

Mary and Ralph can also very easily live on a considerably less expensive scale—and need to, though at this point they certainly do not know that. They will be well advised to sell that second home, saving unnecessary upkeep and taxes, and to start to build much more liquid savings and investments. They do not need three cars and expensive vacations. For that matter, they probably will soon not need their very expensive and highly taxed home, and might do far better in a smaller, far less expensive, and far less "prestigious" community. At every step of the way, they are overspending, and courting catastrophe; a little common sense can take them several long steps back from the brink.

PERSONAL SITUATION 15
SAM BERGER

What had attracted him to selling in the first place was the freedom, the independence, the feeling of being entirely on your own, make or break, sell or not. Also that selling required no academic credentials, and paid pretty well. Those things were important at the time, as they are today.

Maybe they were particularly important to Sam, because he had seen what it meant to his father—to the whole family—to lose a secure white-collar job back in the 1930s. In 1929, Sam's father was the respected assistant manager of the tool-and-die works that was the main industry of the little Iowa town where Sam grew up. In 1930, Sam's father was part of the army of unemployed that clogged the roads and waste places of an America that had suddenly and quite completely gone bust. For 10 years, until the plant reopened just before World War II, Sam's family lived on what his father made in a series of odd jobs, the small earnings his mother was able to bring in from time to time, and what they all made as pickers at harvest time.

Which meant no education for Sam or his brothers and sisters. He finished high school, though, in 1940, and his first job was that of sweeper in the just-reopened plant his father had worked in long ago.

Sam—and his high school sweetheart, Nancy—knew what they wanted. It wasn't much, actually; a piece of the American dream they had been taught was their birthright, consisting of a family, a home, children, and a car that worked. They married late in 1940, after Sam had been on his sweeper's job for a few months and Nancy had found a job in a local retail store. Their first child, Sam, Jr., was born late in 1941.

And then the war came. To no one's surprise, Sam volunteered for the Marines on December 8, 1941, and was accepted. Nancy and Sam, Jr., moved in with her parents and stayed there for the duration of the war. Sam spent a little over four miserable years in the Pacific, emerging as a much-decorated master sergeant with absolutely no skills other than the ability to lead men to death and possible glory; Nancy counted the days and worked in the plant, making war materials.

After the war, their piece of the dream began to emerge, and kept on coming for most of the next 40 years. They had their children, home, a car that worked, and a good deal more, besides.

Sam had no taste for going back to school after the war. He and Nancy felt as if four years of college would mean deferring too much for too long. Instead, they used their savings and Sam's severance pay to put a down payment on a house, buy a car and a little furniture, and pay the doctor who delivered their second child. And Sam went to work in selling, for the same company his father and he had worked for before the war.

He turned out to be quite good at it—and machine tools were not a bad thing to be selling to a country and world getting over depression and war. It was the start of what turned out to be a very substantial career. He moved from machine tools to farm equipment and from their home town to Des Moines in the late 1950s, and has spent his whole working life since then very happily and effectively pursuing the kind of independent work he had always dreamed of. He did move into management once, in the early 1960s, but that turned out to be a mistake. It was a good company, with good people on top, and not very bureaucratic back then. But there was company politics to take into account, and a good deal of paperwork, and success that depended on how well others sold, rather than on how well he sold. He didn't fail at sales management, but he didn't succeed, either; and his company had traded a star performer for a mediocre regional manager, which nobody wanted. So it was back into a territory, with relief; and he had been a perennial sales leader ever since.

Nancy and Sam had four children, and every single one of them went all the way through a four-year college; two of them went through graduate school, besides. It cost a lot, but that was part of the dream, too; providing the kind of education that had not been possible for Sam and Nancy during the depression. And there were "cars that worked"—more than one. And a big house in Des Moines, and a country club membership, some vacations, a camper, and a good many of the other things that material success brought. Make no mistake about it; Sam was in financial terms an outstanding success, making just as much money as all but a very few of the managers, doctors, and dentists he and his family met at the club.

Now Sam and Nancy are up to that part of the dream that is retirement. They have long planned to quit when Sam turns 65, sell the house, and move to Florida. Sam has accumulated some optioned stock in his company over the years, and there is a pretty good pension plan payout, as well as Social Security. They don't have much in the way of savings, though; college costs and living standards saw to that. In fact, they don't have very much equity in their house, either; they had to remortgage to pay college costs, as did most of their friends at the time.

Now, at 63, taking a good hard look at their whole financial picture two years before retirement, it has become perfectly clear that their plans just won't work. And that is a considerable shock.

There are several problems. One of them should be a boon, but also poses a problem; it is long life, which means that they have to plan to support themselves for decades beyond retirement. Another is inflation, which has been a constant tendency, though at varying rates, all their working lives. Their savings and public and private pension payouts will be worth less and less in real money as the long retirement years go by. In addition, their savings are small, and, given the state of the economy, they have begun to understand that promised private pension payouts may not be all there some years down the line. When you add to all this the constant pressure they see to reduce real dollar Social Security payments and the fact that the company stock they own really isn't worth much, their concern can easily be seen as entirely justified.

After a long series of conversations, in which they involved their oldest daughter, Harriet, now an accountant in Chicago, they have decided not to retire and not to go to Florida to live. Instead, Sam is going to keep on doing what he does so well, and Nancy is going to go back to work, something she has wanted to do for years.

Sam's sales management is delighted by his decision. Sam is going to stay on in his territory as long as he can handle it well, and he will be the first to know it when he no longer can. At that point, he is likely to be offered less demanding work; perhaps telephone selling or some special account handling.

Nancy is going to become a tax preparer, training at the expense of one of the national tax preparation firms. She also plans to take a course in bookkeeping, and develop bookkeeping and tax preparation into a sound later-years career, which she can practice just about as long as she likes.

Sam has his eye on the further future, too. He is going to talk to some of his best customers—people he has known for decades—and see what other opportunities may be out there for him. After all, he has been a top sales professional and effective independent operator for a long time. He would not be at all surprised if he came up with a piece of a distributor-ship, or of an independent representative's firm, or found himself repre-senting several smaller manufacturers on a part-time basis later on. All he and Nancy really know right now is that they are going to continue to work out their part of the dream as best they can for the rest of their lives, and stand a very good chance of successfully doing so.

PART V

LANGUAGE FOR SALES PROFESSIONALS

Every profession has at least to some extent a language of its own, developed partly to satisfy language created by special concepts, techniques, and materials; and partly because its practitioners have long since discovered that professional status is enhanced by the existence and rather free use of a special language to which others have only limited access.

Selling has a number of such terms; rather less than most other professions, as those who sell have a strong need to communicate simply and effectively in the many languages of business and finance in order to sell well.

We include here definitions and comments on a considerable number of terms used wholly or mainly in sales and marketing. We also include many terms in general use in business and finance, and especially some dealing with new concepts encountered by sales professionals. We have also included some terms commonly encountered in career and financial planning.

We have focused here more on concepts than on techniques and materials, which are normally far better reached through a good, concise general dictionary of business and finance, as discussed in Part 6, Sources of Information. The glossary that follows is in no way intended to be a substitute for that kind of dictionary, which we strongly urge you to purchase and use routinely; we do not here define more than a small fraction of the special terms you encounter during a life in selling. Rather, we here attempt to discuss terms needing the clarification that is best achieved by more extended discussion than is possible in a concise dictionary. Please note that many of these terms have also been discussed in *Personal Financial Survival* by David M. Brownstone and Jacques Sartisky, and also in our own The Manager's Career Companion: A Personal and Practical Handbook (Wiley, 1983). Some of the commentaries are identical, though in many the commentaries differ considerably, reflecting the tilt of this book toward the needs of the working sales professional. Note also that these terms are not cross-indexed within this section; however, to locate any term used here or in context throughout this book, you need only turn to the Index.

Following this glossary are some practical aids to your writing. First, Notes on Grammar and Usage, which focuses on trouble spots faced by most writers. Following that are a Checklist of Commonly Misused and Misspelled Words, a table of Proofreading and Editing Marks, and a Phonetic Alphabet, for use in giving dictation.

Advertising. Advertising is the dissemination of selling material, whatever the form and media chosen; also the material disseminated.

It comes in many forms, and is therefore variously described. In geographic terms, it may be *local, regional, national,* or *international advertising,* depending upon its spread. In form, it may appear as *broadsides* printed on one side and distributed one by one, *brochures, booklets,* printed *display* or *classified advertisements* in *print-on-paper* media, *billboards* in outside media, *spot advertisements* and more generally *commercials* in broadcast media, *point-of-purchase (p-o-p)* advertising in retail establishments, messages printed on premium items, and in whatever other ways advertising specialists can devise.

It should be noted that in a sales professional's hands a piece of advertising material may play several roles. A brochure, for example, may be advertising material alone when mailed to or left with a prospect; but it may also be preapproach material, and thereby part of the direct selling process, or even be used as a basic presentation from which to work face-to-face with the prospect. Certainly, it is better to have presentation materials tailored for the face-to-face selling situation, but many a professional has sold from many a brochure quite successfully in the absence of better selling aids.

Affirmative action, discrimination. *Affirmative action* is an antidiscrimination concept that grew to maturity in the socially conscious 1960s, was embodied in the Equal Opportunity Act of 1972, and has for almost two decades been the subject of intense and often painful controversy on the American scene. It proposes that a long history of discrimination against minority groups and women requires redress, and that real redress consists not only of cessation of discriminatory actions, but in positive actions aimed at bringing groups formerly discriminated against into positions of real equity with others. Therefore, in many instances the policy requires that special steps be taken on their behalf. In economic terms, that has been interpreted to mean such actions as special training programs, super-seniority to afford job protection, accelerated promotions, and active re-cruitment of minorities and women, especially for jobs from which they had formerly been barred or in which they had been relegated to inferior positions because they were women or members of minority groups.

Many kinds of *discrimination* are barred by law and public policy, including most racial, sexual, age, and religious discrimination in employ-ment, and a good deal of political, ethnic, and other discrimination. How-ever, it is the attempt to help minorities and women catch up by means of affirmative action that has caused charges of *reverse discrimination;* that is, discrimination against the majority in favor of minority groups and women, and at least one major Supreme Court case, the Bakke case, has set some limits on the expansion of the concept of affirmative action.

In the same general area is the concept of *tokenism,* that is the place-ment of minority group members and women into jobs in which they will be conspicuous, but often powerless, and not at all typical or indicative of a general move by people like themselves into those kinds of jobs. For example, a single woman or a Black on a sales force composed otherwise of all white males; a single Hispanic on a sales force that has no other Hispanics, and no more than one or two women and Blacks; a single Black, a Hispanic, a Jew, and a Protestant or Catholic woman in a group numbering hundreds—all can and often are attacked as examples of toke-nism.

Alcoholic, workaholic. The old folk definitions apply rather well here. An *alcoholic* is someone who "can't leave the stuff alone," in this case, alcohol. Quantification helps little in these kinds of areas. For some, a little alcohol, taken as a matter of habit and then need, may grow very little in quantity and yet become a damaging and sometimes disabling habit. For others, considerably larger quantities are needed to addict and disable. Little matter; the net is the same for tens of thousands of American sales professionals, joined together by the single most common and serious illness in the world of selling.

Similarly, a *workaholic* is someone who can't leave the work alone, but must continue at it beyond all need or reason, as a matter of habit verging upon or passing over into addiction. The stresses that result from this kind of addiction can be and often are life-threatening; this addiction is no more a matter for jesting than is alcoholism. It should also be noted that many professionals are mislabeled as workaholics, due to widespread misunder-standing as to the legitimate time demands placed upon practitioners by their professions. The sales professional who spends 10–30 hours a week at work beyond normal field selling hours is not necessarily a workaholic, but may indeed only be a top-notch professional practicing his or her trade as it should be practiced.

Approval sale.   This is not really a firm sale at all, for it is a sale in which the customer has the right to nullify the purchase agreement at will, often within a specified time, or within an imprecisely stated time frame. When used by mail marketers, as it often is, it makes a good deal of sense in situations in which experience indicates a low and acceptable rate of return for products sold on this basis. But when used as a refuge by weak sellers, it is a recipe for personal disaster, and never more so than when it is used covertly, against company policies. It is also known pejoratively as a *maybe sale.*

It is not a *conditional sale,* which is just as weak and therefore just as dangerous, but which can be encountered as an industry-wide practice, and then must be lived with. In the sale of books by publishers to book-stores for resale, for example, the bookstores have the right to return unsold books for credit under stated conditions, meaning that most such sales are not really closed at all, but are a matter of goods being placed, in practical terms, as if on consignment. On the conditional sale, though, title to the goods passes to the retailer and passes back on return, while on a *consignment sale,* title generally passes from owner to ultimate purchaser, when the real sale is made.

These kinds of sales carry great hazards for professional sellers, who must be able to sell well and consistently throughout their careers. Where they occur in substantial numbers they force professionals into very bad selling habits, and away from professional excellence.

Assets.   In the widest colloquial sense, anything carrying any kind of positive value—from such tangibles as office equipment, rolling stock, and factory buildings to such intangibles as future royalties, love, and happiness—can be described as an asset. In the economic and financial sense, although assets can be as tangible as office equipment or as intangible as a future interest in royalties, they must be capable of producing wealth that can be measured in financial terms now or at some future time—and that lets out love and happiness.

Assets can be liquid—that is, cash or near cash—such as notes minus an allowance for uncollectibles, or quickly marketable securities and commodities, including listed common stocks, some bonds, and gold. Some assets are considerably less liquid, including a large number of such business assets as real estate, buildings, and equipment. Others may be extremely difficult to make liquid in a way that is useful in ongoing business operations, such as future interests and equity in a wholly owned business that is not readily salable. Yet all of these are assets, to which a value may be attached, ultimately if by no one else but the tax authorities.

When a company is described as *asset-rich,* but *cash-poor,* it may be in considerable difficulty, especially in a period of high interest rates and tight money—and a company ripe for acquisition. And when you are with such a company, be wary, for you may not survive such an acquisition. When two previously competing sales organizations merge, those who have been acquired may also be those who are let go.

Automation. *Automation* is the replacement of human-controlled processes with machine-controlled processes. That is a step beyond *mechanization,* which is the replacement of humans by machines, and which is as old as the replacement of the horse-drawn wagon by the railroad train. Automation has, in the latter part of the twentieth century, mainly been used to describe the introduction of machine-controlled production processes, such as machine-controlled lines of presses or assembly lines, with humans performing only machine-watching and repair functions. In recent years, however, some have also begun to use automation as a synonym for mechanization, as when a computer performs arithmetic functions formerly performed by human clerks. That is not a correct or incorrect use of the term; the meaning of the term has simply changed somewhat. But that change of meaning can cause some confusion as to much that is happening in many countries, where mechanization and automation are together causing *technological unemployment,* as people are replaced by machines. In developed countries, such as the United States, automation is a very significant factor in the development of technological unemployment; but in much of the world the main question is still mechanization, as when hundreds of pick-and-shovel workers are replaced by a single digging machine.

But—ready or not—we are now beginning to move into the era of *robotics,* in which robots operated by *machine intelligence*—the developing name for computers that operate machines—will begin to replace very large numbers of human workers who perform a wide variety of tasks in all countries.

As these processes continue and accelerate, many companies and whole industries and therefore many jobs in selling are and will be deeply affected. No, sales professionals are unlikely to be replaced by robots; but many will need to leave failing and obsolete companies and industries. Those who can do so flexibly, demonstrating that they can sell in any company or industry will continue to be highly prized sales professionals; those who see themselves too narrowly and thereby impede their own mobility may be in trouble.

Bait and switch.   This is one of the oldest tricks in the repertoire of the unscrupulous seller. It involves advertising or otherwise promoting items at prices that are "too good to be true," which they are. The crooked seller gets a prospect inside his or her door that way, and then proceeds to try to sell something else, usually claiming that the advertised item is for some reason no longer available. The something else is invariably far more expensive, or of far lower quality, or both.

It is a form of misrepresentation that is actionable as fraud, if provable. But, like so many other actionable frauds in the world of commerce, the question of proof is often difficult, and the penalties for such fraudulent practices are very modest indeed, compared to the rewards such practices can bring.

Except for sales professionals, that is; for them, the practice of fraud and misrepresentation means the slow death of professionalism, which depends first of all upon belief in one's own integrity.

Balance.   *Balance* is a term with two quite distinct meanings and many business and financial uses.

In its first sense, balance deals with equilibrium. A tightrope walker keeps balance, or equilibrium, while traversing a rope, in order to avoid falling off. An accountant brings books of account into equilibrium by equalizing debits and credits, and calls it "balancing the books."

A *balance sheet* is a financial statement, derived from a double-entry bookkeeping system, of the financial condition of a business entity or individual as of a given moment, including all assets, liabilities, and ownership equities. To achieve a frozen moment—describing a living entity at a particular time, much as a still photo describes its living subjects—the accountant "closes" the books of the entity as of a stated moment, and makes such adjusting entries as are necessary to produce a document accurately portraying that moment.

For smaller entities, balance sheets are often quite detailed and therefore tell a great deal about the entity; for larger entities, such as substantial corporations, they will normally be only brief summaries, requiring that a great deal of additional data be added before they become very useful tools of financial analysis. In summary or detailed form, though, they are basic to any kind of financial analysis. As an essential element of quarterly and year-end reports to directors and stockholders, they are, with other financial statements, the focus of very considerable management attention.

The *balanced budget*—so dear to the hearts of all politicians, and the unmet goal of the United States government for most of this century—is a budget that not only forecasts equal expenditures and income for a given period, but actually works out that way, without additional net borrowing during the budget period.

A *balance of payments* is a summary of all transactions between a single country and the rest of the world in a given period, including all business, government, individual, and other institutional transactions. It is made of these components: the *current account,* which includes all imports and exports of goods and services; the *capital account,* which includes all exports and imports of investment capital; and the *gold account,* which includes all financial reserves exported or imported to bring total exports and imports into balance, or equilibrium.

In its second sense, balance means remainder or net, that which is left after other transactions have taken place. A *balance due* is the remainder of what is owed. A *bank balance* is what the depositor owns in a bank account; again what is owed, but this time by the bank to the depositor.

A *balance of trade* is the net of all merchandise transactions between a single country and the rest of the world during a given period. More exports than imports net a *favorable balance of trade;* more imports than exports net an *unfavorable balance of trade.*

A *balance of indebtedness* is the net of all owed amounts between a single country and the rest of the world during a given period. If amounts owed by a country and its citizens are greater than amounts owed them by the rest of the world, the country is an *international debtor;* if the reverse, an *international creditor.*

Boom and bust. Prosperity and depression—the rapid expansion of the 1920s followed by the Great Depression of the 1930s, after the Crash of 1929—are the classic *boom* and *bust.* We often think of the unrestrained operation of the boom-and-bust business cycle as a purely historical matter, living as we do in a far more managed economy. But recession is only a euphemism for depression, and there have been many depressions of lesser impact than the Great Depression, both before and after the 1930s. We are not yet done with the business cycle and its impacts; indeed, one of the major economic phenomena of our time is the fluctuation of managed economies around stagnation, expanding as economies are manipulated by governments and contracting as resulting inflationary pressures cause governments to manipulate differently. The main feature of the American economy before this current period was not the business cycle; it was prolonged, meteoric growth, punctuated by the recurrent temporary contractions. The main feature of this period is the economic stagnation around which the business cycle continues to move.

Bottom line.   In its narrow and original sense, the *bottom line* is literally the final line on a profit-and-loss statement, showing a specific result for the period covered by the statement. In this sense, it also is used to refer to the result on other financial statements organized to show a *balance,* where balance means remainder rather than equilibrium, as in a cash flow statement.

In recent years, the term has also come to be used synonymously with *net results* or *net–net,* meaning the ultimate result of any single action or group of actions, whether or not business and financial in nature.

Net also means result, but not necessarily ultimate result, or net–net, though it very often is so used. For example, there may be several net, or summary, figures on a financial statement, each in turn relating to further entries; only the bottom line of the statement will be the ultimate, or net–net, result.

Budgets and budgeting.   *Budgets* are income and expenditure forecasts; the process of developing those forecasts is *budgeting.*

The *operating budget* is a forecast of income and expenditures for a given period, usually a year. In most large organizations, and in many small ones as well, it is by no means a frozen instrument, but rather a forecast that is formally revised as often as quarterly, with reviews monthly, and extraordinary revisions in order at any time conditions make such revisions necessary. Operating budgets also are developed for specific one-time projects, for the project period, in such segments as seem desirable by project managers.

The *capital budget* is a forecast of capital expenditures, usually on a longer term basis than a year. Although often generated for as long as 5- and 10-year periods, it too is subject to periodic revision, although long-term fixed capital commitments are often less malleable than are operating budget items.

Budgeting is a major operational tool. To set forecasts is to set goals, and to meet or better forecasts is to reach or better goals. To bring in more revenue than forecast at or near expenditure forecasts is to bring in higher-than-forecast profit. To bring in a project or come through a period with lower-than-forecast expenditures, while meeting forecast revenue goals, is to bring in higher-than-forecast profit. Conversely, to spend more than forecast while selling no more than forecast is to cut profits; to sell less than forecast while spending as much as predicted is also to cut profits.

Those who have done better than forecast are presumed to have functioned well, in the absence of very special circumstances. The sales professional who has done worse than forecast is presumed to have functioned less than well. And those presumptions, though qualified by dozens of different factors in each specific situation, are extremely important. For, in the long run, a record of successful performance is a base without which no sales professional can hope to move ahead. All the good relationships in the world are worthless if they are not accompanied by a basic high performance record. Excellent sales professionals are superachievers; there is no better measure of achievement than meeting performance goals.

That is especially true in selling, for most sales professionals actively participate in developing their own forecasts. Oh, often with great pressure for higher goal-setting and cost-cutting from management—that is a basic, and must always be considered part of the game—but still with full personal participation.

Burn-out. Burn-out is a very spongy term, indeed, when used to describe a human being rather than some portion of an electrical system. It is generally used to describe someone who is thought to be no longer capable of energetically pursuing personal and organizational goals, but is rather coasting along dispiritedly, hoping only to survive.

But the term itself embodies a foolishly wrong equation of people with machine parts. People regenerate; machines do not. Tired people are often perfectly capable of rest, recuperation, and return to creative contribution. People caught in inimical situations are often capable of startlingly rapid creative regeneration upon successful job change. And while sales professionals do get tired and discouraged, especially in difficult times, they very seldom deteriorate so badly that they self-select out of the profession.

Business ethics. No ethical questions in business are any different, or more or less important, than those ethical questions encountered in personal life and in the larger local, national, and world communities within which we function. And, as in the larger communities, ethical constructs vary widely. Participation in a combination in restraint of trade within the United States is illegal and highly unethical; participation by oil producers in a cartel that combines to set prices and restrain trade is pursuit of legitimate national interest.

Nor is it necessarily true that good guys triumph in the end—or finish last. Good guys finish first, in the middle of the pack, and last; it depends on the facts of the case. It may or may not be true that wholly unethical styles work best in the American—and other—corporate and political worlds; but it cannot be said that to reach material goals they work any worse than other, highly ethical styles. And that is so for both organizations and individuals. It should be borne in mind that, in the main, victors write histories, and that today's sanctified founder or statesman (or woman) may be yesterday's buccaneer or robber baron.

Yet for us, individual Americans working in the late years of the twentieth century, the ethical questions are crucially important. The fact is that for most of us, out of our time and place, the question of personal integrity is a make-or-break one. For most of us, our view of ourselves as ethical human beings, in business and in the larger world, is central to our self-respect, and without that self-respect we are not worth much to ourselves or anyone else. Some of us are exceptions to that rule; not many.

Buzz words. Buzz words are the fashionable terms that everyone in business uses for a season or two, and that thereafter may become part of one of the special languages of business management, if they have proved intrinsically useful. Every language or sublanguage has its own slang; whether a new word continues to be part of that language can only be a matter of conjecture when the term bursts upon the scene. One learns them because they are there; people use them in daily conversation, and they pass into our own language. Some leap to the use of new, trendy terms, feeling that knowing and using the latest terms will make them seem somehow au courant trendsetters. Some resist because they feel that most slang debases the language, not realizing that their insistence on what they think of as "correct" English would in the long run perhaps make English a dead language. Others resist, somewhat, feeling that some new terms make communication harder than necessary, and that simple business English, with the addition of any really new technical terms, will do very well for most purposes. The main rule of thumb should be to take what is useful among the new terms, and leave fashions to live or die of their own accord.

Call. For field sales professionals, a *call* is a face-to-face contact with a prospect or a prospect's organization. It is in this field sales context not a telephone call; that is a matter of custom and practice rather than of logic. In telephone selling, a call is a telephone call; but on a call report prepared by a field seller, it must be face-to-face contact.

That contact may only be with a receptionist or a secretary, as when *cold calling* (also called *canvassing* and *smokestacking*) is being done.

When you are driving down a country road, see a factory you didn't know was there, and on impulse convert the sighting into a cold call, that's smokestacking. When you start at the top of an office building, and work your way down through that building, or do the same on a strange street or in a strange town, calling on everyone who might remotely be a prospect, that's cold selling or canvassing. It is about the least productive and uninformed kind of activity a seller can engage in, and is thoroughly unprofessional.

A call may also be an *interview,* face-to-face with a prospect. And a call that is an interview may also result in a *presentation,* a full-scale sales situation in which seller and prospect engage in the selling process.

A call may also be a second or subsequent call, and then be a *callback.* Or it may be for other purposes than primarily to sell—though every call is properly regarded as a sales opportunity—and then be, for example, an *installation call* to orient customer and staff on previously sold items; or a *service call;* or a *reinstatement call* to attempt to resell a lost customer.

Call report.   In one form or another, this is a report required by most sales managements of their field sales staff. It is often onerous; there are very few chores quite as annoying as filling out reports of the day's activities while sitting in a motel room far from home, exhausted after an unproductive day in the field, and wanting only to forget it all and start fresh tomorrow. It is often time consuming; many call reports are poorly constructed, and require far more time than they should. It is also the most basic of all sales management tools, and the management that dispenses with call reports because "the field staff doesn't like them" is quite unwise to do so. And, if properly perceived and used, it can be as basic a self-management tool as it is a sales management tool, for close analysis of your own call reports can tell you a great deal about what you are doing right and what you could be doing better.

Cash and credit.   In the world of the consumer, a *cash purchase* is one in which payment is made in currency or by negotiable instrument at the point of purchase. A *cash customer* is one making such a cash purchase, and a *cash price* is the price paid in such a transaction. Any transaction involving goods delivered now and payment later then involves extension of *credit* by seller to purchaser.

But in the world of business—and that is the world in which most sales professionals function—most cash purchases, customers, and prices involve the use and extension of credit, with the rough dividing line between cash and credit extension being at 30 days after purchase. Therefore, whether a sale is called a credit sale or a cash sale, good business practice regarding new customers requires *credit investigation.* This results in a *credit report* and a *credit rating* through such organizations as *credit bureaus.* Then *credit approval* is granted by the selling organization before a *credit account* is set up or a *credit line* maximum up to which a customer may purchase is fixed. All of this adds up to an assessment of *credit risk* by the seller. Sometimes, a seller will hedge credit risks by purchasing *credit insurance.*

Those purchasing within 30 days are often granted a *cash discount,* such as 2% off for paying within that time; therefore the standard invoice offer—terms net 2% within 30 days.

Credit is also used in a different sense, as when a return or refund results in seller owing purchaser goods or services to be purchased, up to a specified sum.

Cash budget.   A *cash budget* is purely a forecast of cash revenue and expenditures for a given period without accruals or deferrals. In contrast, operating budgets, other than those for very small companies, are organized as profit-and-loss forecasts, with results generating an operating profit-and-loss statement.

Most people working in medium-sized and large companies work with operating budgets rather than cash budgets. However, in difficult times, when the question of cash flow can become extraordinarily important— and especially in times characterized by extremely high interest rates— many find themselves working with cash budgets, and watching cash as closely as they watch profit and loss.

Caveat emptor and caveat venditor.   *Caveat emptor* and *caveat venditor* are Latin phrases, which are often put as polar opposites, but are far better understood as general principles to be observed in all business transactions.

Caveat emptor is usually translated as "Let the buyer beware," and is often taken to mean that "anything goes" in commercial transactions, short of provable fraud. But that is not really so; it has not been so for centuries, and is even less so today. The term is better translated, "Let the buyer take care," which places the burden of care upon the buyer without removing the obligation of the seller not to misrepresent or fail to honor warranties.

Caveat venditor, which means "Let the seller beware," or "Let the seller take care," has bound the seller to represent honestly and to honor warranties. A body of common law has been built slowly, case by case and precedent by precedent, setting and interpreting that maxim. In recent decades, a good deal of legislation, regulation, and interpreting case law has created a new balance between the two maxims, especially in the area of consumer protection, with unstated or implied warranties obligating sellers to take care far more than was necessary under common-law rules.

The term *caveat* is in this period also finding considerable acceptance outside the law, and is being used as a synonym for *reservation,* as when someone who has a slight disagreement or feels that a situation may not be quite as stated, says "I have a caveat in that area."

Close. Whatever technique is used and whatever has gone before in the selling situation, a *close* is a serious attempt to get a favorable buying decision right now. Whether that happens once or a dozen times during the course of an interview, each such attempt is a close. A close is also the securing of that favorable buying decision. "I closed six times, and just couldn't get the order," uses the first meaning of the term. "I closed the sale," uses the second meaning.

There is also the *trial close,* which is not a close at all, but rather an attempt to take a prospect's temperature, and often an attempt to warm up a prospect by getting some kind of agreement, as well. "Doesn't that make sense to you?," delivered early in a presentation, by someone hoping only to get an approval nod from a prospect, is scarcely a serious closing attempt, and should not be mistaken for a close.

Common stock and preferred stock. *Common stock* is an unrestricted ownership share in a corporation; it is the kind of stock that is normally traded in investment markets, and the kind of stock usually found in such fringe benefits as stock option and stock purchase plans. Common stock is by far the main form such ownership shares takes, its owner sharing fully in risks and opportunities and voting its proportion of ownership in the issuing corporation. It fluctuates with the varying fortunes of its corporate issuer and with the stock markets within which it is traded as a whole.

Preferred stock is a form of ownership share in which the stock is literally preferred over common stock in terms of the issuance of dividends, which must be distributed to preferred shareholders before dividends can be distributed to common shareholders. It sometimes also carries a preferred position in voting on some corporate affairs. Preferred stock dividend amounts are specified by the terms of original issue; they may be *cumulative*—that is, payable in subsequent years if not paid in a given year or years; or *noncumulative*—that is, if a dividend is passed, or not paid, in a given year, it is lost. Some preferred stocks can, to a limited extent, share profits beyond stated dividends with common stocks, which have neither guarantees nor limits placed on their shares of profit participation.

As a practical matter, most preferred stocks today represent equity ownership and what amounts to a debt obligation, since almost all corporate boards must pay them before common stocks and at the same time literally must pay some dividends to common stockholders. However, preferred stocks generally present neither the profit nor the growth possibilities inherent in common stock ownership, which is why the overwhelming majority of stocks traded are common stocks.

Compensation package. The total compensation paid a modern sales professional often consists of far more than direct pay and a few fringe benefits, such as paid vacations, life and health insurance, and some kind of pension plan. Those basics are certainly part of the total compensation package; but a good many other elements are often included as well, such as stock options, profit-sharing, overrides, tuition assistance, college financing aid for the families of company employees, dental insurance, and early vesting and retirement. In addition, there are sometimes relocation funding, mortgage assistance, and a good many expense account allowances that cannot be described as anything but disguised fringe benefits aimed at tax sheltering part of incomes.

All the elements together are the total compensation package; all together are what need to be comparatively evaluated when choosing between available positions.

Many compensation elements are very hard to quantify, although personnel departments and insurance companies try their best to do so on some kind of averaging basis. You cannot really know how many dollars a major medical plan will save you, or whether or not you will take advantage of tuition or college financing assistance. You cannot know the value of a profit-sharing plan until the profits to be shared are or are not made. You cannot even know the real value of a fixed-payment pension plan until the years of payout—the real value of the dollars paid then will depend upon the rate of inflation between now and then. A wonderful stock option plan can yield enormous tax-deferred gains, or can be worthless if the stock falls or barely holds its own over the years.

Yet estimates must be made, and company estimates can be extremely helpful, though they are no substitute for your own estimates. At the same time, it is always hazardous to rely too much on compensation elements paying off in the future, and not at all a bad idea to err, if necessary, on the side of current direct cash compensation. A new deferred compensation wrinkle, a rise in status, and a new insurance benefit may all be very welcome, but they should not be allowed to substitute for more cash now.

Competition.   Rivalry for advancement, for recognition, for markets, for acquisitions—competition is a fact of American economic life. Sales professionals are covertly and overtly engaged in competition every day.

Competition among sellers may and often does involve selling substantially similar and sometimes identical products to the same buyers; for example, the differences between brand-name formulations of the same basic drug are often so insignificant as to be effectively nonexistent. Or it may involve competition between products or services that satisfy similar needs but are quite different; or between quite different kinds of products and services, for a dollar that may be spent one way or the other.

Computers of several kinds.   *Minicomputers, microcomputers, personal computers, home computers, small business computers*—they all used to be a little different, to some extent justifying their differing names. Micros had somewhat smaller memories and capabilities than minis; therefore micros tended to be called personal or home computers and minis tended to be used by small businesses. But they are all tending to merge in size and function as the years go by, and as that happens the nomenclature stops being very meaningful and instead becomes confusing. It is and will soon become even more confusing, as very powerful small computers begin to be routinely hooked up together into networks capable of handling the kinds of tasks previously done only by large standard, or *main frame* computers. Then we will probably call all of them just computers, and distinguish between them directly by function and capability.

Computer terminal.   The *computer terminal* has about as many names as it has uses. It is a video display device, commonly called a *video display terminal (VDT),* which is in construction a *cathode ray tube (CRT),* that is hooked up to a computer, so that material put into the computer and coming out of the computer—*input* and *output*—can be seen by whomever is working at or viewing the screen. The terminal may variously be called a *word processing terminal, videotext terminal, layout terminal, editing terminal,* or *teaching terminal,* or for that matter it may be named after whatever other kind of major use it is designed for. Later on, all will probably be called simply terminals, and sometimes further qualified by form and function.

Consumer Price Index.   The *Consumer Price Index,* maintained by the Federal Bureau of Labor Statistics and updated monthly, used to be called the Cost of Living Index, and is just that. Economists have some dispute as to whether or not it accurately reflects the real pace of increase in the cost of living, and there is considerable reason to believe that it does not. For example, it makes no serious attempt to allow for hidden inflation, which is a matter of cutting the quantity and quality of goods sold, as opposed to raising prices, which is more obvious. However, this index is the best tool we have for rough measurement of the cost of living, which, in turn, can be used for measuring our own individual situations.

This index is used as a base figure for a wide range of calculations, such as the indexing of Social Security payments and wage increases mandated by some collective bargaining contracts.

Costing.   *Costing,* also called *costing out,* is the process of assessing the tangible cost of something; for example, the cost of a proposed new building program, or of a set of new tools. In some instances, costing seeks to determine the best available price of a projected purchase that is consistent with other specifications. In others, it includes estimates of relevant factors, such as overhead and the cost of money borrowed. That branch of accounting called *cost accounting* is devoted to the collection of cost information, its reporting to management, and the use of that information to develop cost control methods.

Cost–price squeeze.   When costs go up, prices must rise commensurately, if profit margins are to maintain constant levels. But neither costs nor prices are always that obliging, even when a single company or group of companies dominates a national market, for prices are responsive to such factors as international competition, internal competition from within an industry and from competing industries, government regulations, and consumer resistance. When costs are forced up, and the price must be kept down for whatever reason, the company or industry in that situation is caught in a cost–price squeeze.

While large companies may be caught in such a squeeze, small companies are far more vulnerable. A major steel or automobile company, faced with successful competition from abroad, may cut back production and even look forward to being bailed out by government if the squeeze becomes a stranglehold. On the other hand, a small parts supplier, an automobile agency, or a restaurant, caught between costs over which it has no control and prices that must be kept too low to be adequately profitable is often driven out of business.

In an environment that forces small profit margins on some kinds of businesses, effective cost control can be a life or death matter for a business.

Customer, account.   In the widest sense, anyone who buys from a seller is a *customer* of that seller, whether the purchase is that of a single sausage at a market stall or purchase of tens of millions of dollars worth of goods and services over a period of decades.

In professional selling, it is useful to further define the nature of buying relationships, and that definition normally uses the term *account* (as in this context) as an exact synonym for customer, implying also that the buyer may only buy once but is thought to be one with whom a longer term relationship may be developed.

An account may be an *active account,* meaning that the customer has been buying and will probably continue to buy in the current period; therefore, an active account is also called a *current account.* Or it may be described as an active account because it buys relatively often in the current period. And, if it buys not so relatively often, it may be called an *inactive account.* Of course, one company's active account is another's inactive account; these are relative matters.

Many accounts will be called only that, connoting regular or unexceptional status. But some will be *special accounts,* for any of a substantial number of reasons, among them size of purchases, nature of business, and geographical spread, as when an account sold to or using goods and services in many locations is a *regional account* or a *national account.*

Discount.   In sales and marketing, a price reduction, usually stated as a percentage but sometimes as a flat amount, usually with the discounted sum taken off the price before sale but sometimes with the discounted sum returned after sale in the form of a *rebate.*

A cash discount as between businesses normally involves a price reduction if payment is made within a specific time after purchase, normally 30 days. As between seller and consumer, it normally involves a reduction for payment in currency or by check rather than by such instruments as credit cards.

A *discount store* or *discount house* is usually a retailer selling at what are claimed to be deeply discounted prices; the terms have been considerably overused, though, and are falling into disrepute.

Easy and tight money.   Quite simply, *easy money* is easy-to-get credit, and *tight money* is hard-to-get credit. Before manipulation of the federal money supply became a dominant feature of the economic landscape, money was easy to borrow during a period of booming expansion, although interest rates tended to rise, reflecting the exuberance of the economy and the optimism of the time. Then, during a period of economic contraction—whether labeled a depression, recession, or, as it was often called before 1929, a panic—money became very hard to borrow, although lenders tended to lower interest rates somewhat in order to attract those who were still good lending risks and who wanted to borrow.

In recent years, federal intervention has changed that pattern considerably. Money is still relatively easy to borrow during a period of relative prosperity, although that is often not a period of real expansion, but rather a period of high inflation rates. However, money can become very hard to borrow and can feature skyrocketing interest rates because of federal manipulation of the money supply and of interest rates late in such a period, as the federal government makes an attempt to diminish the rate of inflation. Then, as that manipulation helps develop the recession phase of the cycle, further manipulation can cause interest rates to fall and money to become much easier to borrow during that recession, in an attempt to bring about relative prosperity.

Economic indicators. The economy fluctuates between prosperity and recession, whether in the context of a sustained long-term expansion, such as between 1945 and 1968, or a period of economic stagnation, such as in the 1970s. In an attempt to help track and predict the course of fluctuations, the federal government has identified a substantial number of economic factors, which, when measured, are thought to be helpful in indicating the direction of economic fluctuation; such economic indicators include construction starts, prices, wages, profits, industrial capacity used, and scores of others. Those factors thought to give indications well in advance of major cyclical economic fluctuations are called *leading indicators;* those thought to move at the same time as those fluctuations are called *coincident indicators;* and those thought to move after fluctuations are called *lagging indicators.*

These indicators do not, however, indicate quite as well as they might, because they do not allow for sudden, sharp swings up and down within a stagnant economy, caused by federal manipulation of the economy in pursuit of the economic goals of the moment—which are all too often deeply affected by the political goals of the moment.

Empathy, rapport. Here are two similar, but often misused and misunderstood terms. *Empathy,* as encountered in selling, is achieving understanding of a prospect's thinking so well that you are able to "put yourself into the other guy's shoes"; and that is an indispensable basis of selling success. *Rapport,* in this context, is the achievement of warm mutual trust between seller and prospect, and that is not necessary or in most instances really possible in the business situation. To reflexively reach for empathy is essential; to reflexively reach for rapport may in many situations cause a prospect to back away from unwanted familiarity and at the same time make it more difficult to see and use selling clues, for which a certain professional distance is required.

Equity. In finance, *equity* is the value of an ownership share. That sounds rather straightforward, but it is often very difficult to determine. If a company has issued stock that is publicly traded, and you own some of that stock, its market price rather easily determines the value of your ownership share, or equity, at any given time and also indicates the total market value of the company at that time. On the other hand, the same company may sell for more or less than the total of all its shares outstanding, and the shares themselves will soon reflect the difference in a sale situation. Similarly, you can estimate the value of your ownership interest in a dwelling by estimating fair market value and subtracting outstanding mortgage debts, but you will not be able to find the real worth of that equity until an actual sale. In taxation, the value of a closely held business is often a hotly disputed matter between tax authorities and heirs, much affecting the taxes levied on many estates.

Forecasting. Attempting to predict the course of future business, economic, and financial events and trends is not unlike modern weather forecasting, in that it is systematic, uses a set of analytical tools that include computer models, and is far, far better on long-term trends—the farther away the better—than on short-term trends and specific events. Like everyone in the prediction business, forecasters understand well that, to stay in business, they must hedge their predictions in as many ways as possible, while seeming to make hard, specific forecasts. They must also be prepared to call attention to those forecasts that turned out well, while ignoring those that proved inaccurate.

Yet forecasting is a major business activity, and for good reason, for there can be no planning without informed guessing—that is, prediction —as to the shape of the future. In the kind of forecasting commonly called budgeting, that future is forecast at least yearly, and is often routinely reevaluated quarterly and at other times, as necessary.

Fringe benefits. *Fringe benefits* are usually described as all elements of compensation other than direct compensation, and direct compensation has normally been thought to include salaries, wages, commissions, bonuses, and expenses.

But the term is really far less precise than that, as more and more non-direct-cash items become extremely important elements of compensation, as mandated both by tax avoidance strategies and by increasing concern for the total life and health of those who work. Health and life insurance plans, pensions, profit-sharing plans and stock option plans, to mention only a few of the standard "fringes" available, are widely viewed as part of a *compensation package*, rather than as optional fringes. Professionals today are far better advised to try to see the total compensation package clearly, rather than to think of its elements as direct compensation and fringe benefits. (See also *Compensation package.*)

Head hunter, executive recruiter.   *Head hunters* recruit executives, including sales representatives and sales and marketing management people, on behalf of client companies. Actually, the label is rather unfair to *executive recruiters.* Although originally coined to describe unethical recruiters, who were allegedly willing to use any means to get desired people for their clients, it is now generally applied to all executive recruiters. They should not be confused with employment agencies, variously describing themselves as counselors and executive placement organizations of all kinds, which are in the business of attempting to place you only after you have paid a considerable fee. Such agencies are just that—agencies; they are not executive recruiters.

Executive recruiters often prove to be quite valuable people to know. Many very successful people, who might be receptive to job offers, understandably hesitate to look aggressively for new positions, on the quite correct theory that their management may learn that they are looking and be unhappy about it. The executive recruiter searches for proper people to fill available client jobs, and has a considerable stake in preserving the anonymity of those approached. Oh, some executive recruiters do talk too much, but they are very much the exception rather than the rule in their trade.

It can be flattering and illuminating to talk to an executive recruiter who approaches you with a job offer—as long as you look very hard before you leap. Recruiters are, in the long run, paid for producing results and, like most people who have something to sell, are often adept at convincing themselves that the jobs they are trying to fill are far better than they really are. Remember, you can always listen and refuse; but if you move to a new job, you are the one who has to live with it, not the executive recruiter.

Hyperbole, puffery.   In selling, *hyperbole,* or *hype,* is considerable exaggeration on the part of the seller; an adaptation from the wider meaning of hyperbole, which is any kind of great exaggeration in colorful language.

Puffery more precisely refers to exaggeration by sellers in order to enhance sales success.

Unfortunately, exaggeration is so much part of the selling and advertising scene that such embellishment—all too often leaning toward fraud and misrepresentation—is a constant temptation, on the theory that you will not be heard in a crowd unless you shout. But there is a sharp distinction to be made between advertising, mailing, and the other broadcast forms on the one hand, and face-to-face selling on the other. In the field, it is very easy to go over from modest and easily understood and forgiven embellishment to what is perceived by prospects as the kind of willful misstatement that kills sales and sales relationships—and that is a hazard to be carefully avoided.

Incremental sale.   This is also called an *add-on sale* or *expansion sale,* as when seller, just after a successful close, suggests that purchaser buy more of the same or complementary items, and purchaser agrees. It also can happen on installation of recently purchased items, on early service calls, and as a result of buyer satisfaction after a period of use, if the seller has wit to ask for an expanded order. It is akin to trading up, when buyer moves to more expensive items in line in later purchases, as is so often the case in automobile and computer selling.

Indexing.   An *index* can be a measuring device, such as the Consumer Price Index, or a guide to the contents of a database or book. Indexing can be the creation of such a guide; an investment technique that tries to get investment results as good as that of a selected stock index; or the linking of variations in a selected index, such as the Consumer Price Index, with other voluntary changes in such matters as wage increases and Social Security payments.

In the last sense, indexing has been increasingly widely used throughout the world in the late 1970s and early 1980s; much of Israel's economy is indexed; so are United States Social Security benefit payments and many other kinds of payments. The choice of index and the extent and frequency of indexing are the subjects of great political and economic pressures; since those matters affect millions of people who receive public and private payments, those pressures are very likely to continue for most of the rest of our lives.

Inflation.   *Inflation* involves a general rise in prices throughout an economy, and in varying amounts in several linked economies, resulting in a lowering in the real or purchasing power value of the currency units used in that economy. It is a long-term trend, at least in the economies of all industrial countries; but the main mischief caused in the United States in these years (and in other economies around the world) stems from the *rate* of inflation, which has been exceedingly high. It has also been true in this period—unlike many other periods of even rapid inflation—that inflation has in general risen faster than incomes, resulting in losses in real income for most of the population. While not necessarily a complete view, the process has been seen by many as a spiral—the *inflationary spiral*—with many pressure groups contending for advantage and thereby forcing prices and wages steadily upward. The gravity of the situation has been thought by some to be rather understated, as it does not take into account the impact of *hidden inflation,* which is lessened quality and diminished quantity in many goods and services. The causes and possible cures of inflation are the subject of worldwide speculation and argument, and we do not deal with those matters here.

Deflation, which involves a general decrease in prices throughout one or more economies, with a consequent rise in the real purchasing power of currency, can occur when a recession or depression forces prices downward. That does not always happen, however; many periods of recession since World War II have also been periods of continued, though usually somewhat moderated, inflation. Deflation can also occur by government fiat, as when currency reevaluation raises the value of currency by a prescribed amount, artificially and in one stroke.

Disinflation describes a lowering of the pace of inflation, as when double-digit inflation becomes single-digit inflation for some period. In periods of protracted inflation, the term is very often used as a synonym for deflation, although deflation involves actual decreases in prices, rather than a moderating pace of inflation.

Reflation is a matter of economic policy, and is an effort by government to get a stagnant and depressed economy moving by the application of such stimuli as tax cuts and increases in money supply, resulting in a resumption of inflation.

Information explosion.   In this country, and especially since World War II, a great deal more information has been generated throughout the world than ever before. During the last three decades, the process has accelerated due to the development of computer technology, which enables the storage and relatively easy retrieval of far larger bodies of documents than in earlier periods. The result has been characterized as an *information explosion.*

It should be noted that much of the material generated is not so much information as it is analysis, interpretation, and prediction, for that is the main content of the tens of thousands of newspapers, magazines, journals, newsletters, and annuals that comprise the main bulk of available information sources.

Lean.   When used in the business world, *lean* usually describes a state of mind as much as it does a state of company affairs. A management that is attempting to minimize what it considers to be wasteful expenditures is often characterized as one "running a lean company," the connotation being that fat has been trimmed from company operations. It should be noted that in difficult times, such as those encountered by many companies in the late 1970s and early 1980s, the main attempt being made is to maximize profit—in some instances to make any profit at all. Leanly run companies, then, are often companies that are doing far more than trimming unnecessary fat from operations and overhead; rather they are cutting deep into the kind of bone and sinew that is essential for the long-term growth and even survival of their organizations. A short-term profits approach that makes no adequate provision for reinvestment in modernization of plant and development of new products can and often does doom a company—and sometimes an entire economy and nation—to early obsolescence and disastrous inability to compete with other companies and economies.

The term is also used somewhat more objectively, as when adverse times are described as "lean times," or tight buying in pursuit of a low inventory policy is described as "lean buying." In these contexts, the opposite of lean, which would be "fat," is seldom encountered, but rather only implied.

Macro, micro.   *Macro* means large; *micro* means small, as when *macroeconomics* means the study of large economic units and *microeconomics* means the study of small economic units.

But the terms are also used to distinguish something from a norm. The term *computer* means both any one of a host of computing machines of all sizes, and a machine on the large side of the range. *Micro* is added to distinguish it from a normal large computer; so a *microcomputer* is a small computer. Similarly, *time and motion study* refers to all kinds of such studies, but *micromotion study or analysis* examines individual motions with the help of freeze frames and slow-motion replays provided by film editors. And a *microform* or *microfilm* is any of several kinds of reduced photographic images, such as *microfiche* and *microdots*. The full-sized photographic image is not called a macrofilm; it is already thought of as full-sized.

Management. Any process, function, or organization may be operated and controlled, that is, managed; in this book, for example, we pay considerable attention to the management of time and other personal resources. Regarding human organizations, however, the term has a separate and quite distinct meaning; it is the operation and control of organizations, with *managers* seeking to maximize organizational performance toward stated goals.

Most managers operate within business organizations, in which goals include maximizing profit and often growth as well; some operate in other institutional frameworks, such as those provided by nonprofit organizations and governments, where some goals differ but organizational performance goals are basically the same. In organizational terms, management is management; managers are managers, whether working in or out of government, for profit or not for profit. Managers are generalists, though skills and knowledge differ from industry to industry, and country to country. Yet, after allowing for differences, the basic tools of inquiry, problem-solving techniques, people- and process-handling are general rather than particular in nature.

Managers are, in theory and sometimes in practice, ultimately responsible to those who own the organizations, through elected or otherwise designated boards of directors in private organizations. As a practical matter, especially where stock ownership is widely diffused, top managers exercise many decision-making functions, affecting the long-term directions of the organizations they control and operate.

Management is also a body of theory and practice, to some extent codified and transmitted through a substantial body of business schools, teachers, and writers. But it is a body of often-conflicting theories and practices, with no single set of guidelines within which all or even most managers work. It may be science or art, or both; its practitioners are usually highly pragmatic people, who care little about academic definitions and a great deal about making plans and working their plans to maximum organizational advantage.

Margin, marginal. The terms *margin* and *marginal* have several different business meanings.

In one sense, they are synonymous with incremental, describing the effect of adding one or more elements to an existing entity. In this sense, a *marginal cost* is a cost added to an existing body of costs. Although the precise impact of a new cost factor is often very difficult to calculate exactly, the concept is useful, making it possible to attempt to relate new costs to new benefits in order to assess properly the impact and desirability of the added cost. In new product evaluation, the concept of *marginal costing* or *incremental costing* is used; in assessing profitability only determinable new costs are allocated to the revenues produced by the new product during a period designated as a product introduction period, the full share of existing overhead and other applicable costs not being allocated to the new product. The term is also applied in this sense to any change in factors, and the process of attempting to evaluate the results of specific changes is called *marginal analysis.*

In a somewhat different but related sense of the term, the sales revenue resulting from additional sales at varying prices and terms is called *marginal revenue.* For example, if 10 identical items sold at $10 each yield $100 in revenue, and a quantity price break at that point takes the price of each down to $9.50 each for 11 or more, the revenue from a sale of 11 of the items is $104.45; in this case the marginal revenue from the eleventh sale is $4.50.

In quite a different sense, the term is applied to collateralized loans, such as a bank loan in the form of a mortgage secured by property, or brokers' loans secured by stock in a margin account, which have available collateral value beyond the value of the outstanding loans; the value of the collateral above the loan amount is its *margin of safety.* In this sense, the term is often used more loosely to describe the amount of risk thought present in a given situation.

Margin is also used as a synonym for profit, and in this sense also a synonym for net, as when a financial statement calls any of the net figures appearing on it "margin."

And in yet another meaning, a *marginal business* is one showing little profit and not very likely to do much better, for reasons intrinsic to the nature of the business or its operators.

Market, marketing.   A *market* is a marketplace, anywhere that trading takes place. To market is to take whatever is for sale to its marketplace or marketplaces. *Marketing* is the process of doing so. Although marketing sometimes refers to the whole set of distribution functions, it generally describes the sales and sales-related functions, including direct selling, advertising (which may not always sell directly), and a miscellany of other promotional functions. The term also often includes customer service, which shades off into manufacturing functions, not so much as a matter of reporting relationships but as of functional necessity.

Marketing terms are often very spongily used in practice; perhaps that is because people involved in the selling functions, much like those involved with computers, greatly enjoy coining new terms and expanding old terms to include new meanings. It is very easy—seductively so—to move from the coining of selling slogans to the coining of new words in the everyday language of the workplace. And, as all who sell know, to implant a term is often to implant an idea, and that is often a most important step on the way to a sale.

Sales professionals can find themselves discussing several related marketing terms in a single meeting, some seeming to be used interchangeably with others that should—and often do—have other meanings. For example, *marketing plan* and *marketing mix* are sometimes used as synonyms, although a marketing plan is marketing management's total and detailed plan of operations for a given period, while the marketing mix is, in fact, the working out of that plan. A new product may be described as having great *market potential,* enhanced by the company's *marketing power,* and its *market penetration* or *market share* in the main market to which the product is addressed, particularly as the company occupies preeminent *market position* in that market. That means the new product probably will sell well, because the company has a demonstrated ability to sell well in the right markets, as indicated by previous success, which has caused it to occupy first rank among those selling to that market.

Marketing concept.   This idea indicates that a company should primarily be interested in producing goods and services tailored to perceived customer wants and needs, and that the company that adopts this orientation will triumph in the marketplace, thus achieving better profitability and growth than its competitors. It therefore asserts the primacy of the marketing functions and of the people who perform those functions. Unfortunately, those pressing the concept in an unbalanced way all too often have failed to pay equal attention to quality, financial stability, and economy, with results all too painfully apparent in the American automobile industry. Studying customer wants and needs is useful, but is no substitute for hard and early analysis of all the relevant factors; wants and needs can change very rapidly, as when economic necessities force national belt-tightening.

Media.   The avenues through which advertising and promotion flow are all *media,* or *advertising media,* or *communications media;* in this context they are all used synonymously. These general terms embrace newspapers, magazines, and other print-on-paper forms; and such broadcast forms as radio and television. The term *media hype* has developed in recognition of the tendency of some using these forms to exaggerate their claims in pursuit of mass audiences.

These terms are most often used to describe *mass media,* which are forms reaching mass audiences. However, media seeking to reach narrower audiences are very often used by advertisers and direct sellers, as when a publisher of a handbook directed to sales professionals attempts to sell that book by advertising it in a publication directed to sales professionals.

Mergers, acquisitions, divestitures, and all that. In this age of the multinational corporation and the conglomerate, the language of corporate combination is an important part of the language of business.

When a company, partnership, or individual—that is, any business entity—takes over or acquires a controlling interest in all or a discrete portion of another business entity, that is an *acquisition.* It is also a *takeover,* for the terms are synonyms; the term acquisition is favored in the United States, and the term takeover is favored in Great Britain. It is also one variety of *merger,* for (with rare exceptions) one of the parties to a merger is taking over the other party or parties.

The controlling interest acquired may be 100%, or as little as a bare majority of ownership shares. What is acquired is often a business entity, such as a company, division, or one of its subsidiaries. But other assets, such as a line of products, an inventory, or a trade name can also be acquired, and described as acquisitions. When a business entity is so acquired, it then becomes a *subsidiary* of the acquiring company, as is every wholly owned legal entity belonging to a parent company.

But when less than a majority interest, but essentially a controlling interest, is acquired, the acquired entity's status is that of an *affiliate,* as is every such entity controlled by a parent company. In terms of day-to-day control, the differences are often rather insubstantial; but there are substantial differences for the acquirers in terms of freedom of action toward the acquired entity, and as to tax treatment of acquirer and acquired. Both subsidiaries and affiliates are sometimes also called *controlled companies.*

Acquisitions can be painless, resulting in considerably enhanced prospects for those in the company being acquired. They can also be extremely painful, as when acquirer and potential acquiree are in an adversary relationship, with the management of the company being sought vigorously resisting takeover, while public charges and counter-charges effectively hamstring the day-to-day operations of the company and its relationships with many of its customers and suppliers.

Those in a company that may be acquired are often personally in a certain kind of limbo during acquisition proceedings, even if all goes smoothly. For whatever the assurances made by current management and potential new owners, there are enormously adverse personal possibilities in many acquisition situations. Positions achieved after decades of work can be destroyed for those unlucky enough to be in a portion of an acquired company scheduled for actual merger with a portion of the acquirer; when two sets of employees exist, those of the acquired company are highly likely to be those thought redundant. Also, someone in a division or group thought not profitable enough, or at variance with the new management's main goals, may soon be out of a job.

A company that is being seriously considered for acquisition or take-over is often described as an *acquisition candidate* or *takeover candidate*, whether or not its management has indicated that it wants the company to be acquired. Once a potential acquirer has decided to attempt to acquire it, the company becomes a *target company*. The use of the word *target* would seem to connote probable adverse relations between acquirer and acquiree; that is often, but not always, true.

An *asset play* is an attempt by a potential acquirer to take over an ailing but asset-rich company for a purchase price smaller than the liquidation value of its assets.

A kind of speculator who specializes in takeover situations is called a *takeover arbitrageur.* These arbitrageurs speculate in the stock of companies involved in acquisition situations, betting that the acquisition will (or will not) occur, and therefore on the coming stock prices of the companies involved.

A *divestiture* is the opposite side of the coin from acquisition. Here a company gives up ownership of an economic entity, such as a subsidiary, affiliate, or division, usually by sale whole, but sometimes by sale and liquidation piecemeal. In addition to normal business reasons for doing so, companies may sometimes be forced to divest themselves of operations by court action taken by antitrust regulators or by consent agreements in settlement of such actions.

Mergers are the result of acquisitions or divestitures, with one of the organizations involved taking complete control of the other; the organization taken over may then lose its existence as a legal entity or may retain that existence but still be completely controlled by its acquirer. Rarely, two merging organizations will both lose their identities in the merger and be succeeded by a new organization; that is generally described as a *consolidation,* rather than a merger.

There are some short-term joinings of interest between organizations that do not involve transfer of control over all or any part of the organizations involved. They are generally described as *joint ventures;* that term describes only the principle involved, as the ventures themselves may take any of the various business forms. One commonly used international joint venture form, usually describing large joint ventures in which several major companies and often financial institutions are involved, is the *consortium.* Those engaged in joint ventures are often described as having engaged in a *pooling of interests.*

When companies or financial institutions openly pursue joint monopolistic activities in the United States, they are called *trusts,* and are therefore organized in a form prohibited by United States antitrust laws. However, when such common interests are pursued internationally by nations or organizations outside United States jurisdiction, as by a group of coffee or oil producers, it is called a *cartel,* and as such is a normal business form used throughout the world.

Narrowcasting. In the early 1980s the jargon term for marketing activities directed toward a relatively small, sharply definable and reachable market or related group of markets has been *narrowcasting.* During the 1960s, the term was *special interest marketing;* in the 1970s, it became *special marketing,* and *segmented marketing.* Narrowcasting is probably more appropriate than the other terms, as it seems somewhat more descriptive of the prospect selection and selling efforts involved. By the time you read this paragraph, the jargon may have changed again; it matters little, for the concept will in all probability have not changed at all.

Networking, network. *Networking* is a nice new name for something that has been done quite reflexively by most professionals for as long as anyone can remember. It is the process of building a web of supportive contact—a *network*—with others, inside and outside of current employment, with the aim of being able to develop information, contact, and action directed toward personal and business objectives, and to do so consistently and over the course of a lifetime. To some extent, networking happens naturally, but it happens far more quickly and effectively if a network is built carefully and consciously, with the seeking of compatible resource partners continuing as a personal and career-building activity in all seasons.

The term *network* is also used in an entirely different sense, relating to the creation, collection, and distribution of data. In a very wide sense, it is used to describe the information and communications web resulting from the tying together of such equipment as word processors, computer terminals, facsimile machines, copiers, teleconferencing facilities, and PBX systems, and the creation and reaching of both local and remote bodies of data. Such a network may be called a *distributed* or *distributive data processing system,* although that term normally describes a smaller system using computer terminals and printers distributed throughout a single office complex. When a comprehensive network is used only in a local area, as in a single office complex, it is usually called a *local area network,* and is tied together through either a coaxial cable installed throughout the complex or a private telephone system.

Performance appraisal. A *performance appraisal* is a formal review of employee progress, engaged in by an employee and his or her immediate supervisor and sometimes by other superiors and personnel staff people as well. It attempts to provide a rational basis for evaluation of such matters as pay raises, increased responsibilities, and promotions, and functions in essence as a kind of auxiliary and interim employment interview. In some instances, it also functions as a preseparation interview, when perceived negatives so far outweigh positives that warnings of peril to continuing employment accompany such evaluations. In most instances, it functions as little more than a ritual, as employee and immediate superior are so close as to make the distancing necessary for this kind of formal appraisal impossible to accomplish, while top management insists on the appraisal being conducted. Then it becomes a time-waster.

Preapproach. A seller often does a good many sales-related things after identifying a possible prospect and before coming face-to-face with that prospect. There are telephone approaches aimed at securing an interview and a presentation opportunity; additional research on prospect and company; and promotional activities such as *preheat letters,* aimed at making a prospect more receptive. All are generally described as *preapproach* matters, to distinguish them from both prospecting, and the direct face-to-face selling situation. These are not matters in a single simple sequence, though; a sales professional keeps on researching and *reheating* after an initially unsuccessful presentation, and in this sense preapproach can also describe a multiple set of customer and prospect contacts outside the direct sales situation.

Premium. In selling, it is something extra, in the form of a gift, prize, or some other noncash incentive to buy. It may be a piece of merchandise given away by a bank as an inducement to open an account, a gift offered in a coupon printed on a box of goods, or any of thousands of other goods and services offered by sellers to prospective buyers and recommenders of their products. Premiums are also widely used as sales incentives, in the forms of merchandise, travel, and other prizes for excellent sales performance.

Presentation.   A formal attempt by seller to convince prospect to buy; usually, but unfortunately (for some sellers) not always, a *planned presentation,* with a coherent body of thought presented in a planned sequence and often accompanied by prepared visual materials and language aimed at helping tell the selling story and make the sale.

Some planned presentations are *fully memorized presentations,* often called *canned presentations,* in which every word, inflection, and use of visual materials is rehearsed in advance, and delivered with no significant deviation from the script. Some such presentations are really canned, being presented on film and with complete soundtrack, with the sales professional's role a matter of objection handling and closing after the presentation. Most planned presentations, though, allow the professional much more room than that, recognizing that empathy and selling success depend much more upon what occurs between seller and prospect than upon material presented in canned form. Many planned presentations supply sellers with key words and visual materials to work with and around; these are sometimes called *talkthrough presentations.*

Product line.   This term is used in two senses in the field. In one sense, it is a group of related products sold to a set of related needs, as when an office machine seller has several models of the same kind of copier, a body of equipment peripheral to the copiers, and such materials as ink and paper, to be used by the copiers.

In another, spongier sense, it is all the products a seller has to sell, related or not. Most sales professionals use the term in the first sense, and will describe themselves as selling several product lines if products and groups of products are unrelated.

Profit sharing.   *Profit sharing* is an element of employee compensation that is tied to the current profit performance of a business. Quite often it takes the form of a straightforward monthly, quarterly, or year-end bonus, with the year-end by far the most common form of bonus given.

However, the American tax system invites tax-avoidance and tax-deferral efforts, and such bonuses are entirely taxable as current income. Therefore, many businesses are heavily involved in tax-deferred profit-sharing arrangements, in which portions of current profits are held in tax-deferred, IRS-qualified profit-sharing plans until retirement or termination of employment.

Prospect.   A *prospect* is a prospective purchaser. Which means that he or she must be someone who might reasonably be expected to have desire or need for what you are selling and the wherewithal to buy what you are selling. Until you have found those things out, a possible prospect may be properly described only as a *suspect.*

But even someone with desire or need may not have the ability to buy; one who works for a company, and uses the kinds of office machines you are selling may not have the authority to buy; only someone with that authority is a *qualified prospect,* and it is only to qualified prospects that you can sell.

The whole process of identifying possible prospects and then qualified prospects is called *prospecting,* and the indispensable and enormously valuable set of prospective purchasers that develops from sound and consistent prospecting—often supplemented by home office efforts—is the *prospect file.* Without a good prospect file, no matter how good you are at the rest of selling, you are dead in the water.

Psychic income.   The emotional satisfaction derived by doing a job is sometimes called *psychic income;* maximizing that is a matter of considerable management interest, often being the particular focus of people in human resources development and personnel.

For the overwhelming majority of those in the world of work, it is hardly ever just the money that brings job satisfaction. Oh, money is basic, both as current need and goal, but it is not the whole story at all. There are many other factors, including such basics as competition—winning or losing whatever the game is—pride in your work; the esteem of co-workers; and family factors related to work. All have to do with the amount of psychic income derived from work.

Quota.   In selling, a *quota* is a goal or set of personal selling goals determined by sales management, often in consultation with the individual for whom goals are to be set. Quotas are a normal feature of the selling landscape; the real hazard presented by quotas is that they may come to be regarded as maximums, rather than minimums. If a sales professional is doing nothing more than making quotas, then there is either something very wrong with those quotas, that company, or the professional, and something that is best looked into by all concerned as soon as possible.

Referrals.   When a customer or prospect gives you the names and telephone numbers of two of his or her best business friends, and tells you to mention who suggested that you call, you have received two *referrals.*

But such a referral is not necessarily a *recommendation,* nor should it be misunderstood or put forward as such unless that too has been specified. If it is a recommendation you are getting, then it must be understood that those business friends will hear the same recommendation you are hearing when they call or see your recommending customer. If there is any doubt at all on that score, don't put it forward as a recommendation, but only a referral, for the false recommendation can destroy the possibility of a sale, while a good referral can help it enormously.

You may also get what amounts to a broadcast endorsement, in the form of a *proof letter,* which is *third-party material.* This means that a third party, presumably without any kind of axe to grind on your behalf, recommends in writing what you have to sell, and perhaps you, as well.

Sales professional. In the modern period, we have not yet quite solved the problem of finding a single word to describe one who combines self-definition as a selling professional with a substantial bundle of skills transferable to the sale of all kinds of goods and services. In an earlier day, such professionals were called *peddlers,* and then the travelers among them called *drummers,* and later simply *travelers,* all three terms being admirably asexual and thereby quite up to late twentieth-century needs and standards as to sexual equality in language. Unfortunately, peddler and drummer have quite negative connotations now, and traveler in these times, while still applied to some sales professionals, neither describes all or is limited to those who sell.

Men who sell have been called *salesmen,* which was for most of this century the standard term for sales professional, with women who sell called *saleswomen;* that, too, seems not quite right, as perhaps too sex-differentiated. So in this period we tend to rather awkwardly say *sales professional,* or *seller, sales representative, account executive,* or *salesperson,* the last satisfying no one, since it has long been identified with retail store selling, rather than outside selling.

We also differentiate further, describing sellers by geography and function. A sales professional may sell *inside,* generally meaning the practice of *retail selling* or *telephone selling,* though lately the telephone seller may be rather pretentiously called a *telemarketer.* Or a seller may practice *outside selling,* which characterizes the main bulk of sales professionals. A seller may be an *independent representative* (or *rep*), who works for or is someone representing rather than being employed by the originators of the goods and services being sold. Earlier, and to some extent still today, the independent representative was called a *manufacturer's representative.* Even further differentiated, a seller employed by a dealer may be called a *dealer representative,* and one employed by a distributor a *distributor representative.* And there are also those sales professionals who do everything but sell, convincing and training sellers who work for independents, dealers, wholesalers, jobbers, and retailers to sell the products of their employers; these are called *missionaries.*

Saturation campaign.   This is an attempt to blanket a specified geographical or functional area with promotional and selling efforts aimed at securing excellent sales results. Sometimes, it represents a highly skilled direction of major expenditure into the designated area; alas, all too often it eventuates only in the placement of some quantities of advertisements and press releases, which may or may not prove helpful to field sales efforts.

Seller's market, buyer's market.   When supply is short, and many buyers are clamoring for what you sell at the prices you are asking, that is a *seller's market.* When buyers are in short supply, sales are low, and your previously firm prices turn out to be very, very negotiable, that's a *buyer's market.* But when a sales professional in a rather normal set of markets is heard to mutter repeatedly that he or she is bucking a buyer's market, that's probably just a personal slump.

Selling.   *Selling* comes in several forms, its varieties having quite a number of descriptors. There are the old traditional functional names: *inside selling* and *outside selling,* the former being a matter of prospects coming to you and the latter being a matter of you finding and going to prospects, and both involving face-to-face personal selling. Most kinds of inside selling, but not all, are *retail selling.* Outside selling is variously named, usually by main perceived function, as in *systems selling, industrial selling,* and *institutional selling,* among others; all such perceived functions overlap, and for the face-to-face professional, selling continues to be selling.

Some sell by telephone, rather than face-to-face; they are *telephone sellers* in the older nomenclature, and more recently *telemarketers.* Others sell by mail and other broadcast means; as those means have expanded, so has their description. *Mail marketers* and *direct mail marketers* have become *direct marketers,* which could be rather confusing if anyone bothered to reflect and conclude that both face-to-face selling professionals and broadcast marketers are in their own ways direct marketers.

Sex discrimination.   Discrimination against women in favor of men has long been a feature of the American business landscape, ameliorated only to a small extent during the world wars, and then seriously attacked starting in the 1960s—an attack that continues today, although somewhat weakened by new conservative political trends in the United States in the early 1980s.

Like similar discriminations against minorities, such acts of discrimination as failure to hire qualified women for available jobs in management, sales, and elsewhere is now illegal, as is—in general—failure to pay equally for equal work performed. Unlike other minorities, women all too often also face sexual harassment on the job, and this too is illegal, though often extraordinarily difficult to prove.

(*See also:* Affirmative action, discrimination.)

Soft sell, hard sell.   As generally used, a *soft sell* is thought to be a sales effort that rather gently but empathically goes about the business of convincing prospects to buy, seeking agreement every step of the way and successfully assuming sale or adopting some other way of easing into the buying decision at the close. A *hard sell,* on the other hand, is generally thought to be a sales effort that bludgeons rather than attempting to convince, with seller depending upon domination of prospect and situation for success, and boldly asking for the order again and again, until gasping prospect gives in.

Nonsense, of course; a set of misperceived seeming differences. Professionals who bludgeon soon self-select out of the selling profession; so do professionals who fail to ask for the order again and again, in every possible way, when that asking is right. There are differences in personal style as between professionals, and several styles work equally well. But at the heart of the matter and in the long run there is only empathy, the finding of desire and need, and the skillful development of the selling situation into a successful close, in all conditions and with all products, again and again and year after year.

Stock option: When a corporate employee has an option to buy company stock at a fixed price, often a favorable price, within a stated period, that is a *stock option.* Unlike many other kinds of options, which are intrinsically valuable and often actively traded, the employee stock option has no intrinsic value, must be exercised by its owner, and is therefore not tradable.

Stock options can be enormously valuable fringe benefits, and for some may be a key element in the total compensation package—when the stocks in question are going up. That was true of many stocks in the booming stock markets of the 1960s, and became much less true in the stagnant markets of the 1970s and early 1980s. There is no particular reason to exercise an option in a stock that is going nowhere; the money is better invested elsewhere. However, there are always some stocks that will go up, such as some of the high technology and genetic engineering stocks of the early 1980s. Those employed by such companies were often able to take advantage of very advantageous stock options, even in falling or stagnant stock markets. At this writing, stock options are considerably tax-advantaged, providing even more incentives to use them in some companies.

Time management: A term coined in recent years, *time management* describes a considerable body of techniques aimed at helping people to most effectively use the limited time at their disposal to accomplish identified tasks and goals. None of the approaches and techniques offered by the wide variety of advisors working in this area are particularly new; all require the same kind of self-discipline and consistency that successful people have always needed.

Trainee.   A *trainee* is not necessarily a neophyte. Someone just starting out in selling may be both trainee and neophyte, but someone starting a new selling job may be a thoroughly experienced sales professional and yet regarded by a new company as in many respects a trainee. That can be demeaning, but only if you or your new employer misperceive the situation. The truth is that on a new job even excellent professionals can benefit from a good deal of training time and attention, in terms of product knowledge, use of sales materials, approach to new markets and kinds of prospects, and orientation to a new company. In different ways, both formal training classes and field training can be useful.

A sales professional sometimes does have to clarify status, though, as when an inexperienced home office or field trainer takes an ego trip and treats a group of new hirees condescendingly. Sales professionals need accept nothing less than respect.

Undersold, oversold.   Here are two related and very imprecise terms indeed. They are usually encountered in the forms of criticism and alibi; the sales manager charging that a customer has not been sold enough, or the sales representative ascribing failure to sell more or to hold a previous level of sales to an overloaded market or specific customer condition. Both characterizations are suspect; each more often than not can be seen quite otherwise; neither characterization is worth much, either as analytical tool or motivating device.

Underselling also has a second business meaning, as when one seller may price products lower than competitors to gain competitive advantage. A twist upon this form of price competition is *lowballing,* in which a seller quotes an unrealistically low price and then seeks to raise prices during the course of contract fulfillment, or to quote higher prices on future contracts, once competitors have been defeated and perhaps put out of business.

Vested interest. A *vested interest* is a person's interest, or equity, in receiving payments from a pension plan or profit-sharing plan, which covers that person even if employment or association with the organization providing the plan is terminated before retirement. For example, an employee covered under a pension plan may go to work with a company at the age of 30, stay for 10 years, leave at age 40, retire 25 years later at age 65, and still be legally entitled to a modest, continuing pension payment from the company's pension plan after 65. Given that example, the payments will indeed be modest—taking into account the amount of time worked and the impact of inflation after a quarter of a century—but payments will be legally due then. If the employee had stayed 25 years, until age 55, and then moved on, the payments due 10 years later, at age 65, might be quite substantial.

Zero base. *Zero base* is a planning concept, widely used in American companies, which points out that nothing in a plan should be taken as a given solely because it is carried over from a previous plan or has previously been a feature of group thinking. Each planning period is looked upon as a whole new ball game, with each element in each plan evaluated afresh.

The concept has achieved greatest impact as applied to budgeting. *Zero-based budgeting* sets out to examine each budget element as if it were brand new, no matter how much of it is fixed by previous decisions; for example, long-term fixed plant costs and basic debt service costs are treated as carefully and as if they were as reachable as short-term advertising and promotion costs. In this context, the approach makes planning far more flexible than is possible when major cost factors are thought of as frozen, mandated, and unreachable, and at the same time makes possible more balanced decisions between alternatives, so that new possibilities will not be forced out by the deadweight of older choices.

The other main application of the zero-based concept has been in quality control, where it is put forward as a *zero-defects* concept, which essentially refuses to accept any defects rate as a given, arguing that all too often an acceptable defects rate becomes in practice a minimum defects rate, with even higher defects rates actually treated as acceptable. The zero-defects rate concept treats no defects as acceptable, while of course recognizing that in real life defects do occur. If taken too far, the concept can become absurd, and can itself become unacceptable to those who try to use it; but if taken as a general guide to better quality control, it can be very useful indeed.

NOTES ON GRAMMAR AND USAGE

Clarity is greatly prized in all business writing—clarity of image as well as content. For communication of a professional image is often as important as communication of a particular message, and has a great deal to do with whether or not readers listen to that message.

And that is why grammar and usage are important. You will find no grammatical purists here. We are well aware that language changes. New words come into the language constantly, while others pass away; and rules that were immutable to an English teacher of some decades ago are being bent daily or are disappearing before our eyes. But it is still true that people judge you by how you express yourself. Not only by how clearly and effectively you get your ideas across, but also by your style of writing. That does not mean a literary style of writing, which is out of place in business communications. It does mean that your writing should fall within the standard ranges of acceptability. We leave correctness to the grammarians and purists; indeed, a piece of business prose that was perfectly "correct" might very well be stilted, and draw attention away from your content as much as ungrammatical writing that reflected negatively on your education and background. As in so many other areas, you should aim for a middle ground between the two extremes.

The following material is aimed at helping you do just that. Grammar alone, of course, will not ensure effective writing. It will not save faulty logic or a weak argument. But sound grammar is an important part of the overall picture. If your writing is sloppy, it will not be very appealing. Misspelled or improperly used words, dangling modifiers, or a singular verb with a plural subject can communicate negative messages about you to the reader. Even small grammatical errors can do a lot to undermine your writing—and your credibility.

So, while you are editing your copy for its clarity and organization, you should also check for errors in grammar and usage. When in doubt about the spelling of a word, always look it up; it pays to doublecheck. (The

Checklist of Commonly Misused and Misspelled Words will help you there; beyond that, rely on your dictionary—make sure it is up to date.) It is also a good idea to have a thesaurus handy. If you have overused a word and would like to substitute another, a thesaurus will help you find it. Use words only when you are certain of them; do not guess, as some words may seen synonymous when they really are not.

It is best to avoid colloquialisms, slang, and too many informal contractions in business writing. What passes as acceptable in speech or in casual notes to friends is not necessarily appropriate for your business correspondence and reports. You want to present as polished an image as possible; your writing style is your public relations representative.

Here we will just hit the highlights, focusing on those areas where writers are most likely to have trouble. We will use a minimum of grammar—our concern is with practical usage. While a few grammatical terms are inevitable in some discussions, we have not belabored them; even if those terms are Greek to you we hope the examples will be useful. First, some general problem areas.

PROBLEM AREAS

Many writers unwittingly make errors in subject–verb agreement, before they ever have a chance to dangle a modifier or split an infinitive. It is easy to see why. Compound nouns and modifying clauses can cause real confusion.

The rule for subject and verb agreement is simple: Singular subjects require a singular verb, and plural subjects require a plural verb.

The announcement is late.
The customers are resisting the price.

What could be simpler? But the following sentence is trickier:

This collection of articles give us a clear picture of the military policies in South America.

The subject of this sentence is *collection,* not *articles.* The phrase *of articles* simply describes the subject. The correct subject–verb agreement is shown here:

This collection of articles gives us a clear picture of the military policies in South America.

Here is another example of subject–verb disagreement:

The first example are the methods used to control crop diseases.

Here the plural word *methods* can easily confuse matters. But the subject of the sentence, *example,* is singular and needs a singular verb:

The first example is the methods used to control crop diseases.

Modifiers—single words or groups of words—can also cause problems, especially when they dangle by not referring logically to a noun or pronoun. Here is an example of a misplaced modifier:

Along with daily workouts, Jones watches for muscle soreness.

Surely the writer does not mean that Jones watches for both muscle soreness and daily workouts. This sentence should be rewritten.

Jones works out daily and watches for muscle soreness.

Here is another example:

While on vacation, the car was stolen.

That sounds like the car was stolen while it was on vacation. The sentence is better this way:

While I was on vacation, the car was stolen.

or

The car was stolen while I was on vacation.

Infinitives pose another problem area. Infinitives are verbs in plain form, usually preceded by to, as in *to go, to eat.* In school you were probably admonished never to split infinitives. But times have changed. It is now generally acceptable to split them when necessary, although it is wise not to separate the elements too much.

Not split: He was told to inspect the units carefully.
Split: He was told to carefully inspect the units.

Both of the above are acceptable, although the first is still preferable to purists.

The real problems arise when too much material splits an infinitive, resulting in a clumsy, vague sentence; as here:

I had to for several reasons take my car into the shop.

It is better to rejoin the infinitive, as here:

I had to take my car into the shop for several reasons.

or

For several reasons, I had to take my car into the shop.

Negatives also require careful handling. It is easy to avoid the obvious double negatives, as in:

Do not use no double negatives.

But beware of sentences—even grammatically correct ones—that contain too many negative words; they can confuse the reader, as here:

The Supreme Court declined to hear an appeal seeking to overturn a law that prohibits . . .

It would be better to rewrite such a sentence, so that it has no more than two negatives, as here:

The Supreme Court let stand a lower-court ruling that a law prohibiting gun sales on Sundays is constitutional.

Parallelism requires a bit more care. Clarity and conciseness—as well as correctness—are enhanced when items in a series match each other in grammatical form. Elements of sentences should be parallel; that is, of equal rank. It is easy to lose parallelism when describing a series of actions or characteristics. The examples below illustrate some common mistakes in parallelism, and how to correct them.

Unparallel: The Therm-O-Warm space heater is compact, light-weight, and will heat up to 800 cubic feet.

Parallel: The Therm-O-Warm space heater is compact and lightweight. It will heat up to 800 cubic feet.

or

The Therm-O-Warm space heater is compact, lightweight, and capable of heating up to 800 square feet.

In the unparallel example, *compact* and *lightweight* are both adjectives describing the heater, and parallelism would lead the reader to expect another adjective as to the third item in the series. Instead we get a verb that takes the sentence off in quite a different direction. Such a lack of parallelism is distracting because it generally causes readers to circle back to the beginning of the sentence. The problem can be solved quite easily, as shown in the two parallel examples, either by breaking apart the two parts of the original sentence or by changing the odd item in the series into a form that matches the others. The same solutions apply to the additional examples below:

Unparallel: His new job responsibilities include work on the task force and preparing a marketing plan.

Parallel: His new job responsibilities include work on the task force and preparation of a new marketing plan.

or

His new job responsibilities include working on the task force and preparing a new marketing plan.

Unparallel: Sales of the women's sportswear and separates were down in the third quarter due to these factors:

- Sidewalk construction that hampered entrance to the store and reduced store traffic;
- Advertising was cut back for several weeks;
- Lack of popularity of the new label.

Parallel: Sales of the women's sportswear and separates were down in the third quarter due to these factors:

- Sidewalk construction hampered entrance to the store and reduced in-store traffic;
- Advertising was cut back for several weeks;
- The new label lacked popularity.

Handling of clauses also can cause some difficulties. While there are a number of types of clauses, the primary ones are independent and dependent. Independent clauses can stand by themselves as complete sentences, while dependent clauses cannot function alone.

The report was copied. While he waited.

In this example, the independent clause *The report was copied* can stand alone as a complete sentence, but *while he waited,* the dependent clause, cannot. It should be joined to the independent clause, like this:

The report was copied while he waited.

Dependent clauses may be used to begin sentences, although they may weaken them. When used at the beginning, introductory dependent clauses are followed by a comma, as here:

While he waited, the report was copied.

Clauses are often joined together by *conjunctions,* such as *and, but, for, or,* and *while.* These can join two independent clauses together, or an independent clause with a dependent one. Often, two short independent clauses are joined to make a longer, smoother sentence, as here:

I am going on vacation but Mary is attending the conference.

Without judicious use of conjunctions, writing can be choppy.
While it is acceptable to begin sentences with conjunctions, do so sparingly. Sentences beginning with conjunctions frequently develop thoughts expressed in previous sentences or add emphasis; for example:

The Therm-O-Warm can cut your heating bill up to 30 percent. And it's easy to install.

Correlative conjunctions are used in pairs and join elements that are equal. Examples of correlative conjunctions are *either . . . or, neither . . . nor,* and *both . . . and.*

Both the Model 30 and the Model 40 meet our data processing needs.
Neither the Model 30 nor the Model 40 meets our data processing needs.

Neither the Model 30 nor the newer models meet our data processing needs.

Note that *both . . . and* takes a plural verb, while *either . . . or* and *neither . . . nor* require a singular verb, unless the second item mentioned is plural.

Many of the writer's problems in editing a piece of writing, especially in punctuation, revolve around appositives and relative clauses. Appositives are nouns or noun phrases that act as nouns; they further define or rename another noun. Relative clauses modify nouns and are usually introduced by pronouns such as *that, who, which,* and *whose.* Both have two types: nonrestrictive and restrictive.

Nonrestrictive appositives and relative clauses add information but are not essential to the meaning of the sentence; they may be omitted without changing the meaning, and they are set off with commas. Here is an example of a nonrestrictive appositive:

Jane Smith, the controller, is in the hospital.

Controller further defines or renames Jane Smith, but can be left out without altering the meaning of the sentence.

Jane Smith is in the hospital.

Here is an example of a nonrestrictive relative clause:

The committee, which usually meets on Tuesdays, canceled its meeting this week.

Without the clause, the sentence reads:

The committee canceled its meeting this week.

Restrictive appositives and relative clauses are essential to the meaning of the sentence and are not punctuated with commas. Here is an example of a restrictive appositive:

A committee on policy planning was formed.

Which committee? The one *on policy planning,* and no other.

Similarly, a restrictive relative clause:

The woman who won the contract has left town.

Which woman? The one who *won the contract.*
That leads us directly to the whole question of punctuation.

PUNCTUATION MARKS

The comma is the most frequently used and abused punctuation mark. There are so many rules governing its usage, and so many exceptions to the rules that many writers use either too few or too many commas. Generally, commas are inserted where there is a natural pause and where elements of a sentence must be separated to avoid misunderstanding.

The erroneous omission or placement of a comma can wreak havoc with the meaning of the sentence. Consider the following examples:

If you must take the last copy.
If you must, take the last copy.

Commas help make order out of chaos; without them sentences can be nothing but a jumble of run-on words. Of course, a misplaced comma can sometimes create chaos by twisting the meaning of a sentence. The trend nowadays is to use commas sparingly. "When in doubt, leave it out" is the rule of thumb followed by many writers, especially by journalists, who drop certain commas in order to make the news snappy, fast reading.

Of all the punctuation marks, the comma indicates the briefest of pauses—much less than the semicolon, colon, or dash. The lack of commas in the following sentence will cause the reader to rush pell-mell through it—and probably to double back to make sense out of it:

As you go through the intensive demanding seminar you'll take a close look at who you are at what you really want out of life and at what obstacles are standing in the way of your success.

With commas, the reader pauses, and the sentence readily makes sense:

As you go through the intensive, demanding seminar, you'll take a close look at who you are, at what you really want out of life, and at what obstacles are standing in the way of your success.

Each comma has been inserted for a different reason. The first, between *intensive* and *demanding,* separates coordinating adjectives. The second, between *seminar* and *you'll,* sets off a dependent clause that begins the sentence. The third and fourth, between *are* and *at,* and *life* and *and,* separate a series of three prepositional clauses.

Here are some basic rules—and exceptions—that govern the use of commas, in various situations:

- *In a series.* Commas are needed to separate series (three or more) of words, phrases, or clauses. In formal writing, a comma is required after all elements in a series:

The board room was decorated in black, gold, and white.

However, in much modern writing, the comma is omitted before the *and:*

The board room was done in black, gold and white.

Be careful that omitting this final comma does not create an awkward sentence; retain that final comma if it helps avoid misunderstanding, as in the example below:

Breakfast consisted of toast, bacon, tea and ham and eggs.

Note that the final element in the series is compound: *ham and eggs.* Without a final comma between *bacon* and *and,* the sentence sounds as though the tea and ham and eggs were mixed. The final comma avoids that problem, making the meaning clearer.

In the previous example the comma inserted before the final *and* creates a desirable pause before the last clause in the series. Note that, without it, the last two clauses would have run together.

As you go through the intensive, demanding seminar, you'll take a close look at who you are, at what you really want out of life and at what obstacles are standing in the way of your success.

No comma is needed if all elements in a series are preceded by a conjunction, such as *and, but,* and *or,* as here:

Tom or Dick or Harry can handle the order.

While grammatically correct, however, that sentence has a singsong tone to it. A little rewriting and a comma make it flow more smoothly:

Either Tom, Dick or Harry can handle the order.

• *Between coordinating adjectives.* Coordinating adjectives can be interchanged or separated by *and* and without altering the meaning of the sentence. In general, a comma should be used to separate them, as here:

The new model has a handsome, readable display.

Note that this sentence fits the above requirement; *readable and handsome,* or *handsome and readable.* Where adjectives are not interchangeable and cannot sensibly be separated by *and,* the comma is not used, as here:

This is our new four-color model.

• *With introductory, transitional, and interpolated expressions.* Words and phrases that introduce a sentence, make a transition, or are interjected in a sentence are set off by commas:

The results, as we expected, confirm our original findings.
However, we can't afford to underwrite the project.
We can't, however, afford to underwrite the project.
We can't afford to underwrite the project, however.

Note the different shades of emphasis achieved by shifting the position of *however.*
Expressions such as *i.e., et al.,* and *e.g.* are set off by commas. The word *too* also is set off, although many writers currently choose to omit the comma if *too* falls at the end of the sentence. Either way is considered correct.

He, too, was promoted.
He was promoted, too.
He was promoted too.

• *With certain clauses and appositives.* Grammar rules call for insertion of a comma between two independent clauses—that is, clauses that could each stand alone as a separate sentence—joined by a conjunction, as in the following examples:

The packages are wrapped, and I will deliver them.
They called his name, but he had already gone.

However, some writers feel that a comma between independent clauses interrupts the flow of the sentences and is not necessary. The best rule is: If a pause is beneficial to the reader, it is best to use a comma. With short clauses, the comma may be safely dropped, as here:

The sun set and the tide came in.

Dependent clauses, which include nonrestrictive relative clauses, cannot stand alone as complete sentences. Whether they introduce a sentence or interrupt one, they should be set off by commas, as in these examples:

Because it was raining, he missed his delivery.
The band, while they were playing, remained seated.

No comma is needed if a dependent clause falls at the end of a sentence.

He missed his delivery because it was raining.
The band remained seated while they were playing.

Appositives that are nonrestrictive need comma punctuation, as in this example:

Mr. Hughes, the financial analyst, recommends selling this stock short.

With dates, use a comma with a full date but not a partial one. December 1865 requires no comma, but December 5, 1865, does. If a full date falls in the middle of a sentence, separate it with a second comma:

The treaty was signed on December 5, 1885, a month after the battle.

With numbers set off every thousand with a comma:

1,000
23,000

For clarity, it is best to use the comma even with four-digit numbers, saying 2,000 rather than 2000, for example.

- *With names, degrees, and titles.* With names, commas precede the designates Sr. and Jr., but not III or IV; for example:

Tom Smith, Sr.
Tom Smith, Jr.
Tom Smith II

Commas are also used to separate names from titles:

Jane Jones, D.V.M.
Robert Adams, Ph. D.
Richard Simpson, president, Acme Electric Co.

However, no comma is used when the title precedes the name.

President Richard Smith

- *With addresses.* Commas separate cities and towns from states, including the District of Columbia; for example:

She lives in Tulsa, Oklahoma.

Note the use of a second comma when city and state fall in the middle of a sentence:

She lives in Tulsa, Oklahoma, but wants to move to Washington, D. C., soon.

If quoting an address that includes street, city, and state, use commas this way:

Send your order to Ajax Cosmetics, 333 Park Ave., New York, NY 10017.

- *Inside quotation marks.* Commas *always* fall within quotation marks:

He said he "couldn't do it," but I don't believe him.

Before an extensive quotation use a comma:

He said, "I don't think I can do it." I don't believe him.

If the quotation is partial and follows a preposition such as *that,* omit the comma:

Shakespeare said that "reputation is an idle and most false imposition."

A full quotation would read:

Shakespeare said, "Reputation is an idle and most false imposition."

While commas are the most common separating marks, others are used for different effects and emphases. The *semicolon* is a mark of separation stronger than a comma but not as strong as a period. It can be used to separate independent, related clauses that otherwise might be two short, choppy sentences.

Choppy: I wanted the contract. Charles won it instead.
Smoother: I wanted the contract; Charles won it instead.
Choppy: The study began two weeks ago. A report is due in a month.
Smoother: The study began two weeks ago; a report is due in a month.

Semicolons are useful in separating elements in a series, particularly if the elements are varied or are themselves punctuated with commas.

Participants included Martha, my sales manager; George, my assistant; and Raji, my counterpart from abroad.

Colons commonly are used with formal salutations instead of the more casual comma. When used in text, colons bring a sentence almost to a halt and raise the reader's expectations about the material that follows. Colons can be used for drama and emphasis, as here:

His announcement was shocking: He would not seek another term.
The reason Sandra quit the project was simple: She had just grown tired of it.

Note that the material following the colon is capitalized when it is a complete sentence. Colons often are used to introduce lists and formal quotations, as here:

The contest has three categories: beginner, intermediate, and advanced.

I have six favorite flavors of ice cream: chocolate, strawberry, butterscotch, almond, maple, and cherry.

Use colons to introduce direct quotations of more than one sentence.

Nietzsche said: "Every tradition grows continually more venerable, and the more remote its origin, the more this is lost sight of. The veneration paid the tradition accumulates from generation, until it at last becomes holy and excites awe."

Use commas with short quotations.

Matthew Arnold once said, "Calm's not life's crown, though calm is well."

Parentheses are used to set off explanatory material, comments, and asides, and usually contain essential, but secondary, information. Parentheses are always used in pairs. Periods fall outside the parentheses, unless the aside is a complete sentence standing on its own; then the period falls within the parentheses.

He said (and I agree wholeheartedly) that we must pursue the project.

He said we must pursue the project. (I agree wholeheartedly.)

Parenthetical asides are interruptions to the main thought, and should be kept few and brief. If your parenthetical comment is longer than a short sentence, consider rewriting to work it in—or excising it.

If you wish to document sources of information and are not footnoting your material, enclose the source in parentheses.

Last year, cosmetics sales across the nation totaled $20 million (*Beauty News,* June 19xx, p. 66).

Dashes can also be used to set off parenthetical material that interrupts a sentence, as well as to indicate a break in thought or to provide emphasis. Dashes, which may be used singly or in pairs, are stronger than commas. They are not as formal as colons and may be used in place of them.

Here pairs of dashes set off parenthetical elements for emphasis:

He said—and I agree wholeheartedly—that we must pursue the project.
The hurricane—the first to hit this area in a decade—caught many unprepared.

Single dashes are also used to create breaks that cause readers to pause, in addition to providing emphasis, as here:

He was fired from his job—the third in a year.
I won't give him the camera—it wouldn't be fair.

If you find that you are using many dashes, reexamine your material to see if commas or a colon might not suffice and perhaps be more appropriate. In the following example, dashes are overused:

In his inaugural address, the governor said what everyone had expected—that a tax increase would be necessary to balance the budget. He also asked legislators—and the public—to support his proposal to raise income and business taxes. He said there was no strong argument not to raise the taxes—despite what opposition members of the House claim.

The paragraph reads more smoothly with some of the dashes omitted:

In his inaugural address, the governor said what everyone had expected: that a tax increase would be necessary to balance the budget. He also asked both legislators and the public to support his proposal to raise income and business taxes. He said there was no strong argument not to raise the taxes—despite what opposition members of the House claim.

Remember that dashes cause readers to make significant pauses. Use them only when you wish to call extra attention to something.

Brackets have two purposes: First, they allow a writer to explain or comment on material within original quotations, as here:

"The quality of the mass mind does not matter because he [the dictator] rules."
"Incidents and situations of 1933 do not coincide with those of last year [1980], though parallels may be drawn."

Second, brackets enclose parenthetical matter within parentheses. This use usually occurs with citations of sources. Brackets are always used in pairs.

The research findings upheld those previously published (see The Molecular Structure of Crabgrass [Erudite Publications, Boston, Mass., 1955] for a comparison of studies).

The *ellipsis*, which is three spaced periods, denotes words omitted from quotations, incomplete thoughts, and pauses. To show omission, the ellipsis can be used at the beginning, in the middle, or at the end of a quotation.

He that loves not his wife . . . broods a nest of sorrows.
According to Tolstoy, ". . . every happy family is unhappy in its own way."

When a quotation is incomplete at its end, place the ellipsis after the period of the last sentence:

Fiction is not a dream. . . .

If the last word of the quotation is followed by a comma, omit the comma. If a quotation breaks off in the middle of a sentence that ends with a question mark or exclamation point, place the ellipsis between the last word and the final punctuation mark.

"That he survived the flood is amazing . . . !"

Finally, an ellipsis can be used to indicate a pause. Generally, however, a dash is more effective for this purpose.

She heard no more footsteps behind her . . . and slowly exhaled in relief.
He said he would arrive early . . . but he came late instead.
He said he would arrive early—but he came late instead.

Question marks should always be used with direct questions, but not with indirect.

Direct: Can we make the deadline? I think we can.
Indirect: Bill wonders why we're doing this.

Exclamation points indicate intense, strong emotion, but when overused, their effect dulls. So does the reader, who becomes exhausted from overreacting to ordinary sentences, like this one:

We spent our vacation in the Bahamas! We loved it! It was hot! We ate seafood every day!

Use exclamation points sparingly.

Quotation marks are used to enclose the exact wording of someone else's writing or speech. With long quotations, it is preferable to indent the material and introduce it with a colon, rather than use quotation marks. Quotation marks are used with partial and complete quotations, but are not necessary for single words unless the word is significant or unusual. Quotation marks are used to show dialogue.

She said, "Give me the keys to the house."
He said he entered a room "filled with wonderful paintings."

When quotations continue from one paragraph to another, marks are placed at the beginning of each new paragraph but at the end of only the last paragraph:

"These new systems are designed to meet the needs of persons who are not accustomed to using video display terminals.
"Functions such as storing, retrieving, editing, and printing of documents can be performed with a single command.
"The systems will be sold at all distributor outlets throughout the country."

Quotations within quotations take single and double marks, respectively.

The lawyer said, "My client told me, 'I'm innocent.' "
"She said, 'You're crazy,' " he told us.

Periods and commas always fall within quotation marks, whether they are double or single. Other punctuation marks, such as question marks, exclamation points, colons, semicolons, and dashes, appear inside quotation marks if they are part of the quotation.

What does he mean by "instant readiness"?
The committee chairwoman stated she would "never consider such
a risky financial move"!

Do not use quotation marks if you are simply paraphrasing someone
else's words.

Hyphens are used to divide words at the ends of lines and to join related
words into compounds.

When you must hyphenate a word at the end of a line, divide it according to its syllables, which are marked in dictionaries. Never divide words
of one syllable, after single-letter syllables, or before single-letter syllables.

Use: itin-erant

Not: i-tinerant

Avoid dividing short words, such as *icy, maybe,* and *legal.*

Many words may be divided between double consonants, except when
the consonants are part of an original word with a suffix.

Use: suf-frage

But use: stuff-ing

Not: stuf-fing

Divide full dates between the day and the year.

May 15, 1975

Do not divide dates that are only months and years, or months and days,
as here:

May 1975
May 15

Whether or not to use hyphens in compound words is more troublesome, partly because they tend to be dropped from terms in common
usage. For example, most words with the prefix *multi* are hyphenated;
multimillionaire is not. Nor is *multinational.* When you are uncertain,
consult a dictionary—but make sure it is an up-to-date one, that reflects current usage. In any case, here are a few general guidelines to
follow:

A temporary adjective compound that modifies a noun is hyphenated when it falls before the noun, but not after.

He was a well-built athlete.
He was an athlete who was well built.
This is a first-rate hotel.
This hotel is first rate.
A five-pound package arrived.
A package arrived that weighed five pounds.

Some compounds are hyphenated regardless of where they are in a sentence. For example:

She was a slim, light-footed dancer.
As a dancer, she was slim and light-footed.

While the hyphen remains in *light-footed,* it has been dropped from *lighthearted.* This is where a dictionary comes in handy.
Compound modifiers with adverbs ending in -ly are not hyphenated:

It was a quickly produced play.
The company is a wholly owned subsidiary.

When two compound words sharing the same second element are used together, the second element is dropped from the first, leaving an "open-ended" hyphen, as here:

The part includes two- and seven-inch rods.
Both short- and long-term effects have been studied.

When you improvise compounds, use hyphens between all words; for example:

This is a take-it-or-leave-it offer.

The apostrophe is used in place of omitted letters and numbers, as in contractions, and in possessives. It also is optional with certain plurals.

• *Omissions.*   When letters or numbers are omitted, insert an apostrophe, as here:

don't (do not)
o'clock (of the clock)
'33 (1933)

Do not confuse *it's,* the contraction of *it is,* with *its,* the personal pronoun possessive.

It's going to rain.
The dog licked its paw.

• *Possessives.*   For singular nouns, the possessive is formed by adding an apostrophe and *s.*

Tom's notebook
the president's committee

When a singular noun ends in an *s,* two styles of possessives are acceptable:

Janis' perfume
Janis's perfume

Plural nouns require only an apostrophe at the end:

the contractors' convention
states' rights

In combined possessives, use a single apostrophe added to the last element:

Smith and Simpson's Jewelry Co.

In a series of individual possessives, use an apostrophe with each element:

Ted's, Bill's, and Bob's reports are done.

• *Plurals.*   Apostrophes are optional with certain plurals, as in the following examples:

Energy costs will continue to rise in the 1980s.
Energy costs will continue to rise in the 1980's.
Sometimes an apostrophe is needed for clarity:

Poor: The Four As announced a membership drive.

Better: The Four A's announced a membership drive.

HANDLING NUMBERS

A few simple guidelines suffice for handling numbers in text material. You should spell out the numbers zero through nine and use figures for numbers 10 and above. However, use figures for all percentages, even 1 percent. Use commas to denote every thousand, as in 1,000 and 1,000,000. You may, however, wish to spell out very large numbers, as in:

We sold one million units last year.
The deficit is nearly one trillion dollars.
The star is three billion light years away.

Do not mix figures and numbers that are spelled out in the same sentence. Use one or the other style, whichever seems more appropriate or readable.

Poor: The children's zoo featured 12 goats, 5 pigs, and three ducks.

Better: The children's zoo featured twelve goats, five pigs, and three ducks.

When numbers begin a sentence, always spell them out. Years are an exception to this rule. Numbers ending in -y should be joined by a hyphen to any other numbers following them. Do not insert commas or *and* between words that are part of the same number. (As in writing out a number on a personal check, *and* stands for the decimal point.)

Forty-four students enrolled in the course.
One hundred twenty-five students enrolled in the course. (Not "one hundred and twenty-five.")
1978 was a good year for California wines.

If a sentence begins with a large, ungainly number, rewrite it so that you can use figures instead.

Three thousand four hundred thirty-six books were delivered yesterday.
Yesterday 3,436 books were delivered.

The large number is much easier to grasp when presented in figures.

Always use figures for percentages. Fractional percentages are best presented in decimal form. In text, it is best to spell out *percent,* except in informal memos or when the text is full of percentages. It is acceptable to use the percent symbol (%) in tables and charts.

3 percent
10.8 percent

Spell out fractions that stand alone or are preceded by *a* or *an.*

one-half mile
a fourth of a gallon

When expressing fractions in figures, use a slash between numerator (the upper number of the fraction) and denominator (the lower number).

7 ¾
21 8/19

If you are using few fractions, consider converting them to decimals, when it is practical to do so. Decimals are easier to read.
    Always use figures for decimals; do not spell out the numbers.

Use: 4.5
Not: four-point-five

Avoid mixing decimals and fractions in the same sentence, except occasionally in percentages.
    Hyphenate numbers if they are combined with adjectives to modify nouns.

Hyphen needed: a 30-mile race
Not needed: The race will be 30 miles long.
Hyphen needed: a 10-inch ribbon
Not needed: a ribbon 10 inches long

CAPITALIZATION

When to capitalize confounds many a writer. When in doubt, many writers tend to err with unnecessary capitals. Here are some general guidelines to follow for using capital letters:

- *With proper names.*   Capitalize the proper names of people, places, and things. Places include major geographic areas as well as designations that are part of a proper name.

> Susan went to the West Coast to seek a job in Hollywood.
> The Department of Human Resources has issued new guidelines.
> In Paris, I visited the Louvre. Later, I traveled south to the Riviera.
> The convention will be in North Carolina.
> He organized an expedition to the North Pole.

Capitalize common nouns that are part of a proper noun, such as *street, avenue,* and *river;* but use lower case if the common nouns are plural.

> The shop is at the corner of James Street and Martin Avenue.
> The shop is at the corner of Main and Hall streets.

In general, use lower case in casual second references to proper nouns.

> The Hanson Dance Company will be at the Center for the Performing Arts. Appearing later at the center will be the Six String Ensemble.
> The Society of Flower Growers meets tomorrow. Those who wish to join the society are invited.
> The president formed the Committee to Halt Bureaucracy. Members of the committee include . . .

- *With titles.*   In general, capitalize a person's title when it appears before the name but not after it.

> Vice president Mary Jones
> Mary Jones, vice president

If a person has a long title, it is best to place it after the name. A long string of capitalized words preceding a name looks awkward.

> *Use:*   Mike Smith, assistant manager of product development
> *Not:*   Assistant Manager of Product Development Mike Smith

Exceptions to this rule are titles for heads of state, such as presidents and prime ministers; royalty; and major religious leaders. Always capitalize those titles whether they precede or follow a name. Use lower case on second reference when a title refers to the person.

Treasurer William Penny released the quarterly earnings statement yesterday. The treasurer said . . .

It is acceptable to abbreviate certain titles before complete proper names, including Rev., Hon., Dr., Sen., Rep., Gov., and most military titles. Do not abbreviate vice president, president, assistant, or secretary.

Gov. Big Spender
Sen. Pork Barrel

However, spell out titles if they are used only with last names or if they are enclosed within direct quotations.

Governor Spender
Senator Barrel
"I told Reverend Harry Smith . . ."
"I told Reverend Smith . . ."

Do not capitalize job descriptions.

Ruth Barton, computer programmer
Jack Grieve, contractor

Capitalize the major words in the titles of books, publications, articles, stories, plays, movies, and works of art. Conjunctions, prepositions, and articles (*a, an,* and *the)* customarily are lower case unless they are the first word of the title.

The Old Man and the Sea
Of Mice and Men
Beethoven's *Ninth Symphony*

ITALICS

That brings up the last item: italics. Italics are used for titles, foreign words, and emphasis. In typewritten or handwritten copy, indicate italics by underlining words. Use italics for book titles and names of publications, but not for titles of magazine articles (use quotation marks for those). Italicize the titles of plays, movies, and works of art.

The notes in this section can, of course, only give you general guidelines to follow in your writing. If you do a good deal of writing in your job (and most managers do), you will be wise to supply yourself with some basic reference books—at least a current dictionary, a modern thesaurus, and a basic guide to usage—so you can check out troublesome problems when they arise. That way you can produce the kind of finished writing that not only communicates your ideas but also speaks on your behalf to all your readers.

CHECKLIST OF COMMONLY MISUSED AND MISSPELLED WORDS

accept/except: *Accept* means *to receive willingly* or *to agree to. Except* means *to leave out; but.*

accommodate: Not accomodate.

accumulate: Not accummulate.

adverse/averse: *Adverse* means *hostile* or *unfavorable,* while *averse* means *unwilling* or *opposed to.* People are usually averse and conditions are adverse.

affect/effect: *Affect* is a verb that means *to alter* or *to have influence on. Effect* is a noun meaning *the result of an action or condition.*

Inflation affects us . . .
The effect of inflation is . . .

aggravate: *Aggravate* means *to make worse.* It is often used when *irritate* is meant. Colloquially, *aggravate* is often used as a synonym for *irritate* or *burdensome,* but it is best to avoid this in business writing.

all right/alright: *All right* is the preferable form; *alright* is considered colloquial.

allude/elude: *Allude* is *to refer indirectly* to something, while *elude* means *to avoid or evade.*

She alluded to her profits.
He eluded detection.

amid/amidst: Both are accepted to mean *in the middle of,* though *amid* is generally preferred for business writing.

among/between: In general, use *among* when referring to more than two persons or objects, and *between* when referring to two.

Among the three of us . . .
Between the two of us . . .

amount/number: *Amount* generally refers to mass quantity, while *number* denotes quantities that can be counted individually.

A large amount of money was stolen . . .
A large number of customers gathered . . .

as/like: *Like* has been gaining acceptance as a conjunction, but *as* is still considered more correct and preferable.

Poor: It is concise, like a memo should be.
Better: It is concise, as a memo should be.

awhile/a while: *Awhile* means *a short time; a while* is *a period of time that needs further defining,* as in "for a long while."

barbiturate: Not barbituate.

bellwether: Not bellweather.

biannual/biennial: A *biannual* event happens twice a year; a *biennial* event every two years.

bimonthly/semimonthly: *Bimonthly* is every two months; *semimonthly* twice a month.

beside/besides: *Beside* means *near* or *at the side of; besides* means *in addition to.*

She sat beside me.
Besides Bill, Ray came to the meeting.

between/among: See *among.*

capital/capitol: *Capital* generally refers to money or principal, or a seat of government. A *capitol* is the place where a legislature convenes. The nation's Capitol building is a proper noun.

We have enough capital to buy them out.
The capitol is getting a new wing.

censor/censure: A *censor* is someone who reviews material for objectionable matter. *Censure,* as either a noun or verb, means *blame* or *condemnation.*

The censor killed the script.
He was censured for the failure.

compare to/with: Both are correct, although there is a fine difference
   between them. *Compared to* means *likened to; compared with* is used
   when people or objects are noted for similarities and differences.

complementary/complimentary: *Complimentary* remarks are *in praise
   of,* and *complimentary* refreshments are *free. Complementary,* however, means *making complete.*

He complimented her on the fine report.
His field experience complemented her planning ability.

compose/comprise: *Compose* means *to make up the whole. Comprise*
   means *to consist of* or *to include;* although it is increasingly being
   used as a synonym for *compose,* that usage is best avoided.

Poor: That division is comprised of six departments.
Poor: Six departments comprise that division.
Better: That division is composed of six departments.
Better: Six departments compose that division.
Better: That department comprises six departments.

connote/denote: *Connote* means *to suggest* or *convey,* as in meaning;
   denote means *to signify* or *designate.*

continual/continuous: *Continual* activities happen frequently or periodically; *continuous* activities go on without break or end.

criterion/criteria: These are singular and plural forms, respectively.
   Match verbs accordingly.

datum/data: Singular and plural forms, respectively; *datum,* however,
   is seldom used. *Data* has come to be acceptable with either a singular
   or plural verb, but is most frequently used with a single verb.

The data is available.

or

The data are available.

denote/connote: See *connote.*
diminution: Not dim*u*nition.

disinterested/uninterested: A *disinterested* person is *impartial* or *neutral;* an *uninterested* person is *apathetic* or *bored.*

She is a disinterested party in the dispute.
He was uninterested in the topic.

effect/affect: See *affect.*

e.g./i.e.: These two terms are often confused. *E.g.* stands for *exempli gratia,* meaning *for example. I.e.* is an abbreviation for *id est,* meaning *that is.*

The items on the agenda, e.g., the report, . . .
The subject of the meeting, i.e., the report, . . .

elude/allude: See *allude.*

elusive/illusive: *Elusive* means *evasive* or *difficult to grasp mentally; illusive* means *unreal* or *illusory.*

The concept is elusive.
The theory is illusive.

embarrass: Not embarass.

emigrate/immigrate: One *emigrates* by leaving a country or region to settle in another; one *immigrates* by arriving in a new country or region to settle.

He emigrated from Austria and immigrated to the United States.

eminent/imminent: *Eminent* means *distinguished; imminent* means *about to happen.*

She is an eminent scientist.
An eruption is imminent.

enquire/inquire: Both mean *to ask about,* and both are acceptable. *Inquire* is the more common usage.

ensure/insure: Both mean *to guarantee* or *protect. Insure* is generally used only with insurance matters.

I am ensured of making the sales club.
The package is insured against damage.

except/accept: See *accept.*

farther/further: The terms, both meaning *more distant,* are frequently interchangeable. *Farther* generally is used when referring to *space,* while *further* is used with *degree, addition,* and *time.* Also, *further* means *to advance.*

The car traveled farther away.
My goals seem to be getting further away.
The promotion will further my goals.

fewer/less: *Fewer* is used with persons and things, while *less* is used with quantities.

Fewer people came than I expected.
Less money is available for prizes this year.

finalize: This term, which means *to finish* or *bring to conclusion,* is popular with jargon-users and bureaucrats. Try to avoid it.

Poor: We've finalized our plans.
Better: We've finished our plans.

fitful: *Fitful* means *restless,* as in "a fitful night." It is often erroneously used to mean *fit,* as in "physically fit."

flaunt/flout: *Flaunt* means *to show off,* while *flout* means *to scorn.* One flaunts success but flouts the law.

forcible: Not forceable or forcable.

foreword: See *forward.*

forsake: Not foresake.

forward/foreword: When referring to direction, the term to use is *forward.* A *foreword* is a preface or introduction to a document.

headquarters: *Headquarters* is a noun, and is best not used as a verb.

Poor: The company is headquartered in Maine.
Better: The company's headquarters are in Maine.
Better: The company is based in Maine.

hemorrhage: Not hemorrage or hemorhage.

historic/historical: An *historic* event is important or significant; an *historical* event is in the past.

hopefully: *Hopefully* means *it is hoped that.* It is overused by writers and is often vague in terms of who is hoping.

> *Poor:*   Hopefully he'll find a solution.
> *Better:* We hope that he'll find a solution.

i.e.: See *e.g.*

illusive/elusive: See *elusive.*

immigrate/emigrate: See *emigrate.*

imminent/eminent: See *eminent.*

implausible: Not implausable.

imply/infer: *Imply* means *to hint; infer* means *to conclude from information already known. Infer* is loosely used as *imply,* but if you mean *imply,* use it.

She implied that he was ready for promotion.
He inferred the answer.

importantly: *Importantly,* which is an adverb meaning *in an important manner,* is often wrongly used where the adjective *important* would be more appropriate. *Importantly* is a favorite of jargon-users who strive for emphasis or to dress up a sentence.

> *Poor:*   Importantly, we must solve this problem.
> *Better:* It is important that we solve this problem.

incredible/incredulous: An *incredible* event is *improbable.* Someone who is *incredulous* is *disbelieving.*

indiscriminately: Not indiscriminantly.

indispensable: Not indispensible.

innocuous: Not inocuous.

inquire/enquire: See *enquire.*

in regards to: Avoid using *in regards to.* In this context, *regard* means *in relation to,* but *regards* means *best wishes.* It is correct to say *in regard to* or *regarding.*

> *Poor:*   In regards to your application.
> *Better:* Regarding your application.
> *Better:* In regard to your application.

insure/ensure: See *ensure*.

in terms of: This phrase adds little to a sentence; it is better to avoid it.

>   *Poor:*   In terms of a conservative, he'd make a good candidate.
>   *Better:*   He'd make a good conservative candidate.

irregardless/regardless: *Irregardless* is a nonword—one of its two negatives is redundant. *Regardless* is the correct term.

its/it's: *Its* is a possessive term; *it's* is a contraction of *it is.*

>   The committee met its deadline.
>   It's a sure thing.
>   It is a sure thing.

-ize: This is a suffix jargon-lovers love to hang onto nouns, thus transforming them into verbs. There are legitimate words that end in *-ize,* such as *formalize* and *maximize,* but generally a shorter word will be sharper and clearer. Beware of creating nonwords, such as *dollarize* and *solutionize* by adding *-ize* to nouns indiscriminately.

judgment: Not judgement.

knowledgeable: Not knowledgable.

lay/lie: Relating to position, *lay* means *to cause to recline* or *to place; lie* means *to recline.*

>   I think I'll lie down.
>   I think I'll lay the book on the table.

legible: Not ledgible.

less/fewer: See *fewer*.

liaison: Not liason.

likable: Not likeable.

like/as: See *as*.

literally: *Literally* means *really* or *in the strictest sense.* It is effective when used sparingly for emphasis, but too often writers use it unnecessarily. You generally can drop it without altering your meaning.

>   *Poor:*   We received literally dozens of proposals.
>   *Better:*   We received dozens of proposals.

livable: Not liveable.

-ly: It is easy—too easy—to create an adverb out of any adjective simply by adding *-ly.* Resist the temptation. It may be passable in pulp fiction, but not in business prose.

>   *Poor:* Firstly, we have to consider . . .
>   *Better:* First, we have to consider . . .

manageable: Not managable.

medium/media: *Media,* the plural form, has become the accepted term for singular or plural when referring to print and electronic journalists. Both singular and plural verbs are used with *media,* although the plural is considered more correct.

>   *Poor:* The media has hounded him.
>   *Better:* The media have hounded him.
>   *Poor:* The print media is worried about cable TV.
>   *Better:* The print medium is worried about cable TV.

minuscule: Not miniscule.

nuclear: Not nucular.

number/amount: See *amount.*

occasion: Not occassion.

occupy: Not occuppy.

orient/orientate: Both terms mean *to adjust to a situation; orientate* also often means *to turn toward the east,* as a church. *Orient* is preferable.

parallel: Not paralell.

pejorative: Not perjorative.

permissible: Not permissable.

personally: *Personally,* which means *directly by oneself,* is often misused for emphasis, much in the same way *literally* is misused. In most cases, it is unnecessary.

>   *Poor:* I personally recommend . . .
>   *Better:* I recommend . . .

phenomenon/phenomena: Singular and plural forms, which take singular and plural verbs, respectively.

phony: Not phoney.

possess: Not posess.

presently: *Presently* means both *soon* and *now.* To avoid ambiguity, select another term that is more precise.

principal/principle: A *principal* is *someone or something first in importance;* a *principle* is a *standard, law,* or *truth.*

She is a principal in the company.
He stands by his principles.

prioritize: Like *finalize, prioritize* is jargon, meaning *the assigning of an order of importance.* It is most often found in business and government communications, and is best avoided.

privilege: Not privil*i*ge or privil*ed*ge.

questionnaire: Not question*n*aire.

rebut/refute: *To rebut* is *to oppose* or *to argue to the contrary; to refute* is *to prove wrong.*

Will you rebut the argument?
Have you enough evidence to refute the charge?

regardless/irregardless: See *irregardless.*

resistible: Not resis*ta*ble.

salable: Not sal*e*able.

seize: Not *sieze.*

semimonthly: See *bimonthly.*

set/sit: *Set* means *to place* or *to arrange; sit* means *to occupy* or *to rest upon.*

I'll sit here.
I'll set the books here.

sizable: Not siz*e*able.

solution: *Solution* is a noun meaning *an answer to;* it is not correct used as a verb.

Poor: We must solution this soon.
Better: We must find a solution to this soon.

supersede: Not super*c*ede.

that/which: Both are pronouns for objects and animals without names. Generally, *which* is used in nonrestrictive relative clauses, which are set off with commas. *That* is used in restrictive relative clauses, which are not punctuated with commas.

He bought a minicomputer, which was portable.
He bought the minicomputer that was portable.

threshold: Not thres*h*hold.

tortuous/torturous: *Tortuous* means *winding* or *twisting,* sometimes *devious; torturous* means *severely painful,* generally relating to torture.

The halls in the new headquarters are tortuous.
The questioning of the board was torturous.

totally: *Totally* is an adverb used to overkill. It is usually redundant when coupled with adjectives, as in *totally unnecessary, totally false,* and *totally destroyed.* Avoid it.

uninterested: See *disinterested.*

utilize: *Utilize* means *to make productive use of;* its meaning is more limited than *use,* which means *to put into action or service.* Synonyms for *utilize* are *employ* and *appropriate.*

weird: Not w*i*erd.

which: See *that.*

who/whom: Both are pronouns for people and animals with names. *Whom* is used as the object of a verb or preposition—as in "for whom this is intended"—but is dropping from common usage.

who's/whose: *Who's* is a contraction of *who is; whose* is possessive.

Who is coming?
Who's coming?
Whose office is this?

-wise: This is another suffix jargon-lovers are fond of attaching to nouns. Resist the urge.

Poor: Profit-wise, this is a good move for us . . .
Better: Profits can make this a good move . . .

Symbol	Meaning	Example
ℰ/	Delete	~~managers~~ℰ/ manager𝒔/
∧	Insert at this point	the∧report *(unedited above ∧)*
⌗	Begin new paragraph	The lease expired. ⌗ It does . . .
ℂ or No ⌗	Do not begin new paragraph	today.⟩ ~~Don't hesitate.~~ℯ/ ⌐Sign up now.
		today. Don't hesitate. No ⌗ Sign up now.
∿	Transpose	wa∿nt ⟨report⟩ annual⟩
stet and ----	Let it stand as was	Please bring ~~with you~~ℯ/ *(stet above, dashes under)*
⌗	Insert space	all⌗sessions
⌒ or ◡	Close up space	non⌒combustible l◡ess
✓	Space evenly	the ✓ annual ✓report
⊙	Insert period	The plan is on target⊙ ~~and~~ℯ/ ~~we expect~~. ⊙. ℯ/
⌄	Insert comma	February⌄ June and July
⊙	Insert colon	The list includes⊙four volunteers, two staff . . .
⌄;	Insert semicolon	after the meeting⌄ we will ;
⌄⌄	Insert quotation marks	❝The reason the plan is . . .
⌄ʾ	Insert apostrophe	David⌄s report
[	Move to the left	[If any of this
]	Move to the right	List of Symbols] List]of Symbols

Figure 1. Proofreading and Editing Marks

Symbol	Meaning	Example
][	Center	] Chapter One [
≡	Make upper case	president Smith (with ≡ under p)
/	Make lower case	Ɍecycling Ᵽroject
⋎³	Insert superior letter or figure	100^{3}
⌄₂	Insert inferior letter or figure	$CH_{2}O$
═══	Straighten lines	$M_{a}^{n}ag_{e}^{m}e^{n}{}^{t}p^{o}licy\ is$
‖	Align copy vertically	‖Fiscal Year Ending
ital or ────	Set in italic type	*Daily News* ital Daily News
bf or ∿∿∿	Set in boldface type	make this **stand out** bf make this **stand out**
rom	Set in Roman type	daily news rom
?	Doublecheck point queried	capacitance technology ?
⬭→	Move copy as shown	today. Don't hesitate. Sign up now, without delay.

Figure 1. (*Continued*)

464

Energy Conservation at Widget Works

Since the Arab oil embargo of 1973, energy and its
availability remains an important issue. ~~These days~~ at
constantly   e
Widget Works, energy specialists ~~are~~ investigating energy
                    of which   innovative
alternatives, some are innovative. One alternative is

solar power.
            beat the increasing   of
~~When out of necessity~~ to ~~avoid sky-high~~ prices ~~for~~
fuel, ~~the company has turned to solar energy~~ Widget Works
built
~~has~~ one of the country's largest solar systems private
          and
~~and~~ collectors are mounted on the roof of the
          and face   In five years,
main building ~~facing~~ south with a 35 degree tilt. The
solar system ~~in operation for five years~~ has ~~provided a~~
saved the company
~~cost avoidance of~~ $20 million.
                                     s
Widget works energy specialist also are ~~having some~~
            considering
~~talk about the feasibility of using~~ windmills as a source
                a decision on them may be years away.
of power, but ~~its still uncertain~~
                              realized
Energy savings also have been ~~made possible~~ with more
efficient boilers that shut off during the night, saving
                              addition,
30,000 gallons of oil a year. In ~~parallel with this,~~
lighting levels were reduced and thermostats on air
conditioners are adjusted seasonally.
                    comes
"Energy conservation ~~derives~~ from energy consciousness,"
says Walter Widget, company president. The success of our
energy program depends ~~largely~~ on how much each employee
    educated about
is ~~sensitized to~~ the values of energy."

Figure 2. Example of How to Use Proofreading and Editing Marks

PHONETIC ALPHABET

A—Alpha	N—November
B—Beta	O—Oscar
C—Charlie	P—Page
D—Delta	Q—Quebec
E—Echo	R—Romeo
F—Foxtrot	S—Sierra
G—Golf	T—Tango
H—Hotel	U—Uniform
I—India	V—Victor
J—Juliet	W—Whiskey
K—Kilo	X—X-ray
L—Lima	Y—Yankee
M—Mike	Z—Zulu

PART VI
SOURCES OF INFORMATION

Sales professionals reach out for several different kinds of information, including hard and very specific prospect and company information, wider insights into trends within their own industries, and more general information, interpretation, insight, and guidance as to main trends in business and society. That is why they find so many different kinds of information sources useful, read so much, and continually attempt to expand relevant available sources and refine their abilities to tap those sources.

Working sales professionals seeking information are usually attempting to find current information. That will often include recent history, but will seldom include the kind of research information desired by, for example, someone working in the field of business history. Most sources of meaningful information are therefore found in forms that make it easy to update bodies of existing material or to supply bodies of new material—forms such as newspapers, newsletters, magazines, looseleaf reports, annuals, serials, and computerized databases. Some materials are in hardcover book form, such as dictionaries, handbooks, and encyclopedias, but those, too, are forms capable of being updated in new editions.

We should distinguish here between two quite different kinds of information needs. One is the specific answer to a specific question. When a sales professional needs to know who are the logical prospects for a new line of products, he or she reaches for the appropriate national, state, or local industrial directories, identifies the right companies, and then proceeds to identify the right individual prospects within those companies, often also using a wide range of "people" directories, such as Standard and Poor's and a variety of "who's who" books. If an identified prospect must be researched further, the same tools are turned to, and the process is the same.

This is usually done in a public or business library; the sources of information in these areas are usually too large and expensive to warrant individual purchase.

The other kind of need is a general need, shared by all professionals, for ongoing hard information and insight. An excellent sales professional stays informed as to the multiple contexts within which he or she performs tasks and pursues a career. And that means a bookcase full of both basic works and periodicals of several kinds, as well as a lifelong commitment to keeping abreast of world, national, industry, company, and selling trends and events. There can be no lifelong commitment to professional and personal development without a parallel commitment to sources of information and insight.

The sources of information discussed and listed in this section should meet both of these kinds of information needs.

Lifelong access to information and insight starts with your own book-shelf and sources of day-to-day information, and the key to it all is habit. There is no mechanical substitute for the habitual turn to a dictionary, almanac, encyclopedia, catalogue, or looseleaf service to get a timely answer to a current question. And although refresher courses, briefing meetings, and the like may be useful means of keeping up to date—when they do not waste too much valuable time for the benefits derived— nothing is as valuable as the habit of reading relevant material every day of every year. That is the best way to gather, ingest, and distill an ever-growing body of information and insight into that complex, erratically functioning, yet seemingly infinitely capable little chemical computer we all carry with us every day of our lives—the human brain.

Yet there are tens of thousands of sources of business information and insight published in English throughout the world every year, and some thousands of them may be in some way relevant to your working life. No single human being can possibly keep up with even a significant fraction of the information that began exploding around us after World War II and continues to explode at an accelerating pace as the century draws nearer its close. What can be done, however, is to identify a small number of basic works that should be available and used on a day-to-day basis, to suggest certain other works that can be enormous time-savers, and to provide a substantial group of key reference sources. All of which we will do now, starting with a suggested basic bookshelf.

We suggest that you should have and habitually use the following books and subscriptions. In some instances, we will suggest specific publications; in others, we will suggest kinds of publications, for the specifics will depend upon your individual circumstances.

To begin, a good general desk dictionary, one containing a considerable body of language, including many commonly used modern words, and attempting to provide as many modern usages as possible, without a great deal of attention as to which usages are "permissible." In the business world, great concern over matters of "correct" usage is inappropriate and sometimes even offensive to those with whom we work, who are concerned with communicating clearly and precisely, rather than with the requirements of pedants attempting to freeze our fast-growing language into a dreary, static set of fixed forms.

Such a dictionary should be easy to handle. One such good all-purpose dictionary is *The American Heritage Dictionary of the English Language,* published jointly by American Heritage and Houghton-Mifflin. Whatever dictionary you buy, get the thumb-indexed edition, which generally has somewhat larger type than the student edition; it costs a few dollars more, but in the long run will save your eyes and help save your equanimity. You will also probably find it useful to carry a paperback dictionary on the road.

But such a dictionary is not enough to meet your business needs. You should also have a good, concise, clearly written general business dictionary. There are several such, one of which is our own, *The VNR Dictionary of Business and Finance,* published by Van Nostrand Reinhold and Company, written by David M. Brownstone, Irene M. Franck, and Gorton Carruth. But authors should be wary of recommending their own works, unless they are the only works of their kind, so let us also recommend Jerry M. Rosenberg's *Dictionary of Business and Management,* published by John Wiley and Sons.

Do not hesitate to reject a dictionary—or any other reference work, for that matter—if you pick it up, read into it a little, and find that you cannot make head or tail of it. Normally, that is in no way your fault, but rather the fault of those who wrote and edited it badly. The widespread notion that business and technical material must, by its very nature, be written opaquely is nonsensical; it makes all the sense in the world to trust your own insight in these matters. Do not let yourself be cowed into acceptance of turgid, unclear prose as some sort of standard; if you do, you will reach for that unacceptable kind of standard in your own writing.

In addition to a good, up-to-date general dictionary and a clear, concise business dictionary, you may need one or more highly specialized dictionaries, to fit your current work. For example, someone selling in the computer industry will need a computer dictionary. Each area of specialization has its own special sublanguage, which needs to be referred to and worked with. Some of it is just the jargon of the moment but, jargon or enduring language, it is the mode of communication in your field; it is indispensable to know and use it well.

You will also find it useful to buy a paperbound almanac every year, to answer general questions of current fact. We have no specific recommendation in this area, but do suggest that you rotate your purchases, buying a different one of the three or more basic almanacs each year, thereby getting the benefit of marginally superior coverage by one over another, and in no way sacrificing the basic current facts supplied by all major almanacs equally.

Those who travel a good deal, such as national account representatives, will find two sources of great value. The first is a periodically updated hotel directory; the other a subscription to the official airline guide. Both together make it possible to handle travel arrangements with a minimum of inconvenience. Business travelers often find it necessary to make last-minute changes, the kinds of changes that travel agencies cannot easily handle, but that you can readily handle directly with the right tools.

For ongoing current general business information *The Wall Street Journal* is an indispensable tool. It is quite strong on most domestic matters, and fairly strong on international matters, but whatever its strengths and weaknesses it stands alone in acceptance as the national daily business newspaper. Therefore, much of the material it carries is taken into account daily by American businesspeople, and current familiarity with its content is useful for talking with customers, prospects, and colleagues. In addition, you will probably routinely purchase a major local or regional newspaper, which will devote some of its space to local and regional business news, as well as supplying somewhat more expanded context for national and international news than does *The Wall Street Journal.*

Many sales professionals read such general, business, and financial periodicals as *Business Week, Fortune, Forbes, Newsweek,* and *Time,* in pursuit of analysis of the fast-moving events of the time. If you find any such publications useful—and you should examine several and take short-term subscriptions to several over the years—by all means subscribe to them; but we think that these are quite optional purchases.

Beyond these general books and periodicals are a whole world of special interest publications appearing in every publishing form known, including books, magazines, newsletters, looseleaf services, catalogues, and computerized databases. You will need to keep up with those that relate to the field in which you are selling, at least as much as you need any of the basic books and periodicals discussed previously. Most fields have a few periodicals that "everybody reads," and that fairly inexpensively provide a substantial body of information on people, companies, trends, and technical matters. They are worth subscribing to and following carefully. If you have any doubt as to which ones to follow on entering a new field, your sales management will know; so will your customers. If you need help beyond that, you will find Brownstone and Carruth's *Where to Find Business Information* (Second Edition, Wiley, 1982) in most libraries.

Whatever information sources we are following, we all find ourselves with the need to read, and read—and read. In addition to the sources we have described here as basic, there are masses of computer-generated internal materials, letters, and memos. There are also articles and books on selling—and sales professionals must continually seek to upgrade skills and find new insights into the selling process. The flood of words on paper seems never to end, but rather to multiply as the years go by and our interests expand.

For most of us, the remedy scarcely lies in a speedreading course; cramming in more reading only leads to a kind of indigestion, as we become secretly and quite completely convinced that we are experiencing creeping personal obsolescence, and that it will be all right only if nobody else learns how little we are able to keep up with it all. Many of us go through our working lives convinced that we should be able to read and carefully ingest far more than we are currently able to handle, and envying those who seem to be able to handle far more reading material than we can.

We should dispel that illusion. In most instances the trick is not to be able to read more and more, but to read less and less—only considerably more effectively. And the keys to that lie in a wide view of information sources and insights; skillful and consistent selection of essentials; reflexive application of a few techniques you have probably known since school days, having to do with such matters as scanning, note-taking, and marking relevant passages; and the putting in of enough of the right kind of time, beyond the field selling day.

But no matter how much time you put in, it will all come to naught without selection. The person who takes pride in being an omnivore and "reading everything," only exhibits arrogant pride and very bad management of information and other written materials. Careful selection means taking a newspaper like *The Wall Street Journal* or *The Washington Post* and skimming it for matters of interest, both contextual and specific. Between the front page and the general index to each issue, you will be able to get a broad overview and also to identify items directly relating to current business and personal interests. It means taking magazines like *Time, Newsweek,* and *Barron's,* as well as special-interest industry periodicals and doing essentially the same thing, usually going in through the table of contents. The same procedure should hold for all the periodicals you see. Many will help you to do this, by providing some kind of highlighting device worked into the format of the periodical. For example, a magazine like *Fortune* will supply a summary of the main points in each article, so that you will quickly be able to see whether or not you want to read further.

Careful selection also means selection while reading. An article of interest is best scanned for a little distance first; a reading of the first paragraph or two and a scan to get the sense of what immediately follows will usually tell you whether or not you want to read all or most of the article. If you decide to really read it, then it is appropriate to return to where you started scanning, for a closer reading. Information-packed material can be read for meaning, but the information read will not be retained as memorized fact. Nor should it; key facts are best underlined, taken separately as notes as we did in school, and then retrieved as necessary from filed articles.

Materials generated in-house and through correspondence must often be handled a little less rationally, for such materials must often be read, whether or not they are of any value. Responses must be made, based on such materials; here scanning, note-taking, and highlighting serve us all well. "Reading" such materials should involve much scanning and internal selection of portions to be carefully studied, if you want to avoid burial in a sea of documents.

Now follows a group of information sources, drawn from the second edition of Brownstone and Carruth's *Where to Find Business Information*. The information sources cited have been drawn from the 5,000 entries in the book itself, and seem to us to be those sources most generally useful for working sales professionals. Please note that, due to inflation, the prices of most of these information sources have undoubtedly risen since the data was gathered. Many will be consulted in libraries; we include prices here only to supply some sense of the range of expenditure that will be required if you consider buying any of the sources listed. Clearly, we regard the book itself as a necessary tool; this group of sources merely begins to illustrate the scope of the matter available.

Abbreviations Dictionary

American Elsevier, 52 Vanderbilt Ave, New York, NY 10017. Telephone (212) 867-9040.

Dictionary of shortened and abbreviated usage, including contractions, nicknames, signs, symbols, and abbreviations used in business and industry. Price $35.00.

ABI/INFORM

Data Courier, Inc, 620 S 5 St, Louisville, KY 40202. Telephone (502) 582-4111. Telex 204235.

Online service. Provides access to business information. Contains abstracts of articles on accounting, economics, information science, marketing, and other related subjects. Price available on request.

ABS

American Building Supplies, 1760 Peachtree Rd, NW, Atlanta, GA 30357. Telephone (404) 874-4462.

Monthly magazine. Reports on home improvement and building materials markets. Focuses on merchandising trends. Price $35.00 per year.

Accent

Chilton Co, Chilton Way, Radnor, PA 19089. Telephone (215) 687-8200.

Monthly magazine. Reports on developments in fashion jewelry business. Price $12.00.

Acronyms and Initialisms Dictionary

Gale Research Co, Book Tower, Detroit, MI 48226. Telephone (313) 961-2242.

Book. Covers shortened and abbreviated usage, including equipment, processes, and names of organizations. Price $82.00.

Ad Day/USA

Executive Communications, Inc, 400 E 54 St, New York, NY 10022. Telephone (212) 421-3713.

Weekly newsletter. Gives terse rundown of advertising and marketing news. Price $55.00 per year.

Adhesives Age

Communication Channels, Inc, 6285 Barfield Rd, Atlanta, GA 30328. Telephone (404) 256-9800.

Monthly magazine. Covers the application, technology, and sale of industrial adhesives. Emphasizes industrial consumer problems and solutions. Price $21.00 per year.

Administrative Digest

Southam Communications Ltd, 1450 Don Mills Rd, Don Mills, Ont, Canada M38 2X7. Telephone (416) 445-6641. Telex 06 966612.

Monthly magazine. Provides information on business products and equipment. Price $35.00 per year.

Advanced Retail Marketing

Downtown Research and Development Center, 270 Madison Ave, Suite 1505, New York, NY 10016. Telephone (212) 889-5666.

Semimonthly newsletter. Discusses marketing strategies, consumer promotion techniques, consumer behavior trends, and advertising techniques for the retailing industry. Price $185.00 per year.

Advertiser's Annual

Kelly's Directories Ltd, Windsor Court, E Grinstead House, E Grinstead, W Sussex, England RH19 1XB. Telephone (44) (01) 0342 26972.

Annual book. Contains material on British advertising agencies and clients, marketing, and direct mail. Also covers newspapers, television and radio stations, and public relations companies. Price £30.00 per copy.

Advertising Age

Crain Communications, Inc, 740 Rush St, Chicago, IL 60611. Telephone (312) 649-5219.

Weekly newspaper. Contains news of advertising campaigns, account changes, personnel shifts, and new products. Discusses pertinent legislation and regulation and includes market research information. Price $40.00 per year.

Advertising and Marketing Intelligence (AMI)

New York Times Information Service, Inc, Mt Pleasant Office Pk, 1719A 10, Parsippany, NJ 07054. Telephone (201) 530-5850. Telex 136390.

Database. Provides information on advertising and marketing fields. Identifies new products, consumer trends, and research. Price $165.00 per hour.

Advertising Techniques

Advertising Trade Publications, Inc, 10 E 39 St, New York, NY 10016. Telephone (212) 889-6500.

Monthly magazine. Reports on professionals' handling of specific advertising campaigns. Focuses on success stories in visual advertising. Price $7.50 per year.

Aerospace Daily

Ziff-Davis Publishing Co, 1156 15 St NW, Washington, DC 20005. Telephone (202) 293-3400.

Daily newsletter. Covers trade news and trends in the aerospace industry. Price $610.00 per year.

Africa Guide

World of Information, 21 Gold St, Saffron Walden, Essex, England, CB10 1EJ. Telephone Saffron Walden 21150 (STD 0799 21150). Telex England 817197 a/b Jaxpress G.

Annual book. Provides analysis of commercial, economic, political, and social developments in Africa, with separate chapters about each country. Price $43.00. ISBN 0-904439-19-4.

Ag-Marketer

Columbia Publishing & Design, PO Box 1467, Yakima, WA 98907. Telephone (509) 248-2452.

Monthly magazine offering marketing information for diversified farm operators in the Northwest. Price $8.00 per year.

Agricultural Outlook

US Dept of Agriculture. ESS Publications, Room 0054-S, Washington, DC 20250. Order from Superintendent of Documents, US Government Printing Office, Washington, DC 20402. Telephone (202) 783-3238.

Report issued 11 times per year. Discusses food and agriculture outlook. Covers commodities, marketing, world agriculture and trade, farm income, and transportation. Tables. Price $19.00 per year domestic, $23.50 per year foreign.

Agricultural Price Report

US Dept of Agriculture, Crop Reporting Board, Economics and Statistics Service (ESS), Room 0005 S Bldg, Washington, DC 20250. Telephone (202) 447-4021.

Monthly report. Indicates prices received by farmers for principal crops and livestock products. Free.

Agricultural Situation

US Dept of Agriculture. Order from ESCS Information Staff, Room 5855-S, USDA, Washington, DC 20250. Telephone (202) 655-4000.

Monthly report. Features articles on trends and research in agricultural field. Includes statistical summaries and economic and marketing developments affecting farmers. Price $5.00 per year.

Agri Marketing

Agri Business Publications, Inc, 5520 Touhy Ave, Suite G, Skokie, IL 60076. Telephone (312) 676-4060.

Monthly magazine and annual directory. Discusses agricultural market techniques, new products for farmers, and farm market research. Is aimed at sellers to farm markets. Directory lists top 150 agricultural companies, farm publications accepting advertising, radio stations with farm programming, and agricultural associations. Price $20.00 per year.

Airconditioning & Refrigeration Business

Penton/IPC, 614 Superior Ave W, Cleveland, OH 44113. Telephone (216) 696-0300.

Monthly magazine. Reports on air conditioning and refrigeration industry. Discusses manufacturing, marketing, installation, and service. Price $24.00.

Airport Services Management

Lakewood Publications, Inc, 731 Hennepin Ave, Minneapolis, MN 55403. Telephone (612) 333-0471.

Monthly magazine. Presents business information for the ground support market for commercial, government, and military aviation. Price $18.00 per year.

Alabama: State Industrial Directory

Manufacturers' News, Inc, 3 E Huron St, Chicago, IL 60611. Telephone (312) 337-1084.

Annual book. Identifies 5,000 Alabama industrial companies. Price $55.00.

America Buys

Information Access Corporation, 404 Sixth Ave, Menlo Park, CA 94025. Telephone (800) 227-8431.

Annual book. Indexes information on over 40,000 products, including evaluations, brand name references, consumer buying information, and brand comparisons. Price $94.00.

American and European Market Research Reports

Frost & Sullivan, Inc, 106 Fulton St, New York, NY 10038. Telephone (212) 233-1080. Telex 235986.

Reports. Analyze market research trends. Offer forecasts for American and European markets for a segment of one industry. Price $600.00 to $1,000.00 each.

American Book Trade Directory

R R Bowker Co, 1180 Ave of the Americas, New York, NY 10036. Order from R R Bowker Co, PO Box 1807, Ann Arbor, MI 48106. Telephone (212) 764-5100.

Annual directory. Gives information about book outlets in the US and Canada. Provides statistics and lists. Price $54.95. ISBN 0-8352-0928-8. ISSN 0065-795X. 1252-1.

American Druggist

Hearst Corp, 224 W 57 St, New York, NY 10019. Telephone (212) 262-4167.

Monthly magazine. Covers trade news and trends in the drug industry. Price $12.00 per year. ISSN 0002-824X.

American Export Register

Thomas Publishing Co, One Penn Plz, New York, NY 10001. Telephone (212) 695-0500.

Annual directory. Lists over 37,000 manufacturers who export products worldwide. Provides 3,033 product classifications and alpha-betical listings in English, French, German, Spanish, and Japanese. Price $60.00.

American Import/Export Bulletin

North American Publishing Co, 401 N Broad St, Philadelphia, PA 19108. Telephone (215) 574-9600.

Monthly report. Discusses US import-export news. Includes information on product sales, marketing, finance, and distribution. Price $15.00 per year.

American Machinist

McGraw-Hill Book Co, Hightstown-Princeton Rd, Hightstown, NJ 08520. Telephone (609) 448-1700. Telex 843449.

Directory with periodic updates. Provides inventory of metalworking manufacturing equipment. Price $30.00.

American Machinist (Magazine)

McGraw-Hill Publications Co, 1221 Ave of the Americas, New York, NY 10020. Telephone (212) 997-1221. Telex TWX 7105814879 WUI 62555.

Monthly magazine. Focuses on metalworking manufacturing industries and engineering. Includes material on plastics technology. Price $30.00 per year US, $35.00 Canada, $60.00 elsewhere.

American Metal Market

Fairchild Publications, Inc, 7 E 12 St, New York, NY 10003. Telephone (212) 741-4130.

Daily newspaper. Covers news of the metals industry, including the latest prices for metals and scrap. Price $215.00 per year.

American Register of Exporters & Importers

American Register, 90 W Broadway, New York, NY 10007. Telephone (212) 227-4030.

Annual directory. Supplies information on US exporters and importers, chambers of commerce, foreign embassies, and foreign trade associations in the US. Contains product indexes in English, Spanish, French, and German. Price $40.00 per copy.

American Salesman

National Research Bureau, Inc, 424 N 3 St, Burlington, IA 52601. Telephone (319) 752-5415.

Monthly magazine. Supplies information about and of interest to American salespersons. Price $19.00 per year. ISSN 0003-0902.

American Statistics Index

Congressional Information Service, Inc, 4520 EW Highway, Suite 800, Washington, DC 20014. Telephone (301) 654-1550.

Service composed of monthly, quarterly, and annual indexes and abstracts. Covers statistical data published by US government departments, agencies, and offices. Price $1,165.00 per year.

American Trucking Trends

American Trucking Assn, Inc, 1616 P St NW, Washington, DC 20036. Telephone (202) 797-5351.

Annual report. Covers trucking industry developments. Notes truck registrations, tonnage and mileage, freight products, and financial data. Tables and charts. Free.

Amusement Business

Billboard Publications, Inc, PO Box 24970, Nashville, TN 37202. Telephone (615) 748-8120.

Weekly newspaper. Reports on mass entertainment business, including facility operations and management, events, spending, promotions, and routes of touring attractions, carnivals, and circuses. Price $2.00 per copy; $35.00 per year. ISSN 08668.

AN, AND & MS Standards

National Standards Assn, Inc, 5161 River Rd, Washington, DC 20016. Telephone (301) 951-1310. Telex 89-8452.

Twenty-volume set. Provides standards for automotive, marine, and aircraft components. Price $590.00 per year.

Anbar Management Publications Marketing & Distribution Abstracts

Anbar Publications Ltd, PO Box 23, Wembley, England HA9 8DJ. Telephone (44) (01) 902 4489. Telex 935779.

Publication issued eight times per year and separate annual index. Contains abstracts of articles from marketing and distribution periodicals, mostly British and American. Supplies copies of articles. Price £67.00 per year. ISSN 0305-0661.

Annual Abstract of Statistics

Her Majesty's Stationery Office, PO Box 569, London, England SE1 9NH. Telephone (44) (01) 928 1321.

Annual service. Provides statistics on British economic subjects, such as wages, consumer expenditure, industrial production, energy consumption, and imports and exports over a 10-year period. Price $11.90 per year.

Annual Book of ASTM Standards

American Society for Testing and Materials, 1916 Race St, Philadelphia, PA 19103. Telephone (215) 299-5400.

Annual book in 48 volumes. Contains 6,400 standards for materials, products, systems, and services. Price $1,750.00 for complete set, prices for individual volumes available on request.

APC Tablet

Alltech Publishing Co, 212 Cooper Ctr, N Park Dr & Browning Rd, Pennsauken, NJ 08109. Telephone (609) 662-2122.

Monthly newsletter. Reports on data processing industry developments. Includes profiles of compa-nies and information on new products and applications. Price $30.00 per year.

Apparel South

Communication Channels, Inc, 6285 Barfield Rd, Atlanta, GA 30328. Telephone (404) 256-9800.

Monthly magazine. Reports on retail apparel news from major cities throughout the South and from the three major apparel marts in Miami, Atlanta, and Charlotte. Includes Southern fashion trends, merchandising displays, and New York fashions. Price $16.00 per year.

Apparel Trades Book

Dun & Bradstreet, Box 3224, Church St Station, New York, NY 10008. Telephone (212) 285-7346.

Book. Provides credit information on 110,000 retail and wholesale clothing outlets. Price on request. Available to Dun & Bradstreet subscribers only.

Appliance Magazine

Dana Chase Publications, Inc, York St at Park Ave, Elmhurst, IL 60126. Telephone (312) 834-5280.

Monthly magazine. Contains current statistics and other information on the appliance industry. Price $24.00 per year, $37.00 per year foreign.

Appliance Manufacturer

Cahners Publishing Co, Inc, 221 Columbus Ave, Boston, MA 02116. Telephone (617) 536-7780.

Monthly magazine. Covers trends and technology affecting the appliance industry. Price $20.00 per year.

Asian Wall Street Journal

Dow Jones & Co, Inc, 22 Cortlandt St, New York, NY 10007. Order from Dow Jones & Co, Inc, PO Box 300, Princeton, NJ 08540. Telephone (212) 285-5000.

Daily newspaper. Discusses business and financial news affecting Asian business and trade. Includes US and foreign stock prices and a review of international money and commodities markets. Price $206.00 per year.

Associated Equipment Distributors (AED) Edition of Construction Equipment Buyers Guide

Associated Equipment Distributors, 615 W 22 St, Oak Brook, IL 60521. Telephone (312) 654-0650.

Annual book. Offers a guide to US and Canadian distributors of construction equipment and the manufacturers they represent. Gives manufacturer and product listings. Price $20.00 per copy.

Association of Executive Recruiting Consultants: Directory

R R Bowker Co, 1180 Ave of the Americas, New York, NY 10036. Order from R R Bowker Co, PO Box 1807, Ann Arbor, MI 48106. Telephone (212) 764-5100.

Directory. Lists 58 member firms of Association of Executive Recruit-ing Consultants. Gives key information and specialization areas, and brief profiles of senior management and professional recruiting personnel of each firm. Price $38.-50. ISBN 0-8352-1256-4. ISSN 0195-6981.

Audiovisual Market Place

R R Bowker Co, 1180 Ave of the Americas, New York, NY 10036. Order from R R Bowker Co, PO Box 1807, Ann Arbor, MI 48106. Telephone (212) 764-5100.

Annual directory. Lists producers, suppliers, and services for audiovisual materials. Covers in a reference section such topics as literature, associations, funding sources, and government agencies. Price $29.95 paperbound. ISBN 0-8352-1201-7. ISSN 0067-0553.

Auerbach Applications Software Reports

Auerbach Publishers, Inc, 6560 N Park Dr, Pennsauken, NJ 08109. Telephone (609) 662-2070. Telex 831 464.

Book, plus monthly reports. Evaluates applications software products. Provides pricing, operational characteristics, and hardware requirements. Price $325.00.

Auerbach Buyers' Guide to Business Minicomputer Systems

Auerbach Publishers, Inc, 6560 N Park Dr, Pennsauken, NJ 08109. Telephone (609) 662-2070. Telex 831 464.

Semiannual book. Analyzes performance capabilities and specifications of major US business minicomputer systems. Describes several classes of systems, and includes directory of suppliers. Price $59.00.

Auerbach Buyers' Guide to Word Processing

Auerbach Publishers, Inc, 6560 N Park Dr, Pennsauken, NJ 08109. Telephone (609) 662-2070. Telex 831 464.

Semiannual book. Reports on the word processing industry. Analyzes different systems and applications. Specification charts. Price $59.00.

Australian Directory of Exports

Peter Isaacson Publications, 46–49 Porter St, Prahran, Vic 3181, Australia. Telephone (61) (03) 51 8431. Telex 30880.

Annual book. Surveys Australia's major industries. Lists products for export, exporters, and services available to overseas companies. Price $28.50.

Australian Key Business Directory

Dun & Bradstreet, Box 3224, Church St Station, New York, NY 10008. Telephone (212) 285-7346.

Annual book. Provides a directory to several thousand of the largest public and private businesses in Australia whose net worth is Australian $100,000. Price on request. Available to Dun & Bradstreet subscribers only.

Australian Market Guide

Dun & Bradstreet, Box 3224, Church St Station, New York, NY 10008. Telephone (212) 285-7346.

Biannual book. Contains over 130,-000 listings of Australian manufacturers, wholesalers, retailers, and agents. Includes credit appraisal. Price on request. Available to Dun & Bradstreet subscribers only.

Australian Trading News

Australian Dept of Trade & Resources, PO Box 69, Commerce Court Postal Station, Toronto, Ont, Canada M5L 1B9. Telephone (416) 367-0783. Telex 06-219762.

Quarterly magazine. Reports on Australian industrial developments and products available for export. Free.

Automotive Fleet

Bobit Publishing Co, 2500 Artesia Blvd, Redondo Beach, CA 90278. Telephone (213) 376-8788.

Monthly magazine. Discusses issues affecting passenger car fleets and the light truck industry. Price $15.00 per year.

Automotive Industries

Chilton Co, Chilton Way, Radnor, PA 19089. Telephone (215) 687-8200.

Monthly publication. Carries information on new automotive manufactured products, design, developments, and production techniques. Price $25.00 per year.

Automotive Marketing

Chilton Co, Chilton Way, Radnor, PA 19089. Telephone (215) 687-8200.

Monthly magazine. Covers buying and retailing of automotive parts. Price $24.00 per year.

Ayer Directory of Publications

Ayer Press, 1 Bala Ave, Bala Cynwyd, PA 19004. Telephone (215) 664-6205.

Annual book. Lists US, US territory, and Canadian newspapers, magazines, and trade publications. Includes names of editor, publisher and national advertising manager, address, periodicity, circulation, and advertising rates. Price $66.00.

Bacon's International Publicity Checker

Bacon's Publishing Co, 14 E Jackson Blvd, Chicago, IL 60604. Telephone (312) 922-8419.

Annual looseleaf book. Provides publicity guide to western European markets. Enables subscriber to reach over 7,500 business, trade, and industrial publications, plus over 600 newspapers in 15 countries. Price $120.00.

Bacon's Publicity Checker

Bacon's Publishing Co, 14 E Jackson Blvd, Chicago, IL 60604. Telephone (312) 922-8419.

Two annual looseleaf books, with quarterly revisions. List over 4,000 business, trade, industrial, professional, farm, and consumer maga-

zines that use publicity material. Includes list of 1,815 daily and 7,429 weekly newspapers. Price $110.00.

Bankers Almanac and Year Book

Thomas Skinner Directories, Windsor Court, E Grinstead House, W Sussex, England RH16 1XE. Order from IPC Business Press Ltd New York, 205 E 42 St, New York, NY 10017. Telephone (212) 867-2080.

Annual directory. Lists and supplies essential information on banks throughout the world. Includes a special section on British banks. Price $120.00 per year. ISBN 611 00647 2.

Bank Marketing

Bank Marketing Assn, 309 W Washington St, Chicago, IL 60606. Telephone (312) 782-1442.

Monthly magazine for bank executives. Covers the marketing of banking services. Includes sales promotion, bank planning, and public relations. Price free to members, $48.00 to nonmembers in US, $60.00 foreign.

Bank Marketing Newsletter

American Bankers Assn, 1120 Connecticut Ave NW, Washington, DC 20036. Telephone (202) 467-4123.

Monthly newsletter. Acquaints user with regulatory and legislative issues relevant to the banking field. Includes coverage of development in competing industries. Price $22.50 per year.

Bank Marketing Report

Warren, Gorham & Lamont, Inc, 210 S St, Boston, MA 02111. Telephone (617) 423-2020.

Monthly report. Focuses on bank marketing techniques. Includes information on advertising, promotions, and innovative banking services. Price $56.00 per year.

Bank of Canada Review

Bank of Canada, Distribution Section, Ottawa, Ont, Canada K1A OG9.

Monthly review. Features graphs and tables on Canadian banking, economic, labor force, foreign trade, and monetary topics. English and French texts. Price $10.00 per year. CN ISSN 0045-1460.

Bank of Hawaii Monthly Review

Bank of Hawaii, Economics Div, PO Box 2900, Honolulu, HI 96846. Telephone (808) 537-8269.

Monthly newsletter. Pertains to business activity in Hawaii. Free.

Bank of Nova Scotia Monthly Review

Bank of Nova Scotia, 44 King St, W, Toronto, Ont, Canada MSH 1H1.

Monthly newsletter. Covers economic and business trends mainly in Canada. English and French editions. Free. ISSN 0005-5328.

Barclays Review

Barclays Bank, Group Economics Depart., 54 Lombard St, London, England EC3P 3AH. Telephone (44) (01) 283 8989.

Quarterly magazine. Expresses the Barclays Bank's views on economic and financial developments in the United Kingdom and other parts of the world. Free.

Barron's

Dow Jones & Co, Inc, 22 Cortlandt St, New York, NY 10007. Telephone (212) 285-5000, 5243.

Weekly newspaper. Provides financial and investment news. Includes information on commodities and international trading. Contains tables on New York Stock Exchange transactions. Price $32.00 per year.

Best's Agents Guide to Life Insurance Companies

A M Best Co, Ambest Rd, Oldwick, NJ 08858. Telephone (201) 439-2200.

Book. Profiles over 1,300 life insurance companies including policyholder ratings. Contains operating and financial facts and lists states and territories where each company is licensed. Price $20.00.

Bio-Medical Insight

International Bio-Medical Information Service, Inc, PO Box 756, Miami, FL 33156. Telephone (305) 665-4856.

Bimonthly newsletter. Covers over 20 annual biomedical trade shows in the US and overseas. Reports on business environment, markets, and technology. Price $320.00 per year. ISSN 0090-161X.

Bio-Medical Scoreboard

International Bio-Medical Information Service, Inc, PO Box 756, Miami, FL 33156. Telephone (305) 665-4856.

Monthly newsletter, plus annual index. Provides financial data on over 450 US-based medical and bi-omedical firms. Price $160.00 per year. ISSN 0095-0971.

Black Enterprise

Earl Graves Publishing Co, Inc, 295 Madison Ave, New York, NY 10017. Telephone (212) 889-8220.

Monthly magazine geared to Black people in business and profession-als. Provides information on money, management, and market-ing. Price $10.00 per year.

Blue Book of Canadian Business

Canadian Newspaper Services In-ternational Ltd, 55 Eglinton Ave E, Suite 604, Dept A, Toronto, Ont, Canada M4P 1G8. Telephone (416) 487-4725.

Annual hardcover book. Contains basic information on over 2,000 major companies doing business in Canada, including company pro-files, rankings, and business index. Price $59.50 per issue.

Boardroom Reports

Boardroom Reports, Inc, 500 5th Ave, New York, NY 10110. Tele-phone (212) 354-0005.

Semimonthly magazine for execu-tives. Discusses new ideas about such subjects as advertising, invest-ments, law, management, person-nel, selling, and taxes. Price $44.00 per year.

Book Marketing Handbook: Tips and Techniques for the Sale and Promotion of Scientific, Technical, Professional, and Scholarly Books and Journals

R R Bowker Co, 1180 Ave of the Americas, New York, NY 10036. Order from R R Bowker Co, PO Box 1807, Ann Arbor, MI 48106. Telephone (212) 764-5100.

Book. Discusses book marketing techniques, including direct mail, space advertising, telephone mar-keting, publicity, outlets, and spe-cialized marketing. Includes profes-sional journals. Appendixes, glossary, index. Price $45.00. ISBN 0-8352-1286-6.

Book of the States

Council of State Governments, Iron Works Pike, PO Box 11910, Lexington, KY 40578. Telephone (606) 252-2291.

Book. Serves as reference for infor-mation on state government. Tables and statistics. Price $28.00 per copy.

Books in Print

R R Bowker Co, 1180 Ave of the Americas, New York, NY 10036. Order from R R Bowker Co, PO Box 1807, Ann Arbor, MI 48106. Telephone (212) 764-5100.

Annual four-volume book. Indexes about 550,000 books by author and title. Includes price, publisher, and other information. Price $110.00. ISBN 0-8352-1300-5. ISSN 0068-0214.

Brad Directories & Annuals

Maclean-Hunter Ltd, 30 Old Burlington St, London, England W1X 2AE. Telephone (44) (01) 434-2233.

Annual publication. Covers all reference books and directories published annually in Great Britain for all consumer, trade, and technical publications. Price available on request.

Bradford's Directory of Marketing Research Agencies & Management Consultants in the US & the World

Bradford's Directory, PO Box 276, Dept E, Fairfax, VA 22030. Telephone (703) 560-7484.

Irregularly revised book. Gives alphabetical listings by state and city of over 750 marketing research and management firms, with information about services available. Provides international listings by countries. Contains an index of agencies, key personnel, and classified service-guide. Price $25.50 per copy.

British Business

Her Majesty's Stationery Office, PO Box 569, London, England SE1 9NH. Telephone (44) (01) 928-1321.

Weekly magazine. Contains statistics on British wholesale prices, retail sales, industrial production, and other economic indicators. Includes commentary from the Departments of Industry, Trade and Prices, and Consumer Protection. Price £18.72 per year.

British Columbia Industry and Small Business News

Ministry of Industry and Small Business Development, Parliament Buildings, Victoria, BC, Canada V8V 1X4. Telephone (604) 387-6701.

Newsletter. Reports on business activity and government programs in British Columbia. Free.

British Columbia Manufacturers' Directory

Ministry of Industry and Small Business Development, Vic, BC, Canada V8V 1X4. Telephone (604) 387-6701.

Annual directory. Lists manufacturers in British Columbia. Indicates products both alphabetically and by product classification. Free.

British Exports

Kompass Publishers Ltd, Windsor Court, E Grinstead House, E Grinstead, W Sussex, England RH19 1XD. Telephone 0342 26972.

Annual book. Furnishes a registry to 18,000 British products available for export. Notes British exporter and corresponding overseas agency. Price £25.00 per copy.

British Rate & Data

Standard Rate & Data Service, Inc, 5201 Old Orchard Rd, Skokie, IL 60077. Telephone (312) 470-3100.

Monthly book. Lists advertising rates and information for British television and radio stations, newspapers, and periodicals. Price $310.00 per year.

Building Supply News

Cahners Publishing Co, Inc, 221 Columbus Ave, Boston, MA 02116. Telephone (617) 536-7780.

Monthly magazine. Provides marketing and management information for retail and wholesale building supply establishments. Price $35.00 per year.

Business America

US Dept of Commerce, 14th St between Constitution Ave and E St NW, Washington, DC 20230. Order from Superintendent of Documents, US Government Printing Office, Washington, DC 20402. Telephone (202) 783-3238.

Report. Covers US and international business developments. Evaluates economic conditions and various US industries. Price $41.00 per year.

Business Asia

Business International Corp, 1 Dag Hammarskjold Plz, New York, NY 10017. Telephone (212) 750-6300.

Weekly newsletter. Covers trade opportunities and business developments in Asia and the Pacific. Price $450.00 per year.

Business Books and Serials in Print

R R Bowker Co, 1180 Ave of the Americas, New York, NY 10036. Order from R R Bowker Co, PO Box 1807, Ann Arbor, MI 48106. Telephone (212) 764-5100.

Book. Gives finding, ordering, and bibliographic data for more than 31,500 titles, which are indexed by author, title, and business subjects. Includes a directory of publishers. Price $37.50. ISBN 0-8352-0965-2. ISSN 0000-0396.

Business China

Business International Corp, 1 Dag Hammarskjold Plz, New York, NY 10017. Telephone (212) 750-6300.

Biweekly report. Discusses opportunities for establishing or expanding markets in the People's Republic of China, Vietnam, North Korea, Cambodia, Laos, Mongolia, and the Soviet Far East. Price $265.00 per year.

Business Conditions Bulletin

Arthur Young & Co, 277 Park Ave, New York, NY 10017. Telephone (212) 922-4724.

Quarterly report. Presents analyses of current and forecasted economic and business conditions in Canada. Free.

Business Conditions Digest

US Dept of Commerce, Bureau of Economic Analysis, Washington, DC 20230. Order from Budget Office, Bureau of Economic Analysis, Washington, DC 20230. Telephone (202) 523-0961.

Information service. Furnishes data on national income and product accounts, employment, production, trade, fixed capital investment, prices, profits, money credit, and foreign trade. Price $100.00.

Business Eastern Europe

Business International Corp, 1 Dag Hammarskjold Plz, New York, NY 10017. Telephone (212) 750-6300.

Weekly report. Discusses new developments on and sales and licensing opportunities in the Union of Soviet Socialist Republics, Bulgaria, East Germany, Czechoslovakia, Hungary, Poland, Rumania, and Yugoslavia. Price $560.00 per year.

Business Europe

Business International Corp, 1 Dag Hammarskjold Plz, New York, NY 10017. Telephone (212) 750-6300.

Weekly eight-page report. Discusses the opportunities and dangers of doing business with, within, and from Europe, emphasizing marketing, finance, taxation and management, and the European Economic Community. Price $690.00 per year.

Business in Brief

Chase Manhattan Bank, Economics Group, 1 Chase Manhattan Plz, New York, NY 10015. Telephone (212) 552-3704.

Bimonthly newsletter. Reports on business and economic developments in the US and abroad. Free.

Business Index

Information Access Corp, 404 6th Ave, Menlo Park, CA 94025. Telephone (800) 227-8431.

Monthly microfilm service. Includes abstracts and index of all articles, reviews, news, and related business material from 325 business periodicals, and over 1,100 general and legal periodicals. Catalogs business books and reports from the Library of Congress MARC (Machine Readable Cataloguing) database. Price $1860.00 per year.

Business Information Reports

Dun & Bradstreet, Box 3224, Church St Station, New York, NY 10008. Telephone (212) 285-7346.

Information service. Reports on businesses' credit ratings. Gives immediate access to rating changes. Price on request. Available to Dun & Bradstreet subscribers only.

Business Information Sources

Lorna M Daniells, University of California Press, 2223 Fulton St,

Berkeley, CA 94720. Telephone (415) 642-4247.

Book. Provides listing of business indexes, directories, publications, and statistical sources. Makes recommendations for a basic bookshelf. Price $14.95. ISBN 0-520-024946-1.

Business International

Business International Corp, 1 Dag Hammarskjold Plz, New York, NY 10017. Telephone (212) 750-6300.

Weekly eight-page report. Discusses worldwide business problems and opportunities, emphasizing international management problems, laws and regulations, and business forecasts. Price $435.00 per year.

Business International Washington (BIW)

Business International Corp, 1 Dag Hammarskjold Plaza, New York, NY 10017. Telephone (212) 750-6300.

Fortnightly report. Provides information for executives concerned about the impact of US Government on international corporate operations. Covers trends in taxation, trade restrictions, export financing, restrictive business practices, and incoming-outgoing investment. Price $195.00 per year.

Business Latin America

Business International Corp, 1 Dag Hammarskjold Plz, New York, NY 10017. Telephone (212) 750-6300.

Weekly analysis of regional developments throughout Latin America. Price $435.00 per year.

Businessman & The Law

Man and Manager, Inc, 799 Broadway, New York, NY 10003. Telephone (212) 677-0640.

Semimonthly report. Presents legal cases and their effect on day-to-day business decisions. Annual index. Price $48.00 per year.

Businessman's Guide to Brazil

Guides to Multinational Business, Inc, Harvard Sq, Box 92, Cambridge, MA 02138. Telephone (617) 868-2288.

Annual book. Provides information about Brazil. Notes government, finance, transportation, and shipping data. Is designed to aid the foreign businessperson. Price $20.00.

Businessman's Guide to the Arab World

Guides to Multinational Business, Inc, Harvard Sq, Box 92, Cambridge, MA 02138. Telephone (617) 868-2288.

Annual book. Provides information about Arab countries for foreign businesspersons. Includes government, shipping, finance, and insurance data. Price $40.00.

Business Periodicals Index

H W Wilson Co, 950 University Ave, Bronx, NY 10452. Telephone (212) 588-8400.

Monthly publication (except August) with quarterly cumulations and a bound annual. Provides an index to 272 business publications. Covers economics, finance, investments, management and personnel administration, transportation, and related subjects. Price available on request.

Business Publications Rates & Data

Standard Rate & Data Service, Inc, 5201 Old Orchard Rd, Skokie, IL 60077. Telephone (312) 470-3100.

Monthly book. Indicates advertising rates and information for 3600 business, trade, and technical publications. Price $125.00 per year.

Business Report

Manufacturers Hanover Trust Co, Corporate Communications Dept, 350 Park Ave, New York, NY 10022. Telephone (212) 350-3300. Telex 232337, 420966, 62814, 82615.

Quarterly report. Analyzes US business conditions. Statistics. Free.

Business Review and Economic News from Israel

Israel Discount Bank of New York, 511 5th Ave, New York, NY 10017. Telephone (212) 551-8500. Telex 420250.

Quarterly booklet. Reviews Israeli economic, industrial, and stock market developments. Notes Israel Discount Bank news. Free.

Business Studies

Touche Ross International, 1633 Broadway, New York, NY 10019. Telephone (212) 489-1600.

Series of 20 books. Each describes investment factors, business practices, accounting and auditing, taxation, and other factors affecting business in a country. Also included in this series is *Tax & Trade Profiles,* similar in content but each book covers 10–15 countries. Price available on request.

Business Travel Costs Worldwide

Guides to Multinational Business, Inc, Harvard Sq, Box 92, Cambridge, MA 02138. Telephone (617) 868-2288.

Book. Offers guide to business travel and entertainment expenses for over 70 countries. Includes data on hotel accommodations, restaurants, transportation, entertainment, secretarial, and translation services. Price $125.00.

Business Week

McGraw-Hill Publications Co, 1221 Ave of the Americas, New York, NY 10020. Telephone (212) 997-1221. Telex TWX 7105814879 WUI 62555.

Weekly magazine. Reports on US and international business and economic topics. Is aimed at business management personnel. Includes industrial, European, international, and five US regional editions. Price $34.95 per year.

Buying Offices and Accounts

Salesman's Guide, Inc, 1140 Broadway, New York, NY 10001. Telephone (212) 684-2985.

Book. Lists paid and commission resident buying offices serving 11,000 accounts connected with sporting goods and men's, women's, and children's wear. Price $35.00.

California International Trade Register

Times Mirror Press, 1115 S Boyle Ave, Los Angeles, CA 90023. Telephone (213) 265-6767.

Biennial book. Lists California businesses involved in foreign trade. Includes import and export sections. Price $59.95.

California Manufacturers Register

Times Mirror Press, 1115 S Boyle Ave, Los Angeles, CA 90023. Telephone (213) 265-6767.

Annual book. Lists 19,000 manufacturers in California. Notes branch plants, products, and number of employees. Price $85.00.

California Services Register

Times Mirror Press, 1115 S Boyle Ave, Los Angeles, CA 90023. Telephone (213) 265-6767.

Annual book. Lists 12,000 service companies in California. Covers construction, insurance, real estate, finance, and other industries. Price $60.00.

California: State Industrial Directory

Manufacturers' News, Inc, 3 E Huron St, Chicago, IL 60611. Telephone (312) 337-1084.

Annual book. Identifies 14,000 industrial firms in California. Notes executives and number of employees. Price $70.00.

Canada Commerce

Dept of Industry, Trade and Commerce, 235 Queen St., Ottawa, Ont, Canada K1A OH5. Telephone (613) 995-7489.

Monthly magazine. Reports on Canadian trade. Free.

Canada: Scott's Atlantic Industrial Directory

Manufacturers' News, Inc, 3 E Huron St, Chicago, IL 60611. Telephone (312) 337-1084.

Biennial book. Identifies industrial firms in Canada's Atlantic provinces (New Brunswick, Nova Scotia, Prince Edward Island, Newfoundland). Price $57.75.

Canada: Scott's Ontario Industrial Directory

Manufacturers' News, Inc, 3 E Huron St, Chicago, IL 60611. Telephone (312) 337-1084.

Biennial book. Contains information on 14,500 industrial companies in Ontario. Price $98.50.

Canada: Scott's Quebec Industrial Directory

Manufacturers' News, Inc, 3 E Huron St, Chicago, IL 60611. Telephone (312) 337-1084.

Biennial book. Lists 11,000 industrial firms in Quebec. Includes information about executives. Price $98.50.

Canada: Scott's Trade Directory, Metro Toronto

Manufacturers' News, Inc, 3 E Huron St, Chicago, IL 60611. Telephone (312) 337-1084.

Book published every 18 months. Lists manufacturing and non-manufacturing companies in the metropolitan Toronto area. Price $90.00.

Canada: Scott's Trade Directory, Toronto Vicinity

Manufacturers' News, Inc, 3 E Huron St, Chicago, IL 60611. Telephone (312) 337-1084.

Book published every 18 months. Lists businesses and manufacturing companies in 11 cities in the vicinity of Toronto. Price $60.00.

Canada: Scott's Western Canada Industrial Directory

Manufacturers' News, Inc, 3 E Huron St, Chicago, IL 60611. Telephone (312) 337-1084.

Biennial book. Lists industrial firms in western Canada (Manitoba, Saskatchewan, Alberta, and British Columbia). Price $98.50.

Canadian Book of Corporate Management

Dun & Bradstreet, Box 3224, Church St Station, New York, NY 10008. Telephone (212) 285-7346.

Directory. Lists names, titles, and functions of key officers and managers in Canada's 6,000 leading companies. Price available on request.

Canadian Key Business Directory

Dun & Bradstreet, Box 3224, Church St Station, New York, NY 10008. Order from Dun & Bradstreet of Canada, Marketing Services Div, Suite 1107, 415 Yonge St, Toronto, Ont, Canada M5B 2E7. Telephone (212) 285-7346.

Directory. Provides marketing guide to Canada's major companies. Gives name and title of each company's key executives, annual sales volume, and primary and secondary lines of business. Price $125.00.

Canadian Trade Index

Canadian Manufacturers' Association, 1 Yonge St, Toronto, Ont, Canada M5E 1J9. Telephone (416) 363-7261.

Annual book. Index lists more than 13,000 Canadian manufacturing companies alphabetically, geographically, by products manufactured, and by trademarks and/or brand names. Services section. Price $63.00 per year.

Caribbean Business News

Caribook Ltd, 1255 Yonge St, Toronto, Ont, Canada M4W 1Z3. Telephone (416) 925-1086.

Monthly newspaper covers business news of 30 Caribbean countries. Includes government activity, real estate news, analysis of economic trends and reports on industry, finance, trade, shipping, and others. Price $17.50 per year. ISSN 0045-5792.

Caribbean Year Book

Caribook Ltd, 1255 Yonge St, Toronto, Ont, Canada M4W 1Z3. Telephone (416) 925-1086.

Annual book covering all Caribbean and West Indies countries. Includes business directories, history, geography, government, population, trade and industry statistics, directory of exporters, and shipping. Price $30.00. ISSN 0083-8233.

Carpet & Rug Industry

Household & Personal Products Industry, Box 555, 26 Lake St, Ramsey, NJ 07446. Telephone (201) 825-2552.

Monthly magazine. Reports on carpet and rug industry developments. Notes design and color trends, new equipment, and industry meetings. Price $18.00 per year.

Catalog Showroom Business

Gralla Publications, 1515 Broadway, New York, NY 10036. Telephone (212) 869-1300.

Publication. Provides news of developments in catalog showroom field. Price available on request.

Central Atlantic States: Manufacturers Directory

Manufacturers' News, Inc, 3 E Huron St, Chicago, IL 60611. Telephone (312) 337-1084.

Biennial book. Covers manufacturers in Maryland, Delaware, Virginia, West Virginia, North Carolina, and South Carolina. Price $50.00.

Chain Merchandise Magazine

Chain Merchandiser, 65 Crocker Ave, Piedmont, CA 94611. Telephone (415) 547-4545.

Bimonthly periodical. Covers merchandising and sales for chain retail and direct sales markets and their suppliers. Price $3.00 per year.

Chain Store Age, Executive Edition

Lebhar-Friedman Publications, Inc, 425 Park Ave, New York, NY 10022. Telephone (212) 371-9400.

Monthly report. Reports on retail operations and capital expenditures for specialty, drug, discount, department, home center, shopping center, and supermarket stores. Price available on request.

Chain Store Age, General Merchandise Edition

Lebhar-Friedman Publications, Inc, 425 Park Ave, New York, NY 10022. Telephone (212) 371-9400.

Monthly report. Discusses merchandising and operations of department stores and chain stores. Price $7.00 per year.

Chain Store Age, Supermarkets Edition

Lebhar-Friedman Publications, Inc, 425 Park Ave, New York, NY 10022. Telephone (212) 371-9400.

Monthly report. Provides coverage of trade news and trends in the supermarket industry. Price available on request.

Chemical Marketing Reporter

Schnell Publishing Co, 100 Church St, New York, NY 10007. Telephone (212) 732-9820.

Weekly newspaper. Contains industry news and lists 3,000 current prices of chemicals and associated materials. Price $45.00 per year.

Chemical Week

McGraw-Hill Publications Co, 1221 Ave of the Americas, New York, NY 10020. Telephone (212) 997-1221. Telex TWX 7105814879 WUI 62555.

Weekly magazine. Pertains to chemical process management. Includes data on technical and nontechnical developments, environmental issues, and financing trends. Price $26.00 per year.

Chicago: Geographic Edition

Manufacturers' News, Inc, 3 E Huron St, Chicago, IL 60611. Telephone (312) 337-1084.

Biennial directory. Contains information on 12,000 Chicago firms and 50,000 executives. Includes maps. Price $49.95.

China Letter

Asia Letter Ltd, PO Box 54149, Los Angeles, CA 90054. Telephone (213) 322-4222.

Monthly newsletter. Covers economic, political, trade, and social developments and trends in the People's Republic of China. Provides background, commentary, and current major business deals. Price $175.00 per year.

College Placement Annual

College Placement Council, Inc, PO Box 2263, Bethlehem, PA 18001. Telephone (215) 868-1421.

Annual occupational directory containing career information about approximately 1,300 employers. 512 pp. Price $5.00 per copy.

College Recruiting Report

Abbott, Langer & Assoc, PO Box 275, Park Forest, IL 60466. Telephone (312) 756-3990.

Annual report. Provides information on starting salaries of college graduates in engineering, scientific and technical, and nontechnical fields. Price $75.00 per copy.

Colorado: Manufacturers Directory

Manufacturers' News, Inc, 3 E Huron St, Chicago, IL 60611. Telephone (312) 337-1084.

Biennial book. Lists 3,500 Colorado manufacturers. Notes executives and number of employees. Price $38.00.

Commerce Business Daily

US Dept of Commerce, 14th St between Constitution Ave and E St NW, Washington, DC 20230. Order from Superintendent of Documents, US Government Printing Office, Washington, DC 20402. Telephone (202) 783-3238.

Daily newspaper. Lists US government procurement invitations, contract awards, subcontracting leads, sales of surplus property, and foreign business opportunities. Price $105.00 per year.

Commercial Bulletin

Curtis Guild & Co Publishers, Inc, 88 Broad St, Boston, MA 02110. Telephone (617) 357-9450.

Weekly newspaper. Covers wool, lumber, building materials, energy, and recycling trades. Price $16.00 per year.

Commercial Directory for Puerto Rico and the Virgin Islands

Dun & Bradstreet, Box 3224, Church St Station, New York, NY 10008. Telephone (212) 285-7346.

Directory. Publishes information on 10,000 retailers and 2,000 wholesalers in Puerto Rico and Virgin Islands. Prices on request. Available to Dun & Bradstreet subscribers only.

Community Publication Rates and Data

Standard Rate & Data Service, Inc, 5201 Old Orchard Rd, Skokie, IL 60077. Telephone (312) 470-3100.

Semiannual book. Reports on advertising rates and related information for weekly newspapers and shopping guides in metropolitan and other areas. Price $18.00 per year.

Compensation Review

American Management Assns, 135 W 50th St, New York, NY 10020. Telephone (212) 586-8100.

Quarterly report. Provides information on developments in compensation. Price $24.75 per year.

Compmark Data Services

Standard & Poor's Corp, 25 Broadway, New York, NY 10004. Telephone (212) 248-2525.

Information service in variety of formats. Provides facts on more than 37,000 US and international corporations. Also covers 405,000 corporate executives, with 72,000 biographies. Price available on request.

Compustat

Standard & Poor's Compustat Services, Inc, 7400 S Alton Ct, Englewood, CO 80112. Telephone (303) 771-6510; (800) 525-8640.

Annual service provides computerized library of financial information on approximately 6500 companies. Includes industrial, bank, utility, and special files. Price available on request.

Computerworld

CW Communications, Inc, 375 Cochituate Rd, Box 880, Framingham, MA 01701. Telephone (617) 879-0700.

Weekly newspaper. Covers EDP/MIS business industry, including hardware products, software systems, data communications, and industrial trends. Price $36.00.

Connecticut-Rhode Island: Directory of Manufacturers

Manufacturers' News, Inc, 3 E Huron St, Chicago, IL 60611. Telephone (312) 337-1084.

Annual book. Identifies manufacturing firms in Connecticut and Rhode Island. Price $59.50.

Connecticut: State Industrial Directory

Manufacturers' News, Inc, 3 E Huron St, Chicago, IL 60611. Telephone (312) 337-1084.

Annual book. Names 6132 Connecticut businesses. Identifies executives and products. Price $50.00.

Construction Equipment

Cahners Publishing Company, Inc, 221 Columbus Ave, Boston, MA 02116. Telephone (617) 536-7780.

Monthly magazine reports on purchase, maintenance use, and management of heavy construction equipment. Price $25.00 per year.

Construction Plant & Equipment

Morgan-Grampian Ltd, Morgan-Grampian House, Calderwood St, London, England SE18 6QH. Order from Morgan-Grampian Publishing Co, 2 Park Ave, New York, NY 10016. Telephone (44) (01) 855-7777. Telex 896238 MORGAN G. New York (212) 340-9700. Telex 425592 MGI UI.

Monthly magazine. Pertains to use of construction plants and equipment. Is geared to specifiers and buyers. Price $45.00 per year.

Consultants and Consulting Organizations Directory

Gale Research Co, Book Tower, Detroit, MI 48226. Telephone (313) 961-2242.

Directory providing information on firms and individuals offering business, industrial, and governmental consultation services. Price $190.00. ISBN 0352-3.

Consumer Magazine & Farm Publication Rates & Data

Standard Rate & Data Service, Inc, 5201 Old Orchard Rd, Skokie, IL 60077. Telephone (312) 470-3100.

Monthly magazine. Provides profiles and advertising rates for consumer and farm magazines. Includes analysis of markets. Price $106.00 per year.

Contract

Gralla Publications, 1515 Broadway, New York, NY 10036. Telephone (212) 869-1300.

Report. Covers furnishing and interior architecture for commercial interiors. Is aimed at specifiers, buyers, and users of contract furnishings. Price available on request.

Contractor

Morgan-Grampian Ltd, Morgan-Grampian House, Calderwood St, London, England SE18 6QH. Order from Morgan-Grampian Publishing Co, Circulation Dept, Berkshire Common, Pittsfield, MA 01201. Telephone (413) 499-2550. Telex 425592 MGI UI.

Semimonthly magazine. Covers US air conditioning, heating, and plumbing industries. Price $36.00 per year.

Course Catalog—Management Development Guide

American Management Association, 135 W 50th St, New York, NY 10020. Telephone (212) 586-8100.

Catalog. Lists management development courses, home-study programs, on-site training program, and special American Management Association services. Groups career opportunities by subject and region. Indexed. Price $4.25.

Creative Selling

Januz Marketing Communications, Inc, PO Box 1000, Lake Forest, IL 60045. Telephone (312) 295-6550.

Semimonthly newsletter. Provides tested sales techniques for professional salespersons and other self-help ideas. Price $48.00 per year, $96.00 per two years, $120.00 per three years. ISSN 0163-1748.

Croner's Reference Book for World Traders

Croner Publications, Inc, 211-03 Jamaica Ave, Queens Village, NY 11428. Telephone (212) 464-0866.

Looseleaf books with monthly updates. Contains sources of information on trade and marketing in countries throughout the world. Price $85.00 per year.

C-Store Business

Progressive Grocer Pub Co, 708 3rd Ave, New York, NY 10017. Telephone (212) 490-1000.

Bimonthly publication. Covers news and trends in the convenience store industry. Price $18.00 per year. ISSN 0193-919X.

Current African Directories

CBD Research, Ltd, 154 High St, Beckenham, Kent, England BR3 1EA. Telephone (44) (01) 650-7745.

Book. Offers guide to directories concerned with Africa and sources of information on business enterprises in Africa. Price $38.00. ISBN 900246-11-1.

Current British Directories

CBD Research, Ltd, 154 High St, Beckenham, Kent, England BR3 1EA. Telephone (44) (01) 650-7745.

Book published every three years. Supplies guide to directories of all kinds published in Great Britain, Ireland, British Commonwealth, and South Africa. Price $105.00. ISBN 900246-31-6.

Current European Directories

CBD Research, Ltd, 154 High St, Beckenham, Kent, England BR3 1EA. Telephone (44) (01) 650-7745.

Book. Provides guide to international, national, city, and specialized directories and reference works for all countries of continental Europe. Price available on request. ISBN 900246-02-2.

Daily Traffic World

Traffic Service Corp, 1435 G St NW, Suite 815, Washington, DC 20005. Telephone (202) 783-7325.

Daily newspaper. Reports on transportation industry news. Covers legislative and regulatory developments. Price $340.00 per year.

Dairy Industry Newsletter

Federal State Reports, Inc, 5203 Leesburg Pike, #1201, Falls Church, VA 22041. Telephone (703) 379-0222.

Biweekly report. Covers Washington developments affecting producers, processors, and retailers, as well as dairy industry representatives. Price $95.00 per year.

Dartnell Direct Mail and Mail Order Handbook

Dartnell Corp, 4660 Ravenswood Ave, Chicago, IL 60640. Telephone (312) 561-4000.

Book. Practical guide to direct mail and mail order operations. Price available on request.

Dartnell Marketing Manager's Handbook

Dartnell Corp, 4660 Ravenswood Ave, Chicago, IL 60640. Telephone (312) 561-4000.

Book. Covers theory and practice of marketing management. Price available on request.

Dartnell Sales Manager's Handbook

Dartnell Corp, 4660 Ravenswood Ave, Chicago, IL 60640. Telephone (312) 561-4000.

Book. Theory and practice of sales management. Price available on request.

Dartnell Sales Promotion Handbook

Dartnell Corp, 4660 Ravenswood Ave, Chicago, IL 60640. Telephone (312) 561-4000.

Book. Theory and practice of organizing a sales promotion campaign. Price available on request.

Data Channels

Phillips Publishing, Inc, 7315 Wisconsin Ave, Bethesda, Md 20014. Telephone (301) 986-0666.

Monthly newsletter. Covers the data communications industry, including regulations, technology, and trade shows. Price $97.00 per year.

Datamation

Technical Publishing Co, 1301 S Grove Ave, Barrington, IL 60010. Order from Technical Publishing Co, 666 5th Ave, New York, NY 10019. Telephone (212) 489-2200.

Monthly magazine. Covers international electronic data processing industry. Reports on new equipment and techniques. Price available on request.

Defense & Economy World Report

Government Business Worldwide Reports, PO Box 5651, Washington, DC 20016. Telephone (202) 966-6379.

Weekly report. Contains information on armament and military procurement in the US and abroad. Surveys defense policy, equipment, and requirements and votes international cooperative projects and arms exports and controls. Price $265.00 per year. ISSN 0364-9008.

Delaware: State Industrial Directory

Manufacturers' News, Inc, 3 E Huron St, Chicago, IL 60611. Telephone (312) 337-1084.

Annual book. Identifies 584 Delaware industrial firms by name, location, and product. Price $15.00.

Dental Industry News

Harcourt Brace Jovanovich Publications, 757 3rd Ave, New York, NY 10017. Order from Harcourt Brace Jovanovich Publications, 1 E 1st St, Duluth, MN 55802. Telephone (218) 727-8511.

Monthly magazine. Reports on dental products and practice. Price $10.00 per year.

Department Store Jewelry Buyers Directory

Newsletters International, 2600 S Gessner Rd, Houston, TX 77063. Telephone (713) 783-0100.

Annual book. Contains a directory of department stores selling fine and costume jewelry. Notes buyers' names and stores' addresses and telephone numbers. Price $150.00 per copy.

Developing Business in the Middle East and North Africa

Chase Trade Information Corp, 1 World Trade Center, 78th Floor, New York, NY 10048. Telephone (212) 432-8072.

Five books covering the Persian Gulf states, Algeria, Iraq, Egypt, and Saudi Arabia. Each study covers critical issues, including economic and social conditions, government development plans, and official policy on foreign investment. Price $375.00 for Gulf states, $185.00 for four other books.

Dialog

Dialog Information Retrieval Service, 3460 Hillview Ave, Palo Alto, CA 94304. Telephone (415) 858-2700. Telex 334499.

Information service with more than 100 databases. Provides access to references to articles and reports on science, technology, business, medicine, social science, current affairs, and humanities. Price available on request.

Digest of Executive Opportunities

General Executive Services, Inc, Park St Bldg, New Canaan, CT 06840. Telephone (203) 966-1673.

Weekly report. Describes executive job opportunities in general management, sales and marketing, manufacturing, finance, and other fields. Price $95.00 for 20 weeks.

Direct Mail List Rates & Data

Standard Rate & Data Service, Inc, 5201 Old Orchard Rd, Skokie, IL 60077. Telephone (312) 470-3100.

Quarterly book. Indicates the source of 50,000 business, consumer, farm, and cooperative mailing lists and rental rates. Price $92.00 per year.

Direct Marketing

Hoke Communications, Inc, 224 7th St, Garden City, NY 11535. Telephone (516) 746-6700.

Monthly magazine. Emphasizes direct mail advertising and other direct marketing techniques for any kind of business. Price $30.00 per year.

Direct Marketing Marketplace

Facts on File, Inc, 460 Park Ave S, New York, NY 10016. Telephone (212) 265-2011.

Directory. Lists alphabetically by category company name, address, phone number, key executives, product, and other specific direct marketing data. Price $40.00.

Directory of American Firms Operating in Foreign Countries

World Trade Academy Press, Inc, 50 E 42nd St, New York, NY 10017. Telephone (212) 697-4999.

Annual book. Provides a guide to 4,200 US corporations operating overseas. Includes information on subsidiaries, branches, products, and services. Price $125.00.

Directory of Associations in Canada

University of Toronto Press, Front Campus, Toronto, Ont, Canada M5S 1A6.

Directory. Lists Canadian associations alphabetically and by subject. Includes company, name, address, and top executive. Price $37.50.

Directory of British Associations

Gale Research Co, Book Tower, Detroit, MI 48226. Telephone (313) 961-2242.

Directory. Lists the interests and activities of Great Britain and Ireland. Provides a listing of the publications for associations in these countries—including trade, scientific, technical, and professional. Price $125.00.

Directory of British Importers

Dun & Bradstreet, Box 3224, Church St Station, New York, NY 10008. Telephone (212) 285-7346.

Directory. Lists 470 importers in Great Britain. Price available on request, to Dun & Bradstreet subscribers only.

Directory of Business and Financial Services

Special Libraries Assn, 235 Park Ave S, New York, NY 10003. Telephone (212) 477-9250.

Directory. Presents a guide to more than 1,000 business and financial services in the US and Canada. Subject index and publishers index. Price $18.80. ISBN 0-87111-212-4.

Directory of Colorado Manufacturers

University of Colorado, Graduate School of Business Adm, Business Research Div, Boulder, CO 80309. Telephone (303) 492-8227.

Book revised approximately every 18 months. Lists Colorado manufacturing firms alphabetically and by city and product. Price $30.00. ISBN 0-89478-031-X.

Directory of Corporate Affliations

National Register Publishing Co, Inc, 5201 Old Orchard Rd, Skokie, IL 60077. Telephone (312) 470-3100.

Book, with five bimonthly updating reports. Offers a directory to 4,500 US parent corporations. Gives their domestic and foreign divisions, subsidiaries and affiliates, with subsidiaries and affiliates cross-indexed. Price $109.00. ISBN 0-87217-002-0.

Directory of Counseling Services

American Personnel and Guidance Assn, 2 Skyline Place, Suite 400, 5203 Leesburg Pike, Falls Church, VA 22041. Telephone (717) 820-4700.

Book. Lists over 300 accredited counseling services and agencies in the US and Canada. Price $6.00.

Directory of European Associations

Gale Research Co, Book Tower, Detroit, MI 48226. Telephone (313) 961-2242.

Directory. Contains information on over 9,000 European industrial, trade, and professional associations (excluding Great Britain and Ireland). Price $175.00.

Directory of Executive Recruiters

Kennedy & Kennedy, Inc, Templeton Rd, Fitzwilliam, NH 03447. Telephone (603) 585-2200.

Annual book. Lists members of the Association of Executive Recruiting Consultants and other firms and individuals doing executive recruiting. Price $12.00.

Directory of Importers and Manu-facturers' Agents in British Co-lumbia

Ministry of Industry and Small Business Development, Parliament Buildings, Victoria, BC, Canada V8V 1X4. Telephone (604) 387-6701.

Directory. Provides a roster of im-porters and manufacturers' agents in British Columbia. Includes prod-uct lines. Free.

Directory of Industrial Distribu-tors

Morgan-Grampian Ltd, Morgan-Grampian House, Calderwood St, London, England SE18 6QH. Order from Morgan-Grampian Publishing Co, 2 Park Ave, New York, NY 10016. Telephone (212) 340-9700. Telex 425592 MGI UI.

Book published every three years. Provides marketing guide for in-dustrial distributors in the US. Price $300.00.

Directory of Manufacturers and Products

Kansas Dept of Economic Devel-opment, 503 Kansas Ave, Room 626, Topeka, KS 66603. Telephone (913) 296-3481.

Annual directory. Lists Kansas manufacturers and products. Price $20.00.

Directory of Manufacturers, State of Hawaii

Chamber of Commerce of Hawaii, Dillingham Transportation Bldg,

735 Bishop St, Honolulu, HI 96813. Telephone (808) 531-4111.

Biennial publication. Lists all Ha-waiian manufacturers. Includes brand, trade, and manufacturers' names. Price $15.00.

Directory of Maryland Manufac-turers

Maryland Dept of Economic & Community Development, 2525 Riva Rd, Annapolis, MD 21401. Telephone (301) 269-2041.

Book. Contains data on more than 3096 Maryland manufacturers, in-cluding addresses, personnel, and products. Price $18.00.

Directory of Michigan Manufac-turers

Pick Publications, Inc, 8543 Puri-tan Ave, Detroit, MI 48238. Tele-phone (313) 864-9388.

Annual directory. Lists about 15,-000 Michigan manufacturers al-phabetically, geographically, and by product. Mailing labels and lists available. Price $95.00.

Directory of Nebraska Manufac-turers

Nebraska Dept of Economic Devel-opment, Box 94666, 301 Centennial Mall S, Lincoln, NE 68509. Tele-phone (402) 471-3111.

Directory. Lists manufacturing firms in Nebraska. Price $10.00.

Directory of Oregon Manufactur-ers

Oregon Economic Development Dept, 155 Cottage St NE, Salem,

OR 97310. Telephone (503) 373-1200.

Biennial book. Lists all manufacturers in Oregon alphabetically, geographically, and by product. Supplies employment data. Price $25.00.

Directory of the National Association of Personnel Consultants

National Assn of Personnel Consultants, 1012 14th St NW, Washington, DC 20005. Telephone (202) 638-1721.

Annual directory to private personnel placement services. Lists over 2,500 services, noting employment specialties. Price $8.50.

Directory of US and Canadian Marketing Surveys and Services

Charles H Kline & Co, Inc, 330 Passaic Ave, Fairfield, NJ 07006. Telephone (201) 227-6262. Telex 13-9170 KLINECO.

Looseleaf book. Provides a directory to 2,500 marketing services and published studies covering US, Canadian, and international industrial and consumer markets. Two updated supplements. Price $125.-00.

Discount Merchandiser

Charter Publishing, Inc, 641 Lexington Ave, New York, NY 10022. Telephone (212) 872-8430.

Monthly report. Covers industry news and gives statistics on some companies. Price $20.00 per year. ISSN 0012-3579.

Discount Store News

Lebhar-Friedman Publications, Inc, 425 Park Ave, New York, NY 10022. Telephone (212) 371-9400.

Fortnightly report. Covers news and trends in discount store industry. Price $7.50 per year. ISSN 0012-3587.

Doing Business in Brazil

Matthew Bender & Co, 235 E 45th St, New York, NY 10017. Telephone (212) 661-5050.

Looseleaf book. Examines business practices in Brazil. Includes information on changes in pertinent laws. Price $135.00.

Doing Business in Canada

Matthew Bender & Co, 235 E 45th St, New York, NY 10017. Telephone (212) 661-5050.

Two volumes, book with periodic updates. Discusses how to establish a business in Canada. Notes federal and provincial legislation affecting business transactions. Price $215.00.

Doing Business in Europe

Commerce Clearing House, Inc, 4025 W Peterson Ave, Chicago, IL 60646. Telephone (312) 583-8500.

Looseleaf book, plus monthly reports. Provides an overview of company, tax, labor, and financial requirements for business operations in Europe. Price $325.00 per year.

Doing Business in Japan

Matthew Bender & Co, 235 E 45th St, New York, NY 10017. Telephone (212) 661-5050.

Five-volume looseleaf book. Provides information on Japan's business world. Includes information on statutes, laws, and court cases. Price $625.00.

Doing Business In Mexico

Matthew Bender & Co, 235 E 45th St, New York, NY 10017. Telephone (212) 661-5050.

Two volumes. Discusses opportunities for US investment in Mexico. Covers taxation and legal aspects. Price $200.00.

Doing Business with Eastern Europe

Business International Corp, 1 Dag Hammarskjold Plz, New York, NY 10017. Telephone (212) 750-6300.

Ten-volume, continuously updated reference service. Analyzes, in separate volumes for each East European country, the national market, political context, economy, foreign trade, sales promotion, financing, and trademarks. Price $1,700.00 per year.

Drop Shipping Source Directory of Major Consumer Product Lines

Consolidated Marketing Services, Inc, PO Box 3328, New York, NY 10017. Telephone (212) 688-8797.

Directory. Lists firms that will make drop shipments of single units of over 57,000 products direct to consumer for retailers, mail order firms, and other establishments. Lists products that are divided into 25 classifications. Price $7.00. ISBN 0-917626-01-X.

Drug & Cosmetic Catalog

Harcourt Brace Jovanovich Publications, 757 3rd Ave, New York, NY 10017. Order from Harcourt Brace Jovanovich Publications, 1 E 1st St, Duluth, MN 55802. Telephone (218) 727-8511.

Annual catalog. Lists the sources of raw materials, equipment, packaging components, and services for drug and cosmetic manufacturers and distributors. Price $10.00 per copy.

Drug & Cosmetic Industry

Harcourt Brace Jovanovich Publications, 757 3rd Ave, New York, NY 10017. Order from Harcourt Brace Jovanovich Publications, 1 E 1st St, Duluth, MN 55802. Telephone (218) 727-8511.

Monthly magazine. Covers developments in the drug and cosmetic industries. Notes regulatory action and new products. Price $10.00 per year.

Drug Store News

Lebhar-Friedman Publications, Inc, 425 Park Ave, New York, NY 10022. Telephone (212) 371-9400.

Fortnightly report. Covers trade news and trends in the chain drug store industry. Price $10.00 per year.

Dun & Bradstreet Composite Register

Dun & Bradstreet, Box 3224, Church St Station, New York, NY 10008. Telephone (212) 285-7346.

Annual book. Lists over 200,000 British businesses representing all industries and trades. Provides bank of account and credit recommendation. Price available on request, to Dun & Bradstreet subscribers only.

Dun & Bradstreet Metalworking Marketing Directory

Dun & Bradstreet, Inc, Box 3224, Church St Station, New York, NY 10008. Telephone (212) 285-7346.

Annual book. Offers a list of US metalworking, producing, and distributing operations, with descriptive details on each. Price available on request, to Dun and Bradstreet subscribers only.

Dun & Bradstreet Reference Book

Dun & Bradstreet, Box 3224, Church St Station, New York, NY 10008. Telephone (212) 285-7346.

Bimonthly book. Lists and rates the financial strength of companies. Notes new business and credit ratings. Price available on request, to Dun & Bradstreet subscribers only.

Dun & Bradstreet Standard Register

Dun & Bradstreet, Box 3224, Church St Station, New York, NY 10008. Telephone (212) 285-7346.

Annual book. Lists over 200,000 businesses. Includes the date of formation, ownership, bank of account, and credit information. Price available on request, to Dun & Bradstreet subscribers only.

Educational Marketer

Knowledge Industry Publications, 701 Westchester Ave, White Plains, NY 10604. Telephone (914) 694-8686.

Biweekly newsletter relevant to the educational market. Gives sales of textbooks and audiovisual materials and reports on federal education funding and school enrollment trends. Price $115.00 per year. ISSN 0013-1806.

Electrical Construction and Maintenance

McGraw-Hill Publications Co, 1221 Ave of the Americas, New York, NY 10020. Telephone (212) 997-1221. Telex TWX 7105814879 WUI 62555.

Monthly magazine. Provides information on electrical design, installation, maintenance, construction modernization, repairs, and equipment. Price $50.00, Canada $60.00 per year.

Electrical Construction and Maintenance (Annual)

McGraw-Hill Book Co, Hightstown-Princeton Rd, Hightstown, NJ 08520. Telephone (609) 448-1700. Telex 843449.

Annual book. Provides a buying guide to electrical equipment. Emphasizes new products. Price $12.-00.

Electrical Marketing Newsletter

McGraw-Hill Publications Co, 1221 Ave of the Americas, New York, NY 10020. Telephone (212) 997-1221. Telex TWX 7105814879 WUI 62555.

Semimonthly newsletter. Contains material on electrical equipment marketing and sales trends. Notes personnel changes. Price $300.00 per year.

Electrical Wholesaling

McGraw-Hill Book Co., Hightstown-Princeton Rd, Hightstown, NJ 08520. Telephone (609) 448-1700. Telex 843449.

Directory. Provides a register of electrical wholesale distributors. Includes a market planning guide. Price $7.00.

Electrical Wholesaling (Magazine)

McGraw-Hill Publications Co, 1221 Ave of the Americas, New York, NY 10020. Telephone (212) 997-1221. Telex TWX 7105814879 WUI 62555.

Magazine issued seven times a year. Provides electrical equipment marketing information. Notes specific products, such as minicomputers and pertinent legislation. Price $18.00 per year.

Electric Vehicle News

Porter Corp, PO Box 350, Westport, CT 06881. Telephone (203) 226-4600.

Quarterly report. Covers electric vehicles industry. Discusses engineering, marketing, and applications. Price $12.00 per year.

Electric Vehicle Progress

Downtown Research and Development Center, 270 Madison Ave, Suite 1505, New York, NY 10016. Telephone (212) 889-5666.

Semimonthly newsletter. Provides management news, technical developments, marketing, research, manufacturing, and government actions on electric vehicles. Aimed at management and technical people in industry and government. Price $210.00 per year.

Electronic Business

Cahners Publishing Co, Inc, 221 Columbus Ave, Boston, MA 02116. Telephone (617) 536-7780.

Monthly magazine. Provides reports and commentary on business and marketing aspects of the electronics industry. Price available on request.

Electronic Component News

Chilton Co, Chilton Way, Radnor, PA 19089. Telephone (215) 687-8200.

Monthly magazine. Covers new products and technology in the electronics market. Price available on request.

Electronic Design's Gold Book

Hayden Publishing Co, Inc, 50 Essex St, Rochelle Park, NJ 07662. Telephone (201) 843-0550. Telex TWX 710 990-5071.

Annual four-volume directory. Describes products in electronics industry. Price $45.00–$60.00.

Electronic Distributing

Electronic Periodicals, Inc, 33393 Aurora Rd, Cleveland, OH 44139. Telephone (216) 248-4955.

Magazine published 10 times per year. Focuses on marketing and selling electronic components and equipment through electronic distributors. Free to qualified recipients.

Electronic Market Data Book

Electronic Industries Assn, 2001 I St NW, Washington, DC 20006. Telephone (202) 457-4950.

Annual book. Contains current and historical sales data on the electronics industry. Covers a full range of products, world trade patterns, employment, industry earnings, and government needs for electronics. Price $50.00.

Electronic Market Trends

Electronic Industries Assn, 2001 I St NW, Washington, DC 20006. Telephone (202) 457-4950.

Monthly journal. Contains articles on the electronics markets, new technologies, international developments, and policy issues. Provides monthly statistics on domestic sales and foreign trade. Price $150.00 per year.

Electronic Office Management and Technology

Auerbach Publishers, Inc, 6560 N Park Dr, Pennsauken, NJ 08109. Telephone (609) 662-2070. Telex 831 464.

Two-volume service, updated monthly. Provides information on planning, purchasing, implementing, and managing electronic office technologies. Includes equipment vendors, prices, and evaluations. Price $350.00.

Electronics Buyers' Guide

Dempa Publications, Inc, 380 Madison Ave, New York, NY 10017. Telephone (212) 867-0900.

Annual directory. Lists electronics products and manufacturers in Japan, Korea, Taiwan, Hong Kong, and Singapore. Price $54.00.

Electronics-Buyers' Guide

McGraw-Hill Book Co, Hightstown-Princeton Rd, Hightstown, NJ 08520. Telephone (609) 448-1700. Telex 843449.

Annual publication. Provides an inventory of electronics production equipment and products. Price $30.00 per year.

Electronic Technician Dealer

Harcourt Brace Jovanovich Publications, 757 3rd Ave, New York, NY 10017. Order from Harcourt Brace Jovanovich Publications, 1 E

1st St, Duluth, MN 55802. Telephone (218) 727-8511.

Monthly magazine. Reports on the sales and service of television, radio (including citizens' bands), and other home entertainment electronic equipment. Price $9.00 per year.

Encyclopedia of Associations

Gale Research Co, Book Tower, Detroit, MI 48226. Telephone (313) 961-2242.

Book. Contains information on over 13,000 associations in the US. Provides an index by subject, key word, and proper name. Price $120.00. ISBN 0133-4.

Encyclopedia of Business Information Sources

Gale Research Co, Book Tower, Detroit, MI 48226. Telephone (313) 961-2242.

Book. Provides an information source for 1280 business-oriented topics. Lists reference books, periodicals, organizations, and other kinds of information sources. Price $98.00. ISBN 0372-8.

Encyclopedia of Governmental Advisory Organizations

Gale Research Co, Book Tower, Detroit, MI 48226. Telephone (313) 961-2242.

Book. Provides a guide to US federal advisory committees, task forces, conferences, and similar bodies. Price $190.00. ISBN 0251-9.

Encyclopedia of Information Systems and Services

Gale Research Co, Book Tower, Detroit, MI 48226. Telephone (313) 961-2242.

Book. Describes 1,750 organizations involved in information products and services, including publishers, computer companies, and data banks. Price $175.00. ISBN 0939-4.

Energy Directory Update

Environment Information Center (EIC), Inc, Catalog Order Dept, 292 Madison Ave, New York, NY 10017. Telephone (212) 949-9494.

Looseleaf books, with bimonthly updates. Provide information on organizations and officials involved in the energy field. Includes indexes. Price $125.00.

Energy Executive Directory

Carroll Publishing Co, 1058 Thomas Jefferson St, NW, Washington, DC 20007. Telephone (202) 333-8620.

Book published three times per year. Lists energy related offices and personnel of the federal, state, and local governments. Identifies trade association personnel and newsletters. Price $60.00 per year.

Energy Information Abstracts

Environment Information Center (EIC), Inc, Catalog Order Dept, 292 Madison Ave, New York, NY 10017. Telephone (212) 949-9494.

Monthly report. Contains informative abstracts from varied publications on energy and related subjects. Includes a listing of upcoming conferences and newly published books. Price $350.00 per year.

Energy Information Locator

Environment Information Center (EIC), Inc, Catalog Order Dept, 292 Madison Ave, New York, NY 10017. Telephone (212) 949-9494.

Looseleaf report, with annual updating. Provides a directory to information sources on energy, including indexes, directories, computerized service libraries, and research centers. Includes five indexes. Price $35.00.

Engineering and Mining Journal— Annual Buyers' Guide

McGraw-Hill Book Co, Hightstown-Princeton Rd, Hightstown, NJ 08520. Telephone (609) 448-1700. Telex 843449.

Annual directory. Provides a buyer's guide to metal and non-metal mining, milling, smelting, and refining equipment. Free with an *Engineering and Mining Journal* subscription. Price $18.00 per year.

Engineering Index

Engineering Index, Inc, 345 E 47th St, New York, NY 10017. Telephone (212) 644-7615.

Monthly and annual publications. Provide bibliographic reference service with complete abstracts and subject index to all fields of engi-

neering. Draw on worldwide sources. Annual is also available on microform. Prices available on request.

Enterprise

National Assn of Manufacturers, 1776 F St NW, Washington, DC 20006. Telephone (202) 626-3700.

Monthly magazine. Reports on American business issues, including economic, labor, energy, and environmental developments. Price $10.00 per year.

Enterprising Women

Artemis Enterprises, Inc, 525 West End Ave, New York, NY 10024. Telephone (212) 787-6780.

Monthly magazine. Addresses itself to women's role in the economy and professions. Discusses taxes, insurance, and personal finances as well as management issues. Price $18.00 per year.

Equipment Market Abstracts

Predicasts, Inc, 200 University Circle Research Center, 11001 Cedar Ave, Cleveland, OH 44106. Telephone (216) 795-3000.

Monthly set of abstracts. Covers developments in the equipment, electronics, and hard goods industries, as reported in journals and government reports. Indexed by product, company, country, and trade name. Price $500.00 per year.

Europa Year Book

Europa Publications Ltd, 18 Bedford Sq, London, England, WC1B 3JN. Telephone (44) (01) 580-8236.

Yearbook. Offers detailed information on every country in the world and 1650 international organizations. Price $180.00.

European Compensation Survey

Business International Corp, 1 Dag Hammarskjold Plz, New York, NY 10017. Telephone (212) 750-6300.

Annual computerized comparisons of wages, fringe benefits, and allowances in eight European countries, distinguished by industry and by managerial, technical, sales, clerical, and blue-collar job classifications. Price $1,190.00 for series; $230.00 per country.

European Directory of Business Information Sources & Services

Center for Business Information, 7 Rue Buffon, 75005 Paris, France. Telephone 707-26-14. Telex 204320.

Annual looseleaf book, with monthly updating service. Monitors international and European sources of information to provide data on such subjects as finance, economics, insurance, banking, law, marketing, and communications. Price $180.00 per year, plus postage.

European Journal of Marketing

MCB Publications, 200 Keighley Rd, Bradford, W Yorkshire, England BD9 4JQ. Telephone 0274 499821.

Three journals and three monographs per year. Present articles on marketing and market research in Great Britain and Western Europe. Price $168.00 per year.

European Marketing Data & Statistics

Euromonitor Publications Ltd, 18 Doughty St, London, England WC1N 2PN. Telephone (44) (01) 242-0042. Order from Gale Research Co, Book Tower, Detroit, MI 48226.

Annual. Offers vital statistics on Eastern and Western Europe, including data on population, employment, trade, food and energy consumption, prices, and taxation. Price $150.00.

Europe's 5,000 Largest Companies

Guides to Multinational Business, Inc, Harvard Sq, Box 92, Cambridge, MA 02138. Telephone (617) 868-2288.

Annual book. Presents a guide to 5,000 European industrial companies and 1,500 European banks, trading, transport, and insurance companies. Price $150.00.

Executive Living Costs in Major Cities Worldwide

Business International Corp, 1 Dag Hammarskjold Plz, New York, NY 10017. Telephone (212) 750-6300.

Annual survey. Compares the living costs for executives and their families in 77 cities throughout the world. Price $160.00 per city; $3715.00 for all cities.

Executive Woman

Executive Woman, Box 3101, Grand Central Station, New York, NY 10017. Telephone (212) 661-7139 or (914) 528-2256.

Monthly (except June and July) newsletter for business and professional women. Contains information on credit, investments, education, career opportunities, and business trends. Price $28.00 per year.

Exporters Directory

Twin Coast Newspapers, Inc, 110 Wall St, New York, NY 10005. Order from US Buying Guide, 445 Marshall St, Phillipsburg, NJ 08865. Telephone (201) 859-1300.

Directory. Lists 40,000 exporters and identifies products. Price $175.00.

Exporters' Encyclopedia—World Marketing Guide

Dun & Bradstreet, Box 3224, Church St Station, New York, NY 10008. Telephone (212) 285-7346.

Annual book, with semimonthly bulletins. Contains data on world export regulations. Price available on request, to Dun & Bradstreet subscribers only.

Facts on File Weekly News Digest

Facts on File, Inc, 460 Park Ave S, New York, NY 10016. Telephone (212) 265-2011.

Weekly newsletter. Covers current events. Includes cumulative index. Price $315.00 per year.

Fairplay World Shipping Yearbook

Fairplay Publications Ltd, 301 E 64th St, New York, NY 10021. Telephone (212) 879-4418.

Annual book. Provides detailed data on shipping companies, organizations, and associations. Lists ship sale and purchase brokers. Index and statistics. Price $56.00.

Far East and Australasia

Europa Publications Ltd, 18 Bedford Sq, London, England, WC1B 3JN. Telephone (44) (01) 580-8236.

Annual book. Surveys South Asia, Southeast Asia, Australasia, and the Pacific Islands. Covers history, geography, economy, and major personalities. Price $100.00.

Farm Industry News

The Webb Co, 1999 Shepard Rd, St Paul, MN 55116. Telephone (612) 690-7200.

Magazine issued nine times per year. Reports on agricultural products. Includes information on machinery, fertilizers, and pesticides. Price available on request.

Farmline

US Dept of Agriculture, ESS Publications, Room 0054-S, Washington, DC 20250. Order from Superintendent of Documents, US Government Printing Office, Washington, DC 20402. Telephone (202) 783-3238.

Magazine issued 11 times per year. Gives overall picture of trends in agriculture. Covers developments in rural life, natural resources, farm finances and other topics affecting farm families. Price $10.00 per year domestic, $12.50 per year foreign.

Fast Service

Harcourt Brace Jovanovich Publications, 757 3rd Ave, New York, NY 10017. Order from Harcourt Brace Jovanovich Publications, 1 E 1st St, Duluth, MN 55802. Telephone (218) 727-8511.

Monthly magazine. Pertains to fast-service restaurant management. Price $15.00 per year.

Federal Executive Directory

Carroll Publishing Co, 1058 Thomas Jefferson St, NW, Washington, DC 20007. Telephone (202) 333-8620.

Bimonthly directory. Lists federal personnel and offices. Notes titles and phone numbers. Price $96.00 per year.

Federal Yellow Book

Washington Monitor, 499 National Press Bldg, Washington, DC 20045. Telephone (202) 347-7757.

Looseleaf directory with bimonthly updates. Lists federal department and agency employees. Provides titles, addresses, and phone numbers. Price $120.00 per year.

Feed Industry Review

Communications Marketing, Inc, 5100 Edina Industrial Blvd, Edina,

MN 55435. Telephone (612) 835-5888.

Quarterly magazine. Contains information on the production and distribution of livestock and poultry feeds. Aimed at executives in the field. Price $12.50 per year.

Fence Industry

Communication Channels, Inc, 6285 Barfield Rd, Atlanta, GA 30328. Telephone (404) 256-9800.

Monthly magazine. Covers all types of fencing and new developments in installation and related products. Price $21.00 per year.

Fiber Producer

American Building Supplies, 1760 Peachtree Rd, NW, Atlanta, GA 30357. Telephone (404) 874-4462.

Monthly magazine. Covers developments in fiber production and textile industries in US and abroad. Price $25.00 per year.

Financial Post Directory of Directors

Financial Post, 481 University Ave, Toronto, Ont, Canada M5W 1A7. Telephone (416) 596-5585.

Annual book. Provides a directory to Canada's top executive personnel. Covers 13,000 people and 2,100 companies. Price $45.00.

Financial Post Newspaper

Financial Post, 481 University Ave, Toronto, Ont, Canada M5W 1A7. Order from Financial Post Circulation, Box 9100, Postal Station A,

Toronto, Ont, Canada M5W 1V5. Telephone (416) 596-5148.

Weekly newspaper. Covers Canadian business, investments, and public affairs. Includes about 52 special reports with an annual subscription. Price $29.95 per year (Canadian).

Financial Times Newspaper

Financial Times Business Information Ltd, Bracken House, 10 Cannon St, London, England EC4P 4BY. Order from Financial Times Ltd, 75 Rockefeller Plz, New York, NY 10019. Telephone (44) (01) 248-8000. Telex 886341-2.

Daily newspaper. Covers British and world financial and economic news. Price $200.00 per year.

Financial Times of Canada

Financial Times of Canada, 920 Yonge St, Suite 500, Toronto, Ont, Canada M4W 3L5. Telephone (416) 922-1133.

Weekly newspaper. Covers Canadian business, government, industry, and investment. Includes some European and American coverage. Price $15.00 per year, $26.00, foreign outside Canada. ISSN 0015-2056.

First Chicago World Report

First National Bank of Chicago, Business and Economic Research Div, 1 First National Plz, Chicago, IL 60670. Telephone (312) 732-3779. Telex 253801-3.

Monthly newsletter. Discusses worldwide economic trends, such as unemployment, gas shortages, and international pricing systems. Includes an evaluation of foreign economies. Free.

Flooring

Harcourt Brace Jovanovich Publications, 757 3rd Ave, New York, NY 10017. Order from Harcourt Brace Jovanovich Publications, 1 E 1st St, Duluth, MN 55802. Telephone (218) 727-8511.

Monthly magazine. Discusses the flooring industry. Includes information on wall and related interior-surfacing products. Price $8.00 per year.

Florida: Industries Directory

Manufacturers' News, Inc, 3 E Huron St, Chicago, IL 60611. Telephone (312) 337-1084.

Annual book. Identifies 10,000 industrial companies in Florida by name, location, and product. Price $45.00.

Flying Annual & Buyers' Guide

Ziff-Davis Publishing Co, 1156 15th St NW, Washington, DC 20005. Order from Ziff-Davis Publishing Co, One Park Ave, New York, NY 10016. Telephone (212) 725-3680.

Annual book. Provides information on aviation equipment and maintenance. Includes a listing of manufacturers. Price available on request.

Focus Japan

Japan Trade Center, 1221 Ave of the Americas, New York, NY 10020. Telephone (212) 997-0400.

Monthly magazine. Covers Japanese economic and trade issues. Includes government policies and book reviews and gives a glimpse of the Japanese outside the work environment. Price $28.00 per year.

Food Industry Newsletter

Profit Press, Inc, 400 E 89th St, New York, NY 10028. Telephone (212) 534-0366.

Semimonthly newsletter. Covers trends and developments among food manufacturers, primarily management, marketing and sales aspects. Price $95.00 per year.

Food Management

Harcourt Brace Jovanovich Publications, 757 3rd Ave, New York, NY 10017. Order from Harcourt Brace Jovanovich Publications, 1 E 1st St, Duluth, MN 55802. Telephone (218) 727-8511.

Monthly magazine. Reports on the institutional food service industry, including educational and health care institutions. Price $15.00 per year.

Forbes

Forbes Inc, 60 5th Ave, New York, NY 10011. Telephone (212) 620-2200.

Biweekly magazine. Covers general business, economic, and financial news. Reports on various corpora- tions, executives, stocks, and indus- tries. Price $30.00 per year.

Foreign Tax and Trade Briefs

Matthew Bender & Co, 235 E 45th St, New York, NY 10017. Telephone (212) 661-5050.

Looseleaf volumes with monthly updating. Supply tax and trade in- formation for over 100 foreign countries. Give every class of taxa- tion for each country. Price $180.00 for two volumes; $150.00 per year.

Fortune

Time, Inc, Time & Life Bldg, New York, NY 10020. Order from Time, Inc, 541 N Fairbanks Ct, Chicago, IL 60611. Telephone (212) 586-1212.

Semimonthly magazine. Covers business and economic develop- ments. Evaluates specific industries and corporations and notes banking and energy news. Price $20.00 per year.

Foundation Directory

Foundation Center, 888 7th Ave, New York, NY 10106. Order from Columbia University Press, 136 S Broadway, Irvington, NY 10533. Telephone (212) 975-1120.

Directory. Describes 3,218 of the largest US foundations. Includes subject index, grant application procedures, and statistical profiles of foundations. Price $41.50.

Franchising

Matthew Bender & Co, 235 E 45th St, New York, NY 10017. Telephone (212) 661-5050.

Two-volume set of books. Provides a guide to franchising. Includes such topics as contracts, trademarks, taxation, and equipment provisions. Price $150.00.

Friday Report

Hoke Communications, Inc, 224 7th St, Garden City, NY 11535. Telephone (516) 746-6700.

Weekly newsletter. Contains reports on direct response advertisers and market data centers organizing direct marketing. Price $84.00 per year.

Gallagher Report

Gallagher Report, Inc, 230 Park Ave, New York, NY 10017. Telephone (212) 661-5000.

Weekly report. Presents news and trends in the fields of marketing, advertising, media, and sales. Price $84.00 per year.

Georgia: State Industrial Directory

Manufacturers' News, Inc, 3 E Huron St, Chicago, IL 60611. Telephone (312) 337-1084.

Annual book. Contains information on Georgia industrial companies. Price $50.00.

Geyer's Dealer Topics

Geyer-McAllister Publications, Inc, 51 Madison Ave, New York, NY 10010. Telephone (212) 689-4411.

Monthly magazine. Provides information of interest to office machines, furniture, and stationery dealers. Price $14.00 per year.

Gibson Report

D Parke Gibson International, Inc, 475 5th Ave, New York, NY 10017. Telephone (212) 889-5557.

Monthly report. Deals with marketing for and communications with minority groups. Discusses new products and advertising. Price $25.00. ISSN 0016-9784.

Gifts & Housewares Buyers

Salesman's Guide, Inc, 1140 Broadway, New York, NY 10001. Telephone (212) 684-2985.

Directory, with quarterly supplements. Lists top department, chain, and specialty stores carrying giftware and housewares. Notes the names of buyers and merchandise managers of giftware and housewares. Price $95.00.

Graduate Study in Management

Graduate Business Admissions Council, PO Box 966, Princeton, NJ 08540.

Book. Provides information on 886 graduate management school programs, public and educational administration, hospital administration, and urban planning. Includes, also, information on the Graduate Management Admission Test. Price $7.70.

Guide to American Directories

B Klein Publications, Inc, PO Box 8503, Coral Springs, FL 33065. Telephone (305) 752-1708.

Book. Offers a listing of 7,000 directories organized by subject. Describes contents of the directories, noting the publisher, date of publication, and cost. Price $55.00.

Guide to Irish Manufacturers

Dun & Bradstreet, Box 3224, Church St Station, New York, NY 10008. Telephone (212) 285-7346.

Biannual book. Describes 4000 Irish manufacturers. Notes the line of business, number of employees, and names of directors. Price available on request, to Dun & Bradstreet subscribers only.

Guide to Key British Enterprises

Dun & Bradstreet, Box 3224, Church St Station, New York, NY 10008. Telephone (212) 285-7346.

Annual book. Describes large and middle-range companies in the United Kingdom. Contains lists of products, services, and company subsidiaries. Price £40.00. ISSN 0072-856X.

Guide to Travel and Residence Expenses for the Multinational Executive

Guides to Multinational Business, Inc, Harvard Sq, Box 92, Cambridge, MA 02138. Telephone (617) 868-2288.

Book. Offers a guide to travel and residence expenses for 55 countries.

Includes data on hotel accommodations, restaurants, transportation, apartments, and food. Price $50.00.

Guide to US Government Publications

Andriot, John L, Editor, Documents Index, Box 195, McLean, VA 22101. Telephone (703) 356-2434.

Books with quarterly update supplements. List publications of US Government agencies. Price available on request.

Happi

Household & Personal Products Industry, Box 555, 26 Lake St, Ramsey, NJ 07446. Telephone (201) 825-2552.

Monthly magazine. Contains news of household and personal products industry. Includes information on cosmetics, soaps, detergents, waxes, and polishes. Price $18.00 per year.

Hardware Age

Chilton Co, Chilton Way, Radnor, PA 19089. Telephone (215) 687-8200.

Monthly magazine. Covers consumer buying trends that aid in successful marketing of products in the hardware/hardlines industry. Price $35.00.

Harvard Business Review

Harvard University, Graduate School of Business Adm, Teele 314, Soldiers Field, Boston, MA 02163. Telephone (617) 495-6800.

Bimonthly review. Provides an analysis of conditions and problems in all areas of business. Price $24.-00.

Hawaii: Manufacturers Directory

Manufacturers' News, Inc, 3 E Huron St, Chicago, IL 60611. Telephone (312) 337-1084.

Biennial book. Identifies 487 Hawaii manufacturing firms by name and product. Price $35.00.

Health Care Product News

Gralla Publications, 1515 Broadway, New York, NY 10036. Telephone (212) 869-1300.

Publication. Carries news on new products in the health care field. Price available on request.

Home Video Report

Knowledge Industry Publications, Inc, 701 Westchester Ave, White Plains, NY 10604. Telephone (914) 694-8686.

Weekly newsletter. Reports on the production and distribution of video programming and video discs, television advertising, pay television, CATV, and video technology. Price $225.00 per year. ISSN 0300-7057.

Hong Kong Enterprise

Hong Kong Trade Development Council, 548 5th Ave, New York, NY 10036. Telephone (212) 582-6610.

Monthly magazine. Surveys various Hong Kong industries. Includes photographs and descriptions of products available for export. Price available on request.

Housewares

Harcourt Brace Jovanovich Publications, 757 3rd Ave, New York, NY 10017. Order from Harcourt Brace Jovanovich Publications, 1 E 1st St, Duluth, MN 55802. Telephone (218) 727-8511.

Magazine issued 18 times per year. Provides information on housewares and small electrical appliances. Notes sales and marketing trends. Price $8.00 per year.

Idaho: Manufacturing Directory

Manufacturers' News, Inc, 3 E Huron St, Chicago, IL 60611. Telephone (312) 337-1084.

Biennial book. Names 900 Idaho manufacturing firms. Includes information on executives and number of employees. Price $30.00.

Identified Sources of Supply

National Standards Assn, Inc, 5161 River Rd, Washington, DC 20016. Telephone (301) 951-1310. Telex 89-8452.

Annual two-volume book. Lists manufacturers and distributors of products conforming to 12,000 military, federal, and aerospace standards. Price $130.00.

Illinois: Manufacturers Directory

Manufacturers' News, Inc, 3 E Huron St, Chicago, IL 60611. Telephone (312) 337-1084.

Annual book. Provides information on 27,000 Illinois manufacturing firms. Notes location, product, and executives. Price $99.50.

Illinois: Services Directory

Manufacturers' News, Inc, 3 E Huron St, Chicago, IL 60611. Telephone (312) 337-1084.

Annual book. Lists 15,270 service companies in Illinois. Price $70.00.

Impact

Tasco Publishing Corp, 305 E 53rd St, New York, NY 10022. Telephone (212) 751-6500.

Semimonthly newsletter. Covers US alcoholic beverage industry developments. Contains marketing, economic, and research news. Price $78.00 per year.

Incentive Marketing

Bill Communications, Inc, 633 3rd Ave, New York, NY 10017. Telephone (212) 986-4800.

Monthly magazine. Covers specialized research, product planning evaluation, and marketing consultation. Price $25.00 per year.

Incentive Travel Manager

Brentwood Publishing Corp, 825 S Barrington Ave, Los Angeles, CA 90049. Telephone (213) 826-8388.

Monthly magazine. For sales and marketing executives involved with incentive travel programs. Price $30.00 per year.

Industrial Distributor News

Ames Publishing Div, Chilton, 1 W Olney Ave, Philadelphia, PA 19120. Telephone (215) 224-7000.

Monthly magazine. Reports on sales, marketing, and technical developments within commodity areas for firms engaged in distribution of industrial equipment and supplies. Price $24.00 per year.

Industrial Equipment News

Thomas Publishing Co, 1 Penn Plz, 250 W 34th St, New York, NY 10001. Telephone (212) 695-0500.

Monthly newsletter. Discusses new and improved industrial equipment and parts. Offers editions for Europe, Japan, Brazil, and Spanish-speaking Latin America. Free.

Industrial Marketing

Crain Communications, Inc, 740 Rush St, Chicago, IL 60611. Telephone (312) 649-5385.

Monthly newspaper. Discusses business marketing plans. Analyzes effective advertising campaigns. Price $20.00 per year.

Inform

American Personnel Guidance Assn, 2 Skyline Place, Suite 400, 5203 Leesburg Pike, Falls Church, VA 22041. Telephone (703) 820-4700.

Monthly periodical. Provides information on sources of career information, plus Career Resource Bibliography. Price $25.00 per year.

Information Bank I and II

New York Times Information Service, Inc, Mt Pleasant Office Pk, 1719A Route 10, Parsippany, NJ 07054. Telephone (201) 539-5850. Telex 136390.

Database. Provides abstracts of articles from *The New York Times* and 60 other newspapers and magazines. Includes 1.9 million abstracts dating back to January 1969. Price available on request.

Information Guide for Doing Business in Countries Abroad

Price Waterhouse & Co, 60 Broad St, New York, NY 10004. Telephone (212) 489-8900.

Series of reports. Contains information on running a business in a particular country. Price available on request.

Information Industry Market Place: An International Directory of Information Products and Services

R R Bowker Co, 1180 Ave of the Americas, New York, NY 10036. Order from R R Bowker Co, PO Box 1807, Ann Arbor, MI 48106. Telephone (212) 764-5100.

Annual directory. Lists 400 database producers, as well as information centers that collect, analyze, evaluate, and process raw data. Also lists other support services and suppliers, organizations, conferences and courses, reference books, periodicals, and newsletters in the field. Price $32.50. ISBN 0-8352-1291-2. ISSN 0000-0450.

InfoWorld

CW Communications Inc, 375 Cochituate Rd, Box 880, Framingham, MA 01701. Telephone (617) 879-0700.

Biweekly newspaper. Provides information on personal or desktop computers. Price $25.00 per year.

Innovation World

Raymond Lee Organization, Inc, 230 Park Ave, New York, NY 10017. Telephone (212) 661-7000.

Bimonthly magazine. Covers product ideas, including marketing, research and development, packaging, and trademark news. Price $24.00 per year.

Insurance Marketing

Bayard Publications, Inc, 1234 Summer St, Stamford, CT 06905. Telephone (203) 327-0800.

Monthly magazine. Covers all branches of insurance. Price $10.00 per year.

Insurance Sales

Rough Notes Co, Inc, 1200 N Meridian St, Indianapolis, IN 46204. Telephone (317) 634-1541.

Monthly magazine. Covers life and health insurance, with an emphasis on sales. Price $8.00 per year.

International Businessman's Who's Who

Kelly's Directories Ltd, Windsor Court, E Grinstead House, E Grinstead, W Sussex, England RH19 1XB. Telephone (44) (01) 0342-26972. Telex 95127 INFSER G.

Annual directory. Contains biographical data on outstanding businesspeople to 1980. Price £40.00. ISSN 610-00526X.

International Directory of Executive Recruiters

Kennedy & Kennedy, Inc, Templeton Rd, Fitzwilliam, NH 03447. Telephone (603) 585-2200.

Directory. Lists 600 executive recruiting firms in 150 countries. Price $15.00.

International Intertrade Index

International Intertrade Index, PO Box 636, Federal Sq, Newark, NJ 07101. Telephone (201) 623-2864.

Monthly newsletter. Lists new products shown at foreign trade fairs. Notes new foreign processes, licenses, and patents. Price $45.00 per year.

International Market Guide—Continental Europe

Dun & Bradstreet, Box 3224, Church St Station, New York, NY 10008. Telephone (212) 285-7346.

Annual book with two supplements per year. Lists over 375,000 European firms in 19 countries. Notes their lines of business and provides general appraisal. Price on request. Available to Dun & Bradstreet subscribers only.

International Market Guide—Latin America

Dun & Bradstreet, Box 3224, Church St Station, New York, NY 10008. Telephone (212) 285-7346.

Biannual book. Contains listing of Latin American firms, their lines of business, and general appraisal. Covers 33 countries. Price on request. Available to Dun & Bradstreet subscribers only.

International New Product Newsletter

Transcommunications International Inc, 426 Statler Office Bldg, Boston, MA 02116. Telephone (617) 426-6647.

Monthly newsletter. Provides information on new industrial products and processes, primarily from foreign sources. Notes products immediately available for manufacture under license. Offers Japanese edition. Price $90.00 per year.

International Reference Manual

Coopers & Lybrand, 1259 Ave of the Americas, New York, NY 10019. Telephone (914) 489-1100.

Looseleaf book. Contains information on doing business abroad. Arranged by country. Price available on request.

International Series

Ernst & Whinney, 2000 National City Center, Cleveland, OH 44114. Telephone (216) 861-5000.

Series of reports. Contains analysis of climate for investment and trade in a particular country. Price available on request.

International Who's Who

Europa Publications Ltd, 18 Bedford Sq, London, England, WC1B 3JN. Telephone (44) (01) 580-8236.

Annual book. Contains bibliographies of approximately 15,000 of world's most eminent men and women. Price $90.00.

Investing, Licensing, and Trading Conditions Abroad

Business International Corp, 1 Dag Hammarskjold Plz, New York, NY 10017. Telephone (212) 750-6300.

Monthly, updated reference service. Rules and laws of 56 countries are interpreted with respect to finance, labor, taxes, remittances, licensing, and trade. Price $685.00 per year.

Iowa: Manufacturers Directory

Manufacturers' News, Inc, 3 E Huron St, Chicago, IL 60611. Telephone (312) 337-1084.

Biennial book. Identifies 3,900 Iowa manufacturing companies. Indicates executives and number of employees. Price $26.00.

Irish Export Directory

Irish Export Board, Strand Rd, Sandymount, Dublin 4, Ireland. Order from 10 E 53rd St, New York, NY 10022. Telephone (212) 371-3600. Telex 420012 IREXUI.

Directory. Lists 1,700 Irish manufacturing companies and products

they manufacture. Products are listed in English, French, German, Spanish, and Italian. Price £3.00 per copy.

Januz Direct Marketing Letter

Januz Marketing Communications, Inc, PO Box 1000, Lake Forest, IL 60045. Telephone (312) 295-6550.

Monthly newsletter. Presents direct mail marketing ideas, case histories, and special reports. Price $96.00 per year, $192.00 two years, $240.00 three years.

Japan Company Handbook

Oriental Economist, 1-4 Hongokucho, Nihonbashi, Chuo-ku, Tokyo 103, Japan. Telephone (81) (03) 270-4111.

Annual book. Provides data on 1,000 major Japanese corporations, including financial and stock information. Forecasts future growth. Price $49.00 Seamail, $65.00 Airmail.

Japan Letter

Asia Letter Ltd, PO Box 54149, Los Angeles, CA 90054. Telephone (213) 322-4222.

Bimonthly newsletter. Covers Japanese economic and political developments, and regulations affecting foreign business. Price $55.00 per year.

Jewelers' Circular-Keystone

Chilton Co, Chilton Way, Radnor, PA 19089. Telephone (215) 687-8200.

Monthly magazine. Covers jewelry industry and its outlets. Provides jewelers with information to improve store management and merchandising. Price $16.00.

Jewelry Newsletter International

Newsletters International, 2600 S Gessner Rd, Houston, TX 77063. Telephone (713) 783-0100.

Monthly newsletter. Reports on international jewelry business in retail, wholesale, and manufacturing areas. Price $75.00 per year.

Journal of Marketing

American Marketing Assn, 222 S Riverside Plz, Chicago, IL 60606. Telephone (312) 648-0536.

Quarterly journal. Furnishes articles concerned with the practice and teaching of marketing. Price $12.00 per year member, $24.00 nonmember.

Journal of Marketing Research

American Marketing Assn, 222 S Riverside Plz, Chicago, IL 60606. Telephone (312) 648-0536.

Quarterly magazine. Reports on fundamental research in marketing. Price $15.00 per year member, $30.00 nonmember.

Journal of Retailing

New York Univ, Inst of Retail Management, 202 Tisch Hall, Washington Sq, New York, NY 10003. Telephone (212) 598-2286.

Quarterly journal. Discusses retailing practices, problems, and research. Price $15.00 per year.

Journal of the Electronics Industry

Dempa Publications, Inc, 380 Madison Ave, New York, NY 10017. Telephone (212) 867-0900.

Monthly journal. Reports on electronics industry. Provides information on technological advances, production and sales statistics, and trade. Price $92.00 per year airmail.

Kansas: State Industrial Directory

Manufacturers' News, Inc, 3 Huron St, Chicago, IL 60611. Telephone (312) 337-1084.

Annual book. Lists 4,989 Kansas industrial firms. Identifies 26,556 executives. Price $40.00.

Kelly's Manufacturers & Merchants Directory

Kelly's Directories Ltd, Windsor Crt, E Grinstead House, E Grinstead, W Sussex, England RH19 1XB. Telephone (44) (01) 0342 26972.

Annual book. Gives listing of British manufacturers, merchants, and wholesalers, alphabetically and by product. Contains rundown of British importers and European exporting manufacturers and producers by product. Price £35.00 per copy.

Kentucky: State Industrial Directory

Manufacturers' News, Inc, 3 E Huron St, Chicago, IL 60611. Telephone (312) 337-1084.

Annual book. Lists 2,580 Kentucky industrial companies by name, location, and product. Price $40.00.

Kiplinger Washington Letter

Kiplinger Washington Editors, Inc, 1729 H St, NW, Washington, DC 20006. Telephone (202) 887-6400.

Weekly newsletter. Supplies briefings on business trends. Includes pertinent government policies and information on employment, investment, and interest rates. Price $42.00 per year.

Korean Trade Directory

Korean Traders Assn, Inc, 460 Park Ave, Room 555, New York, NY 10022. Telephone (212) 421-8804. Telex KTANY 425572.

Annual book. Offers directory to South Korean trade, banks, insurance, export, and shipping companies. Price $10.00 per copy.

Lawn & Garden Marketing

Intertec Publishing Corp, 9221 Quivera Rd, PO Box 12901, Overland Pk, KS 66212. Telephone (913) 888-4664. Telex 42-4156.

Magazine published 10 times per year. Offers information on lawn and garden products, markets, and merchandising practices. Price $20.00 per year.

Lloyd's List

Lloyd's of London Press Ltd, Sheepen Pl, Colchester, Essex, England CO3 3LP. Telephone 0206 69222. Telex 987321.

Daily newspaper. Contains shipping, insurance, transportation, energy, and finance news. Price $570.00 per year.

Louisiana: State Industrial Directory

Manufacturers' News, Inc, 3 E Huron St, Chicago, IL 60611. Telephone (312) 337-1084.

Annual book. Contains information on industrial companies in Louisiana. Indicates county, city, and product. Price $30.00.

Magazine Index

Information Access Corp, 404 6th Ave, Menlo Pk, CA 94025. Telephone (800) 227-8431.

Monthly microfilm service, with two looseleaf supplements. Provides author, title, and subject indexes to 375 US magazines. Covers articles, news, product evaluations, editorials, poetry, recipes, reviews, and biographies. Price $1,480.00 per year.

•Maine: State Industrial Directory

Manufacturers' News, Inc, 3 E Huron St, Chicago, IL 60611. Telephone (312) 337-1084.

Annual book. Lists 1,500 Maine industrial firms by location and product. Price $20.00.

Maine, Vermont, New Hampshire: Directory of Manufacturers

Manufacturers' News, Inc, 3 E Huron St, Chicago, IL 60611. Telephone (312) 337-1084.

Biennial book. Provides information on manufacturing firms in Maine, Vermont, and New Hampshire by name, location, and product. Price $39.50.

Mainly Marketing

Schoonmaker Associates, Drawer M, Coram, NY 11727. Telephone (516) 473-8741.

Monthly newsletter. Presents surveys and material relevant to marketing of technical products in the electronics field. Price $144.00 per year. ISSN 0464-591X.

Major Mass Market Merchandisers

Salesman's Guide, Inc, 1140 Broadway, New York, NY 10001. Telephone (212) 684-2985.

Directory. Lists discount, variety, drug, supermarket, and off-price stores. Notes buyers of men's, women's, and children's wear and accessories. Price $60.00.

Management Compensation in Canada, and The Remuneration of Chief Executive Officers in Canada

H V Chapman Consulting & Compensation Ltd, Box 8, 24th Fl, One Dunas St W, Toronto, Ont, Canada M5G 1Z3. Telephone (416) 598-1700.

Annual books, three volumes. Present for key management positions the latest figures on annual salary, total cash bonus, and car allowances. Report on salaries, bonuses, total compensation, and company cars for chief executive officers only in second volume. Price $450.00, $282.00, and $245.00, respectively.

Management Contents

Management Contents, 3014 Northbrook, IL 60062. Telephone (312) 564-1006.

Biweekly service issued 26 times per year. Contains tables of contents of latest issues of business and management periodicals. Price $68.00 per year.

Manufacturers' Agents' Guide

Manufacturers' Agent Publishing Co, Inc, 663 5th Ave, New York, NY 10022. Telephone (212) 682-0326.

Biennial book. Lists more than 11,-500 manufacturers who distribute through agents, classified by industry. Price $27.00.

Manufacturing Directory of Idaho

Univ of Idaho, Center for Business Development and Research, Moscow, ID 83843. Telephone (208) 885-6611.

Book. Lists 1,104 Idaho manufacturers alphabetically, geographically, SIC code, and product. Includes brief product descriptions. Price $22.50.

Marketing

Inst of Marketing, Moor Hall, Cookham, Maidenhead, Berkshire, England SL6 9QH. Telephone Bourne End (062 85) 24922.

Weekly journal. Gives news and trends within specific industries and case histories with special emphasis on the UK. Furnishes Institute of Marketing news. Price $57.00 per year airmail.

Marketing & Media Decisions

Decisions Publications, Inc, 342 Madison Ave, New York, NY 10017. Telephone (212) 953-1888.

Monthly magazine. Interprets trends in marketing and media as they affect national advertisers and agencies. Price $36.00 per year.

Marketing Communications

United Business Publications, Inc, 475 Park Ave S, New York, NY 10016. Telephone (212) 725-2300.

Monthly magazine. Discusses marketing communications ideas and applications. Price $13.50 per year.

Marketing Economics Institute (MEI) Marketing Economics Guide

Marketing Economics Inst Ltd, 441 Lexington Ave, New York, NY 10017. Telephone (212) 687-5090.

Looseleaf book. Gives information to help develop effective marketing strategy. Price $15.50.

Marketing Economics Key Plants

Marketing Economics Inst Ltd, 441 Lexington Ave, New York, NY 10017. Telephone (212) 687-5090.

Biennial directory. Lists 40,000 plants that have more than 100 employees. Aimed at salespeople seeking industrial markets. Price $80.00 per copy. ISBN 0-914078-23-2. ISSN 0098-1397.

Marketing for Sales Executives

Research Inst of America, Inc, 589 5th Ave, New York, NY 10017. Telephone (212) 755-8900.

Biweekly newsletter. Deals with marketing news for high-level management. Provides sales advice. Price $36.00 per year.

Marketing Ideas

Predicasts, Inc, 11001 Cedar Ave, Cleveland, OH 44106. Telephone (216) 795-3000.

Weekly newsletter. Reports on marketing trends, advertising news, and market research. Price $132.00 per year.

Marketing in Europe

Economist Intelligence Unit Ltd, Spencer House, 27 St. James's Pl, London, England SW1A 1NT. Order from Economist Intelligence Unit Ltd, 75 Rockefeller Plz, New York, NY 10019. Telephone (212) 541-5730. Telex 148393.

Monthly journal. Reports on consumer markets in Europe, with emphasis on the original six EEC countries. Price $310.00 per year.

Marketing Information Guide

Hoke Communications, Inc, 224 7th St, Garden City, NY 11535. Telephone (516) 746-6700.

Bimonthly bibliography lists books, articles, and other sources of information on marketing. Indexed by subject and geographical area. Price $30.00 per year.

Marketing Letter

Alexander Hamilton Inst, 1633 Broadway, New York, NY 10019. Telephone (212) 397-3580.

Monthly letter. Reports on sales and marketing techniques, new trends that affect marketing and international marketing terminology. Price $63.00 per year.

Marketing News

American Marketing Assn, 222 S Riverside Plz, Chicago, IL 60606. Telephone (312) 648-0536.

Biweekly newspaper. Covers activities of American Marketing Association and other marketing news. Price included with membership, $20.00 per year nonmember.

Marketing Science Institute Newsletter

Marketing Science Inst, 14 Story St, Cambridge, MA 02138. Telephone (617) 491-2060.

Newsletter issued three times per year. Pertains to research and activities of Marketing Science Institute in marketing sciences. Free.

Marketing Times

Sales and Marketing Executives International, Inc, 380 Lexington Ave, New York, NY 10017. Telephone (212) 986-9300.

Bimonthly magazine. Covers variety of marketing topics such as new product research and product performance. Price $10.00 per year.

Market Research Abstracts

Market Research Society, 15 Belgrave Sq, London, England SW1X 8PF. Telephone (44)(01) 235-4709.

Biannual information service. Abstracts from 40 journals cover marketing and advertising research. Price £25.00.

Market Research Handbook

Supply and Services Canada, Canadian Govt Publishing Centre, Hull, Que, Canada K1A 0S9. Telephone (819) 994-3475, 2085.

Annual book. Provides information on Canadian markets. Includes statistics on population growth, income distribution, and changes in consumer consumption patterns. French and English. Price $30.00.

Market Share Reports

US Dept of Commerce, Industry and Trade Adm, Bureau of Export Development, Washington, DC 20230. Order from National Technical Information Service, 5285 Port Royal Rd, Springfield, VA 22161. Telephone (202) 377-2000.

Annual pamphlet. Provides product-by-product comparison of exports from the US and competing industrial nations. Includes a five-year analysis of the international export market. Price $4.75 each country series, $3.25 each commodities series.

Maryland: State Industrial Directory

Manufacturers' News, Inc, 3 E Huron St, Chicago, IL 60611. Telephone (312) 337-1084.

Annual book. Lists 4,000 Maryland industrial firms by name, location, and product. Includes information on District of Columbia. Price $35.00.

Massachusetts: Service Directory

Manufacturers' News, Inc, 3 E Huron St, Chicago, IL 60611. Telephone (312) 337-1084.

Biennial book. Contains information on 6,000 service firms in Massachusetts. Price $38.00.

Massachusetts: State Industrial Directory

Manufacturers' News, Inc, 3 E Huron St, Chicago, IL 60611. Telephone (312) 337-1084.

Annual book. Lists 10,000 industrial firms in Massachusetts and identifies executives. Price $60.00.

Media Guide International: Business/Professional Publications Edition

Directories International, 1718 Sherman Ave, Evanston, IL 60201. Telephone (312) 491-0019.

Four-volume annual book. Provides advertising rates and data for more than 8000 business, professional, and trade publications. Covers 90 countries. Offers regional issues for Europe, Asia, Australia, and USSR, Latin America, Middle East, and Africa. Price $220.00 per year. ISBN 0-912794.

Media Guide International: Newspapers/Newsmagazines Edition

Directories International, 1718 Sherman Ave, Evanston, IL 60201. Telephone (312) 491-0019.

Annual book. Supplies data and advertising rates for newspapers and news magazines in 110 countries. Arranges editions by continent and includes special section and multicontinental media, and advertising tax information for each country. Price $65.00 per copy. ISBN 0-912794.

Medical & Healthcare Marketplace Guide

International Bio-Medical Information Service, Inc, PO Box 756, Miami, FL 33156. Telephone (305) 665-4856.

Book. Contains data on over 2,000 US-based manufacturers and dealers connected with medical field. Includes drug, medical electronic equipment, and dental supply companies. Tables. Price $200.00. ISSN 0146-8022.

Meeting News

Gralla Publications, 1515 Broadway, New York, NY 10036. Telephone (212) 869-1300.

Monthly magazine. Covers convention, trade show, and professional meeting planning. Pricc available on request.

Michigan State Industrial Directory

Manufacturer's News, Inc, 3 E Huron St, Chicago, IL 60611. Telephone (312) 337-1084.

Annual book. Lists 14,500 industrial companies in Michigan. Identifies executives, location, and products. Price $70.00.

Middle East and North Africa

Europa Publications Ltd, 18 Bedford Sq, London, England,WC1B 3JN. Telephone (44) (01) 580-8236.

Annual book. Gives vital statistics on 24 countries in Middle East and North Africa. Covers such topics as population, employment, finance, trade, government, and religion. Includes information on major personalities in region. Price $80.00.

Middle Market Directory

Dun & Bradstreet, Box 3224, Church St Station, New York, NY 10008. Telephone (212) 285-7346.

Annual book. Lists all US businesses with net worth of $500,000 or more. Includes about 31,000 companies. Price available on request. Available to Dun & Bradstreet subscribers only.

Million Dollar Directory

Dun & Bradstreet, Box 3224, Church St Station, New York, NY 10008. Telephone (212) 285-7346.

Annual directory. Lists all US businesses with net worth of $1 million or more. Notes officers and directors and interlocking affiliations. Price available on request. Available to Dun & Bradstreet subscribers only.

Minnesota: State Industrial Directory

Manufacturers' News, Inc, 3 E Huron St, Chicago, IL 60611. Telephone (312) 337-1084.

Annual book. Lists 5,508 industrial firms in Minnesota and 35,048 executives. Indicates location, products, and number of employees. Price $50.00.

Mississippi: State Industrial Directory

Manufacturers' News, Inc, 3 E Huron St, Chicago, IL 60611. Telephone (312) 337-1084.

Annual book. Provides information on 2,271 industrial firms in Mississippi. Indicates executives, products, and number of employees. Price $35.00.

Missouri: State Industrial Directory

Manufacturers' News, Inc, 3 E Huron St, Chicago, IL 60611. Telephone (312) 337-1084.

Annual book. Contains information on 7,040 industrial companies in Missouri. Lists products, executives, and number of employees. Price $50.00.

Modern Paint & Coatings

Communication Channels, Inc, 6285 Barfield Rd, Atlanta, GA 30328. Telephone (404) 256-9800.

Monthly magazine. Provides information on paint technology, production techniques, marketing, and management for personnel in the paint, varnish, lacquer, and allied synthetic coatings industry. Price $21.00 per year.

Money

Time, Inc, Time & Life Bldg, New York, NY 10020. Order from Money, Time-Life Bldg, 541 N Fairbanks Ct, Chicago, IL 60611. Telephone (212) 586-1212.

Monthly magazine. Reports on personal finance. Includes topics on stock market◆trends, estate planning, taxes and tax shelters, and consumer affairs. Price $14.95 per year.

Montana: State Industrial Directory

Manufacturers' News, Inc, 3 E Huron St, Chicago, IL 60611. Telephone (312) 337-1084.

Annual book. Contains information on 750 Montana industrial companies. Identifies executives, products, and number of employees. Price $25.00.

Monthly Catalog of US Government Publications

Superintendent of Documents, Government Printing Office, Washington, DC 20402. Telephone (202) 783-3238.

Monthly list of recently issued government publications. Annual cumulative index available. Price $80.00 per year. ISSN 0362-6830.

Moody's Industrial Manual and News Reports

Moody's Investors Services, Inc, 99 Church St, New York, NY 10007. Telephone (212) 267-8800.

Two-volume manual plus twice-weekly reports. Gives ratings for and details on all firms listed on New York and American stock exchanges, plus those listed on regional exchanges. Price $350.00 per year.

Moody's Over-the-Counter (OTC) Industrial Manual and News Reports

Moody's Investors Service, Inc, 99 Church St, New York, NY 10007. Telephone (212) 267-8800.

Manual plus weekly looseleaf reports. Offers ratings for and details on 3,200 firms not listed on major exchanges. Price $320.00 per year.

Moody's Transportation Manual & News Reports

Moody's Investors Service, Inc, 99 Church St, New York, NY 10007. Telephone (212) 267-8800.

Book plus twice-weekly looseleaf reports. Covers domestic transportation companies. Includes maps and details of ownership and operation. Price $280.00 per year.

Motor/Age

Chilton Co, Chilton Way, Radnor, PA 19089. Telephone (215) 687-8200.

Monthly magazine. Provides technical and merchandising information about service and repair of automobiles and trucks. Price $12.00.

Multinational Executive Travel Companion

Guides to Multinational Business, Inc, Harvard Sq, Box 92, Cambridge, MA 02138. Telephone (617) 868-2288.

Book. Provides information on 160 countries for business travelers. Lists government and business offices. Notes transportation, hotels, and restaurants. Price $40.00.

Multinational Marketing and Employment Directory

World Trade Academy Press, Inc, 50 E 42nd St, New York, NY 10017. Telephone (212) 697-4999.

Annual directory. Lists 7,500 US corporations operating in US and abroad. Indicates main headquarters, foreign operations, and products and services. Price $100.00.

National Hardware Wholesalers Guide

Southern Hardware, 1760 Peachtree Rd, NW, Atlanta, GA 30357. Telephone (404) 874-4462.

Annual directory. Lists hardware manufacturers. Notes home office and regional sales personnel. Price available on request.

Nation's Business

Chamber of Commerce of the US, 1615 H St, NW, Washington, DC 20062. Telephone (202) 659-6231.

Monthly magazine. Forecasts, analyzes, and interprets trends and developments in business and government. Price $18.75 per year.

Nation's Restaurant News

Lebhar-Friedman Publications, Inc, 425 Park Ave, New York, NY 10022. Telephone (212) 371-9400.

Biweekly report. Discusses trends in food-service and restaurant industries. Price $15.00 per year.

Nationwide Directory of Sporting Goods Buyers

Salesman's Guide, Inc, 1140 Broadway, New York, NY 10001. Telephone (212) 684-2985.

Book with three supplements. Lists top retail stores with buyers' names for all types of sporting goods, athletic apparel, and footwear. Price $80.00.

Nationwide Men's and Boys' Wear

Salesman's Guide, Inc, 1140 Broadway, New York, NY 10001. Telephone (212) 684-2985.

Book with three supplements. Lists department, clothing, and specialty stores, together with the names of buyers and merchandise managers of mens' and boys, apparel and accessories departments. Price $65.00.

Nationwide Women's and Children's Wear

Salesman's Guide, Inc, 1140 Broadway, New York, NY 10001. Telephone (212) 684-2985.

Book with three supplements. Lists top department, family clothing, and specialty stores. Notes the names of buyers and merchandise managers of women's and children's apparel and accessories departments. Price $65.00.

Nebraska: State Industrial Directory

Manufacturers' News, Inc, 3 E Huron St, Chicago, IL 60611. Telephone (312) 337-1084.

Annual book. Provides information on 2,501 Nebraska industrial firms and their executives. Price $25.00.

Nevada: Industrial Directory

Manufacturers' News, Inc, 3 E Huron St, Chicago, IL 60611. Telephone (312) 337-1084.

Biennial book. Lists Nevada manufacturers, wholesalers, and public warehouses. Price $8.00.

New Business Report

Executive Communications, Inc, 400 E 54th St, New York, NY 10022. Telephone (212) 421-3713.

Monthly newsletter. Provides new business leads, sales tips, and other solicitation strategies for advertising agency top executives and new business specialists. Price $50.00 per year.

New From Europe

Prestwick International, Inc, PO Box 205, Burnt Hills, NY 12027. Telephone (518) 399-6985.

Monthly report. Gives information on new products from Western Europe available for license, franchise, purchase for resale, or acquisition. Includes new process data. Price $275.00 per year.

New From Japan

Prestwick International, Inc, PO Box 205, Burnt Hills, NY 12027. Telephone (518) 399-6985.

Monthly report. Gives information on new products from Japan available for license, franchise, purchase for resale, or acquisition. Includes new process data. Price $275.00 per year.

New Hampshire: State Industrial Directory

Manufacturers' News, Inc, 3 E Huron St, Chicago, IL 60611. Telephone (312) 337-1084.

Biennial book. Contains information on 900 industrial companies in

New Hampshire. Notes executives. Price $20.00.

New Jersey: Directory of Manufacturers

Manufacturers' News, Inc, 3 E Huron St, Chicago, IL 60611. Telephone (312) 337-1084.

Biennial book. Lists 12,000 manufacturing firms in New Jersey by name, location, and product. Price $59.50.

New Mexico: State Industrial Directory

Manufacturers' News, Inc, 3 E Huron St, Chicago, IL 60611. Telephone (312) 337-1084.

Annual book. Provides information on 1,000 industrial companies in New Mexico. Identifies executives and lists number of employees. Price $25.00.

New York: Manufacturers Directory

Manufacturers' News, Inc, 3 E Huron St, Chicago, IL 60611. Telephone (312) 337-1084.

Annual book. Covers 16,000 manufacturing firms in New York. Identifies key executives. Price $39.00.

New York Times

New York Times, 229 W 43rd St, New York, NY 10036. Telephone (212) 556-1234.

Daily newspaper. Contains articles on business, financial, and economic news, along with general news coverage. Includes securities price statistics. Price $150.00 per year.

New Zealand Business Who's Who

Fourth Estate Group, PO Box 9344, Wellington, New Zealand. Order from Fourth Estate Group, PO Box 9143, Wellington, New Zealand. Telephone (64) (4) 859-019.

Annual book. Provides information on 10,000 New Zealand companies, executives, products and services, and marketing. Furnishes index of subsidiaries. Price $40.00 (New Zealand).

Nonwovens Industry

Household & Personal Products Industry, Box 555, 26 Lake St, Ramsey, NJ 07446. Telephone (201) 825-2552.

Monthly magazine. Covers nonwoven fabric industry. Reports on manufacturing, converting, and marketing developments. Price $18.00 per year.

North Carolina: Manufacturers Directory

Manufacturers' News, Inc, 3 E Huron St, Chicago, IL 60611. Telephone (312) 337-1084.

Biennial Book. Provides information on 8,000 North Carolina manufacturing firms by name, location, and product. Notes executives. Price $39.00.

North Dakota: State Industrial Directory

Manufacturers' News, Inc, 3 E Huron St, Chicago, IL 60611. Telephone (312) 337-1084.

Annual book. Contains information on 903 industrial firms in North Dakota. Identifies 5412 executives. Price $15.00.

Occupational Outlook Handbook

US Dept of Labor, Bureau of Labor Statistics, 441 G St, NW, Washington, DC 20212. Telephone (202) 523-1221.

Biennial book. Covers employment outlook, nature of work, training, entry requirements, line of advancement, location of jobs, earnings, and working conditions for 850 occupations and 30 major industries, including farming. Price $8.00.

Official Industrial Directory for Puerto Rico

Dun & Bradstreet, Box 3224, Church St Station, New York, NY 10008. Telephone (212) 285-7346.

Annual directory. Lists 9,000 manufacturers and exporters in Puerto Rico. Price available on request. Available to Dun & Bradstreet subscribers only.

Ohio: Industrial Directory

Manufacturers' News, Inc, 3 E Huron St, Chicago, IL 60611. Telephone (312) 337-1084.

Annual book. Lists 17,000 Ohio firms. Indicates executives, number of employees, and approximate sales. Price $69.50.

Oklahoma: State Industrial Directory

Manufacturers' News, Inc, 3 E Huron St, Chicago, IL 60611. Telephone (312) 337-1084.

Annual book. Covers industrial firms in Oklahoma. Notes location and products. Price $37.00.

Oregon: Manufacturers Directory

Manufacturers' News, Inc, 3 E Huron St, Chicago, IL 60611. Telephone (312) 337-1084.

Biennial book. Lists 5,000 Oregon manufacturing companies by name, location, and product. Notes executives and number of employees. Price $40.00.

Outlook

Chilton Co, Chilton Way, Radnor, PA 19089. Telephone (215) 687-8200.

Monthly newsletter. Pertains to electronic component products, people, and markets. Price available on request.

Overseas Assignment Directory Service

Knowledge Industry Publications, 701 Westchester Ave, White Plains, NY 10604. Telephone (914) 694-8686.

Annual looseleaf book. Addresses itself to US businesspersons operating abroad. Supplies basic information on about 43 countries.

Monthly updates. Price $325.00 per years including updates.

Overseas Business Reports

US Dept of Commerce, International Trade Administration, Washington, DC 20230. Telephone (202) 377-1470.

Approximately 50 reports per year. Furnishes information on overseas business conditions. Price available on request.

Paper Sales

Harcourt Brace Jovanovich Publications, 757 3rd Ave, New York, NY 10017. Order from Harcourt Brace Jovanovich Publications, 1 E 1st St, Duluth, MN 55802. Telephone (218) 727-8511.

Monthly report. Offers information relevant to paper wholesalers, including sales suggestions. Price $5.00 per year.

Pennsylvania: State Industrial Directory

Manufacturers' News, Inc, 3 E Huron St, Chicago, IL 60611. Telephone (312) 337-1084.

Annual book. Serves as guide to 25,000 industrial companies in Pennsylvania. Identifies 100,000 executives and notes products. Price $90.00.

Pets/Supplies/Marketing

Harcourt Brace Jovanovich Publications, 757 3rd Ave, New York, NY 10017. Order from Harcourt Brace Jovanovich Publications, 1 E 1st St, Duluth, MN 55802. Telephone (218) 727-8511.

Monthly magazine. Discusses pets and pet supplies. Notes merchandising trends. Price $15.00 per year.

Photographic Trade News

PTN Publishing Corp, 250 Fulton Ave, Hempstead, NY 11550. Telephone (516) 489-1300.

Semimonthly magazine. Covers photographic industry news and trends. Discusses new products and successful retail techniques. Price $6.00 per year.

Plastics World

Cahners Publishing Co, Inc, 221 Columbus Ave, Boston, MA 02116. Telephone (617) 536-7780.

Monthly magazine. Contains articles on adaptation of systems, materials, and equipment to increase efficiency in plastics processing. With annual Buyers Guide. Price available on request.

Polk's World Bank Directory

R L Polk & Co, 2001 Elm Hill Pike, PO Box 1340, Nashville, TN 37202. Telephone (615) 242-1694.

Semiannual directory with updates. Lists banks of the world. Includes financial statistics and other information. Price $67.50 per issue.

Potentials in Marketing

Lakewood Publications, Inc, 731 Hennepin Ave, Minneapolis, MN 55403. Telephone (612) 333-0471.

Magazine issued nine times per year. Covers marketing tools such as premium and incentive products, awards, training aids, meeting and convention sites, and advertising. Price $10.00 per year.

Practical Solar

Business Publishers, PO Box 1067, Silver Springs, MD 20910. Telephone (301) 587-6300.

Monthly newsletter. Discusses marketing and installation of solar energy systems. Price $67.00 per year.

Predicasts Source Directory

Predicasts, Inc, 200 University Circle Research Ctr, 11001 Cedar Ave, Cleveland, OH 44106. Telephone (216) 795-3000.

Annual book with three quarterly supplements. Gives bibliographic information on business information sources, including newspapers, trade journals, government publications, and bank letters. Price $100.00 per year, plus three quarterly supplements.

Premium, Incentive and Travel Buyers

Salesman's Guide, Inc, 1140 Broadway, New York, NY 10001. Telephone (212) 684-2985.

Directory with quarterly supplements. Contains register of over 16,000 buyers of premium and incentive merchandise and travel incentive programs. Price $110.00.

Premium/Incentive Business

Gralla Publications, 1515 Broadway, New York, NY 10036. Telephone (212) 869-1300.

Publication. Deals with premium and incentive sales and buying. Price available on request.

Principal International Businesses

Dun & Bradstreet, Box 3224, Church St Station, New York, NY 10008. Telephone (212) 285-7346.

Annual book. Serves as world marketing directory to over 49,000 of world's leading enterprises in 133 countries. Gives addresses, sales volume, number of employees, and lines of business. Prices available on request to Dun & Bradstreet subscribers only.

Product Marketing

Charleson Publications, 124 E 40th St, New York, NY 10016. Telephone (212) 953-0940.

Monthly magazine. Provides news and industry information for marketing/management executives and retailers. Focuses on cosmetics, toiletries, fragrances, and proprietary drugs. Price $20.00 per year.

Professional Furniture Merchant

Gralla Publications, 1515 Broadway, New York, NY 10036. Telephone (212) 869-1300.

Monthly magazine. Presents articles on furniture merchandising and trends. Price $20.00.

Progressive Grocer

Progressive Grocer Publishing Co, 708 3rd Ave, New York, NY 10017. Telephone (212) 490-1000.

Monthly publication. Covers news and trends in the grocery business. Price $30.00 per year. ISSN 0033-0787.

Progressive Grocer Marketing Guidebook

Progressive Grocer Publishing Co, 708 3rd Ave, New York, NY 10017. Telephone (212) 490-1000.

Annual publication. An encyclopedia covering 79 markets for the retail and wholesale food industry. Gives profile of major US chains, wholesalers, and convenience stores. Price $159.00. ISBN 0-911790-20-9.

Puerto Rico: Official Industrial & Trade Directory

Manufacturers' News, Inc, 3 E Huron St, Chicago, IL 60611. Telephone (312) 337-1084.

Annual book. Lists 5,000 industrial firms in Puerto Rico. Includes companies involved in trade. Price $60.00.

Quick Frozen Foods

Harcourt Brace Jovanovich Publications, 757 3rd Ave, New York, NY 10017. Order from Harcourt Brace Jovanovich Publications, 1 E 1st St, Duluth, MN 55802. Telephone (218) 727-8511.

Monthly magazine. Reports on frozen foods industry. Notes equipment, packaging, and distribution. Price $15.00 per year.

Rand McNally Commercial Atlas & Marketing Guide

Rand McNally & Co, 8255 N Central Park, Skokie, IL 60076. Telephone (312) 673-9100.

Annual book. Provides geographic and economic information for each state, county, and zip code area within US. Maps and charts. Price $135.00 per copy.

Reference Book of Corporate Managements

Dun & Bradstreet, Box 3224, Church St Station, New York, NY 10008. Telephone (212) 285-7346.

Annual book. Contains biographical sketches of about 30,000 executives in more than 2400 large companies of investor and general business interest. Prices on request. Available to Dun & Bradstreet subscribers only.

Reference Book of Manufacturers

Dun & Bradstreet, Box 3224, Church St Station, New York, NY 10008. Telephone (212) 285-7346.

Biannual book. Offers 355,000 listings of manufacturers, with sales, credit, and purchasing data on each. Prices on request. Available to Dun & Bradstreet subscribers only.

Reference Book of Transportation

Dun & Bradstreet, Box 3224, Church St Station, New York, NY 10008. Telephone (212) 285-7346.

Book. Provides credit and marketing facts on Class I, II, and III motor carriers, as well as air, rail, water, and bus carriers. Includes freight forwarding and pipeline companies. Prices on request. Available to Dun & Bradstreet subscribers only.

Register of Corporations, Directors and Executives

Standard & Poor's Corp, 25 Broadway, New York, NY 10004. Telephone (212) 248-2525.

Three-volume directory. Provides listing of 37,000 private and public companies, 405,000 executives by function, plus principal products. Biography volume gives brief accounts of 72,000 executives. Indexes. Price available on request.

Rent All

Harcourt Brace Jovanovich Publications, 757 3rd Ave, New York, NY 10017. Order from Harcourt Brace Jovanovich Publications, 1 E 1st St, Duluth, MN 55802. Telephone (218) 727-8511.

Monthly magazine. Reports on rental equipment industry, including party supplies, lawn and garden equipment, tools, and campers. Price $15.00 per year.

Republic of Ireland Reference Book

Dun & Bradstreet, Box 3224, Church St Station, New York, NY 10008. Telephone (212) 285-7346.

Annual book. Lists approximately 6,000 business establishments in Irish Republic. Gives proprietors and associates, primary line of business, and credit appraisal. Prices on request. Available to Dun & Bradstreet subscribers only.

Retailing Today

Robert Kahn and Associates, PO Box 249, Lafayette, CA 94549. Telephone (415) 254-4434.

Monthly newsletter. Discusses retail trade trends and research on retailing. Suggests ways executives can improve ethical standards. Price $24.00 per year.

Retail Operations News Bulletin

National Retail Merchants Assn, 100 W 31st St, New York, NY 10001. Telephone (212) 244-6780.

Quarterly magazine. Reports on retail store operations, including security, maintenance, and delivery. Price $14.50.

Rhode Island: State Industrial Directory

Manufacturers' News, Inc, 3 E Huron St, Chicago, IL 60611. Telephone (312) 337-1084.

Annual book. Contains information on Rhode Island industrial companies, including location and products. Price $20.00.

Sales & Marketing Management

Sales & Marketing Management, Sales Builders Div, 633 3rd Ave, New York, NY 10017. Telephone (212) 986-4800.

Magazine issued 16 times per year. Presents articles on sales and marketing operations. Includes information on packaging, advertising, and distribution of products. Price $25.00 per year.

Sales Manager's Bulletin

Bureau of Business Practice, 24 Rope Ferry Rd, Waterford, CT 06386. Telephone (203) 442-4365.

Semimonthly looseleaf newsletter. Covers techniques of conducting sales campaigns, including managing a sales force, conducting market research, and improving customer relations. Price $72.00 per year.

Salesman's Opportunity Magazine

Opportunity Press, Inc, Suite 1405, 6 N Michigan Ave, Chicago, IL 60602. Telephone (312) 346-4790. Telex 25-6138.

Monthly magazine. Emphasizes direct sales and individually owned business opportunities. Notes new products and sales tips. Aimed at salespersons. Price $8.00 per year.

Sales Prospector

Prospector Research Services, Inc, 751 Main St, PO Box 518, Waltham, Boston, MA 02154. Telephone (617) 899-1271.

Monthly report. Contains market research on sales prospects in US and Canada. Price $82.00 per year.

Savvy

Savvy, PO Box 2495, Boulder, CO 80321.

Monthly magazine. Discusses management issues from a woman's viewpoint. Offers investment advice. Price $12.00 per year.

Scott's Industrial Directory. Atlantic Manufacturers

Scott's Industrial Directories, PO Box 365, Oakville, Ont, Canada L6J 5M5. Telephone (416) 845-8881.

Biennial directory. Lists manufacturers, identifying their executives and products and classifying them by type of product. Covers the Canadian Atlantic provinces. Price $57.75 per copy.

Scott's Industrial Directory. Ontario Manufacturers

Scott's Industrial Directories, PO Box 365, Oakville, Ont, Canada L6J 5M5. Telephone (416) 845-8881.

Book issued every 18 months. Supplies a directory to 15,500 Ontario manufacturers, noting their products, executives, and other company information. Classifies manufacturers by type of product. Price $98.50 per copy.

Scott's Industrial Directory. Quebec Manufacturers

Scott's Industrial Directories, PO Box 365, Oakville, Ont, Canada

L6J 5M5. Telephone (416) 845-8881.

Directory issued every 18 months. Furnishes a registry to Quebec manufacturers. Classifies the manufacturers, by type of product and provides other information on firms. French and English. Price $98.50 per copy.

Scott's Industrial Directory. Western Manufacturers

Scott's Industrial Directories, PO Box 365, Oakville, Ont, Canada L6J 5M5. Telephone (416) 845-8881.

Biennial book. Provides a list of manufacturers in Canada's western provinces, classifying manufacturers by product. Notes other company information. Price $98.50 per copy.

Security Distributing & Marketing (SDM)

Cashners Publishing Co, 5 S Wabash Ave, Chicago, IL 60603. Telephone (312) 372-6880.

Monthly magazine. Covers marketing and installation of security products. Includes technical information. Price $24.00 per year. Product directory $20.00 per issue.

Service World International

Cahners Publishing Company, Inc, 221 Columbus Ave, Boston, MA 02116. Telephone (617) 536-7780.

Monthly magazine. Covers food service, lodging, transportation, and related industries serving world tourism. Price $15.00 per year.

South Carolina: Industrial Directory

Manufacturers' News, Inc, 3 E Huron St, Chicago, IL 60611. Telephone (312) 337-1084.

Annual book. Provides information on 3,300 South Carolina industrial firms listed by name, location, and product. Price $34.00.

South Dakota: State Industrial Directory

Manufacturers' News, Inc, 3 E Huron St, Chicago, IL 60611. Telephone (312) 337-1084.

Annual book. Contains information on 850 industrial firms in South Dakota. Notes 5,109 executives. Price $22.00.

Specialty Salesman

Communication Channels, Inc, 6285 Barfield Rd, Atlanta, GA 30328. Telephone (404) 256-9800.

Monthly magazine. Covers facets of sales techniques for direct salespersons who work for themselves. Price $10.00 per year.

Specialty Salesman & Business Opportunities

Specialty Salesman Magazine, Div of Communication Channels Inc, 6285 Barfield Rd, Atlanta, GA 30328. Telephone (404) 256-9800.

Monthly magazine. Contains articles about business opportunities in direct selling. Price $10.00 per year.

Sporting Goods Business

Gralla Publications, 1515 Broadway, New York, NY 10036. Telephone (212) 869-1300.

Publication. Provides news for sporting good retailers on industry-related topics. Price available on request.

Standard Directory of Advertisers

National Register Publishing Co, Inc, 5201 Old Orchard Rd, Skokie, IL 60077. Telephone (312) 470-3100.

Annual directory. Offers a register of 17,000 corporations responsible for 95% of US advertising. Notes their sales volume, advertising budgets, and agencies. Nine yearly supplements. Price $153.00 per copy. ISBN 0-87217-000-4.

Standard Directory of Advertising Agencies

National Register Publishing Co, Inc, 5201 Old Orchard Rd, Skokie, IL 60077. Telephone (312) 470-3100.

Book published three times per year. Provides a directory to 4400 advertising agencies. Catalogs agencies' gross billings by media, annual billings, and clients. Supplies periodic supplements that carry agency news. Price $52.00 per copy, three issues $127.00. ISBN 0-87217-003-9.

Standard Industrial Classification Manual, 1972

US Dept of Commerce, Bureau of the Census, Washington, DC 20233. Order from Superintendent of Documents, US Government Printing Office, Washington, DC 20402. Telephone (202) 783-3238.

Manual. Defines industries in accordance with the composition and structure of the US economy. Includes conversion tables for 1972 and 1967 standard industrial classification codes. Price $8.80.

Standard Periodical Directory

Oxbridge Inc, 40 E 34th St, New York, NY 10016. Telephone (212) 689-8524.

Provides the name, address, circulation, and other data for 65,000 US and Canadian periodicals. Price $120.00.

State Executive Directory

Carroll Publishing Co, 1058 Thomas Jefferson St, NW, Washington, DC 20007. Telephone (202) 333-8620.

Directory published three times per year. Identifies state government offices and personnel. Supplies phone numbers and titles. Price $84.00 per year.

State Sales Guides

Dun & Bradstreet, Box 3224, Church St Station, New York, NY 10008. Telephone (212) 285-7346.

Book. Gives information on companies, by individual states and some large cities, for traveling salespersons. Price, available on request, to Dun & Bradstreet subscribers only.

Statistical Abstract of the United States

Bureau of the Census, US Dept of Commerce, Washington, DC 20233. Order from Superintendent of Documents, US Government Printing Office, Washington, DC 20420. Telephone (202) 783-3238.

Annual report. Contains tables of economic, industrial, political, and social statistics for the US as a whole as well as some areas and regions. Includes lists of publications. Price $9.00.

Stores

National Retail Merchants Assn, 100 W 31st St, New York, NY 10001. Telephone (212) 244-6780.

Monthly magazine. Focuses on retail issues in the areas of merchandising, operations, credit, store design, information systems, and related topics. Price $10.00 per year.

Successful Meetings

Bill Communications, Inc, 633 3rd Ave, New York, NY 10017. Telephone (212) 986-4800.

Monthly magazine. Covers association meetings, seminars, and expositions around the world. Price $37.50 per year.

Success Unlimited

Success Unlimited, Inc, 401 N Wabash Ave, Chicago, IL 60611. Telephone (312) 828-9500.

Monthly magazine. Discusses successful salespersons and sales techniques. Includes tax information and book reviews. Price $14.00 per year.

Supermarket News

Fairchild Publications, Inc, 7 E 12th St, New York, NY 10003. Telephone (212) 741-4224.

Weekly newspaper. Covers news of the supermarket trade. Price $24.00 per year. ISSN 0039-5803.

Survey of Buying Power

Sales & Marketing Management, Sales Builders Div, 633 3rd Ave, New York, NY 10017. Telephone (212) 986-4800.

Annual survey magazine. Provides estimates of population, income, and retail sales for US states, metropolitan areas, counties, cities, and for Canadian provinces and metropolitan areas. Price $55.00.

Survey of Current Business

US Dept of Commerce, 14th St between Constitution Ave and E St, NW, Washington, DC 20230. Order from Superintendent of Documents, US Government Printing Office, Washington, DC 20402. Telephone (202) 783-3238.

Magazine. Reports on US economic conditions. Contains information on corporate profits, gross national product, employment, plant and equipment expenditures, and US international transactions. Price $35.00 per year.

Survey of Selling Costs

Sales & Marketing Management, Sales Builders Div, 633 3rd Ave,

New York, NY 10017. Telephone (212) 986-4800.

Annual survey issue. Provides selling costs index and cost-per-call estimates for 80 metropolitan markets. Notes sales meetings and sales training rates and facilities in major cities. Price $25.00.

Swiss Export Directory

Consulate General of Switzerland, 444 Madison Ave, New York, NY 10022. Telephone (212) 758-2560.

Periodically revised book. Supplies information on over 10,000 Swiss export products, trademarks, 7000 export firms, and service enterprises. Indicates products in English, German, and French. Price $30.00 per copy.

Target Twenty

Chilton Co, Chilton Way, Radnor, PA 19089. Telephone (215) 687-8200.

Monthly newsletter. Furnishes an overview of the food and beverage market. Discusses advertising, market research, and industry trends. Price available on request.

Tax and Trade Guide Series

Arthur Andersen & Co, 69 W Washington St, Chicago, IL 60602. Telephone (312) 580-0069.

Series of 20 guides direct attention to running a business in a particular country. Free.

Telephone Marketing Report

Januz Marketing Communications, Inc, PO Box 1000, Lake Forest, IL 60045. Telephone (312) 295-6550. Semimonthly newsletter. Gives advice on improving effectiveness of telephone sales and marketing. Notes ways to reduce telephone costs. Price $96.00 per year, $192.00 two years, $240.00 three years. ISSN 0270-9635.

Tennessee: State Industrial Directory

Manufacturers' News, Inc, 3 E Huron St, Chicago, IL 60611. Telephone (312) 337-1084.

Annual book. Lists 4,901 industrial companies in Tennessee by name, location, and product. Identifies executives. Price $40.00.

Texas: Manufacturers Directory

Manufacturers' News, Inc, 3 E Huron St, Chicago, IL 60611. Telephone (312) 337-1084.

Annual book. Identifies 12,000 manufacturing companies in Texas and their executives. Price $68.00.

Textile World—Fact File Buyers' Guide

McGraw-Hill Publications Co, 1221 Ave of the Americas, New York, NY 10020. Telephone (212) 997-1221. Telex TWX 7105814879 WUI 62555.

Annual magazine. Lists over 3,300 textile supplier companies and 2,000 different products. Notes textile production and marketing trends. Price available on request.

Thomas Grocery Register

Thomas Publishing Co, 1 Penn Plz, 250 W 34th St, New York, NY 10001. Telephone (212) 695-0500.

Three-volume set. Provides directory of food industry manufacturers and distributors. Lists chains, wholesalers, brokers, exporters, warehouses, food and nonfood products, services and brand names. Price $75.00.

Thomas Register of American Manufacturers

Thomas Publishing Co, 1 Penn Plz, 250 W 34th St, New York, NY 10001. Telephone (212) 695-0500.

Annual set of 16 volumes. Provides listing of over 100,000 US manufacturers, their products and services, brand names, and catalogs. Price $120.00.

Time

Time, Inc, Time & Life Bldg, New York, NY 10020. Order from Time, Inc, 541 N Fairbanks Ct, Chicago, IL 60611. Telephone (212) 586-1212.

Weekly magazine. Covers international and US political developments, economic conditions, medical, educational, and energy issues. Includes books, theater, and motion picture reviews. Price $26.00 per year.

Toys, Hobbies & Crafts

Harcourt Brace Jovanovich Publications, 757 3rd Ave, New York, NY 10017. Order from Harcourt Brace Jovanovich Publications, 1 E 1st St, Duluth, MN 55802. Telephone (218) 727-8511.

Monthly magazine, with annual directory. Focuses on toys, hobbies, and crafts. Considers manufacturing and retail developments. Price $7.00 per year.

Trade Directories of the World

Croner Publications, Inc, 211-03 Jamaica Ave, Queens Village, NY 11428. Telephone (212) 464-0866.

Looseleaf directory, plus monthly supplements. Lists approximately 3,000 trade, industrial and professional directories. Includes import/-export directories. Price $55.00 per year.

Trade Names Dictionary, 1st edition

Gale Research Co, Book Tower, Detroit, MI 48226. Telephone (313) 961-2242.

Two books. List 106,000 trade and brand names. Contain information on manufacturers, importers, marketers, and distributors. Price $160.00 per set. ISBN 0692-1.

Ulrich's International Periodicals Directory

R R Bowker Co, 1180 Ave of the Americas, New York, NY 10036. Order from R R Bowker Co, PO

Box 1807, Ann Arbor, MI 48106. Telephone (212) 764-5100.

Annual book. Gives information on 62,000 periodicals, arranged according to subject. Bibliography. Price $69.50. ISBN 0-8352-1297-1. ISSN 0000-0175.

United Kingdom-Guide to Key British Enterprises I

Dun & Bradstreet, Box 3224, Church St Station, New York, NY 10008. Telephone (212) 285-7346.

Annual book. Provides detailed data on 10,000 companies, representing one-third of the British labor force and richest available markets. Price available on request to Dun & Bradstreet subscribers only.

United Kingdom-Guide to Key British Enterprises II

Dun & Bradstreet, Box 3224, Church St Station, New York, NY 10008. Telephone (212) 285-7346.

Annual book. Contains information on 11,000 middle sector British companies. Price available on request to Dun & Bradstreet subscribers only.

United Kingdom Kompass Register

Kompass Register Ltd, Winston Court, E Grinstead House, E Grinstead, W Sussex, England RH19 1XD. Telephone 0342 26972.

Annual register. Gives information on British raw materials, manufactured products, and services. Includes business data for over 33,000

public and private companies. Price £60.00 per copy.

United States-Brazil Business Listing

Brazilian–American Chamber of Commerce, Inc, 22 W 48th St, New York, NY 10036. Telephone (212) 575-9030.

Directory. Provides names and addresses of 1,000 firms, subsidiaries, and affiliates operating in or having interest in the US and Brazil. Notes products and activities. Price $20.-00.

United States Industrial Directory

Cahners Publishing Co, Inc, 221 Columbus Ave, Boston, MA 02116. Telephone (617) 536-7780.

Annual directory (in four volumes). Lists industrial suppliers, products, trade names, and catalogs for all US industries. Price available on request.

US News and World Report

US News and World Report, PO Box 2629, Boulder, CO 06830.

Weekly magazine. Provides news and analysis of national and international political and economic developments. Price $31.00 per year.

Utah: State Industrial Directory

Manufacturers' News, Inc, 3 E Huron St, Chicago, IL 60611. Telephone (312) 337-1084.

Biennial book. Covers 2,100 industrial companies in Utah. Notes location, products, and executives. Price $15.00.

Vending Times

Vending Times, Inc, 211 E 43rd St, New York, NY 10017. Telephone (212) 697-3868.

Monthly magazine. Discusses vending and food service topics. Price $15.00 per year.

Verified Directory of Manufacturers' Representatives

Manufacturers' Agent Publishing Co, Inc, 663 5th Ave, New York, NY 10022. Telephone (212) 682-0326.

Biennial directory. Lists 16,000 manufacturers' agents in the United States, Puerto Rico, and Canada. Notes sales territory covered and product lines carried. Price $52.90.

Vermont: State Industrial Directory

Manufacturers' News, Inc, 3 E Huron St, Chicago, IL 60611. Telephone (312) 337-1084.

Annual book. Contains information on 1,500 industrial firms in Vermont and 3,000 executives. Price $20.00.

Virginia: State Industrial Directory

Manufacturers' News, Inc, 3 E Huron St, Chicago, IL 60611. Telephone (312) 337-1084.

Annual book. Lists 5,100 Virginia industrial companies by name, lo-

cation, and product. Identifies executives. Price $60.00.

Vision—The Inter-American Magazine

Vision, Inc, 13 E 75th St, New York, NY 10021. Telephone (212) 744-9126.

Published 24 times a year. Contains articles on business in Latin America. Price $44.00 per year.

VNR Dictionary of Business and Finance

Van Nostrand Reinhold Co, 135 W 50th St, New York, NY 10020. Telephone (212) 265-8700.

Book. Contains definitions of over 4,500 terms drawn from all areas of business and finance, with examples of modern usage. Price $18.95.

Wall Street Journal

Dow Jones & Co, Inc, 22 Cortlandt St, New York, NY 10007. Telephone (212) 285-5000.

Daily newspaper. Contains news articles on business and finance and includes statistics on securities, commodities, and exchange rates. Price available on request.

Washington Information Directory

Congressional Quarterly, Inc, 1414 22nd St, NW, Washington, DC 20037. Telephone (202) 296-6800.

Annual directory. Serves as guide to information sources in Congress, the executive branch, and private associations. Includes subject and agency indexes. Price $25.00.

Washington: State Industrial Directory

Manufacturers' News, Inc, 3 E Huron St, Chicago, IL 60611. Telephone (312) 337-1084.

Annual book. Covers 5127 industrial firms in the state of Washington. Indicates location, products, executives, and number of employees. Price $45.00.

West Virginia: State Industrial Directory

Manufacturers' News, Inc, 3 E Huron St, Chicago, IL 60611. Telephone (312) 337-1084.

Biennial book. Provides information on 2000 industrial firms in West Virginia. Notes location, products, and executives. Price $25.00.

Where to Find Business Information

John Wiley & Sons, Inc, 605 Third Ave, New York, NY 10158. Telephone (212) 850-6418.

Directory. Covers over 5,000 sources of business information and insight, drawn from all over the world, and is itself the source from which the entries in this section of this book are taken. Price $45.00.

Who's Who

St Martin's Press, Inc, 175 5th Ave, New York, NY 10010. Telephone (212) 674-5151.

Annual book. Covers living persons of note worldwide. Includes up-to-date biographical data on 28,000 distinguished people. Price $99.50.

Who's Who in America

Marquis Publications, 200 E Ohio St, Rm 5604, Chicago, IL 60611. Telephone (312) 787-2008.

Biennial book. Contains more than 73,500 biographical sketches of outstanding American men and women. Price $89.50. ISBN 0-8379-0141-3.

Who's Who in Finance and Industry

Marquis Publications, 200 E Ohio St, Rm 5604, Chicago, IL 60611. Telephone (312) 787-2008.

Biennial book. Gives information about top executives from America's largest corporations, plus data on leaders of small- and medium-size firms. Price $62.50. ISBN 0-8379-0322-X.

Who's Who of American Women

Marquis Publications, 200 E Ohio St, Rm 5604, Chicago, IL 60611. Telephone (312) 787-2008.

Biennial book. Presents more than 21,000 biographical sketches of outstanding American women. Price $62.50. ISBN 0-8379-0412-9.

Who's Who (United Kingdom)

St Martin's Press, Inc, 175 5th Ave, New York, NY 10010. Telephone (212) 674-5151.

Annual book. Covers living persons of note in Great Britain. Includes biographical data. Price $67.50.

Wisconsin: State Industrial Directory

Manufacturers' News, Inc, 3 E Huron St, Chicago, IL 60611. Telephone (312) 337-1084.

Annual book. Contains information on 4,500 industrial companies in Wisconsin and 27,109 executives. Lists firms by name, county, city, and product. Price $50.00.

Women in Business

American Business Women's Assn, 9100 Ward Pkwy, PO Box 8728, Kansas City, MO 64114. Telephone (816) 361-6621.

Magazine issued six times per year. Provides information about legislation, finance, business technology, communications, taxes, and association news for the working woman. Price $8.00 per year. ISSN 0043-7441.

Women's Work

Women's Work, 1302 18th St, NW, Suite 203, Washington, DC 20036. Telephone (202) 223-6274.

Bimonthly magazine. Discusses career opportunities for women. Notes employment trends in major cities and includes interviews and book reviews. Price $9.00 per year individuals, $18.00 per year institutions.

Working Woman

Hal Publications, Inc, 1180 Ave of the Americas, New York, NY 10036. Telephone (212) 944-5250.

Monthly magazine. Offers career advice for women. Appraises job market and provides information on personal finances. Price $9.00 per year.

World Aviation Directory

Ziff-Davis Publishing Co, 1156 15th St NW, Washington, DC 20005. Telephone (202) 293-3400.

Semiannual book. Lists aviation companies and personnel, air carriers, manufacturers, support services, government agencies affecting the aviation and aerospace industry, and international organizations. Price $60.00 per issue.

World Directory of Marketing Communications Periodicals

International Advertising Assn, 475 5th Ave, New York, NY 10017. Telephone (212) 684-1583.

Directory. Provides a guide to 350 publications in 34 countries relevant to the marketing field. Contains in the Introduction a code for interpreting listings in English, French, German, and Spanish. Price $8.00 per copy.

World Guide to Abbreviations of Organizations

Gale Research Co, Book Tower, Detroit, MI 48226. Telephone (313) 961-2242.

Book. Gives the full name behind initials and abbreviations used for companies, international agencies, and government departments throughout the world. Price $100.00. ISBN 2015-0.

World Guide to Trade Associations

R R Bowker Co, 1180 Ave of the Americas, New York, NY 10036. Order from R R Bowker Co, PO Box 1807, Ann Arbor, MI 48106. Telephone (212) 764-5100.

Book. Provides information on 26,-000 trade- and industry-related organizations in 153 countries. Lists chambers of commerce, artisan guilds, trade unions, and employers' and employees' groups in the US and abroad. Subject index. Preface and headings in English and German; entries in language of country of origin. Price $72.50. ISBN 3-7940-1032-9.

World Marketing

Dun & Bradstreet, Box 3224, Church St Station, New York, NY 10008. Telephone (212) 285-7346.

Semimonthly report. Focuses on overseas marketing developments and trade possibilities throughout the world. Price available on request to Dun & Bradstreet subscribers only.

World Products

Dun & Bradstreet, Box 3224, Church St Station, New York, NY 10008. Telephone (212) 285-7346.

Monthly report. Provides information on new products available from overseas suppliers. Price

available on request to Dun & Bradstreet subscribers only.

World Trade Information Center

World Trade Information Center, 1 World Trade Center, Suite 86001, New York, NY 10048. Telephone (212) 466-3069.

Service. Handles trade information requests through data collection. Has direct access to major on-line databases, worldwide individual and organization contacts, and customized reports and surveys. Price varies.

Worldwide Guide to Medical Electronics Marketing Representation

International Bio-Medical Information Service, Inc, PO Box 756, Miami, FL 33156. Telephone (305) 665-4856.

Book. Lists over 400 medical electronics marketing organizations throughout the world, excluding the US. Furnishes demographic and medical data for 100 nations. Indexes. Price $195.00 US, $200.00 elsewhere. ISSN 0146-8014.

Wyoming: Directory of Manufacturing and Mining

Manufacturers' News, Inc, 3 E Huron St, Chicago, IL 60611. Telephone (312) 337-1084.

Annual book. Covers manufacturing and mining companies in Wyoming. Notes executives, products, and number of employees. Price $15.00.

INDEX

Numbers in *italics* refer to definition of term in glossary.